CULTURAL ANTHROPOLOGY

CULTURAL ANTHROPOLOGY

DAVID HICKS
MARGARET A. GWYNNE
STATE UNIVERSITY OF NEW YORK AT STONY BROOK

HarperCollins*College*Publishers

Senior Editor: Alan McClare
Developmental Editors: Kirsten Olson, Carol Einhorn
Project Editor: David Nickol
Art Director: Teresa Delgado
Text Design: Baseline Graphics
Cover Design: Baseline Graphics
Cover Photos: *Front cover, left to right*: © David R. Frazier
   Photolibrary; (c) Harvey Lloyd/Peter Arnold, Inc.; © S. J.
   Krasemann/Peter Arnold, Inc. *Back cover, left to right*:
   Odyssey Productions, Chicago; © Robert Frerch/Odyssey
   Productions, Chicago; Brian North/Leo de Wys Inc.; Mark
   Harris/© Tony Stone Worldwide.
Photo Researcher: Rosemary Hunter
Production Administrator: Jeff Taub
Compositor: Black Dot Graphics
Printer and Binder: R.R.Donnelley & Sons Company
Cover Printer: The Lehigh Press

To Emma and Paul
And to the Memory of Margaret Spencer Wood Anderson

Library of Congress Cataloging-in-Publication Data

Hicks, David, 1939–
   Cultural anthropology / David Hicks, Margaret A. Gwynne.
      p. cm.
   Includes bibliographical references and index.
   ISBN 0-06-501072-8
   1. Ethnology.   I. Gwynne, Margaret Anderson.   II. Title.
GN316.H52   1994
306—dc20

93 94 95 96 9 8 7 6 5 4 3 2 1

CONTENTS

PREFACE

Before we embarked on the preparation of *Cultural Anthropology,* neither of us had ever found a textbook entirely suitable for our first-year anthropology students, and colleagues sometimes mentioned encountering the same problem. Some available textbooks seemed unnecessarily pedantic; others dwelt on material that was obviously remote from students' interests; still others seemed to us to be too abstract. We were looking for something that was clearly and engagingly written; that was as comprehensive as any single textbook could reasonably be, covering the basic subjects to which instructors would wish to expose their introductory students; that would introduce certain materials commonly shortchanged in current textbooks (such as women and culture, the human body as a vehicle for cultural expression, and sexuality from a cross-cultural point of view); and that would genuinely interest and even excite its undergraduate readers.

We wrote *Cultural Anthropology* to address these needs. We were guided by two related and equally fundamental premises: that American college students are interested in their own cultural experience, and that the comparative study of their own culture with others will result in a deeper appreciation of all cultures. In *Cultural Anthropology* we quite consciously focus on familiar aspects of Western culture that find parallels in other cultures, since we believe this will foster readers' awareness of, and tolerance for, the ethnic diversity that constitutes an ever-increasing element in the lives of American students.

••

THEMES

Cultural Anthropology is designed around four distinctive themes that we regard as fundamental to the education of anthropology students in the last decade of the twentieth century.

1. *Cultural relativity.* Most introductory cultural anthropology texts promote the notion that some invisible dividing line separates Westerners from non-Westerners. In *Cultural Anthropology* we reject what we consider the improper distinction between "us" and "them," and following from this general stance, consistently advocate what we take to be the most important lesson cultural anthropology has contributed to human understanding: cultural relativity, the ability to evaluate a culture in terms of its own

values rather than those of another culture. Throughout the book, we contrast this ideal with its opposite, ethnocentrism.

2. *Holism.* Despite its traditional fragmentation into four subfields customarily treated in separate courses, anthropology remains a holistic discipline, and "American anthropologists . . . credit the quality of their insights, research and teaching in one field to past and present influences of the remaining three. Trained in one subdiscipline, they still are affected by other parts of the whole. The persistent power of holism continues today as American anthropology's essential and coveted reality" (Givens and Skomal 1992:1).

   The same concept is also used by anthropologists to convey the idea that the various aspects of any culture are closely interrelated, even as the different but interconnected parts of a car's engine work together to keep the car running smoothly. Anthropologists study cultures holistically because the synchronic interconnections between the different aspects of a given culture help to impart meaning to it. We continue this tradition here.

3. *Women and Anthropology.* A major theme of *Cultural Anthropology* is that lifeways, the beliefs that encapsulate them, and the institutions by which they are brought into action belong not to one gender but to both. Until recently, even though much anthropological fieldwork was carried out by women, most published work in anthropology was dominated by the presumption that culture was male culture and society was male society. This unrealistic (not to say outmoded) stance is currently in the process of being replaced by one that emphasizes the complementary influences of males and females in fashioning the communal worlds in which they live. While not wholly uncritical of contemporary feminist research, we draw upon it frequently in our attempt to fashion a coherent, balanced account of the contributions of women to the cultures they have helped create.

4. *The Value of Applied Anthropology.* In the 1980s, the proportion of anthropology graduates who applied their training outside of academia increased to such an extent that these anthropologists now outnumber their academic colleagues. However, applied anthropology continues to take a back seat to academic anthropology in the majority of textbooks. In contrast, *Cultural Anthropology* emphasizes this newly recognized and growing subdiscipline and gives it special attention in three chapters (Chapters 1, 9, and 16).

THEORETICAL APPROACH

Cultural Anthropology has no theoretical axe to grind; we treat the most influential perspectives and approaches used in our discipline with an even hand. Still, as teachers of anthropology we have found that we can best express our holistic view of culture through two approaches, the structural-functionalist and the cultural materialist. Since holism is a lesson we regard as fundamental to understanding cultures, and therefore an essential one for our readers to grasp, we emphasize these two approaches rather more than, say, the psychological or structuralist approaches. This is perhaps especially true for Chapters 5 and 9, which provide cultural-materialist treatments of subsistence strategies and economics, and Chapters 7 and 12, which provide structural-functionalist interpretations of marriage and religion.

SPECIAL FEATURES

Unique Coverage

While generally following the now-standard format and range of topics found in other major introductory anthropology textbooks, *Cultural Anthropology* offers additional materials not available in any introductory text with which we are familiar.

◆ *Unique chapters on sexuality and the human body.* We devote an entire chapter (Chapter 8) to a cross-cultural look at social constructions of sex, gender, and sexuality, and another (Chapter 15) to considering how people in different cultures reconstruct the human body to reflect their own cultural images.

◆ *"The Anthropologist at Work" boxes.* Over the past twenty-five years our students have told us that they are perhaps more interested in learning about how anthropologists gather their information than in any other topic discussed in introductory anthropology. So in addition to devoting a full chapter (Chapter 2) to a discussion of fieldwork and the professional and personal lives of anthropologists, we have created boxes entitled "The Anthropologist at Work" in most chapters. Each of these focuses on a practicing anthropologist and her or his work, or else suggests a way students might apply an undergraduate education in anthropology toward a specific career path.

◆ *"Ask Yourself" boxes.* We believe a good textbook

should provide intellectual challenge, actively encouraging its readers to think for themselves. To promote independent thinking, we have placed inserts, entitled "Ask Yourself," throughout each chapter. These boxes ask readers to formulate their own personal answers to questions—many of them of an ethical nature—related to the text. We hope they will also stimulate discussion in class.

Student Accessibility

Unfamiliar material, especially when combined with technical jargon, can intimidate newcomers to anthropology. We have taken pains to ensure that our special features and style of writing will make this book accessible to undergraduate students.

- ◆ *Chapter-opening vignettes.* Each chapter of *Cultural Anthropology* opens with a brief vignette, selected from Western culture, calculated to evoke immediate interest and recognition in student readers. Many of these vignettes are drawn from the popular press. The chapter on marriage, for instance, begins with a back-page news story about a brother-sister marriage in Massachusetts, and discusses this episode in the context of familiar Western marriage customs before going on to consider the different forms of marriage encountered cross-culturally.
- ◆ *Student-oriented writing.* We have taken to heart our students' preferences for brevity, informality, and even humor. Each chapter is short enough to be read comfortably at a single sitting; our writing style is nonpedantic; and here and there, we hope, the material will bring a smile to our readers' faces.
- ◆ *Personality profiles.* We have also learned that students relate much more directly and meaningfully to the experiences of individuals (particularly other young adults) than to analytical abstractions. Accordingly, our focus is consistently on people, their behavior, their ideas, and their feelings. To underscore this focus, we include fictionalized profiles of three contemporary, non-Western people, each of whom reflects a particular culture, socioeconomic setting, and world view.

Cultural Anthropology is the result of our combined teaching experience of over forty years. Our hope is that students who read it will become considerably better informed about the contemporary world and the place of a wide range of cultures, theirs and others, within "the world system."

ACCOMPANYING SUPPLEMENTS

We have written our own *Instructor's Manual and Test Bank* to aid instructors in the classroom use of *Cultural Anthropology*. Each chapter of this manual includes suggested additional lecture topics with substantial discussion; a suggested class activity; recommended reference materials; full citations for related audiovisual materials, including source information; essay-type exam questions; and a test bank of multiple-choice questions.

To assist students in their review and comprehension of the text material, a *Student Study Guide* has also been developed by Peter Aschoff at the University of Mississippi. Each chapter of the study guide contains a chapter outline, chapter learning objectives, key points for review, identification exercises, a practice test of multiple-choice questions (including an answer key), and three practice essay questions which require the student to synthesize the chapter material.

A NOTE TO SPECIALISTS

Cultural anthropology poses special challenges to scholars seeking to synthesize its theories, hypotheses, and philosophical approaches. On the one hand, we see our discipline as holistic. On the other, we acknowledge that its elements may not only be disparate but controversial or even contradictory as well.

One problem is definitions. Anthropologists are notorious for disagreeing, and nowhere is this more obvious than in their attempts to define terms such as "marriage" or "religion." The more general a definition, the more specific instances it can accommodate; the more precise the definition, the fewer. Broad or narrow: which to choose?

Another problem is empirical generalizations. Anthropologists have been conditioned by experience to avoid these, yet in interpreting features of social life we find it impractical to do so. Topical and geographic specializations are essential, but paradoxically they must be transcended if our discipline is to progress, for without cross-cultural generalization cultural anthropology would have no academic justification. So we generalize, but our generalizations almost invariably result in some distortion.

We ask colleagues who may be concerned—and rightly so—about the distortions that our particular definitions or generalizations may have introduced into *Cul-*

tural Anthropology to help us find our way through the semantic or conceptual minefields we have no doubt wandered into by interpreting our material for their students in their own way.

◆◆◆

ACKNOWLEDGMENTS

We owe a great debt of thanks to the following colleagues, friends, and family members, whose generous support and in many instances painstaking labor have helped us immeasurably.

For editorial help we enthusiastically thank Alan McClare, Kirsten Olson, Carol Einhorn, and David Nickol, all at HarperCollins.

For thoughtful criticism of the manuscript we are grateful for the help of Leo Wiegman, formerly of Dorsey Press; the late John Sturman; as well as Peter Aschoff, University of Mississippi; Stephen Childs, Valdosta State College; John Coggeshall, Clemson University; Vernon Dorjahn, University of Oregon; Charles Ellenbaum, College of DuPage; John Fritz, Salt Lake Community College; James Garber, Southwest Texas State University; K. Godel Gengenbach, Arapahoe Community College; David Glassman, Southwest Texas State University; Priscilla Jackson-Evans, Longview Community College; Linda Kaljee, University of Maryland; Ester Maring, Southern Illinois University; Mac Marshall, University of Iowa; Susan Meswick, St. Johns University; Barry Mitchie, Kansas State University; John Mock, Rose-Hulman Institute of Technology; Richard Moore, Ohio State University; Michael Olien, University of Georgia; Zenon Phorecky, University of Saskatchewan; and Richard Scaglion, University of Pittsburgh.

More often than not, we incorporated the suggestions of these reviewers, whose opinions and criticisms we valued highly, into the final version of *Cultural Anthropology*. Lack of space and our inability to reconcile the diversity of reviewers' opinions made it impossible to include every suggested change or addition, but this does not at all lessen our appreciation of each reviewer's efforts.

For specialist advice we are grateful to our colleagues Najwa Adra, W. Arens, Michael Clatts, Shirley Fiske, Nancie Gonzalez, Roger McConochie, Lorna McDougall, Maria Messina, Dolores Newton, Loretta Orion, John Shea, Elizabeth Stone, Dan Varisco, Zhusheng Wang, and Patricia Wright.

For photographic help we appreciate the invaluable assistance of Rosemary Hunter at Scott, Foresman, and our talented spouses.

For constant and stimulating feedback we affectionately salute our undergraduate students at SUNY/Stony Brook since 1968.

For personal support we acknowledge, with love and gratitude, our spouses and children: Maxine, Tom, Cathy, Ellen, Emma, Lizzie, Meg, Nik, Paul, and Thad.

David Hicks

Margaret A. Gwynne

ABOUT THE AUTHORS

David Hicks studied anthropology at the University of Oxford, where he earned his Ph.D after carrying out nineteen months of field research on the island of Timor, in eastern Indonesia. He has taught at the State University of New York at Stony Brook since 1968, and he has returned to Indonesia for further research on several occasions. He has received research awards from the National Science Foundation, the Wenner-Gren Foundation for Anthropological Research, and the American Philosophical Foundation. He has also served as a consultant for the World Bank.

Margaret A. Gwynne received her Ph.D. in Anthropology from the State University of New York at Stony Brook. She has taught anthropology at the State University of New York at Stony Brook and Dowling College, and as a specialist in international health and development has worked as a consultant, mainly in Eastern Caribbean countries, on projects sponsored by the World Health Organization, the United States Agency for International Development, private foundations, and consulting firms. She is the recipient of two teaching awards from the State University of New York at Stony Brook and of research grants from the State University of New York at Stony Brook and the Pew Charitable Trusts.

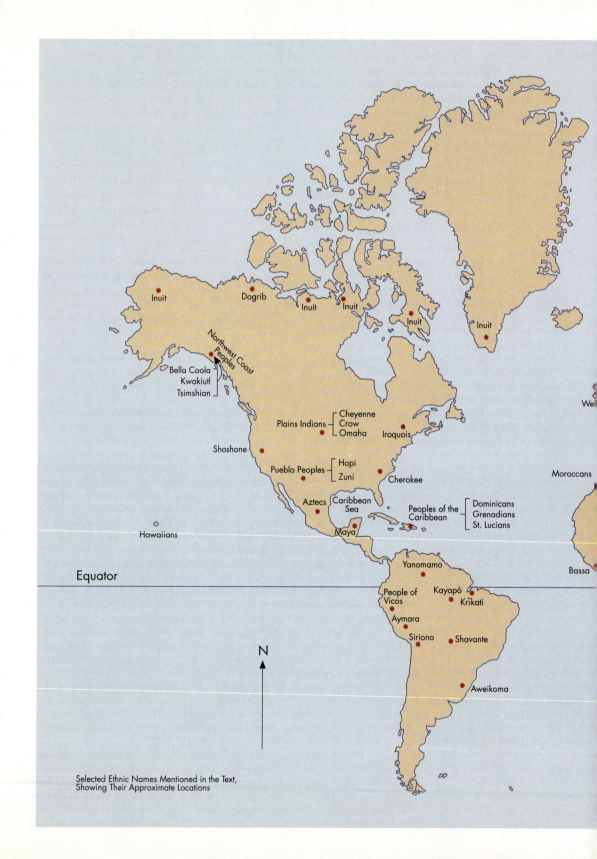

Inuit

Dogrib

Inuit

Inuit

Inuit

Inuit

Northwest Coast Peoples

Bella Coola
Kwakiutl
Tsimshian

Plains Indians { Cheyenne
Crow
Omaha

Iroquois

Shoshone

Pueblo Peoples { Hopi
Zuni

Cherokee

Moroccans

Aztecs

Caribbean Sea

Peoples of the Caribbean { Dominicans
Grenadians
St. Lucians

Wel

Hawaiians

Maya

Equator

Yanomamo

Bassa

People of Vicos

Kayapó

Krikati

Aymara

Siriono

Shavante

N

Aweikoma

Selected Ethnic Names Mentioned in the Text,
Showing Their Approximate Locations

Lapps

Northern Tungus

Chukchee

Chinese

Ukrainians
Croatians
Sarakatsani

Koreans
Japanese

Israelis

Qashgai

Villagers of
Golpalpur

Jingpo

Taiwanese

Bedouin

Yemeni

Nayar

Nuer

...ako
Azande
Konso

Sri Lankans
Minangkabau

Tasaday

Maloh
Iban

Peoples of
New Guinea

Dani
Etoro
Kwoma
Sambia

ng
Mbuti

Maasai
Gogo

Javanese
Tetum

Alorese

Trobrianders

Tikopians

Ndembu

Peoples of
Ranomafana
Park

Betsileo
Tanala

Yolngu

!Kung San
Tswana
Zulu
Xhosa

Maori

CHAPTER 1

Anthropology is the study of people and all the things they do, think, say, and make. The behavior, ideas, language, and appearance of these little girls, enjoying ice cream in a village in central Iran, would all be of interest to an anthropologist.

INTRODUCTION

College student, standing in doorway of anthropology professor's office: "I found this really weird-looking rock on the beach, and I was wondering if you could identify it for me."

Medical technician, making small talk while taking patient's pulse: "I see on your personal history form that you're an anthropologist. Doesn't that have something to do with old bones?"

Small nephew, climbing into aunt's lap: "Mom told me you're an anth-ro-pol-o-gist, so I wanna show you my model dinosaurs."

Irate father to college student daughter: "Your mother and I spend all this money on your education, and now you want to major in *anthropology?* Why don't you study something that will help you find a job!"

As the old saying goes, if we had a nickel for every time we heard a comment reflecting some misconception about anthropology, we'd be rich. The confusion stems from the fact that there are several different kinds of anthropologists, and they study many different things. Some are interested in rocks and bones (if not dinosaurs), but only insofar as these can reveal something about people. The word *people* is the key to understanding what anthropology is about: it is the study of people, from the time of their emergence on this earth up to the present day, and of anything and everything that sheds light on their existence and behavior.

Almost every anthropologist is a specialist in some particular aspect of the study of people. On a given day, one anthropologist may be asking a resident of the Amazon jungle how she and her neighbors determine the boundaries of their banana gardens, another anthropologist may be sitting in a university laboratory peering through a microscope at a sample of human blood, and a third may be interviewing the patrons of a run-down urban bar. Yet another may be admiring an ancient stone arrowhead just dug out of the ground, and still another may be sitting cross-legged in a tent, entering into a portable computer the different terms by which the inhabitants of a Pacific island refer to their cousins. A sixth may be delivering a lecture to college students on the evolutionary ideas of Charles Darwin, and a seventh, binoculars and notebook in hand, may be stalking a group of wild chimpanzees through the forests of Zaire.

Different jobs, but all anthropologists. What do they have in common? *Each of them—in his or her own way—is engaged, directly or indirectly, in the study of people.*

While all anthropologists study people, each anthropologist has his or her own specific interests. In Brazil, an Apinayé woman demonstrates a traditional knitting technique, unique to the New World, to anthropologist Dolores Newton.

●●●

Theories and Hypotheses

The accumulated knowledge of a science is contained in its body of **theories** and **hypotheses.** The scientific meaning of the term *theory* is rather different from its meaning in common usage. If you're halfway through a murder mystery and you remark, "I have a theory that the butler did it," you're using the word to mean an educated guess, or what we might call a "hunch." In science, however, a theory is a statement about some phenomenon (such as an event or thing or the relationship between two or more events or things) that has been examined repeatedly and is widely accepted as true. Einstein's theory of relativity is a classic example.

A *hypothesis* comes much closer to a hunch. It's a reasonable statement about a phenomenon or the relationship between phenomena that is based on, and does not contradict, already-established theory. Scientists formulate hypotheses and then test them to determine whether or not they hold true. If the validity of a hypothesis is proven, the predictive value of the theory from which the hypothesis was drawn is increased, and our confidence in the theory similarly increases. If testing shows that a hypothesis doesn't hold water, either the theory requires rethinking or the testing was carried out improperly.

●●●

THE DISCIPLINE OF ANTHROPOLOGY

Natural or Social Science?

Science may be broadly defined as the attempt to discover the laws of nature by formulating and testing ideas called hypotheses, systematically collecting and analyzing data, and attempting to establish theories. Or science may be much more narrowly defined in terms of its specific objects of inquiry, such as the stars and planets, the chemical elements of which matter is composed, bacteria and viruses—or people. By either definition, anthropology can be considered a science.

Another way to define science is in terms of the procedures used to pursue scientific knowledge. In every scientific endeavor, information is collected, examined, analyzed, and classified in a systematic and—as far as possible—objective manner. Most anthropologists view their work in these terms. However, they distinguish between two different kinds of science: **social science** and **physical (natural) science.**

One distinction between the two lies in the relationship of the scientist to the subject under study. In physics, chemistry, or other natural sciences, the subjects of study are things or events, and the researcher and the phenomena under observation are clearly separated (Holy 1984:14). In psychology, sociology, or other social sciences, the subjects of study are human beings,

and often no such separation exists or it is blurred. Either way, the social scientist may affect the object of research and may in turn be affected by it. The greater subjectivity of social science is what most sharply divides it from physical science.

Another distinction between the social and physical sciences is that theories in the former are often less rigorous than in the latter. Some social scientific theories are more like viewpoints needed for interpreting data (see Chapter 2).

Anthropology is at once a physical and a social science, depending on the specific focus of study. When

●●

theory a statement about some observable, testable phenomenon that has been examined repeatedly and is widely accepted as true

hypothesis a reasonable statement about some phenomenon or the relationship among phenomena that is based on, and does not contradict, theory

science the attempt to discover the laws of nature

social science the more subjective kind of science in which the researcher and the phenomena being observed may not be distinctly separated

physical (natural) science the more objective kind of science in which the researcher and the phenomena being observed are more clearly separated than is usual in the social sciences

anthropologists study bones or stones, they can perhaps be more objective than when they study living people, and their work most closely resembles physical science. (Remember, though, that even "objective" interpretation is based on presuppositions that provide a particular frame of reference. Without this frame of reference we can observe nothing, yet with it we are condemned to some degree of subjective bias.)

When anthropologists analyze living people, the way they interpret the data reflects their subjective evaluation of the relative importance of various people and events, and their work is termed *social science.* Indeed, the subjective nature of some anthropological research and interpretation allies it more closely with the humanities, such as history, literature, and philosophy, than with the sciences. In some cases, the patterns that emerge from a body of data may be so unique to the anthropologist who collected and is studying the data that the portrait he or she finally draws of the people under study resembles a realistic novel or an historical narrative more than a scientific treatise. Subjective interpretation, however, can contribute a different and important dimension to the study of people.

The Branches of Anthropology

An academic discipline as broadly defined as "the study of people and whatever sheds light on their exis-

tence and behavior" obviously covers a lot of territory. No single individual can be an expert in every aspect of such a broad discipline, so anthropology is usually divided into four major fields. These are **cultural anthropology, anthropological linguistics, archaeology,** and **physical (biological) anthropology** (Figure 1.1). Much of the research that cultural anthropologists and anthropological linguists do is thought of as social science (often with a dash of humanistic flavoring, depending on the researcher), whereas much of what archaeologists and most of what physical anthropologists do is considered to be physical science.

In addition to their common focus on people, the four fields of anthropology share a major philosophical perspective. They are all comparative (rather than dedicated to the study of any one group of people) and comprehensive (in that they exclude no group). Yet even though the four fields sometimes overlap, the specific subjects they address are quite different. Most anthropologists consider themselves to be specialists in only one field of anthropology.

Cultural Anthropology. Cultural anthropology is the study of **culture,** which can be defined as everything that people collectively do, think, make, and say (see Chapter 3). More specifically, cultural anthropology focuses on the culture of contemporary people—those living today—and "historic" people—people of the rela-

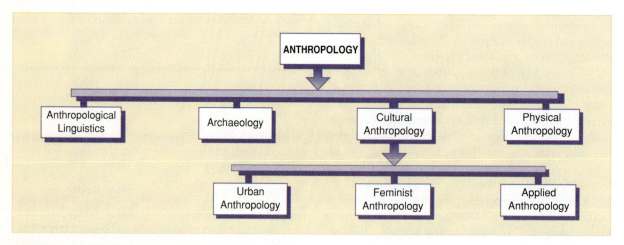

Figure 1.1
Fields and Subfields of Anthropology. We usually divide anthropology into four major fields, each of which focuses on a different subject. This book is about cultural anthropology, a field that embraces a number of subfields, such as urban anthropology, feminist anthropology, and applied cultural anthropology.

A society's members live in the same place and interact with one another, but they may or may not be similar in other ways. North American society incorporates people from many different cultural backgrounds. Chinese society is much more uniform.

tively recent past, about whom written information exists. (The study of the culture of people who lived in the past, as reflected in their material remains, is archaeology.)

Another focus of cultural anthropology is something called **society,** but this term has been defined in so many different ways that even anthropologists don't agree about its meaning. For our purposes, a very simple definition will do. A society is a group of people whose members live in the same place and whose lives and livelihoods are interdependent. This is not to say that the members of a society must be alike. They may come from one or more traditions, their skin color may be the same or different, and they may speak the same or different languages. Thus we may refer to "North American society," which incorporates many different traditions, shades of pigmentation, and languages, just as we speak of "Trobriand society," referring to people who live on several tiny islands in the Pacific and share a single tradition, skin color, and language.

In England, where anthropologists traditionally preferred to focus on societies and the relationships among people within them rather than on culture, one

cultural anthropology the anthropological study of contemporary and historic people

anthropological linguistics (linguistic anthropology) the field of anthropology that focuses on languages

archaeology the field of anthropology that focuses on the material remains of people of the past

physical (biological) anthropology the field of anthropology that focuses on the biological aspects of being human

culture everything that people collectively do, think, make, and say

society a group of people whose members live in the same place and whose lives and livelihoods are interdependent

◆ ASK YOURSELF

As a member of a particular society, what makes you similar to other members of this society? Do you see yourself as different in some ways? If so, what ways? Is it possible for a person to be a member of more than one society at the same time?

often hears the term **social anthropology.** It was given prominence by A. R. Radcliffe-Brown (1881–1955), who advocated the analysis of **social structure,** the web of relationships that binds members of a society together. Since social anthropology and cultural anthropology overlap considerably, you may also encounter the term **sociocultural anthropology.** In this book we avoid this cumbersome term; our use of *cultural anthropology* is sufficiently flexible to include the British concept of society.

Alternatively, cultural anthropology is sometimes called **ethnology** because of its focus on **ethnicity**—the identification of individuals with particular groups called **ethnic groups.** These are groups whose members share basic cultural traditions and values and a common language and who identify themselves (and are identified by others) as distinct from other groups. All of us belong to one or more of these groups.

Central to cultural anthropology, and deriving from the concept of ethnicity, is the notion of **ethnocentrism,** the misguided belief that one's own ethnic group (or more broadly, one's own society or culture) is superior to all others. This concept has an opposite, **cultural relativity**—perhaps the most important concept in this book and central to modern cultural anthropology. This is the idea that a culture must be evaluated in terms of its own values, not according to the values of another culture.

Sometimes the concept of cultural relativity has been interpreted narrowly, implying that anthropologists must suspend all of their own moral and cultural values when studying the cultures of others. We don't like this narrow interpretation since it amounts to saying that people are justified in engaging in any practice, however reprehensible, simply because it is "part of their culture" (Maybury-Lewis 1988:378). In the broader sense in which we see it, *cultural relativity* means that anthropologists should temporarily suspend judgment of other peoples' customs and practices until those customs and practices have been understood in their own cultural

terms (378–379). Under this definition, the Holocaust could never be justified because it was part of Nazi culture, nor the racism practiced in South Africa because it was part of South African culture.

Although some of our colleagues may draw fine distinctions among the terms *cultural anthropology, sociocultural anthropology,* and *ethnology,* we use them interchangeably. Their practitioners—cultural anthropologists, sociocultural anthropologists, or ethnologists—are all interested in much the same kinds of questions about people. Why do different people behave so differently? Why does one group of people insist on political equality, whereas another prevents it? Why does one worship many gods, whereas another worships a single diety? Why does one prohibit premarital sex, whereas another encourages it? Why does one applaud obesity, whereas another deplores it? Are any of the things people do and believe universal? Does kissing occur everywhere, are babies rocked to put them to sleep all over the world, and do members of every human group eat three meals a day? Is there such a thing as "average" human behavior? Is there any kind of behavior that occurs only among members of one ethnic group and no other?

Traditionally, cultural anthropology has focused on societies that are small-scale and **nonliterate**—lacking a tradition of reading and writing. (The term *nonliterate* distinguishes such people from **illiterate** people, who do not read or write either but who live in societies in which others are literate.) Nonliterate societies used to be called *primitive* societies, but because Westerners are inclined to equate that word with "inferior," most anthropologists today prefer either *nonliterate* or *small-scale* when referring to such societies. Nonliterate societies are in no way inferior to others, nor should they be equated with prehistoric societies (as scholars of the Victorian period believed). Their technology may be simpler than that of contemporary industrialized societies, but in other ways—their kinship systems, for example—they may be considerably more complicated.

A second traditional focus of cultural anthropol-

◆ ASK YOURSELF

Do you identify yourself as a member of a particular ethnic group? Have you ever had the rewarding experience of questioning older relatives about your ethnic background? If so, whose ethnic identity is stronger, yours or your older relatives'?

Small-scale, nonliterate societies are characterized by simple technologies. On the island of Flores in eastern Indonesia, a Manggarai man, wearing a hat made from half a coconut shell, sets a rat trap.

ogy has been **peasant** societies (see Chapter 5). These societies are more difficult to categorize than nonliterate societies, for the term *peasant* can be defined in many ways. Much of the reason for this is that peasants are typically found within the geographical and ideological contexts of larger and more technologically complex societies, whose traditions they share. Still, to generalize, peasants are people whose principal unit of economic production is the household and whose subsistence technologies are usually simpler than the ones used in industrialized societies. Once largely illiterate, peasant societies today are increasingly apt to include formally educated members.

Today, cultural anthropology includes a number of subfields, which may overlap. Three important ones are urban anthropology, feminist anthropology, and applied cultural anthropology.

Urban Anthropology. Since the late nineteenth century, when anthropology started to become an academic discipline, the number of small-scale, nonliterate societies around the world has decreased rapidly, and peasant societies have become increasingly Westernized. At the same time, cultural anthropologists discovered that their theories and research methods were as useful for studying human behavior in literate, urban societies as in nonliterate and peasant societies (see Gmelch and Zenner 1980). Thus an additional focus of cultural anthropology, **urban anthropology**—the anthropological study of urban dwellers—was born (see Chapter 5).

Feminist Anthropology. By the 1970s, it was becoming increasingly clear within anthropology that the discipline had not previously incorporated women equally with men, either as practitioners or as a focus of

social anthropology especially in England, the brand of anthropology focusing on societies rather than on culture

social structure the web of relationships binding members of a society together

sociocultural anthropology a term for cultural anthropology that emphasizes society

ethnology an alternative term for cultural anthropology

ethnicity the identification of individuals with particular ethnic groups

ethnic group a group whose members share basic cultural traditions and values and a common language and who identify themselves (and are identified by others) as distinct from other such groups

ethnocentrism the belief that one's own society or culture is superior to all others

cultural relativity a central idea in modern cultural anthropology—that a culture must be evaluated in terms of its own values, not according to the values of another culture

nonliterate lacking a tradition of reading and writing

illiterate lacking the ability to read and write while living in a literate society

peasants typically agricultural people who share the same general cultural tradition as members of the larger and more technologically complex societies in which they live

urban anthropology the anthropological study of urban dwellers

Since the 1970s, the attention of anthropologists—many of them female—has focused increasingly on women. On the island of St. Lucia in the West Indies, female farmers gather in town on market day to sell their produce.

research. Part of the reason for this was that most early anthropologists were men, mainly because of a general lack of equal educational opportunities for women. Much anthropological research thus had a male bias, and women's contributions to culture were inadequately documented.

To rectify this bias, cultural anthropologists in the 1970s and beyond, many of them women, focused their research on women and the part they play in culture and society. Eventually, an Association for Feminist Anthropology was established within the American Anthropological Association. Today, feminist anthropology is a major area of research for both female and male cultural anthropologists (Mukhopadhyay and Higgins 1988) who "seek to understand and dismantle gender hierarchies in

their intellectual as well as personal worlds" (Wolf 1992:1). Throughout this book, you'll find numerous examples drawn from feminist anthropology.

Applied Cultural Anthropology. In the past, many anthropology majors either did not make direct use of their anthropological training or eventually became teachers of anthropology. Today, however, teaching is only one of many opportunities for anthropologists to apply their expertise professionally, a fact that might relieve the dismayed parent upon whom we eavesdropped at the beginning of this chapter. To give only a few examples, an increasing number of women and men with undergraduate majors or advanced degrees in anthropology are working outside the academic community as health care professionals, law enforcement agents, ministers and rabbis, businesspeople, environmental conservationists, and journalists. Applying anthropological ideas and methods to achieve practical ends is termed **applied anthropology.**

It's a subfield that is growing rapidly. As recently as 1972, only an estimated 2 percent of anthropologists worked outside of academics. The remainder were teachers (Dunkel 1992:10). Today, over half of all graduates holding B.A., M.A., or Ph.D. degrees in anthropology work outside of academics, many as applied anthropologists, and the range of jobs from which they can choose is immense. Some work 40 hours a week as employees of businesses, government agencies, or nonprofit groups. Some serve as independent consultants to such organizations. Some have established and work for their own consulting firms. Some work for the media. Some apply their anthropological skills and insights to **development anthropology** (see Chapter 16), working with professionals in other countries, in areas such as health care, education, or agriculture, to improve the well-being of people in what is often called the Third World. The potential list of nonacademic anthropological occupations would seem to be limited only by anthropologists' imaginations.

In most of the chapters of this book, you'll find sections entitled "The Anthropologist at Work" containing examples of how the *discipline* of anthropology—the pursuit of anthropological knowledge—is translated into the *profession* of applied anthropology. These sections contain short profiles of applied anthropologists and the work they have accomplished. Together, they will give you some idea of the inexhaustible range of job opportunities for anthropologists outside of academia.

THE ANTHROPOLOGIST AT WORK

As a graduate student in anthropology at the University of Michigan, cultural anthropologist Roger P. McConochie carried out three years of predoctoral fieldwork among German-speaking peasants in the Italian Alps. Even before finishing his dissertation, however, he had decided to apply his specialized knowledge not in academics but in the hectic world of business. Founding his own consulting firm, Corporate Research International, he set up shop as a business consultant and began publishing *Global Business: The Newsletter of Corporate Anthropology*.

Right from the start, McConochie realized that his solid grounding in the academic discipline of anthropology had provided him with the skills and credentials needed for business. As he puts it, "In my work, I use all my training in each of the traditional four subfields of anthropology, but rather than pursuing knowledge for its own sake my focus is pragmatic and applied. On a daily basis, I'm having measurable effects on the lives of real people" (McConochie 1992).

McConochie carved out a career for himself by "combining two things I loved." One was anthropology; the second was aviation. This combination led him to specialize in the area of cross-cultural factors in aviation safety. His distinctively anthropological talent for bridging cultures then led him into the field of intercultural training. "Tomorrow," he remarks, "it will be something else" (McConochie 1992). He acknowledges that want ads specifically seeking "corporate anthropologists" are few, but he thinks opportunities are "uncountable"—limited only by anthropologists' ability to translate their insights into products, processes, and services with direct and immediate effect on people's lives and work.

Perhaps some of you who read this book will decide to major in anthropology. Based on his own successful experience, McConochie's advice to you is "don't wait." Get some immediate, practical experience, paid or volunteer, so that you can move as quickly as possible beyond the status of "student" and into the status of "professional anthropologist." Then, continue to pick up skills from other areas. Cultivate your uniqueness, he further suggests. And, because it worked for him, "Find novel ways of combining two things you love." If you thrive on challenge, novelty, and unpredictability, you may be able to follow in the footsteps of this internationally recognized pioneer by carving out your own niche as a practicing anthropologist.

You'll discover that, far from being an ivory-tower discipline focusing exclusively on the obscure or the exotic, cultural anthropology has everything to do with our own world.

Anthropological Linguistics. Anthropological linguistics (sometimes called linguistic anthropology) is the study of languages, ancient and modern, written and unwritten, from the anthropological point of view. Among the many interests of anthropological linguists are how certain sounds combine to make up a language, how ancient languages developed and changed through time, and how language and culture interact. We devote an entire chapter of this book to the work of anthropological linguists (Chapter 13).

Archaeology. Archaeology is the anthropology of people who lived in the past, as reflected in their material remains.[1] The goal of archaeologists is fundamentally the same as that of other anthropologists: to understand people. But the specific ways in which archaeologists pursue the answers to questions about people are different from the methods other kinds of anthropolo-

applied anthropology the use of anthropological ideas and methods to achieve practical ends outside of the academic community

development anthropology anthropological work intended to improve the well-being of people in developing countries

---

[1]Some of our colleagues would define *archaeology* as the study of the material products of all people, whether past or present.

gists use. Archaeologists concentrate on **artifacts**—material things, from tools and pottery to garbage to huge walled cities—that people of the past made and then discarded or left behind when they died or moved. Since these artifacts are apt to be buried under layers of dirt by the passage of time, the primary research method of archaeologists usually involves digging.

Archaeology may be either prehistoric or historic, depending on whether or not the people under study kept written records, ranging from information carved on

◆ ASK YOURSELF

Have you ever taken the time to record in a diary a description of your home, the names and ages and occupations of your relatives, the foods you eat, the kinds of transportation you most often use, or other such ordinary details of your life? Why or why not?

tombstones to historical accounts by great writers. You may think that when studying historic societies there would be no reason for practicing archaeology. Yet information that is well known to members of a society is often so familiar that it is taken for granted, so the written records left by societies of the past never provide a complete picture of ancient life. And in the case of non-literate cultures, if it were not for the efforts of prehistoric archaeologists there would be no record at all of our roots in those cultures.

Physical Anthropology.   Physical anthropology focuses more specifically than the other major fields of anthropology on the biological aspects of being human (which is why it is sometimes called biological anthropology). All living things are members of a specific category of living creatures with a specific scientific name—in the case of human beings, *Homo sapiens sapiens*. What defines the members of this category? Where did we come from and when, and what evolutionary

Archaeologists are anthropologists who study the material things left by people of the past. In Iraq, archaeologist Elizabeth Stone excavates the site of Mashkan-Shapir, an ancient city that had been forgotten for nearly four thousand years.

changes occurred along the way that resulted in what we are today? Why are our heads, bodies, and limbs shaped as they are? What accounts for our intelligence, size, upright posture, and manual dexterity? In what ways are we different from one another, and why? What characteristics do we share with nonhuman creatures? How have we adapted physically to the many different environments in which we live?

This book does not treat either archaeology or physical anthropology, topics that have an important bearing on our subject but which are almost always studied in courses exclusively devoted to them. However, given the overlap among the four fields of anthropology, you may discover, if you have previously taken courses in archaeology or physical anthropology, that some of the ideas in this book are already familiar to you.

Anthropology's broad-based approach to the study of people gives it a range and depth of interest and understanding unique among academic disciplines. A major assumption of anthropology is that its different perspectives and fields cannot be separated from one another if we are to try to understand fully what it means to be human. Because it combines two different ways of looking at people, the biological and the cultural, anthropology is sometimes described as a *biocultural* discipline. Likewise, because it is concerned with all aspects of human activity—past and present, physical and cultural—anthropology is sometimes described as *holistic*, meaning "all-encompassing." So even though different kinds of anthropology are usually taught in separate courses, "American anthropologists . . . credit the quality of their insights, research and teaching in one field to past and present influences of the remaining three. Trained in one subdiscipline, they still are affected by other parts of the whole. The persistent power of holism continues today as American anthropology's essential and coveted reality" (Givens and Skomal 1992:1).

••

PIONEERS

The First Anthropologists

Anthropology as a formal academic discipline is only a little over a hundred years old, but from the beginning of recorded history (and probably before that as well) people have been observing their neighbors and obtaining information on them. Much of this informa-

tion was collected to serve the ends of warfare, trade, conquest, or missionary work, but some of it—more and more as time went on—was gathered to further people's understanding of themselves. Human beings are endlessly curious, and much of our curiosity is focused on ourselves.

No one knows who the first anthropologist was, but the honor is usually given to the Greek historian Herodotus (ca. 485–425 B.C.). In the fifth century B.C., Herodotus traveled widely, living among and learning firsthand about the cultures of others and comparing people's natural environments, physical appearances, laws, politics, religions, and languages. Since his purpose was to provide his own government with information to guide its interaction with foreign countries, we might view him not only as the first anthropologist but also as the father of applied anthropology. He earned another, more dubious distinction as well. Because he dismissed all non-Greeks as barbarians, Herodotus may have been the first anthropologist to be guilty of ethnocentrism.

After Herodotus but still before the time of Christ, Romans traveled to Gaul (now France); seventh-century Arabians journeyed northeastward to Persia and northwestward to France; eleventh-century Norsemen traveled westward to America; and Genghis Khan and Marco Polo traveled west and east, respectively, in the twelfth and thirteenth centuries. In the fifteenth and sixteenth centuries, an Age of Exploration began, as western Europeans fanned out around the globe, coming into contact with other human beings who up until then simply hadn't existed for Westerners, even in their imaginations.

By the eighteenth and early nineteenth centuries, numerous systematic attempts had been made to explain the origins and organization of human societies, the extraordinary variety of people's customs, and how societies changed through time. If these attempts can collectively be considered the childhood of anthropology, the nineteenth century witnessed the discipline's rapid adolescent growth. As the colonial empires of Great Britain, France, the Netherlands, and Germany expanded all over Africa, the East Indies, South America, and Asia, so did data accumulate on foreign cultures. This information was gathered by administrators, merchants, missionaries, and soldiers, who rapidly expanded the West's knowledge of nonliterate people.

•••

artifact *any material thing created by people*

One reason for the explosion of interest in and information about other people and other ways of life was that such information had some very direct, practical applications. Western European governments hungered for information collected by travellers to foreign places, in part because it could be used in the colonization of foreign lands and in the exploitation of their people. Similarly, in the United States, the government established the Bureau of American Ethnology (BAE) in 1872 to study native Americans,[2] whose activities the government wished to control and whose welfare it felt it had the right to oversee. One famous study carried out with the support of the BAE was James Mooney's 1895 investigation of the Ghost Dance ritual of the native Americans of the Great Plains. The U.S. government feared that this religious ritual might herald a military uprising, and Mooney's mission was to advise the Department of War how to respond to it. We cannot duck the fact that some of anthropology's roots lie in Western efforts to exploit, contain, or control other societies.

The quest for genuine understanding of what it means to be human also motivated anthropology in the late nineteenth and early twentieth centuries. Among the greatest contributors to the development of the new academic discipline in America were three men[3] whose curiosity, perseverance, and insight are still admired in our discipline.

Frank Hamilton Cushing (1857–1900)

Although the nineteenth-century American ethnologist Frank Hamilton Cushing was untrained in anthropology, which was not yet being taught in colleges and universities in the United States as a formal course of study, his contribution to our discipline was enormous.

As a young man, Cushing was appointed to a U.S. government post in the BAE and settled down to what he anticipated would be a desk job. But four years later, the Smithsonian Institution underwrote an expedition to the American Southwest to collect native American artifacts, and Cushing was sent along as the expedition's official ethnologist. His instructions were generous: he could choose for himself where to collect his anthropological data, and he could use his own methods. All he had to do was "get the information," which could probably be done, said his boss, in three months (Grönewald 1972:38).

Five years later, Cushing still hadn't returned to his desk in Washington. The region of the Southwest to which he had been sent included the lands of the Pueblo people, and Cushing's insatiable curiosity about the culture of the Zuni, the very first Pueblo group he met, prompted him to devote the next several years of his life to anthropological research (Cushing 1990).

Arriving in Zuni territory, the Smithsonian expedition made camp. Cushing, without benefit of formal training in collecting anthropological data, cautiously began collecting data by observing, sketching, and mapping the local Zuni village and beginning to learn the Zuni language. The Zuni treated their uninvited ethnologist with aloofness. When he asked for permission to sketch scenes of ceremonial activities, he received a curt refusal. He later wrote that the Zuni's suspicion of him resulted from the fact that his party had unwittingly set up camp on the property of the local missionary, whom the Zuni heartily disliked. Naturally, they associated Cushing with the despised missionary, whose nickname was "Dust-eye."

Cushing realized that to win the confidence of the Zuni he must not only observe them but also participate in their lives. So he abandoned his expedition tent mates and hung his hammock in the house of a Zuni politician, the man who held the highest office in the village. But no sooner had Cushing begun to overcome the mistrust that kept the Zuni from confiding their customs and ideas to him than the expedition leader announced plans to move to another Pueblo group, the Hopi. With his Zuni acquaintances just beginning to warm up to him, Cushing couldn't bear to leave. He decided to remain with the Zuni until his party returned from Hopi country.

Trouble soon arose. Although the expedition had left supplies for its temporary defector with "Dust-eye," the unscrupulous missionary told Cushing that everything left behind was now *his* property—compensation for the use of his land as a campsite. The leader of the expedition, the missionary claimed, had said nothing about any supplies for Cushing, who would now have to fend for himself. Under the circumstances, Cushing had

---

[2]Some people object to the term *native* because they feel it implies being non-Western, or worse, inferior. For us, it suggests neither. We use the term to refer to people who are members of a given local culture by both birth and tradition.

[3]Virtually all practicing anthropologists at this time were men. Among the few exceptions was Alice Fletcher (1845–1923), who studied the native Americans called the Omaha.

In the late nineteenth century, pioneering American ethnologist Frank Cushing studied the pueblo-dwelling Zuni people of the American Southwest. Cushing lived with a Zuni family and adopted Zuni dress.

little choice, in that era before motels, restaurants, cars, or even telephones, but to throw himself on the generosity of the Zuni.

We don't know just what combination of ingenuity and naiveté was involved on Cushing's part (Grönewald 1972:40), but the Zuni eventually developed a great fondness for their ethnologist. Perhaps his run-in with the reprehensible missionary had something to do with it. At any rate, the Zuni politician with whom Cushing was living actually adopted him into his family and gave him a Zuni name, Medicine Flower. From then on, Cushing ate Zuni food and wore Zuni clothing. He received instruction in every aspect of Zuni culture,

much as though he were a child. His hosts even pierced his ears as a sign of their acceptance of him.

Cushing's Zuni education was just beginning to produce some fascinating anthropological results when the Smithsonian expedition returned from Hopi country. By now, Cushing was living comfortably among the hospitable Zuni and had learned enough about their ideas and customs to want to know a great deal more. When the expedition departed for Washington, he decided to remain with his new family. Later, he may have doubted the wisdom of that decision. One day, for example, one of his hosts prepared a Zuni delicacy for him, a soup made from rat intestines. How his Zuni friends must have snickered as he tried to convince them he was enjoying this exotic fare! Natural ethnologist that he was, Medicine Flower downed it all.

According to Zuni marriage practices, a bachelor who accepted a gift of cornmeal from an unmarried girl was officially betrothed to her. On two separate occasions, Zuni girls offered the handsome Cushing presents of cornmeal, but by the time of the first such marriage proposal he had already learned enough about local customs to insist on paying for these offerings, and so avoided marital entanglement.

Cushing attended Zuni ceremonies no outsider had ever witnessed, and it has been said that he felt himself one of the Zuni to such a degree that he never published data on customs he knew his hosts wished kept secret. Some anthropologists think this explains why Cushing actually published very little on the Zuni. The truth may be less romantic: he may have thought there was no hurry about doing so. Soon after leaving the Zuni, he switched anthropological fields and began to practice archaeology, excavating the remains of ancient lake dwellings in Florida. (In those days, the dividing lines between the fields of anthropology were less distinct than they are now.) He must have believed he had plenty of time to pursue various kinds of anthropological research and to publish the countless facts he had collected. But he miscalculated. In April 1900, at the age of 43, Cushing choked to death on a fish bone.

Cushing practiced **participant observation**—sharing in people's lives as well as observing them—long before that method had become established as an

participant observation cultural anthropology's major research tool—sharing in people's lives as well as observing them (see Chapter 2)

At the turn of the century, anthropologist Franz Boas assembled a huge collection of artifacts while studying the native Americans of British Columbia, Canada. Now housed at the American Museum of Natural History in New York, the collection includes household utensils, hats, boxes, ceremonial blankets, totem poles, and even a war canoe.

essential tool for cultural anthropologists. Indeed, we might say that he was one of the inventors of this important anthropological technique. When it came to publication, his scholarly contributions were insignificant compared with those of other anthropologists and sadly underrepresentative of what he had learned from his research. Today, publishing research data so that other anthropologists can compare them with their data from other societies is considered a basic requirement for a good cultural anthropologist, for only in this way can anthropologists add to what is known about different cultures. But in research techniques Frank Hamilton Cushing was one of the best, and all the more remarkable a man for the early date of his contribution to anthropological methods.

Franz Boas (1858–1941)

If you visit the American Museum of Natural History in New York City, be sure to spend some time admiring the huge collection of objects made around the turn of the century by the native Americans of British Columbia on the Pacific coast of Canada. Dominated by towering totem poles carved with animal faces, the collection also includes kitchen utensils, boxes, hats, decorated ceremonial blankets, and even an enormous, high-prowed war canoe bearing the model figures of more than a dozen men in traditional costumes. This impressive collection is only one of the legacies left to anthropology by the foremost American anthropologist of his time, Franz Boas.

Boas was born in Germany, where in 1881 he obtained his doctorate in geography. Two years later this interest prompted him to join a geographical expedition to eastern Canada. There Boas encountered a group of native Americans, the Central Eskimo or Inuit,[4] and he

---

[4]Although *Eskimo* is by far the more familiar term, some people prefer *Inuit* because the word *Eskimo* means "eater of raw meat" in the language of a neighboring society.

became so intrigued by their way of life that he abandoned geography and began an anthropological career that eventually focused on the nonliterate people of the northwest coast of North America.

Boas delved into anthropology, reading up on the ideas that in the nineteenth century were believed to shed light on the astonishing variety of human behavior. He found many of these ideas unsatisfying. How could sweeping statements about humanity be made on the basis of so little data? It was clear to Boas that before anthropologists could hope to understand human behavior a huge amount of detailed information about specific cultures was needed. Determined to contribute to this effort, Boas traveled in 1886 to the west coast of Canada to begin an intensive study of one of the groups of people native to British Columbia, the Kwakiutl. For years afterward, Boas collected information about Kwakiutl culture, eventually amassing an enormous amount of information, much of it very detailed.

Boas's reputation as a prolific compiler of Kwakiutl customs earned him eminence, but this was not his only contribution to anthropology. He also contributed to anthropological theory. In the late nineteenth century, many scholars were attracted to **cultural evolution,** the idea that in human culture, as in biology, a gradual but continuous process of adaptive change occurs. Some evolutionists believed that this process involved a set series of stages through which all cultures must eventually pass and that similar natural environments, similar economic systems, and similar population sizes would produce similar cultural results. Boas disagreed, and proposed an alternative theory to explain why human cultures differed. Each culture is unique, Boas argued, for each is the individual product of unique historical circumstances. This approach is known as **historical particularism.**

Boas also developed a new and important research method. While living among the Kwakiutl, he realized he would be unable to absorb single-handedly the enormous amount of anthropological data these people could provide. He needed help. So Boas trained a local Canadian man, a part native American, part English speaker of Kwakiutl named George Hunt, to record anthropological information—the first time a member of a group being studied by an anthropologist had been recruited as a research assistant. In 1893, Hunt began to record, on Boas's behalf, information given to him by other Kwakiutl individuals.

Today, we recognize the use of local residents as research assistants as one way of overcoming barriers between the researcher and those who provide information (Goldman 1980:335). The latter are usually called **informants,** although some anthropologists, fearing that this term may carry negative connotations, prefer to call them "assistants." We'll stick with the traditional term, but we want to make it clear that an anthropological informant is not an "informer" or spy!

Adding Hunt's material to the results of his own inquiries, Boas was able to provide detailed information, often in the actual words of Kwakiutl informants, on many different topics, including hunting, fishing, local myths, food gathering, recipes, the life cycles of men and women, marriage, songs, prayers, death, sweat baths, the status of women, art, curses, names, the significance of dog hair, spirits, tributes to chiefs, blood revenge, wars, family quarrels, village organization, kinship, chieftainship, and social status. His goal was no less than to document every aspect of Kwakiutl culture. Long before he was finished, he had amassed so much information that it seemed to Boas that—if similar amounts of data were available for other societies—no unified explanation of human behavior could ever emerge. His idea that every culture must be the unique product of its own particular circumstances was thus reinforced by his research.

Unlike Cushing, Boas published much of his data (see especially Boas 1897). He never abandoned the historical particularist approach, believing, throughout a career of almost four decades, that anthropology should focus on the multiplicity of human cultures rather than seek grand patterns that applied to all of them. For many years, Boas *was* American anthropology, teaching the "Boasian approach" to students who became notable in their own right. His influence has waned over the years as other ideas about human behavior have arisen, but no one has ever had a greater impact on American anthropology.

◆◆

cultural evolution the notion that in human culture there is a gradual, continuous process of adaptive change

historical particularism the idea that every culture, because it is the product of specific historical circumstances, is unique

informant an individual who provides an anthropological researcher with information

Bronislaw Malinowski (1884–1942)

Like Boas, Bronislaw Malinowski came into anthropology almost by accident. He began his career by studying physical science in his native Poland, but his interests ranged well beyond that field. One day he picked up an early edition of Sir James George Frazer's (1890) *The Golden Bough,* which describes the myths and magical rites of nonliterate peoples, as well as their impact on contemporary religion and science. Malinowski was hooked. From that point on his heart was set on anthropology, and in 1908, with a doctorate from the University of Cracow in his pocket, he left Poland for England and the career that was to propel him into anthropological immortality.

In 1914 Malinowski pitched his tent in a tiny village in the faraway western Pacific—Omarakana, in the Trobriand Islands off New Guinea. Life must have been difficult for him at first; none of the familiar comforts of England were to be found in this remote place, and he didn't speak a word of the local language. He immediately found himself an interpreter, but after six months or so he felt sufficiently confident in the native language to discard this help and thereafter carried out his inquiries in the Trobriand tongue.

Anthropological research methods in 1914 were still not sufficiently established for Malinowski to have learned how to conduct research in a nonliterate, non-Western community, but obviously there was more than one way to accomplish this goal. Like Cushing, he rejected the alternative of remaining aloof from the daily lives of the Trobrianders as he collected his data, choosing instead participant observation. In addition to questioning informants, he took part in community events to

Early twentieth-century anthropologist Bronislaw Malinowski, one of the first to practice participant observation, spent over two years with the Trobriand Islanders of the South Pacific. Rather than studying the Trobrianders from a distance, Malinowski lived among them and learned to speak their language.

a much greater extent than Boas, behaving more like Cushing. He closely scrutinized the activities going on about him and listened carefully to anecdotes and local gossip, so that later he could provide much fuller accounts of Trobriand customs than would have been possible had he relied on the formal questioning of informants alone.

The many books and papers resulting from Malinowski's Trobriand work were an enormous success. With his gift for placing himself squarely in the center of things, he was able to integrate the details of Trobriand customs into a broad mosaic of island life. The effect, on paper, is not one of abstract analysis removed from daily life but "a picture of the living reality of Trobriand society which brings to mind the novels of Émile Zola" (Evans-Pritchard 1951:94). The titles Malinowski chose for his books didn't discourage either scholarly or popular interest; he had a fancy for eye-catching names such as *Crime and Custom in Savage Society* (1978, originally published in 1926) and *The Sexual Life of Savages in Northwestern Melanesia* (1962, originally published in 1929).

Malinowski lived among the Trobriand Islanders for 26 months between 1914 and 1918. Later, while a professor at the University of London, he did research in Africa, Latin America, and the United States, but it was his Trobriand work that established him as one of the most influential of anthropologists. Thanks to Malinowski, we know far more about the culture of the Trobriand Islanders than about those of most other nonliterate people.

Malinowski's reputation isn't based solely on his reports about the Trobriand Islands, for he contributed to anthropological ideas as well. Living among the Trobrianders not just for a few months at a time but throughout the year, he had been impressed with the fact that the customs of the islanders all served their needs—for food, shelter, companionship, and so on—very well indeed. At first, some Trobriand customs seemed quite useless, but Malinowski eventually came to see their significance. This idea—that customs function to fulfill the biological and psychological needs of individuals—is known as **functionalism.**[5] Malinowski's ideas and work earned such high esteem that in 1939 he was of-

---

[5]Since Malinowski's day, the term *functionalism* has been applied to other, somewhat different ideas, proposed by other anthropologists. We distinguish between two different kinds of functionalism in Chapter 4.

fered a post as a visiting professor at Yale University, where he died in 1942.

CONCLUSION

You are about to embark on a course of study in which *people* are the object of interest and the focus of research. Since we are all people, we're actually studying ourselves. Can we hope to learn things that we don't already know? If the answer to that question was not altogether clear in the days before anthropology was born as an academic discipline, it is now. The more we learn about people, the more there is to learn. For example (to raise just one unanswered, but particularly interesting, question), why, despite the intelligence it takes to put a human being on the moon, do large numbers of us continue to make war, starve, and die of preventable diseases? Can we really say that we know ourselves until we have found the answers to questions such as this?

Bronislaw Malinowski (1984:517–518) eloquently summed up both the urgent need for and the desired result of the anthropologist's quest. His words were written over sixty years ago, and we leave it to you to judge whether or not we have yet learned all the lessons that anthropology can teach. Tasting of the almost infinite variety of human experiences is important, Malinowski wrote, yet

> there is . . . one point of view deeper and [even] more important . . . , and that is the desire to turn such knowledge into wisdom. . . . our [ultimate] goal is to enrich and deepen our own world's vision, to understand our own nature and to make it finer, intellectually and artistically. In grasping the essential outlook of others, with . . . reverence and real understanding . . . we cannot help widening our own. We cannot possibly reach the final Socratic wisdom of knowing ourselves if we never leave the narrow confinement of the customs, beliefs, and prejudices into which every man is born. Nothing can teach us a better lesson . . . than the habit of mind which allows us to treat the beliefs and values of another man from his point of view. [Anthropology] should lead us to such knowledge, and to tolerance and generosity, based on the understanding of other men's point of view.

functionalism the idea that aspects of culture function to fulfill the biological and psychological needs of individuals

SUMMARY

Anthropology, the study of people, can be considered a scientific discipline. Unlike most other sciences, however, anthropology is both a physical science and a social science, depending on exactly what is being studied and with what degree of objectivity or subjectivity. Indeed, some anthropological research is so subjective that it seems to be more humanistic than scientific.

Anthropology is a uniquely wide-ranging discipline. Because of its twin perspectives, the biological and the cultural, it is often described as *biocultural*. Since it includes every aspect of human existence and activity, anthropology is sometimes described as *holistic*. It is also *comparative,* in that it seeks to compare the similarities and contrast the differences among human groups, and *comprehensive* since no human group is excluded.

Anthropology is divided into four major fields: cultural anthropology, also termed sociocultural anthropology or ethnology (the study of the culture of contemporary and historic people); anthropological linguistics (the study of languages); archaeology (the study of people of the past through their material remains); and physical anthropology (the study of the biological aspects of being human).

Although we devote a chapter to anthropological linguistics, this book is mainly concerned with cultural anthropology. This field is distinguished by its traditional interest in nonliterate and peasant societies, but today it is devoting increasing attention to such groups as urban dwellers and women and to applied work. Central to cultural anthropology are the opposing concepts of ethnocentrism—the belief that one's own ethnic group, society, or culture is superior to all others—and cultural relativity—the idea that a culture must be evaluated in terms of its own values rather than according to the values of another culture.

This chapter illustrates, through the lives and anthropological work of Frank Cushing, Franz Boas, and Bronislaw Malinowski, how anthropology as an academic discipline originated and grew during the late nineteenth and early twentieth centuries. These three portraits also open the door to two topics as important to anthropology as to any academic discipline: its methods and theoretical perspectives. So far, we have given you only a glimpse of how two important anthropological research methods, participant observation and interviewing local informants, were invented, along with a peek at three different theoretical perspectives—cultural evolution, historical particularism, and functionalism. We'll discuss these methods and theoretical perspectives in more detail in later chapters.

KEY TERMS

anthropological linguistics (linguistic anthropology)
applied anthropology
archaeology
artifact
cultural anthropology
cultural evolution
cultural relativity
culture
development anthropology
ethnic group
ethnicity
ethnocentrism
ethnology
functionalism
historical particularism
hypothesis
illiterate
informant
nonliterate
participant observation
peasants
physical (biological) anthropology
physical (natural) science
science
social anthropology
social science
social structure
society
sociocultural anthropology
theory
urban anthropology

SUGGESTED READINGS

Birdsell, Joseph B. 1987. Some Reflections on Fifty Years in Biological Anthropology. *Annual Reviews of Anthropology* 16:1–12. A personal view of some of the key developments in the field of physical anthropology by an eminent scientist.

Diamond, Stanley (ed.). 1980. *Anthropology: Ancestors and Heirs*. The Hague: Mouton. Twenty essays presenting topics, personalities, and interests from most of the countries where anthropology is an academic subject. The collection gives an excellent idea of the different anthropological traditions worldwide.

Greenberg, Joseph H. 1986. On Being a Linguistic Anthropologist. *Annual Review of Anthropology* 15:1–24. A leading linguistic anthropologist describes how he became a practitioner of this field of anthropology, and in doing so provides useful insights into the study of languages in their cultural context.

Kaplan, Abraham. 1984. Philosophy of Science in Anthropology. *Annual Reviews of Anthropology* 13:25–39. In this chapter we have addressed the problem of whether anthropology should be considered a science or not. Kap-

lan provides a brief overview of some of the issues involved.

Silverman, Sydel (ed.). 1981. *Totems and Teachers: Perspectives on the History of Anthropology.* New York: Columbia University Press. This book describes the contributions of eight major figures in anthropology, with an emphasis on American anthropologists.

CHAPTER 2

FIELDWORK

During the course of a long-term research project that began in 1964, anthropological fieldworker Napoleon Chagnon spent over four years among the Yanomamo of South America. Chagnon's headband, the tail of a black monkey, is traditional headgear for Yanomamo visitors.

INTRODUCTION

Late on a summer afternoon, a professorial-looking, middle-aged man carrying a battered leather briefcase dropped in at a small café in a town somewhere in the American Southwest. Seating himself at the counter, he began to spread around him numerous loose-leaf notebook pages and index cards. Next he drew from his briefcase a portable tape recorder, to which he listened intently as he sipped his coffee and added to his already voluminous notes. The curious proprietor, never at a loss for words, asked the man whether he might be an agent for the Internal Revenue Service or perhaps even the Federal Bureau of Investigation, but the man shook his head with a smile. "No," he replied, "I'm an anthropologist, and I'm interested in studying changing speech patterns among Navaho youths. This town is the place I've chosen for my fieldwork."

The next day it rained. The café was disappointingly empty until lunchtime, when a damp threesome of local women, whom the proprietor recognized as members of the church's morning sewing group, entered in the company of an unfamiliar younger woman. Curious about the stranger, the proprietor kept his ears open as he served the women dessert. "All of you have been enormously helpful," the young woman was saying to the others. "But my search for data on the changing roles of rural women is getting more complicated than I had expected. I'm beginning to think I should extend my fieldwork by a couple of months." Now the café owner was truly confused. In *his* day, "fieldwork" meant getting out of bed early, grabbing a hoe, and spending a hot morning weeding the corn. He wished he understood what was going on.

In Chapter 1, we pointed out that anthropology isn't limited in time or space; the anthropologist is interested in *people,* no matter where or when they live or lived. The process of collecting information about people, ancient or modern, is called **fieldwork,** a catchall term for a number of different anthropological data-collecting strategies. No matter how different they seem, these strategies are all designed to yield information about people.

You'll recall from Chapter 1 that cultural anthropologists usually gather information from living people, called informants. Typically they seek this information in small-scale, often nonliterate societies or among ethnic or other groups in large-scale societies. The young anthropologist studying the changing roles of rural women in contemporary North America was collecting cultural anthropological data. Recall, too, that anthropologists whose research focuses on language are called anthropological linguists. They collect data from living informants too; the professor studying Navaho speech patterns is a case in point.

◆◆

KINDS OF FIELDWORK

Collecting and recording anthropological data within a particular society is called **ethnography,** and an anthropologist who is actually in the process of collecting anthropological data is called an **ethnographer.** Whatever its specific focus, modern ethnographic fieldwork is an attempt to find out something about people. It isn't the case that ethnographers with time on their hands and cash in their wallets randomly pick interesting places in which to live for awhile to see if they can discover anything new and different. Rather, anthropological ideas suggest specific fieldwork projects, and these projects in turn sometimes lead to additional interesting ideas. Although early fieldworkers such as Cushing, Boas, and Malinowski (see Chapter 1) were strongly motivated by a desire to collect information about populations unknown to the outside world, social scientists today usually go "into the field" for more specific reasons.

Two very common reasons are (1) to test specific hypotheses, either new ones or previously tested hypotheses that may have been insufficiently tested or may no longer be valid because of change; and (2) to apply anthropological principles and methods to achieve specific, practical ends. A fieldwork expedition may combine these aims; testing new ideas, checking up on old ones, and achieving practical goals are not incompatible. No matter what the impetus, fieldwork is the primary way in which anthropologists get data, which they use to add to our knowledge of how people all over the world live and think.

Hypothesis Testing

Since a major goal of modern anthropological fieldwork is to provide new insights into human behavior, many fieldwork projects are selected on the basis of their potential contribution to anthropological knowledge. As you know from Chapter 1, the accumulated knowledge of any science is contained in its body of theories and hypotheses. Given that human behavior is almost infinitely variable, there is an ongoing debate about whether any legitimate anthropological theories actually exist. Most anthropologists, however, are willing to use

◆ **ASK YOURSELF**

Can you see yourself doing either of the kinds of fieldwork mentioned above? Which kind appeals to you most, and why?

the term *theory* in the somewhat generous sense in which we defined it in Chapter 1. Thus, cultural evolution, the idea that in all human cultures there is a gradual, continuous process of adaptive change, is widely referred to as an anthropological theory.

Hypotheses, in contrast, are more like educated guesses. Thus an anthropological hypothesis is an educated guess about what people will do, and why. An example of a hypothesis based on the theory of cultural evolution could be this: introducing a daily National Weather Service radio broadcast into a village of rural Iranian peasants will result in the abandonment of traditional but less accurate methods of weather prediction and a new reliance on the radio since more accurate weather information is highly adaptive for such farmers. (Most hypotheses worthy of field testing are more complex than this; we intentionally chose a simple example.) Whether or not it is proven valid, an anthropological hypothesis, when tested, has the potential to shed new light on human behavior.

Much anthropological research centers on the testing or retesting of specific hypotheses among particular groups of people. Using the methods described below, fieldworkers collect the data they need to test specific hypotheses and then analyze these data to see whether or not the hypotheses hold true. The results aren't always perfect, but they should at least suggest some anthropological truth. In the case of the hypothesis about peasant farmers, will or will not the anthropologist's expectation—that the radio broadcast will quickly replace former methods of weather prediction—be upheld strongly enough to support increased confidence in the predictive value of cultural evolutionary theory (Agar 1980:64)?

Not all anthropological fieldwork revolves around specific hypotheses. For some anthropologists, collecting ethnographic data about some interesting institution or set of beliefs or gathering information about a culture never before studied is a sufficient motivation for fieldwork. And sometimes, in the course of doing this kind of fieldwork, anthropologists collect data that invite later cross-cultural comparisons or even generate hypotheses.

Checking up on previously tested hypotheses, one's own or another researcher's, also takes anthropol-

ASK YOURSELF

What changes have taken place in the community of people into which you were born in the time that has passed since then? What factors best account for these changes?

ogists into the field. Most are eager to return, sooner or later, to the places where they carried out earlier work. Sometimes they are unsure of certain facts and want to do a follow-up study. Sometimes there are data they missed the first time around. Or in the process of mulling over their own or others' field data and comparing them with data from other cultures, they may think of ways to rework their original hypotheses or even develop new ones altogether.

A lot of what motivates this desire to follow up on earlier work is the pace of change in today's world. Technologically complex cultures are affecting technologically simpler ones at an ever-increasing rate. In response, the thrust of ethnographic research has changed. A great many anthropologists today are interested in studying the process of change at "their" research sites. At the end of this chapter you'll meet Napoleon Chagnon, who in the course of his anthropological career has revisited his original fieldwork site in the Amazon jungle some twenty times.

Applied Anthropology

As you know from Chapter 1, anthropological ideas and methods are sometimes applied to specific problems in order to achieve practical ends. You also know that the first anthropologists, although perhaps primarily motivated by curiosity about other cultures, also provided anthropological data to governments or other sponsoring agencies, typically in situations of colonialism or economic expansion. The fieldwork of the nineteenth-century anthropologist Frank Cushing, for example, was paid for by a U.S. government agency, the American Bureau of Ethnology, whose mandate was to administer to the native Americans of the American Southwest. Cushing was one of the first applied anthropologists.

Since Cushing's time, ethnography for practical ends has grown in importance. Today, in the roles of data gatherers and advisors, many anthropologists work either full time or as consultants on projects intended to

fieldwork the process of collecting information about people, ancient or modern, where they live or lived

ethnography the process of collecting and recording information within a particular society

ethnographer an anthropologist in the process of doing ethnography

During fieldwork, anthropologists collect the data they need to test specific hypotheses. Later they analyze these data to see whether or not the hypotheses hold true. Anthropologist Loretta Orion uses a computer to analyze the data she collected during fieldwork in North America.

Tylor's Hypothesis

In his book *Primitive Culture* (1873:133–136), the nineteenth-century anthropologist Edward Burnett Tylor (1832–1917) raised an interesting question. Why do many people around the world believe in magic, whereas others (including Tylor himself) are certain that magical power doesn't really exist? Based on the theory that people all over the world, literate or nonliterate, think in much the same logical manner, Tylor proposed several hypotheses. One was that in societies with strong beliefs in magic, "magical" rituals are performed at the same time as other, more mundane activities, and it is these other activities that really make the wished-for "magical" results occur. For example, magicians might "help" their predictions of life or death come true with medicines that cure or kill.

But Tylor was an **armchair anthropologist.** Instead of carrying out fieldwork, he collected his data second-hand from books, articles, and letters written by others. His hypothesis that magicians combine their "magic" with other actions that have more predictable results waited 50 years to be tested in the field. In 1926, E. E. Evans-Pritchard went to live among the Azande of Central Africa, with testing of this hypothesis one of his several goals. Evans-Pritchard (1985:203) learned that Azande leaders use "magic" to attract followers, but they hand out free food at the same time. His findings supported Tylor's hypothesis.

serve the needs of governments, other public institutions, or private agencies (such as charitable organizations or relief agencies).

◆◆◆

FIELD METHODS

In this section, we'll describe and explain the arsenal of time- and field-tested methods and tools anthropologists use to collect their data. Later, in a section on what it's like to do fieldwork, we'll show how this arsenal can be configured to the kinds of data sought and the nature of the field situation, whether a remote village or a modern city. At the end of the chapter, we'll describe what two modern anthropologists actually did in the field, not only to collect information but also to cope with the unexpected problems that always seem to crop up in fieldwork.

Participant Observation

As you know from Chapter 1, participant observation is the major strategy used by ethnologists to collect data in the field. Rather than read about or briefly visit the people they are interested in studying, fieldworkers reside among them, usually for many months or even years. They attempt to live the way members of the community under study live, speak their language, eat their foods, observe their customs, and share to the fullest extent possible in their daily activities. This strategy is so important in anthropological fieldwork that we devote a separate section to it, entitled Doing Fieldwork.

Other Research Tools and Procedures

In addition to participant observation, anthropologists use other ethnographic methods and tools, some in conjunction with participant observation and some not. Participant observation is a highly effective way to undertake a holistic study of a culture; but sometimes, rather than attempting to provide such a broad-brushed picture of a society, an ethnographer may want to focus on a more restricted problem: why people emigrate from rural areas to cities, for example, or why some societies reject modern birth control methods. These are legitimate topics for anthropological research, but they do not necessarily require total immersion in communal life. They may be researched by studying documents, collecting information from a single informant rather than a

whole community, or distributing questionnaires (Clammer 1984:63–85).

Among the most useful research tools and procedures ethnographers have at their disposal, whether in conjunction with participant observation or not, are the following.

Interviewing. Probably the most commonly used ethnographic field method, an **interview** is a conversation between an ethnographer and one or more informants. Almost any member of a community under study is a potential informant, and the type and quantity of information each can offer vary tremendously (Cohen 1984:224–225). Most people will be **casual informants,** from whom an ethnographer obtains general or specialized information from time to time. Certain individuals, however, will be **key informants,** upon whom the ethnographer relies more heavily. They may be "key" because they have specialized knowledge or just because they know more than others about what is going on. Or, although not especially knowledgeable themselves, they may be politically powerful and thus able to help the ethnographer obtain information from those who might otherwise be reluctant to share it. Or they may be popular characters, at the center of social activities or networks of gossip, and hence in constant touch with other people. Most ethnographers try to assemble a mix of informants, both casual and key.

The ethnographer may ask an informant a series of prearranged questions on preselected topics or engage the informant in a free-ranging, open-ended interview. Usually the ethnographer records the informant's answers in writing (often with the help of a portable computer) or on tape. The length, content, and scope of interviews vary greatly, depending on the number of questions asked, the degree of predetermination in the questions, the broadness of the questions, the type of in-

◆◆◆

armchair anthropologist an anthropologist who analyzes data from documents written by others rather than carrying out fieldwork

interview a conversation between an ethnographer and one or more informants

casual informant an informant from whom an ethnographer obtains information from time to time

key informant an informant on whom, because of specialized knowledge or influence, an ethnographer relies heavily

One commonly used ethnographic field method is the interview, a conversation between an ethnographer and one or more informants. In Botswana, Africa, anthropologist Richard Lee interviews informants living a gathering-and-hunting way of life in the Kalahari desert.

terview (individual or group), the interviewer's personal style, and the informant's willingness to cooperate.

If a group of informants is involved, it is usually small, consisting of no more than four or five people, so that the ethnographer can accurately record all of the informant's answers and opinions. A small group of informants brought together to shed light on a particular topic of interest to an ethnographer is called a **focus group.**

In general, the more informal and casual the interviewer's style, the more "negotiable" the interview (Agar 1980:90) because "the informants can criticize a question, correct it, point out that it is sensitive, or answer in any way they want to"—including turning the interview around and questioning the ethnographer (Clammer 1984:231–232). In addition to the interviewer's demeanor, an informant's willingness to cooperate is also affected by his or her natural degree of reticence or forthrightness, the setting (e.g., is the interview private or might others overhear?), the topic (are the

questions politically or socially sensitive?), and the informant's sense of coercion (did the informant volunteer to be interviewed, or did he or she feel somehow pressured into it?).

Sometimes (for reasons ranging from a need to keep certain information private to a wish to have some fun at a visitor's expense) informants may deliberately mislead ethnographers. You'll find an example of purposeful deception in our account of the fieldwork of Napoleon Chagnon, later in this chapter.

Sampling. A fieldworker undertaking our hypothetical research project among Iranian peasants would immediately be challenged by several methodological questions. Should the population studied consist of *all* of the farmers in a village or only some of them? Should only wheat farmers be studied, or should people with small kitchen gardens also be included? To provide comparative data or cross-check data provided by the farmers, should another group of farmers, similar in size and composition, be chosen, perhaps from a second village, as a **control group**? Every fieldworker must decide whether to base his or her research on an entire population or to "sample" it. The decision depends on the scope of the research and the size of the population. The technique of **sampling**—in which only a small part of something, representative of a larger whole, is investigated—is used more and more frequently as anthropologists become increasingly computer-literate since computers are well suited to assessing the statistical validity of sample results.

Genealogies. **Genealogies** are essential to the study of descent (Chapter 6) and marriage (Chapter 7). Genealogical research involves tracing the genealogical links between individuals to discover who is related to whom and in what way. When written records are not available, genealogical data are limited by what present-day members of a community can recall.

Life Histories. A **life history** is the personal story of an informant's life and the cultural and economic influences on it (Clammer 1984:75). Life histories can provide very personal, very vivid pictures of a culture from within, through the eyes of its own members. One of the best, the story of an African woman named Nisa who lived a gathering-and-hunting way of life, is listed in the Suggested Readings at the end of this chapter.

Case Studies. An anthropological **case study** focuses on a single individual or episode rather than on the wider actions of whole families or communities of people. A detailed narrative about how a conflict between two people was resolved in the context of a given culture is an example of a case study. By analyzing several case studies from the same society on the same topic, we can learn much about the society—in this case, its rules for conflict resolution.

Film and Taped Records. Photographs and videos are excellent ways to record ethnographic information. Photos capture details of daily life, such as styles of dress or housing, and record the memberships of extended families, clubs, or teams. Videos accurately preserve public or private performances, such as religious rituals, for later study and analysis. Showing group photographs to informants is one way of identify-

ing individuals and tracing genealogies. A tape recorder is also essential if a fieldworker wants to record precise information from informants in certain contexts, such as storytelling sessions or meetings. Some ethnographers use tape recorders to take their own notes. Finally, the camera-toting anthropologist is often asked to take portraits. A Polaroid photo is an effective way to repay informants for the help they have provided.

Studies of Material Culture. Occasionally a research hypothesis involves the study of objects produced by a group of people. Such objects are part of every society's **material culture,** the physical things that members of the society create. Baskets, pottery, fishing gear, ceremonial headdresses—all are examples of objects that may reveal a great deal about the culture of the people who made them. Such objects may be studied in their original contexts or in museums or university study collections.

Team research. Most commonly, the ethnographer goes into the field alone. (By "alone," we mean unaccompanied by other specialists. It is not uncommon for anthropologists to take their husbands, wives, and perhaps children with them into the field since fieldwork typically lasts for many months or even years.) Sometimes, however, the ethnographer is part of a team that includes either fellow anthropologists or specialists in other disciplines, such as medicine, agriculture, or economics. Multidisciplinary field teams are increasingly common, especially on large-scale applied projects. Be-

focus group a small group of informants brought together to shed light on a particular topic

control group a group similar in size and composition to a group under study, used for comparison or as a cross-check on the data provided by the study group

sampling using a small part of something to represent a larger whole

genealogy a record of a person's relationships by descent or marriage

life history an informant's story of his or her life and the influences on it

case study a detailed ethnographic study focusing on a single individual or episode

material culture the physical things people create

Cameras of various kinds are useful pieces of equipment for fieldworkers. In central China, villagers look at a Polaroid photo of themselves.

ing a member of such a team can be particularly rewarding since the anthropologist has much to learn from and share with his or her teammates.

Surveys and Questionnaires. Large-scale opinion polls—in which a researcher asks questions over the phone—are routinely used by sociologists and political scientists but little used by anthropologists. Still, surveys and questionnaires can be useful tools for ethnographers since almost all fieldwork includes collecting some sort of statistical information.

In a **survey,** items or events or opinions are counted and classified (Wallman and Dhooge 1984:257). If it's a **personal survey,** a researcher personally counts items or events—for example, by standing at the entrance to a village market and counting the number of people of a certain ethnic group who enter—and then tallies the results. In a **respondent survey,** a pre-

arranged series of questions, spoken or written in questionnaire form, is asked of informants called **respondents,** and the results are then tallied (Mitchell 1984). For example, an ethnographer might visit all of the heads of households in a community to collect information about household composition or the educational status of family members.

In conducting a respondent survey, the wording of questions is crucial. They must be precise enough to leave little room for individual interpretation (by the interviewer or the respondent) and neutral enough to avoid tilting respondents toward positive or negative answers (Wallman and Dhooge 1984:261–262). The degree of openness of the questions is also important. There is a big difference between the open-ended question "What are your religious beliefs?" and the much more restricted question "Do you believe in God?" accompanied by the choices "yes," "no," or "don't know."

THE ANTHROPOLOGIST AT WORK

Large, multidisciplinary field teams require close coordination, both among the researchers in the field and between the fieldwork site and the home office. For this reason they usually include a field coordinator, who takes care of the fieldworkers' basic needs, juggles their schedules, provides secretarial and other services, administers funds, and maintains contact with the project's directors and sponsors. If the field coordinator can also help out with the research, so much the better.

A multidisciplinary field team recently spent three months in an African nation, helping its government analyze and control the ever-increasing costs of its public hospital system. The team consisted of a political economist, a doctor, a hospital cost accountant, an anthropologist, and a field coordinator. Her job included renting hotel rooms and offices for the team members, hiring a car and driver, arranging appointments with hospital administrators and government officials, recording the team's daily meetings, transcribing field notes, and reminding team members to take their malaria pills. She also coped with various unexpected emergencies, even managing to find someone to repair an American-made portable computer. If this kind of work appeals to you, an anthropology major and language minor, plus some business skills and perhaps travel experience, might help qualify you for the job of field coordinator.

Network analysis. **Network analysis** is a way of gathering and organizing information about communities by focusing on individuals or small groups and their relationships with others. Its goal is to establish patterns of association among people and assess their effects (Mitchell 1984:267–272).

Networks may be of two kinds. **Set-centered** networks assume the existence of groups, or sets, of individuals with contacts or links with one another. Participant observation is the best way to get information on set-centered networks. Details for subsequent network analysis are abstracted only after the broader ethnographic data have been collected (Mitchell 1984:270). **Ego-centered** networks focus on a particular individual (called "ego") and include all of the links between this person and other individuals in the community under investigation. Data are typically provided by interviews with ego.

Complementing the fieldwork activities described above is a growing list of specialized field techniques, some of them highly sophisticated technologically and borrowed from other disciplines. Depending on the project, garbage may be studied, inkblot or other psychological tests administered, census data studied, or blood analyzed. In addition, most fieldworkers search their field sites for documents such as maps, censuses, government reports, and local histories. Data derived from these sources can provide field research with some historical depth.

DOING FIELDWORK

In this section, we'll try to convey our personal experience of fieldwork, both its highs and its lows. We ask you to imagine, for a moment, that you're a graduate student in anthropology, and you've just been awarded a grant from a foundation to support field research that will be the basis of your doctoral dissertation. (Since

survey the counting and classifying of items, events, or opinions

personal survey a survey undertaken personally by a researcher

respondent survey a survey consisting of a prearranged series of questions, in questionnaire form, asked of respondents

respondent a person who provides information for a respondent survey

network analysis gathering and organizing data by focusing on individuals or small groups and their interrelationships in order to establish patterns of association

set-centered network a network based on groups of individuals linked to one another

ego-centered network a network centering on a particular individual and including all the links between this person and others in his or her community

Network Analysis in London

Until Elizabeth Bott and her co-researcher, J. H. Robb, came along, there had been few anthropological studies of Western families inside their homes. In a pioneering study using network analysis, Bott (1971:17–22) and Robb studied families in London to formulate hypotheses about how family members interact with people outside their homes and what effect these relationships have on family life. The researchers visited 20 families an average of 13 times each, exploring in each family the relationship between wife and husband and the radiating networks of relatives and nonrelatives in which the spouses were involved.

Bott and Robb found that each wife had her network of social ties outside the family, and each husband had his. These extrafamilial ties both strengthened and weakened the families. They strengthened them in that wives and husbands tended to deal with the outside world as a couple. At the same time, they weakened families in that both wives and husbands were sometimes more interested in and involved with members of their networks than with their spouses. Several interesting hypotheses emerged from these observations. One was that the denser the network of ties, the weaker the bond between wife and husband, and vice versa.

some sort of fieldwork is usually required before the degree of Ph.D. in anthropology is awarded, much first-time fieldwork is undertaken by graduate students in anthropology.) Of course, you're elated. At the same time, however, you're apprehensive. You can think of dozens of reasons why the idea of living among strangers, far from home, is sheer madness. You'll miss your best friend's wedding, your stomach gets upset easily by foreign foods, you didn't do very well in your language lessons, you can't afford a portable computer, and you hate to fly!

Getting There

Tourists may enter most foreign countries without special consent from the national governments involved; the visitor usually needs only a passport and sometimes a tourist visa. To do fieldwork in most foreign countries, however, an anthropologist must have not only the government's consent but also, because of the length of time usually spent in the field, a special residence visa. Sometimes both the approval and the visa are easily and swiftly obtained, but delays of up to a year are not unheard of, and occasionally one cannot obtain permission for fieldwork at all.

Why would an anthropologist have a hard time getting permission to do fieldwork? Patriotic, ethical, and other considerations affect whether or not a country will grant a foreigner a residence visa for fieldwork. With educational levels generally rising all over the world, the governments of some countries consider local scholars better suited than foreigners for anthropological studies in their own countries. Governments may also be concerned about outsiders' interference in their citizens' lives or about the health and safety of fieldworkers. Fortunately for anthropology, these concerns are usually dealt with successfully (Hicks 1984:192–197).

The Problem of Culture Shock

Upon entering a totally unfamiliar setting, the ethnographer is immediately faced with strange faces, sights, sounds, and smells, a babble of foreign words, a different climate, and people acting in ways that may seem very peculiar.

The anthropologist Rodney Needham (1975:vii–ix) compared the feelings of an ethnographer newly arrived in the field to those of a person who has been blind since birth but who has just gained the gift of sight. Such a person doesn't see the world as it exists for someone who has never been blind. Instead, he or she is overwhelmed by a chaos of forms, movements, and colors, a "gaudy confusion of sensual impressions," none of which seems related to the others.

We call this unpleasant sense of confusion and disorientation upon entering the field **culture shock.** It may be heightened by loneliness, homesickness, anxiety, or even depression, suspicion, or anger. Occasionally, these feelings are so intense that a fieldworker cannot handle them and chooses to return to a more familiar

Culture Shock at Home

Culture shock can occur even in the context of an ethnographer's own culture. Consider the experience of Jack Haas, who carried out field research among construction workers in a North American city. These daring men, who build our cities' skyscrapers, perform their daily—and deadly—jobs while balancing, hundreds of feet above the ground, on steel beams only a few inches wide. Haas's field project was designed to answer such questions as how these workers could apparently ignore the perils of "running the iron."

On the first day of Haas's nine months of fieldwork, a superintendent waved him through the construction gate, gave him a hard hat, and wished him good luck (1984:104–105). "Directly ahead were five incomplete levels of an emerging 21-story office building . . . [where] workers were . . . putting steel beams into place. These were the [informants] I had come to participate with and observe. This chilling reality filled me with an almost overwhelming anxiety. I began to experience a trepidation that far exceeded any usual observer anxiety encountered in the first days of field research . . . the risks of [participant observation] were profoundly obvious. It was with fearful anticipation that I moved towards the job site." It's no wonder that before commencing his fieldwork, Haas took out a $50,000 accident insurance policy and "forgot" to tell his wife precisely what his ethnographic research involved!

Not all anthropologists study exotic, foreign people and their cultures; some pursue their fieldwork close to home. Fieldworker Jack Haas studied the lives of American construction workers, like these Chicago steelworkers, whose specialty is building skyscrapers.

setting. Usually, however, he or she manages to remain in the field and discovers that culture shock is only temporary. Gradually and with great effort, the fieldworker begins to feel more comfortable, to discern order amid disorder, and to classify things and ideas along the lines of the host society.

Stages of Fieldwork

Each fieldwork experience is unique, yet many ethnographers find that, broadly speaking, their field research might be thought of as dividing into fairly distinct stages. With the warning that we risk oversimplify-

ing what is always more complicated in reality, we outline three stages. Again we ask you to imagine that you are an anthropologist just entering the field.

Adjustment. During the first few months of your project, you expend much of your energy simply adjusting to your new environment and overcoming culture shock. Your inquiries are cautious since you are in all probability an uninvited stranger. Even with prior study, you are unlikely to know the local language well

culture shock the sense of confusion and disorientation fieldworkers may experience upon entering the field

TABLE 2.1 THREE STAGES OF FIELDWORK

Stages	Sample Activities
Stage One: Adjustment	Coping with culture shock; beginning to learn the local language; establishing contacts; learning to schedule activities; making maps; taking photographs
Stage Two: Involvement	Continuing with language acquisition; collecting data relevant to research hypothesis; strengthening friendships
A SHORT BREAK FROM THE FIELD	
Stage Three: Achievement	Strengthening ties with community; widening range of topics; reflecting on the reflexive nature of your fieldwork

enough to enter into detailed discussions about anything; people seem to treat you as somewhat dimwitted, and indeed you feel as if you are. In any case you take pains to steer clear of topics likely to offend, embarrass, or arouse hostility in your informants. Personal contacts are few; you rely mainly on your eyes for information. You learn to find your way around, you map the area, you take photographs, because these are activities that do not require the assistance of local people or involve more conversation than you're capable of. You spend a lot of time writing letters home and eagerly awaiting return mail.

You also learn to schedule your activities. Since ethnographers usually go into the field not only with definite goals in mind but also with a limited amount of time in which to achieve them, most construct rough timetables. Few fieldwork plans are more certain to be overturned than those contained in such timetables, so they have to be flexible enough to allow for unforseen events. But they are nevertheless necessary. The "let's see, what should I do today?" attitude is no substitute for a systematic plan of inquiry.

Just how long this period of adjustment, contact making, language learning, and preliminary data gathering lasts depends on local circumstances and your particular talents and personality. Some fieldworkers are "adopted" into a local host family during this first stage, which helps immeasurably in establishing rapport, friendships, and a group of informants on whom to call for help.

Involvement. Most likely, after a few months you will have entered a second stage of fieldwork. Increasingly involved in and dependent on your informants' daily round of activities, you alter your own schedule to fit theirs. By now you know the most favor-

able times of the day to approach informants. At work they will not usually wish to talk, so during the day you visit old people or children at home. A convenient time to engage the workers of a community in conversation is after the evening meal, so the evening loneliness you experienced at the beginning of your fieldwork is lessened, but you'd still kill for a hamburger and some french fries.

Your second-stage questions, focusing directly on your research hypothesis, are organized around specific themes—local death rituals, perhaps, or the rules of land ownership or some other topic relevant to your hypothesis. By gearing your conversations with informants directly to the hypotheses you have come all this way to address, your time in the field—always too brief—is allocated economically.

Although you have by now weathered culture shock, some continuing strain is inevitable. You feel you are always on stage, your schedule of meals and rest is not what you are used to, you feel dependent on people's willingness to cooperate, and you worry that your work is not coming along fast enough or that the data you are getting are not of sufficient interest or depth. A break from the tension is usually called for after several months of this stage. If your budget doesn't permit returning home, you retreat for some well-earned rest to a city or town where things are more comfortable and less stressful than at your field site. Your short vacation comes as a welcome alternative to both the strains and the boredom that accompany ethnographic research.

Upon returning to the field, you may well find you are now welcomed as a friend, rather than merely tolerated as a stranger, and that your informants are pleased to strengthen ties established earlier.

Achievement. With your more confident command of the language, your greater familiarity with your

In an unfamiliar setting, it may be easier for a visitor to establish initial rapport with children than with other adults. On Woodlark Island in the Trobriand Island chain, a Westerner makes friends with children dressed for a dance.

informants, and your ever-deepening roots in the community, you may now feel more capable of achieving your fieldwork goals. You discover that the quantity and quality of the data you are acquiring are far greater than seemed possible when you were stumbling along in the first or second stages. Now, although you must still exercise caution, topics once too sensitive to introduce with strangers can be put, gently, to carefully chosen members of the community.

By now you will have come to appreciate the intensely personal nature of anthropological research. You will have had an emotional and intellectual impact on the people around you; they, in turn, will have had an impact on you. Fieldwork, you realize, is not just about collecting facts waiting "out there" for you to write down in your notebooks. Your informants are your companions, associates, teachers, and friends. How is the character of your relationships, you wonder, being reflected in the kind of questions you are now asking?

How is your involvement in the lives of people around you affecting the way you perceive the customs and beliefs you are trying to understand? Does the very fact of asking questions that may never have been asked before change, in however modest a way, your informants' own thinking about their culture? Reflections such as these will certainly influence your research. Far from seeming a straightforward job of collecting data, fieldwork emerges as an extremely interactive activity.

Fieldwork is thus a two-way street, a dialogue between the ethnographer and local people that affects everyone concerned. This feedback process is known as **reflexivity.** You may think about it again later, when you sit down to analyze and write up your field notes and realize just how subjective your account is. Today, acutely aware of reflexivity, some ethnographers are ex-

reflexivity the feedback process by which ethnographers and informants mutually affect one another

perimenting with ways to represent more accurately what it means to live in the cultures they attempt to describe. In addition to "facts," the ethnographer may describe his or her inner thoughts, feelings, or emotional reactions to local people's words or actions, thus giving readers a better "feel" for the culture being portrayed. (We'll return to this topic in Chapter 4.)

As the third stage progresses, you ask questions, record responses, and ask new questions in a cycle without apparent end. But suddenly, you realize time is running out. You take more notes or transcribe more tapes at a furious pace, your new feeling of ease in the community offset by the pressure of time. All too soon, you must leave.

The Problem of Gender

Does the sex of an anthropological fieldworker make any difference to the collection of ethnographic data? People in some cultures, perhaps most notably Muslim cultures, will not permit easy relationships between female ethnographers and male informants, and vice versa. But sometimes being female is an advantage. A woman can enter women's public bathhouses or other traditionally "female" settings that are strictly prohibited to men, while at the same time being at least tolerated in sports arenas or other traditionally male spheres. A man, although able to move freely within the world of men, is more apt to be completely excluded from the world of women (Sarsby 1984:124).

Even when excluded from the male domain, the female anthropologist may still have an edge. Describing how gender influenced her fieldwork in Greece, one anthropologist (R. Hirschon in Sarsby 1984:124) wrote,

> Often . . . I could not be involved in specified "male" activities or areas [like] coffee shops [or] football matches, [but] the limitations were not nearly as severe as they might seem. . . . I had the great advantage of free access to homes. Here it was possible to get to know *all* members of the family, male and female. In this respect, a single woman field worker has a distinct advantage over the male counterpart. . . .

Later in this chapter, we'll describe the fieldwork experience of Nancie Gonzalez and how being female affected her work in the Dominican Republic.

The Ethics of Fieldwork

Not long ago, a female ethnologist, interested in feminist issues and funded by a grant from a private ed-

Female anthropologists can sometimes gain access to fieldwork settings where males would be unwelcome. In Morocco, parties at which a bride's hands are decorated with henna prior to marriage are women's affairs.

ucational foundation, worked for a year in a rural West African society in order to study gender differences. One way in which females reinforced their self-identity in this society was by being initiated into adulthood, a process all girls of 11 or 12 seemed eager to undergo. In different stages of the long initiation ritual, girls symbolically "died," were removed for a time from other members of the society, were then "reborn" and given new names, and finally were accepted back into their community as marriageable adult women. The ceremonies accompanying the initial phases of this series of symbolic activities were fascinating, and the anthropologist enthusiastically observed, interviewed, scribbled notes, and took photographs for a future comparative study.

Then a dilemma arose. In the next stage of the

proceedings, the anthropologist learned, the young initiates were to undergo a surgical procedure, without anaesthesia, to alter the outward appearance of the genitalia. The anthropologist was surprised; she had read about such procedures but didn't know they were still practiced in her area.[1] What, if anything, should she do? Could she stand by and observe this event silently? Should she intervene, and if so, how? Should she try to impose her personal feminist values on the people who had permitted her to share their lives? Did her responsibilities to her grant-making organization, or to anthropology, outweigh her responsibilities to the initiates, or vice versa?

Cultural anthropology, to a far greater extent than most other sciences, involves intimate contact between researchers and those who are the focus of anthropological inquiry. Thus, also to a far greater extent than most other sciences, the behavior of the researcher as a human being counts. No matter how objective the researcher tries to be, there is always the possibility that any of the

---

[1]Female genital mutilation was officially condemned by the World Health Organization in 1979 but continues to be practiced, although its incidence is apparently declining. For more information, see Lightfoot-Klein (1989).

many relationships that can exist between individuals—secrecy or openness, affection or dislike, trust or mistrust—may develop and may color the research. And the data collected, if made known to outsiders, may have the potential to embarrass or perhaps even to harm the members of the society under study.

Those who practice cultural anthropology know that research involves more than collecting and publishing as much accurate information about people as possible. We have to balance our responsibilities to the people we are studying, to our sponsors, to the governments of countries that permit us to undertake research, to the profession of anthropology, and to our own consciences. Most cultural anthropologists would probably agree that on the whole, responsibility to the people they study should come first. But this is easier said than done: de-

◆ ASK YOURSELF

What would you do if faced with the fieldwork dilemma described above? Would you decide what to do yourself or consult someone else for advice? If you learned that the surgery would not actually be performed, but the initiates would not know this ahead of time, how would this change your response?

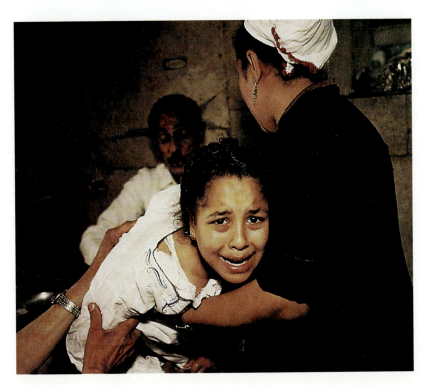

Fieldworkers may face situations that challenge their objectivity by presenting difficult ethical dilemmas. In Egypt, a young girl undergoes a traditional but dangerous procedure known as female circumcision.

Boas and Anthropological Ethics

The first public statement on ethics as an anthropological concern was contained in a letter written in 1919 by Franz Boas to *The Nation* (Weaver 1973:51–52). Boas claimed that several North American anthropologists, hired as U.S. government agents and using anthropology as a cloak, were spying against other governments. Boas was outraged. Anyone who "prostituted science" in this way, he declared, forfeited the right to be considered a scientist. The American Anthropological Association (AAA) did not agree. Stating that Boas's scathing letter was "unjustified," the AAA censured him and stripped him of his membership in its governing council.

Nearly half a century later, in 1965, a research project devised by the U.S. Department of Defense reopened the Pandora's box of controversy over the ethics of social scientific research (Horowitz 1967). Beginning in Latin America, "Project Camelot" was to call on social scientists to investigate the conditions under which social unrest arose in foreign countries and collect information on how to prevent uprisings against pro-American leaders. Such gross interference in the internal politics of other countries angered many anthropologists, who were among the most vocal opponents of the project. Project Camelot was canceled, and partly in response to the controversy, the AAA commissioned an inquiry into the relationships between sponsors and anthropologists, created a Committee on Research Problems and Ethics, and passed a Statement on Problems of Anthropological Research (Ackroyd 1984:135). In 1971, it finally established an official code of ethics (American Anthropological Association 1971).

Even the AAA code of ethics has not made anthropologists' ethical choices easy. As J. A. Barnes (1981:2, 22–23) puts it, "Ethical and intellectual compromise is an intrinsic characteristic of social research." Compromises must be made between commitment to the people one is studying and impartiality; between openness and secrecy; between honesty and deception; and among the pursuit of scientific knowledge, the public's right to know and the individual's right to privacy and protection.

ciding how best to protect the interests and welfare of a society under study may not be at all simple.

CONTEMPORARY FIELDWORKERS

In Chapter 1, we discussed the work of three pioneering anthropologists: Frank Cushing, Franz Boas, and Bronislaw Malinowski. Each undertook ethnographic research many decades ago and contributed significantly to the development not only of anthropology in general but also to ethnographic field methods in particular. Bear the fieldwork experiences of these three pioneers in mind as you share the experiences of two contemporary fieldworkers.

Napoleon Chagnon (1938–)

Napoleon Chagnon is well known for his fieldwork among the Yanomamo, who live in the Amazon region of South America. For his first visit to the Yanomamo in the mid-1960s, Chagnon was part of a multidisciplinary team assembled by a university department of human genetics to conduct medical research. At that time, the Yanomamo had had little contact with other cultures. They lived in small villages scattered widely throughout the remote tropical forest, and they spoke only their own language. Many had never seen anyone of European descent.

In the 1960s, the world knew little about the Yanomamo, yet given the pace at which small-scale societies were becoming swallowed up by larger ones, it was inevitable that the Yanomamo way of life would eventually change; indeed, it was already changing. Thus one of Chagnon's most compelling goals as the anthropologist on the team was to compile ethnographic data about this threatened culture. More specifically, his research hypothesis addressed the question of Yanomamo settlement patterns. Why were all those Yanomamo villages scattered throughout the jungle, how had this pattern come into being, and how long was it likely to last?

Chagnon also wanted to collect data on genealogical ties, information that would help him discover whether or not family relationships provided the basis of Yanomamo village composition. This proved difficult since the Yanomamo observed a strict taboo against mentioning aloud the names of individuals, living or dead. Chagnon (1992:20) nevertheless set to work constructing elaborate family trees, and after five months "smugly thought I had cracked the system" of Yanomamo family organization. But his "anthropological bubble burst" when he discovered that the names he had been so carefully writing down in his notebooks were inventions. Not only were the "names" entirely fictional; many were Yanomamo insults! Chagnon describes the reactions, from "stunned silence" to "uncontrollable laughter," that afflicted one group of villagers when he "named" the wife of a community headman (21). He had to begin all over again. Having originally collected names during public interviews, he now began conducting private sessions, thereby reducing his informants' clowning.

As his command of the Yanomamo language improved and his informants grew more comfortable with his "pesky" questions, Chagnon's body of data increased, until at last he was able to shed some light on his initial research problem. He discovered that many currently occupied Yanomamo villages were recent colonies, splintered off from larger villages. An interesting pattern began to emerge. There appeared to be cause-and-effect connections among the size of villages, their genealogical compositions, the age and sex distributions of their members, and marriage alliances between families. Warfare emerged as a factor controlling the size and distribution of villages. Chagnon (1992:31–32) realized he must visit many villages to document the genealogical aspects of Yanomamo society, make detailed censuses, and map the locations of existing villages and others that had been abandoned. He adjusted his research strategy and began visiting village after village, collecting oral histories about Yanomamo wars, village breakups, and migrations.

Following the lead of Cushing and Malinowski, Chagnon committed himself to full participant observation. On one occasion, he was working on notes for a genealogy in his hut when two of his Yanomamo friends appeared at the door. The local Christian missionary, they reported, had been telling the villagers that unless they stopped their traditional custom of chanting to the *hekura* (spirits), God would destroy them. Chagnon, whose attitude toward the missionary appears to have resembled that of the Zuni toward Dust-eye (Chapter 1), was angry. To show the missionary how he felt, Chagnon (1983:207) said to his friends, "Let's *all* go chant to the hekura!"

Preparations for the chant began. The Yanomamo decorated Chagnon (1983:208) with feathers and painted his face and chest so he would look his best for the spirits. Then, just like a Yanomamo, he permitted his companions to puff a hallucinogenic powder into his nostrils through a long wooden tube. It was painful. Coughing and retching, he rubbed the back of his head to reduce the pain. More powder; more retching, but the pain diminished. The Yanomamo, too, were taking the drug, but bit by bit Chagnon lost interest in them. His knees grew rubbery and his peripheral vision faded. Soon he began to feel as if he were filled with a strange power. Yanomamo songs began to whirr through his brain, and "almost involuntarily" he began to sing. Blips of light flashed before his eyes. He began to dance in the manner of Yanomamo men, calling to the spirits, inviting them

A Yanomamo Victory

In November 1991, after a 20-year struggle by various activists, the president of Brazil moved to reserve a stretch of the Amazon rain forest as a homeland for the Yanomamo. This new reserve, together with a somewhat smaller area across the border in Venezuela, would allow the Yanomamo to range freely over 70,000 square miles of Amazon wilderness. Interviewed by the *New York Times,* Napoleon Chagnon, who had taken on the role of an anthropological advocate (see Chapter 16) to help bring this about, said, "This will go a long way to making cultural survival of the [Yanomamo] a real possibility" (Brooke 1991:A3). Thus, despite the objections of mining corporations, the cultural resources of the Yanomamo will be conserved, together with the natural resources on which these people depend.

to come into his chest and dwell within him. Feeling great confidence, he sang louder and danced with more complex steps. Taking up a friend's arrows, he struck magical blows, searching the horizon for spirits, sensing "intimately why [some Yanomamo] went daily through the pain of taking their drugs, for the experience was exhilarating and stimulating" (208–209).

As it happened, a German visitor was present, clicking photos of the "mad anthropologist going native." Chagnon (1983:209–210) couldn't care less. As his "high" reached ecstatic proportions, he broke the arrows over his head (to the groans of the arrow makers) and pranced wildly with the splinters clutched tightly in his fists. Later he reported that what thrilled him most about this episode was "the freedom to give complete reign to the imagination . . . to shed my cultural shackles and fetters, to cease being a North American animal up to a point and be Yanomamo" (209). Participant observation cannot go much further.

Chagnon was interested in change in Yanomamo society. After collecting baseline ethnographic data during 15 months of fieldwork between 1964 and 1966, he repeated his visits until by 1992 he had spent a total of about 60 months among the Yanomamo. Between 1964 and 1983, as more and more missionaries, settlers, and miners ventured into Yanomamo territory (an area rich in gold, diamonds, and zinc), the Yanomamos' original way of life began to change very rapidly. Chagnon took a filmmaker on subsequent visits and helped shoot over 80,000 feet of ethnographic film. By 1983 he had completed some twenty documentaries on the Yanomamo. Together with numerous articles and several books, Chagnon's films have transformed one of the least known nonliterate peoples into one of the best known.

Nancie L. Gonzalez (1929–)

In the mid-1960s, few anthropological field studies had yet dealt with the problems posed by the migration of rural people to urban communities and the cultural changes that result in both countryside and towns. Nancie Gonzalez decided to study these topics, choosing the Dominican Republic, which shares the large Caribbean island of Hispaniola with Haiti, as her field site. Combining features of Latin American and Caribbean urbanization, previously studied only in Puerto Rico, the country's political atmosphere and social setting seemed well suited to anthropological work (Gonzalez 1974:21).

Gonzalez began her 14 months of fieldwork in July 1967, in the city of Santiago de los Caballeros, at that time home to some 85,000 people. Far from being the typical lone ethnographer, she was accompanied by her two sons, seven and nine years old, as well as a pair of married graduate students who were collecting data for their doctoral theses.

Gonzalez originally found a humble place to live on the outskirts of the city, but this soon proved to be a mistake. Although surrounded by immigrant neighbors, she soon realized that to incorporate herself into the life of the city as a whole she needed to live in the center of town, for only there could she be around when things happened. So Gonzalez and her sons moved into a once fashionable but now deteriorating neighborhood only a block from the main plaza. Wealthier informants remembered the area's former prestige and even the splendor of the mansion she rented, and poorer ones did not feel uncomfortable visiting. Moreover, her new house had a telephone, indispensable for urban research.

Taking her sons with her into the field had its advantages, too. Gonzalez (1974:24) enrolled them in school, where they were quickly accepted into a local gang of neighborhood children. From this "insider" position they were able to enlighten their mother on aspects of life in Santiago she could never have learned had she been alone. As informal field assistants, the boys gave their mother data on children's games, problems, and attitudes toward adults. For example, Gonzalez knew that members of the city's middle and upper classes celebrated Christmas with Christmas trees, Santa Claus, and gifts. But until her youngest son told her, she did not know that poor children had to wait until January 6 (King's Day) to receive their presents because, they said, their working mothers did not get paid until January 1.

Since she was also interested in the effects of immigration into Santiago on the rural communities the immigrants had left, Gonzalez (1974:25) had to pick a second suitable research site, a rural village. Her two graduate students moved into this community, beginning their field research with a census of the local population. In this way they were able to learn the names and addresses of local people who had emigrated to Santiago, so Gonzalez could look them up and collect information about family and marital patterns, household economics, and reasons for migration (26).

As her fieldwork progressed, Gonzalez realized that Santiago's elites controlled the social and economic opportunities available to the immigrants. Thus she could not restrict her inquiries to informants of lower

In the Dominican Republic, fieldworker Nancie Gonzalez's young sons acted as their mother's informal assistants. Gonzalez's two sons were practically indistinguishable from their Dominican playmates.

status; studying the elites would be just as important. But this presented problems. Her previous experience as a participant observer had been in rural areas, and she was unprepared to work among urban elites. Her fieldwork wardrobe, for example, consisted mainly of jeans and casual shirts, but silk dresses would have been more suitable for dealing with upper-class people. Having learned to dress in a particular style, speak in a certain way, and use one kind of table manners, she was now obliged to "acquire different patterns in order to establish rapport with another group in the population" (Gonzalez 1974:27–28).

Gender, too, affected her social status. The elites of heavily Catholic Santiago, among whom divorce was almost nonexistent, were unused to the idea of a single female as the head of a household (Gonzalez 1984:104). Upper-class women in particular, perhaps viewing Gonzalez as a competitor for the attentions of the local males of their class, were reluctant to accept a young, attractive, unattached American woman. Her relationships with middle-class women were somewhat closer, but only among lower-class women could she truly relax.

Working with the elites of Santiago also raised an interesting ethical problem. Gonzalez's upper-class informants were both relatively few in number and promi-

nent in city life. Moreover, on occasion they shared information with her that she felt was politically sensitive. If she was not very careful with her research data, the anonymity of her informants might be compromised, to their embarrassment. So concerned was Gonzalez to protect her informants that she decided not to publish the book she later wrote about her Santiago research. In an article resulting from her fieldwork, she carefully disguised her informants' identities (Gonzalez 1972).

Some of the "special psychological problems" that confronted Nancie Gonzalez during her fieldwork resulted from the circumstances peculiar to urban research. Unlike most nonliterate people or peasants, for instance, Santiago's residents stayed up late, and the activities Gonzalez wanted to study would often last far into the night. Other problems were caused by the "extreme pressures" of her particular circumstances. Trying to fulfill many different and even contradictory roles—researcher, mother, teacher, friend—and having to shift quickly and frequently from one form of behavior to another were emotionally exhausting. To add to these problems, Gonzalez's intended study of immigrants' interactions with their home communities proved impossible. (This is not a rare experience for fieldworkers; many a research hypothesis has had to be adjusted in the field or even abandoned for a new one.) The final results of her fieldwork bore little resemblance to the research design she had initially planned (Gonzalez 1974:34).

Despite these difficulties, Gonzalez's fieldwork produced findings of considerable importance to urban anthropology. She was able to demonstrate that to understand how cities work, ethnographers need to pay more attention to the roles of upper- and middle-class inhabitants (Gonzalez 1974:19). More specifically, she demonstrated that rural-urban differences in the Dominican Republic were far less marked than social scientists had generally assumed. And she showed that in the ranking system of this particular urban center, differences in life-styles and the associated values and expectations of immigrants and long-time city dwellers were the result not so much of the contrast between rural and urban origins as between the haves and the have-nots, regardless of where they came from (38).

Nancie Gonzalez's experience offers a good lesson in urban fieldwork methods. Like all cultural anthropologists, urban anthropologists rely heavily on participant observation, but they also use other research techniques sometimes denied to ethnographers of isolated, nonliterate people. First, urban anthropologists have access to written documents, which in a few cases go back as much as 6,000 years, to the time when urban centers first appeared. Second, because urban communities are large, geographically concentrated, and usually literate, the field technique of using surveys and questionnaires is particularly helpful. And third, because of its great quantity and comparability, information collected in surveys and from documents and questionnaires lends itself especially well to statistical analysis.

CONCLUSION

As the work of Napoleon Chagnon and Nancie Gonzalez shows, the modern techniques by which anthropologists collect information about cultures have come a long way since Cushing, Boas, and Malinowski. But if jet travel, computers, and network analysis have made the job of fieldwork easier, the impetus behind fieldwork, the kinds of information ethnographers seek in the field, and the main strategy they use to go about getting this information all remain much the same. The discipline is still concerned with finding, describing, and explaining human behavior—and the more anthropologists learn about this subject, the more, it seems, there is to discover.

SUMMARY

This chapter describes the way in which many ethnographers obtain their data: by going into the field and, using a particular strategy designed to obtain the kind of information being sought, testing specific hypotheses to learn more about why human beings behave as they do.

The chapter outlines the way in which modern ethnographers select their goals, locales, and methods, always with specific hypotheses in mind. It describes participant observation, the major strategy of ethnographers, and discusses the techniques that accompany (or sometimes substitute for) this strategy: interviewing; sampling; collecting genealogies, life histories, and case studies; filming and taping; studying material culture; using team research; and employing surveys, questionnaires, and network analysis.

Fieldwork is often fraught with difficulties, and the chapter describes some of the problems that commonly bedevil ethnographers—obtaining permission for research, culture shock, difficult gender relations, and either affection or mistrust on the part of both researchers and informants. A particularly thorny problem is that ethnographic data, if not handled appropriately, may embarrass or even harm the people under study. Anthropologists must strike a balance among competing responsibilities to the people they study, their sponsoring institutions, the governments of countries that give permission for anthropological research, the profession of anthropology itself, and their own consciences. Most fieldworkers are able to surmount these problems and successfully pursue their goals through stages of fieldwork that we have called adjustment, involvement, and achievement.

The chapter ends with a description of the ways in which two modern fieldworkers, Napoleon Chagnon and Nancie Gonzalez, obtained their research findings.

KEY TERMS

armchair anthropologist	key informant
case study	life history
casual informant	material culture
control group	network analysis
culture shock	personal survey
ego-centered network	reflexivity
ethnographer	respondent
ethnography	respondent survey
fieldwork	sampling
focus group	set-centered network
genealogy	survey
interview	

•••

SUGGESTED READINGS

Agar, Michael H. 1980. *The Professional Stranger: An Informal Introduction to Ethnography.* New York: Academic Press. An account of how research in anthropology is carried out. The author brings his own experiences into his suggestions to the reader. We have made extensive use of Agar's book in this chapter.

Ellen, Roy (ed.). 1984. *Ethnographic Research: A Guide to General Conduct.* ASA Research Methods in Social Anthropology 1. London: Academic Press. A comprehensive guide to carrying out ethnographic research, with contributions from experts in various specialties. As with Agar's book, we have used Ellen's book extensively in this chapter.

Mead, Margaret. 1972. *Blackberry Winter.* New York: Simon & Schuster. An autobiography describing the early fieldwork of one of the world's most famous anthropologists.

Parkin, Frank. 1986. *Krippendorf's Tribe.* New York: Dell. A comic novel about an anthropologist whose fieldwork documents the strange customs of a particularly unusual group: members of his own family.

Rabinow, Paul. 1977. *Reflections on Fieldwork in Morocco.* Berkeley: University of California Press. This short but perceptive book argues cogently that the fieldwork setting and the individuals the fieldworker encounters strongly affect the fieldworker, the material collected, and its interpretation.

Russell, Bernard H. 1988. *Research Methods in Cultural Anthropology.* Newbury Park, CA: Sage Publications. An excellent and enjoyable manual on research, focusing on preparing for field research, collecting data, and analyzing data.

Sanjek, Roger (ed.). 1990. *Fieldnotes: The Makings of Anthropology.* Ithaca, NY: Cornell University Press. A well-balanced collection of articles illustrating the fieldwork not only of traditional but also of feminist and postmodernist anthropologists.

Shostak, Marjorie. 1983. *Nisa: The Life and Words of a !Kung Woman.* New York: Vintage Books. An evocative portrayal of a woman's life among African gatherers and hunters.

Whitehead, Tony L., and Mary Ellen Conaway (eds.). 1986. *Self, Sex and Gender in Cross-Cultural Fieldwork.* Urbana: University of Illinois Press. Sixteen case studies dealing with the reciprocal impact of fieldworkers' personalities and behavior and those of people under study. A special focus is how the sex of the ethnographer affects this interaction.

CHAPTER 3

Acculturation is the process of change that results from contact between cultures. In Brazil, a member of the Kayapó culture uses a videocamera, a product of the culture of the industrialized Western world, to record a political rally.

INTRODUCTION

In 1799, a strange, filthy, nearly naked boy was found wandering in the wooded countryside near the village of Aveyron, France. He appeared to be perhaps 11 or 12 years old and had apparently been living alone in the woods for many years. Brought to Paris, this "dirty, scared, inarticulate creature who trotted and grunted like the beasts" became an object of great curiosity (Itard

1962:vi). Because he could neither speak nor behave like a normal person, he was assumed by Parisians to be an incurable idiot. But a young French doctor, Jean-Marc-Gaspard Itard, doubted that the child, dubbed the "Wild Boy of Aveyron," was simply mentally deficient. Itard thought that if the child had grown up in isolation from other humans, deprived of culture, this might explain his odd behavior. Itard made up his mind to try to cure the "idiot."

Itard attempted to introduce the Wild Boy to French culture by giving him language lessons, dressing him like a typical French boy, and trying to persuade him to imitate the behavior of others, whether at the dinner table, in the classroom, or on the dance floor. Sadly, however, the doctor's treatment was not a great success. Despite five years of devoted effort, Itard was unable to teach the Wild Boy to behave like a normal human being. For one thing, the boy may indeed have had less than normal intelligence, although various observers disagreed on this point. But the main reason why Itard was unable to transform the Wild Boy into a typical nineteenth-century Parisian was because of the boy's apparently total lack of exposure to culture during his impressionable early years, a time when the "ordinary child is learning to be a human being" (Itard 1962:xi). It seems as though we humans must absorb culture early, or we will not absorb it at all. For the Wild Boy, the opportunity came too late.

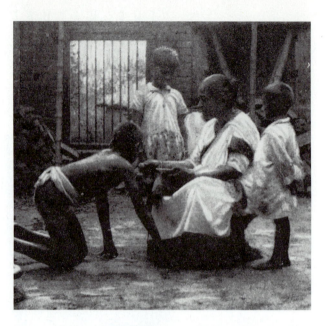

Because they are deprived of culture, children who grow up in isolation behave differently from other human beings. Kamala, found living alone in the jungle in India, may have been deprived of culture since babyhood. She moves about on all fours and eats from her guardian's hand.

THE CONCEPT OF CULTURE

What Is Culture?

In Chapter 1, we defined culture as all the things people think, do, say, and make—in other words, their ideas, behaviors, languages, and artifacts. These include institutions (such as marriage), political ideas (such as democracy), religious beliefs (such as witchcraft), customs (like decorating Christmas trees), rituals (like

saluting the flag), art styles, games, stories, and much more.

Except for physical anthropology, which is devoted to the biological rather than the cultural aspects of what it means to be human, each of the fields into which anthropology is divided focuses on one or more of these aspects of culture. Cultural anthropologists are most concerned with the customs and ideas of living human beings, although they are also interested in people's artifacts and languages. Archaeologists focus on the artifacts of people who lived in the past, which they usually find buried in the ground, using these objects to shed light on the customs, ideas, and even the languages of ancient people. Anthropological linguists study languages, both ancient and modern, within the context of people's customs, ideas, and artifacts. The concept of culture is the theme that unites all three fields of anthropology.

Because the concept of culture is both complex and absolutely fundamental to anthropology, we'll refine our definition by describing and analyzing culture's various characteristics.

Culture Is Collective. Not everything that any given individual thinks, does, says, or makes can be con-

◆ **ASK YOURSELF**

What does the word culture mean to you? Sometimes it is defined in terms of certain activities, such as going to the opera or reading poetry. What is the relationship between that definition and the one we are proposing?

sidered a part of that person's culture, for culture is collective—shared by the members of a group—rather than individual. Culture thus consists of all the customs, ideas, artifacts, and languages that human beings *share with* and *learn from* one another, collectively and down through the generations.

Culture Is Compulsory.   Individuals who wish to get along successfully have no option but to take their society's culture into account in their dealings with others. Even individuals who don't accept one or more aspects of their culture usually behave the way most others behave because the penalty for not doing so may be stiff. You may not believe personally in representative government, an important aspect of mainstream Western culture, but to barge into the U.S. Senate and insist on representing yourself would probably land you in jail.

Culture Is Essential for Social Life.   Culture isn't shared only when the members of a group feel like cooperating; it is essential for people's very existence as members of a group. A mechanism for solving the problems of human existence, culture enables people to establish families and form communities, to communicate with one another, to work cooperatively to make a living, to maintain order in their lives, to give meaning to life by believing in something, to express themselves creatively, and to raise new generations of people who can continue to live and work together. We can view a given culture as a complex set of problem-solving strategies for satisfying people's needs within a particular social environment, which itself exists with a given natural environment.[1]

Culture Is Integrated.   Essential to the concept of culture is the idea of holism. We used the term *holistic* in Chapter 1 to describe anthropology as an all-encompassing study of humanity from four different points of view. But anthropologists also use the term to convey the idea that the various aspects of any culture are closely interrelated, even as the different but interconnected parts of a car's engine work together to keep the car running smoothly. Anthropologists study cultures holistically because it is the interconnections among the different aspects of a culture that give the culture mean-

ing. Well over a hundred years ago, the English armchair scholar Sir Edward Burnett Tylor (1873:1) defined culture as "that complex whole which includes knowledge, belief, art, morals, law, custom, and any other capabilities and habits acquired by man as a member of society." In his use of the word *whole,* Tylor recognized the thorough integration of the different aspects of any culture.

Culture Is Dynamic.   Both cultures and car engines are dynamic; they constantly change rather than remain static. Even a small change to one of the parts of an engine—a little wear and tear, perhaps—may cause the whole engine to operate differently. Likewise, a change in one aspect of culture may produce much broader cultural changes.

What might cause a culture to change? This question is so important in anthropology that we devote an entire chapter (Chapter 16) to it, but just to give you an idea, a culture might change in response to internal or environmental factors, or influences exerted on it by another culture through trade, war, population movements, missionary activity, or (nowadays) worldwide communications systems. The process by which major changes take place within a culture in response to the influences of another is called **acculturation.** The mosaic of cultures existing in the world today reflects the past and present spread of ideas among the world's people. In what is perhaps the most dramatic instance of acculturation, Western cultures began spreading their influence to all corners of the world around 1500. Sometimes this influence has been beneficial (as with the spread of Western medicines); sometimes, it has resulted in the destruction of cultures. In Chapter 2 we provided an example of destructive acculturation among the Yanomamo.

Culture Is Unique to Humans.   When a society is defined simply as a group whose members live in the same place and whose lives and livelihoods are interdependent (see Chapter 1), even animals may be said to form societies. Troops of baboons, for instance, may be likened to societies. From a biological point of view, baboons and other nonhuman higher primates (all the monkeys and apes) are humans' closest animal relatives, and some students of animal behavior have argued that these primates—monkeys of various kinds, chimpanzees, orangutans, and gorillas—possess culture of an elemen-

---

[1]We need to distinguish clearly between "culture" as we defined it in Chapter 1, and "the culture" of a particular society, which is all the cultural things that characterize that particular society.

♦♦

acculturation the process by which important changes take place in a culture as the result of contact with another culture

tary type. Most cultural anthropologists would probably not agree. We'll take this subject up again in a moment (see Animal Symbols? below). For now, we do not consider the behavior of any nonhuman creatures to be cultural.

Culture Versus Nature

Besides identifying and examining the characteristics of culture, a second way to understand this concept is to compare it with nature. If culture is all the things people think, do, say, and make, *nature* (as the term is applied to humans) is all the things people inherit biologically and can't change. Your eye color is natural; your haircut is cultural. The shape, size, and health of your body is a combination of both natural and cultural influences such as genes, diet, and exercise.

Although human beings are, of course, products of both nature and culture, some societies have deemphasized the natural aspects of what makes us human, dis-

 ASK YOURSELF

Are there aspects of Western culture you really don't like or of which you disapprove? Do you behave as if you accept these cultural features? What would the penalty be if you publicly rejected them?

tinguishing themselves from all other forms of life on the basis of their cultural attributes, which are often seen as superior to natural attributes. Westerners thus speak of "conquering" nature, in this way forging an opposition between the two concepts.

But Western societies aren't the only ones to identify culture as that which makes humans special and superior to all other forms of life. Fascinated with the concept of culture as long ago as 2000 B.C., the ancient Babylonians apparently conceptualized culture as the opposite of nature too. In the earliest story to have come down to us in written form, the *Epic of Gilgamesh,* the Babylonians contrasted culture with nature in a sprawling tale consisting of 72 poems written over the course of 1000 years. On its surface, the epic recounts the strange adventures of Gilgamesh, a great hero-king who ruled the city of Uruk (Warka in Iraq today). Symbolically, however, the epic is a parable that chronicles the separation of what is human or cultural (embodied in the person of Lullu-amelu, the first human being) from what is wild or natural (Gardner and Maier 1985:15).

THE TRANSMISSION OF CULTURE

Culture, as the Wild Boy of Aveyron illustrates, is not genetic; it has to be learned. We call the process by

---

Marriage in America

Marriage exists, in some form or another, in virtually every society known to anthropology. As practiced in mainstream Western culture, marriage is a legal and social union, intended to be permanent, between two—and only two—people of opposite sexes. (In Chapter 7 you'll see that this definition does not apply to marriage in all cultures.)

This particular kind of marriage is a Western cultural institution, with all the cultural characteristics discussed above. It's collective because the rules that govern it are learned by members of younger generations from members of older ones; people don't reinvent marriage in every generation, nor is the institution the product of any one person's mind. It's compulsory in that people who wish to function successfully in Western society have no choice about

whether to recognize it or not. If a Westerner ignores his society's marriage customs and asks a married woman for a date, her husband is likely to punch him in the nose. Because it functions to regulate sexual access, marriage is essential for group life; imagine the problems that would occur in Western society if there were no rules about who could have sex with whom! It is intimately related to other aspects of culture—residential arrangements, for example, or child rearing—thus providing an example of the integration characteristic of all cultures. Finally, marriage is a dynamic institution, changing in response to other changes in Western culture. One need only compare the rates of marriage and divorce now with those of the past to appreciate how much this institution has changed over the last couple of decades.

The institution of marriage is part of the culture of every society, although the details of what marriage entails differ from society to society. In North America (but not everywhere), marriage is a legal and social union between one man and one woman.

which an individual absorbs the details of his or her particular culture, starting from the moment of birth, **enculturation.** (Don't confuse this term with *acculturation,* which we defined previously.) There are three main, and

somewhat overlapping, ways in which the process of enculturation takes place: through symbols, through imitation, and through experience.

Symbols

> The flag of the United States of America . . . should be displayed on all days when the weather permits. . . . No disrespect should be shown to the flag; [it] should not be dipped to any person or thing. . . . The flag should never be carried flat or horizontally, but always aloft and free . . . [and] when the flag is passing . . . all persons present should face the flag, stand at attention, and salute.
>
> *Public Law 623 of the 77th Congress of the United States of America*

A **symbol,** to use the simplest definition of the term, is something that stands for something else (Needham 1979:7). A rectangular piece of cloth imprinted with a design consisting of a certain arrangement of stars and stripes in specific colors symbolizes the United States of America; and when you display this object, recite the Pledge of Allegiance to it, or salute it, you are symbolizing your loyalty to your country and your

enculturation the process by which an individual absorbs the details of his or her particular culture, starting from birth

symbol something that stands for something else

THE ANTHROPOLOGIST AT WORK

Some anthropologists combine their interests in both culture and nature by focusing on the relationship between people and the natural environments in which they live. Applied anthropologist Shirley Fiske is one of them. As an employee of the U. S. government's National Oceanic and Atmospheric Administration (NOAA), she oversees research on coastal environmental issues that is used to help local governments, businesses, and the owners of beachfront homes decide how best to manage

The barrier islands off the coast of Rhode Island are densely populated, but homeowners face the loss of their property in the near future due to erosion. After a severe coastal storm, anthropologist Shirley Fiske assesses the extent of the damage and talks with a marine extension specialist about how to help constituents protect their vulnerable shoreline.

coastal processes such as flooding and erosion, while at the same time protecting the natural environment. In this way she helps integrate culture and nature in the coastal zone.

agreement with the ideals on which the government is based. From this everyday example we can draw two important conclusions about symbols. First, a symbol can be an object (such as a flag), a series of words (such as a pledge), or an action (such as a salute), and any of these symbols can represent an abstract idea (freedom). Second, to use a symbol is to communicate something—a concept, an attitude, or a feeling.

In every society, symbols are the most important vehicles by which culture is transmitted. Whether in the form of language, actions, or objects, people constantly employ symbols in doing, thinking, saying, and making things. Moreover, the symbols used by members of a so-

ciety often form integrated symbolic systems. A language, for instance, is the integrated use of many sounds, many gestures, and many tones of voice, every one of which is a symbol in its own right. Hence a language is an integrated system of symbols.

Animal Symbols?   If symbols are things that stand for other things, the capacity to use symbols is not uniquely human. Although they do not use human beings' most common symbols, words, animals often use sounds, colors, scents, and body movements to stand for other things. With a flash of colorful plumage, a male bird-of-paradise sends a message about its maleness; a dog purposefully urinates to mark the edges of its turf; a horse whinnies with alarm to signal the approach of a dangerous snake. To distinguish the kinds of symbolic behavior of which animals are capable from human symbol making, anthropologists use the word *signs* (or sometimes *signals*) for nonhuman symbols (see Chapter 13).

An argument *can* be made for the occasional use of symbols, as we have defined them, by our nearest relatives in the animal kingdom, the apes. Researchers studying primates' ability to acquire language have taught captive chimpanzees and gorillas to communicate with humans by using some symbolic system, such as sign language (the language of the deaf), colored plastic shapes, or typewriter or computer keys.

Apes, then, do have some capacity to use symbols, but this capacity is a product of human culture. Apes do not communicate with one another by these methods in the wild, although they might occasionally use objects to represent concepts. An angry chimpanzee may snatch up a stick and wave it threateningly over its head. Is the stick a symbol, and must we therefore concede that noncaptive animals use symbols as well as signs? Or are the ape's threatening posture and movements, including its seizing of a stick, merely what we have defined as signs?

Although one might argue for either side of this issue, an important difference between the symbolic behavior of animals and that of humans exists. We use symbols much more frequently and in a far wider range of situations than animals. Rather than repeating the same symbols over and over again, as animals do, we constantly vary and elaborate on our symbols, and we frequently invent new ones. And our symbols are mostly arbitrary: there is no direct or obvious connection between the thumb-out gesture of a hitchhiker and the

A symbol is something that stands for something else. A flag bearing a particular arrangement of stars and stripes symbolizes the United States of America, and saluting this flag symbolizes loyalty to the United States.

The Evil Eye

Depending on their differing environmental, social, or economic conditions or their cultural traditions, members of different cultures often attach different meanings to similar experiences. The everyday human experience of illness or other misfortune is a case in point. In most of the Western world, if your baby gets the measles or your car breaks down, these are *your* problems, not society's; illness and misfortune are seen as quite separate from social life. But in much of the non-Western world, this attitude is very rare. Instead, illness and misfortune may be seen as resulting from the deliberate or unintentional actions of members of your community.

One widespread belief of this type, found around the Mediterranean and extending over an enormous range southward into Africa, eastward into South Asia, and northward into Europe, is that someone can cause misfortune to befall another merely by *looking* at that person or at his or her property (Dundes 1981). Where this belief prevails, the human eye is a symbol of evil or of the potential for evil.

In many cultures, the evil eye embodies the feeling of envy. To ward off the evil eye, individuals, depending on their cultures, may display charms such as chili peppers, snakeskins, shoes, or horns. These are believed to distract the evil eye or to absorb the evil directed toward a person or object. One Middle Eastern way of diverting the evil eye is to display a blue bead, sometimes with a painted eye. Often, the first gift a baby receives, this is pinned to the inside of its cradle. Blue beads are also used to protect animals and property. You can see them decorating the radiator grilles of cars, trucks, and busses or dangling from the harnesses of donkeys.

Since, in many cases, the evil transmitted by the evil eye consists of envy, anything excessively desirable, such as a pretty child or your best milking ewe, stands out as a tempting target. To ensure yourself from becoming its victim, and to avoid casting the evil eye yourself, you neither accept nor give compliments, and you avoid displaying perfection or good fortune at all costs. It is considered very poor form, for example, to tell a mother what a beautiful baby she has; instead, you neutralize your compli-

The belief that people can cause harm to other people or their property with an evil glance is widespread, and various symbols are used to ward off this "evil eye." In India, vehicles are protected from the evil eye by old shoes or, as on the truck above, pictures of shoes.

ment by couching it in some oblique phrase. For her part, the mother may protect her child from the evil eye by smudging its forehead with dirt so that it is less than perfect (Maloney 1976:103).

Why should the eye have become a symbol for misfortune in so much of the world? Anthropologist Joe Delmonaco (1986) argues that the evil eye symbolically expresses some of the problems inherent in human interaction. In many societies, Delmonaco claims, the evil eye is associated with a fear of the violation of privacy, and consequently with the loss of the self-control and security that privacy creates in social life. He sees the evil eye as an *exposing* eye, and has found that frequently it is the overly curious person—the busybody—who is suspected of casting the evil eye. This person can be someone familiar, such as the neighborhood gossip, but the individuals most strongly suspected are outsiders who exhibit excessive curiosity—such as ethnographers!

Our closest nonhuman relatives, the apes, occasionally employ symbols to convey ideas. Using sign language taught him during a study of primates' ability to use language, a chimpanzee tells his trainer he's thirsty.

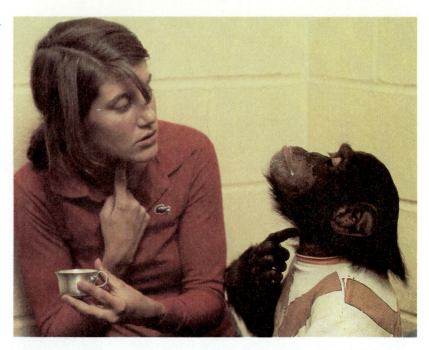

message "I need a ride."[2] Finally, human symbols are conventional; they are widely understood among members of the same group. So distinctive is our symbolic behavior that we might define *Homo sapiens sapiens* as the only species of animal capable of frequent, infinitely varied, constantly elaborated, and widely understood symbolic behavior.

Symbolic Anthropology. Given that symbols are the most common transmitters of culture, it's obvious that studying the symbols used by a particular community of people will help us to understand their culture. Indeed, so important are symbols that there is a special subfield of cultural anthropology, called **symbolic anthropology,** devoted to the cross-cultural study of symbols. Symbolic anthropologists have shown that an analysis of the symbols used by members of a society helps us decipher whatever significance lies hidden in their behavior and discover patterns of meaning within and among cultures. Language, art, games, rituals, colors, and fables are all subjects for symbolic analysis, now considered a major avenue by which to approach an understanding of culture.

Symbolic anthropologists sometimes focus on the

use of just one symbol, such as the evil eye, either within a single culture or cross-culturally. More frequently, they address themselves to the study of systems of symbols, analyzing how symbols are used in concert to communicate messages. In his analysis of the symbolism of the Ndembu, a south-central African society, anthropologist Victor Turner (1967:48–55) chose the local "milk" tree to illustrate how symbols of at least three different kinds—objects, actions, and institutions—can be coherently combined into a meaningful part of Ndembu culture.

The Ndembu see that when you scratch the thin bark of the milk tree, a milky, white sap oozes out. For them, this sap is the tree's most important physical property, and on it they base an ever-widening series of symbols that ultimately entails six different referents: the white sap (actually beads of latex) symbolizes human milk (1), which symbolizes the female breast (2), from which human milk flows. The breast in turn symbolizes the suckling of infants (3), which symbolizes the mother-child bond (4). This important tie symbolizes a social group crucial to Ndembu society, the family (5), and the family, finally, symbolizes Ndembu society (6) in its entirety.

The Ndembu have thus incorporated into their culture a series of symbols in which each object, action, or institution can serve as a symbol for another (see Figure 3.1). The chain starts with tangible symbols—beads of

---

[2]In parts of the Middle East, the thumb-out hitchhiking symbol Westerners are familiar with is an obscene gesture.

latex, milk, the female breast—and progresses to abstract ones. The breast symbolizes an action—nursing a baby—which in turn stands for something more abstract—a social institution, the relationship between two individuals. This tie symbolizes a wider social institution, the family, which ultimately symbolizes yet another, Ndembu society as a whole. There is in this symbolic system a logical progression from material symbols through a series of increasingly abstract symbols to the ultimate referent. No single referent alone can convey the full symbolic meaning of the milk tree to the Ndembu, for the tree's meaning lies in the combination of all six referents, and any particular referent can be fully understood only within the holistic context provided by all referents.

Because it does not depend on language, imitation is a particularly important way of enculturating the young. In Zaire, Africa, an Efe child learns to prepare leaves for thatch by imitating her mother.

Imitation

We human beings also transmit culture by wordless, nonsymbolic, imitative behavior. Because it does not depend on language, imitation is an important way in which infants and children are enculturated. When a rural Caribbean mother washes clothes in a stream, her small daughter may gravely imitate every motion. The mother is communicating an aspect of her culture to her daughter, and the daughter is learning it, yet neither is using symbols. Learning by imitation is not confined to children. If you have a driver's license, you know that

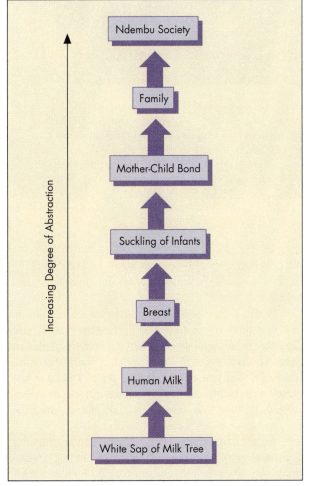

Figure 3.1
In the Ndembu series of symbols, each object, action, or institution can serve as a symbol for another.

symbolic anthropology the anthropological study of symbols

Right Versus Left

In all cultures about which we have the relevant information, *right* is considered to be superior to *left*. Further, *right* usually symbolizes goodness and strength, whereas *left* is associated with evil and weakness. This symbolism may date back to our Paleolithic ancestors. In Kenya, Stone Age skeletons were discovered in a cave, with the males lying on their right sides, the females on their left sides, suggesting that females might have been considered the inferior sex in this society (Turner 1967:78).

This universal association of left/inferior and right/superior isn't good news for left-handed people, and in fact in some cultures "lefties" are disadvantaged. In Western culture, for instance, we write from left to right, which is more difficult for left-handed people. Ordinary scissors as well as baseball gloves fit the hands of right-handed but not left-handed people. Among the Nuer of Africa, the right hand symbolizes what is strong, virile, and vital, and the left hand symbolizes evil (Evans-Pritchard 1956:233–235). Nevertheless, left-handed Nuer are not discriminated against and are certainly not thought of as inherently evil. The Nuer simply say of a left-handed person that his left hand is his right.

All over the world, "right" symbolizes goodness and strength, whereas "left" represents the opposite. Thus, in cultures in which greetings take the form of handshakes, the right hand is used, never the left. Former U.S. President George Bush greets his successor, President Bill Clinton, with a handshake.

learning to drive was as much a matter of watching others drive and then imitating their behavior as it was of listening to your instructor or studying your driver's manual.

Experience

A third way we transmit culture is by experience, whether negative or positive, gained through trial and error. Negative experience is the flip side of imitation. Instead of learning by doing what others are doing, one learns by avoiding doing what others don't do. In Tibet, it's polite for a person to stick his tongue out at others, as a sign of respectful greeting. However, it does not take Tibetan visitors to America very long to discover that this behavior is not part of American culture. Nega-

tive experience quickly teaches them to avoid sticking out their tongues; imitation teaches them to smile and shake hands instead.

Positive experience, too, promotes enculturation. As a first-time visitor to a Middle Eastern bazaar, you turn away in disappointment when a merchant quotes an excessive price for a silver bracelet. "Wait!" the merchant calls after you, and lowers the price. You have just learned that in this particular culture, prices are negotiable. Next time you need to buy something, you'll be ready to haggle over its cost.

Enculturation may rely on a combination of modes of cultural transmission. Instruction (including formal education), for example, enculturates through a combination of symbols (speech) and imitation (demonstration).

THE TRANSLATION OF CULTURE

In Chapter 2, on fieldwork, we described the process of learning about, and making sense of, another culture. It's a difficult task and one that doesn't end with fieldwork. Back home, the fieldworker must somehow interpret the collected data in such a way as to make the culture that was investigated intelligible to members of his or her own culture. In anthropology, this attempt at cross-cultural explanation is sometimes called the *translation* of culture since the anthropologist must translate the ideas, values, symbols, and institutions of one culture for members of another.

It's not simply a matter of presenting the facts, for when a culture is being analyzed, meaning and interpretation count as much as or more than facts. The English anthropologist Edward Evans-Pritchard (1902–1974), who considered sociocultural anthropology to be more akin to the humanities than to the sciences, stressed the importance of interpretation as early as 1950:

> Social anthropology is a kind of . . . philosophy or art, [which] implies that it . . . is interested in design rather than in process, and that it therefore seeks patterns and not scientific laws, and interprets rather than explains (Evans-Pritchard 1962:26).

Anthropologists have a habit of coining new phrases for established ideas. In the 1970s, 20 years after Evans-Pritchard argued for interpretation over explanation, Clifford Geertz (1973) popularized this view by coining the term **interpretive anthropology** to convey the idea that the ethnographer's job is not merely to describe but also to interpret cultures, to discover what members of the culture being studied have made meaningful and why. A culture may be regarded, said Geertz, as a sort of text that its members constantly "read" and which ethnographers must interpret.

In seeking to make sense of what the people in a society are doing, the ethnographer has to distinguish among four perspectives. First, there are guidelines for ideal behavior in every culture, a set of cultural ideals understood by members of the society by which they agree to run their collective lives. These ideals enable them to predict what behavior to expect from their fellows. Without some notion of what to expect from others in a particular situation, social life would be chaotic. So the ethnographer asks local informants to explain the society's ideals.

Second, far from being cultural robots, individuals have their own personalities, desires, and goals. Thus, although they may accept their culture's ideals as targets to shoot for, they don't necessarily obey them. If a non-Western ethnographer asked you, a Westerner, to describe marriage in your culture, you'd probably say something like this: "Well, a man and a woman fall in love, get married, set up a household, sometimes have children, and spend their lives together. When one of them dies, the marriage is considered to be over." But this is only ideally, not actually, true. In reality, almost half of all U.S. marriages collapse in divorce. The contradiction between the ideal (what *should* happen) and the real (what actually happens) gives the ethnographer a second perspective on culture: what the people actually do.

Third, the ethnographer, like the members of a

interpretive anthropology the view that the ethnographer's job is to describe and interpret what members of the culture being studied find meaningful

Color Symbolism

Colors have different symbolic meanings the world over. In Western culture, brides traditionally wear white, and black is associated with death. In India, white symbolizes death, and brides dress in red. Cross-culturally, white, black, and red are the colors most widely used as symbols, but the three colors have different meanings in different parts of the world (Turner 1967:72–77). The same seems to have been true in the past; archaeologists have discovered evidence of the symbolic use of these colors in a prehistoric South African Stone Age burial site, which contained half an ostrich eggshell, coated internally with a black substance and externally with red, lying beneath the arms of a skeleton (78–79).

culture under study, is also an individual, with a certain kind of personality, certain preconceptions perhaps, certain desires and goals. Inevitably, the ethnographer will put his or her own "spin" on what can be learned about a culture. No matter how thorough or objective the field-worker tries to be, the results of fieldwork will, in the end, always reflect the fieldworker; and no two field-workers, investigating the same culture at the same time, could possibly come up with exactly the same interpretation. So the third perspective is the ethnographer's idea of what is actually going on in the culture.

Finally, individuals in any society will have their own view of what is going on. Usually well aware of the ideal, they may feel that deviations from it are justified at times, or they may not even realize that ideals are being ignored. So the fourth perspective from which to understand a culture is what the people themselves *think* is really going on.

Each of the four perspectives—the ideal (what the people say should go on), the real (what actually goes on), the ethnographer's view (what the ethnographer thinks actually goes on), and the people's view (what the people themselves think actually goes on)—is important to the ethnographer struggling to find meaning in another culture. Only by coming to terms with all four perspectives can an ethnographer attain the level of awareness so essential if the full richness of a culture in all its shades of meaning is to be appreciated.

Individuals don't always follow their society's rules. At a cricket match in England, a nude "streaker," breaching cultural rules regarding proper dress, is apprehended by the police.

CULTURE AND PERSONALITY

The nineteenth-century Austrian psychoanalyst Sigmund Freud claimed that things that occur in childhood, even things we don't remember, strongly influence our adult personalities. Freud's ideas had a considerable impact on early twentieth-century anthropology, and for good reason. It seemed possible to some anthropologists that a close link could be found between a person's culture and his or her psychological makeup. Not only could one's cultural surroundings influence one's personality, they supposed; the personalities of individuals could also help to shape a culture.

The idea gained followers in the first few decades of this century, and by the 1930s members of the **culture and personality** school of anthropology, were already in the field testing their hypotheses. Early advocates of this approach to the understanding of culture believed that each culture could be characterized in terms of specific cultural attributes and a typical personality type, and moreover they believed that such attributes and personality types could be compared cross-culturally.

Among the most influential members of the culture and personality school were Ruth Benedict and a student of hers, Margaret Mead. From among limitless possibilities, Benedict wrote, every society selects the cultural attributes that characterize it and ignores others. Is money important to members of the culture or not? How are adolescents treated? Is warfare encouraged, tolerated, or not engaged in at all? (Benedict 1989:35). A society's cultural choices give it a distinct flavor. Benedict claimed that the Zuni of New Mexico (see Chapter 2), for example, were a sober, moderate, formal, somewhat puritanical, nonviolent, and restrained people, who placed the good of society above that of the individual.

The Kwakiutl, on the other hand, seemed to Benedict to be almost the direct opposite.

Many members of the culture and personality school were interested in the effects of childhood experiences and child-rearing practices on the adult personality. One of them was Cora DuBois (1903–1991), who earned her doctorate in anthropology in 1932. In the spring of 1936 DuBois sat in on a university seminar that was to change her life. It was chaired by Abram Kardiner, a prominent psychoanalyst who believed that how adults treated young children in a given society— how long they are breast-fed, how they are toilet trained, and so on—affected the personalities of those children when they became adults, thus providing a basic "personality structure" for the society (Kardiner 1945).

DuBois decided to put this hypothesis to the test in the field. In 1937 she traveled to Alor, an island in eastern Indonesia, where she lived for nearly a year and a half while studying Alorese personality (DuBois 1961). In addition to gathering what had by this time become the customary types of ethnographic data, DuBois also administered psychological tests to her Alorese hosts, collected some of their children's drawings, and recorded their dreams in detail.

On the island of Alor, anthropologist Cora DuBois noted that parents seemed to give their children little love, a tendency she associated with the hostile personalities of Alorese adults. Frightened by the photographer, an Alorese child clings to its mother, whose response seems to lack warmth.

DuBois's data yielded a picture of Alorese society that surprised some Americans. Alorese mothers typically resumed their full-time gardening work shortly after childbirth, leaving their infants in the care of others, such as grandmothers or aunts (DuBois 1961:34). If they could, these nannies sometimes breast-fed their charges in the mother's absence. Otherwise they fed the babies soft or liquid foods "more or less conscientiously," but to DuBois this feeding was "neither very effective nor satisfactory" (35). As the children grew up, it seemed they were given little consistent direction and little love. Aggressive teasing was common, and punishments often harsh (61).

What was the effect of this kind of child rearing on the Alorese? DuBois claimed that adults tended to be hostile, suspicious, jealous, and given to temper tantrums. Married couples seemed to share little warmth. People took great delight in teasing one another but otherwise seemed apathetic. These traits, DuBois concluded, resulted from the local child-rearing practices. She went on to suggest that certain features of any society, such as widespread mutual hostility and suspicion, could be explained with reference to the **modal personality**—the statistically most common personality type—of that society (DuBois 1961:xix).

In the 1950s and 1960s, the culture and personality school branched out to include studies of national character, group personality, the differences between "normal" and "abnormal" personality, and the effects of culture on mental illness and vice versa. A series of cross-cultural studies, spearheaded by anthropologists

 ASK YOURSELF

When you were a child, how did your mother and father punish you? How did they show affection? Do you think these aspects of your childhood helped to make you the person you are today? With your own children, will you handle these matters the way your parents did or differently?

culture and personality an area of special interest in anthropology whose practitioners see a significant link between culture and human psychology

modal personality in any culture, the personality type that is statistically the most common

Beatrice and John Whiting and Irvin Child (Whiting and Child 1953, Whiting 1963), revealed two distinct human patterns of child rearing, only one of which is usually found in a given culture: dependence training and independence training. In cultures that train children for dependency, adults tend to be compliant, conformist, and dependent on their families or other social groups. In cultures that train children for independence, adults tend to be more self-reliant, achievement-oriented, and individualistic. It is not difficult to choose which best characterizes the ideal North American personality.

Although the idea that psychology can help us to understand culture continues to inspire anthropological interest (Paul 1989), many anthropologists today think that the culture and personality school went too far in its interpretations. They consider that besides psychological explanations, additional or different explanations for cultural differences may be found. Thus, not all of today's anthropologists accept this perspective as valid. Nevertheless, because of the research of Benedict, Mead, DuBois, and their successors, the connection between culture and personality remains an area of contemporary anthropological interest.

CULTURE, RACE, AND PLURALISM

The term **race** is sometimes used to identify groups of people based on certain physical attributes such as skin color, hair texture, and facial features. In the past, anthropologists, too, used the term as though human beings could be classified into various categories based on such physical attributes. Physical characteristics, however, are continually being combined and recombined in the human species, and do not invariably converge to define clear-cut races. As a biological category, "race" does not exist.

The term has also been used to distinguish groups of people based not only on their physical attributes but also on cultural similarities. This use of "race" as a cultural category is prevalent today but is of limited applicability because the term's meaning changes to suit the cultural context in which it is used.

One cultural anthropologist (Pohorecky 1992) served recently as an expert in a court case involving racial discrimination by whites against darker-skinned Pakistanis. According to various "scientific" sources

National Character

The idea that people in certain ethnic groups have certain psychological dispositions is embedded in Western social thought. The French are seen as excitable, the Germans as industrious, the English as reserved, the Spanish as proud, and so on. Sometimes, a group of people is said to display contrary characteristics: although the English are considered to be reserved, they are also supposed to be eccentric. Such stereotypes may have no basis in fact, yet they are hard to refute (Bock 1988:79–80).

A number of studies of national character were undertaken in the U.S. around the time of World War II to gain insights into the cultures of the country's enemies, the Japanese and the Germans. In 1939, a group that included Margaret Mead worked with the Committee for National Morale "to consider ways in which the sciences of anthropology and psychology . . . could be applied to the problems of morale building in wartime" (Bock 1988:80). Later, other American anthropologists, among them Ruth Benedict,

moved to Washington, where they took part in these national character studies. After the war ended, research was extended to include the Russians.

But trying to isolate distinct personality types supposedly characteristic of large-scale, sometimes pluralistic cultures is difficult—some say impossible—and the validity of the attempt was increasingly questioned. By the 1960s, national character studies were becoming less popular among anthropologists, although sociologists and political scientists continued to undertake such studies into the 1980s. Anthropologists had discovered that there was just too much variation among individuals to make sweeping generalizations about national character. However, even if national character stereotypes were proven false, they were still of anthropological interest, for they were often used to justify exploitation and discrimination, to the advantage of those employing them (Bock 1988:80).

cited in court, Pakistanis are categorized as members of the "white" race, raising an interesting legal question: how can "racial discrimination" occur between members of the same race? The anthropologist argued that the court should rely not on the supposed biological classification of Pakistanis as "white" but on the common usage of the term *white* since it was this particular community's *cultural* interpretation of the term that was relevant in this context. The anthropologist's view prevailed, and the court found that "racial" discrimination had indeed occurred.

Victorian armchair anthropologists thought they could detect causal links between "race" and such cultural attributes as literacy, religious beliefs, and economic development. Since then, the world has witnessed attempts to correlate "race" with various intellectual, psychological, and behavioral attributes: Intelligence Quotient (IQ) is a well-known example. But since race is an idea with different meanings in different contexts, and since intellectual, psychological, and behavioral characteristics have nothing to do with skin color, hair texture, facial features, or any other physiological attribute, these attempts were doomed to failure. The subsequent history of cultural anthropology has shown that **racism**, the belief that some "races" are inherently superior to others and are therefore justified in exploiting them, is not based on any fact of nature or culture.

When people with different physical characteristics or cultural traditions come together in a single society, the result is **cultural pluralism** or **multiculturalism.** It is most characteristic of large-scale, modern societies. The U.S., the world's nineteenth-century "melting pot," is among the most multicultural of contemporary societies. Black Americans, Italian-Americans, Irish-Americans, WASPs (white Anglo-Saxon Protestants), and others all live not only within the context of one broad culture but within their own **subcultures** as well. This term describes small groups, always found within larger ones, that distinguish themselves (or are distinguished by others) from other such groups on any basis, including biological similarities, cultural traditions, or even common interests.

How do multicultural societies handle the prob

◆ ASK YOURSELF

Do you see yourself as a member of any subculture? If so, do you feel members of other subcultures should be compelled to avoid giving you offense on the basis of your membership?

lems deriving from cultural pluralism? In some, political or religious regulations control the behavior of people of different races, religions, sexual orientations, and classes. In modern democracies, democratic ideals tend to limit the number of such regulations. Yet the biases that characterize modern democracies show that these societies don't yet know how to handle cultural pluralism so that no subculture is handicapped. Some Western nations have laws to protect members of subcultures from discrimination, but in no multicultural society have these been wholly successful.

One response to cultural pluralism, and a recent subject of debate on college campuses, is "political correctness" (see Berman 1992). The idea behind political correctness may sound reasonable: people should avoid saying or doing anything that demeans members of another subculture. But this idea raises a troubling question. Should we give equal treatment to members of every subculture, or would such extreme "sensitivity" lead to the further fragmentation of American culture into subcultures; the nondiscriminatory affirmation of any person, behavior, or view (even, of course, the reprehensible); and the neglect of cultural and historical realities?

Those favoring political correctness argue that demeaning another subculture is inconsistent with the American ideal of equality. Those who oppose it point out that special treatment for certain groups, such as creating special college curricula for minority students, is in itself demeaning and that political correctness, with its implicit guidelines about what one may and may not say, restricts free speech. The continuing debate may have an important impact on how we view subcultures in our culturally pluralistic society.

◆◆◆

race a term commonly used to identify groups of people supposedly sharing certain specific physical attributes or, alternatively, physical plus cultural similarities. The word is not useful for distinguishing either biological or cultural categories of people

racism the belief that some "races" are inherently superior to others

cultural pluralism the meeting of many cultural traditions in a society, particularly a large-scale, modern society

multiculturalism another term for cultural pluralism

subculture a small group, within a larger one, whose members distinguish themselves (or who are distinguished by others) as culturally different from others

CONCLUSION

Animals don't need culture to survive. They adjust to their physical environments, over the long term, by evolving physical traits that favor their survival—a covering of hair to keep them warm in cold climates, a specialized set of teeth for chewing raw foods, or eyes that permit them to see in minimal light. Human beings, too, adapt physically over time, but more important, we adapt culturally, employing cultural means, such as fire for warmth, cooking to soften raw foods, and electric lights for night vision, to achieve not merely our long-term survival as a species but also our short-term comfort, safety, health, and well-being as individuals.

So flexible is culture that, unlike other species, which typically inhabit particular environmental "niches," human beings have been able to adapt to life in Arctic regions, hot deserts, tropical rain forests, and temperate zones, as well as places where temperature, rainfall, and climate vary widely from season to season. We have not simply found our special niche and managed to hold our own in the world of nature; we have also expanded into almost every environmental niche and exploited the world of nature to our own advantage.

Thus, human beings are unique. Originally creatures of nature like all other living things, we are now the only species on the planet that depends for its continued existence on something other than nature, something we ourselves invented: culture. So dependent have we become on our own invention that we could not, as a species, survive without it.

SUMMARY

At the heart of cultural anthropology is the concept of culture, which we define as the customs, ideas, artifacts, and languages that human beings in groups share with and learn from one another. Culture is collective rather than individual, compulsory in the sense that we have no choice but to take our society's culture into account if we wish to get along with others, and essential for human social life. Because the various aspects of a culture are closely interrelated and constantly changing, culture can also be described as integrated and dynamic. Finally,

Politically Correct—Not!

Beginning in the fall of 1991, ardent Atlanta Braves baseball fans have cheered their team on to victory with a slicing motion of the forearm they call the "tomahawk chop," in honor of their team's mascot, the Indian brave. Many fans were surprised when this gesture elicited outrage in the national media. Editorials pointed out that the "tomahawk chop" was not, in the parlance of the day, "politically correct." It demeaned native Americans who, they asserted, should never have been chosen as a mascot for a baseball team in the first place; after all, no one would dream of naming a sports team the Palefaces!

"Political correctness" demands that we avoid saying or doing anything to demean the members of any subculture. Fans of the Atlanta Braves baseball team felt they were honoring their team's mascot, the Indian brave, with a gesture called the "tomahawk chop," but critics thought the gesture was demeaning to native Americans.

culture is a uniquely human response to the challenge posed by the difficulties of surviving, a mechanism for solving the problems of human existence. Not even our closest animal relatives can be considered to possess culture.

The primary means of transmission of culture, both among people who are contemporaries and from one generation to the next, is through symbols, things that stand for something else. Words are perhaps human beings' most important symbols. But symbols are not the only vehicle for the transmission of culture. Imitation and experience also contribute to enculturation, the process by which we learn how to become functioning members of our culture.

Anthropology's task is to "translate" the ideas, values, symbols, and institutions of cultures so members of other cultures may understand them. This is not simply a matter of reporting facts but also one of interpretating meanings. Interpretive anthropologists translate cultures by describing and interpreting what their members find meaningful. To do so, they must distinguish among four perspectives: the ideals by which the members of a society say they should lead their collective lives; the real behavior of the society's members; the reality the ethnographer perceives; and the reality the people themselves perceive.

One way of exploring the subject of culture is to investigate how it might affect, and be affected by, personality. Early members of the culture and personality school, including Ruth Benedict and Margaret Mead, proposed that cultures could be characterized in terms of specific cultural attributes and common personality types. Others examined the effects of childhood experiences and childrearing practices on adult personality or attempted to identify a modal personality—the statistically most common personality type—for particular cultures. The culture and personality school later went on to study national characters. Today, not all anthropologists have confidence in the reliability of this perspective, although it remains an area of anthropological interest.

Our discussion of culture touched on the question of race and the related problem of multiculturalism, or cultural pluralism, the inclusion of many subcultures within large-scale societies. The term race is not particularly useful either as a biological or a cultural category since its definition varies according to context. Racism, the belief that persons of one race are inherently superior to those of another, is not founded on facts but on prejudice. Some nations have laws to prevent discrimination against people who are biologically or culturally different from others, yet racism and other forms of bias still characterize multi-

cultural societies. Human beings have not yet found the best way to cope with cultural pluralism in large-scale societies, but "political correctness" is one recently devised way of dealing with the problem.

Culture is our mechanism for solving the problems of human existence. It enables us to form families and communities, to communicate, to make a living, to maintain order in our lives, to find meaning in life, to express ourselves creatively, and to continue our species into the future. So dependent have we become on culture, our own creation, that without it we could not survive.

KEY TERMS

acculturation
cultural pluralism
culture and personality
enculturation
interpretive anthropology
modal personality
multiculturalism
race
racism
subculture
symbol
symbolic anthropology

SUGGESTED READINGS

Barnouw, Victor. 1985 (1963). *Culture and Personality* (4th ed.). Belmont, CA: Wadsworth. A good introductory text to this topic, covering all the basic information.

MacLaury, Robert E. 1992. From Brightness to Hue: An Explanatory Model of Color-Category Evolution. *Current Anthropology* 33 (4) :137–186. The most recent contribution to the controversy about whether the meanings of certain colors vary cross-culturally or are similar for all cultures. The author adopts an in-between position.

Turner, Victor. 1967. *The Forest of Symbols: Aspects of Ndembu Ritual.* Ithaca, NY: Cornell University Press. Ten essays dealing with the use of symbols in ritual in a Central African society, by one of the most eminent contributors to symbolic anthropology.

White, Leslie A. (ed.)., with Beth Dillingham. 1973. *The Concept of Culture.* Minneapolis: Burgess Publishing Company. An overview of the culture concept by one of its most famous interpreters.

CHAPTER 4

ANTHROPOLOGICAL PERSPECTIVES AND SPECIALTIES

The diets of some Hindus in India are protein-deficient, yet Hindus neither kill nor eat cows, which are considered to be sacred and are allowed to wander in the streets. From one anthropological perspective, the cultural materialist, cows, which pull plows and provide dung for fertilizer and fuel, are worth more to Hindus on the hoof.

INTRODUCTION

Once upon a time, so the old story goes, there was a city in which all the inhabitants were blind. One day an elephant was brought into town, and word of its presence spread rapidly. Eventually, three of the most curious—none of whom had any idea of how an elephant looked—approached the beast and began to grope about, gathering information by touching various parts of its body. Soon each blind man was convinced that he had discovered just what an elephant was. The one who had chanced to seize an ear exclaimed, "It's obvious that an elephant is a large, rough thing, flat and wide. It's very much like a rug." Another, who had handled the trunk, disagreed. "Not at all," he remonstrated. "An elephant is like a big, flexible pipe." A third, who had grasped one of the legs, announced as confidently as his fellows, "You're both wrong. An elephant is upright, sturdy and straight, like a pillar!"

Though only a children's fable, this story illustrates an important point: if we wish to understand a subject fully, we must examine it from as many angles as we can, for no single point of view is likely to afford a comprehensive interpretation. This is as true of culture as it is of elephants. In this chapter, we look at various **anthropological perspectives,** different philosophies or viewpoints from which anthropologists try to understand culture, and **anthropological specialties,** topical areas in which major groups of anthropologists have done interesting and important research. Each perspective and specialty has something significant to contribute to our understanding of culture.

SYNCHRONIC VERSUS DIACHRONIC APPROACHES TO THE STUDY OF CULTURE

One way to learn about an elephant (see Figure 4.1) is to examine its ears, trunk, and legs carefully, attempting to find out how these are related to one another and how they work together to keep the whole beast going. We call this approach **synchronic,** meaning "at one point in time," because it seeks to understand how the various parts of the elephant fit together at a particular moment in time, rather than looking at how it developed through time. To understand and interpret a culture using this approach, an anthropologist collects data on the different institutions, ideas, and customs of the culture and attempts to fit them together into a general, comprehensive picture.[1] This is a practical way of organizing, summarizing, and understanding data on cultures that lack written or other records of the past.

---

[1]This point in time may be contemporary with the anthropologist or not. The French scholar Emmanuel LeRoy Ladurie (1979) wrote a book about life in a village in southern France in the early 1300s, and the fact that the community he studied existed 700 years ago made his study no less synchronic.

A very different approach, the **diachronic,** takes a dynamic, historical point of view. The term *diachronic* means "through time." The diachronic approach is based on the assumption that to understand the elephant fully, we must not only examine its ears, trunk, and legs but also study how it was conceived, was born, and grew. Followers of the diachronic approach believe that we cannot understand cultures unless we know something of their origins and how they developed through time.

Which approach is better? Neither one; each is valid, and the choice of which to use depends on the circumstances. Using both is preferable to using only one, and modern fieldworkers often do just that. In Chapter 2 we described the fieldwork of Nancie Gonzalez, who studied rural-urban migration into the city of Santiago de Cabelleros, Dominican Republic. Gonzalez began her research with a synchronic study of a single neighborhood, soon expanding her work to encompass many neighborhoods and eventually organizations, methods of transportation, economics, and politics. She incorporated all this information into what was emerging as a holistic but still synchronic portrait of an entire city. But studying Santiago as it existed in the present proved insufficient for a full understanding of immigration into the city; she needed to understand its roots. Switching to the diachronic approach, Gonzalez (1974:26) completed her research with a study of historical events affecting migration, to discover how the city "had become what it was in 1967."

Most contemporary anthropologists would make use of both the synchronic and diachronic approaches if they could. But for many cultures, no archaeological data and no historical documents—books, letters, diaries, legal papers, maps, and religious or civil records—are available to help us understand change and development through time. Anthropologists studying such cultures are therefore limited to the synchronic approach. Throughout this book, we'll make as strong a case as we can for the use of both approaches, whenever possible.

SOME ANTHROPOLOGICAL PERSPECTIVES

Cultural Evolution

In Chapter 1, we introduced the theory of cultural evolution, the idea that cultures tend to undergo a grad-

Synchronic

Looks at a Culture at One Point in Time

• What are its customs and beliefs like?

• How are these customs and beliefs
  related to one another?

*APPROACH OFTEN USED WITH CULTURES
THAT LACK WRITTEN HISTORICAL RECORDS*

Diachronic

Looks at a Culture Through Time

• How did culture's customs and beliefs
  begin?

• How did they grow and change?

*APPROACH OFTEN USED WITH CULTURES
THAT HAVE WRITTEN RECORDS*

Figure 4.1

*Synchronic and Diachronic Approaches to Studying a Culture. Two approaches to studying a cul-
ture are the synchronic, in which the culture is viewed at a single point in time, and the diachronic,
in which the culture is viewed as it developed through time.*

ual, continuous process of adaptive change. This idea, first proposed in the nineteenth century, owed much to the biological evolutionism of Charles Darwin. When they compared the many cultures about which they had read, the cultural evolutionists—foremost among whom were the British anthropologist Edward Tylor and the American lawyer-anthropologist Lewis Henry Morgan—thought, ethnocentrically, that some cultures seemed exceedingly "primitive," others somewhat more advanced, and still others (especially their own) quite civilized indeed. They concluded that cultures must progress through stages, from "savagery" to "barbarism" and finally to "civilization."[2]

The initially rather rigid concept of cultural evolution in the nineteenth century has been greatly modified in the twentieth century to produce several new ideas, collectively called **neo-evolutionism.** Thus cultural evolution (which is not just a theory about culture but also a

perspective on the study of culture) still has many followers in anthropology.

One important contribution of the neo-evolutionists was a refinement of the concept of culture change. To

 ASK YOURSELF

In your view, are there any societies in existence today that you would consider "primitive"? What are the features that make them so? Can you think of anything "primitive" about your own society?

anthropological perspectives different viewpoints from which anthropologists try to understand culture

anthropological specialties topical areas in which major groups of anthropologists have done interesting and important research

synchronic approach the study of how aspects of societies and cultures fit together at any given time

diachronic approach the study of societies and cultures as they move through time

neo-evolutionism any of several twentieth-century variations on cultural evolution

---

[2]The historical particularism of Franz Boas, described in Chapter 1, was in part a reaction to cultural evolution, with its generalizations about human progress. Rather than passing through predictable stages, Boas thought, every culture is unique. We have not included a discussion of historical particularism in this chapter because this perspective has few contemporary proponents.

neo-evolutionists, the term *change,* when applied to a culture, does not necessarily imply progress or betterment; whether a culture is "better" today than it was in the past is a value judgment best avoided. Indeed, modern evolutionists recognize that cultures, far from inevitably getting "better" or more technologically advanced through time, may remain stable for long periods or even move toward forms less capable of adaptation to changing circumstances. This is as true of North American culture as of any other. Our twentieth-century tendency to degrade our natural environment, for instance, hardly seems adaptive in the long run. So the neo-evolutionists prefer to avoid using terms like *change* and *progress.* Instead, they use the term **cultural process** to describe what happens to cultures through time, whether this is change or stability, greater complexity or greater simplicity.

A second contribution of the neo-evolutionists was to modify the nineteenth-century idea of **unilineal evolution,** the notion that all cultures follow the same trajectory, from savagery to civilization. There did seem to be some empirical support for unilineal evolution: ancient cultures between which there had apparently been no contact and which thrived at different times (such as the cultures of long-ago Egypt and Mexico) nevertheless shared some similar cultural characteristics, such as the building of pyramids. To explain this, Julian Steward (1955) proposed that the natural and cultural environments in which a given society exists contribute heavily to its particular developmental trajectory. He termed his perspective **multilineal evolution,** after the multiple, but similar, lines along which different cultures seem to evolve. Although societies in similar settings may evolve along parallel tracks, Steward added, any society, at any given time, will be at a particular point along its track, a point at which its cultural institutions are appropriate to its particular circumstances. Steward called these points "levels of sociocultural integration."

Most contemporary anthropologists would probably agree that evolutionary trends in the direction of more and more complex and adaptive cultural character-

◆ **ASK YOURSELF**

Native American culture today is characterized not only by increasing involvement in mainstream American culture but also by disproportionately high rates of poverty and alcoholism. Do you think Native American culture is "better" than it was before western European contact?

istics *can* be observed in many societies. Does this notion help us to understand a given society? Let's look at a familiar phenomenon of contemporary American culture. Since the 1970s, an increasing number of long-distance truckers have been using citizens band (CB) radios. A modern cultural evolutionist might declare that this phenomenon can best be explained as an adaptive response to certain environmental changes, both general (such as the country's increasing population and the development of a national system of linked superhighways) and specific (such as the 1973 fuel crisis and the 55-mile-an-hour speed limit). This view is evolutionary in that a more complex, more adaptive, more efficient cultural characteristic—instant communication among truckers by CB radio—is understood to have developed out of a less adaptive, less efficient one (headlight blinking, horn honking, and hand waving). In Steward's terms, CB radio is a particularly efficient, effective method of communication among long-distance truckers, given American society's level of sociocultural integration.

Functionalism

Another viewpoint from which to understand cultures is the anthropological perspective called functionalism. We introduced this perspective in Chapter 1, in our discussion of the pioneering fieldwork of Bronislaw Malinowski among the Trobriand Islanders of the South Pacific. Malinowski was a founder of the functionalist school in anthropology.

Malinowski viewed culture as a system, somewhat like (to continue with the analogy we used in Chapter 3) the engine in a car, which runs (or "functions") when its various parts work both individually and interactively. But while an engine is made up of parts like spark plugs, cylinders, and pistons, a culture is made up of such components as a certain kind of social organization, a political ideology, and an economic system. Change one part of the system, and you change the whole thing. Malinowski thought that even seemingly baffling aspects of Trobriand culture could be understood if one could see how they functioned. How did each cultural component actually work, together with others, in the context of Trobriand society? All aspects of culture, he believed, functioned to satisfy particular biological or psychological needs, such as the need for food, sex, shelter, security, or prestige. And each contributed to the maintenance of the whole culture.

One of the most interesting aspects of Trobriand

Cultures tend to become more complex and adaptive through time. From a cultural-evolutionary point of view, long-distance truckers' increasing use of CB radios is an adaptive response to environmental changes such as the development of a national superhighway system and the 55-mile-an-hour speed limit.

culture was inter-island trading voyages, which involved—in addition to boat building—seemingly useless activities such as elaborate magical rituals lacking any obvious, tangible result. (The Trobrianders, of course, were not alone in undertaking apparently "useless" activities. In our own culture, to cite only one example, people sometimes expend much money and effort on restoring antique cars not intended for transportation, a seemingly nonfunctional endeavor.) How might one explain the Trobrianders' magic rituals? From a Malinowskian functionalist perspective, these complex rites and spells can be understood as serving a psychological function: reassurance. Magic helped to relieve the islanders' anxiety about traveling over dangerous seas in canoes, in the face of uncertain weather conditions and without navigational aids (Malinowski 1954:90). If this explanation seems reasonable to you, you can see why the idea that aspects of culture should be viewed as functional parts of a whole is a compelling one.

Malinowski's influence was considerable, as the important work of his followers demonstrates. *We, the Tikopia* (1963), a classic in anthropology by Malinowski's student Raymond Firth (1901–), begins with a description of family life among the Tikopians, technologically simple agriculturalists living on a South Pacific island. Firth presented the Tikopian family in terms of its primary "functions," reproduction and enculturation. Later, his study branched out to other Tikopian institutions with links to the family, and from these institutions to still others. *We, the Tikopia* contains no unifying theme; Firth simply moved from one aspect of culture to another, examining each as it interlaced with others. Since it lacked any theoretical framework that would help the reader appreciate what was relevant and what was marginal to the understanding of the Tikopian way of life, the book was criticized as "undisciplined." Firth later acknowledged that the way Malinowskian functional analysis led ethnographers from one aspect of culture to another, on the assumption that everything in a society is related to everything else, constituted a basic conceptual flaw. One critic wondered why, in a book that runs to hundreds of pages, Firth felt the need to stop at the particular point he did (Kuper 1985:73).

◆◆

cultural process what happens to cultures through time, whether this means change or stability, increasing or decreasing complexity

unilineal evolution the notion that all cultures follow the same trajectory, from savagery to civilization

multilineal evolution the notion that different cultures evolve along multiple, if similar, lines, depending on their natural and cultural environments

Apparently nonfunctional activities occur in all cultures. In North America, for example, some people spend a great deal of money and effort on restoring antique cars not intended for transportation.

Like cultural evolution, functionalism has been rethought and reshaped since Malinowski's time. A couple of decades after Malinowski, another, less descriptive brand of functionalism emerged. Because it was more abstract, it was destined ultimately to be of greater use to anthropologists. The origins of this modified functionalism lay in the work of the French sociologist Émile Durkheim (1858–1916), but it was popularized by the English anthropologist A. R. Radcliffe-Brown. It dominated anthropology in Britain during the 1940s and 1950s.

Like Malinowskian functionalism, Radcliffe-Brown's version was based on a synchronic approach to culture. But if Malinowski found the function of some aspect of culture in the fulfillment of specific biological and psychological needs, Radcliffe-Brown (1965:190) saw the function of the same aspect of culture in the part it played in maintaining the social structure, which we defined in Chapter 1 as the sum total of the social relationships of all the individuals in a society at a given moment in time. Because of its emphasis on social structure as opposed to biopsychological needs, Radcliffe-Brown's functionalist perspective is often referred to as **structural-functionalism.**

When Radcliffe-Brown's view of social structure caused some controversy, he explained the concept in the following way:

When I pick up a particular sea shell on the beach, I recognize it as having a particular structure. I may find other shells of the same species which have a similar structure, so that I can say there is a form of structure characteristic of the species. . . . I examine a local group of Australian aborigines and find an arrangement of persons in a certain number of families. This, I call the social structure of that particular group at that moment of time. Another local group has a structure that is in important ways similar to that of the first. . . . By examining a number of different species [of shell], I may be able to recognize a certain general structural form. . . . By examining a representative sample of local groups in one region, I can describe a certain form of structure (quoted in Kuper 1985:53–54).

As it turned out, finding cultural groups that were "representative" of a "certain form of structure" proved virtually impossible: too many cultural phenomena were peculiar only to one society. Nevertheless, other anthropologists took up the structural-functionalist perspective. The best known was Edward Evans-Pritchard, who studied a nonliterate group of people in Africa called the Azande.

The Azande believe that some people are witches. If a Zande person dies, and the death cannot be logically explained by an obvious illness or injury, it is assumed that the person has been bewitched. To avenge the death, the witch must be killed by relatives of the deceased.

But before the avenger can kill a witch, he must ask permission to do so from his local village headman (Evans-Pritchard 1985:6–7). Every time someone asks a headman for permission to kill a witch, the headman's authority is reinforced. If the people's belief in magic were to be destroyed, for instance because of acculturation, the authority of the headman would decline. From a structural-functional point of view, one function of Zande magic is that it helps maintain the political authority of the village head. In sum, in Evans-Pritchard's view, the complex of beliefs surrounding Zande witchcraft functions to prop up the society's political organization.

As useful a tool as it has become, the structural-functionalist perspective has been criticized within anthropology for two reasons. First, its synchronic emphasis makes culture change (a constant feature of human life) impossible to understand clearly. And second, it did not live up to the claim made for it by Radcliffe-Brown: that it would eventually enable us to discover laws governing human social behavior. Despite these limitations, however, functionalism in general remains a major theoretical orientation in anthropology, for a very good reason: functionalists have produced numerous field studies that have revealed much about individual societies, how they function and what makes them unique. Either functionalist perspective—Malinowskian functionalism or structural-functionalism—can contribute to our understanding of a given society.

Cultural Materialism

Some anthropologists think that concrete, measurable things, such as the natural environment, technology, population size and distribution, and the ways people get food and shelter, are more responsible for specific aspects of culture than other factors. According to this perspective, even nonmaterial aspects of a culture, such as family organization or spiritual beliefs, develop in response to these material realities. If this makes good sense to you, you are a proponent of **cultural materialism.** (The idea is by no means a new one. The German philosopher Karl Marx, who found explanations for social customs in the way a culture produced the goods it needed, would have agreed with it in the nineteenth century.) The modern-day anthropologist with whom the idea is most closely associated is Marvin Harris (1927–).

The cultural materialist perspective offers us yet another vantage point for helping to understand a cul-

The Azande of Africa believe that illness or injury may be caused by witchcraft. To redress it, a victim's relatives must seek vengeance against the offending witch, but only with the permission of the village headman. From a structural-functionalist point of view, the need to seek permission reinforces a headman's authority. Above, a Zande village headman.

ture. We return once again to the Trobriands, and to one particularly interesting but seemingly nonfunctional aspect of Trobriand culture, the kula ring (see Figure 4.2). This is a ritual exchange of certain gifts between people

structural-functionalism an anthropological perspective in which aspects of culture are viewed in terms of the part they play in maintaining the social structure

cultural materialism the idea that concrete, measurable things, such as the natural environment or technology, are more responsible for specific aspects of culture than other factors

living on different Pacific islands. What was most baffling to Westerners about the kula ring was that the very same gifts—always shell necklaces and armbands—were given away over and over again. These objects circulated endlessly among island traders, sometimes eventually winding up in the same hands that had given them away years ago. Even though the recipient of a kula gift was only its temporary "owner," the transfer of a particularly desirable shell necklace or armband from one person to another won both donor and recipient great prestige. What could explain the islanders' compulsion to make dangerous canoe trips between islands in pursuit of purely ceremonial objects?

Malinowski viewed this seemingly irrational activity in subjective terms. For him, the kula trade satisfied certain psychological needs, such as the islanders'

craving for prestige. But an ethnographer of the region, R. F. Fortune (1989:206–210), pointed out that in addition to their ceremonial component kula voyages also had an economic function, in that food, tools, and other necessities of life were distributed along with ritual objects. This practical exchange was important because nature had distributed the necessities of life unevenly throughout the Trobriand Islands. Many of the islands in the Trobriand Island chain specialized in producing particular commodities. Some produced yams, others stone for ax heads, still others pottery, all of which needed to be distributed through some sort of exchange system. The kula ring provided the context in which the purely economic exchange of important, everyday necessities could take place in a friendly fashion, among islanders who did not have equal access to everything they

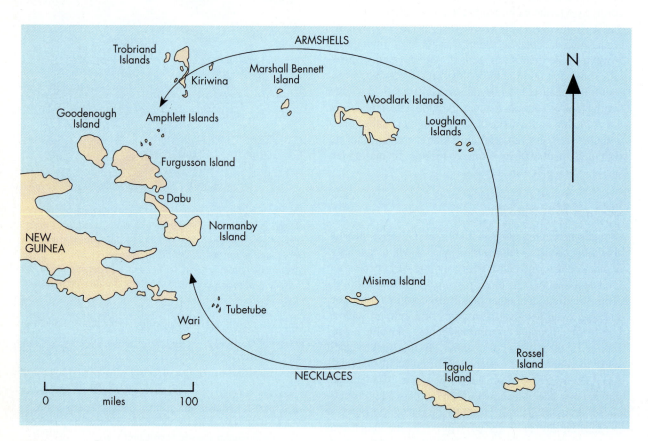

Figure 4.2
The Kula Ring. In the kula ring, residents of different islands in the western Pacific give one an-
other the same gifts—shell necklaces and armbands—over and over again. Necklaces always pass
from hand to hand in one direction, armbands in the other. Giving or receiving these items wins
prestige for both givers and receivers.

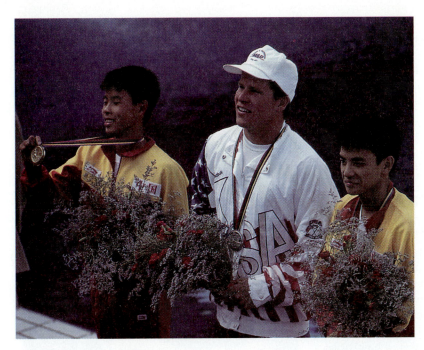

The idea that certain objects are desirable for reasons other than their monetary value is common cross-culturally. To Scott Donie (center), a champion diver, the medal he won at the 1992 Olympics in Barcelona is worth much more than its weight in silver.

needed. From the cultural materialist perspective, then, the kula ring can be understood in economic terms, as a matter of production and distribution.

Cultural materialists look for the adaptive advantages of various aspects of culture. How does a particular idea, institution, or custom help the people in a given society to adapt more efficiently to their natural and social environments and their particular level of technological expertise? Viewed from a cultural materialist perspective, the kula ring was certainly adaptive. It brought politically independent communities together for their mutual benefit.

Cultural materialism overlaps considerably with the other anthropological perspectives we have considered. Although the cultural materialist's view is often diachronic while the functionalist's is synchronic, both perspectives attempt to pin down the reasons people behave as they do, one finding these reasons in material things such as environment or technology, the other

◆ ASK YOURSELF

Cross-culturally, the idea that certain objects are desirable not simply because of their monetary worth but for other reasons as well is a common one. Can you find similarities, or differences, between kula ring objects and American football players' Superbowl rings or Olympic champions' medals?

finding them in immaterial, psychological, or social phenomena. It's important to recognize that the two perspectives aren't necessarily mutually exclusive; the kula ring might have served *both* economic and psychological functions. Likewise, cultural materialism overlaps with cultural evolution in that both focus on environmental and technological variables as explanations for cultural process.

There are several different kinds of materialist perspectives on the study of culture, depending on what aspect of the real, material world is emphasized. One of them, in which there is a particular focus on the natural environment as a factor influencing the things human beings do, think, make, and say, is **cultural ecology** (see especially Vayda and McKay 1975; Ellen 1982). This is the study of how cultures adapt to their particular natural environments. Introduced into American anthropology by Julian Steward in 1955, this perspective won many followers in the environmentally conscious 1960s, for it provides a useful framework within which to examine otherwise puzzling human behaviors.

From the cultural-ecological point of view, a human group and its environment are viewed as part of an integrated system (in this regard, cultural ecology has much in common with functionalism). Why, for example, did some migratory Inuit (Eskimo) groups abandon

cultural ecology a materialist perspective focusing on the natural environment as a factor influencing culture

The Witches of Salem

Like the twentieth-century Azande, the late seventeenth-century residents of Salem, Massachusetts, believed in witchcraft. Over a hundred villagers were accused of being witches, and 20 were executed for their alleged activities. Unlike the Azande, however, the villagers of Salem were literate and kept various kinds of records. Thus, whereas Evans-Pritchard was limited to a synchronic interpretation of Zande witchcraft, Paul Boyer and Stephen Nissenbaum (1974), by analyzing historical records detailing changes that had taken place in Salem in the late 1680s and early 1690s, were able to bring a diachronic perspective to what had happened there. They came to understand how Salem's explosion of witchcraft accusations began, intensified, and eventually died down. Evans-Pritchard's approach to Zande witchcraft was structural-functionalist, a highly useful approach when analysis must be synchronic, whereas Boyer and Nissenbaum were able to use what some anthropologists would call a diachronic cultural materialist approach.

At the time of the witchcraft accusations and trials, the economic strength and prestige of one of Salem's families, the Porters, was on the rise. Porter lands, compared to the holdings of some other families, were concentrated nearer to the growing commercial prosperity spreading out from the town of Boston. At the same time, the economic status and prestige of a more established family, the Putnams, was decreasing, in part because the location of their lands denied them ready access to commerce. When Boyer and Nissenbaum tried to discern some pattern in the Salem witchcraft accusations, they realized that those who brought the accusations were related to or allied with the economically deteriorating Putnam

In seventeenth-century Salem, Massachusetts, over a hundred villagers were accused of witchcraft, and 20 were executed. Historical records describing changing economic relationships among the villagers permit an analysis of the witchcraft accusations that is at once synchronic, diachronic, and cultural materialist.

family, and the accused were allied with the economically successful Porters. In the face of their declining power and influence in the village, the Putnams were striking out against members of a family benefiting from the economic changes taking place.

elderly and infirm members, allowing them to die alone in the frigid arctic? From the cultural-ecological perspective, such abandonment is seen as a product of an especially harsh environment, in which feeding and transporting an elderly family member would lessen the survival chances of the rest of the group. Clearly this is a materialist perspective, with emphasis on a particular aspect of the real, material world.

SOME ANTHROPOLOGICAL SPECIALTIES

In addition to its various theoretical perspectives, three of which we have just described, cultural anthropology also incorporates a number of topical specialties. There are many more of these than we can discuss here, so we have chosen four that we think are especially sig-

Ecology

PLEASE HELP CONSERVE ENERGY
Before leaving the room
1. Close all windows
2. Turn off all lights
3. Close the door

The above is an official notice posted in classrooms and offices at the State University of New York at Stony Brook. If one takes this directive literally, it isn't at all clear how one is supposed to get out of the room! What *is* clear, however, is that this injunction is what we would call "ecologically sound"—it is intended to help preserve natural resources.

In the United States in the 1960s, there arose a new social consciousness that incorporated a long-overdue awareness that our natural resources were not only valuable but also limited. Americans were urged to conserve their resources by recycling reusable materials and avoiding air and water pollution. The term *ecology* entered the vocabulary of many Americans at this time. As it has been popularly used since then, ecology implies conservation efforts: people who remember to turn out the lights before leaving the room, or who recycle their aluminum cans and plastic bottles, are described as "ecologically aware," and such acts are said to be "good for the ecology."

The real meaning of the term is far broader than this. Ecology is actually the study of the relationship between living organisms—any living organisms, from insects to plants to people—and their environments. The specific study of the relationship of human beings to their environment is called **human ecology.**

nificant—cognitive anthropology, structural anthropology, psychological anthropology, and postmodernism. Each specialty is a focus of interest for a whole group of like-minded anthropologists who have organized their research around that specialty, in many cases over a whole lifetime of anthropological work.

Cognitive Anthropology

One anthropological specialty, **cognitive anthropology,** attempts to explain cultures by examining the different categories people create to organize their universe. Since these categories affect how people learn and think, cognitive anthropologists are also interested in how people perceive, organize, evaluate, and use information.

The origins of cognitive anthropology go back to the seventeenth century, when the human mind became a topic of great interest to scholars. Most (e.g., Locke 1979 [1690]) believed that people were born with minds empty of content. Later, the German Adolf Bastian (1826–1905) disagreed, arguing in support of what he called the "psychic unity" of all humankind (Needham 1970:1xxii). According to Bastian, **mental universals,** or fixed patterns of thought, were common to human beings all over the world. The details of the universal ideas and institutions shared by all of us differ from society to society because so do the natural environments and the stages of cultural evolution different cultures have reached. Bastian thus conceded a place for cultural evolution and cultural materialism but felt these operated hand in hand with mental universals.

Is there any validity in this notion? Yes, the cultures of people who are widely separated, temporally or geographically, often contain striking similarities. This observation has suggested to some scholars that human behavior is indeed affected by mental universals. Similarities among myths from around the world—the story of a great flood wiping out most of humanity is one example—lend some support for this possibility.

human ecology the study of the relationship between human beings and their environment

cognitive anthropology a specialty whose practitioners attempt to explain cultures by examining the different categories people create to organize their universe

mental universals fixed patterns of thought believed to be common to human beings all over the world

◆◆

Noah and the Flood

The biblical story of Noah and the flood is familiar to most Westerners, but what is not so well known is that other cultures also have stories describing great floods caused by divine actions. Typically, the deluge causes the subsequent extinction of most of humanity, but the few people who are saved eventually repopulate the earth. The ancient Greeks, for instance, told a story in which the god Prometheus foresees that Zeus, the mightiest of all gods, plans to flood the earth. Prometheus warns his son Deucalion of the coming deluge, instructing him to build an ark

in which to save his life and that of his wife, Pyrrha. Just as the vessel is completed, torrential rains begin, which flood the earth and drown all life except for the occupants of the ark. When the rain stops, Deucalion and Pyrrha emerge from their ark into an empty world. They thank Zeus for their lives and are instructed by him to throw their "mothers' bones," the rocks of Mother Earth, over their shoulders. As they do so, human beings spring up where the stones land, and the earth is repopulated.

Most cognitive anthropologists believe that human beings want order in their lives. Not only does order govern our daily lives; we *must* order things to survive—to distinguish things that are edible from things that are not, things that are safe from things that are dangerous, and so on (Gombrich 1979a; see also Gombrich 1979b). If this idea seems so obvious that it is below our threshold of attention, this is only because nature itself is so regular. Although sometimes virtually unnoticed, the procession of the seasons, the regularity with which the sun revolves around the earth, and other natural phenomena reflect an unchanging orderliness. The order perceived in the natural world can serve as a convenient analogy for the order created in the social world. Indeed, many societies are patterned on regularities people believe they can observe in nature, and their sense of this order is reflected in their artifacts, "from tools to buildings and from clothing to ornaments" (Gombrich 1979b:60).

Although not an anthropologist, the Swiss psychologist Jean Piaget contributed to cognitive anthropol-

◆ ASK YOURSELF

It has been said that the number three has assumed a special importance in American culture (Dundes 1968). One example is the Holy Trinity—the Father, Son and Holy Spirit—of Christianity, this culture's predominant religion. Can you think of other examples of important groupings of three in American society? Is there another number that seems to you to be more important, culturally?

Swiss psychologist Jean Piaget contributed to cognitive anthropology with studies of how young children develop their capacity to classify and therefore to think. No matter what their culture, children go through the same stages of cognitive development.

◆◆◆

Classification by Sevens: The Zuni

The Zuni, whom we met in Chapter 1 as hosts to the pioneering fieldworker Frank Cushing, illustrate how the order that members of a society perceive in the natural world can be reflected in their social order. Cushing (1896) noted that the Zuni viewed most natural phenomena as divided into sevenths of some larger whole. For example, they believed that the physical world was divided into seven spatial regions or sectors: north, south, east, west, the zenith (or heavens), the nadir (or depths), and the center. Everything in the world belonged in one or another of these seven regions.

Zuni social life was organized to reflect this principle. Society consisted of seven subtribes. In the past, the subtribes had occupied seven towns, but by the time of Cushing's fieldwork they had congregated into a single village organized into seven sectors, each corresponding to one of the seven divisions of space (Cushing 1896:367). Zuni rituals, held in an orderly sequence based on a yearly calendar, dramatized the sevenfold natural world.

So comprehensive was the Zuni system of division by sevens that it penetrated all corners of their lives. This "mythic division of the world," as Cushing (1896:369) later came to call it, was so comprehensive and integrated that "not only the ceremonial life of the people, but all their governmental arrangements as well" were thoroughly systematized according to the same pattern. Cushing concluded that "something akin to written statutes" resulted from all this coherence: "the people employing such devices may be said to . . . be writing their statutes and laws in all their daily relationships and utterances" (372).

ogy in studies of how young children develop their capacity to classify and therefore to think. Beginning in the 1920s, Piaget examined children's concepts of time, space, numbers, and logic to discover whether or not their intellectual development occurred in fixed stages. He suggested that all children, no matter what their culture, go through the same stages of cognitive development. First, they learn about reality by perceiving what is going on around them; next, they physically explore their world. Piaget's ideas have proven to be particularly valuable for cognitive anthropologists, who are interested in discovering whether and to what extent Piaget's stages of learning can be modified by culture (Bock 1988:176–177).

All cultures have some system of order, and in many of these systems, numbers play an important part. In cultures in which the predominant religion is Christianity, things are often organized into threes. At left is sixteenth-century Flemish painter Joos van Cleve's three-part Crucifixion with Donors.

Structural Anthropology

Closely related to cognitive anthropology is a subfield called **structural anthropology,** pioneered by Claude Lévi-Strauss, a French anthropologist. Lévi-Strauss analyzed cultural phenomena such as languages, myths, and kinship systems to discover what ordered patterns, or structures, they seemed to display. These, he suggested, could reveal the structure of the human mind. In any society, the same minds that create myths also create the organization of social relationships, the political system, religious beliefs, magical rituals, pottery—in fact, everything cultural. Hence, Lévi-Strauss suggested, the orderly patterns used to structure myths may be replicated in these other areas of culture.

Lévi-Strauss (1983) chose the discipline of linguistics (see Chapter 13) to help develop his structural anthropology. According to linguists, any language consists of a set of sounds and the rules (grammar) governing their organization, plus a limitless number of meaningful utterances. The sounds and rules we call language, and the utterances, speech. Lévi-Strauss likened people's language rules to the "rules" that govern society, in that the governed are largely unconscious of what they know. He likened speech—the *use* of the sounds and rules, mainly in the form of sentences—to the actual ideas and behaviors that result from the application of social rules. Members of a society are much more likely to be conscious of their actual ideas and behaviors than they are of the deeply structured rules that made these ideas and behaviors possible. Therefore, Lévi-Strauss reasoned, the ideas and behaviors of a given group of people can be understood if the unconscious structures in their minds can be discovered.

Psychological Anthropology

Anthropologists who believe that culture can best be accounted for by understanding intangibles, such as feelings, dreams, and artistic impulses, have developed an important specialty in contemporary anthropology called **psychological anthropology.** Like cognitive anthropology, it focuses on what is going on in people's heads, and indeed the two specialties overlap. The major difference between them lies in the difference between sensations and perceptions. Psychological anthropology stresses feelings and experiences, whereas cognitive anthropology stresses the different categories people create to organize their universe and, therefore, how they learn and think. By focusing on topics such as the interrelationship of personality and culture (see Chapter 3) or people's concepts of self in different cultures (see below), psychological anthropology explores the relationship between culture and the psychological makeup of individuals and groups.

◆◆◆

Opposition

Opposition, or thinking in terms of opposed categories, is of interest to both cognitive and structural anthropologists. To think, we must classify, which means we must be able to discriminate or distinguish between things. Thinking of two things as opposites is the simplest way to distinguish between them. So important is opposition to thinking that we may refer to it as a basic component of human thought. Long ago, the ancient Greek philosopher Heraclitus observed that many things in the natural and social worlds had opposites. Good was opposed to bad, life to death, right to left, male to female, and so on. He suggested that we could think of the entire world as being organized in a dualistic way. Others have agreed: human beings, regardless of what society they belong to, do tend to think in terms of opposites. Much of Chinese philosophy, for example, is based on the idea of two opposing life forces: yin (the passive, female principle or force) and yang (the active, masculine principle or force).

Much more recent thinkers than Heraclitus have made use of the idea that human beings have a natural tendency to think in dualistic patterns. The German philosopher George Hegel (1770–1831) proposed that every idea implied its opposite and that by uniting an idea and its opposite (a process termed *synthesis*), the two of them would create a single new idea, which in turn would give birth to *its* opposite, and so on. This *dialectic* process was later employed by the influential German philosopher Karl Marx.

One focus of psychological anthropology is the notion of selfhood. Human infants develop a sense of self when they perceive their own bodies as separate from those of others. Self-absorption is apparently common to infants of all cultures.

From our discussion of culture and personality in Chapter 3, you already know something about what was once an intense focus of psychological anthropology. Beginning in the 1930s, some anthropologists of this school compared child-rearing practices cross-culturally, and others searched within cultures for modal personalities. Still others tried to explain why people in different cultures valued different personal characteristics such as aggressiveness or meekness. They even labeled whole cultures with such adjectives as "warlike" or "peace loving" on the basis of what was perceived to be some dominant personality type.

A more recent focus of psychological anthropology has been the concept of selfhood. The term **self** refers to the individual person as the object of his or her own perception (Murphy 1966:523). Human infants seem to develop a sense of self from an early perception of their own bodies as distinguished from those of others, especially their mothers'. The self becomes a source of emotional satisfaction, and self-love appears to be common to infants of all cultures. As they mature, their concept of self changes gradually, through involvement with others.

The notion of self is very much a product of enculturation, and a number of contemporary anthropologists are interested in understanding if, and how, selfhood differs from culture to culture (Bock 1988:198). However, they come at this subject from different points of view.

From the culture and personality perspective, for example, differences in people's concepts of self are established by early patterns of interaction between young children and their caretakers. Another possibility is that developing a selfhood is a universal human process on which cultural differences are superimposed.

Cultural differences in naming newborns illustrate this possibility. In some American hospitals, newborn babies are referred to for administrative purposes as "Infant So-and-So," which indicates a baby's family membership while denying his or her individuality (Bock 1988:198). In other cultures, particularly those with high infant mortality, babies are not given names until they are several weeks old and considered likely to survive. And in societies with a belief in reincarnation, a child may not receive a name until it has been established

structural anthropology an anthropological specialty whose followers attempt to discover orderly patterns common to languages, myths, kinship systems, and other aspects of culture

psychological anthropology an anthropological specialty focusing on the relationship between culture and the psychological makeup of individuals and groups

opposition thinking in terms of opposed categories

self the individual person as the object of his or her own perception

which dead ancestor's soul has entered the child's body. How children's names are assigned in different cultures reflects differences in how different cultures interpret the notion of self.

Some cross-cultural studies undertaken by psychological anthropologists have focused on the analysis of dreams and how their content may be influenced by the culture of the dreamer. People's brains are very active during sleep regardless of their culture. However, the content of dreams varies. In some cultures, solutions to personal problems are expected to come during sleep, and often they do. In other cultures, the dreamer's hidden enemies are revealed. In still others, people wake with ideas for songs, poems, or visual images they later fulfill in artistic creations.

Yet another area of interest to psychological anthropologists is the relationship between the psychology of the individual and symbolic meanings shared widely within his or her culture. While working in Sri Lanka, an island off the south coast of India, psychological anthropologist Gananath Obeyesekere (1981:6–7) brought Freud's ideas about the unconscious motivations of individuals together with the anthropological notion that culture imposes meaning on every aspect of human existence. Obeyesekere was able to show how certain cultural symbols—not all, but some—can become "personalized" by individuals, for whom they take on highly individualized meanings. Such meanings are typically marked by intense emotion, an aspect of the individual in culture rarely discussed by previous ethnographers.

Obeyesekere's first analytical focus was the possible hidden meaning behind the long locks of matted hair worn by Sri Lankan priestesses of a Hindu-Buddhist cult. When Obeyesekere first saw a priestess of this cult, her hair reminded him of snakes, and he was seized with anxiety. Immediately he thought of a paper by Freud in which the snake-covered head of a mythical female character named Medusa was linked to the terror of castration. Was it this association that caused Obeyesekere's anxiety? Did Sri Lankan people have similar feelings when they saw the matted locks of hair worn by priestesses? Could Obeyesekere utilize his own feelings and reactions to learn something broader about Sri Lankans—or about human psychology in general?

Obeyesekere (1981:9) soon learned that Sri Lankans "are indeed often anxious when they see the matted hair" of their religious practitioners. From this experience, he realized that his own reactions were useful for understanding "what goes on in the minds of oth-ers." He went on to analyze symbols that acted at both the personal and the cultural levels in Sri Lankan society. Such symbols, because they have meaning at both levels, help to integrate culture and the individuals who share it.

Postmodernism

In Chapter 2, we described how some modern fieldworkers, aware of the subjective nature of ethnography and how the relationship between ethnographer and informant can affect the ethnographic process, have described the feelings they experienced in the field, their personal relationships with their informants, and sometimes other subjective observations as well—anything they think will enable readers to understand what the culture under study is like.

This reflexive kind of ethnography is closely tied in with a wider development in cultural anthropology called **postmodernism,** which emerged during the 1980s. Like feminist anthropologists, with whom they share the desire to rethink anthropology's traditional assumptions, postmodernists are a diverse group. In general, however, postmodernism's leaders—James Clifford, George E. Marcus, and Stephen Tyler—distinguish far more clearly than do most of their predecessors between two processes: doing field research and writing up the data collected in the form of books or articles.

Postmodernists believe that a more accurate description of what is going on in a particular culture would be possible if ethnographers adopted more self-conscious attitudes about their own methods, assumptions, and ideas. Instead of regarding ethnographic reports based on field research as accurate reflections of a culture, for example, postmodernists view ethnographies as the unique products of particular researchers, informants, and field methods. In addition, they believe that ethnographic writing itself is a legitimate focus of an-

 ASK YOURSELF

We have included several fictional "profiles" in this book, hoping that our made-up characters will give you a better sense of what their cultures are like than would portraits of real individuals, with all their distinctive personal peculiarities. Does this "postmodernist" approach help you to get a feel for what the fictional characters' cultures are all about?

Psychological anthropologists are interested in the relationship between the psychology of individuals and the symbolic meanings shared by individuals of the same culture. One anthropologist felt anxious when he first saw the long, matted hair of a Sri Lankan priestess. On learning that Sri Lankans have similar feelings, he concluded that his own reactions could help him learn something about Sri Lankan culture.

thropological analysis (Marcus and Cushman 1982: Clifford 1986).

Writers of **realistic ethnographies,** such as Malinowski, Evans-Pritchard, and Chagnon, have been sharply criticized by postmodernists, who claim the cultural "realities" these writers sought to portray never really existed. Traditional ethnography claims to paint a realistic picture of a culture, often a holistic one. It sug-

gests that the different aspects of that culture can be organized in a systematic, understandable way and that the ethnographer's representations of his or her findings is a more or less objective analysis of what is really going on in the culture. By contrast, in distinguishing the process of fieldwork from the ethnography produced, postmodernists use the ethnography itself as their central object of study, not the culture it portrays. For example, they analyze the style in which an ethnography is written and determine whether individuals in the society under study have been allowed to voice their own feelings—or whether the ethnographer has either chosen not to mention individuals at all or edited what they said, thus only *appearing* to give them their own voice.

A number of postmodernists have experimented with the process of creating ethnographies. Some, for instance, have written portraits of fictitious members of a culture under study or included descriptions of fictitious incidents, in the belief that somehow these efforts will provide a greater sense of reality than the mere presentation of data. Such fictionalization must be clearly labeled as such, of course, but the effort strikes us as worthwhile.

Margery Wolf (1992), who carried out fieldwork in Taiwan, an island off the coast of mainland China, has sought to bring together certain of the experimental ideas of postmodernism and feminist anthropology, combining a long, fictionalized account of a Taiwanese woman with her "real" fieldwork data. The result may lack the coherence of traditional realist ethnography, but one gets some vivid insights into what being a female Taiwanese villager is all about.

As with most advocates, postmodernists tend to oversell the novelty of what they claim to have discovered, and some anthropologists are put off by the unnecessary jargon that confuses much of what the postmodernists are attempting to say (Sangren 1992). But by emphasizing that the analysis of how ethnographies are written is as valid a type of research as the more traditional analyses of the cultures these ethnographies claim to describe, postmodernists are encouraging us to rethink the very foundations of cultural anthropology.

postmodernism an anthropological specialty, developed in the 1980s, that encourages anthropology to focus on the analysis of ethnographies, examining them from a reflexive point of view

realistic ethnography an ethnography that claims to represent a "real" portrait of a culture or society

CONCLUSION

"The Blind Men and the Elephant" illustrates the important point that no narrow explanatory approach, no single perspective, suffices when one's goal is a thorough understanding of some multifaceted whole. We think the most useful approach to culture is to consider any and all potential ways of understanding it and to use one or another approach as the particular conditions of a study suggest. Often a certain aspect of culture will yield secrets when looked at multidimensionally, for every idea, institution, mode of behavior, or artifact occurs within many different, overlapping contexts. What is the historical or evolutionary context in which a particular custom or artifact occurs? What are the material correlates of the setting in which it is found? What is its functional meaning; that is, how does it connect with other aspects of culture? What meaning does it have for its members and for its ethnographer?

One reason such an all-inclusive point of view appeals to us is that it does not necessarily depend on the hope that theories that can explain human behavior exist and will one day be discovered. In truth, the long anthropological search for theories of human behavior has not proven particularly successful, partly because human behavior is so varied. Thus, as soon as one anthropologist comes up with what appears to be a custom or idea or institution that can be found in human societies everywhere, another anthropologist points to a society in which this generalization about people doesn't hold true.

Looking at culture through a series of lenses enables us to use any perspective that involves the quest for orderly cultural patterns (recall Gombrich on the importance of order in human existence) and encourages us to look for multiple ways in which ideas and institutions can be understood. It does not limit us with evolutionary, materialist, functionalist, cognitive, structural, psychological, or postmodernist assumptions or preconceptions.

After looking at a particular idea or institution from as many angles as possible, an anthropologist might well decide that one perspective reveals most of its properties. Naturally, he or she will stress that perspective as a general interpretive framework. But you can be sure that no matter what aspect of culture is under consideration, it will reveal at least some of its secrets from other angles, and these need to be taken into account. The cultural elephant is a many-sided creature.

SUMMARY

To reach as full an understanding of culture as possible requires examining this complex subject from as many different angles as possible, for it is unlikely that any single point of view will be able to afford us an unchallenged interpretation. In this chapter, we have considered three different (if at times partially overlapping) perspectives on the study of culture: cultural evolution (in several different forms), functionalism (in two varieties, Malinowskian functionalism and structural-functionalism), and cultural materialism. In addition, we have looked at four anthropological specialties, each a topical area in which groups of anthropologists have done interesting and important research: cognitive anthropology, structural anthropology, psychological anthropology, and postmodernism. All of these perspectives and specialties are in use today in the interpretation and explanation of cultural phenomena.

KEY TERMS

anthropological perspectives
anthropological specialties
cognitive anthropology
cultural ecology
cultural materialism
cultural process
diachronic approach
human ecology
mental universals
multilineal evolution
neo-evolutionism
opposition
postmodernism
psychological anthropology
realistic ethnography
self
structural anthropology
structural-functionalism
synchronic approach
unilineal evolution

SUGGESTED READINGS

Harris, Marvin. 1977. *Cannibals and Kings: The Origins of Cultures.* New York: Random House. The well-known cultural materialist explains how human behavior can be explained through the cultural-ecological approach.

Kuper, Adam. 1980. Great Britain: Functionalism at Home, a Question of Theory. In Stanley Diamond (ed.), *Anthropology: Ancestors and Heirs,* pp. 293–315. The Hague: Mouton. An excellent summary statement of functionalism.

Roland, Alan. 1988. *In Search of Self in India and Japan: Toward a Cross-Cultural Psychology.* Princeton, NJ: Princeton University Press. In this series of case studies, an American psychoanalyst explores the notion of self among Japanese and Indians and concludes that there are fundamental differences between their selfhoods and those of Westerners.

Sahlins, Marshall D., and Elman R. Service (eds.). 1960. *Evolution and Culture.* Ann Arbor: University of Michigan Press. Neo-evolutionists distinguish specific from general evolution.

CHAPTER 5

MAKING A LIVING

One way to make a living is pastoralism—raising herd animals that provide subsistence necessities such as meat, milk, and hides. In Norway, where pastoralists herd reindeer for a living, a Lapp woman tries to corral a frisky young animal.

INTRODUCTION

"Tennessee," panhandling on a busy downtown Los Angeles street corner, tells any passerby who will listen that he's trying to collect money to buy a bus ticket back home to the state that gave him his name (Corwin 1984:3). His friend "Tom" asserts proudly that he hasn't looked for steady work in years; occasionally he unloads trucks to make a few dollars, but he prefers just to "hang out." Tennessee and Tom are members of a group of homeless men whose base of operations is a Los Angeles park. By begging, scrounging, eating some of their meals free at local churches, wearing used clothing, and protecting themselves from the elements with newspapers, cardboard boxes, sheets of plastic, and an occasional night in a city-run shelter, these homeless men not only survive but also claim to be enjoying life.

Many of the homeless in America's cities are victims of a weak economy, unable to find the steady work they need to obtain permanent homes and reliable sources of food, clothing, and other necessities of life. Some are alcoholics (see Spradley 1970); some have AIDS or other diseases; some are mentally ill. But others, like Tennessee and Tom, are apparently content with their unusual way of life. Determinedly self-reliant, they have purposefully chosen their hand-to-mouth existence. Their strategy for procuring the things they want and need is very different from that of most Americans, but it seems to work for them.

This chapter is about the different ways in which people obtain the necessities of life and how different natural environments, technologies, social relationships, activities, and ways of thinking all come together to produce very different kinds of cultures. We call the complex of technologies, activities, and ideas that together add up to a particular way of making a living within a particular environment an **adaptation** to that environment.

COLLECTING VERSUS PRODUCING

Subsistence refers to all of the ways in which people get the basics they need to live—food and drink, clothing, shelter, security, and warmth. There are two main subsistence methods: people can *collect* things that have already been provided by nature, or they can *produce* the things they need. Subsistence based entirely on collecting is now extremely rare, but it is by far the older

Many homeless people in the United States want permanent homes and steady jobs. But others, like this California man who says he prefers the outdoors to a shelter, claim they have developed a satisfactory strategy for procuring the things they want and need.

of the two ways of making a living, having been practiced for over 2 million years. Tennessee and Tom are modern-day examples of this way of life.

Subsistence based on producing food and other necessities did not begin until relatively recently. We can't provide a precise date since this way of life began at different times in different places. But all over the world, the drama unfolded something like this. After thousands of generations of collecting, people began to manipulate their natural environment to make it more productive. The first steps must have been simple. Perhaps someone noticed that certain bushes produced more berries after a forest fire, and set a fire intentionally in order to have more berries to pick. Or perhaps someone noticed that wild rice plants produced more rice when they weren't surrounded by other plants, and removed the competing plants from places where wild rice grew. Over many generations, human beings added to their stock of such inventions as they tried to shape the environment to their own needs. Eventually, probably after thousands of years, both plants and animals were domesticated for food and other uses.

The change from collecting to producing was a gradual process rather than a single event. Producing did not become widespread anywhere in the world until some ten thousand years ago. Subsequently, more and more wild plants and animals were domesticated, until people could pretty much decide for themselves just where various species would reproduce and how much reproduction would take place. The impact of producing on human life and culture was so revolutionary that the shift from a life-style based on collection to one based on production is called the **Neolithic** ("new stone") **revolution,** after the kinds of stone tools people were making at the time.

When people began living in towns, their way of adapting to their environment became more complex. Some, for instance, didn't produce any subsistence necessities at all but instead produced goods or services that they could exchange for the things they needed. This kind of specialization remains with us today.

The nineteenth-century cultural evolutionists correctly identified a general trend in human history from collecting (**gathering and hunting**) to simple methods of production (such as growing crops and rearing animals by simple methods) to more complex methods of production (such as mechanized agriculture and industrialism). There are variations on these ways of life, but they all fit under one of the two basic subsistence methods: collecting or producing. Shellfishing, for instance,

can be considered either collecting or—if shellfish are being encouraged to reproduce in certain places and then are harvested like crops—simple food producing.

Not every society has moved from one method to the next, much less at the same rate, so over the last ten thousand years many different adaptations have existed simultaneously. This remains true today. Nor do clear-cut dividing lines separate one way of life from another. Members of a single society can gather food, hunt game, and grow crops. To make our description clearer, we'll discuss the major adaptations as if they were distinct from one another, answering such questions as how long the adaptation in question has been used, what societies practice it now and in what environments, how people get the things they need, how the work of getting them is shared, and (most important) what it would be like to live in a society that bases its livelihood on a given adaptation.

•••

COLLECTING

Gatherers and Hunters

Out of a current world population of more than 5 billion people, only some .25 million, about 1/20,000 of the world's total, rely on gathering and hunting. Despite their rarity, however, gatherers and hunters are of exceptional interest to anthropologists, for three reasons.

First, theirs is by far the oldest adaptation; indeed, for most of human history, it was the only one. People have been gatherers and hunters for so long that we can state with certainty that 98 percent of your direct ancestors (and those of every other person on this earth) pursued this way of life.

Second, during the almost inconceivably long period of time in which all people were gatherers and hunters, they established some basic behavior patterns that are still with us today. In every society, for example,

•••

adaptation a complex of ideas, activities, and technologies that add up to a particular way of making a living

subsistence all the ways in which people get the things they need to subsist

Neolithic revolution the shift in human subsistence from collecting to producing subsistence needs

gathering and hunting the nonproducing method of subsistence

it is customary for males and females to pair off, live together, and contribute jointly to the rearing of their offspring. Likewise, all over the world people eat their food with others who are sharing the same food. Since they seem so obvious, we take these behaviors for granted. We say it's just "human nature"; after all, who wants to live or eat alone? Yet there really is no reason why we shouldn't live or raise our children differently or get our nourishment in some other setting. Customs such as food sharing were established by our gatherer-and-hunter ancestors and have persisted ever since. To understand why people behave as they do today, it's helpful to look at our gatherer-and-hunter roots.

A third reason why anthropology focuses so much attention on gatherers and hunters is that their small numbers are rapidly becoming even smaller. There were many more of them in the last century than now, but even the nineteenth-century anthropologists could see that if they did not study gatherers and hunters promptly and thoroughly, the opportunity would be forever lost.

Studying gatherers and hunters is difficult because today all of them live in inhospitable, marginal environments—such as the arctic, deserts, and jungles—in which subsistence is at best uncertain. In the past, most gatherers and hunters lived in temperate surroundings, but over the years they have disappeared from their traditional homelands. Some moved and some adopted an-

other way of life, but most became extinct. In every case the reason was competition from other people who practiced a different adaptation. The absence of contemporary gatherers and hunters from the temperate zone makes it difficult for us to know how earlier gatherers and hunters lived in such environments, although archaeology can help.

Gatherers and hunters share certain features. First, since they must move from time to time in search of food (often with the seasons), they live in temporary sites, called **camps.** They can accumulate little beyond the clothes on their backs, tools, and perhaps a few ornaments, as they must carry any possessions with them when they move. Thus individual ownership of property, common among more settled people, is not well established among gatherers and hunters, and the few objects they do have are apt to be temporary rather than permanent possessions. They make their tools and shelters when and where required, and when these things have served their functions, they are abandoned, to be replaced when needed. Food, too, is generally collected when needed; storing it would tie the group to one place.

Second, gatherers and hunters live in **bands,** small social units of 25 to 50 people, all practicing the same subsistence strategy and all related to one another by kinship or marriage. A band's size is limited by the **carrying capacity** of its environment—the maximum num-

Of the world's population of over 5 billion people, only about a quarter of a million rely solely on gathering and hunting to get the things they want and need. In the Kalahari desert of Botswana, Africa, a San gatherer and hunter collects berries.

●●

Ice Age Gatherers and Hunters of Western Europe

We think of the "Cave Man" of cartoon fame as having inhabited a bleak, glacial world, devoid of warmth and comfort. Clad in animal skins and shouldering knobby clubs, men won mates by unceremoniously grabbing women by the hair and dragging them into cold, dank caverns. There Ice Age families spent their days huddled beside their campfires, grunting at one another and gnawing hungrily on animal bones.

According to modern researchers, this view of prehistoric gatherers and hunters is inaccurate. Based on evidence from sites in France and Spain, archaeologists have discovered that environmental conditions in long-ago western Europe were much more hospitable than the term *Ice Age* suggests (Hadingham 1979:85). Vast grasslands were home to herds of reindeer, horses, and cattle, whose bones litter Ice Age sites. The remains of bear, deer, and wild pigs show that our Ice Age ancestors also exploited forests, where they surely gathered nuts, fruits, and other plant foods as well. (The remains of these foods do not often survive for archaeologists to dig up.) Cave paintings of leaping salmon show that nearby streams were also a source of food (Pfeiffer 1982:61–2). In short, some Ice Age environments, far from being marginal, offered gatherers and hunters an extraordinary range of plant and animal life to exploit. From this comfortable subsistence base, they were able to develop a rich and long-lived culture of great technological sophistication and artistic accomplishment.

---

ber of people who can live indefinitely within a given area at a given level of technology (Zubrow 1975:15). Actually, most gatherer-and-hunter groups contain fewer people than their environments could theoretically support, perhaps because gatherers and hunters are aware of the great hardship that could result from overpopulation. They keep their numbers low by using various forms of birth control. The size of a band often fluctuates considerably, as births, deaths, and marriages add or subtract members or as resource scarcities or conflicts cause band members to split up.

Third, gatherers and hunters allocate the tasks that need to be done according to sex and age. Women usually gather fruits, nuts, seeds, and berries, and sometimes small animals, shellfish, eggs, or insects as well. This work provides most of the band's calories (Dahlberg 1981). Women also prepare the meals. Adult men hunt, although hunting is usually less important than gathering as a means of getting food. It does have other important functions; for example, it may be a way for males to enhance their personal prestige, or when it requires collective effort, it may strengthen social bonds. One efficient method of hunting is the drive, in which able-bodied adult males join forces to goad their prey into waiting traps, using fires or shouts or beating the bushes.

Females do not hunt big animals, although they sometimes hunt small game. Big-game hunting is dangerous, and hunters sometimes get killed. A society with few members needs to protect its females from premature death since it is they who produce the children that perpetuate the group. Even if most of a small group's males were to die in hunting accidents, those remaining, even if they were few in number, could father many children. But should many of a small group's females die, the few remaining females, giving birth at the average rate of less than one child per year, could not ensure the continued existence of the group. Perhaps another reason why females don't hunt big game may be that this activity is incompatible with looking after children.

Most bands are characterized by **egalitarianism,** meaning not that everyone is equal but that everyone of the same sex and age has roughly the same standing in society. Among middle-aged men, for example, there is

●●

camp a temporary residential site for gatherers and hunters

band a group of gatherers and hunters

carrying capacity the maximum number of people who can live indefinitely within a given area at a given level of technology

egalitarianism a condition in which all people of the same sex and age have a roughly equal social position

In gatherer-and-hunter bands, men do the big-game hunting. This activity may not provide as much food as the gathering done by women, but it can strengthen social bonds. A nineteenth-century painting shows native American Hidatsa hunters working together to kill buffalo.

no boss who can command his fellows because of his superior social status, education, or wealth. Perhaps because property cannot be accumulated, no one can be "richer" or "better" than the next person. Then, too, since a person's job is usually the same as that of everyone else of the same age and sex, no superior positions exist for the ambitious to seek. Thus the only major differences in social position are those based on sex or age (usually the older you are, the higher your position).

When it comes to relations between bands, gatherers and hunters tend to be relatively peaceful, for several reasons. Property, a major cause of conflict between societies, is far less important to band members than to other people. Bands or their members don't "own" land, for example. Instead, members of different bands acknowledge one another's rights to exploit any area. Peaceful relations are also encouraged by the fact that band members typically marry members of other bands,

so people in one band are likely to have relatives in others. This is not to say that conflict never arises between gatherer-and-hunter groups, but when it does, it is more likely to be resolved by the disputing parties moving further apart than by fighting.

Anthropologists used to assume that all gatherers and hunters lived in want and misery. A wandering life-style and a lack of material goods suggest poverty and a constant struggle for existence. But recent studies have shown that some gatherers and hunters, particularly those who occupied hospitable environments in the past, may have enjoyed a comfortable life-style (Sahlins 1974). In many parts of the temperate zone, nature provided food, water, and the materials for shelters and clothing so abundantly that it was probably unnecessary for people to work more than a few hours a day. Even some gatherers and hunters today seem to have plenty of time for napping, telling stories, and playing with their children. If "affluence" is defined as having everything you want and need, then, as anthropologist Marshall Sahlins points out, gatherers and hunters are "the original affluent society." Still, the majority of today's gatherers and hunters are hardly affluent because of the marginal environments they have been shunted into by people of more powerful societies. Many must work very hard just to survive.

How Production Began

Anthropologists are puzzled over why, where, when, and how the production of subsistence necessities began. Some argue that people were domesticating animals as early as the end of the last Ice Age, which if true would make "cave people" the world's first producers. Others think the title should go to the gatherer who first realized that there were ways in which she could alter the natural environment to encourage the growth of certain plants. Selective burning, weeding, pruning, and transplanting are all effective, nonagricultural ways to produce food crops (Bender 1975). One authority has even suggested that people may have transplanted and cultivated flowers for the pleasure of their appearance and smell before they discovered how to grow crops for more practical reasons, and playing with pets may have provided the knowledge necessary for animal domestication (Smith 1975).

So the origins of domestication remain a mystery, as are the reasons behind it. Perhaps worsening climatic conditions, maybe a long drought, forced some hungry gatherers and hunters to develop other ways of getting food. Perhaps some bands grew to exceed the carrying capacity of their local environments, prompting their members to experiment with ways to feed more people.

Archaeologists think the idea of domestication occurred in at least three different areas of the world and at three different times. Many of the domesticated plants and animals Westerners regularly use—wheat and barley, for instance, as well as goats and pigs—originated in present-day Iraq and Iran some ten thousand years ago. In Central America, people grew corn, beans, peanuts, avocadoes, sweet potatoes, and tobacco as early

◆ **ASK YOURSELF**

Do you agree with Sahlins's definition of affluence? As a college student, what goods or other resources would you need to consider yourself affluent?

as nine thousand years ago. And approximately six thousand years ago, in places that are now parts of China and Thailand, people first domesticated rice and soybeans. Because of pronounced environmental differences among these regions of the world, anthropologists have not been able to agree on any one model explaining how domestication occurred (Flannery 1973), and we are still "far from a complete understanding of the transition" to food production (Pryor 1986:892).

SIMPLE PRODUCTION METHODS

The various ways of life based on simple methods of production share two significant characteristics: they are small-scale, and they use no machinery. Beyond these similarities, however, there are considerable differences between the two major types of simple production: horticulture and pastoralism.

Horticulturalists

The impact of the Neolithic revolution on human life can hardly be overestimated. With domesticated plants and animals, people were no longer totally reliant on natural resources. Growing food and filling a storehouse full of grain for the coming winter may seem far preferable to collecting food. Still, it's often said that everything in life is a trade-off; and for their peace of mind, people doing simple gardening, or **horticulture,** had to give up many of the advantages of the gatherer-and-hunter way of life—among them mobility, egalitarianism, and a good deal of leisure time.

Horticulturalists till the earth with hand-held tools, using stone or metal hoes or wooden digging sticks to plant seeds in holes dug in the ground. They care for the resulting crops without chemical fertilizers, complex irrigation systems, or farm machinery. They don't even use animals or plows to help in the sometimes back-breaking labor of planting and harvesting. Their only domesticated animals are usually small food animals like chickens or pigs. It's a technologically simple way of life that has been going on, in various places around the world, for ten thousand years and still exists today in some parts of South America, Africa, and Asia, among other areas.

horticulture a method of subsistence based on growing crops with simple tools and technologies

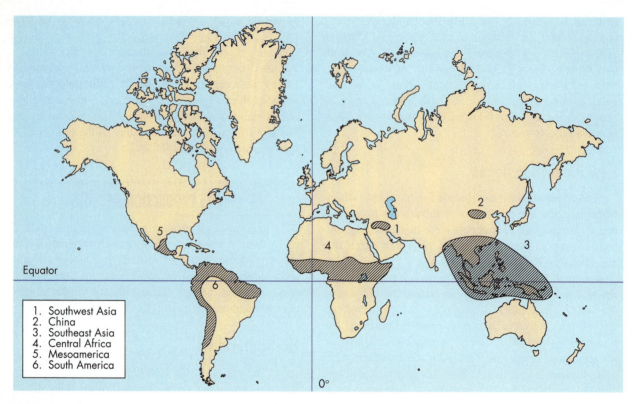

Figure 5.1
Probable Locations of Early Plant and Animal Domestication

The most widespread horticultural technique goes by three different names: **swidden, slash-and-burn,** or **shifting cultivation.** Gardeners clear a patch of forest land by cutting down any large trees and slashing away the undergrowth. After allowing the remaining tangle of branches and weeds to dry, they set fire to it. (This method of clearing land is most often practiced in damp, tropical areas, where there is little chance of setting fire to the whole forest.) Often they leave the charred tree trunks where they have fallen and plant crops of many different species—perhaps corn, yams, sweet potatoes, manioc, and coconuts—among the debris. As untidy as a plot such as this looks, it is actually a very productive garden since the ash from the burned vegetation provides a natural fertilizer for the soil. The gardeners harvest their crops at different times, so there are always some plants in the soil.

After the ground has been prepared and the crops planted, the gardeners' chores are minimal. They may stand watch to make sure the growing crops are safe from predators, human or otherwise. They may even do a little weeding, although in tropical areas this is a thankless job because new weeds appear virtually overnight. In general, though, this kind of farming involves relatively little work between planting and harvesting. But there's a catch: after a couple of years, the nutrients in the soil become depleted, and underbrush begins to take over. At this point, the horticulturalists abandon the plot, shifting their efforts to a newly burned area. After allowing the plot to lie undisturbed for a time so fresh nutrients in the form of rotting plant life can restore fertility to the soil, the cultivators may return to begin the cycle all over again.

Unlike gatherers and hunters, horticulturalists usually live in permanent or semipermanent villages, for it's hard to be a successful planter unless you stay close to your crops. But like gatherers and hunters, they tend to live very near their relatives. Big families, consisting of grandparents, aunts, uncles, and cousins as well as parents and their offspring, are particularly important

Using hand-held tools, horticulturalists clear forest land for planting by felling trees and burning away undergrowth. They then plant their crops among the fallen tree trunks. In Brazil, taro, a starchy root crop, grows in a Yanomamo garden.

among horticulturalists because, in addition to forming a kinship group (see Chapter 6), these relatives often own land jointly and work side by side.

For the amount of energy put into horticulture, many more calories' worth of food are produced than can be gathered and hunted with the same amount of effort. Horticulture is thus a more efficient way to get food than gathering and hunting, and communities of horticulturalists can be larger than gatherer-and-hunter bands. However, it takes more people to clear garden plots, guard and weed them, and harvest and store crops than it takes to forage for nuts or stalk and kill an animal. So at the same time that it requires a larger community, the horticultural way of life also makes a larger community possible. Horticulturalists' villages may contain as many as several hundred people.

Although sex and age largely determine jobs in bands, horticultural societies also allocate jobs according to individual talent, interests, and family heritage. Thus, if you are particularly good at textile weaving or if your father was a weaver, it's likely you'll be a weaver too.

Women in horticultural societies do a great deal of the sometimes hard work of gardening, and in some of these societies cultivation is solely women's work. Perhaps for this reason, the position of women is, on the average, higher in horticultural than in gatherer-and-hunter societies (see Quinn 1977:199).

Although warfare is uncommon among gatherers and hunters, this is not the case with horticulturalists, among whom warfare and other kinds of violence may be small-scale but reap a severe toll in lives. What is the reason for this bloodshed? Horticulturalists, unlike gatherers and hunters, own property: land, crops, houses. People are distinguished from one another on the basis of who has what, a situation that seems to provoke envy and hostility that may erupt into conflict.

Horticulturalists also tend to be less egalitarian than gatherers and hunters. Leaders, almost always

swidden, slash-and-burn, or shifting cultivation a form of horticulture in which a plot of land is cultivated for some years and then abandoned in favor of a new one

Slash-and-Burn Horticulture among the Tetum

The Tetum people of Indonesia are horticulturalists whose yearly cycle of plant cultivation begins in the fall (Hicks 1988). The dark blue skies over Timor grow cloudy in the last weeks of October, and by early November the rainy season has begun, with downpours persisting for up to six hours at a time. By the end of the month, the tawny covering of grass and trees that blanketed the island during the preceding dry season has given way to dazzlingly green foliage.

Even as the first showers are falling, you can see Tetum families hurrying to their garden plots, eager to thrust their digging sticks into the damp soil. The women and girls do the actual planting, dropping their corn, sweet potato, yam, and vegetable seeds in shallow holes. A family usually seeds its garden in about two days, camping out in a crude lean-to at night. When the job is done, the family moves on to its next plot; most families have two or three. As soon as the planting is finished, the planters return to their villages.

By about the middle of December, the rains are at their heaviest, and the corn is already 3 feet high. Getting from one place to another is no longer as easy as it was in the dry season, for even when the rain ceases for a few hours, raindrops from overhanging trees plop onto travelers' heads as they plod along paths knee-deep in mud. To avoid a mud bath, they must from time to time leave the path and force their way through soggy undergrowth that seems always to be well protected by sharp thorns. No wonder Tetum families prefer to remain in the dry comfort of their own villages during December. The women weave cloth, make clay pots, and plait mats from dried palm leaves. Men talk politics and make gardening tools. Social gatherings, frequent during the dry season, are rare, for whenever a family takes advantage of a brief dry spell it is to weed its gardens rather than to socialize.

Families harvest their corn on dry days in February, normally taking two days per garden. Planting is women's work, but now time is of the essence, so men and women join together in the job of harvesting. In March, rain returns in force, and rice is planted in the same gardens. In April, the Tetum

In Indonesia, after the rainy season has yielded to the dry season, Tetum horticulturalists harvest their corn and rice. Young people help thresh the rice harvest by stamping on the grain with their feet.

plant a second corn crop, once again spending most of their days at home, venturing forth only to weed and protect their fast-growing crops from birds and help themselves to vegetables that can now be pulled from the soil as needed. By June, the rains are nearly over, and as the dry season approaches, social activities pick up. Weddings, parties, cockfights, and visits from distant relatives are interrupted only by the harvesting of corn and rice. Children join adults in the cheerful job of threshing the harvest with their feet.

By September, the harvesting is over, and men tramp to their gardens to burn the stubble and weeds that have accumulated over nearly twelve months of gardening. Curling up from hundreds of fires, smoke bathes Timor in a blue haze. Men don't like missing the fun at home, so they spend as little time as possible looking after the fires they have started, and the flimsy lean-tos they have erected in their gardens are occasionally destroyed. Soon it is October again, and families prepare their gardens for another wet season, trooping from plot to plot, raking up the ashes left by the September burn-off, and turning over the soil with their digging sticks. Men repair fences and rebuild any garden lean-tos that have burned down. By the end of the month, most families have returned home, where they wait for the rainfall, and the garden work, to begin once more.

male, may have more wealth and power than other people. Where there are leaders, there must of course be followers; so horticulturalists are distinguished from one another by social position, whereas gatherers and hunters generally are not. The reason is that horticulturalists are tied, by gardening, to specific places. They can make use only of land near their villages, which limits the amount of land available. With limited land, there must be rules about who has the right to clear or plant what plots; otherwise there could be continual quarreling. So in horticultural societies, some individuals are landowners and some are not, making them unequal to each other.

Pastoralists

Pastoralists depend for their subsistence mainly on herds of animals that provide meat and milk and sometimes transportation, wool, or hides. Today, most pastoralists are found in places where it is difficult to raise crops. The Qashgai of Iran, for instance, raise sheep, goats, and camels in an arid climate, and the Northern Tungus of Siberia herd reindeer in a very cold one.

Because the needs of their herds come first, and because their herds sometimes can't find food in one location all year round, many pastoralists practice **transhumance,** a way of life in which people move their homes and herds from one grazing area to another, depending on the season. In the spring, for example, the Qashgai move their animals from the warm lowlands where they have spent the winter to the cooler slopes of the Zagros Mountains, where fertile summer pastures can be found (Beck 1980). In the fall, they move back to the lowlands. Other pastoralists, called **nomads,** are on the move year-round to provide their animals with adequate grazing.

Pastoralists live in **herding camps,** temporary places of residence where families that herd and travel together live in tents or other simple shelters. Usually, camp members are related by blood or marriage to individuals in other camps in the same region; and although they may separate to find suitable grazing for their animals, they typically join together for mass migrations. During migrations, everything the pastoralists own—tents, clothing, food, pots and pans, weaving looms, religious articles, and family treasures—is loaded onto the backs of animals. Babies, the sick, and the elderly are allowed to ride, but everyone else walks, prodding the herds along on trips that may last several weeks and cover hundreds of miles.

A pastoralist household is apt to be relatively large. A married couple and their offspring commonly share their shelter with other family members, perhaps unmarried siblings of the wife or husband or a widowed aunt or two. Although individual households may be large, camps tend to be small, consisting of only a few related families. However, the number of pastoralists who consider themselves members of the same culture and society may be enormous. The hillsides of southwestern Iran are peppered with herding camps, each numbering only six or eight tents but adding up to many thousands of people who consider themselves Qashgai.

Like gatherers and hunters, pastoralists usually allocate daily work by sex and age rather than skill or preference. Women perform household tasks, such as preparing food, caring for babies, and weaving rugs, while men look after the herds. Men may also hunt or farm part time.

Far from being self-sufficient, pastoralists are part of the larger economy of the area in which they move, and they maintain strong ties with local nonpastoralists.

pastoralists those who practice a method of subsistence based on herd animals

transhumance a pastoral way of life in which people move with their herds according to the seasons

nomads pastoralists who travel constantly throughout the year, within a large area, to provide their animals with grazing land

herding camp the pastoralist residence, consisting of the temporary homes of families that herd and travel together

Their mobile way of life does not permit them to collect or manufacture all of their subsistence necessities, so they must trade their wares—cheese, rugs, or whatever else they produce—with settled people living near their camps or with merchants who serve as middlemen. Thus a pastoralist may travel with a load of wool or cheese to the urban shop of a merchant who stocks household goods, and trade his wares for the things he and his family need.

Over the course of history, pastoralists have tended to be warlike. A cultural materialist would say this is because their livelihood has always depended on the availability of good grazing lands for their animals. Land is worth fighting for, and herders have a reputation for doing just that. The fearsome Mongols of ancient Central Asia, for instance, were pastoralists. Pastoralist societies are not as egalitarian as gatherers and hunters, but neither are they highly stratified. Usually there is a

◆ **ASK YOURSELF**

During their long semiannual migration, Qashgai women use umbrellas to protect themselves from the sun. When they encounter strangers, they lower the umbrellas to shield themselves from view. Do you think this behavior can be related to the idea of the evil eye (Chapter 3)? How would an ethnographer, female or male, best approach these women?

leader who makes important decisions in consultation with other men. But this leader is not a political specialist; he is a herder like every other man.

COMPLEX, CONTEMPORARY PRODUCTION METHODS

Peasants

If you visit the Middle East, China, Africa, South America, India, or even some parts of Europe, you'll see peasants plowing fields and threshing grain with the help of animals rather than machines. This adaptation, **nonmechanized agriculture,** differs from horticulture in that not all the work of cultivation is done by hand. Instead, peasants use wooden or metal plows pulled by horses, donkeys, or water buffaloes. Their cultivated lands may be irrigated by water pumped up from wells, drained from tanks, or diverted from streams and run through man-made channels. They may enrich the soil with chemical fertilizers purchased in a nearby town, or they may use natural fertilizer—dung from their domestic animals. Because they have frequent contact with people in towns and cities, they are geographically and economically less isolated than gatherers and hunters and horticulturalists—so much so that they are usually considered integral parts of larger societies (Redfield 1956:11–14).

The pastoralist Qashgai, who herd sheep, goats, and camels in south-central Iran, set up temporary herding camps each time they move their animals to new grazing land. Families live in large black tents made from goat hair.

THE ANTHROPOLOGIST AT WORK

The Ngorongoro Conservation Area in northern Tanzania, East Africa, is a natural and cultural legacy for the entire world (Århem 1985:12ff). Its wildlife is among the most plentiful of any region on our planet, and Olduvai Gorge, where physical anthropologists found human fossils that changed our understanding of human evolution, is located there. The Ngorongoro Conservation Area is also home to about fifteen thousand cattle-herding Maasai people.

The government's Ngorongoro Conservation Area Authority (NCAA), which manages the region, has two major policy concerns: environmental conservation and the economic development of local communities—two aims that concern many other governments and development agencies. Many of these organizations assume that pastoralism and environmental conservation are incompatible.

In 1980, the NCAA hired Swedish anthropologist Kaj Århem to explore the relationship between pastoralism and the environment in the Ngorongoro Conservation Area. Århem visited the area to collect data on local land use, settlement patterns, population trends, and living conditions. He studied the Maasai not only synchronically but also diachronically, examining statistical data collected by earlier researchers. Combining findings obtained from both approaches, Århem discovered that in contrast to the assumptions of the NCAA, the land use system of the Maasai was both environmentally sound and economically rational. Even though they ranged widely, Maasai cattle were controlled, thus reducing pressure on natural resources. The Maasai social system proved to be a resource of great development potential because it included an elaborate system of rights that regulated access to specific grazing areas and water sources.

Århem (1985:102–103) found that the Maasai had a "profound knowledge of the semi-arid savanna environment they called home." His applied anthropological work resulted in reports to the NCAA showing that environmental conservation and the subsistence needs of Maasai pastoralists could be integrated into a comprehensive development strategy that would also be environmentally sound.

What Are Peasants? Anthropologists find it difficult to agree on what peasants have in common because the details of their adaptation, their social relations, and their economic and political lives can vary considerably from region to region and culture to culture. This great variety is not surprising when you consider that there are literally millions, perhaps even billions, of peasants around the world today.

One authority, Raymond Firth (1950:503) adopts as the defining characteristic of a peasant the scale of production rather than the product. "Many a peasant farmer," writes Firth, "is also a fisherman or craftsman by turns, as his seasonal cycle or his cash needs influence him." Most anthropologists, however, would probably side with another authority, Robert Redfield (1956:26) who restricts the term *peasant* to agricultural people. Peasant authorities agree that most peasants share a particular set of features: nonmechanized agriculture, a distinctive outlook on life, and perhaps most important, an economic and social relationship with nonpeasants who live in the same area and share the same general cultural tradition.

Peasants are self-reliant. They grow most of their own food, make their own clothes, build their own houses, make their own farm tools, and rely on their own skills to satisfy other subsistence needs. Their adaptation, like that of the homesteaders of the early American West, requires long hours of exhausting, repetitive chores. Sometimes this drudgery produces barely enough to keep the peasants alive. And despite the fact that they produce most of what they need and perform their own labor, they are by no means independent. Since they exist within the context of a national culture, they are subject to their nation's laws, involved in its markets, obliged to pay taxes, and eligible to be drafted into the armed forces.

At the same time, however, peasants are usually isolated from the mainstream of national political, economic, and social life. Some, those who can't read and don't own radios or television sets, may be very much in the dark about what is going on nationally or interna-

nonmechanized agriculture agriculture using wooden or metal plows, pulled by animals

tionally. Others, who do read newspapers and listen to the radio, may know what is happening nationally and internationally, but they rarely organize to present whatever opinions they may have to the outside world. Sometimes they are simply too overburdened to have time for political involvement. Sometimes they have been exploited for so long by their economic and political superiors that they fail to recognize their potential power. This could be considerable in situations in which the peasants produce food for their urban countrymen. But caution is advisable here, for the political situation of peasants differs widely depending on the nation-state in which they live.

Peasants grow food mainly to support their own households, but because they must pay for some of their needs with cash, they must also produce a surplus to sell. If they own land, they can grow extra food and sell it to neighboring urban dwellers. If they do not own land

 ASK YOURSELF

Peasants depend on their own children for labor, so families tend to be large, and children may have little formal education. The need of peasants for extra hands to help with the farming is in direct conflict with the aims of those national governments that wish to limit population size and educate children. Do you see any way in which national-level policymakers could resolve these conflicting aims?

Peasant Life

From sixteenth- and seventeenth-century European painters such as Peter Bruegel and Jan Steen to the advertising executives of today who dream up romanticized wine and cereal commercials for television, peasant life has been portrayed as earthy, comfortable, sunny, and secure. Peasants are pictured as merry, healthy, ruddy-cheeked, relaxed characters.

This pleasant image is actually a romantic ideal. In many countries, especially in Latin America and India, today's peasants often do not get enough to eat, and because grains are more readily available than other kinds of food, their diets are often unbalanced nutritionally. In reality, because of the hard lives they live, peasants are typically tough, wiry people who spend their days and nights working rather than feasting and dancing.

Twelfth Night, *by seventeenth-century Dutch painter Jan Steen, romanticizes peasant life. Real peasants are much less apt to spend their time feasting and merrymaking than working at exhausting, repetitive chores. Even so, some produce barely enough to live on.*

and the means with which to farm it, they must use some of their surplus to pay various rents, which may be high. In past times in Iran, for example, wealthy landowners had vast farms that were divided into plots farmed by peasants. A peasant sharecropper could keep only one-fifth of the produce from a plot of land (Jacobs 1966:137). Meanwhile, the landowner, the owner of the irrigation system that watered the plot, the owner of the ox that was used to plow it, and the supplier of the seed each took a fifth also. Since the landowner usually owned the irrigation system and provided the seed, he got 60 percent, the ox owner 20 percent, and the peasant 20 percent—scarcely enough to feed his family.

The Worldview of Peasants. Because of their ethnic variety and geographical spread, it's hard to generalize about how peasants view the world, but we do find some features shared by most. They tend to identify strongly with their land, their families, and the ethic of hard work (Redfield 1956:112). They also tend to view the world as a place in which there are not enough good things—wealth, happiness, good health—to go around, a view termed the **image of the limited good** (Foster 1965, 1972; Kennedy 1966; Piker 1966; Gregory 1975). Inherent in this view is the idea that if one person accumulates more than his or her share of good things, another will have less than a full share. This idea tends to make peasants jealously protective of what they have, suspicious rather than open in their relationships with others, and wary of change. These attitudes are reinforced by the self-sufficiency of peasant families. Most do not need to share much with or rely much on their fellows.

Some peasants seem passive, a result of their traditional economic, political, and social inferiority. Denied opportunities to advance themselves, many believe they are powerless to change things. Sometimes their religious beliefs encourage them to think that whatever happens to them is the will of God. In some cases, their passive acceptance of whatever life throws at them seems to have been intensified by colonialism. Latin American peasants, for example, were for many generations under the direct domination of Spanish or Portuguese overlords, and to this day few have risen above poverty.

Perhaps the feature that most helps us to understand peasants is their relationship to larger, more powerful cultural traditions. As we suggested earlier, peasants are always found in the context of a wider, literate

In addition to supporting their own households, peasants must also produce a surplus to sell for cash. The constant farm labor required makes peasants a lean, hard, sunburned lot. An Indian peasant's thin frame and weathered face attest to his long years of hard outdoor work.

culture, which Redfield (1956) terms a **Great Tradition.**[1] Usually peasants speak the same language as other members of their Great Tradition, partake in its artistic genres, recognize its history as their own, tell its myths, sing its songs, and honor its culture heroes. If a nation-state is Muslim, for example, its peasants are Muslims too. Thus peasants can be viewed as less sophisticated, more impoverished, smaller-scale, rural reflectors of a Great Tradition rather than as the bearers of their own distinctive culture.

---

[1]Because they are found in literate societies, peasants cannot be viewed as nonliterate; many, however, are illiterate (see Chapter 1 for definitions of these terms).

◆◆◆

Great Tradition the wider, literate culture in which peasants exist

image of the limited good the view that the world is a place in which there are not enough good things to go around

The Great Tradition in Iran

In 1978–1979, the culturally diverse Iranian people—rich and poor, male and female, urban dweller and peasant, young and old—joined together under the religious and political leadership of Ayatollah Ruhollah Khomeini to overthrow the government of Shah Reza Pahlavi. The Iranian revolution stunned Western political analysts, who had sorely underestimated the depth of Iranians' feelings for their traditional culture. The concept of the Great Tradition helps us understand the forces that brought the Iranian people together under Khomeini.

Iranian urban dwellers, peasants, and pastoralists all share a common religious heritage, Islam. Ninety percent of them are of the Shi'a Islamic sect. Iranians also share artistic traditions whose roots are deeply buried in their ancient and universally respected past. Writing poetry, composing and playing music, and engaging in traditional crafts such as tile work, bone inlay work, carpet making, and metalworking are all still commonly practiced and greatly admired activities. Considered in the light of their Great Tradition, the solidarity of economically, socially, and ethnically diverse Iranians in their effort to oust their Western-oriented shah becomes more understandable.

Kinds of Peasants. One expert on peasants, Eric Wolf (1955, 1957, 1966), distinguishes between **closed peasant societies** and **open peasant societies.** This distinction is useful for understanding the differences between traditional peasants of the past and modern-day peasants, many of whom no longer live lives as isolated or as traditional as their ancestors.

In a closed peasant group, outsiders are unwelcome, and there is no doubt about who is and who is not a member of the community. Crops feed families and pay the rent. Little if anything is left over for sale, which keeps peasants in closed societies isolated from the mainstream of city life. Their technology is old-fashioned, and they resist change. They live in poverty (relative to urban members of their Great Tradition) and what Wolf (1966) calls "defensive ignorance"; that is, they remain uneducated in order to protect their traditional way of life. Finally, their culture discourages the accumulation and display of wealth; those who manage to gain some wealth are pressured to return to the economic level of everyone else by sharing with relatives or by spending lavishly on community events.

The open type of peasantry, according to Wolf (1966), arose in response to the rising demand around the world for crops that could readily be sold for cash, a product of the rise of capitalism. An open peasant society is therefore geared to a national or international economy, and the peasants may sell half or more of what they produce rather than using it all to feed themselves or pay rent, as in closed peasant societies. The coffee growers of Latin America, familiar from TV advertising,

"Open" peasants—for example, Latin American coffee growers—raise crops not mainly to feed themselves and their families but also to sell for cash. Colombian peasant "Juan Valdez" has become familiar to North American coffee drinkers.

grow coffee not mainly for themselves but for outsiders. Open peasants own their land and sometimes borrow money, although on a small scale. They are much more integrated into the larger society than closed peasants, and they may welcome changes from the outside. They do not frown on accumulating and displaying wealth. In fact, they expect it of the more successful among them. But open peasants can and do revert to traditional forms of subsistence agriculture in hard times.

Urban Dwellers

Living in cities forces people to develop indirect and complex means of obtaining food and satisfying other needs. We'll say relatively little about the adaptation on which modern urbanization rests—large-scale, mechanized agriculture (agrobusiness) combined with industrial production—because anthropologists usually consider the holistic study of large-scale societies at this level of technological complexity to be more within the scope of sociology than anthropology.

Still, increasingly since World War II, anthropologists have turned their attention to cities, developing the branch of anthropology called urban anthropology (Chapter 1; see also our description of the work of urban anthropologist Nancie Gonzalez in Chapter 2). Although it got off to a late start, urban anthropology has expanded rapidly in popularity, and today ethnographers can be found studying such varied urban subpopulations as street gangs, corporate executives, ethnic minorities, and prison inmates. Of the many topics of current interest to urban anthropologists, two are particularly timely and interesting: urban migration and poverty.

Urban Migration. Increasingly over the last 150 years or so, peasants have been forced from their land by overpopulation or seduced by the promise of greater economic opportunities in cities. Urban migration was encouraged by the nineteenth-century Industrial Revolution and the rapid pace of technological development in the twentieth century. With more efficient farm machinery and more intensive agricultural production, it takes fewer farmers to feed the world's nonfarmers; thus, increasing numbers of peasants have been unable to sustain themselves economically. In search of an alternate adaptation, they have flocked to cities in huge numbers. What has happened in Peru is typical. In 1940, the country's agricultural interior was home to 65 percent of the population, and the coast, where the major cities are located, held less than 30 percent. Today, more

than half the people of Peru live in its few coastal cities, many of them in slums, whereas fewer than 40 percent live in the interior (CNP 1984).

What happens when people who used to live in villages try to adapt to city life? What new customs and ideas are adopted or developed as former peasants attempt to solve the problems of urban existence? To what traditional ideas and behaviors do they cling, despite their move? There are, of course, wide geographical and ethnic differences in the adaptations of urban migrants, but we can offer some generalizations.

First, peasants don't usually improve their lot by migrating to cities. Instead, they are apt to be even more impoverished, at least to begin with. They may have less (and less healthy) food, smaller living quarters, poorer sanitation, and poorer health. Jobs are difficult to find because former peasants have little or no training for urban work. To ease their poverty, most try out new professions requiring little experience or training. Many become souvenir peddlers, taxi drivers, shoeshine boys, gardeners, or maids.

Second, urban dwellers' lives are not, in general, as socially rich as peasant villagers' lives. Some anthropologists suggest that when peasants move to cities, family ties loosen, religion declines in importance, and interpersonal relationships become increasingly superficial. In the impersonal atmosphere of a city, former peasants are apt to feel isolated, sometimes so isolated that not even clubs or new business relationships can help. Yet the social isolation of urban migrants has an adaptive aspect. One authority on urban dwellers, Oscar Lewis (1966b), claims that in urban slums, where essential resources are scarce, permanent relationships such as marriage can be a handicap. Being able to break off relationships easily improves a person's chances of survival.

Third, a sense of hopelessness prevents some people who immigrate to cities from seizing whatever political, economic, and educational opportunities may exist. Some suffer a **dependency mentality,** the feeling that

••

closed peasant society a type of peasant society characterized by production for household use, old-fashioned technology, isolation from mainstream city life, and resistance to change

open peasant society a type of peasant society characterized by substantial participation in a national or international economy

dependency mentality a feeling of powerless dependency on some superior person or group such as a landlord or a charitable organization

In search of a better way of life, peasants have flocked to the cities of the Third World, but often their dreams of better jobs and more money are frustrated. In Lima, Peru, an urban slum has sprung up in the middle of an upper-middle-class neighborhood.

they cannot and should not be responsible for themselves, that their superiors—formerly their landlords, now the church, state, or private charities—should take care of them. They feel powerless; if anything can be done to improve their lot, they believe, it must come from above, not from within. Over the last several decades, aid organizations established to help poor immigrants "pull themselves up by their bootstraps" often discovered that their efforts did not have the intended effect. Instead, aid seemed to encourage some immigrants to be passive.

This isn't true of all urban immigrants. Some band together to form self-help groups called **voluntary associations** to meet specific needs. These political, recreational, religious, or occupational groups thrive in many areas of the world. In Nigeria, urban immigrants from many different ethnic groups have created voluntary associations called tribal unions, modeled on traditional, rural mutual aid groups (Little 1982:192). As they become police officers, traders, and laborers, formerly rural people discover that they have to band together to protect themselves from other urban dwellers. Tribal

unions provide financial support for jobless members, and sympathy and financial assistance in times of illness or death (178–179). For Nigerian urban migrants, they have helped greatly to reduce the harshness of city life.

Recent migrants to the Peruvian coastal city of Lima typify the problems and prospects of urban migrants everywhere (Stein 1985). Extreme poverty is nearly universal among them. Many live in slums, where their housing may consist of straw matting, an abandoned automobile, or a sewer pipe, and where there are no sanitary facilities, electricity, or clean water. Old customs have died slowly, and many migrants still cling to traditional ideas. When they get sick, for example, some continue to visit a traditional curer rather than a doctor. They also cling to the traditional idea of family labor; in little sweatshops all over Lima, family members, including children, work together to produce small articles for sale on the streets.

As elsewhere, self-help organizations have sprung up in Lima's immigrant neighborhoods. In one neighborhood, migrant families banded together to bring electricity into their homes by ingeniously (if illegally) tap-

What Is Poverty?

A wholly satisfactory definition of poverty is difficult to provide, for we need to avoid using standards that apply only to some cultures. Many non-Westerners, for example, lack the material things Westerners have, yet they cannot be termed impoverished since they have most of the things they want and need; recall Marshall Sahlins's (1974) definition of gatherers and hunters as "the original affluent society."

Various attempts have been made to define poverty in terms of U.S. dollars or their equivalent. However, many people around the world today transact their business without the use of cash; some, for example, barter for goods and services (see Chapter 9). Thus, using dollar figures to define a poverty level is not only inadequate but ethnocentric as well. We prefer to define poverty as a state of want rather than of scarcity.

ping into power lines in neighboring communities. They had no running water, so they organized a water delivery service. Trucks bring water to the entrance of the community, and residents carry it home in pots and jugs. They also organized themselves to achieve political and economic goals. Each city block elected a representative to a neighborhood board of directors, which presents issues of community concern to local authorities. And recently, a group of young mothers formed a collective to combat malnutrition in children. The group collects money from residents to buy inexpensive powdered milk in bulk for the community's children.

Urban Poverty. In any cultural setting, "poverty" includes lacking the means to obtain life's necessities. But urban poverty is quite different from rural poverty. It is more apt to include feelings of deprivation and despair, undernutrition, impermanent residence, and unstable sexual relationships. Oscar Lewis (1961, 1966a, 1966b), who studied urban poverty in Mexico, Puerto Rico, and New York, coined the expression **culture of poverty** for the ideas and behavior poor people in some capitalist societies develop as they adapt to the circumstances in which they find themselves. Among the features of the culture of poverty are a lack of involvement in the institutions of the wider society (except for the armed services, courts, prisons, and welfare organizations); financial circumstances that include a shortage of cash, lack of savings, borrowing, and pawning; inadequate education and virtual illiteracy; mistrust of the police and government; social relationships that include early experience with sex, widespread illegitimacy, wife abandonment, and mother-centered families; and a lack of privacy (Lewis 1966b:xliii–xliv).

Patrick Moynihan (1965), who wrote about poor American blacks, suggests that the culture of the poor is essentially different from that of the well-off. Black culture, Moynihan claims, is not a "failed" white culture but a genuine culture in its own right, transmitted from generation to generation. The idea that there is a distinct culture of poverty has been criticized by Charles Valentine (1968), among others. Although agreeing that poor people develop attitudes that enable them to adapt to their situation, Valentine suggests that in the United States no substantial differences separate the culture of poor people from that of others. He claims that the poor fail to live up to the ideals of the wealthy mainly because they lack the same educational opportunities. This means that the jobs available to the children of richer families are closed to the poor.

Thus there are at least two very different views of urban poverty. Supporters of the first view claim that the urban poor develop their own unique adaptation, which is fundamentally different from the larger society's way of doing things. Supporters of the second view argue

◆ ASK YOURSELF

In this chapter, we've tried to give you a feel for a variety of different life-styles. Did any of them seem familiar, or is your own life-style very different from all of them? If you had to choose one, which adaptation described here would best suit you?

voluntary association a self-help group

culture of poverty the ideas and behavior of poor people in some capitalist societies

•••

Tally's Corner

Elliot Liebow, an authority on urban dwellers, carried out field research on the street corners of a Washington, D.C. ghetto. In his famous study, *Tally's Corner* (1967), he provides support for the notion that one reason poor urban blacks develop patterns of behavior distinct from those of the broader American culture is that they lack the educational opportunities available to wealthier Americans. Without educations to prepare them for personally satisfying jobs and without jobs that provide enough money to support themselves and their families, urban blacks are forced to develop their own culture.

Liebow writes of men who are able and willing to work but simply can't earn enough money to support themselves and their families. A man's chances of securing regular employment are good only if he is prepared to work for less money than he can possibly live on. The few good jobs available are hard to get and insecure when they are obtained. Construction work is desirable because it pays better than many other occupations, but it suffers from uncertain weather, seasonality, changes in the requirements of specific building projects, and business ups and downs. In addition, many of the highest-paying construction jobs are beyond the physical capacities of some urban men. Liebow adds that the wages for some jobs are kept artificially low because employers assume that workers will make up the difference between their wages and their minimum financial requirements by stealing.

that the urban poor share many values with members of the larger society around them, whose behavior and life-style they envy. Their adaptation is different only because they lack the education and money to conform.

Which interpretation is correct? Urban anthropologists haven't yet solved this puzzle, but recent research in several cities in the United States suggests one possible approach to a solution. As working-class residents move away from impoverished city neighborhoods, they leave behind only the poorest and most socially isolated residents. Their neighborhoods then decay rapidly, and the behavior and culture of those who remain—which had not previously been the standard behavior and culture for the neighborhood—become standard and even spread to neighboring communities (Wilkerson 1987). Perhaps the "culture of poverty" develops as a response to the success of some poor urban dwellers in overcoming it.

•••

CONCLUSION

What factors determine the life-style a group of people will pursue? Among the many possibilities are the natural environment (climate, terrain, and available natural resources), the level of technology available to the group (including not only a society's productive capacities but also its level of economic and political development), tradition (including the society's organization and system of values), the society's interaction with other societies, and its population size (in turn affected by its fertility rate and health status). Some theorists might even add psychological or genetic predispositions to this list.

The view that a single factor accounts, either solely or largely, for a particular adaptation is a kind of determinism. Those who view the environment as not just affecting but as actually determining cultural features, for instance, are called environmental determinists.

Although various determinist explanations have been proposed in the past to explain the great variety of human adaptations, most anthropologists today agree that no way of life can be attributed to a single cause. The adaptations discussed in this chapter are brought about by combinations of all the factors we mention, and no doubt others as well.

•••

SUMMARY

In this chapter, we discuss the different methods people have developed to obtain food and satisfy their other needs. A system of technologies, ideas, and behaviors by which to do this within a particular natural environment is called an adaptation.

Two principal methods dominate humanity's quest to satisfy its needs: collecting the products of nature or producing the things that are needed. Collecting is by far the older of the two methods, but it is very rare today; only a tiny fraction of the world's population, called gatherers and hunters, pursue this way of life. Producing necessities is far more common. The particular adaptation made by producers may be simple, as our descriptions of horticulturalists (technologically simple gardeners) and pastoralists (animal herders) show; or it may be complex, as illustrated by our descriptions of peasants and urban dwellers.

Although the world's gatherers and hunters and horticulturalists continue to decline in numbers, peasants are numerous and widespread. While diverse, they nevertheless have a lot in common: nonmechanized agriculture; a household-based economy set in the context of a larger economic system; a political life of subordination to wealthier and more powerful groups; a unique worldview that focuses on family and community; the idea of limited good; elements of conservatism and passivity; and perhaps most important, a crucial cultural bond with nonpeasants, with whom peasants share a wider cultural tradition called the Great Tradition. The chapter distinguishes between two types of peasantry, closed and open, based on how much of what peasants produce is for household use versus sale in an external market.

The study of urban dwellers is a rapidly growing field in anthropology. This chapter touches on two topics related to this adaptation: peasant immigrants to urban settings and the subculture of the urban poor. Urban immigrants share certain features all over the world: poverty, the retention of certain peasantlike attitudes and values, general feelings of helplessness, and (sometimes) a dependency mentality. The urban poor are sometimes prevented by these features from bettering their lot and participating fully in the urban cultural mainstream, but in other cases they are able to help themselves by banding together in voluntary self-help associations. Some urban dwellers' "culture of poverty," characterized by a lack of involvement in many of the institutions of the wider society and by impermanent social relationships, may be functional and adaptive for them.

KEY TERMS

adaptation
band
camp
carrying capacity
closed peasant society
culture of poverty
dependency mentality
egalitarianism
gathering and hunting
Great Tradition
herding camp
horticulture
image of the limited good
Neolithic revolution
nomads
nonmechanized agriculture
open peasant society
pastoralists
subsistence
swidden, slash-and-burn, or shifting cultivation
transhumance
voluntary association

SUGGESTED READINGS

Auel, Jean M. 1980. *The Clan of the Cave Bear.* New York: Crown. A best-selling novel about "cave" people. The main character is a woman whose many adventures, inventions, and feats require a considerable stretch of the imagination to be believed, but the book nevertheless presents an accurate portrait of the late Ice Age gatherer-and-hunter way of life.

Dragadze, Tamara. 1988. *Rural Families in Soviet Georgia.* New York: Routledge. Among the many excellent studies available on peasants, this short book describing a traditional Russian village is particularly interesting since less is known about Russian peasants than others.

Howells, William H. 1985 (1977). Requiem for a Lost People. In David E. K. Hunter and Phillip Whitten (eds.), *Anthropology: Contemporary Perspectives* (4th ed.), pp. 259–263. Boston: Little, Brown. A particularly moving account of the extermination of a gatherer-and-hunter group.

Mullings, Leith (ed.). 1987. *Cities of the United States: Studies in Urban Anthropology.* New York: Columbia University Press. A nonspecialist's introduction to urban research in the United States. Topics include wage labor, welfare, unemployment, kinship among city dwellers of lower socioeconomic status, and minority education.

Rigby, Peter. 1985. *Persistent Pastoralists: Nomadic Societies in Transition.* Totowa, NJ: Biblio Distribution Center. A discussion of rural development and management in the context of the economic conditions found among East African pastoralists, including the Maasai

CHAPTER 6

FAMILY AND DESCENT

Although it occurs in many different versions, the family is virtually universal in human culture. One version consists of a married couple and their offspring, like this northern Indian family.

UNSOLVED MYSTERY: WHO'LL GET THE RICHES HOWARD HUGHES LEFT BEHIND?

Newspaper Headline, 1976

When the industrial tycoon Howard Hughes died in April 1976, he left behind what was described as "the second largest accumulation of riches ever piled up by a single American citizen"—something over $2 billion. But Hughes, an eccentric, reclusive figure in his later years, had left neither a clearly authentic will nor any immediate family to whom his wealth should obviously go—no wife, no children, no grandchildren, no sisters or brothers. His closest known relatives at the time of his death were an 85-year-old aunt and several cousins.

The laws of the state of Texas, where Hughes lived, dictate that in such cases, "any relative, no matter how distant, is a potential heir" (Shoumatoff 1985:280). When someone dies without a will, his or her estate, after the U.S. government takes its share, is divided among relatives according to family ties. Suddenly, **descent** (a relationship defined by a connection to an ancestor through a series of parent-child links) became of overwhelming concern to a number of people who believed they had a legitimate claim to part of Howard Hughes's vast fortune. By August 1976, four months after his death, some 33 Hughes "wills" had surfaced, bequeathing millions to "relatives" Howard Hughes didn't even know he had. Eventually a total of 22 legitimate Hughes relatives were found.

Descent was important in the Hughes case because a great deal of money was at stake, but for most North Americans it doesn't have the same legal significance. People in many non-Western societies, in contrast, are greatly concerned with family ties, not just because they might inherit something of value but also because other important personal matters, from their social status to their choice of spouse, are affected by descent. North Americans—brought up on the Judeo-Christian notion that every human being is a worthy individual in his or her own right, not just a member of a particular family (illustrious or otherwise)—are sometimes surprised to learn that in much of the world who you are, what your job is, who you marry, and just where you fit into your society are largely determined not by your own character and accomplishments but by the family to which you belong and the ancestors from whom you are descended.

In those parts of the world where descent determines your position in society (see Chapter 11), if you are born into a noble family, you are automatically a member of the nobility, entitled to certain privileges denied to commoners. And no matter who you are, noble or commoner, you're acutely aware of the names, occupations, marriages, and status of your ancestors, for they quite literally made you what you are today. In contrast, most North Americans can't even name their eight great-grandparents, let alone more remote ancestors—a

In many non-Western societies, family ties are more important than they are in North America. A young Korean shows off part of his family tree, which extends back to the sixth century and occupies five thick volumes.

lack of interest that an Australian aborigine, who can recite the names of his or her ancestors five generations deep, might find incomprehensible. Family ties among the living are important to most of us, but who is related to whom or descended from what ancestor just doesn't concern us much on a day-to-day basis.

Descent involves relatives by birth, or "blood" relatives,[1] in contrast to relatives by marriage (see Chapter

descent a relationship defined by a connection to an ancestor through a series of parent-child links

---

[1]The term *blood relative* has been used since long before we knew that our biological inheritance is determined by genes rather than blood.

An example of how kinship ties in with religion is provided by the Members of the Church of Jesus Christ of the Latter Day Saints, better known as Mormons. Mormons believe that to enter the kingdom of heaven after death, one must have been baptized a Mormon. Thus no one born before 1830, when the Mormon church was founded, can gain entrance to heaven unless he or she is baptized by proxy. Following the advice of their founder to "seek after your dead," Mormon genealogists have embarked on a monumentally ambitious project to collect the names and relationships of the dead all over the world in order to identify their ancestors and to perform for them, by proxy, the ordinances that will ensure their entry into the "Celestial Kingdom." Since all Mormons have non-Mormon ancestors, these genealogists aim for no less than a complete compilation of the names and lines of descent of every member of the human species for whom some record exists—an estimated 6 or 7 billion people (Shoumatoff 1985).

In the 1960s, by tunneling 700 feet into a granite mountain in Utah, the Mormons constructed six huge bombproof vaults for the storage of genealogical records. In one of these is already stored, on microfilm, over a billion names, a prodigious proportion of what the Mormons hope will eventually be a complete archive of human genealogy, "wherein the name and vital records of every man and woman born on earth is collected, indexed, computerized, and, ultimately, baptized into the . . . family of saints" (Stewart 1980:8).

To make its compilation of names and genealogies as thorough as possible, the Mormon Genealogical Society is laboriously searching through old birth and death records, family histories, church rosters, marriage licence applications, land sale documents, and censuses in 44 countries, both Western and non-Western, around the globe. Realistically, the genealogists have little hope that they will eventually record the name of everyone who ever lived, since so many people lived and died before the time of recorded history, but they do expect to ferret out records for most of the people who lived between 1500 and 1900, eventually adding the names and records of all twentieth-century people. Whenever possible, they will augment this stupendous list with ancient records, oral or written, extending deep into the past. Some Chinese clan histories, for example, go back to 1000 B.C. (Stewart 1980:8).

By now, the Mormons "have done enough genealogy to realize that *everybody,* in the end, is kin" (Shoumatoff 1985:13). The stunning fact of the matter is that there is no human being now alive anywhere on this earth who is more distantly related to any other human being than the degree of fiftieth cousin. "The 'family of man' which has been posited by many religions and philosophies . . . actually exists" (244).

The Mormon genealogists pursue their quest largely for religious reasons, but the amassing of names has other useful functions as well. Genetic researchers, for example, have used the work of the Mormons to learn more about hereditary diseases, and lawyers have resorted to the records stored in the Mormon's "mountain of names" to settle legal claims (Shoumatoff 1985:280–281). But perhaps the most important function of the Mormon genealogists' work is to satisfy for the many individuals who consult it what some people believe is a "basic human need for kinship" (14).

THE ANTHROPOLOGIST AT WORK

Following the advice of their church's founder to "seek after your dead," Mormons are searching through documents all over the world in an attempt to collect the names and genealogies of everyone who has ever lived. They do their genealogical research in bombproof laboratories dug into a mountain in Utah.

7). Blood relatives are also known as **consanguines (consanguinal kin)** because they are related by **consanguinity,** a relationship based on the tie between parents and children that also includes more distant relatives. As we mentioned in Chapter 2, the complete set of such relationships for any single individual forms that person's genealogy. In every society, these relationships pass (or as anthropologists say, "descend") from one generation to the next following certain rules.

In this chapter, we'll take a cross-cultural look not only at how descent contributes to an individual's social identity but also at how it fits into our holistic picture of culture, strongly influencing individuals' attitudes and behavior and linking up synchronically with such important cultural features as rights and duties, inheritance, religion, marriage, political authority, and residence.

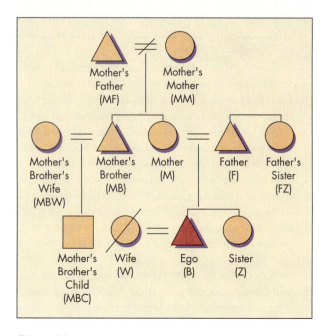

Figure 6.1

Kinship Diagram. In a typical kinship diagram, ego is the point of reference from which we define all relatives. With triangles, circles, vertical lines, horizontal lines, extended "equals" signs, and abbreviations, we have the basic tools to reduce a tangle of complex kinship connections to a relatively simple diagram.

KINSHIP DIAGRAMS

Anthropologists use kinship diagrams to help them describe and explain descent. These diagrams may look somewhat daunting, but they are quite logical in their construction, and they enable us to display relationships between relatives more conveniently than is possible with verbal description alone.

Figure 6.1 contains triangles, circles, squares, vertical lines, extended "equals" signs, horizontal brackets, and a variety of letters. Combined, these symbols represent the family relationships of a particular figure, the person from whose perspective the diagram has been constructed. In any kinship diagram, this person is called **ego,** and ego is always represented by whichever triangle, circle, or square is darkened. In Figure 6.1, ego is the darkened triangle at the bottom of the diagram. All of the other shapes represent people who stand in particular relationships to ego. For instance, there is a triangle labeled "father," but this person is "father" only with respect to ego. From the perspectives of other individuals represented in the diagram, this person may be a brother, uncle, husband, or other male relative. Because a kinship diagram is always constructed from the perspective of a single person, it follows that there can't be two or more egos in the same diagram.

Using only a few different symbols, we can easily

◆ **ASK YOURSELF**

Can you name all eight of your great-grandparents? Can you name any of their parents?

diagram most kinship relationships. Triangles stand for males, circles stand for females, and squares are used when sex is irrelevant for the purposes of the diagram. In this particular diagram, ego is male, but we could just as easily have constructed the diagram from the point of view of a female or an ego whose sex is irrelevant.

To keep kinship diagrams uncluttered, a triangle, circle, or square may represent not just one individual but a category of relative. In other words, all individuals related to ego in the same way are represented by the same triangle, circle, or square. For example, in Figure 6.1 there is a circle representing ego's "father's sister" (the person English speakers would call ego's aunt). If ego's father has several sisters, all of them are represented by this one circle because they all stand in exactly the same relationship to ego.

The other commonly used symbols in kinship diagrams—vertical lines, extended equals signs, horizontal brackets, and slashes—represent relationships rather than categories of relatives. A vertical line stands for descent. In Figure 6.1, lines of descent link individuals in three generations. An extended equals sign stands for the tie created by marriage. A horizontal bracket stands for the relationship between siblings: the figure shows that ego has a sister, represented by a circle connected to ego's triangle by a bracket. A slash through a triangle, circle, or square indicates that the individual represented is dead, as in the case in Figure 6.1 of ego's wife. Finally, a slash through an equals sign shows that a marriage has ended in divorce, as between the couple at the top of the diagram (ego's mother's father and mother's mother).

Whereas categories of individuals and their relationships are represented by these various signs, specific individuals are represented in kinship diagrams by *letters*. Some are represented by the first letters of their kinship terms. Others are represented by two or more letters, combinations of the letters that stand for the basic terms. Some possibilities are

F = father; FF = father's father (or paternal grandfather)

M = mother; MM = mother's mother, MF = mother's father

D = daughter; DD = daughter's daughter (or granddaughter)

S = son; SS = son's son (or grandson)

FB = father's brother; FBC = father's brother's child

MB = mother's brother; MBC = mother's brother's child

C = child

H = husband; W = wife

We run into some potential confusion when it comes to sons and sisters since both begin with the same letter. To avoid this problem, anthropologists use the letter Z to designate sisters, reserving S for sons. Thus,

FZ = father's sister

FZS = father's sister's son . . .

and so on.

Figure 6.1 shows some of ego's relatives. We can see from the diagram that ego has one or more sisters but no brothers. His mother has at least one male sibling (MB), and his father has at least one female sibling (FZ). Ego's mother's brother is married, and he and his wife (MBW) have a child (MBC)—represented by a square since we do not wish to be specific about this child's sex. Ego's grandparents on his mother's side, MF and MM, are shown at the top of the diagram.

In kinship diagrams, an uncle is typically specified more precisely as either FB (father's brother) or MB (mother's brother). A cousin can be many different people: FBD, FBS, FZD, FZS, MBD, MBS, MZD, or MZS. We avoid terms like *uncle, aunt,* and *cousin* because they can refer to any one of several different people.

Your "cousin," for example, can be either a male or female and related to you either through your mother or your father. Moreover, a person who stands in the relationship of "cousin" to you, in the context of Western society, might not be classified as your cousin at all if you were a member of a different society, despite the fact that the genealogical relationship between you and this person is identical in both cases.

Some anthropologists use a different convention for representing individuals in kinship diagrams. Instead of using the first letter of the word for each relative, they use the first two letters. Thus, a father is Fa, a mother is Mo, and a daughter is Da. Other relatives are represented by a combination of these symbols: father's sister is FaSi, and mother's brother is MoBr.

FAMILIES

In the stereotypical (and idealized) Western view, a family consists, at a minimum, of a father, a mother, and their unmarried children. Today, however, the majority of "families," in both North America and the rest of the world, take some other form. To be as inclusive as possible of these many alternate forms, we'll define a **family** as two or more individuals who consider themselves related, who are economically interdependent, and who share the responsibility for rearing any children in their group. This definition is broad enough to include not only individuals who are related by blood or marriage but also those unrelated in either of these ways but who nevertheless consider themselves related (a homosexual couple, for instance, or an adult with an adopted child). Members of a family usually live together, but since this is not always the case we do not include common residence as a criterion for a family.

The functions of the family may (but don't always) include attending to the physical, psychological, economic, linguistic, and social needs of infants and

consanguines (consanguinal kin) individuals related by ties of consanguinity

consanguinity a relationship based on the tie between parents and children that also includes more distant relatives

ego the individual from whose perspective a kinship diagram is drawn

family two or more individuals who consider themselves related, who are economically interdependent, and who share responsibility for rearing any children they have

Cousins

In North America, we usually use kinship terms such as *cousin* without worrying about their imprecision, but in many cultures precision is essential since distinctions among kinship terms may reflect differences in how rights and duties are allocated. To take the usages of such cultures into account, anthropologists distinguish between two basic types of cousins (Figure 6.2). **Parallel cousins** are children of siblings of the same sex. Your mother's sister's child (either male or female) is your parallel cousin because your mother and her sister are siblings of the same sex. Your father's brother's child is also your parallel cousin because your father and his brother are of the same sex. **Cross cousins** are children of siblings of the opposite sex. Your mother's brother's child (male or female) is your cross cousin because your mother and her brother are of the opposite sex. Your father's sister's child is also your cross

cousin since your father and his sister are opposite-sex siblings.

Cousins linked to you through your mother (e.g., your mother's brother's child) are your **matrilateral cousins,** and those linked to you through your father (e.g., your father's sister's child) are **patrilateral cousins.** Thus, although in English we lump them indiscriminately under the broad term *cousin,* each type of cousin actually has its own anthropological name: matrilateral cross cousin, matrilateral parallel cousin, patrilateral cross cousin, or patrilateral parallel cousin. Distinguishing among these cousins is not important for the allocation of rights and duties in Western society, but in certain non-Western societies it is very important indeed, for certain cousins can be ideal marriage partners and others absolutely prohibited as marriage partners (see Chapter 7).

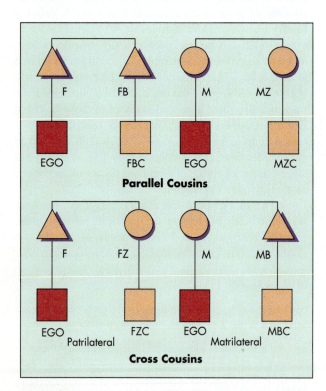

Figure 6.2
Parallel and Cross Cousins

children and providing adults with the resources they need to cope with the problems of living. These resources include psychological benefits such as security and a feeling of being loved.

Family Types

Anthropologists use specific terms for the different forms a family can take. A **nuclear (elementary** or **simple) family** is a unit consisting of a father, a mother, and unmarried children. Many people belong to two nuclear families: the one into which they were born or adopted and the one they created by having or adopting children. In some societies, a man may have more than one wife at the same time, and a woman may have more than one husband at the same time (see Chapter 7). Such a union is best considered as two or more nuclear families sharing one member in common rather than as a single nuclear family.

The nuclear family in most societies has vital economic, sexual, psychological, child-rearing, and legal functions to fulfill. These functions could be managed by other institutions, but the family is a very convenient way of combining all of them.

An **extended family** is a larger family group,

◆◆◆
"Family Values": How "Traditional" Is the North American Family Today?

During the 1992 presidential campaign, the vice-president of the United States, Dan Quayle, repeatedly promoted the virtues of the "traditional" nuclear family as the ideal social unit. To emphasize his point, he condemned the TV sitcom "Murphy Brown" for advocating unwed motherhood by choice.

Quayle may not have approved of single-parent families, but U.S. government figures show that they are becoming increasingly common. In 1991, only 26 percent of all U.S. households consisted of married couples with children, in contrast to 40 percent in 1970. The number of families headed by single, never-married women increased at an annual rate of almost 15 percent during the 1970s. It dropped to just under 10 percent between 1980 and 1991, but female-headed households still constitute the fastest-growing type of family in the United States. Single mothers— never married, separated, divorced, or widowed— now head about 25 percent of all families with chil-

dren; single fathers head about 4 percent (Sturo 1992). So much for the "traditional" American family!

Quayle disapproved of Murphy Brown's unmarried status, but the rate of marriage, too, has decreased. Fewer Americans married in 1991 than in any year since 1965. One explanation links marriage with economics: perhaps more marriages are postponed when the national economy is weak. Another explanation may be that many modern American women either choose to have jobs outside their homes or have to have them for economic reasons, yet at the same time many wish to be mothers. Since both activities are time-consuming, some women try alternate ways of sequencing babies and careers. Some marry, then have babies, then start careers; others establish careers first, then marry, then have children. Others, like Murphy Brown, choose careers and babies prior to or without marriage (Barringer 1992).

---

more variable than the nuclear family in the relatives it may include. Your extended family, for example, might include the members of the family you were born into plus married children of this family and the families those married children created through their own marriages. Or an extended family might consist of two brothers, their wives, and their children.

Do nuclear or extended families occur in all societies? This appears to be the case in the vast majority of societies, but there are some interesting alternatives. Among the Nayar of southwest India in traditional times, a family "was in no sense a legal, residential . . . productive, or distributive group" (Gough 1962:363). A husband-father did not live with his wife and children, did not eat regularly with them, and did not work with or for them, nor did he customarily distribute goods to his children. Instead, he lived with or near his sisters, and his children and wife resided with the wife's brother, who provided for them. Thus the Nayar residential group comprised children, their mother, and the mother's brother.

Another variation on the family is found in Israel, where some people live in a **kibbutz** (plural form: *kibbutzim).* A kibbutz is an agricultural collective whose

main features include communal living, collective ownership of all property, and communal child rearing (Lavi 1990). The nuclear family, as defined above, does not exist in the kibbutz, any more than it does among the Nayar. A wife and husband do not form an economic unit. Instead, each works for *all* members of the kibbutz. Women cook, sew, launder, and carry out other domestic chores not only for their husbands but also for the whole kibbutz. Men grow agricultural produce for

◆◆◆

parallel cousins children of siblings of the same sex

cross cousins children of siblings of the opposite sex

matrilateral cousin a cousin on the mother's side

patrilateral cousin a cousin on the father's side

nuclear (elementary or simple) family a social unit consisting of a father, a mother, and unmarried children

extended family a larger family group than the nuclear, whose membership is more variable

kibbutz an agricultural collective in Israel whose main features include communal living, collective ownership of property, and communal child rearing

S. GROSS

"I guess we'd be considered a family. We're living together, we love each other, and we haven't eaten the children yet."

The 1950s TV show "Ozzie and Harriet" portrayed an idealized North American family, consisting of a father, a mother, and their children. This kind of family is becoming less and less common.

everyone, not just for their wives. Children live apart from their parents, eat together, and are supervised by nurses, visiting their parents for a few hours every day.

Family Property

Family ties may grant certain rights over the property of relatives, especially in non-Western societies. "Property" sometimes means tangible property such as houses, fields, buffaloes, or like Howard Hughes, 2 billion dollars' worth of your society's kind of money. But the "property" regulated by descent may also consist of intangible wealth you can neither see nor touch but that nonetheless has value.

Intangible property that can be regulated by descent is not something with which Westerners are familiar. We don't think of the privilege of running for a certain political office or of wearing certain ornaments as rights granted through inheritance, much less as property. But other types of inheritable, intangible property *are* familiar to Westerners. These include the right to use a family surname or eligibility for membership in a certain social class, both of which pass to children through their parents. So perhaps the idea that intangibles as well as material wealth can be transferred through descent is not so foreign after all. Descent may also impose certain *duties* on relatives, duties that may again involve both types of property. The obligation to help a relative build a house involves something tangible, while the obligation to refrain from speaking in the presence of a superior is intangible.

Kindreds

Even larger than the extended family is the circle of relatives known as the **kindred,** a group of individuals who have at least one living relative, ego, in common (Figure 6.3). Your kindred comprises all relatives on both your mother's side and your father's to whom you consider yourself related. Potentially, this group of people could be enormous, but in practice each individual

kindred a group of relatives who have at least one living relative, ego, in common

---

How Kindreds Are Used: The Iban of Borneo

The Iban of the island of Borneo in Indonesia live in large houses called longhouses, each containing from 30 to 350 inhabitants (Fox 1983:160). Extended families occupy separate apartments in this building, with as many as 50 in the same longhouse. Members of these extended families are related to one another either by consanguinity or marriage, so that any given individual has many members of his or her kindred living in the same building.

The many people living together in an Iban longhouse do not form an economic group, yet in the past parties of Iban men pursued common economic goals, joining together on large-scale trading and head-hunting expeditions. They managed to field such large forces by exploiting the only kinship group of any size they had, the kindred. An Iban man's personal kindred might include his father, father's brother, mother's brother, son, brother, and other consanguines up to and including his first and second cousins, from whom he had the right to demand help and to whom he had the duty to reciprocate when they needed his help. But a single kindred rarely had enough members to help a man with a full-scale trading or raiding venture. More were needed. So the consanguines of ego's consanguines would be called on. Each member of ego's kindred had *his* own kindred and could call on its members to join forces with the original ego's kindred. Each new recruit, in turn, recruited members of *his* kindred to join the expedition, and so on. In this way, more and more men were drawn into the network until eventually there were enough to carry out the task, be it trading or head-hunting. If the venture succeeded, all of the participants enjoyed the spoils.

In Borneo, members of a number of Iban extended families live together in a single longhouse. Each occupant is related to every other occupant, either by consanguinity or affinity. Thus, every occupant lives with numerous members of his or her kindred.

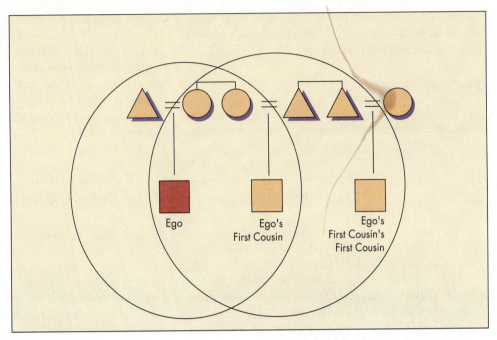

Figure 6.3
Partial Kindreds. Not every member of ego's kindred has the same ancestors; only siblings of ego have the same ancestors and hence belong to the same kindred as ego (After Fox 1983: 165).

limits the number of relatives from whom mutual rights and obligations are expected by just forgetting about, or not keeping in touch with, the more distant.

Kindreds are *ego-focused* groups—that is, their members don't have a common ancestor; instead, ego is the group's point of reference. Ego's kindred are not all related. You may include your cousins on your mother's side and your cousins on your father's side as members of your kindred, but in *their* own respective kindreds they may not include each other. Apart from your siblings, therefore, you do not share exactly the same kindred with anyone else. Because kindreds are personal, they cannot have any legal, economic, or political functions outside of the perspective of ego. Your children do not inherit membership in your kindred; they have their *own* personal kindreds. Your kindred is yours (and your siblings') alone. When you die, it goes out of existence.

DESCENT GROUPS

Every society has a system of descent. For many, although not Western society, the most prominent expression of this system is the **descent group,** a group of consanguines, male and female, who believe they can

trace their relationship to one another back to a common ancestor who founded their group. Descent groups can be of enormous importance in the lives of their members. Some non-Western societies refuse full legal recognition to anyone not belonging to such a group. Because descent groups can be of such great practical and psychological significance in the lives of individuals, we'll examine each different type in some detail, but first we'll take a look at some features common to most of them.

The Corporate Nature of Descent Groups

A descent group is corporate: unlike the kindred, it persists from generation to generation even as its members are born and die. Diagramatically, a descent group is apt to resemble a pyramid, for as the number of de-

 ASK YOURSELF
List and count the members of your kindred. Does this group contain all of your first cousins, or have you lost touch with some of them because of divorce, perhaps, or geographical separation? Does it contain more distant relatives?

scending generations increases through the years, so, too, do the relatives in each. Descent groups are also corporate because they often control resources or own property in common. Besides being legal entities, they may also provide opportunities for members to cooperate in such activities as building houses, making gardens, and protecting common political interests.

Descent Groups and Residence

Often all the adult members of the same sex in a descent group have the same pattern of residence. Either they are all localized (meaning they live with or near one another) or they are all dispersed. There is an advantage to having a descent group that is localized. If descent is through males, men are kept together on their ancestral lands, always at hand to prevent other descent groups from moving in and exploiting their territory's natural resources. And because its members can more easily be assembled in an emergency—a natural disaster or a social upheaval, such as an attack by another descent group—such a group is more cohesive than one whose members are scattered. The advantages of localized groups when descent is through females are not so great since it is not usually females but males who manage land, fight, and hold political office. However, localized females do provide benefits to their descent groups in that they may be jointly responsible for continuing the traditions of their groups.

Descent Groups and Exogamy

Exogamy is the rule that one must marry someone from *outside* one's own group, however that group is defined. The concept is not unfamiliar to Westerners. The Western extended family is an exogamous unit since family members must seek spouses from families other than their own. (In contrast to exogamy, *endogamy* is the practice of marrying a spouse chosen from *within* one's own group. We discuss endogamy in the next chapter.)

Descent groups are often exogamous. When this is the case, their members may not marry one another but must find their spouses outside the group. Sexual relations between group members constitutes incest, even though in large descent groups some members will be only very distantly related. But the ideal and the actual may not converge. Descent groups vary widely concerning the rigor with which their members conform to the ideal of exogamy.

Clans and Lineages

Clans and lineages are the two major types of descent groups. The **clan** is a descent group whose members believe themselves descended from (or in some special way related to) the same founding ancestor, male or female. The founder may have lived so long ago that a member's precise genealogical tie to this ancestor, who may be referred to as the clan's **culture hero,** cannot be calculated. Often, the founder is a mythological being or animal who defies all biological credibility as the literal founder of a human group. Or the founder may be an inanimate object, such as the sun or a lake. The list of choices is limited only by the imagination.

If a clan's founder is believed to have been a plant or animal, that item is often the clan's **totem,** or special symbol. Clan members are usually forbidden to harvest that particular plant or kill that animal for food or other purposes, although the members of other clans in the same society may do so. Should you belong to the Eel Clan, for example, the eel would be your totem, and you would be forbidden to kill or eat an eel, although members of your society's Sun Clan could do so.

Among the intangible property a clan may own is the right to tell an **origin myth** describing how the clan was founded. In describing how the clan came into existence and setting forth the social features that make it distinct from all other clans in the society, this myth is often highly imaginative. But an origin myth isn't just good entertainment. It may also serve as a local constitution, justifying the rights and privileges claimed by

descent group a group made up of individuals who trace their descent to a common ancestor

exogamy the social rule that one must marry someone from outside one's own group, however that group is defined

clan a descent group (patriclan, matriclan) whose members believe they are descended from (or in some special way related to) the same founder

culture hero a mythological being, animal, or inanimate object thought to be associated with the origins of a clan

totem a plant, animal, or object from which members of a clan are believed to have descended or which plays some central role in their history

origin myth a story describing the origins of some feature of the physical environment, of a society, or of a culture; often describes the appearance of a clan's culture hero and how the clan was founded

Clans are descent groups whose members believe they are all related to the same founder. Often, as among the Nuer of Africa, clan members live near one another after they marry. Above, Nuer clansmen—brothers and male cousins—work together to make leather thongs.

present-day members of the clan. Many such myths are fine specimens of oral literature (see Chapter 14).

Lineages consist of consanguines who can trace genealogical links through known ancestors to a genuine human ancestor, who may have lived many generations before. The size of a lineage is limited by the depth of its genealogical ties. Clans, because they don't depend on actual genealogical links, can be much older and many generations deeper. In some societies, lineages are linked together into clans. Figure 6.4 shows the internal division of the Eel Clan of the Tetum people of Indonesia.

The Eel Clan comprises three lineages. Members of all three believe that their clan was founded by a creature who was half eel and half man, whereas each lineage was founded by a real, historical person.

Each lineage has certain rights and duties. Bua

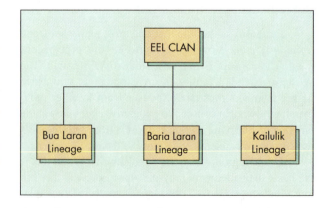

Figure 6.4
Tetum Eel Clan. Many important political and religious functions within the Eel Clan are divided among the three lineages shown here, but all males and females within each of these lineages are clan agnates.

The Origin Myth of the Tetum Eel Clan

One day, seven brothers went traveling in a strange land. At midday, the six oldest brothers commanded the youngest, Ali-iku, to collect water from a nearby stream, but when Ali-iku arrived at the stream he saw that an eel was muddying the water. He returned to his brothers empty-handed and told them what he had seen. The brothers accused Ali-iku of lying and ordered him to go back to collect water. But again Ali-iku found the water so dirty, because of the continued thrashing of the eel, that he returned to his brothers without any. This time they laughed at him, and the eldest, Lela-sou, armed with a chopper, accompanied him back to the stream. There, Lela-sou lifted the eel from the water and hacked it to pieces.

They carried the pieces back to camp, where the older brothers ordered Ali-iku to cook the meat while they went for a stroll. After they had left, the butchered eel, much to Ali-iku's astonishment, began to speak. By sunset, it claimed, Ali-iku, too, would be an eel. Ali-iku ran to find his brothers, but by the time they got back to the camp the eel had stopped speaking. Again the brothers accused Ali-iku of lying, and they continued their stroll. Twice more, in the older brothers' absence, the eel repeated its prediction, and twice more the skeptical brothers scorned Ali-iku's integrity. Finally, the brothers sat down to a meal of well-cooked rice and eel meat, but Ali-iku soon discovered that *his* meat was still raw.

Their meal finished, the seven went to the spring to bathe. When it was time to leave the water, the elder brothers climbed out onto the bank. But Ali-iku was unable to follow them because, although his head remained human, his body had been transformed into that of an eel. From the water he shouted to his brothers, "Today I told you what I had seen and heard, but you wouldn't believe me. Now look at what has happened! But do not feel sorry for me. I want you to go and buy a pig and some rice and cook them."

The startled brothers did as they were instructed. After they had cooked the food, Ali-iku continued giving orders: "Never shall you or any of your descendants eat the meat of eels! Never allow any of your descendants to bathe in this spring again!" Then, after teaching them some songs and dances, Ali-iku struck his head against a rock and was transformed completely into an eel. Thus did Ali-iku leave the world of humanity.

The six surviving brothers divided up their property, split up into two groups of three, and set off in different directions. Lela-sou eventually left his two brothers and established his home at a place called Uma Fatin. In the course of time he married and fathered three sons, each of whom founded one of the lineages of the Eel Clan. Henceforth, each lineage would partake of clan privileges and fulfill clan responsibilities in its own way.

Laran owns most of the Eel Clan's political and economic property, including the office of clan head, and Kailulik owns much of its religious property, including the office of clan priest. Baria Laran, which owns smaller amounts of property, supplies deputies for each of the two leaders. Each lineage is exogamous. Strictly speaking, no Eel person can marry another Eel person, although if the individuals in question belong to different lineages within the clan, marriage may be tolerated. But there is no question about lineage exogamy. Consanguines from the same lineage are always forbidden to marry.

RULES OF DESCENT

Among all societies in the world three forms of descent occur most commonly: (1) patriliny, (2) matriliny, and (3) cognation.

lineage a descent group (patrilineage, matrilineage) made up of consanguines who can trace their precise genealogical links, through known ancestors, to a founding ancestor

Patriliny

Patriliny (patrilineal descent) is a system of descent in which males provide the links by which property descends to the next generation. All male and female consanguines in a patrilineal system are termed **agnates (patrikin).** Agnates trace their descent from a common male ancestor. Since your ties of descent in a patrilineal system are with your father's consanguines only, not your mother's, if you were female you could inherit property from your father but could not pass on any property that was considered to belong to your father's descent group to your children.

As an example of how a system of patriliny works, consider the way family names traditionally pass in Western society. Children inherit them from their fathers, but even though the right to use a name descends to daughters and sons alike, only sons pass it to *their* children. We can say, therefore, that family names (if nothing else) in Western society descend patrilineally.

Other societies patrilineally transfer not just family names but also other property, tangible or intangible. Examples might include the right to live in a certain place after marriage, to own a house there, to succeed to a certain political or religious office when the previous generation's incumbent dies, and to perform certain rituals or recite certain myths. In some societies, the right to belong to a particular patrilineal descent group, or **patrigroup** (a term that covers both clans and lineages), is considered the most desirable right of all. Inheritable duties for members of patrilineal descent groups might in-

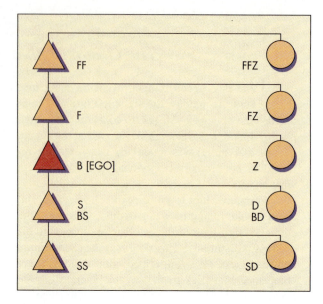

Figure 6.5
A Patrigroup. In patrigroups, the descending ties are all through males, but note how females are "hooked" onto the patriline.

clude helping one's agnates in agricultural work, defending the patrigroup's land and livestock when these are threatened by rival patrigroups, and helping to maintain the patrigroup's prestige in local affairs.

Figure 6.5 shows a tiny patrigroup. If we extended the descent lines to cover more generations we would have a small lineage, and if we went back much further

---

Women in Patrilineal Societies

It may seem that women are devalued in patrisystems, but this is not necessarily so. Sisters and daughters are patrigroup insiders, and for a man to marry a woman from his own patrigroup would violate the rule of exogamy. Thus, if male babies are to be born to ensure the continuance of a patrigroup into the next generation, each man must find a wife from another patrigroup—hence the importance of women for the men of a patrigroup. No wives and mothers, no patrigroup!

The Nuer of Africa provide an example. By residing patrilocally after they marry, male Nuer ag-

nates form localized patrigroups. This means brothers and male cousins are always on hand to look after their patrigroup's local resources, consisting largely of cattle, while the sisters of these men, when they marry, go to live with their respective husbands. Nuer women are thus the *nonlocalized* agnates of their patrigroups. Although these female agnates are dispersed around the territories of their respective husbands' patrigroups, this does not create any problem for Nuer society since the line of descent runs not through them but through their brothers.

we might finish up with a clan. But to avoid complications we limit the group to five generations only. Step into ego's shoes and imagine yourself a member. (Note: ego's triangle in Figure 6.5 is labeled B for brother since ego and his brothers are all represented by that one triangle.) The group includes all male and female agnates directly connected to you through your father (F), his father (FF), and so on—that is, all of the males in a direct line back to the founder of the group. It also includes all males descended from you (since you are male) and your male agnates: your son (S), your brother's son (BS), and your son's son (SS). Finally, it includes all of your female agnates in each generation, from your father's father's sister (FFZ) to your son's daughter (SD).

Earlier we mentioned the advantages of localized descent groups in patrilineal systems. When male agnates continue to live together (perhaps not in the same house but certainly in the same community) after marriage, they can prevent other descent groups from moving in and exploiting their patrigroup's territory and resources. Localized descent groups are common where patrigroups own valuable property. A wife resides with her husband after marriage, while a husband continues to live where he was born and where his father, brothers, and other agnates of his patrigroup live. This form of residence after marriage, called **patrilocal residence,** often occurs with patriliny.

Matriliny

In a system of **matriliny (matrilineal descent),** which is much less common than patriliny, females, not males, provide the links by which property, including intangible property such as rights and duties, descends to the next generation. In Figure 6.6, ego is again male, to enable you to compare matriliny more easily with patriliny. If you were this male consanguine in a **matrigroup** (whether matriclan or matrilineage), your group would consist of all females and males linked to you by matrilineal descent through your mother (M), her mother (MM), her mother's mother (MMM), and so on—that is, all of the females in a consanguinal line back to the female founder of the matrigroup. It would also include all females descended from your sister and your other female relatives, such as your sister's daughter (ZD) and your sister's daughter's daughter (ZDD). As with our patrilineal diagram, these descent lines can be extended through many generations.

In matrisystems both males and females inherit tangible and intangible property from their mothers, but

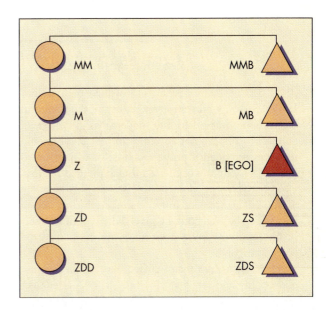

Figure 6.6
A Matrigroup. In matrigroups, the descending ties are all through females, but note how males are "hooked" onto the matriline.

only females pass down this property to the next generation. A male cannot bequeath anything to his own children; instead, his *sisters* provide the links by which his matrigroup's property passes to the next generation.

Thus, as a male in a matrisystem, you are not the legal caretaker of your own children but rather of your *sisters'* children. No doubt you love your children and provide for at least a part of their welfare, but your legal interests lie with your sister's children. It is *their* future

patriliny (patrilineal descent) a system of descent in which males provide the links by which property descends to the next generation

agnates (patrikin) consanguines who trace their descent from a common male ancestor

patrigroup a patrilineal descent group, whether patriclan or patrilineage

patrilocal residence residence for a husband near or with his father after marriage

matriliny (matrilineal descent) a system of descent in which females provide the links by which property descends to the next generation

matrigroup a matrilineal descent group, whether matriclan or matrilineage

Case Study in Matrilineal Descent: The Zuni

Today many of the Zuni of the Southwestern United States, while preserving much of their cultural heritage, are integrated into modern North American culture. But in the not very distant past these pueblo dwellers provided a prime example of a matrilineal descent system at work. A Zuni man divided his loyalties between two women, his sister and his wife. He was a full participant in two families. In the family into which he was born, he played the part of brother; in the family he created by marrying, he played the part of husband.

When a Zuni man married, he left his parents' household and moved to his wife's (Benedict 1989:75–76). There he lived with his wife, her sisters (both unmarried and married), the husbands of his wife's married sisters, his wife's unmarried brothers (her married brothers having moved out to live in *their* wives' households), his father-in-law (who years before would have left his parents' home to live with his wife), and his mother-in-law. The house in which this group lived belonged to the women, who also owned the household's supplies of corn and certain heirlooms and had the responsibility of protect-

ing the secrets of their clan from members of other clans—including their husbands. So the status of Zuni husbands, especially new husbands, was relatively low. Only gradually, as his children grew older, did a husband achieve some standing in his wife's household. A Zuni woman had no such conflict of interest. The only family to which she owed allegiance was her own household, which was one of many that made up her matrigroup.

In economic matters, a Zuni husband was a contributing member of his wife's household, but for religious purposes he remained a member of his sister's. He grew corn for his wife's household, not for his sister's, but returned to his sister's house to officiate at rituals. A man's allegiance as brother carried more weight than his allegiance as husband because of his crucial importance in his sister's home as the performer of her household's rituals. Given this conflict of loyalties, it's not hard to see why divorce was relatively common in Zuni society. An ex-husband would return to his sister's house, leaving his children (who belonged to his wife's matrigroup, not his) with his ex-wife.

(not your own children's) that you work to secure, for your sister's children (unlike your own) are members of your matrigroup and will eventually come into their inheritance from you and your group. No matter how hard you work, your own children will not inherit your estate because they are members of another matrigroup, their mother's. If, for example, you occupy a political office

that descends matrilineally, it is one of your *sister's* sons who has the right to succeed you. If your own son inherits an office, it will be from his mother's (your wife's) side of the family.

With certain reservations, much of what we said about patrigroups also applies to matrigroups. Consanguines in matrigroups are called **matrikin (uterine kin).**

Trobriand Names

The matrisystem of the Trobriand Islanders provides an instructive contrast to our own patrilineal way of handing family names down through the generations. In the Trobriands, ancestral names are transmitted by mothers to their children and then by daughters to their daughters and sons (Weiner

1988:56). The names can be used by sons, but sons cannot transmit them to their own children since the names are regarded as the ancestral property of the matrigroup. The children of a son inherit the ancestral names they receive from their mother.

Although males as well as females are matrigroup members, the core of a matrigroup consists of women of different generations bound together by consanguinal ties. At left are three generations of Navajo women.

Matrikin are consanguines who trace their descent from a common female ancestor, and they include males as well as females, as Figure 6.6 shows. Origin myths tell of a female founding ancestor, and totems and food prohibitions form part of the complex of rights and duties binding members of a matrigroup together.

Yet matriliny is not simply the mirror image of patriliny because in every society about which we have good data, males and females are unequal, with males rather than females generally dominating political and economic life. True, women may be enormously influential in the domestic sphere, and a few individual women, such as Indira Gandhi or Margaret Thatcher, may become important figures in public life, but overall the distribution of political and economic influence in any society heavily favors males. In fact, throughout all human societies there is not a single example of **matriarchy,** a society where women dominate men politically and economically; nor, as far as we know, has there ever been one (Rosaldo and Lamphere 1974:3). All societies fall somewhere between strong **patriarchy** (political and economic domination by men) on the one end of the scale and the egalitarian midpoint between matriarchy and patriarchy on the other.

The relevance of this bias is that mothers in matrilineal societies provide the *links* between female matrikin of different generations, but because they are women they generally are not involved in hands-on management of the property that passes down the matriline. Mothers, for instance, can't transmit their matrigroup's property to their children, so patriliny and matriliny are not mere opposites in this regard. Nor do women occupy whatever political offices their matrigroup controls. But if they don't, who does? The answer is their brothers, who are their *male* matrikin. Hence the great importance, in matrisystems, of the relationship between mothers' brothers and sisters' sons. If you are male, you inherit property from your mother's brother (not your father), and when you die your property passes to your sister's son (not your own child). Your own son inherits property from *his* mother's brother.

Matrigroups and patrigroups view sisters and wives differently. Because in a matrigroup a man's heirs are his sister's children, not those of his wife and himself, it is his *sister,* not his wife, who gives birth to the children whose existence enables his matrigroup to con-

◆◆◆

matrikin (uterine kin) consanguines who trace their descent from a common female ancestor

matriarchy a society in which women dominate men politically and economically

patriarchy a society in which men dominate women politically and economically

◆◆◆

Tsimshian Residence

Matrilocal residence does not always accompany matriliny. Sometimes, a male lives with his mother's brother, a pattern called **avunculocal residence.** This is a more efficient way than matrilocal residence of keeping matrilineal property under the watchful eyes of the males who have a stake in it. If widely practiced in a society, this form of residence also tends to keep brothers together after they have married because unlike matrilocal residence, wives must come to live with their husbands, not vice versa.

Among the Tsimshian, native Americans of the Pacific northwest coast, matriliny prevails. Children of both sexes spend their early years living with their parents. A daughter remains with her parents until she marries, when she goes to live with her husband. A son, however, usually leaves his father's household somewhere between the ages of 8 and 14 to live with his mother's brother. One result of this avunculocal residence is that a core of males, related matrilineally, is geographically established. Since it is these males who control and protect their matrilineage's property, the fact that they live with or near one another is beneficial to the matrilineage (Vaughan 1984:60–61).

tinue into the next generation. A man's sister is therefore more important to the continuance of his matrigroup than is his wife. In a society with patrigroups, in contrast, a man's sister (after she has married) bears children who replenish her husband's patrigroup; it is the man's *wife* who provides children for his patrigroup. This explanation helps us to understand why, in societies with matrigroups, bonds between brother and sister are stronger than those between husband and wife and also why, in societies with patrigroups, the opposite is true.

Yet another difference between patrigroups and matrigroups is residence after marriage. If you are an adult female member of a society with matrigroups, you may spend your whole life living with or near your mother, her sisters, and your own sisters, since these are your matrikin. Your father and any of your brothers who are not yet married will live with you. When you marry, your husband will leave his home and come to live with you and your matrigroup. Since he is in effect living near your mother, we call this form of postmarital residence **matrilocal residence.**

Matriliny sounds much more complicated to Westerners than patriliny, perhaps because—although ours isn't a patrilineal society—we have the traditional transfer of surnames as an example of patrilineality in action. Unfortunately, we have no such handy example of matrilineality in Western society. For many Westerners, it is a conceptual struggle to envision descent through females in conjunction with the control of wealth and the exertion of authority by the male siblings of females.

Cognation

A society like the Nuer or the Trobrianders, which reckons descent through either males or females but not both, is said to have a rule of **unilineal descent.** But most societies reckon descent through both males and females. This is called **cognation (cognatic descent)** and is the most common descent system in the world. It is easily understood by Westerners since it is the system that prevails in the West, although we do not have cognatic descent groups, as some societies do.

In cognatic descent, an individual of either sex can transmit property in any form to individuals of either sex in the next generation, and people see themselves as being equally related to their mother's and their father's families. The rights and duties that may be transmitted in this very liberal fashion are the same as those transmitted under patriliny or matriliny, but descent groups created by cognation are nevertheless quite different from those formed by patrilineal or matrilineal descent.

First, the number of people you consider yourself related to as a member of a cognatic descent group is potentially much larger than the number of your relatives in a matrilineal or patrilineal descent system since you consider yourself a consanguine of both your maternal and paternal kin. As we have seen, in patrilineal and matrilineal systems, individuals automatically belong to either their father's descent group *or* their mother's, but cannot be a member of more than one.

Second, cognatic descent groups overlap; you be-

The Western Residence Pattern

As a matter of course, newlyweds in Western society, if they haven't already established a home before marriage, try to find one in a location separate from those of their families, an arrangement that anthropologists term **neolocal** ("new place") **residence.** Neolocal residence serves the members of our society well since a married couple isn't tied down to either the husband's or the wife's family. Independence is adaptive in a mobile society in which jobs change and people often have to move.

Sometimes, of course, because of economic problems, a couple must live with one or the other set of parents. When couples are permitted to choose whether to live with the husband's relatives or the wife's, this is called **ambilocal residence.** In our society, this arrangement is usually only temporary; the young couple looks forward to the day when they are "out from under" and can move into a home, however modest, of their own. But in other societies, the arrangement is permanent (e.g., the Iban, mentioned above). Although less liberal than neolocal residence, ambilocal residence offers much more freedom of choice than the other residence arrangements we have discussed. The

Some North American newlyweds must live with relatives for economic reasons, but most consider neolocal residence—a home separate from both their families— far preferable, even when they must do without the usual household amenities.

couple moves in accordance with the relative advantages offered by residing with one or the other set of relatives.

long to several of them at the same time. Since theoretically you trace your descent back to all of the ancestors of both of your parents, potentially you are a member of as many cognatic descent groups as you have ancestors. Going back only as far as your grandparents gives you four ancestors (FF, FM, MF, MM). If your society has cognatic descent groups and your four grandparents each belong to a different one, you will belong to all four. This can create conflicts when it comes to rights and loyalties because the rights you are entitled to claim and the duties that claim *you* overlap, just as the descent groups overlap. Consider residence, for example. If you belong to two descent groups, with which do you reside? No one descent group in a cognatic system has a stronger claim on your presence than any other, and a group that decided to keep all of its members together could do so only by depriving other groups of potential members.

avunculocal residence the residence pattern in which male ego resides with his mother's brother

matrilocal residence residence for a husband near or with his wife's parents

unilineal descent a line of descent that runs through either males or females but not both

cognation (cognatic descent) a form of descent reckoned through both males and females

neolocal residence residence for a married couple in a location separate from the residences of their parents

ambilocal residence the residence pattern in which couples choose whether to live with the husband's relatives or the wife's

Another problem involves a common duty of descent group members: the duty to avenge the mistreatment of fellow consanguines (Fox 1983:150). Suppose your society has four cognatic descent groups, and you belong to all four. If a man from one group kills a consanguine of yours from one of the others, which group do you support?

Such problems can be resolved. Some cognatic systems allow individuals to choose the descent group with which to identify. When an individual can choose to join either the father's side of the family or the mother's, this is called **ambilineal descent.** Although ties with the side not selected are still recognized, whatever economic and political resources the chosen descent group owns are made available to the individual.

Combinations of Descent

Until quite recently, anthropologists thought they were justified in labeling entire societies patrilineal, matrilineal, or cognatic on the basis of which rule of descent seemed to predominate. Today we realize that a society does not have to choose an exclusive descent system. It can exploit all three rules of descent to allocate whatever property it has at its disposal. Thus, within a single society, lineage membership and names may descend matrilineally; rights to residence after marriage, patrilineally; and rights to tangible property, cognatically.

In some parts of the world, we find a combination of patriliny and matriliny that is sometimes so well arranged and integrated into the social organization that it has achieved a distinctive fame among anthropologists. We call it **bilineal descent (double descent).** It assigns the responsibility for transmitting certain types of inheritable property patrilineally and other, quite different, types of inheritable property matrilineally.

The Yako of West Africa have both patriclans and matriclans (Forde 1961). These exogamous clans are localized and divided into lineages. All of the males of a lineage live together, their wives forsaking their childhood homes to live with them. A man's rights to a house, land, and protection lie in his patriclan and patrilineage. When he dies, his land and house descend to his sons. However, property that is movable, for example, money and livestock, is inherited matrilineally. In other words, at a man's death his land and house become the property of his sons, and his money and cattle go to his sister's sons.

KINSHIP TERMINOLOGIES

English-speakers use English-language **kinship terms** (or **relationship terms),** such as *father, mother, brother, sister, son, daughter, aunt, uncle, cousin, nephew, niece,* and *grandchild,* to denote relatives. All societies use such terms for classifying relatives. In some cases, a kinship term lumps several or many individuals together as members of a single relationship category; the English kin term *cousin,* a catch-all term into which a number of your relatives (male or female, father's side or mother's side) fit, is an example. In other cases, a kinship term distinguishes between persons; in English, "father" distinguishes one man from all others. In non-Western societies and in languages other than English, the situation may be quite different. Instead of the general term *cousin,* there may be different kinship terms that distinguish among different kinds of cousins. Or a single kinship term may lump the relatives we call *father* and *father's brother* into a single category.

Some societies classify certain relatives together (or "equate" them) because the relatives occupy the same social status or carry out much the same social role. Other relatives are distinguished from one another rather than equated because they occupy different social statuses or carry out different social roles. For example, in some societies a man is encouraged to marry his mother's brother's daughter (MBD). We sometimes find in such societies that the term for MBD is the same as the term for wife (W): MBD = W. (Note that if a man marries his MBD, this is a matrilateral cross cousin marriage.) The Ema of Timor say a man's ideal marriage partner is his MBD, and sure enough, the Ema word for MBD is the same as the word for W (Hicks 1990:76).

In other words, a **kinship (or relationship) terminology**—the complete set of kinship terms by which relatives are known—is one way in which a culture imposes order on the social world of relatives. As children

 ASK YOURSELF

In many societies, including Western society, people who aren't really kin are sometimes addressed using kinship terms. Do you always use kinship terms literally, or do you sometimes "extend" them to include persons who are not really related to you? For example, are all the women you call "aunt" really your aunts?

become enculturated, they learn that different kinship terms are associated with the sort of treatment they can expect to receive from relatives—as well, of course, as how they should behave towards these relatives as they become older and more socially responsible. But there are no hard and fast rules about kinship terminologies. Societies with the same marriage preference as the Ema may use two different words for MBD and W.

Six kinds of kinship terminology have attracted most anthropological interest. Individually, they are labelled the Hawaiian, Eskimo, Omaha, Crow, Iroquois, and Sudanese systems, but they are grouped into three broad categories:

1. nonlineal terminologies: Hawaiian and Eskimo

2. lineal terminologies: Omaha, Crow, and Iroquois

3. descriptive terminology: Sudanese.

Nonlineal terminologies are often found, logically enough, in societies in which descent is cognatic rather than unilineal. In the Hawaiian and Eskimo terminological systems, you don't distinguish relatives on your father's side of the family from those on your mother's. Thus in both of these systems you call your mother's sister and your father's sister by the same term, a term that means "aunt." (If this sounds familiar, it's because most Westerners use the Eskimo system.) Calling these two women by the same term suggests that, from your point of view as ego, both sides of your family are equally important—or unimportant—to you, legally, economically, or politically. Similarly, in these two systems you call a cross cousin by the same term as a parallel cousin.

In lineal terminologies, common in societies with lineal or bilineal descent, you distinguish between parallel cousins and cross cousins and between certain relatives on your father's side of the family and those on your mother's. Lineal terminologies are sometimes called **bifurcate merging** systems because certain relatives are separated (or bifurcated) from one another by the use of different terms, while others are merged under one term. For example, you may "merge" your father and your father's brother, referring to both by the same term, because these two men belong to the same line of descent; but at the same time you may "bifurcate" your mother's brother from your father and your father's brother by using a different term for him, because he belongs to a line of descent different from your father and your father's brother. Similarly, you may classify your mother's sister with your mother, referring to both

women by the same term, but use a different term for your father's sister. It follows logically that in lineal terminologies you refer to your parallel cousins and your siblings by the same term, but you use a different term for your cross cousins.

Descriptive terminologies "describe" individuals by assigning them terms that are used only for them (or others in the same exact genealogical positions), thus distinguishing between relatives in a highly specific way. In English, the term "sister" is a descriptive term; it is used to denote one kind of relative and no other. Merging is less important than bifurcation in descriptive terminologies.

Hawaiian

The **Hawaiian terminology** is the simplest of all kinship terminologies, since it uses the fewest terms (Figure 6.7). Although the Hawaiians provided its name, other societies use it also. In each generation there are only two kin terms: one for males and one for females. Thus—taking the generation above you as an example—you refer to your F, FB, and MB by a single term. The same is true for your M, MZ, and FZ. In your own generation, you classify your male cousins with your brothers and your female cousins with your sisters. The same principle is true for your children's generation. You call your nephews by the same term as your sons, and your nieces by the same term as your daughters.

••

ambilineal descent the kind of descent in which an individual may choose to join either the father's or the mother's side of the family

bilineal descent (double descent) a combination of patriliny and matriliny

kinship (relationship) term a word specifying a specific category of relative

kinship (relationship) terminology the complete set of terms by which relatives are known

bifurcate merging kinship terminology a terminology in which F and FB are known by the same term, whereas MB is known by a different term, and where M and MZ are known by the same term, whereas FZ is known by a different term

Hawaiian terminology a terminology, found in many cognatic societies, in which all relatives of the same sex in the same generation are included under the same term

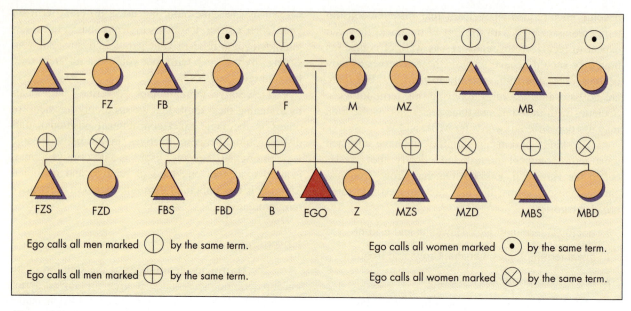

Figure 6.7
Hawaiian Terminology. This nonlineal *terminology uses the least number of terms of any kinship terminology; in each generation, there is one term for males and another for females.*

Eskimo

In the **Eskimo terminology** (Figure 6.8), you refer to the members of your nuclear family (in English: "fa-ther," "mother," "brother" and "sister") by terms used for no other relatives outside this kinship unit. Thus the terms you use to refer to your parents differ from those you use to refer to your aunts and uncles; the terms you

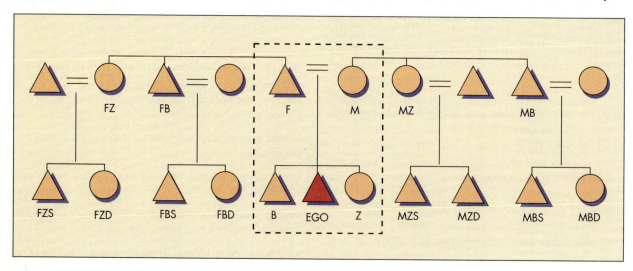

Figure 6.8
Eskimo Terminology. In this nonlineal *terminology one calls members of one's nuclear family by terms that are given to no other relatives outside of this kinship unit. Thus, the terms given to parents differ from those used for uncles and aunts; sibling terms differ from cousin terms; and terms for children differ from those for nephews and nieces. But one does not distinguish cross cousins from parallel cousins.*

call your siblings differ from cousin terms; and terms for your children differ from those for your nieces and nephews. However, as in the Hawaiian system, you don't distinguish your cross cousins from your parallel cousins, referring to all of them by a single term. The system thus verbally distinguishes members of the nuclear family from other relatives, so it is not well suited to societies with lineal descent groups. It is, however, well-suited to cognation, and since cognation is the most common descent system in the world, the Eskimo terminology is the most common terminology. In addition to the Inuit[2], most North Americans and members of other industrialized societies use it. So do members of societies as different from each other as the gathering-and-hunting !Kung of Africa and the pastoralist Sarakatsani of Greece.

Omaha

The **Omaha terminology** is a lineal terminology named after a native American group of the Great Plains, and is usually associated with patrilineal descent

---

[2]Although the people formerly called the Eskimo prefer to be called the "Inuit," the kinship terminological system named after these people continues to be called the Eskimo system.

(Figure 6.9). In effect, you "extend" certain terms across two or more generations in the same patrilineal line. Thus you use a single kin term to refer to your mother's brother, his son, and his son's son. Similarly, you call your mother by the same term as her brother's daughter, and you call your father's sister's child by the same term as your sister's child. Why would a society develop this kind of terminological system? It may happen because of patrilocality, the mode of residence that commonly accompanies patriliny. With patrilocality, your mother's consanguines may not be living near you, so there may be little practical need to distinguish between members of different generations in patrigroups other than your own.

Crow

Another native American society, the Crow, gives its name to this second lineal terminology (Figure 6.10), which, like the Omaha system, may also be associated

••

Eskimo terminology a terminology, found in many cognatic societies, in which members of the nuclear family are distinguished from other relatives

Omaha terminology a bifurcate merging terminology sometimes accompanying patrilineal descent in which, among other identifications, MB = MBS = MBSS

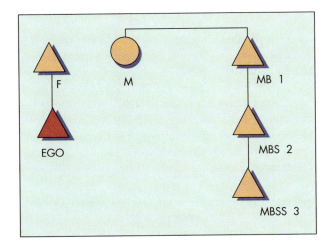

Figure 6.9
Omaha Terminology. In this lineal terminology, one extends some terms across two or more generations in the same patrilineal line. Thus, one calls one's mother's brother, his son, and his son's son by the same term; one's mother by the same term as mother's brother's daughter; and one's father's sister's child by the same term as sister's child.

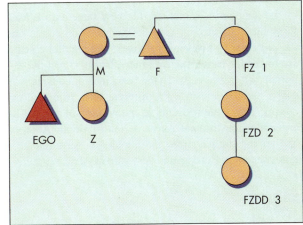

Figure 6.10
Crow Terminology. In this lineal terminology, one extends some terms across two or more generations in the same matrilineal line. Thus, one calls one's father and father's sister's son by the same term; and father's sister and father's sister's daughter by another.

with unilineal descent. Also like the Omaha system, the **Crow terminology** "extends" some terms across two or more generations. But because it usually accompanies matrilineal rather than patrilineal descent, the "extensions" occur in matrilines rather than patrilines. Thus (recalling that in matriliny you are a member of your mother's lineage but not your father's), you call your father and your father's sister's son—two members of a matrilineage other than your own—by the same term. But to your mother's sister and mother's sister's daughter, two members of your own lineage, you give separate terms. Thus in the Crow system you don't necessarily distinguish between members in different generations of matrigroups other than your own (F = FZS; FZ = FZD), but you do distinguish between members in different generations of your own matrigroup because it is the members of your own matrigroup (your mother, your sisters, your sisters' children) who are most important to you, not the members of other matrigroups—even your wife's.

Iroquois

The third lineal system (Figure 6.11), the **Iroquois terminology,** is named after the Iroquois people of upper New York State and is associated with unilineal descent like the Omaha and Crow systems. However, it may occur in societies that have either patrilineal or matrilineal descent. Your cross cousins on both sides of your family, your mother's and father's, are referred to by the same term. Sometimes the very same term is used for spouse, suggesting that cross cousins on either side are preferred as husbands or wives. But parallel cousins are forbidden as marriage partners, and to signal the important difference between the two kinds of cousins, you call a parallel cousin by a different term from a cross cousin. This system occurs in many parts of the world, especially the tropical forest region of South America and among the gatherers and hunters of Australia. It is non-existent in Europe, and very rare in Africa.

Sudanese

Although not considered a lineal terminology because it lacks certain of the distinctions and equations between relatives found in lineal terminologies, the **Sudanese terminology** may be found in societies that have lineal descent (Fig. 6.12). However, unlike the Omaha, Crow, and Iroquois terminologies, it assigns individual terms to relatives such as ego's father, father's brother,

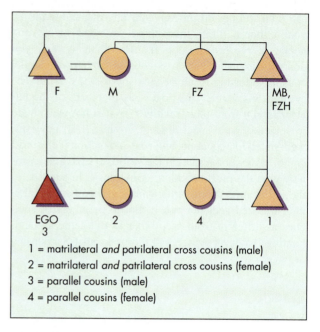

1 = matrilateral *and* patrilateral cross cousins (male)
2 = matrilateral *and* patrilateral cross cousins (female)
3 = parallel cousins (male)
4 = parallel cousins (female)

Figure 6.11
Iroquois Terminology. In this lineal *terminology, which occurs with both patrilineal and matrilineal descent, one calls both cross cousins by the same term. Sometimes this is the same term as that for spouse, suggesting that cross cousins are preferred as husbands or wives. One may not marry a parallel cousin, and to signal this difference between the two kinds of cousin, a parallel cousin is called by a different term from a cross cousin.*

mother's brother, mother's sister, father's sister, siblings, and cousins. There is no merging here; this terminology separates relatives in a highly specific way. For this reason we sometimes call it a descriptive terminology; each relative is associated with a special term that "describes" only that relative. The system may be used in societies in which the different relatives all have different political, economic, or social parts to play in the community.

CONCLUSION

For personal, social, legal, economic, and political reasons, human beings organize themselves into groups based on actual or imagined consanguinal ties. In the West, where genealogical ties result not in membership in descent groups but in loosely organized, self-defined kindreds, such groups have little direct effect on their members' daily lives. You will probably not rely on

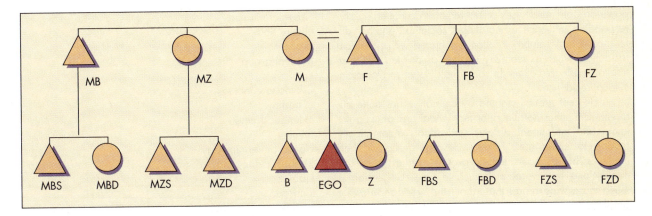

Figure 6.12
Sudanese Terminology. In this descriptive *terminology, one does not merge relatives into a single term; instead, they are separated. Thus, one calls one's father, father's brother, mother's brother, mother's sister, father's sister, siblings, and cousins by distinctive terms.*

family members to dictate to you whom you should marry, where you should live, or what career you should pursue.

But for most people, even Westerners, consanguineal ties are nevertheless fundamental to self-identity. As the genealogical writer Alex Shoumatoff (1985:13–14) says, "The family . . . provides the most intense, intimate, and permanent relationships most of us will have; and this is not likely to change." Without immediate family, Howard Hughes was a sadly isolated figure despite his enormous wealth. He died a lonely man.

SUMMARY

As a minimum, a family is a group of two or more people who consider themselves related, who are economically interdependent, and who share the responsibility for rearing any children in their group. Families can take many forms—single-parent families, nuclear families, extended families, kindreds—but however defined, they help people address their physical, psychological, economic, linguistic, and social needs.

Descent—relationships defined by connections to ancestors through parent-child links—establishes individuals' social identities while spelling out their mutual rights and duties and creating legal, economic, political, religious, and personal bonds. It involves "blood" relatives in contrast to relatives by marriage (treated in Chapter 7). Blood relatives, or consanguines, are related to one another by consanguinity, a bond based on the tie between parents and children but extended to more distant relatives. The complete set of such ties for any single individual is that person's genealogy.

After an explanation of kinship diagrams, which anthropologists use to portray descent systems graphically, this chapter describes major types of descent systems: patriliny, in which one reckons descent through one's father's line; matriliny, in which descent is reckoned through one's mother's line; and cognation, in which descent is reckoned through both parents' lines. These three systems yield three different forms of descent groups: patrilineal, matrilineal, and cognatic.

Some features associated with patrigroups and matrigroups are a corporate nature, a residential pattern based on sex, the principle of exogamy, and a clan or lineage organization (or both). But there are also some significant differences between patrigroups and matrigroups because in no society are males and females precisely equal. In general, males dominate females, politically and economically. Thus, males wield political and economic

Crow terminology a bifurcate merging terminology sometimes accompanying matrilineal descent in which, among other identifications, FZ = FZD

Iroquois terminology a bifurcate terminology associated with unilineal descent in which the matrilateral cross cousin and patrilateral cross cousin are known by the same term, which may sometimes be the same term as that for spouse

Sudanese terminology a terminology often associated with unilineal descent, with separate terms for F, FB, MB, MZ, FZ, siblings, and cousins

power in patrilineal systems, but females do not enjoy corresponding influence in matrilineal societies. Another difference is that patriliny is often associated with patrilocal residence, whereas matriliny is often associated with matrilocal residence, although some matrisystems favor avunculocal residence.

Descent groups created by cognation are quite different from either patrilineal or matrilineal groups. In patrilineal and matrilineal systems, individuals automatically belong to either their father's descent group *or* their mother's, but cognatic descent groups overlap; a person can belong to several at the same time. Cognation is much more widespread throughout the world than either patriliny or matriliny and is a more flexible form of descent.

In ambilineal descent, an individual can choose whether to join the father's or mother's side of the family. Bilineal descent, a rare type, brings together patriliny and matriliny, but each mode of descent is given a different task. For example, immovable property may pass down through localized patrigroups, while movable property is passed down through nonlocalized matrigroups.

Kinship terms are important for anthropologists because they reveal how societies classify relatives. They may also suggest how a society allocates social positions and offer clues about whether cognation, patriliny, or matriliny prevails. And kinship terms suggest the relative importance or unimportance of the father's or mother's side of the family. There are six kinship terminologies: Hawaiian, Eskimo, Omaha, Crow, Iroquois, and Sudanese. The Hawaiian and Eskimo often accompany cognatic descent, whereas the others typically accompany unilineal descent. More specifically, the Omaha is often found with patriliny, the Crow often accompanies matriliny, the Iroquois hints at a preference for marriage with a cross cousin, and the Sudanese suggests subtle differences in the social positions of ego's relatives.

Crow terminology
culture hero
descent
descent group
ego
Eskimo terminology
exogamy
extended family
family
Hawaiian terminology
Iroquois terminology
kibbutz
kindred
kinship (relationship) term
kinship (relationship) terminology
lineage
matriarchy
matrigroup
matrikin (uterine kin)
matrilateral cousin
matriliny (matrilineal descent)
matrilocal residence
neolocal residence
nonlocalized (dispersed) descent group
nuclear (elementary or simple) family
Omaha terminology
origin myth
parallel cousin
patriarchy
patrigroup
patrilateral cousin
patriliny (patrilineal descent)
patrilocal residence
Sudanese (descriptive) terminology
totem
unilineal descent

KEY TERMS

agnates
ambilineal descent
ambilocal residence
avunculocal residence
bifurcate merging kinship terminology
bilineal descent (double descent)
clan
cognation (cognatic descent)
consanguines (consanguinal kin)
consanguinity
cross cousin

SUGGESTED READINGS

Bohannan, Paul, and John Middleton (eds.). 1968. *Readings in Kinship and Social Organization*. Garden City, NY: Natural History Press. A collection of wide-ranging, often classic essays. Many are useful for understanding marriage as well as descent.

Coontz, Stephanie. 1992. *The Way We Never Were: American Families and the Nostalgia Trap*. New York: Basic Books. A sociologist argues that America has known many different family forms, yet none has ever adequately addressed universal problems like poverty, child abuse, or gender inequality.

Gailey, Christine Ward. 1987. *Kinship to Kingship: Gender Hierarchy and State Formation in the Tongan Islands.* Austin: University of Texas Press. A feminist perspective on the differing influences exerted by men and women on the South Pacific Tonga islands. Gailey casts her net wide, describing male and female influences on many aspects of Tongan culture, from economic exchanges to marriage to disputes about who should fill political offices. This is a distinctly holistic study of descent.

Graburn, Nelson (ed.). 1971. *Readings in Kinship and Social Structure.* New York: Harper & Row. A collection of some of the classic papers on descent and marriage. Indispensible for comparing the views of a number of anthropologists.

Hicks, David. 1988 (1976). *Tetum Ghosts and Kin.* Prospect Heights, IL: Waveland Press. A synchronic study showing how descent is integrated with marriage, ecology, and religion in a technologically simple society.

Keesing, Roger. 1975. *Kin Groups and Social Structure.* New York: Holt, Rinehart & Winston. An introduction to descent and marriage from a clearly written structural-functionalist perspective.

T he mile-high central Iranian plateau is a hostile land—arid, virtually treeless, sand-colored, searingly hot in summer and breathtakingly cold in winter. There are a few meager rivers, fed by snow meltwater from the mountains, but their beds are dry for part of the year. The ground, hardly the flat tableland that the word *plateau* might suggest, is tortuously uneven, its desertlike expanses interrupted frequently by rocky outcroppings. Sandstorms often whip the area, and travelers are quickly resigned to journeying in shrouds of dust.

Even so, sitting on the roof of an ancient bus as he bumps along an unpaved road and clings for dear life to his bundle of supplies, Ali marvels at the beauty of the world around him, a gift from Allah to the faithful: nearby, the green tops of a row of poplar trees peering over a mudbrick wall surrounding an irrigated garden; a bit further off, the bright blue-green dome of a mosque surmounting an otherwise fawn-colored village; on the horizon, mauve shadows lying in the crevices of the mighty Zagros mountains, behind the glamorous city of Isfahan.

Ali left Isfahan a couple of hours ago, to return to Hassanabad, his village. Over the last five years—ever since he was 16 and his father decided to quit farming—he has made this trip several times a year, to trade and shop. Each time, he has been awed by the beauty and enormity of the city's mosques and palaces, minarets and columns, rose gardens and reflecting pools. On each visit, he has also been overwhelmed by the four- and five-story buildings; the enormous main square built at the pleasure of a long-ago shah; the broad avenues crowded with cars, buses, donkeys, and people; the strong smell of diesel exhaust and sewage; the boulevards lined with trees so precious each one bears a numbered plaque; the wonderful variety of things for sale in the dim passageways of the bazaar. Today's trip has been a good one; he purchased fertilizer, a pair of shoes, and a copper pot for his mother. The money he got for his sacks of barley and pistachio nuts was just enough.

Ali's thoughts turn to home and quickly to Shereen. Still unmarried at 16, she is, as all of Hassanabad acknowledges, a beauty; she moves gracefully in her flowing chador, and her eyes—the only part of her face he has ever seen—are lovely. She is also bright and curious and would probably love to see something of the world beyond Hassanabad. Someday, if her father agrees to give her to Ali in marriage, he may take her along on one of his trips, although the streets and alleys of cities and towns are not the proper place for women to be seen. Ali's choice of a local girl will surprise no one; village endogamy has always been the norm in Hassanabad. And if Shereen is not the most traditional choice he could make—a daughter of his father's brother would have been the ideal bride—well, that particular marriage doesn't really take place very often, and after all, Shereen is his second cousin on his father's side. Under Islamic law, Ali could theoretically have as many as four wives, but he doesn't expect to; since the Koran teaches that a man must provide equally for all of his wives, polygyny is too expensive to be very common.

As the bus rolls into Hassanabad's single street, children come running, oblivious to the cloud of diesel exhaust blanketing the road. Ali throws his bundle to the ground and leaps down after it, not waiting for the bus to come to a stop. The remaining passengers peer out at a row of small, single-story, closely placed mud-brick houses, their unpainted walls exactly the same color as the surrounding terrain. There is an occasional glimpse into a courtyard; otherwise, high walls block all views. Roofs are domed, for wood is scarce and a domed roof doesn't need wooden supports, as flat ones. A single power line droops from pole to pole down the street, paralleling an open sewer. Formerly the sewer was used for drinking water in addition to laundry, dishwashing, and garbage disposal; now Hassanabad's residents get their drinking water from a public well. The town's little central square contains a mosque; a public bath; a bakery, where Ali's mother buys bread three times a day; and a small shop selling soft drinks, farm tools, and plastic articles. The departing bus passes a gas station and a two-room school near the edge of the village.

Ali's mother and father remember the time before Hassanabad got its power line, well, and school. These gifts of the late shah, whose picture used to hang in every home and shop, changed life in Hassanabad forever. Thanks to the power line, Ali can listen to news and religious broadcasts on the radio, water is pumped electrically from wells into their fields, and the Muslim call to prayer blares five times a day from a speaker atop the local mosque. Thanks to the well, Hassanabad's drinking water is clean, so fewer babies die. Thanks to the school, where his consistently valiant defense of the soccer goal made him somewhat of a local hero, Ali can read newspaper headlines and add numbers.

The shah is of course long gone, his portrait torn down and replaced with images of the Ayatollah Khomeini, the holy *imam* and savior of Iran, even as Ali's fame as a soccer player has given way to a new notoriety in the village based on his stirring religious performances. Ali is proud that he was named after an earlier Ali, the cousin and son-in-law of the Prophet Mohammad, and proud that the faithful of Hassanabad have seen fit to cast him centrally in their annual passion play. This somber pageant commemorates the long-ago tragedy at Kerbala, when Hossein, the original Ali's son, and his family were martyred at the hands of the evil caliph of Damascus. One day a year, consumed by his Shi'ite faith, Ali is overcome by the horror of this event. He cries aloud and beats his own back with a chain until the blood flows.

The rest of the year, however, Ali is a farmer, like most of Hassanabad's men. From his father he has inherited several plots of land plus a thriving pistachio orchard, also walled. He grows mostly garden vegetables for his family to eat but uses his largest plot for cash crops—wheat and barley. He cultivates these grains with the help of a wooden plow pulled by an ox or mule, whichever he can rent more cheaply. He counts on his male relatives to help him with the heavy work of harvesting, as he helps them in turn. Like most other farmers, Ali also owns a few sheep and goats, which graze on a common pasture at the edge of town.

Ali feels fortunate that he is an only son and that his father was a beneficiary of Iran's 1962 land reform law, under which huge agricultural estates were parceled out to the farmers who had been working on them on a crop-sharing basis. Previously, farmers had been able to keep only about

a fifth of what they produced. Under the 1962 law, a farmer was entitled to purchase the plots of land he was working on at the time the law was passed and was given 15 years to pay for it. Ali knows a number of unlucky farmers who were not eligible for land in 1962 and whose sons are still landless. While the shah retained power, most of them worked as day laborers; more recently, these young men have become members of the Ayatollah's Revolutionary Guards or Reconstruction Crusade.

Ali's father, once an admirer of the shah, now grumbles that land reform did not change anyone's way of life in Hassanabad very much. True, the family doesn't have to pay rent any more, but they have to pay taxes, and they are still constantly in debt to moneylenders and merchants. For that matter, neither did the more recent political revolution change their lot. Even if Khomeini did manage to punish the greedy, pro-American city dwellers who seemed to run things before the shah's downfall, new and different palms must still be filled with silver. Just consider the size of the bribe that had to be paid during the war with Iraq to keep Ali, then only a boy, out of the army's ranks of young martyrs! And an entire nation's revitalized faith has not lessened the constant threat of earthquakes and duststorms and droughts. "Inshallah," Ali's father sighs wearily and frequently; "It's Allah's will."

Ducking under the low, arched doorway between the street and his family's courtyard, Ali greets his little sister, Farah. She has lugged her loom out of the house to take advantage of the late afternoon light and is hard at work making a carpet. Although only 10, she has already learned a proper and becoming modesty. Just in case it had been someone other than Ali entering the courtyard, someone outside the family, she demurely holds her floor-length veil across the lower half of her face with her teeth. Only her eyes say she's glad to see him. Farah will be a good wife one day, Ali thinks. She will never allow her veil to slip from her head.

As for Ali, he is content with the thought of marrying Shereen and living the rest of his life in Hassanabad. Not for him the siren call of Isfahan or Teheran, where some of Hassanabad's sons have sought wealth and high-status jobs, abandoning their village, land, and kin. Instead, Ali will work hard without complaint, pay off his family's debts, pray to Allah five times a day, and travel twice a year to Isfahan. Except for short trips to the well or shop, Shereen will stay at home, cook, make carpets, and bear children. If Ali is lucky, his children will be strong boys who will help him farm his land and who will raise *their* sons in Hassanabad.

CHAPTER 7

MARRIAGE

Affinity *refers to relationships created by marriage rather than by descent, and* affines *are people related to one another by marriage. At a wedding in a Hispanic community in the United States, the relatives of the bride and groom, now affines, gather for a family photo.*

INTRODUCTION

BROTHER AND SISTER GUILTY OF MARRYING INCESTUOUSLY

—Newsday, *August 2, 1979, p. 13*

It was the kind of headline guaranteed to attract public attention, and curious readers pored through the accompanying article for details of a bizarre episode that had recently occurred in Massachusetts. Shortly after his birth some twenty years earlier, readers learned, a baby named David had been separated from his sister, Victoria, then 2 years old. Given up by their mother for adoption, the two children had been sent to opposite ends of Massachusetts, where each was raised by foster parents. When she reached adulthood, Victoria longed to meet the brother she barely remembered. By researching old birth records, she was at last able to locate him, and in the spring of 1979, when she was 24 and her brother 22, she arranged to meet him at his foster parents' home.

Later, Victoria was to tell a judge, "It was love at first sight." Obviously her brother felt the same way, for a short time later the two siblings, mentioning their blood relationship to no one, were married in Andover, Massachusetts, by a justice of the peace. With different last names and different addresses, there was nothing to suggest that the two were really brother and sister.

The state of Massachusetts got word of the peculiar union it had sanctioned when the bride's adoptive mother discovered the facts of her daughter's marriage

Victoria and her brother, David, given up for adoption as children, were raised apart. Reunited as young adults, they fell in love and were married. When their illegal marriage was discovered, a judge ordered them to end their incestuous relationship—an unenforceable ruling.

and notified authorities. David and Victoria were ordered to appear in court, where they claimed total ignorance of the law against incestuous marriages. They had heard, Victoria admitted, that children born of incestuous unions were apt to be abnormal in some way, but "we had decided before we got married . . . that Dave would get a vasectomy."

Under Massachusetts law, incestuous marriages are automatically void, and incest carries a maximum penalty of 20 years in jail. But Massachusetts was lenient with the young couple. The judge sentenced them to 2 years' probation and ordered both to undergo counseling. They were permitted to continue living together as unmarried housemates on the condition that they end their incestuous relationship. How that edict could be enforced, though, was what their probation officer called "the thousand-dollar question."

In North America, as the tale of Victoria and David illustrates, we believe that marriage should occur only between individuals our society considers to be appropriate partners. We're not alone. Customs governing whom one can and cannot marry are extremely important in other societies, too. In this chapter, we look at the virtually universal human institution of marriage: its functions, the different ways that appropriate marriage partners are defined in different societies, the different kinds of marriages, and what happens when marriage doesn't work out.

◆◆

THE FUNCTIONS OF MARRIAGE

As a minimum, **marriage** is a socially sanctioned contract spelling out the domestic and civic rights and duties of the people (usually one male and one female, but not always) who enter into it. It may, of course, be many other things as well. Our definition is very broad, but we formulate it like this to make it applicable worldwide.

If you're the romantic type, you're wondering why we didn't include what many Westerners consider to be the most important element of marriage: **romantic love**,

◆◆

marriage a socially sanctioned contract spelling out the domestic and civic rights and duties of the people who enter into it

romantic love any intense and sexual attraction in which the person loved is an object of idealization, with the expectation that the feeling will last for some time into the future

Romantic Love: A Human Universal?

Not all cultures exalt romantic love as Westerners do, but two anthropologists recently conducted a cross-cultural study that suggested it is common in most cultures (Jankowiak and Fisher 1992:149), even though it may not be seen as necessary for, or even desirable in, marriage. To determine whether or not romantic love existed in a particular culture, the anthropologists studied informants' claims about their feelings of love, ethnographers' statements that the concept of love was present, and elopements resulting from mutual affection. They also examined folktales, love songs, and other art forms (see Chapter 14).

One source the anthropologists consulted was a series of ethnographic interviews with Nisa, a woman of the !Kung gatherer-and-hunter society.[1] Nisa recognized a clear difference between two kinds of love: the "companionship" she enjoyed with her husband and the more exciting romantic love she shared with her lover. She described her relationship with her husband as "rich, warm, and secure," while her relationship with her lover was "passionate and exciting, although often fleeting and undependable" (Jankowiak and Fisher 1992:152).

The anthropologists reported that romantic love occurred in 147 out of the 166 cultures they studied. Given the fact that anthropology is only now beginning to focus on the subject, the apparent absence of romantic love in the remaining 19 cultures may be due to a lack of relevant data. If so, romantic love may be a human universal.

Findings from physical anthropology may support this suggestion. Anthropologist Helen Fisher

[1]In the spoken language of the !Kung, there are a number of sounds that do not occur in English. One of them is a soft explosive noise, called a "click," that sounds something like a cross between a "k" and an "l" and is made in the throat. The exclamation point in front of the word "!Kung" (and other words expressed in English but derived from this and other African "click" languages) indicates that this word begins with a "click" rather than with any sound that can be represented using the English alphabet.

Romantic love seems to occur in almost all societies, although it is not always considered a necessary ingredient of marriage. Indonesian, Nigerian, Yugoslavian, and native American couples show that the face of love is similar everywhere.

(1992) suggests that romantic love evolved some 4 or 5 million years ago, when human beings began to walk upright and carry their food to places where it was safe to eat. Without help from a partner, mothers could not perform these activities while carrying infants in their arms, so a basic change in reproductive strategies took place: male-female bonding. With the evolution of bonding came changes in body chemistry that stimulated and sustained bonding by producing feelings of infatuation and attachment, the ingredients of romantic love. To this day, humans' romantic feelings are regulated biochemically. Thus all human beings, whatever their culture, have the capacity for romantic love.

that intense and sexual attraction in which the lover idealizes the object of attraction and expects this feeling to last (Jankowiak and Fisher 1992:149). In many societies around the world, whether a married pair are in love with each other or not is relatively unimportant. It's no handicap if it happens, but it isn't necessary for a successful marriage; it's the relationship between the families of the married couple that is most important. To us this seems strange, yet this idea once prevailed among Westerners also. In the Middle Ages (fifth to fifteenth centuries), Europeans regarded romantic love as generally unattainable in marriage and a poor justification for it. Romantic love was a rarified sentiment reserved for someone unattainable—someone already married to another, someone belonging to a different social class, or someone who had died.

Sometimes romantic love is even viewed as potentially dangerous to society. Those who indulge in it refuse to allow the expectations of others to intrude on their happiness. Lovers are known for turning in on themselves and possibly neglecting the world of rights and obligations outside their little island of self-absorption. A relationship of this kind does nothing to further the interests of the lovers' families or their societies, so this kind of love has often been discouraged as a basis for marriage.

As cold and unromantic as it may seem, we cannot include the permanent bonding of lovers as a function of marriage, cross-culturally. The major functions of marriage worldwide are to form new family units, to define the reciprocal rights and responsibilities of married people, to create alliances between the families of married couples, and to spell out how the productive efforts of a couple and the goods and services produced within their marriage should be apportioned for their mutual benefit.

Establish New Nuclear Families

In Chapter 6 we discussed exogamy, the requirement that people must choose their spouses from families (however this term might be defined) other than their own. Joining two representatives of different families usually (but not always) creates a new family for the mutual benefit of its members—not just the husband and wife but also any children who may be born to or adopted by them. The new grouping usually provides each member with basic needs, such as food and shelter; a socially approved role; and in the case of children, protection, nurture, and enculturation.

Specify Rights and Responsibilities

Marriage customs are amazingly diverse, but in every society marriage institutionalizes certain basic rights and responsibilities for married people, and often for their families too. At a minimum, marriage establishes that a husband is the legal father of his wife's children, and she is the legal mother of his; that the husband and wife each have a sexual monopoly over the other (unless the husband has more than one wife or the wife has more than one husband, in which case a spouse shares sexual rights with several cospouses); that the couple have either partial or monopolistic rights to the fruits of each other's labor; that each has partial or total rights over property belonging to the other; and that a joint fund of property is established for the benefit of the children of the marriage (Leach 1963:107–108).

These rights and responsibilities are common to almost all kinds of marriage (and there are many) everywhere in the world. Given such near universality, it's reasonable to suppose that the institution of marriage is just about essential for societies as they attempt to solve universal problems of panhuman importance. Everywhere, for example, the matter of who can have sex with whom must be clearly spelled out (you can imagine the turmoil that would result in a society in which there were no rules about this). Everywhere, arrangements for the care of offspring must be made since human babies and children cannot survive by themselves, and everywhere, the work of men and women, and the property that this work generates, must be divided up in some suitable way. Marriage helps to solve these problems.

Create Alliances

Westerners easily comprehend the notion that marriage establishes a married couple's rights and responsibilities to each other and to their children. But we are less familiar with another aspect of marriage that is extremely common in non-Western societies: marriage creates alliances between the relatives of a married pair. (This idea may not be totally unfamiliar to you if you've heard of marriages between members of very rich or politically powerful families that are contracted for political or economic reasons, perhaps in addition to love.) We may feel that the consanguines of a married couple should have little or nothing to do with the couple's marriage, but the deep and ongoing involvement of relatives is accepted as a matter of course in many societies.

To express the notion of a wider relationship among the relatives of a married couple, anthropologists use the term **affinity.** Whereas marriage refers to the relationship between a married pair, *affinity* refers to this relationship plus the relationships between the married pair and the relatives of both of them. We call people related by marriage **affines.** When affines give wives we call them "wife-givers"; when they take wives we call them "wife-takers."

In societies in which marriage creates ties between the affines of a married pair, these ties, called **affinal alliances,** can serve subsistence, political, legal, economic, and social functions, to the mutual benefit of everyone concerned. In Western society, if you want to build a house or hold a political office, you hire a construction crew or campaign publicly for votes. In a technologically simpler society, however, you would need to call on some group of people for help. You can see how useful a large group of relatives, all obliged to help you, would be.

One common affinal obligation in non-Western societies is to provide affines with subsistence necessities; for example, gifts of food might be required at the time of a marriage, a birth, a death, or other occasions. The custom can be highly functional. If one affinal group has suffered a poor harvest but its partner group living in another region has not, gifts of food may tide the hungry group over its period of famine. Affines may also be required to perform essential ritual services for one another.

Among the Rindi of eastern Indonesia, wife-givers are considered the source of life and spiritual well-being. A man with a long-term illness may move into the house of one of his clan's wife-givers, place himself symbolically under the spiritual protection of the ancestor of this wife-giver, and stay there until he recovers (Forth 1981:292). By contrast, wife-takers are associated with death. If someone dies away from home, "his clan's wife-takers may be called upon to transport the corpse" (291). These customs show how descent, marriage, religion, and symbols come together in a thoroughly holistic way in Rindi society.

Another common obligation of affines is mutual defense. In times past, if you were a Tetum man and your clan were attacked by another clan, not only would you be compelled to join in the defense effort but your affines would also be expected to offer assistance (Hicks 1990). If you refused, they would not come to *your* aid when you and your clan were attacked.

Among the Tetum of Indonesia, the job of making a coffin falls to the affines, rather than the clansmen, of the deceased person. Clan members are prohibited from doing this job for one of their own. Above, members of a wife's patriclan make a coffin for her dead husband, a member of a different patriclan.

Strong affinal alliances require social rules that spell out how suitable matches are made. As you know, the rule of exogamy requires descent group members to choose spouses from groups other than their own, thus bringing two groups into alliance. But most societies do not want people to choose spouses from groups so distant or so alien that useful affinal alliances cannot be formed. So, in addition to rules of exogamy, many societies have rules of **endogamy:** spouses must be chosen from *within* a certain group. Another reason for en-

affinity relationships created by marriage

affines relatives by marriage

affinal alliance ties, created by marriage, between affines

endogamy the custom in which one's spouse must be chosen from within one's own group

Tetum Outcasts

The crucial importance of the affines of married couples in traditional societies is illustrated by what happens when Tetum lovers decide to put individual sentiment before the interests of their respective descent groups. If the couple's consanguines disapprove of their marriage, the consequences can be dire. Usually, a couple will decide not to marry each other rather than alienate their families. However, should the pair decide to elope, publicly affirming their commitment to each other and turning their backs on the web of rights and duties that in ordinary circumstances would bind their descent groups together, both are disowned by their descent groups. The couple is forced to flee from the community, becoming social outcasts, as their future children will be as well. They no longer have kin to call on for help in such basic tasks as gardening, house repair, or health care—a high price to pay for disregarding society's rules.

dogamy is to preserve a religious or ethnic tradition. Usually the endogamous group within which one is encouraged to find one's spouse is relatively large. For example, many people living in Jordan identify themselves as Palestinian rather than Jordanian. They are encouraged to marry other Palestinians, not Jordanians, which helps them to preserve their ethnic identity.

Affinal alliances are so important that when they break down, as may occur with modernization, the consequences can be as extreme as they are unexpected. An example: in the New Guinea highlands, before contact with the outside world, stone ax heads were made by tribes living where suitable stones were available, and interregional trade saw to their distribution. At the same time, intertribal marriages created affinal links that made trade easier between these groups. But after steel axes were introduced from the West, local production of stone ones ceased. As trade declined, so did the opportunity to contract marriages and create affinal ties between tribes. Eventually, as older people died and fewer marriages were arranged between tribes, the network of affinal ties decayed, and conflict and full-scale warfare increased (Podolefsky 1984:85).

Allocate Goods and Services

Once upon a time, a Western woman, visiting in Africa, was invited to attend a wedding. Upon learning that the bride's and groom's families had negotiated the

◆ **ASK YOURSELF**

What are the usual reasons for elopement in Western society? What are some of its social and emotional consequences for the married couple?

The Expansion of Endogamous Groups

As our world grows smaller, figuratively speaking, endogamous groups get bigger. The mountainous island of St. Barts in the French West Indies is divided into a number of sections called *quartiers,* which are separated from one another by topography and distinguished by different dialects (Morrill and James 1990). In the past, the people of St. Barts consistently chose spouses from their own quartier. Today, however, St. Barts has roads, cars, television sets, opportunities for higher education away from the island, and even an airline. People no longer choose their spouses from within their residential quartier, for both their world and the number of possible choices have expanded. The same thing is happening on a grander scale in North America. It is no longer unusual to encounter a married couple who are from different cities or states, of different ethnic heritage, or from different socioeconomic backgrounds.

value of the match and that the groom's family had agreed to pay the bride's a total of two bulls and four milking cows, one with a calf, at the time of the wedding, the Western woman professed shock. "Why, that's barbaric!" she cried. "Can't you see that exchanging a human being for cattle is a dreadful thing to do? It's demeaning to everyone concerned!"

"No, no, not at all," explained her host. "To the contrary, the bride is delighted at the prospect of being given in marriage in return for such valuable goods, for now everyone can see what a remarkable woman she is."

Later, the visitor's host inquired about marriage customs in Western societies. "Tell me," said the host, "are valuable gifts exchanged at the time of a wedding in Western society?" "Oh, yes, indeed," replied the visitor. "And sometimes they are extremely generous gifts. It's not uncommon, for example, for the father of a bride to take the groom aside and press into his hand a check for a rather considerable amount of money." "Why, that's barbaric!" protested the non-Westerner. "Imagine the bride's father *paying* the groom to take the poor woman off his hands! Can't you see that treating a human being in this way is demeaning?"

"No, no, not at all," explained the Westerner. . . .

The point of this anecdote is that in many societies, including our own, marriage may involve the transfer of goods and services among a husband, a wife, and members of their families (Goody and Tambiah 1973). The goods and services may be distributed at the time of marriage or as part of a continuing process that lasts as long as the marriage does. Anthropologists use the terms *bridewealth, bride-service,* and *dowry* to distinguish among the goods and services thus distributed.

Bridewealth. Bridewealth (bride-price) is property transferred from a groom's family to the bride's on the occasion of a marriage. Animals, money, houses, jewelry, or clothing—virtually anything considered of value in a society—can constitute bridewealth. The number and quality of items involved may depend on the wealth of the groom's family, their prestige relative to that of their new affines, and the social importance of the particular marriage.

As our anecdote about the African wedding shows, Westerners sometimes react critically at the thought that in non-Western societies a woman can be "bought" or "sold." But those who give or receive bridewealth see this custom in an altogether different light, as a practice that enhances the repute of both

Bridewealth—property presented to a bride's family by a groom's family when a marriage takes place—consists of money or other goods considered valuable in a society. In Tanzania, East Africa, bridewealth cattle are driven from a Gogo groom's home to that of his bride.

sexes. This doesn't mean that women in societies in which bridewealth is given enjoy equal status with men; often they don't. Still, bridewealth is a custom that both women and men may support. In Zimbabwe, for instance, a new law, intended to give women equal rights, was enacted some years ago. Among other things, it states that a woman can decide for herself whether or not her prospective husband must pay bridewealth. Given the choice, many Zimbabwean women "continue to view [bridewealth] as a symbol of worth and dignity in a male-dominated society . . . " (*New York Times* 1987:A17).

Generally speaking, the more rights the groom's family gets, the larger the bridewealth. This is especially true in patrisystems, in which the most important right a groom's family gets is the right to claim any children the wife may bear as members of its own group. Also com-

◆◆

bridewealth (bride-price) property transferred from a groom's family to his bride's at marriage

mon in patrisystems is the right to expect the bride to live with her new husband and his relatives, rather than vice versa. This custom, patrilocal residence (see Chapter 6), ensures that the groom need not live with his in-laws in an alien place, where he may have few privileges. Following from this right is that of the groom's family to the fruits of the new wife's labor. From her wedding day onward, the bride is a contributing member of her husband's household, not the household into which she was born. If the bridewealth isn't paid, these rights aren't secured and the marriage may be void.

Even though bridewealth is more common in patrilineal societies, it may also occur with matriliny. But in matrilineal societies, any children a married couple produce belong to the wife's descent group rather than the husband's. Since the marriage benefits the husband's group less, the bridewealth is usually smaller.

Bride-service. **Bride-service** occurs when a son-in-law works for his father-in-law to compensate him for the loss of his daughter's services. Sometimes the son-in-law's labor is for a limited period of time, perhaps until his wife gives birth to their first child. Sometimes it lasts until the older man dies. The custom may appear similar to the Western practice in which a bride's father takes his new son-in-law under his wing, as a trainee in the family business, perhaps, or as a junior partner in his law office. There is one big difference, however: a Western groom may decline a junior partnership, but bride-service is obligatory.

Dowry.   Narrowly defined, a **dowry** is the goods given by a bride's family to the family of her groom. As such, the custom is quite rare. More broadly, a dowry is all the goods—jewelry, money, household items, animals, or other valuables—a bride brings with her to her marriage. Once widely practiced in both Asia and Europe, this custom may have originated where land could be inherited only by sons, and thus was a way for parents to include their daughters as beneficiaries of their wealth.

In India, dowries have been declared illegal, in part because of a tendency of some families to view the birth of a daughter as an unwelcome financial burden and to treat girls accordingly. Yet a dowry is still a part of many Indian marriages. Especially among the poor, it may pay for the wedding itself rather than enrich the groom's family or purchase basic household necessities for the married couple.

If bridewealth and bride-service seem alien, the idea of a dowry may be less so since a form of this custom is still practiced in North America, although it appears to be on the wane. At least through midcentury, some teenage girls were given "hope chests," sturdy and decorative boxes into which they would place items collected in the expectation of a future marriage and the establishment of a home. Typically, a well-stocked hope

◆ **ASK YOURSELF**
What purpose does the custom of gift giving at marriage serve in Western culture?

Narrowly defined, a dowry is gifts a bride's family presents to a groom's at the time of a marriage. In northwestern India, to mark the wedding of a member of the nobility, the male consanguines of the bride arrive at the groom's home carrying platters of money.

chest would contain household linens, bedding, silverware and other decorative silver objects, and perhaps small appliances as well. Today, the custom of "registering," in which a bride deposits a list of her household needs with the stores from which she expects her family and friends to purchase wedding gifts, has largely replaced the hope chest.

MARRIAGE PARTNERS: WHO'S OKAY AND WHO ISN'T

As you know, there is a world of difference between having sex and being married, but in almost every society, sex is assumed to be an essential ingredient of marriage, and individuals who are permitted to have sex with each other are generally also allowed to marry. Thus, when we speak of appropriate marriage partners, we are usually talking about appropriate sex partners as well. However, societies differ widely on the subject of who is an appropriate partner and who is not. Moreover, societies regulate these matters, sometimes by prohibiting certain marriages (as in the case of David and Victoria) and sometimes by encouraging or even mandating certain marriages. In some societies, sex or marriage between biological first cousins is considered wrong and is discouraged or even legally prevented. In others, marriage between first cousins is encouraged as the ideal, or preferred, marriage.

Preferred Marriages

If you're North American and married, it's nice if you get along with your in-laws, but the personal relationship between you and your spouse is much more important than your relationship with your spouse's family. However, as you already know, in many parts of the world the affinal relationship between the relatives of a married couple may be even more important socially than the personal relationship between the couple. If you were a member of a society in which strong affinal alliances were important, you might experience great social pressure to marry a specific person or a person from a particular category. In some cases—traditional China, for instance—you'd have no choice at all; you would have been betrothed to a particular person as an infant. Such customs differ widely from the Western ideal of love and free spousal choice as preludes to marriage.

If the idea of a socially dictated marriage partner seems strange, the notion that your preferred spouse should be a certain type of relative may be even more

so. Yet in many societies marriages between certain relatives are not only sanctioned but also strongly advocated. Commonly, one's preferred spouse is a first cousin, which means that the bride and groom have a set of grandparents in common. One powerful reason for such a marriage is to continue the already-existing ties between the bride's family (wife-givers) and that of the groom (wife-takers).

Cross Cousin Marriage. In Chapter 6, we distinguished between two kinds of cross cousins, patrilateral (on the father's side) and matrilateral (on the mother's side). In a society with preferred marriage rules, a person might be strongly encouraged to marry one kind of cross cousin or the other.

In **patrilateral cross cousin marriage** (Figure 7.1), a man is required or at least encouraged to marry his father's sister's daughter, and a woman is required or encouraged to marry her mother's brother's son. As though to express this preference, societies with this form of marriage may use the Crow kinship terminology (see Chapter 6), in which parallel cousins and cross cousins are distinguished from each other, and the kinship term used for the cross cousin who is the preferred marriage partner is often the same term as that for spouse. Thus a man calls his father's sister's daughter by the term *wife*, and a woman calls her mother's brother's son by the term *husband*.

Similarly, in societies that practice **matrilateral cross cousin marriage** (Figure 7.2), in which a man is required or encouraged to marry his mother's brother's daughter and a woman is required or encouraged to marry her father's sister's son, this preference is often revealed in the use of the Omaha kinship terminology (see Chapter 6). Again, the cross cousins are distin-

---

bride-service an arrangement in which a son-in-law is obliged to work for his father-in-law as a way of compensating the father-in-law for the loss of his daughter's services

dowry goods given by a bride's family to the family of her groom

cross cousin marriage a marriage between two cross cousins

patrilateral cross cousin marriage a man's marriage to his father's sister's daughter or a woman's marriage to her mother's brother's son

matrilateral cross cousin marriage a man's marriage to his mothers's brother's daughter or a woman's marriage to her father's sister's son

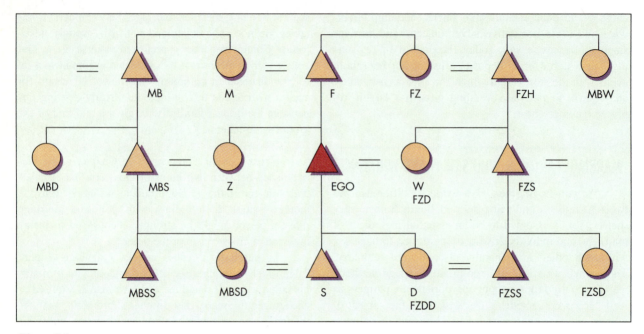

Figure 7.1
Patrilateral Cross Cousin Marriage. In patrilateral cross cousin marriage, a man marries his father's sister's daughter and a woman marries her mother's brother's son.

guished from each other, and the kinship term used for the cross cousin who is the preferred marriage partner is often the same term as that for spouse.

What if you're supposed to marry a particular cousin, but you have no such cousin? This kind of dilemma sometimes crops up in Western society when a

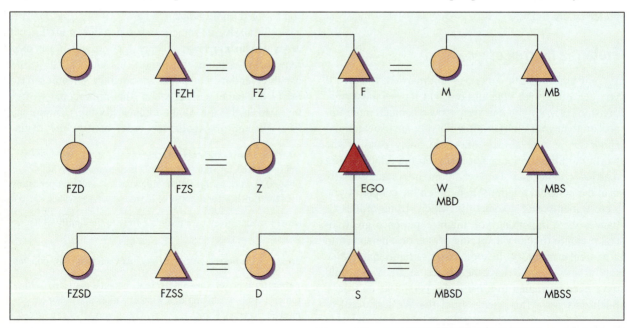

Figure 7.2
Matrilateral Cross Cousin Marriage. In matrilateral cross cousin marriage, a man marries his mother's brother's daughter and a woman marries her father's sister's son.

specific relative is traditionally supposed to perform a specific role. In the Christian tradition, for instance, the father of a bride is supposed to walk her down the aisle at her wedding and "give her away." What happens if the bride's father isn't present for some reason? In that case, another relative—the bride's brother, perhaps, or an uncle—is chosen to fill in, and nobody looks askance. This type of substitution also occurs in societies with preferred marriages. If you're supposed to marry your mother's brother's daughter but your mother's brother hasn't got a daughter, you marry a substitute, whom your society considers just as acceptable.

Patrilateral cross cousin marriage as practiced by the Trobriand Islanders shows just how elastic the notion of a prescribed spouse can be. A Trobriand man is supposed to marry his father's sister's daughter, a woman he calls by the kinship term *tabugu* (Malinowski 1929:534). But while this is the ideal, it is not often the actual practice (Weiner 1976:185). Although a male

Trobriander *says* he would prefer his father's sister's daughter as a marriage partner, census material shows that his actual choice is apt to be a more distantly related woman of his father's clan, perhaps a second or third cousin. In either case, he often ends up marrying into the same clan his mother did. In fact, *all* of the women in this clan are considered *tabugu*. Thus it seems that the preference among Trobrianders is really for a certain *category* of women, *tabugu* women, rather than for a particular individual.

Bilateral Exchange. A third type of preferred marriage is **bilateral exchange** (Figure 7.3), in which men of different nuclear families or descent groups, who

bilateral exchange a form of cross cousin marriage in which the men of two nuclear families or descent groups, related to one another as cross cousins, exchange women in marriage; sometimes called direct exchange

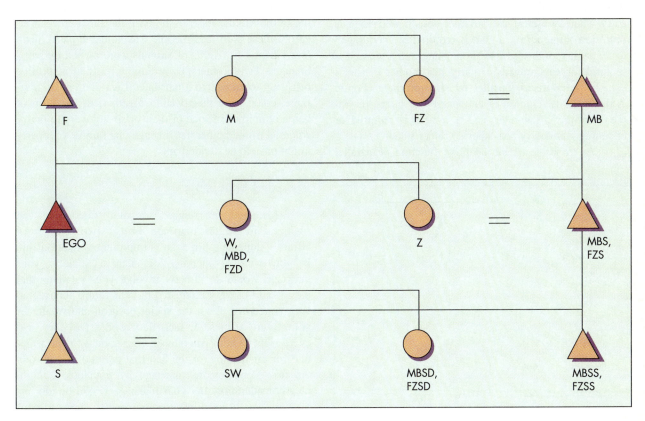

Figure 7.3
Bilateral Exchange. In bilateral exchange, men of different families or descent groups exchange their "sisters" (either their biological sisters or other female relatives classified as sisters) as brides.

are related to one another as cross cousins, exchange their "sisters" as brides (not all at the same time, of course). In this context, the word *sisters* includes not only biological sisters but, more widely, a range of female relatives that one group of men may "give" to another. Because, in effect, men of two groups are exchanging "sisters" directly for "sisters," we sometimes call this custom *direct exchange*. In bilateral exchange, if you were a woman, you might marry a person who is both your mother's brother's son and your father's sister's son. If you were a man, you might marry a person who is both your mother's brother's daughter and your father's sister's daughter. This preference may be suggested by the use of the Iroquois kinship terminology. In a society with bilateral exchange, the cross cousins who are preferred as marriage partners are often known by the same term as that for husband or wife.

Parallel Cousin Marriage. As is the case with cross cousin marriage, there are two kinds of **parallel cousin marriages:** matrilateral and patrilateral. In a society where **matrilateral parallel cousin marriage** is preferred (Figure 7.4), a man is required or encouraged to marry his mother's sister's daughter, and a woman is required or encouraged to marry her mother's sister's son. In **patrilateral parallel cousin marriage** (Figure 7.5), a man is required or encouraged to marry his father's brother's daughter, and a woman is required or encouraged to marry her father's brother's son.

An example of the adaptive function of parallel

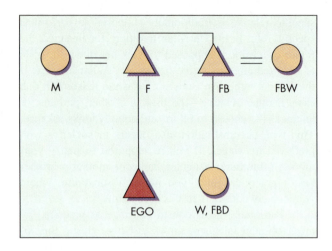

Figure 7.5
Patrilateral Parallel Cousin Marriage. In patrilateral parallel cousin marriage, a man marries his father's brother's daughter and a woman marries her father's brother's son.

cousin marriage is provided by some Muslim groups living in the Middle East. In the past, the subsistence strategy of these patrilineal people was nomadic pastoralism (see Chapter 5). Herds of animals were owned by patrilineages. Two brothers, by arranging for their respective offspring to enter into a patrilateral parallel cousin marriage, could keep their wealth together, in the form of herds of animals. If one of their offspring were to marry a person from another patrilineage, the family's property might have to be divided up.

Arranged Marriages

Arranged marriages are not uncommon in societies in which marriage brings two groups of affines together in an important relationship. If you were a member of such a society, your marriage would so directly involve your relatives that they would be very interested in your future spouse and very concerned about the social position and wealth of your future affines. In fact, they would feel they had every right to help you choose your spouse. Your affection for this person, or the fact that the two of you took the first steps toward marriage by yourselves, might be a consideration, but your marriage would be too important socially to allow your personal feelings to control the future. The opinions of your senior relatives and your future spouse's senior relatives, *not* your own, would be paramount, and these relatives would finalize, if not actually arrange, the match.

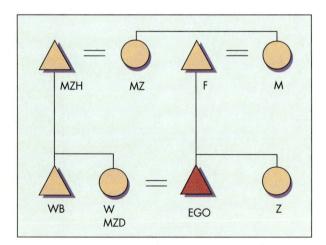

Figure 7.4
Matrilateral Parallel Cousin Marriage. In matrilateral parallel cousin marriage, a man marries his mother's sister's daughter and a woman marries her mother's sister's son.

In many societies around the world, marriages are arranged by the relatives of individuals who do not know each other. In New Delhi, India, the parents of unmarried men and women seek alliances for their children through newspaper ads.

In the many societies around the world in which marriages are arranged for individuals who do not love each other, the hazards threatened by this often-unreliable sentiment are avoided. The cost is personal freedom, but the result may be a satisfying marriage with considerable benefit to the families of the marriage partners. Marriage comes first, and then—who knows?—the mutual respect a couple may develop in a pragmatic union may evolve into love.

Free-Choice Marriages

In Western society and many others, too, no particular spouse is preferred; the selection of one's spouse depends on factors other than kinship, such as love, social status, or wealth (Lévi-Strauss 1969:xxiii). Societies without explicit preferred marriage rules are more common than those with them. And societies without these rules are diverse, including Western, peasant, and nonliterate societies, from North Americans to Iranians to Inuit to !Kung San. In functional and cultural evolu-

tionary terms, this suggests that a lack of rules governing spousal choice must be very adaptive.

Despite the absence of explicit rules, a society may make its preferences felt. Your family and friends may urge you, subtly or not so subtly, to marry into a certain social class, or pick a spouse of a certain religion or one who is well educated. Here in the West we are familiar with the kinds of pressure a family may exert to persuade a person to marry "appropriately."

Prohibited Marriages

David and Victoria's story was newsworthy because sex between members of the same family is considered incestuous in Western society (even though an estimated 10 to 14 percent of American children under 18 have been involved in incestuous acts). Incest between siblings is thought to be the most common type, but father-daughter incest is the most often reported (Shepher 1983). The prohibition against incest is normally restricted to members of the nuclear family, although some countries or states also prohibit marriages between first cousins. But in societies with descent groups, this prohibition can apply to sex or marriage between more distantly related members of the same descent group. Anthropologists call the prohibition of sex between close relatives the **incest taboo.**

Incest seems to be so commonly disapproved of throughout the world that it comes close to being universal. Several explanations, biological and social, have been proposed for this widespread disapproval.

The Genetic Explanation. Victoria and David claimed they had heard that the offspring of closely related parents are more likely to suffer biological defects than other children. This belief underlies a traditional explanation for the incest taboo: incest is forbidden because societies recognize the potential for impaired off-

◆◆

parallel cousin marriage a marriage between two parallel cousins

matrilateral parallel cousin marriage a man's marriage to his mothers's sister's daughter or a woman's marriage to her mother's sister's son

patrilateral parallel cousin marriage a man's marriage to his fathers's brother's daughter or a woman's marriage to her father's brother's son

incest taboo the prohibition of sex between relatives

spring. Advocates of this **genetic explanation** argue that in a society in which there is no prohibition against incest, a high proportion of impaired babies will be born. In prehistoric times, when societies were small and the lives of their members precarious, societies with many impaired members were less able to compete successfully with rival societies that had rules against incest and were thus producing more robust individuals. Natural selection took care of the rest. Societies permitting incest gradually died out, unable to compete successfully for resources against stronger societies, while those in which incest was prohibited thrived. Hence, the argument goes, today (as far as we can tell) all societies have an incest taboo.

The problem with this explanation is that we have no evidence that our remote ancestors saw a link between incestuous mating and future defective children. Moreover, inbreeding isn't automatically harmful to a species. Animals inbred by zoologists often not only perpetuate themselves from generation to generation but actually flourish (Livingstone 1969). Any offspring with defects are exposed to the forces of natural selection and are eliminated from the population before they can pass their genes to the next generation. Presumably this would have been the fate of defective human offspring, too.

The Social Explanation.   Unlike the genetic explanation, the **social explanation** is based on social grounds rather than facts of nature. Were incest permitted within the nuclear family, Malinowski (1927:251) and others have argued, competition for sex among family members would bring about such mutual hostility that families would be destroyed. The incest taboo arose to prevent this. Some anthropologists counter this argument by suggesting that although competition between father and son for the mother, and between mother and daughter for the father, would certainly disrupt the simple family, sibling incest need not do so.

The Instinct Explanation.   Edward Westermarck (1922) argued that girls and boys raised in the same family instinctively find one another sexually unappealing. Research conducted in an Israeli kibbutz disclosed that not a single marriage had occurred among unrelated boys and girls who had been reared together (Talmon 1964), a remarkable finding in view of the fact that the parents of the children had consistently urged them to marry someone from their own group. The same avoidance of familiars was noted in the kibbutz childrens' casual sexual relationships, which did not occur between individuals who had been reared together from birth. Overfamiliarity, said informants, had brought

In a nursery on an Israeli kibbutz, or farming cooperative, unrelated children are reared together, apart from their parents. Scholars interested in incest avoidance have noted that children who grow up on the same kibbutz view one another as siblings rather than potential sex partners.

about a lack of sexual interest. "We are like an open book to each other," one member of a kibbutz said (504).

Critics have charged that this case study does not really support the **instinct explanation.** First, societies do not need to forbid individuals from doing something they are not inclined to do anyway. If childhood familiarity really weakens sex appeal, why do societies expressly prohibit sibling incest? Second, Talmon's (1964) findings concerned only sibling incest, but the incest taboo also prohibits sexual relations between mothers and sons, fathers and daughters. How are *these* prohibitions to be explained?

The Psychoanalytic Explanation. Freud (1918) argued that every boy subconsciously longs to have sex with his mother—an urge Freud labeled the Oedipus complex, after a tragic figure in Greek drama who unwittingly married his own mother. Thus, a son, according to Freud, cannot help but be jealous of and hostile toward his father. Fearing that his father might retaliate against him, the son unconsciously represses his sexual urges. But they continue to haunt him, resulting in feelings of horror at the very thought of having sex with his mother. Freud believed a similar urge and repressive reaction, which he termed the Electra complex (after another figure in Greek drama, who killed her mother), are felt by a daughter toward her father. One problem with this **psychoanalytic explanation** is that the members of at least some societies apparently feel no horror about incest whatsoever. Needham (1974:66) tells us that the Kodi of Indonesia claim to know of individuals who sleep with close relatives, but no one much cares.

The Confusion Explanation. If a man had sex with his daughter, and the daughter later gave birth to a boy, would you consider the child the man's *son* or the man's *grandson?* Some anthropologists assert that the incest taboo exists to prevent this kind of confusion. Against this **confusion explanation** you might note that in such a situation, no confusion would arise if the society already had a rule classifying the child as either son or grandson. Even the absence of a rule need cause no confusion. The society could make up some such rule upon the birth of its latest member.

The Cooperation Explanation. To survive in the demanding environment of prehistoric times, Tylor (1889) and later Lévi-Strauss (1969) argued, nuclear families were forced to cooperate. To encourage cooper-

ation, early humans decided that nuclear families had to practice exogamy, which forced members of one family to look for spouses in other families. The resulting ties between families, established by marriage, bound separate families into societies. Early humans had a choice, as Tylor put it, between "marrying out and dying out." Unfortunately, there are two logical problems with this **cooperation explanation.** First, there are other ways of fostering cooperation between nuclear families, ways that some societies have actually put into practice, such as the exchange of labor or gifts. And second, the "marry out or die out" idea does not explain why members of a nuclear family are forbidden to have *sex* with each other. It explains only why they are forbidden to *marry* each other.

TYPES OF MARRIAGE

Given two sexes, it might appear that there are four theoretical possibilities for marriage: one man and one woman might be married to each other, one man might be married to two or more women at the same time, one woman might be married to two or more men at the same time, or several men and several women might all be married to one another simultaneously. Because of what you already know about the variety of human behavior, you will not be surprised to learn that all four exist. You may be surprised, however, to learn that

genetic explanation an explanation for the incest taboo that emphasizes the genetic advantages of marrying outside the family

social explanation an explanation for the incest taboo that suggests it arose to prevent family disintegration

instinct explanation an explanation for the incest taboo that suggests that members of the same family instinctively find one another sexually unappealing

psychoanalytic explanation an explanation for the incest taboo that suggests its origin in an attempt to control the unconscious desire of children to have sex with the parent of the opposite sex

confusion explanation an explanation for the incest taboo that emphasizes the confusion that would result in the classification of relatives if incest occurred

cooperation explanation an explanation for the incest taboo that emphasizes the social advantages that come from obliging members of the same family to marry outside of it

in some societies, marriage with nonhumans, such as gods or ghosts, is possible.

Monogamy

Today, in most of the industrialized world, a person is allowed to have only one spouse at a time, a form of marriage called **monogamy.** Although some societies sanction other types of marriage, monogamy is so familiar to Westerners that it may seem, somehow, inherently "right." It is also by far the most common kind of marriage found around the world, possibly because in most societies the number of adult males and females tends to be approximately equal. Another possibility is that having more than one spouse at a time may entail considerable expense (in the form of bridewealth, for instance, or the maintenance of two homes), so most people cannot afford to do so.

Monogamy may be the only legal form of marriage in Western society, but as divorce and remarriage become increasingly common a new kind of Western marriage pattern has been identified. This is **serial monogamy,** consecutive marriages to a number of different spouses. The actress Elizabeth Taylor Hilton Wilding Todd Fisher Burton Burton Warner Fortensky may be the Western world's best-known example.

Polygamy

In parts of the non-Western world, it is perfectly acceptable for a person to have more than one spouse at the same time, a practice anthropologists call **polygamy.**

Polygyny.   One form of polygamy is **polygyny,** in which a man has two or more wives at the same time. In Islamic countries, for instance, a man may legally have up to 4 wives. Yet this is moderate compared to what was acceptable in the past among the Tsimshian of the northwest coast of North America: a Tsimshian chief could have as many as 20 wives (Rosman and Rubel 1986:16). Sometimes 2 or more of a polygynous man's wives are sisters, a custom called **sororal polygyny.**

If you were brought up to think of monogamy as "right," you might wonder how any self-respecting woman could tolerate sharing her husband with another wife. Yet from the point of view of the women involved, polygyny may offer some advantages. The first is economic. A household in which several women are working together produces more than one in which one woman is working alone. Since the husband may reap

A new kind of marriage has emerged in twentieth-century Western society: serial monogamy, or consecutive marriages to a number of different spouses. Above, actress Elizabeth Taylor, who had previously married Nicky Hilton, Michael Wilding, Mike Todd, Eddie Fisher, Richard Burton (twice), and John Warner, with her most recent husband, Larry Fortensky.

the rewards of his wives' labor, their work, whether in his fields or among his herds, may make him richer than a monogamous man; and if the wives together produce a large number of offspring, the children, too, may contribute to his household's output. The household may also benefit from the husband's many affines. Some Trobriand chiefs practiced polygyny on a grand scale, their major income coming from annual marriage contributions consisting of goods and services owed them by the brothers of their wives (Malinowski 1929:130–132). One chief had five dozen wives, giving him considerable economic clout.

Women's second benefit in polygynous marriages is social. Cowives may value one another's company and relish the prestige that comes from being married to a man who can afford multiple wives. When fields must

Polygyny, a kind of marriage in which a man has two or more wives at the same time, is permitted in many societies. The 40 wives of Kenyan husband Danja Akuku have borne him a total of 349 children.

be hoed, water carried, and animals milked, extra pairs of hands are welcome. Children, too, benefit socially from this arrangement, often forming close relationships with each of their fathers' cowives. And a child may have half-brothers and half-sisters of about the same age to play with.

Polygynous marriage is also an efficient way for a society to provide for its widowed or otherwise single women. They become cowives, perhaps little begrudging this status in marriage since their only alternative may be living alone, which they may consider undesirable. In rural Iran, one of the authors of this book (Gwynne) visited a family that included an elderly husband and his two wives, sisters who were originally married to two different men. When the husband of the elder died, she became the second wife of her sister's husband. The two women obviously liked each other's company, jointly cooking and serving a meal to their guest, laughing with each other at private jokes, and joining together to tease their husband.

However, polygyny—perhaps especially when not sororal—sometimes creates jealousy among cowives, which not even separate residences can reduce. And in urban settings, polygyny has been cited as a cause of ne-

monogamy the marriage of one husband and one wife

serial monogamy consecutive marriages to a number of different spouses

polygamy a general term that covers both polyandry and polygyny

polygyny marriage between a husband and more than one wife

sororal polygyny the custom in which two or more of a polygynous man's wives are sisters

glect of children because husbands often lack the eco-nomic wherewithal to provide for two or more separate households (see e.g., Coles and Mack 1991:81).

In the United States, polygyny was introduced into the Mormon church in 1843 and became official Mor-mon policy in 1852. Declared illegal under U.S. law in 1887, the practice still survives among some traditional Mormons, despite the fact that the church now excom-municates polygynists. In 1983, Royston Potter, a Mor-mon who was illegally married to three women at once, contended that the law prohibiting plural marriage vio-lated his constitutional right to religious freedom, but a federal judge ruled against him. In a more recent case, the state of Montana decided to turn a blind eye to polygyny, with the result that in tiny Pinesdale, Mon-tana, a man can apparently have as many wives as he wants (*New York Times* 1987:A18).

Polyandry. Much rarer than either monogamy or polygyny is **polyandry,** marriage in which a woman has more than one husband. Like polygyny, polyandry occurs in many places around the world, including Africa and the Americas; but one area in particular—the region around the Himalayas—is famous for polyandry.

Sometimes, the husbands who share a wife are brothers, a form of marriage known as **fraternal**

polyandry. This kind of polyandry accounts for a higher proportion of polyandrous marriages than sororal polyg-yny does for polygynous unions. Cultural materialists claim that fraternal polyandry prevails when it offers some specific advantage to the people involved. In mountainous Tibet, for instance, productive farmland is scarce, yet much of the population depends on farming. If a farmer with a small plot of land and several sons di-vided his land among his sons, none of them would wind up with a plot big enough to support a family (Goldstein 1987). Were the farmer's sons all married to the same woman, however, there would be no need to partition the property into insufficient plots, for the brothers could live and work on it together and pass it along jointly to *their* sons. Also, the number of claimants to the land would be reduced because one woman—even one with several husbands—can produce fewer children in a lifetime than several women can.

Factors other than the scarcity of land (a problem many societies try to handle in other ways) may encour-age polyandry. The Nayar of south India, for example, were professional warriors, which meant that men were often absent from home fighting as mercenaries. Death in battle was a constant risk. Polyandry helped ensure that Nayar descent groups would not become extinct (Gough 1962).

Himalayan societies are famous for polyandry, a form of marriage in which a woman has more than one husband at the same time. Above, a Tibetan wife with her two husbands.

Group Marriage. A fourth, extremely rare, form of marriage involves two or more men and two or more women simultaneously. Anthropologists report this kind of marriage, called **group marriage,** in only a few non-Western cultures, such as the Aweikoma of southern Brazil (Henry 1964). In this society, a marriage might begin with a monogamous or polygynous union. In time, another man or woman or two might be added; meanwhile, some spouses might leave or die. The Aweikoma household was thus a large, flexible unit to which spouses could be added or deleted for a variety of reasons (37).

Other examples of this kind of marriage are the experimental group living arrangements of modern-day North Americans. The "hippie" communes of the 1960s included some arrangements we might term "group marriage," in that sexual and economic bonds existed among two or more women and two or more men simultaneously. Few such arrangements proved long-lasting or particularly rewarding for their participants; many fell apart as tensions developed over responsibilities for the children who were born or the need to earn a living.

The communes of the 1960s were not the original creations of this rebellious period. Similar group "marriages" had existed long before. In the nineteenth century, some fifty idealistic men and women established a commune called the Oneida Community in upstate New York (Farb 1978:406–408). They believed that romantic love between individual males and females would only result in sexual possessiveness and lead to a lack of cooperation among the group's members. So they pledged themselves to one another in a literal group marriage. Unlike their twentieth-century successors, the Oneida Community achieved economic success after its members began producing a line of silverware, which despite the commune's demise is still popular today.

The Oneida commune lasted about thirty years, disbanding when its leader died without leaving an adequately prepared successor, whereupon many members established conventional, monogamous marriages (Farb 1978:408). Despite their avowed commitment to "free love," it seems the commune's members had long ago divided themselves into monogamous pairs.

Other Marriage Customs

The manner in which marriage takes place varies from a complete lack of formality (the bride may simply move in with the groom and the two are henceforth considered married) to a long ritual that unfolds over many days. Most frequently, a marriage is recognized and validated with a modest ceremony, secular or religious, attended by friends and family members.

Unmarried Trobrianders enjoy considerable sexual freedom, as long as they are discreet. A woman enters her lover's house after dark, spends the night with him, and slips out at dawn. When a couple decide to marry, they announce this decision by sitting together on the veranda of the young man's house rather than parting in secret (Weiner 1988:77). Local gossips are quick to note this interesting development, and news of it quickly reaches the girl's mother, who—if she approves—brings the pair a meal of cooked yams. After the couple share this meal, they are officially married.

On the island of Timor, in contrast, the Tetum stage an elaborate ceremony in which as many of the groom's and bride's patrikin as can attend appear at the bride's house, dressed in their best clothes. The bride and groom sit together on a mat woven of dried palm leaves, the same mat they will later sleep on. They hold hands as the bride's mother, acting as priestess for an event of great cosmological, economic, political, legal, and religious significance, prays at length to the ancestral ghosts of both families for the bride's fertility and the compatibility of their respective lineages. She is believed to bring together for their mutual benefit not only the couple, but also their lineages, including the human members and the ancestral ghosts.

Westerners have a variety of wedding ceremonies to choose from. A simple civil wedding in an official's office, attended only by bride, groom, and a few wit-

◆ ASK YOURSELF

How do you feel about communal living arrangements in which sex with anyone is possible? What advantages and disadvantages would be open to the members of such a group? Can you envision yourself as part of such a group?

---

polyandry marriage between a wife and more than one husband

fraternal polyandry the custom whereby two or more of a polyandrous woman's husbands are brothers

group marriage a form of marriage involving two or more men and two or more women as marriage partners at the same time

nesses, suits some couples. Others choose a more elaborate setting and ceremony, often introducing religion as
a central component. In Britain, when a member of the
royal family marries, the event is a state affair, with hundreds of foreign governments represented. But no matter
where a wedding takes place, it is apt to be celebrated
with food, music, and dancing.

We could double the size of this book before exhausting the topic of marriage customs, but we'll address only a few we find particularly interesting.

Bride-capture.   In some societies, even contemporary ones, a man may win his bride by carrying her
off forcibly. Often, however, such **bride-capture
(bride-theft)** is more of a ritual than a literal abduction,
and serves to symbolize social values while cementing
family alliances.

In rural Crete, males should be independent, inno-
vative, aggressive, and smart, while females should be
the passive, chaste objects of male competition. Cretan
bride-theft symbolizes these values (Herzfeld 1985). A
Cretan man who has his heart set on marrying a particular woman asks her father for her hand in marriage, either in person or through agnates acting as his intermediaries. Sometimes the father agrees to the match, on the
condition that the suitor prove himself by a daring act
such as stealing some sheep (28). But the father may
also refuse, perhaps because he feels his daughter is too
young or because he hopes for a better match. If the
suitor is a self-respecting young man, his response to
this refusal is to abduct the woman, often with the help
of his male agnates. The bride may be well aware of,
and not at all opposed to, the impending abduction (23).
Thus she is hardly surprised if, for instance, her suitor
and his crew of brothers and cousins entice her into a car
and drive off with her.

A successful abduction changes the attitude of the
prospective bride's father. "Since the suitor has proved
himself, and has also compromised the bride to the point
where no other self-respecting village male would . . .
make her his bride, his failure to marry her would seriously compromise her natal family" (Herzfeld 1985:29).
The father must now make certain the marriage takes
place, for he can no longer guarantee his daughter's sexual innocence.

Cretans don't worry about the prewedding hostility that the father's initial rejection of the suitor causes
between the families of the groom and bride. They believe that "only those who are worthy of one's rivalry
are also worthy of friendship" (Herzfeld 1985:42). Once

a man has proven his social worth by successfully cap-
turing his bride, the two families resolve their differences (43), converting their enmity, through respect, into
a "cooperative and positively valued relationship" (42).

Ghost Marriage.   In societies with patrilineal
descent groups, the continued existence of these groups
depends on whether or not their male members produce
offspring. Here, marriage and descent come together
very cohesively: marriage provides a man with his wife,
who produces the children who ensure the continued existence of the descent group. The Nuer make sure a
man's name will continue into the next generation
through the custom of **ghost marriage,** which involves
the belief that ghosts are capable of fathering children.
Should a Nuer male die before he has married, his consanguines must find a woman willing to marry his ghost.
After the "wedding," a brother of the dead man sleeps
with the wife, whose future offspring will bear the dead
man's name. If the deceased was already married but his
wife had not yet produced a son, the widow is also expected to sleep with her brother-in-law, and the Nuer assume future offspring were sired by her dead husband's
ghost. If her husband has no brothers or she doesn't have
sex with them, the children of any man she lives with
are considered to be the children of her dead husband
(Evans-Pritchard 1956:163–164).

Levirate and Sororate.   Although not a feature
of American culture, two related marriage customs,
widespread around the world, underscore the importance
of marriage as a way of creating ties between families.
In many societies, when a husband or wife dies and
leaves a spouse behind, the survivor automatically becomes the husband or wife of a sibling of the deceased.
The custom has two different names, depending on
whether a female or male is the survivor. The **levirate** is
the custom whereby a widow marries her dead husband's brother, and the **sororate** is its opposite: a widower marries his dead wife's sister. The original married
couple's two groups of affines continue their affinal relationship. Thus not only does this custom support the un-

◆ **ASK YOURSELF**
*Can you think of additional adaptive advan-
tages of the levirate and sororate? What is your
own feeling about a widower who marries his
dead wife's sister? How about a divorced man
who marries his ex-wife's sister?*

married; the levirate and sororate are also mechanisms through which affinal alliances can be maintained.

DIVORCE

Divorce is not as universal a feature of human culture as marriage, but it is nevertheless legally permissible in most societies (although it may, at the same time, be prohibited by religion). There are as many variations in divorce practices as there are in marriage customs.

Not surprisingly, these variations reflect society's prevailing social, economic, and political priorities. Where descent groups are of paramount importance, for example, divorce is difficult or impossible to obtain. In China, where divorce was traditionally prohibited, one of a wife's functions was to provide children for her husband's patrilineage—too important a duty to permit her to leave him (Freedman 1967, 1970). Where marriage is viewed relatively casually, divorce is a straightforward matter. An Islamic Minangkabau man in western Sumatra may divorce his wife merely by uttering the words "I divorce you" three times. But the Minangkabau view the institution of marriage quite differently from the way Westerners do. After her marriage, a Minangkabau wife continues to reside in the locality where she was born, and her husband continues to live where he was born. The two meet when she brings him lunch while he is cultivating her land (Bachtiar 1967:367), or occasionally in the evenings. Minangkabau wives, by the way, do not enjoy the same right to easy divorce that their husbands do.

The bigger and more technologically sophisticated a society, the weaker its ties of marriage, for several reasons. First, in large-scale societies, especially mobile ones like Western society, individuals continually meet new and interesting people of the opposite sex. Second, people are apt to live longer in technologically advanced societies, and longevity sometimes leads to marital discontent. Third, many of the functions of marriage in such societies are fulfilled by other institutions. A married person's economic support, for example, does not depend on cooperation with a spouse when both spouses earn paychecks outside of their household and can continue to do so even if they part.

The grievances that different societies accept as legal reasons for divorce vary greatly. In the West, adultery is grounds for divorce. In other societies, adultery does not even merit punishment, while in still others, it

is not divorce but death that awaits the adulterer. Among the Sarakatsani, pastoralists of mountainous Greece, the worst thing a wife can do is to have sex with another man. Adultery challenges the authority of her husband, attacks the moral unity of the family, and dishonors it. Adultery is so serious an offense that a husband who spies his wife making love with another man must kill both of them (Campbell 1964:152).

There is a great deal of sexual inequality in this matter worldwide. Surveying 139 societies, Ford and Beach (1951) discovered that in 61 percent, husbands were allowed extramarital affairs though the same licence was prohibited to their wives. But the range of human behavior in this area is very broad indeed. Extramarital sex may be permitted, or even encouraged, for economic or political reasons. Among the Aleuts of the northern Pacific, for example, wife lending was practiced to help men solidify their friendships (Frayser 1985:210).

Beating a spouse, most often a wife, causes many divorces in the West, but it is not a justifiable reason to dissolve a marriage in all societies. Among peasant farmers in Ecuador, wife beating is accepted as marriage's normal accompaniment. Parents transfer farmland, scarce in this mountainous country, to their daughters at marriage, but men must wait until both their parents die to inherit farmland. As a result, a wife's inherited land is the only real property a newly married couple has. But Ecuadorians consider men superior to women and insist that they dominate (McKee 1992:150–151). Men begin marriage as economic inferiors because of their wives' ownership of land, which inevitably creates tension between them. If a husband feels

 ASK YOURSELF

Can you think of other functions of marriage, as it is understood in the West, that make it particularly adaptive within the context of Western society?

bride-capture (bride-theft) the forcible and frequently symbolic carrying off of a bride

ghost marriage the custom in which the ghost of a man who has died "marries" and is considered able to father a child

levirate the custom in which a widow marries her dead husband's brother

sororate the custom in which a widower marries his dead wife's sister

that other villagers view him as a "loser," especially in economic matters, he may take out his frustrations on his wife to prove his manhood and publicly demonstrate his superiority. Provided it is not too extreme, his behavior is condoned by others since the "potential for abuse and wife-beating is built into the . . . cultural system . . ." (151).

◆◆◆

CONCLUSION

We mentioned that marriage is virtually universal (although in a few societies, it is so easily entered into and gotten out of that one could argue against the use of the term *marriage* as we have defined it). What might account for this near universality? One answer is that marriage effectively satisfies so many human needs. It provides a way to house and feed people; it efficiently divides up their labor and property; it fulfills their need for sex, companionship, and love; it helps to prevent sexual jealousy and conflicts; it forges alliances between groups; it nurtures and educates children.

Yet we have pointed out that in many societies there are other institutions, in addition to marriage, that perform these same functions. To use Western society as an example, people can be housed and fed in college dormitories, hotels, prisons, or homeless shelters; their labor is regulated by laws and by supply and demand within a free-market system; property can be allotted by gift giving, inheritance, and taxation; children can be reared by extended kin or in orphanages and educated in schools; and sex can take place as easily outside of marriage as within it. The fact that so many other arrangements can accomplish what marriage accomplishes brings us right back to the original question: why the near universality of marriage? A cultural-materialist approach is perhaps helpful here: marriage is universal not because the functions it performs are unique but because it most efficiently satisfies the most human needs.

◆◆◆

SUMMARY

Marriage, a virtually universal institution, is a socially sanctioned contract, usually between one man and one woman. It typically establishes new nuclear families, specifies the reciprocal rights and responsibilities of married pairs, creates alliances between their families by involving their relatives in social, economic, political, and ritual relationships, and sometimes allocates goods and services among the couple and their affines through bridewealth, bride-service, or dowry.

All societies regulate sex and marriage, some by creating rules that require or encourage certain unions (preferred marriages), some by creating rules that forbid certain matches (prohibited marriages). Preferred marriages are of several different kinds. Arranged marriages (which may or may not be preferred marriages) are found in societies in which the rights and duties that bind affines are so crucial that marriage cannot be left to romantic choice. Marriage partners are often chosen by senior persons in a couple's families.

For many societies, no category of relative is preferred, and the choice of spouse is left to such factors as race, religion, or social status. In most cases, this offers an individual considerable freedom of choice. Nevertheless, no society completely lacks marriage rules since even the most permissive societies incorporate a taboo against incestuous relationships. Which sexual relationships are considered incestuous, however, varies. In some societies, sex or marriage with a biological first cousin is considered incestuous and is forbidden, whereas in others, sex and marriage with a first cousin are encouraged. For certain people in some societies, even the incest taboo is ignored for religious and economic reasons. A number of explanations have been put forward to explain the alleged universality of the incest taboo: the genetic, social, instinct, psychoanalytic, confusion, and cooperation explanations.

Marriage to one spouse at a time is called monogamy, and being married simultaneously to two or more partners is called polygamy. A woman's marriage to more than one man at the same time is called polyandry, and a man's marriage to more than one woman at the same time is called polygyny. The most common types of marriage are monogamy and polygyny. Polyandry and group marriage, in which multiple men and multiple women are married to one another, are much rarer. Other marriage customs include bride-capture, ghost marriage, the levirate and sororate, and a wide range of wedding customs.

Divorce is not as universal a feature of human culture as marriage but is nevertheless permissible in most societies. However, there are as many variations in divorce as there are in marriage customs. These variations reflect social, economic, and political factors.

◆◆◆

KEY TERMS

affinal alliance
affines
affinity

bilateral exchange
bride-capture (bride-theft)
bride-service
bridewealth (bride-price)
confusion explanation
cooperation explanation
dowry
endogamy
genetic explanation
ghost marriage
group marriage
incest taboo
instinct explanation
levirate
marriage
matrilateral cross cousin marriage
matrilateral parallel cousin marriage
monogamy
parallel cousin marriage
patrilateral cross cousin marriage
patrilateral parallel cousin marriage
polyandry
polygamy
polygyny
psychoanalytic explanation
romantic love
serial monogamy
social explanation
sororal polygyny
sororate

SUGGESTED READINGS

Fox, Robin. 1983. *Kinship and Marriage.* New York: Viking Penguin. An excellent guide to the main systems of descent and marriage, written from an ecological/cultural materialist perspective.

Goody, Jack, and S. J. Tambiah. 1973. *Bridewealth and Dowry.* Cambridge: Cambridge University Press. An informative discussion of bridewealth; dowry; and more broadly, property rights in Africa, Eurasia, and South Asia.

Needham, Rodney (ed.). 1971. *Rethinking Kinship and Marriage.* ASA Monographs 11. London: Tavistock Publications. Eleven articles on fundamental aspects of descent and marriage by various anthropologists. Needham's own two contributions are the best summaries of kinship and marriage, and of their histories, that have yet been published.

Spain, David H. 1987. The Westermarck-Freud Incest-Theory Debate: An Evaluation and Reformulation. *Current Anthropologist* 28(5):623–645. An attempt to combine the instinct and psychoanalytic explanations of incest, with commentaries by several anthropologists.

CHAPTER 8

Overt expressions of sexuality are repressed in some cultures, encouraged in others. In the Ukraine, where "kiss-a-girl" is played in traditional Ukranian costume during festivals, a young man makes his move in mid-gallop.

INTRODUCTION

In 1953, many Americans were shocked when an ex-Marine named George Jorgensen announced publicly that he had just undergone surgery that had changed him from a man into a woman (Masters, Johnson, and Kolodny 1985:285–287). At Jorgensen's own request, Danish doctors had removed his external sex organs and had surgically created artificial female genitalia in their

place. Synthetic hormones had already begun to stimulate growth of the patient's breasts and decrease muscu-
larity. Photographed in a dress, nylons, and a blonde wig
to launch a new career as a nightclub performer, Jorgensen announced that hereafter he—now she—would
be known as Christine.

The real marvel of Jorgensen's transformation
from man to woman was the sophistication of the new
surgical and hormonal techniques that had allowed doctors to perform this successful sex change, but in the
newspapers of the day, medical achievement took a back
seat to sensationalism. Besides the details of the surgery
itself, what fascinated most Americans about the case

was that a man would want to become a woman in the
first place. Jorgensen claimed, to general amazement,
that despite his external appearance he had never felt
comfortable in a man's body. Even as a child, he was
sure he had been destined to be a woman.

Jorgensen was a **transsexual,** the term for individuals who decide to adopt the social position of the sex
opposite to their anatomical one, whether or not they
have had sex change surgery. (The term is often used in-
correctly to mean a person who has both male and female physical characteristics; the correct term for such
an individual is **hermaphrodite.**) Although the Jorgensen case astounded and titillated many conservative
Americans, transsexuals—as we shall see later in this
chapter—are often readily accepted, even revered, in
other cultures.

We begin this chapter from the premise that the
human desire for sexual activity is innate and universal.
That said, however, we must add two qualifications.
First, cross-cultural data on human sexual attitudes and
practices, compared to other kinds of anthropological
data, are quite rare and sometimes unreliable because
ethnographers have often brought their own sexual reticence or biases with them into the field. Second, peoples' attitudes toward sexuality, sexual statuses, or sex
practices are not at all uniform. Even though the desire
for sexual activity is a matter of biology, the way that
desire is expressed varies according to culture.

To maintain social order, every society has developed rules by which peoples' desire for sex is directed
and controlled. But these rules vary widely. In determining which individuals make acceptable sex partners and
which do not, for example, one's choice is almost unlimited in some societies, whereas in others (as you learned
in Chapter 7) there are very specific rules—so specific
that a woman might well be limited in her choice of a
husband to a cousin on her father's side of the family.
Sexual intercourse between males and females is recognized as necessary for creating new life in almost all societies (a few, as we'll see, have prohibited even this expression of sexuality), but in some societies, sex for
other purposes is frowned on or even feared. Homosexuality is discouraged for some, whereas in others, it is actively encouraged.

Interestingly, societies that tend to be the most liberal in matters of sex are not modern, industrialized,
Western societies like our own but small-scale, technologically simple ones. In this chapter, we survey the diverse ways in which people in different cultures express
their sexuality.

*Transsexuals—people who adopt the social position of the sex
opposite to their anatomical one—are readily accepted in
some cultures and viewed as oddities in others. Transsexual
George Jorgensen underwent sex change surgery and became
Christine Jorgensen, above.*

SEX VERSUS GENDER

From the point of view of social analysis, the difference between males and females is the most fundamental of all distinctions between people (age differences, which we discuss in Chapter 11, run a close second). In every society, ideas and expectations about the differences between the sexes form the basis of standards around which much of social life is organized. However, the male-female dichotomy is not clear-cut. "Maleness" and "femaleness," as well as the behaviors that are supposedly "male" or "female," are qualities and expectations largely determined by culture rather than by biology. Anthropologists have therefore found it useful when analyzing sexual behavior cross-culturally to distinguish between the *biological* aspects of human sexuality (all those aspects that are chromosomally determined) and its *cultural* aspects (all those aspects that are culturally determined).

The terms *sex* and *gender* are frequently used to make the distinction. There is as yet no consensus among anthropologists regarding the precise meanings of these terms (Gilmore and Gwynne 1985:3), but the word **sex** usually refers to the biological category into which a person is born—male or female. Sex is dictated by chromosomal and anatomical characteristics and is usually permanent. The term **gender** refers to the learned aspects of sexuality and includes sexual orientation (as revealed by one's choice of a sex partner) and sex roles (the behaviors associated, in a given society, with females or males). Culture seems to be even more important than biological differences in determining the sex roles people play. A person's **gender identity**—his or her self-identification as male or female—does not necessarily coincide with his or her sex as defined by anatomy (Money and Ehrhardt 1977).

Most societies classify infants as either male or female at birth, and assign social roles accordingly. Learning to identify oneself as a member of a particular sex and to behave in a manner appropriate to that sex is part of enculturation, and it begins almost immediately. In North America, for instance, gender identification begins the first time a baby boy's father tussles with him gently and addresses him as "tough guy." Observing how his parents behave is perhaps the most important way he learns gender identity. He watches his father to see what he should do to be male, and he observes his mother to see what he must *not* do to be male. The opposite, of course, is true for girls.

The most critical period in determining gender identity is from 18 months to 3 or 4 years. If gender is to be reassigned after this period, the psychological development of the child may be hampered, and after the onset of puberty gender identity is too well established in most human beings to be changed (Money and Ehrhardt 1977:4, 179).

Feminist anthropologist Carol Gilligan (1982) suggests that middle-class American girls are enculturated differently from boys. While girls are urged to maintain ties with their families (particularly their mothers), boys are encouraged to sever these ties. The values of American females thus include social continuity, whereas those of males include independence and aggressiveness. Male values, Gilligan asserts, have long predominated over female ones in America, but as women's power grows, their values—"a different voice"—will have an increasing impact.

However, there's a flaw in this rosy picture of a society becoming "kinder and gentler" by the infusion of feminine values, for women are no less contentious than men when they obtain power in business, politics, or academia. Former political leaders Margaret Thatcher, Golda Meier, and Indira Ghandi neither rose to power nor retained it by insisting on peaceful continuity and refusing to antagonize anyone. If women are really constrained by the desire to keep everyone happy, as Gilligan (1982) supposes, the feminist movement would never have gotten off the ground.

◆ ASK YOURSELF

Among your acquaintances, does a female who displays characteristics usually associated with males encounter disapproval? How about a male who acts like a female? If you answered yes, which sex do you think meets with more disapproval?

transsexual an individual who adopts the social role of the sex opposite to his or her anatomical one

hermaphrodite an individual who has both male and female physical characteristics

sex the biological category into which a person is born, male or female, as determined by chromosomal and anatomical characteristics

gender learned maleness or femaleness, as reflected in "sexual orientation" and sex roles

gender identity an individual's self-identification as male or female

Learning to play the social role associated with one's sex begins early in life. Imitating his father helps an American boy establish his gender identity, his self-identification as a male.

Still, there is some cross-cultural support for the general notion that cultures associate females with social continuity and males with discontinuity. Nancy Chodorow (1974) has shown that in some societies, boys must reject feminine qualities and identification with their mothers to become men. Among the Shavante of Brazil, for example, boys must leave their homes and reside in a special house, where they are taught behavior appropriate to males in their society. Girls, in contrast, continue their early relationship with their mothers as they become women. In his fieldwork among the Tetum, David Hicks discovered that Tetum females were associated with the idea of bringing two parties together, while men were associated with separating them. A woman assumes the role of priest at a wedding, when wife-givers and wife-takers come together. At a death ritual, a man, by drawing his sword, performs the task of driving the soul of the deceased from the community of the living.

◆ ASK YOURSELF

In January 1993, more women entered the U.S. Congress than ever before. In your opinion, will these women be guided by distinctive "feminine" values as they grapple with difficult political decisions and seek to increase their influence as individual politicians? If so, do you expect this to change anything about the way the country is run?

ATTITUDES TOWARD SEXUAL EXPRESSION

Negative versus Positive Attitudes

Although the sex drive is universal, not every society views it as a positive contribution to social life. In some groups, such as the religious society called the Shakers, sex is viewed as negative or even evil, and every effort is made to suppress it. In Western society and many others, sex is considered a positive aspect of life under some circumstances (for instance, when viewed as an expression of love between a wife and husband) and a negative one in others (for instance, when it transfers a venereal disease from one person to another).

A few ethnographic examples will give you some idea of the wide range of cross-cultural attitudes toward sex.[1] The Thonga of Africa believe that sexual activity can adversely affect both nature and humans. Some people, particularly married couples, are considered sexually "hot," and hence dangerous. By having sex too often, "hot" people are likely to upset the fragile balance

---

[1]For many of the examples in this chapter, we rely on Suzanne Frayser's useful book *Varieties of Sexual Experience: An Anthropological Perspective on Human Sexuality* (New Haven, CT: HRAF Press, 1985).

The Shakers

In England, in the mid-eighteenth century, a small group of Quakers left their church to form the United Society of Believers in Christ's Second Coming. During their worship, they would sing, dance, and tremble as they felt themselves filled with spiritual power, so they became known as Shakers. Two of the Shakers' most important principles, both arising from the belief that sex is evil and corrupting, were to avoid sexual relationships and marriage.

Following their leader, "Mother Ann" Lee, whom the Shakers believed embodied the female aspects of God as Christ had embodied the male, the Shakers emigrated in 1774 from England to upstate New York (Henretta et al. 1987:296, 381–382). Here they established a number of economically successful colonies, supported by agriculture and crafts and dedicated not only to avoiding sex and marriage but also to promoting pacifism, the communal ownership of property, seclusion from the outside world, sexual equality, and abstinence from liquor and tobacco. By the early nineteenth century, they had recruited some six thousand members.

Because they abstained completely from sexual relations, the Shakers, of course, produced no successors, relying instead on converts to replace members who had died. But as time passed, and fewer and fewer people agreed that sex was ungodly and could

The Shakers, who numbered in the thousands early in the nineteenth century, abstained from sex, believing it to be evil. Because they produced no successors, the sect virtually disappeared. A nineteenth-century lithograph shows Shakers performing the dance which gave them their name.

be dispensed with, the Shakers gradually declined in numbers. By 1948 fewer than fifty remained. Since then, the sect has all but disappeared.

of nature and injure people who are elderly or sick (Frayser 1985:1). In former times, the Bella Coola of the Pacific Northwest believed that sex weakened people and should therefore be avoided by those wishing to be successful at enterprises like hunting. Bella Coola men refrained from sex for four days before a hunt. In Uttar Pradesh, India, some people believe that sex should be reserved for reproduction only, not for pleasure. The Manus of New Guinea, like the Shakers, consider sexual intercourse to be evil and shameful (1–2).

Until relatively recently, sex outside of marriage in mainstream Western society was severely disapproved of (Stansell 1987; D'Emilio and Freedman 1988). Most Christian churches regarded extramarital sex as immoral; but an even more powerful reason for the long-lasting prohibition against it was probably the

disastrous social and economic consequences of unwed motherhood (Stansell 1987). In the course of only a few decades, however, public attitudes toward sexual activity changed so radically that the change has been termed a *sexual revolution*. Varieties of sexual behavior once considered immoral or even criminal came to be tolerated or even viewed as normal.

This dramatic change actually began well over half a century ago, in the 1920s, when young, middle-class Americans began to dance to a new, black-inspired kind of music called jazz, watch Hollywood sex sirens perform in the movies, read the widely publicized works of sexual theorists such as Sigmund Freud and Havelock Ellis, and "scoff . . . at the sexual prudery" of earlier years (D'Emilio and Freedman 1988:241). World War II, during which huge numbers of American women

Sex and Football

People in many societies in addition to the Bella Coola believe that sex can strip individuals, especially men, of their vitality. They consequently limit sexual activity before tasks requiring skill, strength, or energy. Consider the findings of anthropologist William Arens, who as a college student traveled by chartered bus to a football game with his university's team. Two of the players, noticing that there were some unoccupied seats, asked the coach if their girlfriends could ride to the game with them. Absolutely not, the coach responded—but it would be all right if the girls joined their boyfriends for the ride *home* from the game.

Years later, interested in the cross-cultural analysis of symbolic behavior, Arens (1981) recalled this bus ride while studying the customs of professional football players in the United States. At training camps, football players are often strictly isolated from women. Even married players must live on the camp grounds, apart from their wives, and may visit them only if there is no game or practice the following day. Professional football games are often played on Sundays, and players routinely spend Saturday nights in the company of one another rather than their wives. This custom defies the scientific finding that sexual activity before physical exertion can be beneficial to the extent that it promotes relaxation. But it demonstrates that some Westerners, too, believe that sex strips a man of his strength.

took factory jobs once held by men who had been drafted into the armed services, liberated both men and women from traditional social expectations (Margolis 1984). Then, in the early 1960s, the introduction of "the pill" provided additional leverage for changing America's attitude toward sex. Women in particular, freed from the threat of unwanted pregnancy, now had even greater opportunities to enjoy their sexuality. Their increasing sexual liberation was closely intertwined with the feminist movement of the late 1960s and 1970s. Since they now paid no more of a penalty than men for sexual activity, they began to be viewed as equal to men, not only in the sexual arena but in other respects as well.

Then, beginning in the early 1980s, AIDS (acquired immune deficiency syndrome) began to exert a profound effect on sexual behavior, at least wherever the causes and consequences of this disease were understood. In the West (as elsewhere), other sexually transmitted diseases (**STDs**), such as gonorrhea and syphilis, had been common, sometimes epidemic, for years. Their existence no doubt had had some moderating effect on sexual behavior, but these diseases were either curable or controllable, which diminished their impact on behavior. AIDS, however, is always fatal, and as its incidence increased dramatically through the 1980s and into the 1990s, sexual behavior changed accordingly (D'Emilio and Freedman 1988:357). Although AIDS did not curtail Westerners' generally appreciative, open attitude toward sexuality, it did affect the amount and kind of sexual activity in which people engaged. In other words, AIDS slowed the pace of the sexual revolution. It remains to be seen whether a medical victory over this disease will result in a return to the unbridled sexual activity of the 1970s.

Despite AIDS and other STDs, most members of modern, industrialized Western societies view sexual relations as desirable. They have sex for pleasure as well as procreation, and they consider this activity to be both enjoyable and healthy. In North America, sex for pleasure and for physical and mental well-being is viewed as so desirable that advertisers of products from cars to household cleansers continually promote their wares by associating them with sexually attractive individuals. In response, Americans lavish millions of dollars a year to increase their sex appeal by buying these products.

Children and Sexual Expression

Scientific evidence long ago proved that children are capable of virtually every type of sexual expression found in adults, including erections and orgasms (Ford and Beach 1951:197; Masters, Johnson, and Kolodny 1985:200). Cross-culturally, however, there is as much variety in people's attitudes toward sexual activity among children as toward adult sexuality. These attitudes range all the way from outright denial of child-

Most modern, Western societies view sex as healthy and enjoyable. Advertisers capitalize on this view by associating products—in this case, men's cologne—with sexual attractiveness and pleasure.

hood sexuality to prohibition to condemnation to disinterest, amusement, pride, or even encouragement (see Masters, Johnson, and Kolodny 1985:623).

A few cultures do not accept the view that children have sexual urges (Ford and Beach 1951:180), an attitude that was to a great extent true of Western society until Sigmund Freud's research suggested otherwise. In other societies, children's sexuality is acknowledged but repressed. The Kwoma of New Guinea punish boys so severely for masturbating that they learn not to touch their genitals even while urinating. In most of these restrictive societies, adults maintain a conspiracy of silence about sex while children are present, and children are not allowed to see adults indulging in sex. As in Western society, they may be told fanciful tales about where babies come from, and as a result may remain ignorant of the many culturally determined aspects of sex

until they are married, although there is no evidence to suggest that the normal biological urges of these children are actually repressed (183).

In other societies, childhood sexuality is not only acknowledged but also actively encouraged. The Trobriand and Alorese Islanders, introduced in earlier chapters, allow their children to masturbate freely and to engage in sex play with other children. And in a few other societies, adults not only encourage childhood sexuality but actually participate in it. Parents among the Hopi and the Siriono of Bolivia, for instance, fondle their children sexually (Ford and Beach 1951:188), although some say they are merely soothing them (Masters, Johnson, and Kolodny 1985:632). Societies with liberal attitudes toward childhood sexual activity are apt to be the same ones in which children are permitted to observe adults engaging in sex. Alorese children, for instance, are familiar with all of the details of adult sexual intercourse by the time they are five years old (Ford and Beach 1951:189).

We can view these very restrictive and very permissive societies as representing polar extremes regarding attitudes toward children and sex. Most societies lie between these two poles.

Premarital, Extramarital, and Postmarital Sex

Some societies forbid all premarital sex but many more either permit or encourage it. In fact, the idea that young people should not have sex before marriage is quite unusual, cross-culturally. Western society is one of only a few in which premarital sexual activity short of intercourse is common among the unmarried as a way of preserving virginity and/or avoiding pregnancy (Masters, Johnson, and Kolodny 1985:627). Out of a sample of 863 societies studied by George Murdock (1957), 67 percent placed few or no restrictions on premarital sex; 75 percent of these liberal societies are in the South Pacific. The region of the world in which premarital sex is

◆ ASK YOURSELF

Can you think of any reasons why members of a society would want to prevent young children from learning about sex? If you become a parent, how will you handle this subject with your children?

STD sexually transmitted disease

most repressed is the Mediterranean, where 59 percent of all societies disapprove of sex before marriage.

Trobriand society is one of many that do not regard premarital sex as either evil or shameful but rather as a necessary step in preparing for marriage. From puberty onward, Trobriand girls and boys, whose childhood sex play was unrestricted, are instructed in adult sexual behavior and are given plenty of opportunity to practice what they have been taught (Malinowski 1962:109). If an unmarried Trobriand girl should become pregnant, her relatives regard this as proof of her fertility and therefore marriageability, and when her baby is born they take it under their roof.

In contrast, there are various societies around the Mediterranean where girls must remain virgins until they marry or else suffer public shame and greatly reduced chances of marriage. Since marriage is the "overriding criterion for a fulfilling life" for females in this region (Brandes 1985:113), parents vigorously protect the chastity of their unmarried daughters. In the town of Monteros, Spain, for instance, the "main prerequisite to marriage for women . . . is virginity" (118). Since potential husbands believe that premarital sex for females (but not for males) is somehow defiling, an unmarried woman's chances of marrying are much reduced if she loses her virginity, but a virtuous daughter can readily find a husband. Parents in Monteros tell their daughters, "Good linen, preserved in a trunk, can readily be sold" (118).

Two ideas about premarital sex are encountered worldwide, although by no means universally. The first, called the **double standard,** is the notion that the rules governing sexual behavior should be different for males and females living in the same society. Of a sample of 61 societies compared by Frayser (1985:203), 18 percent sanctioned premarital sexual activity for males but not for females. In contrast, not a single society permitted females to engage in premarital sex while forbidding the same behavior to males. Cross-culturally, then, the double standard is strongly biased in favor of male premarital sex. Frayser adds, however, that in 82 percent of the societies she sampled, no double standard exists. In these societies, members of both sexes must either avoid premarital sex, or else both males and females are allowed to indulge themselves.

The second idea, encountered in many societies in which premarital sex is permitted, is that the females involved must not become pregnant (Frayser 1985:204). Premarital sex is permissible for enjoyment but not for reproduction. Sexual relationships are, in other words, classified as physical rather than social. One might assume that this restriction would characterize modern societies with access to reliable birth control methods, but it applies in many nonindustrial societies as well. Typically, if a girl becomes pregnant her baby must be destroyed, either by abortion or infanticide. Alternatively, by marrying its father the girl may be permitted to transform a physical relationship between two individuals into the social relationship of marriage.

◆ ASK YOURSELF

What is your personal feeling about premarital sex? Does knowing that in many societies premarital sex is encouraged modify your attitude at all?

A Royal Virgin

Today, people in modern, industrialized Western societies seem fairly relaxed about premarital sex as long as couples use adequate safeguards against pregnancy and disease. For most people, sex is considered a private concern rather than a public matter. However, the attitude that it is improper for an unmarried person, especially a female, to engage in sex still has its supporters.

Shortly before she married England's Prince Charles in 1981, the future bride, Lady Diana Spencer, was examined by the royal physician to make sure she was a virgin. The result was affirmative, and the happy tidings were publicly announced on radio and television. As some wit remarked at the time, Diana was a most appropriate match for the future King of England: she was a girl with a *history* (her family's genealogy was long and distinguished) but no *past*.

Premarital Sex among the Maasai

In Kenya, unmarried Maasai men live in cattle camps called kraals. Here they have sexual relationships, not expected to lead to marriage, with young Maasai women. Above, Maasai youths and their girlfriends clasp hands.

After rituals marking the end of boyhood, young males of East Africa's Maasai tribe leave the villages where they were born and go to live in remote camps (*kraals*). For the next ten or fifteen years, which a young man spends as a warrior, the kraal is his home. Older warriors teach him how to fight and to raid other tribes' herds of cattle. The warriors cannot marry, but they are permitted to have sex with young women who live with them in the kraal. Such liaisons are not expected to lead to marriage. A girl who gets pregnant returns to her village, where she marries. She is not stigmatized for having had premarital sex, nor for having become pregnant, for the Maasai welcome children; moreover, at one time or another nearly all Maasai females sleep with the warriors in the kraal. When his period as a warrior comes to an end, a man returns to his village, marries, and assumes the rights and duties of a husband and father (Saibull 1981; Saitoti 1988).

In no society does marriage always satisfy every human sexual urge; everywhere, incompatibility, illness, or absence are sometimes inevitable (Masters, Johnson, and Kolodny 1985:634). Extramarital sex (or adultery), meaning sexual relationships involving at least one person who is married but not to the current sex partner, is understandably quite common cross-culturally, and is by no means universally condemned. Indeed, the number of societies that condone extramarital sex, usually under specific circumstances, is relatively high; in one study of 139 societies, 39 percent permitted or approved of adultery (Ford and Beach 1951:113). Among the Toda of India, for example, both married men and married women are allowed to have extramarital relationships, and the language of these people does not include a word for adultery.

In some societies in which extramarital sex is permitted, one's choice of partner is limited—typically to a brother or sister of one's husband or wife. The Siriono of Bolivia, for example, allow a husband to have extramarital sex with his wife's sisters or his brothers' wives or even these women's sisters (Ford and Beach 1951:114) but not with women outside of these categories.

double standard the notion that within a single society the rules governing sexual behavior should be different for males and females

Since human behavior varies so much, you won't be surprised to learn that there are also many societies that either frown on or forbid extramarital sex, more commonly for women than for men. In the study of 139 societies just cited, 61 percent forbid married women to have sex with men other than their husbands (Ford and Beach 1951:115). Far fewer societies restrict married men in this way (the double standard again). But even in societies in which married men are free to have sex with women other than their wives, these relationships may be hard to come by because married or not all males are competing for the same women. Therefore, although in theory a double standard exists, in actual practice it may be somewhat unusual for a man to be able to "take advantage of his theoretical liberties" (115).

In North American society, extramarital sex is common. Over forty years ago, the famous Kinsey report (Kinsey, Pomeroy, and Martin 1948: 589) revealed that between 27 and 37 percent of American husbands admitted having had one or more extramarital affairs. Since this behavior was (and still is) strongly condemned in our society, Kinsey believed that the proportion was actually somewhat higher. Because of the double standard, American women may be even more reluctant than American men to admit their extramarital relationships despite their recent sexual liberation. This may account for widely differing estimates, since the Kinsey report, of the proportion of wives who have had extramarital relationships—anywhere from 21 to almost 70 percent (397).

Few anthropologists have devoted themselves to studying postmarital sex—sexual activity among people who are widowed or divorced but have not remarried (Masters, Johnson, and Kolodny 1985:634). One reason may be that there is relatively little postmarital sex to study. In many societies, a widowed or divorced person is expected to remarry immediately, often (in societies in which more than one spouse is permitted) to the husband or wife of a sibling (you'll recognize this custom from Chapter 7 as the levirate or sororate, depending on the sex of the widowed or divorced person), or cousin. In other societies, bereaved spouses, especially widows, are forbidden to engage in postmarital sex or to remarry. In a few societies widows' lives are considered to be over, either figuratively or literally.

In modern Western culture, it is assumed that people who have once been married, particularly relatively young people, will continue to have sexual relations, and there is general tolerance of postmarital sexual activity (Masters, Johnson, and Kolodny 1985:635). Even though there is little stigma attached either to remaining single after having been married or to having postmarital sexual relations, most divorced or widowed people in our society eventually remarry.

◆◆◆

A Hindu Sati

India Seizes Four after Immolation
—*New York Times,* September 20, 1987

Some Indian Hindus once thought a woman whose husband died should die as well, by throwing herself onto the funeral bonfire in which the body of her husband was being cremated. Such self-sacrifice, they believed, would guarantee a heavenly reunion for the couple. The practice was outlawed in 1829, but customs are often slow to change, and this one, called *sati,* is still practiced occasionally in rural India.

Recently, in a small village in northwestern India, Maal Singh, a married man of only 24, died of gastroenteritis (*New York Times* 1987:A15). At his cremation, his young widow, Roop Kunwar, 18, either voluntarily placed herself on her husband's bonfire or was forced to do so by her father-in-law and other relatives. She burned to death. Shortly thereafter, Roop's father-in-law and 15-year-old brother-in-law were arrested on charges of murder and abetting a suicide.

The death of Roop Kunwar unleashed the fury of Indian feminists, who felt that the young woman's dreadful death symbolized the ongoing subjugation of Indian women. But devout Hindus by the thousands came to worship at the place where Roop Kunwar died, showing that even today there is widespread respect for a Hindu woman who loses her life in the name of love.

In some societies, widows are expected to wear black clothes and are forbidden to remarry or engage in postmarital sex. Widows in Osijek, Yugoslavia, mourn the deaths of their Croatian husbands, victims of civil war.

SEXUAL STATUSES

Is There a Gender Hierarchy?

Generally speaking, throughout Western history men have enjoyed more privileges, greater respect, and higher social status than women (Lerner 1986). The same is true in many other societies as well. As we mentioned in Chapter 6, societies in which men dominate are termed *patriarchies*. Recently, feminist anthropologists have introduced a new concept, **gender hierarchy,** into the ongoing discussion about patriarchy. The term "refers to the association of what is culturally considered to be 'maleness,' though not necessarily men only, with social power" (Gailey 1987:x). In a gender hierarchy, in other words, there is a difference in status between "maleness" and "femaleness" rather than between specific males and females. Virtually always, maleness is more highly valued.

The concept of gender hierarchy may help us to understand how strong female leaders can be present in societies in which men are generally dominant. Among the Lovedu of Africa, women traditionally served as chiefs (Friedl 1985:228), and it could hardly be said that former British Prime Minister Margaret Thatcher, "the Iron Lady," did not command respect. Yet modern feminists point out that even in Lovedu and British societies, women are, in general, dominated by men.

Late twentieth-century women have shown that there are few activities, beyond biologically determined ones such as breast-feeding, that can be carried out by members of one sex only; yet in most societies men occupy the most important places in public life (if not in the household arena). One cultural-materialist explanation might be that the sex that controls the production and distribution of most of a society's material goods will dominate. Men everywhere tend to control their societies' material wealth, and this seems to determine the relative statuses of men and women and their different roles (Friedl 1984, 1985). But instead of explaining why so many societies consider men superior to women, this observation simply prompts another question. Why is it that men rather than women so often control the production and distribution of a society's material wealth? The answer may lie in the way jobs have historically been assigned according to sex.

The Sexual Division of Labor

As you saw in Chapter 5, the more technologically simple a society, the more likely it is that jobs will be allocated according to sex. In gathering-and-hunting societies, for instance, males and females have very distinct roles which seldom overlap. Having collected a great deal of data from nonindustrialized societies, anthropol-

gender hierarchy a ranking of cultural notions of maleness and femaleness, as opposed to a ranking of individual males and females

••

The Public and Private Domains and Women's Status

Feminist anthropologists disagree about the causes of women's subordination to men (Mukhopadhyay and Higgins 1988). Some suggest that it stems from the contrast they believe exists between two worlds, or domains, within which individuals live—the domestic (or private or household) domain and the public domain. Activity in the **public domain** conveys more status and authority than activity in the **domestic domain.** In many societies, women's activities center about the domestic domain, and men are more active in the public domain.

The notion of two separate spheres of activity helps to put women's relative social status into perspective, and can be linked to other cultural variables, such as subsistence strategies, descent systems, and residence patterns, to form a broader, more holistic

view of cultures. In some horticultural societies, for example, women do much of the actual work of gardening; that is, they play relatively important economic roles outside (as well as inside) of their homes. In these societies, women's status tends to be relatively high. Not surprisingly, in some of these societies descent is matrilineal and residence is matrilocal, both good indicators of women's relatively high status. In most agricultural societies, in contrast, the public domain is dominated by men because harnessing big farm animals to plows and digging irrigation channels is heavy work and is performed mainly by men. Women tend to be more confined to the domestic domain. These societies are often characterized by relatively low status for women and by patriliny and patrilocality.

ogists now generally agree that biological differences between the sexes are the starting point for the rather rigid division of tasks observed in most societies, especially in nonindustrialized settings.[2]

In a cross-cultural study of the division of labor that included 186 societies, Murdock and Provost (1973) discovered that 14 subsistence activities were exclusively allocated to men in all of the societies. These jobs included hunting, mining, boat building, metalworking, and lumbering. Nine other occupations were allocated to men in most of the societies but in some were assigned predominantly or even exclusively to women. These included tilling fields, house building, the care and butchering of large domestic animals, fishing, and rope making. In all 185 societies, there were *no* subsistence activities assigned exclusively to women, and only 9—including collecting fuel and water, gathering vegetable foods, cooking, spinning, and laundering—that were

usually allocated to women. The 50 remaining occupations—including planting and harvesting crops, milking animals, preserving meat and fish, making clothing and leather goods, basket weaving, and pottery making—were performed in some societies by men, by women, or by members of either sex.

Why do societies commonly associate certain jobs with males? Our partial list suggests that "male" jobs are those that require a greater degree of physical strength, endurance, and concentration, involve risk, and are performed publicly. Many women have endurance, muscles, and concentration and are not opposed to taking risks or working in public. But only females can perform one important subsistence activity: nursing infants (White et al. 1975; Burton, Brudner, and White 1977). In nonindustrialized societies, women *must* take the major responsibility for the care of small children, a time-consuming job that if well done strictly limits the type and number of other tasks they can undertake at the same time. This duty eliminates any job that requires intense concentration (such as hunting), for baby-sitters cannot turn their backs on young children, even for a moment. Jobs that would expose children in the care of the workers to physical danger, such as metalworking, must also be avoided.

So women are not often assigned jobs that involve

---

[2]Earlier we pointed out that many basic human behaviors were established during the long period of time in which our ancestors were gatherers and hunters or simple agriculturalists. Thus, studying the division of labor in non-industrialized societies is important for our understanding of contemporary Western society. The assumption that non-industrialized people can shed light on our present situation is common in anthropology.

In many societies, there is a clear distinction between women's and men's jobs. Weaving is a common task for women all over the world. Near Quetzeltenango in the highlands of Guatemala, a Maya woman works at a hand loom.

intense concentration or danger, or for that matter, long-distance travel, sharp tools, potentially dangerous animals, and so on. Instead, women are assigned jobs that are consistent with looking after young children, and, as our list shows, these tend *not* to be the jobs in which the resources or products of society are controlled or distributed. Thus women generally do not have access to the power that controlling and distributing resources conveys.

Supporters of this cultural-materialist hypothesis further assume that societies, like individuals, are efficient and that they therefore consistently minimize the time and effort it takes to train people to perform various jobs. For this reason most individuals—including most women who are beyond their childbearing and baby-sitting years—tend to keep on performing the same jobs throughout their lives rather than retraining for "male" jobs.

Since women must do the tasks necessary for and consistent with child rearing, the occupations remaining to be done by males are usually those that do not involve child care. Men in nonindustrialized societies very rarely care for children, even in those few societies in which women are important politically or economically (Frayser 1985:93–94). Cross-cultural comparisons show that older girls, women whose children have grown up, or women who have no children of their own look after young children far more commonly than men. Feeding

and caring for young children are virtually female monopolies, and this has a profound effect on the division of labor in nonindustrial societies. Frayser's conclusions agree with those of White and his colleagues (1975). Labor is divided on the basis of sex so that all the subsistence activities on which a society depends will be performed in the most efficient way. If a society is to operate as effectively as possible, certain sexual distinctions and restrictions must be made.

Among gatherers and hunters, women are responsible for much of the food collection. The feminist anthropologist Ernestine Friedl (1984:135) notes that in such groups, women's relative power is greatest if women not only provide some of the subsistence necessities but also have a hand in the distribution and exchange of valued goods and services outside of the household, or "extradomestically." In situations in which women either make no contribution to the food supply or do not personally take part in extradomestic distribution, their personal autonomy and influence over others is usually limited.

public domain the social sphere that centers on the wider social world outside of the home and is associated with political and economic activity above the household level

domestic (private, household) domain the social sphere that centers on the home and is associated with such activities as child rearing and food preparation for household consumption

In parts of the Third World, women routinely carry heavy loads on their heads as part of their everyday chores. As village women in Rajasthan, northwestern India, carry pots of water home from a well, they pass men whose work, by comparison, seems less physically demanding.

◆◆◆

Never Underestimate the Power of a Woman

For travelers in parts of the developing world, the sight is a familiar one: barefoot women trudging for miles with enormous loads of firewood or water balanced on their heads. Scientists at the University of Nairobi in Africa, studying human energy expenditure, recently recruited women from the Kikuyu and Luo tribes to carry heavy loads on their heads while walking on a motorized treadmill (*New York Times* 1986). Since oxygen use accurately reflects energy use, the researchers prepared to monitor carefully the extra amounts of oxygen that carrying loads of various sizes would require.

To the scientists' amazement, the women were able to carry loads weighing up to 20 percent of their body weights without any increase in their use of oxygen at all, which meant that loads of this size did not result in any increased expenditure of energy. Carrying an astounding 70 percent of their body weight increased the women's oxygen use by only 50 percent. In contrast, males carrying backpacks equaling 20 percent of *their* body weight increased their oxygen use by 13 percent; loads equal to 70 percent of the carrier's weight increased males' oxygen consumption by nearly 100 percent.

Why was it that the African women could carry heavy loads on their heads so much more efficiently than men could carry equal loads in backpacks? The scientists are still mystified, but they have a couple of hypotheses. Perhaps, they speculate, carrying weight on their heads over a span of many years produces some anatomical change in women that allows them greater energy efficiency. Or perhaps the women walk in such a way as to minimize the up-and-down movement of their loads. Either way, the African superwomen are among the world's most proficient load-bearers, exceeding not only men but even horses in energy efficiency.

◆◆

Sex Roles among the Sarakatsani

Nowhere are sex roles more strongly associated with gender-specific beliefs and ideas than among the Sarakatsani sheepherders of northern Greece. As in other Mediterranean societies, men are dominant (Campbell 1964), and notions of their inherent capability and honor and women's inherent incapability and shame abound. Sarakatsani say that God created males for noble purposes and that females, inferior and even sexually dangerous creatures, constantly threaten to corrupt men's nobility. When men have sex with women, they demean and pollute themselves. Still, because men want children to care for them in their old age and to perpetuate their names, they compromise between their desire to remain untainted by contact with females and their desire for children. Sex is carried out in the utmost secrecy, and afterward a shepherd must wash his hands before milking his sheep.

Although in an emergency someone of either sex may carry out almost any task, the jobs appropriate to Sarakatsani men and women are clearly spelled out. Women look after children, cook, and make woolen clothes and blankets. They cut firewood, raise chickens, carry water, search the mountain slopes for wild vegetables and herbs, and in the summer grow vegetables in small gardens. Men spend most of their time caring for flocks of sheep and making and selling products derived from sheep. They also manage their household finances, engage in local politics, arrange marriages for their children, and protect their wives and daughters from insult and assault. A husband may lift a heavy object to tie it to the back of a mule, but he will never carry a burden on his own back, for this is women's work, and a man who performs a feminine task is viewed as unmanly. A real man must never show shame or excessive modesty. Instead, he must display impatience, pride, and courage. In contrast, the essential feminine virtues are reticence, patience, fearfulness, humility, and most of all a sense of shame for being a woman.

A Sarakatsani husband has absolute control over his wife, who (at least in front of outsiders) is expected to show him great respect. When visitors are present, she does not sit and eat with her husband and his guests but instead stands motionless, ready to administer to the needs of the men. Men eat first, women later. They make do with whatever the men leave, and often this is little. To impress on others that he is master of the household, a husband may bark out commands to his wife. As she scurries to comply, she must remain silent and submissive, neither smiling at her husband nor laughing with him before strangers. (When a married couple is alone, Sarakatsani informants admit, the wife may drop her mask of humility and forthrightly discuss family affairs with her husband.)

Sarakatsani women who are past their childbearing years, and thus, men believe, no longer active sexually, almost manage to overcome the moral weakness inherent in their sex. If all has gone as their husbands hoped it would, they will now be the mothers of adult sons, whose reputation for manliness and whose role as protectors of family honor almost negate the shame of their mothers' earlier sexuality.

The Question of Warfare

Why, in virtually every society (including our own), is the job of making war something that males are thought better qualified to do than females? Even in the few societies in which women participate in combat, men are considered to be better combatants. It has been proposed that warfare is primarily an expression of the aggression that characterizes all humans (Ardrey 1961; Lorenz 1963:236; Morris 1967) and that males are naturally more aggressive than females. In fact, the association of males with aggression and warfare is as strong, cross-culturally, as the association of women with passivity and child care. But the assumption that certain human beings are inherently aggressive (or, for that matter, passive) has been strongly challenged (Montagu 1968; Pilbeam 1972). Moreover, culture plays a part in aggressiveness. In a comparison of societies in New Guinea, Mead (1963) found that one produced children who were insecure and aggressive, whereas children in another were contented, passive, and secure. So the answer to the question of warfare cannot be found in simple psychological explanations based on "natural" aggressiveness or passivity.

We pointed out in Chapter 5 that in gatherer-and-hunter societies, it is the men, not the women, who hunt big game since these small-scale societies cannot afford to put their potential childbearers at risk in a dangerous occupation. The same argument—more functional, more materialist, and less psychological than the "natural male aggression" argument—can be used to explain why women are such infrequent warriors (Friedl 1984:135; Frayser 1985:97–98). Only women can bear children and see them through infancy. If a society sent some of its women to war—presumably its youthful women, at the peak of their fighting strength—some would be killed, and thus their reproductive contribution lost, with possibly catastrophic consequences for the society. The potential number of children any one woman can bear is limited to a maximum of about one per year. A man, however, can father many children per year. Thus the loss of men in warfare would not be as serious, in terms of the continued existence of the group, as the loss of women. The specialization of occupations that mandates that women care for children while men fight—so common around the world—is thus perhaps not as "natural" as it seems. It may be a cultural response calculated to avoid extinction.

◆◆◆

VARIETIES OF SEXUAL BEHAVIOR

There is great variety in the kinds of sexual behavior, both public and private, that are acceptable in different societies. Some societies allow both males and females considerable liberty to express themselves sexually. Others demand restraint—sometimes of the members of both sexes, sometimes of males or females only, sometimes of people of certain social groups or ages. In most societies, sexual behavior that causes physical or psychological harm (rape or child molestation, for example) is prohibited, although there are some exceptions to this generalization. Rape in the course of warfare has been common throughout human history, and rape as an act of social control of women occurs in some societies, including Western society. Sexual practices that may offend some people yet not cause harm to those who engage in them, such as masturbation or homosexuality, are somewhat less widely restricted, although even here we find tremendous variation among societies.

Masturbation

There is relatively little anthropological information on sexual self-stimulation, although the available data seem to suggest that the range of attitudes is as wide in this area of sexual activity as in any other (Masters, Johnson, and Kolodny 1985:627). Around the world, masturbation seems to be more common among children and adolescents, in whom it is generally tolerated, than among adults, in whom it is generally considered a less desirable form of sexual activity, for both males and females, than sex with a partner (Ford and Beach 1951:156–157; Masters, Johnson and Kolodny 1985:627). In some societies, masturbation is considered defiling or, in the case of males, emasculating; in others, it signifies the inability to attract a lover. For adolescents, however, it is considered a "natural and normal activity" in many societies that disapprove of the practice among adults (Ford and Beach 1951:157).

Until about the middle of this century, masturbation was discouraged in Western society because of the mistaken belief that it could cause such harmful conditions as sterility, fatigue, misshapen genitals, memory loss, pimples, or insanity (Masters, Johnson, and Kolodny 1985:359–360). We now know that no physical damage results from masturbation, but every one of a group of American males questioned in a recent study said he believed that if it were practiced "excessively," mental illness would result (Offir 1982:190). Nevertheless, 92 percent of American men and 54 percent of American women masturbate occasionally or frequently (Ford and Beach 1951:153–154). Such figures show that masturbation is a statistically normal kind of sexual behavior and, most authorities now contend, a "legitimate type of sexual activity" (Masters, Johnson, and Kolodny 1985:360).

Homosexuality

Although our ethnographic data on homosexuality are relatively scarce (Carrier 1980:101), the desire of some people, both male and female, to have sexual relations with members of their own sex seems to be common worldwide. In fact, homosexual intercourse seems to be the "most important alternative form of sexual expression utilized by people . . . around the world" (118).

Homosexuality is found all over the world, with a majority of societies viewing it as socially acceptable. In San Francisco, a gay couple celebrates after officially registering their partnership at City Hall.

Western society is unusual in the degree to which homosexuality is seen as abnormal or offensive. Ford and Beach (1951:130) report that in a sample of 76 societies for which information on homosexuality exists, 63 percent regard homosexual activities between adults as normal and socially acceptable. In only 27 percent of these societies is it considered rare or kept secret. In fact, in some societies—classical Greek society is a well-known example (Dover 1989)—homosexuality is, or was, customary and institutionalized (that is, socially accepted and governed by social rules).

The horticultural Etoro people of New Guinea have an intense distaste for sex between males and females (Kelly 1976). Men avoid women as much as possible, for they believe each male has a limited quantity of "life force" within him, and some of it is lost each time he has sex. Men are reluctant to have sex with women for reasons other than reproduction, and the birth of a baby is taken as evidence of a great sacrifice on the part of its father, whose life is believed to have been shortened by the sex act. Etoro women who encourage their husbands to have sex with them may be regarded as witches. Given the belief that intercourse between the sexes is dangerous, it is not surprising that Etoro customs prohibit sex between men and women for more than two hundred days out of the year.

Homosexual relations, however, are condoned by the Etoro. Infant boys are thought to be born without any of the vital "life force," and they must acquire it to grow into men. They do so by engaging in homosexual relations. Their society places no prohibitions on these activities.

In numerous societies, including some native American, Polynesian, Asian, and African societies, homosexual behavior is institutionalized instead of or in addition to being a private matter (Carrier 1980:103). In Siberia, for example, Chukchee men could become powerful religious figures (called *shamans;* see Chapter 12) by assuming the gender role of women (Lewis 1989). These transformed "women" were permitted to marry other men, and they engaged in homosexual intercourse with their husbands. Because they were thought capable

◆ ASK YOURSELF

Try to identify the community of people you feel most a part of. This might be your extended family, high school friends, dorm mates, fellow sorority or fraternity members, or teammates. How is homosexuality viewed within this community? Does your personal view of homosexuality differ from that of this group?

Not Tonight, Dear

The idea that sexual relations should be limited to certain days or times of the year, as they are among the Etoro, may seem bizarre to us, but a similar belief once existed among Westerners. Between the second and sixteenth centuries, the Christian church prohibited sex during the 40-day period before Easter (Lent), in commemoration of Christ's 40-day fast in the wilderness, and during certain other religious holidays as well. Sex was also forbidden for 3 days before one received Holy Communion. Later, during the seventeenth century, the Puritans forbade sex on Sundays. A child born on a Sunday was proof that its parents had had sex on a Sunday, and because of their parents' offense such children were considered ineligible for baptism.

of contacting the spirits and curing the sick, Chukchee shamans enjoyed high prestige. Women, too, could become shamans, as long as they adopted the gender of males. In this role they could marry (biological) males. Similarly, in Africa, some Lango men dressed as women, simulated menstruation, and married other men (Ford and Beach 1951:131).

In contrast, in 27 percent of the societies in Ford and Beach's (1951:129–130) study, homosexuality is reported to be absent, rare, or secret. In these societies, homosexuals are typically punished or ridiculed.

Homosexuality appears to be no more or no less common in North America than elsewhere. Kinsey, Pomeroy, and Martin (1948) estimated that 37 percent of white American men had had at least one homosexual experience, that 10 percent were more or less exclusively homosexual for at least three years of their lives, and that 4 percent were exclusively homosexual all their lives. A later study of 1,200 unmarried women reported homosexual activity among 19 percent of them and a lifelong homosexuality rate of about 2 to 3 percent (Kinsey et al. 1953:487). In part because homosexuality is so frequently practiced, the American Psychological Association removed it from a list of mental illnesses more than a decade ago.

Because in the past the majority of Americans regarded homosexuality as abnormal and therefore offensive, most such relationships were, until recently, conducted privately rather than publicly. But the recent efforts of gay activists to promote the view that homosexuality is normal, and thus should not be seen as shameful, are helping to change our society's traditional view of homosexuals.

Transsexuality and Transvestism

Most Americans would probably say that among anatomically normal people there are two sexes: male and female. But cross-cultural comparisons of ideas about gender identity show that this is not the case in all societies, for it is not uncommon for biological females to identify themselves as cultural males, and vice versa. As we mentioned at the beginning of this chapter, people who adopt the social role opposite to their biological inheritance, as Christine Jorgensen did, are called transsexuals. People who are sexually stimulated by wearing clothing appropriate to the opposite sex—in other words, males who enjoy dressing like females and females who like to dress like males—are called **transvestites (cross-dressers).**

Not all transvestites are transsexuals, and not all transsexuals are cross-dressers. Transsexuality and transvestism occur everywhere, are considered normal in some societies, and are often institutionalized (although we must repeat our earlier caution that the anthropological data, as in the area of sex in general, are skimpy and often confusing).

Berdaches, transvestite and apparently transsexual men who felt they had been prompted in visions to behave like women, were found in some native American societies (Callender and Kochems 1983; Williams 1986).[3] Berdaches had many of the same rights and du-

---

[3]Carrier (1980:106) points out that there is much ambiguity in the anthropological use of the term *berdache,* which has been used as a synonym for *homosexual, hermaphrodite, transvestite,* and *effeminate male.*

Berdaches—transvestite and apparently transsexual men found in some native American societies—wore women's clothes and carried out women's activities. Zuni berdache We'wha wears a woman's ceremonial costume.

CONCLUSION

The subject of sex is ideal for cross-cultural analysis because sexuality is universal but the ways in which it is expressed vary widely from culture to culture. For many years, however, the collection of anthropological data on sex and gender was hampered by Westerners' own conservative attitudes toward the subject. There was little fieldwork focusing on sexuality in women since such a large proportion of anthropologists were men (Masters, Johnson, and Kolodny 1985:621). Nor were sexual activities that were considered abnormal or immoral in Western society often investigated in the field—and when they were, bias was often involved. In discussing homosexuality with informants in New Guinea in the mid-1930s, one anthropologist asked respondents whether they had "ever been subjected to an unnatural practice" (Carrier 1980:101–102). The informants, of course, may not have viewed their homosexual or other sexual practices as unnatural, so the data collected may well have been distorted.

Realizing that our cross-cultural understanding of sexuality was totally inadequate, Gilbert Herdt and Robert Stoller, an anthropologist and a psychoanalyst, decided to pool their expertise in a study of non-Western sexuality. Herdt had carried out fieldwork among the Sambia of New Guinea, and in 1979 he returned to New Guinea with Stoller. The collaborators' goal was to thrust the study of sex more centrally into ethnology (Herdt and Stoller 1989:vii–viii). Their primary research method was not participant observation but interviews, and their perspective was psychological. Women as well as men were interviewed, and the result is perhaps the most exhaustive account of sexuality in a non-Western culture that has yet been attempted.

Thanks to our own culture's changing attitudes toward sex, modern ethnographers are less inhibited than their predecessors from seeking data on the subject. Today, as the work of Herdt and Stoller (1989) shows, *any*

transvestite (cross-dresser) a man who dresses like a woman or a woman who dresses like a man

berdache in some midwestern and western native American societies, a transvestite and perhaps also transsexual male who was prompted by visions to dress and behave like a woman

hijada in northwestern India, a man who cross-dresses, begs for charity, and entertains like a woman at ceremonies

ties as women. They were permitted to dress, style their hair, and speak like women and to cook, do needlework, and carry out other female activities. In northwestern India, males called **hijadas** cross-dress, beg for charity, and dance and sing at ceremonies as women (Carrier 1980:107). The Mohave of California allowed biological females to adopt male gender and biological males to adopt female gender (Martin and Voorhies 1975:96–99). When a Mohave person adopted the social role opposite to his or her biological sex, a ceremony was performed. The person would change names and put on the clothing appropriate to the new gender. So thorough was the transition that the persons involved could marry someone of the same sex because they now had a different gender.

question may be put to a willing informant. As a result, we are starting to learn a great deal about what it means to be a woman or a man and about the sexual behaviors of both. What anthropologists have found in their cross-cultural work on sexuality is that there seem to be no "natural," "normal," or "right" sexual behaviors or attitudes. Instead, the whole spectrum, from prohibitive to conservative to indifferent to permissive, can be found among the world's populations.

SUMMARY

The desire for sexual activity is biological, but its expression and regulation are cultural. This chapter begins with a discussion of biological maleness or femaleness, for which we use the word *sex,* versus cultural notions of maleness or femaleness, termed *gender.* A person's gender identification, by which we mean his or her sexual orientation and sex role, does not necessarily coincide with sex as defined by anatomy.

Although not disputing the importance of early childhood education in the development of male and female values, some feminist anthropologists claim that the way American female children are enculturated encourages them to maintain social relationships, while male children are encouraged to reject such ties in favor of independence. They argue that male values have long predominated over female values to produce in America a society that values independence and aggressiveness over the peaceful maintenance of social relationships. In reality, women in positions of power in business, politics, or academic life, in America and elsewhere, can be as contentious as men. However, as the Tetum examples suggest, certain cultures do associate females with bringing people together and males with separating them.

Attitudes toward sexuality vary widely. Some societies view sex as negative or evil, whereas others consider it a positive aspect of life. There is a wide range of attitudes toward sexual activity among children, premarital sex (which is permitted or even encouraged in many societies), postmarital sex, and extramarital sex. Western society's formerly conservative attitude toward sex has loosened considerably over the last thirty years because of many factors, including the growing empowerment of American women.

In examining sex roles, the chapter treats the notion of male superiority, the sexual division of labor, and the role played by males in warfare. Cross-culturally, men often dominate women. Some anthropologists interpret this domination in the context of public and domestic domains and link it with other aspects of culture such as subsistence strategies, descent, and residence. Others propose a possible cultural-materialist explanation: whoever controls the production and distribution of the material goods produced by a society dominates others. Males everywhere tend to control the material wealth of their societies. Why? The answer may lie in the sexual division of labor. Women must take the major responsibility for the care of children, which limits the other tasks they can undertake at the same time. Jobs that allow women to take care of children tend *not* to be the ones in which the resources or products of society are controlled or distributed.

To explain why men rather than women usually conduct warfare, we again call on the biological fact that only women can bear children. If they are to continue to exist, societies must continue to produce new members. But if a society sent its women to war, some would be slain, and their reproductive contribution lost. Losing males would be less disastrous since a single male can impregnate many women.

Little anthropological information exists on different varieties of sexual behavior, such as masturbation, homosexuality, transsexuality, and transvestism. The available data suggest a wide range of attitudes and behaviors in each of these areas. They occur everywhere, are considered normal in some societies and abnormal in others, and may be institutionalized.

KEY TERMS

berdache
domestic (private, household) domain
double standard
gender
gender hierarchy
gender identity
hermaphrodite
hijada
public domain
sex
STD
transsexual
transvestite (cross-dresser)

SUGGESTED READINGS

Ardener, Shirley (ed.). 1993 (1978). *Defining Females: The Nature of Women in Society.* New York: St. Martin's Press. A collection of articles that view the role of women in a cross-cultural light. It includes discussions of taboos, virginity, education, and birth.

Gilmore, David D. 1990. *Manhood in the Making: Cultural Concepts of Masculinity.* New Haven, CT: Yale University Press. From a psychological perspective, Gilmore examines what it takes to be a man in various societies. Although most societies stress aggressiveness, stoicism, and sexuality, no archetypical male exists. Gilmore concludes that masculinity is learned rather than inherent.

Herdt, Gilbert H. 1987. *The Sambia: Ritual and Gender in New Guinea.* New York: Holt, Rinehart & Winston. A fieldwork study about the use of ritual homosexuality to train warriors among the Sambia. Herdt describes how Sambia culture helps to form gender identity and to stimulate the display of sexuality in a variety of social situations.

Miller, Barbara Diane (ed.). 1993. *Sex and Gender Hierarchies.* New York: Cambridge University Press. An up-to-date inquiry into a topic that has inspired vigorous debate. Is there such a thing as "gender hierarchy"? This book may help you decide.

Morgen, Sandra (ed.). 1989. *Gender and Anthropology: Critical Reviews for Research and Teaching.* Washington, DC: American Anthropological Association. Intended to help college professors bring cross-cultural findings on women into their teaching and research, this edited collection begins with a history of feminist scholarship that shows no single "feminist school" of anthropology exists.

Morris, Jan. 1974. *Conundrum.* New York: New American Library. This autobiography by the well-known English travel writer Jan (formerly James) Morris chronicles the tragedy and joy of the author's psychological and physical transformation from man to woman.

Saitoti, Ole Tepilit. 1988 (1986). *The Worlds of a Maasai Warrior.* Berkeley: University of California Press. A remarkable autobiography by a Maasai man, which includes an intimate account of his experiences as a warrior. Among the topics he discusses are his circumcision and his relationships with young women.

CHAPTER 9

ECONOMICS

In small-scale societies, economic transactions may be based on personal relationships, but in states, they are impersonal and involve the use of money. Thus peasants, who live in state-level societies, are usually involved in their national economies. In a village in northwestern India, a peasant woman uses rupees, the national currency, to buy carrots from a street vendor.

INTRODUCTION

No doubt you've heard about Peter Minuet, the Dutchman who traded a few beads and other small articles worth about $24 to some native Americans in 1626 and received what was eventually to become Manhattan Island in return. Depending on your point of view, this moneyless transaction was either the world's best deal or its worst swindle.

In moneyless transactions, called **barter,** goods as well as services are swapped without the use of money. Barter probably dates back to the earliest human societies and is still common today, not only in traditional societies but also in the West. A California woman wallpapers a room in someone else's house in exchange for hypnotism treatments for her husband, who is trying to give up smoking. Another woman, who loves gardening, weeds and hoes a stranger's yard in exchange for driving lessons for her teenage daughter. A restaurant owner in Austin, Texas, trades meals for a roll of carpeting. In Nova Scotia, a lobster fisherman builds a rowboat for an Irish-moss collector in exchange for help in hauling in his lobster traps. And a major airline based in New York trades airlines tickets for new tires for its aircraft (Sweet 1980:86; *Ms.* 1982:70; *Mother Earth News* 1984:108; *Nation's Business* 1985:18).

In the case of the native Americans of Manhattan, bartering land for beads made a lot of sense. No amount of cash would have been of any value to them, but beads were highly desirable. Since today most North Americans use cash, why does barter thrive in our society? Some people barter because they need things they don't have enough cash to purchase. Others feel they get more for less through bartering. Still others barter to avoid

paying sales or income taxes. Barter is especially attractive in recessions since people can get what they want and need without having to spend money. It can be a most sensible kind of economic behavior.

Economic behavior? Although we're used to thinking of the word *economic* as meaning "having to do with money," in economic anthropology the term doesn't necessarily imply the use of money. In this chapter, we'll discuss what economic anthropologists have learned about different kinds of economic behavior in different societies.

ECONOMICS VERSUS ECONOMIC ANTHROPOLOGY

If you've taken any courses in economics, you may find the material in this chapter somewhat different

◆ ASK YOURSELF

Have you ever taken part in a moneyless transaction? If so, why? Were you offering goods or services for barter? How did you find someone with whom to barter? Were you satisfied with your end of the transaction?

Barter, the exchange of goods or services without the use of money, dates back to the earliest human societies and continues to be practiced today. On a highway near Kiev in the Ukraine, where vodka is plentiful but gas is in short supply, a stranded motorist offers to barter one for the other.

from that in the standard economics textbook. This is because economics as a formal academic discipline was developed by Westerners, and its concepts are based on Western economic behaviors such as maximizing profits, minimizing expenditures, investing, and acquiring surpluses. From a cross-cultural point of view, the Western model is ethnocentric, and may thus be ill suited for explaining what motivates individuals in non-Western societies. Material gain or the idea of accumulating savings may be less important to non-Westerners than to Westerners, for example, and profits may be in the form of prestige rather than material goods. Because of these differences, the theories and concepts of formal economics have not proven especially useful for understanding economic behavior in non-Western societies.

Both anthropologists and economists view the **economy** of a society, whether small- or large-scale, nonindustrialized or industrialized, as all the ways in which its members attempt to fulfill their wants and needs. Any behavior directed toward the fulfillment of wants and needs is economic behavior. But if "the economy" is easy to define in both disciplines, "wants and needs" are less so, for two reasons. First, although anthropologists agree with economists that wants and needs can be things (*goods,* in economic terms) or work (*services*), they also view ephemeral actions, such as songs or rituals, as well as other intangibles, such as love or respect, as wants and needs. Not all economists agree. Second, apart from the basic necessities of life such as food, clothing and shelter, wants and needs vary greatly among societies. Cash, of no use whatsoever to

the native Americans of Manhattan, is of universal value in contemporary North American society. Purple-rimmed clamshells, which contemporary North Americans bypass on the beach without a glance, were once highly prized by native Americans.

Since wants and needs vary so much, people satisfy them in many different ways, but it all boils down to making choices. You weigh what resources are available to you and in what quantity; you choose from among the different goals that you desire and that your resources can gain for you; then you decide what resources, and in what quantity, you wish to expend to achieve what goals.

Economists and economic anthropologists alike call the resources people use to fulfill their wants and needs **means.** These can be either material or nonmaterial: money, labor, raw materials, tools, time, energy, and will are all means. Formal economic theory assumes that means are always limited, or "scarce," but anthropologists have discovered that this does not seem to hold true for all societies. The goals achieved by expending resources are called **ends.** These, too, can be material or

barter economic transactions in which goods and services are swapped without the use of money

economy in the most general sense, all the ways in which the members of a society satisfy their wants and needs

means all the material and nonmaterial resources people use to fulfill their wants and needs

ends the goals achieved by expending resources

nonmaterial: food, shelter, honor, and the class presidency are all ends that can be attained by using various means. Formal economic theory holds that the way people expend means to achieve ends is rational and predictable, an assumption many anthropologists dispute.

Many economic anthropologists doubt that the economic behavior of people in nonindustrial societies can be fully understood in terms of the rational allocation of scarce means toward the achievement of specific ends calculated to satisfy wants and needs. Trobriand yam gardeners work long and hard to fulfill the wants and needs of their wives and children, but they are also strongly motivated by their desire to follow local marriage customs by giving gifts of yams to their married sisters (Weiner 1988:91–92). Such behavior is difficult to account for under formal economic theory. Understanding Trobriand economic behavior requires you to place this behavior within the holistic context of Trobriand values and institutions, a context in which the mutual obligations of certain women and men are of particular importance.

In short, economic anthropologists have observed that different societies, as they attempt to provide for the physical survival and well-being of their members, may develop quite different economic behaviors; different institutions to direct, control, and maintain their economy; and different economic priorities. At first these may not appear "rational," constant, or predictable to the Western economist, but with a dose of cultural relativity they can be seen to make a lot of sense.

••

PRODUCTION, DISTRIBUTION, CONSUMPTION

In studying economic behavior in any society, whatever its subsistence base (see Chapter 5), we're

◆ **ASK YOURSELF**

In her medical practice in upscale Beverly Hills, a successful obstetrician provides health care for rich women. One day a week, she provides prenatal care and delivers babies, without pay, at a clinic in a poor neighborhood in nearby Los Angeles. Is this rational economic behavior? An unknown percentage of the women she treats at the clinic are infected with AIDS, and there is a small but real chance that the doctor will become infected too. Does this danger alter your opinion about whether or not her behavior is rational?

concerned with three separate activities: people produce things, they distribute them, and they use or consume them (Fig. 9.1). Because these activities and all the behavior accompanying them are interrelated, they add up to an **economic system.**

Production

Production occurs when members of a society convert natural resources into things people want and need. A service, such as a rainmaking ritual or a psychiatric consultation, is as much a product as an arrowhead or a jet plane. Whatever the product, production takes place within a particular social context and involves particular human abilities, ideas, and traditions. Therefore production isn't simply economic behavior; in a broader sense, it's cultural. Indeed, production is so essential a feature of culture that the social philosopher Karl Marx regarded it as basic to all societies—a viewpoint that has greatly influenced many anthropologists. It is the cultural aspects of production—the human abilities, ideas, and traditions involved—rather than the products themselves that anthropologists find most interesting.

Among the many variables affecting production are natural resources; the technology, including tools and production methods, available to the producers; the customs that govern the organization of labor in the producing society; and the productive aims and priorities of the society. These aims and priorities may be the most important and are certainly the most difficult to determine.

Effects of the Natural Environment. The natural environment provides the raw materials necessary for production. Some cultural materialists might argue that the environment is the major factor in production, but anthropologists with other perspectives would disagree.

Suppose you're an economic anthropologist trying to understand a society's system of production. For the sake of simplicity, let's assume it's a technologically simple society. You might start by determining whether the society's natural environment is a friendly one with plenty of natural resources or a harsh one with scanty, widely separated, or nonrenewable resources. You would try to discover which resources are available all year around (for instance, flint for tools), which are seasonally renewable (like berries or hibernating animals), which would naturally recur if depleted by humans (such as herds of game animals), and which could not renew themselves if used up (like veins of copper ore).

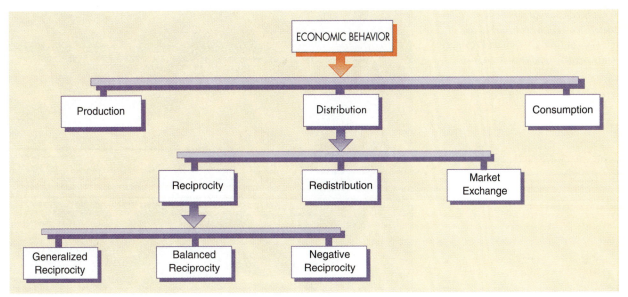

Figure 9.1
One Approach to the Study of Economic Behavior

You'd discover that some depleted resources would renew themselves rapidly (beds of shellfish, for instance), whereas others (such as groves of trees) would recover only after a period of many years.

After you documented the availability of local raw materials, you would explore the people's handling of their resources, determining whether the ones they depend on can be controlled or increased by domestication, whether they conserve their resources and how, and whether they can stay in one place and manage their resources by gardening or herding or have to move to where resources are located. You'd also ask people how they obtained resources that their local environment lacked.

After you had identified all of the resources available and understood how they were managed, your understanding of the effects of the natural environment would still not be complete. You'd also want to learn about the beliefs and values revealed by the people's choices of what resources to exploit. What is considered a resource in one society might not be considered one in another. North Americans don't eat horses and dogs, even though they're aware that these animals are edible and are exploited as a source of food by people in other societies. As important as the natural environment and its resources are, therefore, they alone cannot explain economic behavior.

Technology and Production. Technology includes all the information, expertise, equipment, and traditions that members of a society can draw on to produce what they require to satisfy their needs and wants. A society's level of technological expertise not only influences the ways in which things are produced but also restricts what the society can produce and in what quantities.

Continuing with your effort to understand economic production in a nonindustrial society, you might next explore its technology. First taking the synchronic point of view, you would determine what the people actually *do* with the raw materials their environment provides—how they use natural objects (like stones, pieces of wood, or lumps of clay) or natural forces (like running water, wind, or steam). They may use them in the same form in which nature provides them. A fist-sized stone, picked up from the ground and thrown at an enemy, is being used in its natural form. So is a hot spring in which someone is taking a bath. Simply moving nature's products might make them useful—for example,

◆◆

economic system the interrelated production, distribution, and consumption of goods and services in a society

production transforming natural resources into things people want and need

What is considered a resource in one society may not be considered one in another. In China's Yunnan Province, a man prepares dog meat for a feast.

piling up stones to make a wall. So might reducing natural resources or changing their shape—chipping away at a chunk of stone to fashion a sharply pointed tool, for instance. Or raw materials might be combined, as in making a canoe from wood, bark, and pine pitch; or transformed, as in shaping a piece of clay into a pot and hardening it in a fire.

Next, to follow changes in production through time, you might adopt a diachronic perspective. You'd search for signs that technological developments and changes were occurring or that some aspects of the society's technological capacity were remaining relatively stable. You'd probably find instances of both. Such observations would be easier if you could draw on a written history of the society or an archaeological study of its past. Scholars interested in prehistoric native Americans, for example, can get a good idea of technological change by observing how ancient pots change from one level to the next in stratified archaeological sites. They often find that people became more skillful at making pots through time.

Production and the Organization of Labor. The society's technological capacity would directly affect the organization of work needing to be done. In Chapter 5 we mentioned how some societies allocate jobs according to sex and age. But other criteria can also be used, including skill, personal preference, and family tradition.

Since the society you are studying is a technologically simple one, its members are more likely to reduce or combine natural resources than to transform them. Usually, this means that individuals rather than groups do the producing and that individuals generally carry out the same activities involved in production as other people of the same sex and about the same age. You would find little or no differentiation among people on the basis of who does what—no bosses, no employees, no unskilled as opposed to skilled laborers. This distribution of tasks encourages social equality since there is little reason to view one person as different from or superior to others. If this was a society of gatherers and hunters, you would probably find each female gatherer making her own baskets for collecting wild plant foods.

More complex technologies require different social organizations. A leading authority on peasants, Eric Wolf, one of many anthropologists influenced by the work of Karl Marx, has usefully modified some ideas originally proposed by Marx about how people organize themselves for production. Marx suggested that there are several different kinds of production (he called them "modes of production"), distinguishable from one another by the different kinds of social relationships existing among the producers. Wolf (1982:75) identifies three, although there are others as well. In the **kin-oriented mode of production,** common in many technologically simpler societies, labor is organized on the basis of descent and marriage. For example, household members in a nonmechanized farming society may cooperate to perform tasks too big for individuals to perform themselves.

More complex technological capacities, involving

Technology and Archaeology

Cultural evolutionists point out that technologies generally evolve through time in the direction of greater complexity and efficiency. Chipped stone arrowheads, for example, were used for hunting and warfare long before more efficient, more difficult to produce, metal arrowheads were made. Certain objects—say, metal arrowheads—can therefore imply certain technologies, such as metalworking. But the usefulness of archaeological objects as clues to lost cultures doesn't end here.

Since technology is interconnected with social and political organization, archaeologists can sometimes infer what sort of social or political organization an extinct culture had by determining the kind of technology it used. Arrowheads made of chipped stone, so often found at archaeological sites once occupied by gatherers and hunters, provide a clue to how their makers may have organized themselves po-

litically. Because these artifacts almost always differ somewhat from one another, archaeologists conclude that their makers did not mass-produce them; instead, each person made his or her own. The inference that the artifacts were not made by specialists leads us to suppose that the individuals who made them may have been equal in social rank, which in turn implies an egalitarian kind of social organization and the band type of political organization (see Chapter 5; bands are also discussed in the following chapter). One word of caution, though: although certain kinds of technology are compatible with certain kinds of social and political organization, this association is not invariable enough to support technological determinism, the view that a society's level of technology *determines* either its system of production or its sociopolitical organization.

---

knowledge or techniques that may be difficult or time-consuming to learn, may produce specialists who pursue a single task full time while their basic wants and needs are provided for by others. If you're a full-time canoe builder, you can't be a hunter or a farmer, too. Someone else must provide your food. In societies with specialists, the possibilities for social distinctions already exist, so these societies are apt to have some sort of a ranking system.

Sometimes, to gain access to the things they need for production, producers in non-egalitarian societies must pay tribute to higher-ranking individuals who control these things, politically or militarily. Wolf (1982) calls this a **tributary mode of production.**

Another, still more complex, level of technological capacity may require the cooperation of so many laborers working at the same task that managers are needed to organize their work. Here, individuals are clearly differentiated from one another on the basis of who does what. Some people are lowly laborers, others are higher-ranking supervisors, and still others control the resources needed for production. The pyramids in Egypt could not have been built in an egalitarian society. Too many different and technically difficult jobs, from

stone quarrying to engineering to project management, were involved.

Wolf's (1982) third mode, the **capitalist mode of production,** occurs when **capital** (resources not used up during production, such as factories) is controlled by nonlaboring, decision-making people called capitalists, and other people (workers, who don't own capital) sell their labor to the capitalists to make a living.

Productive Aims and Values. In your anthropological study of production you mustn't forget to examine the economic values of the society you're study-

kin-oriented mode of production a system of production in which labor is organized according to descent and marriage

tributary mode of production a system of production in which producers must pay tribute to people who control the things needed for production in order to gain access to them

capitalist mode of production a system of production in which capital is controlled by capitalists, and workers, denied access to ownership of capital, must sell their labor to the capitalists to make a living

capital resources not used up in the process of production

ing. What worth do its members attribute to the goods, services, and nonmaterial things they produce? The basic material necessities of life are, of course, highly valued in all societies, but beyond these basics it is difficult to generalize about value, for much of what is valuable is culture-bound, or culturally defined.

You'd soon discover that one factor governing the value that members of your society place on various commodities is availability. Easy access to a commodity or service and a plentiful supply of it tend to reduce its value, and vice versa. In North America, cashew nuts are in great demand among members of the cocktail-party circuit, who are willing to pay a relatively stiff price for them. But in rural Iran, where cashew orchards yield great quantities of these delicious nuts, you find enormous burlap sacks of them in every bazaar, and a handful costs you the local equivalent of a few pennies. Not surprisingly, cashew nuts are a staple ingredient in Persian cooking, rather than the expensive gourmet item they are in North America. Because of their easy availability, Iranians value them less highly than do North Americans.

Industrialized societies tend to value the *over*production of goods so that surpluses are maintained, a notion that members of a nonindustrial society might find strange. Surpluses are more apt to be valued in a society in which labor is specialized. With task specialization, a society can increase its production, because dividing production into specialized tasks performed by different workers is more efficient than assigning all of the steps to a single worker, especially when production involves many steps. To manufacture a jet plane, some workers rivet while others install wiring.

In attempting to analyze a society's system of production, the natural environment, technology, the organization of labor, and value are not the only features economic anthropologists study. Other forces may also play a part. Capital, for example, is an important aspect of production in some societies. But in all societies, the different aspects of the productive system are holistically intertwined. None can be understood without reference to the others.

Distribution

Distribution refers to the ways in which people allocate the goods and services they produce. The economist Karl Polanyi (1971) identified three ways in which products could be distributed among a society's members: reciprocity, redistribution, and market exchange.

A plentiful supply of a commodity reduces its value. In North America, cashew and pistachio nuts are sold in small, expensive packages; but in a town in southwestern Iran, where cashews and pistachios grow locally and in abundant supply, a shopper ignores big sacks of very affordable nuts.

Reciprocity. If somebody gives you a birthday present, you feel you should reciprocate when the giver's own birthday rolls around. As anyone who has ever given or received a present knows, gift giving creates a bond between giver and receiver, a bond that is likely to be extended into the future with additional mutual giving and receiving. Moreover, if you and the giver are roughly equal in age, wealth, and social position, the present you received and the one you give should be roughly equivalent in value. If your friend gives you a hand-knit ski sweater on your birthday, you don't feel you can get away with giving her a card on *her* birthday. Some services, too, create these feelings of obligation. A friend does you a favor, and both of you feel you owe him a favor in return.

However, if your social position and that of a person who gives you a present are decidely unequal—let's say you're a doorman and she owns the whole apartment building—both of you assume that any gifts given or received should be and will be unequal in value. She may (if you're lucky) remember your birthday with an extra $20 tucked into your pay envelope, but neither of you will feel there is anything amiss if you merely extend your best wishes on *her* birthday. The inequality of the exchange symbolizes the inequality in social position.

Mutually obligatory behavior, well established in modern Western society, extends deep into human history. In fact, the French anthropologist Marcel Mauss (1990) claimed that mutual gift giving is the most ancient way of distributing products within a social group, and to this day it is the only method of distribution used in some nonindustrial societies. Mauss thought the human compulsion for mutual giving and receiving, or **reciprocity,** underlies much of human behavior in every society. It comes in three different forms: generalized reciprocity, balanced reciprocity, and negative reciprocity (Sahlins 1968). Each can occur in any kind of society, and all three may be found together in the same society.

Generalized Reciprocity. In Western culture as well as in others, people will sometimes give gifts without expecting an immediate return or even any obvious return. When this happens, we are apt to describe the gift giver as generous or altruistic. Actually, however, a seemingly altruistic gift is frequently given in the expectation that sooner or later it will be reciprocated. This kind of gift giving—the kind in which no immediate return is expected but in which both giver and recipient anticipate an eventual balance—is called **generalized reciprocity.** It is related to a person's position in society. Those who can give are expected to; those who cannot give are not.

To use a familiar example, nuclear family members in Western society who give one another presents at Christmas usually expect gifts in return. We don't demand that our gifts be immediately balanced by gifts of identical value; most American parents receive a lot of finger paintings in return for the expensive toys they give their young children. But eventually, children grow up, and they may wind up giving their parents, now on reduced retirement incomes, gifts that are equal or greater in value to those they received as children.

Generalized reciprocity is typical of gatherer-and-hunter economies. Successful food seekers share their bounty with their neighbors without expecting an imme-

Where reciprocity is generalized, those who have valuables share with others without the expectation of any immediate return. In Togiak, Alaska, native American Yupik women fillet red salmon for distribution beyond their immediate families.

diate return. Not only are they paying off their outstanding debts of food, they are also investing in a form of "social security" against the time when they may be too old or too ill to forage. Usually no tally of the gifts given and received is kept, and in some of these societies a generous giver is not permitted to boast about his or her contributions. The Semai of Malaya even forbid the recipient of a gift from expressing gratitude, for to do so

distribution the way in which goods and services are allotted in a society

reciprocity a mutual exchange of gifts or services

generalized reciprocity gift giving with the expectation that sooner or later this act will be reciprocated

!Kung Gifts: A Case of Generalized Reciprocity

In the harsh desert country of southern Africa, the !Kung people eke out a living by hunting small antelopes, birds, rats, snakes, reptiles, and insects and by gathering wild fruits, seeds, roots, and nuts. They are unable to accumulate surpluses for the day when their luck in finding food runs out. Some four thousand !Kung practice this way of life today, in large part because of an effective system of generalized reciprocity.

Richard Lee (1969:58), who carried out field research among the !Kung, describes how each morning up to sixteen of the twenty or so members of a typical !Kung band leave camp for a day's gathering and hunting. In the evening, they return with whatever food they have been able to find, and the entire band shares the total supply of food available. The next morning, the gathering-and-hunting party may be made up of different individuals, who when they return in the evening similarly distribute their spoils among every member of the band. Who went or who stayed behind on either or both days doesn't matter; every member of the band has the right to a share of whatever food is brought into camp, for in time each adult in the band will have brought in food for the others. Thus the balance of giving and receiving among the !Kung may be unequal in the short run, but it evens out over many days and weeks. Everyone knows that in the long run each able-bodied adult will have contributed a fair share toward the subsistence of the band.

would imply that he or she must have calculated the value of the gift (Dentan 1979).

Balanced Reciprocity. **Balanced reciprocity** most often occurs between social equals who are not closely related. Like generalized reciprocity, this form can occur in any kind of society; but as an economically significant kind of behavior, it typically occurs in technologically simple, small-scale societies with political organizations such as the tribe or chiefdom (see Chapter 10) rather than in large-scale societies with the "state" kind of political organization.

Like generalized reciprocity, balanced reciprocity is also based on one's place in society, but in contrast to generalized reciprocity, it involves the immediate (or fairly prompt) return of goods equal in value to what has been given. When giver and receiver are social equals and a gift is not reciprocated, or not reciprocated with a gift of the same value, both parties may feel embarrassed. Both expect that eventually an equitable balance of gifts will be achieved; otherwise the gift-giving relationship will break down. You would not repeatedly give Christmas gifts of expensive jewelry to a friend who reciprocated each year with handkerchiefs; eventually the person who received the jewelry would get nothing more from you than lukewarm wishes for a Merry Christmas.

One interesting form of balanced reciprocity that occurs in some non-Western societies, including the !Kung, is called **silent barter.** Like the examples of modern-day, Western barter we described at the beginning of this chapter, silent barter involves the direct exchange of goods without the use of money. But silent barter is an atypical kind of barter, in that the trading partners never meet each other face to face. Instead, each group of traders leaves its goods to be traded at a prearranged place. Later, the group's trading partners come along, and if they like what they see, they take the proffered goods and leave their goods in return. Silent barter is a convenient method of exchange between hostile communities.

Negative Reciprocity. **Negative reciprocity** characterizes exchanges between strangers or even enemies (Sahlins 1968). Each partner tries to get the better of the other, and their behavior varies from energetic

balanced reciprocity the immediate (or fairly prompt) return of goods equal in value to what has been given

silent barter a kind of barter in which the trading partners never meet each other face to face

negative reciprocity an economic interaction between hostile parties in which each tries to get the better of the other

The Kula: A Case of Balanced Reciprocity

In Chapter 4, we described the Trobriand Islanders' kula ring, a ritual exchange of shell necklaces and armbands. Each gift required the receiver to reciprocate promptly with a countergift of equal or greater value. Armbands and necklaces circulated endlessly around the kula ring, with necklaces traded from person to person, village to village, and island to island in one direction, and armbands in the other. Often these objects would wind up in the same hands that had given them away years ago.

The necklaces and armbands were not currency that the islanders could use to buy whatever they wanted; they were exchanged only for each other. But even though these objects lacked any practical value, their symbolic value was considerable. To be presented with one of these items was to gain prestige, and to give one symbolized a donor's generosity and enhanced his reputation. So eager were the Trobrianders to win prestige and fame that they regularly embarked on dangerous trading expeditions to distant islands, laden with necklaces and armbands to give away. As part of their ritual interaction, traders from different islands (who might otherwise have been hostile toward one another) were obliged to treat one another with great courtesy, each man seeing to the comfort and safety of his trading partners whenever they were in his home territory.

What was really going on here? Were the islanders really so eager to gain prestige that they were willing to befriend potential enemies and risk their lives on dangerous ocean voyages? Marvin Harris (1993:242–243), drawing on the work of Reo Fortune (1989:206–210) to analyze the kula ring from a cultural materialist perspective, pointed out that another, quite different kind of trading, for food and other practical commodities, was going on at the same time. In this way, the residents of naturally well-endowed islands were able to trade their agricultural surpluses to residents of less fertile islands, which specialized in the mass production of nonedible necessities such as pottery and canoes. Long before Malinowski's visit to the Trobriands, inter-island trading partnerships between certain men and particular villages had developed, with food being exchanged on a regular basis for artifacts. Balanced reciprocity made possible a network of relationships that welded the entire group of islands into a single economic unit.

Some anthropologists have concluded that the "real" purpose of the kula ring was therefore not what the Trobriand islanders *themselves* thought—to win prestige by exchanging symbolic artifacts. Rather, it served to place people in a position in which they could trade with one another for such economic necessities as yams, coconuts, canoes, pottery, and fishing nets. In contrast to the symbolic exchanges of armbands and necklaces, trading for essential goods involved a lot of haggling. Were it not for the former, the islanders might well have been too fearful of their neighbors on other islands to attempt any kind of economic relationship (Fortune 1989).

The importance, in economic systems, of social factors—such as the Trobrianders' exchange of ritual objects in pursuit of prestige—reminds us that human beings are rarely so overwhelmed by economic interests as to neglect social ones. "Economic man," a creature whose motivations are economic to the virtual exclusion of social or psychological impulses, is merely an ideal model.

---

haggling to outright theft. The Mbuti of Africa, for example, exchange meat and personal services for other kinds of food and for goods produced by their neighbors, whom the Mbuti heartily dislike (Turnbull 1965). When performing services for these neighbors, the Mbuti work as little as possible, and their neighbors counter with resentful threats intended to increase the Mbutis' productivity.

Redistribution. One way of allocating goods, called **redistribution,** is to designate one individual or group to collect goods and then parcel them out among the members of a society. This form of distribution is

redistribution a way of distributing goods in which the goods are gathered into the possession of a particular individual or group and then parceled out among the members of a society

◆◆◆

Another Day, Another Coconut

In some of the world's nonindustrialized societies, the agent of redistribution was in traditional times a political leader called a chief (see Chapter 10 for the anthropological definition of this term). Like a Western business tycoon, the chief was often a person who made a career of accumulating wealth. But what the typical chief did with his wealth would leave American tycoons scratching their heads in disbelief, for he collected it only to give most of it away.

The Trobriand chief is a case in point. According to Malinowski (1965:46–47), tradition entitled a chief to receive great quantities of tribute, much of it in the form of food (especially yams), from villagers in the district in which he wielded authority. In addition, the chief was (theoretically) the owner of all the coconut trees and pigs in his district, which meant he could claim a portion of the coconuts from each tree and a piece of meat from each pig that was butchered. He was thus able to accumulate supplies of yams, coconuts, and meat far beyond what he and his immediate family could use. But instead of storing these goods for the future or trading them away for his own advantage, the Trobriand chief was obligated by custom to redistribute his accumulated wealth.

Eventually, most of the chief's wealth would be returned to his villagers in the form of payments for a variety of public services. A Trobriand chief could order canoes, houses, and yam storerooms to be built; wars to be waged; wooden sculptures to be carved; kula expeditions to be organized; and village magicians to perform their magic—but he had to pay for all of these services. So in effect, Trobriand villagers were consuming the products of their own labor, but their wealth first had to pass through the hands of their overlord, whose authority was thereby recognized. Malinowski (1965) notes that it was this process of concentration and redistribution of wealth that made it an instrument of political power in Trobriand society.

◆◆◆

common in our own society as well as in certain small-scale societies. In Western society, for example, the heads of individual households may pool the earnings of their productive members (ordinarily the parents) and then redistribute these earnings among all the members of the household, whether productive or not.

Redistribution also occurs between households. In North America, as we're all well aware, state and national governments collect taxes from working people's salaries and then redistribute what has been collected to other members of society based on presumed need. Although it may take the form of money—a welfare payment to an individual, perhaps, or a grant from the National Endowment for the Humanities to a struggling theater group—redistribution may also be in the form of services or goods.

Market Exchange. In common usage, the term *market* refers to the physical site where goods are exchanged. **Market exchange** is something more abstract, a form of exchange in which transactions are impersonal rather than based on one's position in society, on kin-ship, or on political relationships. Unrestricted participation by any and all members of a society is a common feature of market exchange. Because everyone is free to offer goods for exchange in any quantity and to accumulate things in any quantity, shifts in supply and demand are common. These shifts govern the value, and hence the **price**—the worth, expressed in the form of some agreed-on medium of exchange—of the available goods and services. Thus we can say that market exchange is an exchange in which prices are established for whatever is being exchanged. Because each person is theoretically free to sell and buy in any quantity, market exchange is sometimes called free-market exchange, but the concept is more ideal than real. In actuality, market exchange is usually subject to political regulations, including trade barriers, customs regulations, price controls, and rationing, so it isn't really "free."

Market exchange is mostly found in states (see Chapter 10), because it is possible only in societies with dense populations that can produce food efficiently enough to support large numbers of people. For market exchange to develop, a society's food supply must be so

In market exchange, economic transactions are impersonal and open to all, money is used as a medium of exchange, and prices fluctuate. The place where this kind of exchange takes place is called a market. In an Andean mountain town in Ecuador, people from outlying villages gather at an open-air market to buy and sell vegetables.

abundant and dependable that most people can abandon subsistence activities and specialize in other areas of production.

Market exchange usually involves **money**—objects accepted by a society's members as tokens of specific amounts of worth. Paper bills and metal coins serve as most of the Western world's exchange media, but in non-Western societies money can be shells, blocks of salt, or other objects.

Defining *money* is difficult since the term has many shades of meaning. In Western terms, money must be acceptable as a medium of exchange to everyone in the society and able to be used to purchase the entire range of goods and services available to the society. Money that fulfills these criteria is called **general-purpose money.** Money also has to be reasonably durable in a physical sense, sufficiently portable to be moved from one trading transaction to another, capable of being divided into small units, and liquid enough to be easily exchangeable for other things. And money must have the same purpose and value for everyone—blind to social or political or religious or economic differences between its users. The American dollar, the

market exchange the kind of exchange in which transactions are impersonal rather than based on descent, marriage, social position, or political relationships

price the worth, expressed in the form of some agreed-upon medium of exchange, of goods and services

money objects accepted by a society's members as tokens of specific amounts of worth

general-purpose money currency that can be used to buy anything available for purchase

Swiss franc, and the British pound are all forms of general-purpose money.

If we limit the term *money* to objects having these attributes, it is exceedingly rare in technologically simple, nonliterate societies. But if we loosen the definition somewhat, money is not nearly so rare, for the idea of using certain objects to represent certain amounts of value is widespread. The major difference between Western money and the money used in nonliterate societies is that the latter is not comprehensive, meaning that it cannot purchase an entire range of goods and services but only specified items. We call money of this type **special-purpose money.** One kind of special-purpose money, used in New Guinea, consists of shells strung together in units about as long as a man's outstretched arms. With this shell money, you can buy only pigs, nothing else.

George Dalton (1968) suggests that anthropologists might find it useful to classify economies according to the importance they accord to market exchange. He proposes three categories of economic system: (1) economies without markets; (2) economies with **peripheral markets,** or markets of relatively little economic importance in which only objects, as opposed to land or labor, are bought and sold; and (3) economies dominated by markets.

Although many kinds of goods can be exchanged in an economic system lacking market exchange, usually

◆◆

Rossel Island Money

Like the Trobriand Islanders, the people of Rossel Island, which lies near New Guinea just southeast of the islands of the kula ring, place a high value on shells. But unlike the Trobrianders' shells, Rossel Island shells can be viewed as a kind of special-purpose money since they serve as a medium of exchange and a standard of value rather than simply as ornaments for display or prestige (Armstrong 1967).[1]

The people of Rossel Island have 22 different kinds of shells, which they divide into 3 classes. The first class contains shell types 1 to 10; the second class, types 11 to 17; and the third class, types 18 to 22. To buy certain goods, you need a shell of a certain number. A large house will cost you a number 20 shell. You cannot pay for your house with two number 10 shells, for they are not thought of as being equal to a single number 20 shell. Thus the shells of Rossel Island are not convertible, as our money is.

A Rossel Islander who borrows a number 1 shell must repay with a number 2. A person who borrows a number 2 shell must repay with a number 3,

On Rossel Island, shells—like money in Western society—serve as a medium of exchange and a standard of value. However, these shells can be used to purchase only some of the goods and services available on the island. Thus they must be considered special-purpose rather than general-purpose money.

and so on, through shell type number 9. But an islander who borrows a number 10 shell cannot be compelled to return a number 11, for the series 1 to 10 has more generality than the other two series. Finally, the total number of shells used as money numbers no more than one thousand, a feature that severely reduces the money's usefulness.

[1]Armstrong, an economist, carried out only two months' fieldwork on Rossel Island. Since he was unable to do much participant observation, his findings have been challenged.

by reciprocity and redistribution, land and labor are not among them. Instead, these important commodities are allocated among individuals by descent, affinity, and social group membership. Reciprocity and redistribution also characterize economies with peripheral markets, but in this second kind of economy there is in addition a narrow range of things that are exchanged according to market principles. Still, most people don't get the bulk of their income from sales in the market, and land and labor aren't bought and sold; kinship and social position govern most exchanges, and as on Rossel Island, special-purpose money may be used. The third type of economy, dominated by market exchange, is typical of state-organized societies, with or without peasant communities. Land and services as well as goods can be freely bought and sold, and few economic transactions depend on rights and duties derived from descent or affinity.

Consumption

Consumption refers to all the ways in which the goods, services, and nonmaterial things produced within a society are used. Far from merely satisfying basic wants and needs, acts of consumption in most societies have a wide range of purposes, one of the most important of which is to symbolize social prestige. In Western society, you drive a Rolls-Royce not only to transport yourself from one place to another—a bicycle might do just as well for that—but also to demonstrate that you are wealthy enough to buy such an expensive car. In some societies, consumption as a mark of status is a potent device for establishing political clout.

The link between production and consumption has proven particularly instructive to economic anthropologists. In gatherer-and-hunter societies, this link is direct. Since each family accumulates food and other necessities for itself, gatherers and hunters have no need for an institutionalized redistributive system in which goods are amassed by one person or organization and then distributed to the needy. A person fortunate enough to acquire a surplus distributes it directly among the less fortunate, without fanfare, much less a bid for power. In

special-purpose money objects of value that can be used to purchase only specific goods and services

peripheral market a market of relatively little economic importance, in which only objects, as opposed to land or labor, are bought and sold

consumption all the ways in which the goods, services, and nonmaterial things produced in a society are used

potlatch among native Americans of the Northwest coast, a form of institutionalized consumption consisting of a huge party given by a chief for a rival chief and for all the villagers under the sway of both chiefs

Consumption on the Northwest Coast

The kind of consumption that results in increased prestige and power for the consumer is more typical of complex economies than simple ones, but it can occur even in an economy based on gathering and hunting if the natural environment is generous enough to support overproduction. Consumption in the service of prestige was a central value of traditional native Americans of the Northwest Coast. By the time they were contacted by western Europeans in the eighteenth century, they had developed a form of consumption called the **potlatch,** which blended ecology, politics, prestige, law, religion, art, and economics into one holistic phenomenon.

A potlatch was a huge feast, given by a village chief for a rival chief from a neighboring village and for all the villagers under the sway of both chiefs. It was a way for the host to win the support of both sets of villagers, often for some claim, contested by his rival, to certain political rights, the most important the right to be known by a certain chiefly title. The feast required months of preparation, followed by days of feasting, gift giving, dancing, and storytelling. A potlatch host's primary concern was to increase his own prestige relative to that of his rival, and to this end he would throw the most massive, most elaborate potlatch possible, sometimes bankrupting himself in the process, to demonstrate that his wealth and generosity were superior to those of his rival. This was his route to winning community approval for his claim.

The potlatch host would shower his guests with food and gifts—artworks, blankets, fish oil, and household utensils such as carved wooden boxes and spoons. Although potlatch customs differed somewhat among the various Northwest Coast groups, most chiefs would stop at nothing to impress their guests with their wealth and generosity. In one kind of potlatch, the **destructive potlatch** of the Kwakiutl, hosts went so far as actually to destroy their most valued possessions in front of their guests, feeding bonfires with fish oil and furniture, burning houses and canoes, and even slaughtering slaves. They were sending their chiefly rivals the message that they were so wealthy they could afford to indulge in wanton waste.[2] Potlatch guests, for their part, would grumble about their hosts' stinginess, pretend to find the food unsatisfactory, and determinedly refuse to be impressed by the display of wealth around them. All the while, they would be carefully estimating the value of the goods being given away or destroyed and comparing the generosity of one host with that of his rival.

Sooner or later, to counter his host's bid for prestige, a chief for whom a potlatch had been given would have to reciprocate with a potlatch that equaled—or better yet, was superior to—that of his rival. At this counter-potlatch, the former guest would strive to display, give away, or destroy more and superior artifacts and to distribute more abundant and tastier food than his rival. This competition would continue until one chief was too impoverished

_____

[2]Different interpretations of the potlatch depend on the particular economic, political, or religious interests of different analysts. Franz Boas (1966) first identified these lavish parties as a means by which village chiefs could increase their influence. Our description of the potlatch follows that of Boas.

to continue, whereupon both communities would regard the survivor as the legitimate claimant to whatever right was under dispute.

Customs such as the potlatch are possible only when a society can create a surplus of goods, which can then be used not so much for trade but to gain prestige through conspicuous consumption. Again we see that social interests (such as prestige) can motivate a society far more strongly than economic ones.

Like the kula, the potlatch can be viewed from several perspectives. Some anthropologists see it as a mechanism for redistribution, a powerful political symbol, and a means of providing a hedge against hunger. They point out that chiefs amassed food by encouraging villagers to produce surpluses, later redistributing these surpluses to the producers at potlatches. By accepting their chief's gifts, villagers symbolized their subordination to him even as he symbolized his authority over them. Potlatches also helped ensure against occasional famines, which could occur even along the Northwest Coast. Chiefs would give potlatches when they were wealthiest, which was when local natural resources were most abundant. Their guests, however, might live in a different ecological zone, where the climate and natural resources were different, and might be experiencing a temporary shortage of food. So food and goods provided in the course of one village's potlatch may have helped the residents of another through hard times. In this way, shortages and abundances balanced out over the years, with both villages benefiting from their competition in the potlatch (Piddock 1965).

The idea of converting generosity into prestige is hardly foreign to us. In Western society, we appreciate wealthy individuals (or institutions) who give money to charities or found socially beneficial institutions. Private charitable donations to the Guggenheim Museum in New York City and grants by the Mobil Oil Corporation to public television are examples.

more complex societies, in contrast, the link between production and consumption is much less immediate. We've mentioned that in the Trobriand Islands, products moved from producer to consumer through the chief, whose job was to redistribute them. This was no mere

economic service. The chief's power was directly tied to the wealth he collected from and redistributed to his

◆◆

destructive potlatch a variety of potlatch in which Kwakiutl hosts destroyed their most valued possessions

people. In any society, the more remote the connection between production and eventual consumption, the more likely it is that consumption has functions that go beyond the satisfaction of immediate needs.

ECONOMIC DEVELOPMENT

The term **economic development** refers to a variety of strategies designed to increase the capacities of national economic systems to improve human welfare. Although any country can of course develop economically, the term is most often applied to "less developed" or "developing" countries. There is no agreement on what a "developing" country is, but living standards are usually lower than in "industrialized" countries; per capita income tends to be relatively low; the rate of population increase is usually relatively high, meaning that the **dependency ratio** (the number of people in the work force versus those who are too young or elderly to work) is unfavorable; and modern industry and international trade may be just getting off the ground. Most (but not all) developing countries are located in the Southern Hemisphere, and many have histories of colonialism.

The goal of economic development is to satisfy such basic human needs as food, shelter, and health care by stimulating economic growth, redistributing income more equitably, and reducing poverty. More specific aims vary from country to country, but they usually include raising a country's gross national product (GNP) and per capita income; developing its industrial base; increasing productivity; accumulating capital; and improving social services, usually by increasing allocations to public programs such as health, agriculture, public works (road building, for example), and education.

There is no best way to go about achieving these goals, for the histories, traditions, natural resources, and political systems of developing countries vary greatly. Many have chosen to develop modern economies, but political instability, international conditions, tradition, or class structure have inhibited others. Successful economic development also depends on what kind of economy is desired. Socialist economies are centrally planned and controlled, while capitalist economies rely more on market exchange than on central controls.

Given such great variety, it is not surprising that individuals, nations, and international aid agencies have often been at odds over how best to achieve economic development. Different personal, political, religious, and ethnic beliefs and values may be difficult to reconcile.

Many developing countries, for example, have had sharp declines in their death rates because of modern medicine but no corresponding declines in their birth rates, so population growth is rapid (see Figure 9.2). This can be highly detrimental to economic development: a rapidly growing labor force, for example, may result in widespread unemployment. If you were given the job of solving this problem for a particular developing country, you might suggest that the government adopt an official policy of two children per family and impose tax penalties for noncompliance. Or you might encourage an international aid organization to distribute free family-planning services and contraceptives. Or you might urge sexual abstinence. Which solution you would favor would depend on whether you were a government official in the country, a policymaker for an international aid organization, or a religious leader.

Some anthropologists apply their specialized knowledge to promote economic development. An early example of this kind of applied anthropology, begun in 1952, was the famous Cornell-Peru Project, nicknamed the Vicos Project. Vicos was a "hacienda," a huge farm worked by peasants, located in an Andean valley in Peru. Like many other haciendas, it was owned by absentee landlords. The peasants who farmed the land were tenants who contributed three days of labor each week to their landlords in exchange for a house, a small garden plot, and some domestic animals. This arrangement was not a happy one for the 1,700 or so peasants of Vicos. Their plots were small, their crops frequently failed, and often they were unable to feed themselves

◆ **ASK YOURSELF**

In the past, peasants in a certain developing country grew enough food for their own families and sold their surpluses for a little cash. Today, because of economic development and the urbanization and industrialization that accompany it, these peasants live in cities and work in factories. Along with more cash, they now have all the pressures and health problems of urban life. In your opinion, are they any better off?

economic development strategies for improving national economies based on the assumption that they will lead to improvements in human welfare

dependency ratio the number of people in a nation's work force compared with the number who are too young or too old to work

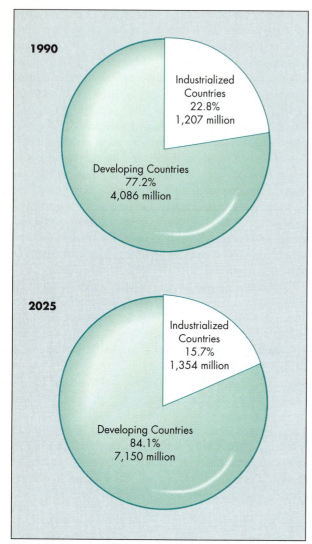

Figure 9.2
*The Increasing Population of the World. Rapid population
growth is a major problem for developing countries because it
slows economic development, but unless present trends are re-
versed, these countries will see huge population increases over
the next generation. By the year 2025, world population may
top 8 billion people, more than 80 percent of them in developing countries. (Source: United Nations Population Division.)*

and their families adequately. Forever in debt to their
landlords, they had little hope for a better life.

Anthropologist Allan Holmberg felt that the Vicos
peasants should have a higher standard of living, be
more involved in decisions affecting the hacienda, and
eventually be economically independent. Hoping to
demonstrate that anthropological research and economic

development could improve their lives, he created the
Vicos Project with the help of Peruvian colleagues
(Mangin 1979:65). His strategy was "participant intervention": he would not simply participate in the project,
as a fieldworker engaged in testing a hypothesis would
do, but also intervene in the peasants' lives to help bring
about what he saw as desirable changes. His approach
was holistic, incorporating not just economic but also
social and cultural improvements—better education, better health care, and increased community participation in
decision making. Holmberg planned to transfer control
of the hacienda gradually to members of the community
as their health and education improved and their self-
esteem, sense of community, and economic decision-
making abilities grew.

After the hacienda's lease was turned over to Cornell and the Peruvian Indian Institute, the peasants were
given improved varieties of seed, fertilizers, and insecti-
cides to use on the owners' land. Success was apparent,
but the peasants lacked money to buy the supplies with
which they could similarly improve the yields of their
own small gardens. So a government-sponsored cooperative credit program, supervised by anthropologists and
other specialists on the project team, was established. In
keeping with Holmberg's holistic approach, the team encouraged other initiatives as well. Education and school
hot-lunch programs were begun. A model garden was
planted to demonstrate better methods of growing vegetables, and sewing machine training was offered so the
peasants could make their own clothes. These lessons
not only taught skills but also gave the peasants a sense
of participation in what was going on around them, the
opportunity to gain new respect as possessors of modern
skills, and a way to increase their families' incomes
(Doughty 1987:456). In addition, the peasants were encouraged to assemble frequently for discussions. As a
result of these meetings, they began to place increasing
trust in one another and to seek cooperative solutions to
common problems.

The community prospered, and in 1962 the tenant
farmers purchased the hacienda from its owners (Mangin 1979:66). By the late 1970s, the peasants were better
fed, better housed, and far better educated than they had
ever been under the old system. And their standard of
living had risen above that of peasants on neighboring
haciendas.

The Vicos Project did not escape criticism. Some
critics pointed out that neighboring communities also
improved their lot somewhat, without help from any
project. Others felt that Cornell and the Peruvian gov-

The Vicos Project, an economic development project aimed at improving the lives of peasant share-croppers on a huge Peruvian hacienda, or farm, raised the standard of living of these peasants, who eventually purchased the hacienda. Above, Vicos peasants cultivate corn.

ernment exaggerated their own contributions and played down those of the people themselves. Still others claimed that the Vicos experiment was unique and therefore could not be replicated in other parts of the world. Although controversy over the project's value remains (Doughty 1987; Mangin 1979), the fact is that after the peasants bought their hacienda, their incomes, literacy rate, and standard of living continued to rise.

As an experiment in economic development and applied anthropology, the Vicos Project was the first holistically designed community development and land reform program that succeeded in improving the lifestyle, sense of self-worth, and rights of impoverished peasants (Doughty 1987:458–459). In a more general way, Vicos showed that anthropologists have the theory, knowledge, and methods required to make significant contributions, at least in certain circumstances, to complicated problems of cultural change and development.

The Vicos Project may have been successful, but other economic development projects have been less so. Recently, for example, the U.S. Agency for International Development (USAID) attempted to promote economic growth in a poor, rural farming village in the Philippines. Most of the farmland in the village contained coconut trees and root crops, important in the local diet. The project's planners believed that by introducing new crops and livestock species aimed at local markets—coffee and pineapples, goats and cows—poor farmers' agricultural output and household incomes would increase and local economic inequalities would be reduced.

Thus, a number of poor households were chosen to participate in the project, the farmers were "educated" about the advantages of agricultural intensification, and the new species were introduced. But after two years, most farmers had seen no significant increase in either agricultural production or household income (Clatts

1991:270). The project's planners had failed to take into account how much labor, land, and capital poor farmers would be willing to invest and what new products the local market could absorb. Moreover, the planners failed to recognize the critical role women played in the agricultural economy, so they didn't teach the new agricultural technologies to the appropriate producers. Even worse than its failure to produce economic growth was the fact that the project aroused hostility by intensifying the same economic inequalities it had been devised to reduce. Designed to help the poorest farmers, the project actually increased the power of the existing political elite.

Failed efforts such as this encourage some anthropologists to oppose the very idea of economic development. Prominent among them is Arturo Escobar (1991), who points out that even though development anthropologists are more sensitive to the traditional values of a "developing" community than nonanthropologists might be, they are nevertheless usually acting on behalf of some international agency; thus their view of what is best for a community may be the agency's rather than that of the local people. Others who criticize anthropologists' involvement in economic development projects note that scientific and development goals are sometimes at odds (Van Willigen 1986:30). Ethnographers testing a hypothesis do not deliberately affect the behavior of the people among whom they carry out research, but anthropologists involved in development projects usually adopt an explicit commitment to bringing about change.

Development anthropology's defenders, among them the Vicos Project's Allan Holmberg, might respond that all ethnographic research influences the community being studied, and this inevitability should be admitted and used for improving people's lives as well as for furthering scientific knowledge (Van Willigen 1986:30). As yet, there is no consensus between those anthropologists who work for development agencies and those who are hostile to development work.

◆ ASK YOURSELF

Some advocates of economic development like to see money, technical assistance, roads, hospitals, or goods freely given to needy developing countries with no strings attached. Others argue that simply giving things to these nations will not promote sustainable development in the long run but only encourage dependency. In a debate, which side of this controversy would you be more comfortable defending?

BUSINESS ANTHROPOLOGY

In Western society, businesses are essentially economic organizations, with both the organizations themselves and the individuals in them dedicated to making as much money as possible in the most efficient way. But businesses are also *social* organizations, each of which has its own unique culture (Young 1986). Like all social groups, businesses are made up of people of both sexes and a wide range of ages, who play different roles, occupy different positions in the group, and display different behaviors while at work. In fact, relationships among a company's employees often extend well beyond the office or factory; many corporations have their own health clubs, after-hours get-togethers, and sports teams, and co-workers are often joined together outside the workplace by friendship or even marriage (Young 1986).

Just as anthropologists carry out fieldwork in nonliterate, peasant, and urban societies, they also apply ethnographic research methods to businesses, both Western and non-Western. The kind of anthropology undertaken by anthropologists who study workers and workplaces and act as consultants to management is called **business anthropology** (Serrie 1986). It's not a new field, having begun as early as 1932 with a study of productivity at a General Electric manufacturing plant. But business anthropology has blossomed only since the early 1980s.

One reason a company might hire a business anthropologist would be to carry out a **cultural audit,** a study of discrepancies between the way the company ideally conducts its business and what really happens (Weber 1986:43). The business anthropologist interviews both workers and managers, sometimes from the position of employee, to discover what problems the workers face and how management might improve its performance.

Business anthropologists also function as market consultants, helping companies design and produce the products that will sell best. They interview consumers, discover their likes and dislikes, determine what values motivate the purchase and consumption of particular products, and try to predict what changes in a company's products or marketing strategy might entice buyers. Market segmentation by sex, age, social class, ethnic group, and subculture are all of interest to business anthropologists (Burkhalter 1986:116).

Some business anthropologists work internation-

Economic development projects are not always successful. In the rural Philippine village of Casiguran, a project intended to decrease economic inequality and increase poor farmers' agricultural yields and household incomes actually widened the economic inequalities it was intended to alleviate.

ally, assisting corporations that conduct business abroad to interact smoothly with people of different cultures. The anthropologist informs managers about the ways in which business is usually conducted in specific cultures and suggests ways to match products with local potential customers (Burkhalter 1986:118). Managers of North American companies rarely know much about the customs of non-Western cultures. And ignorance can be expensive. One company with international ambitions, trying to sell sneakers in the Middle East, embossed a symbol representing Allah, the God of Islam, on the sole of each shoe—a shocking blasphemy that any Middle Eastern ethnographer could have warned against (Varisco 1992).

CONCLUSION

Economic anthropologists see economic behavior as thoroughly embedded in society (Plattner 1989:3–4),

meaning that if we are to understand a society's economy, we must view the society holistically. We cannot separate economic behavior from political, religious, or kinship behavior or, indeed, from any other aspect of the society's culture. Thus, for example, "the reason that the United States stopped buying sugar from Cuba in the 1960s was political, not economic; retail activity peaks in late December for religious, not economic, reasons; and the fact that marijuana is one of the larger cash crops in California is of social as much as economic importance" (4).

But if economic behavior cannot be understood

business anthropology the kind of anthropology undertaken by anthropologists who study workers and workplaces and act as consultants to management

cultural audit in business anthropology, a study of discrepancies between the ideal and actual conduct of business in a company

THE ANTHROPOLOGIST AT WORK

The management of General Motors, a multinational industrial giant, noticed that some employees, on returning to the United States from long-term overseas assignments, had more trouble readjusting than others. Anthropologist Elizabeth Briody, employed by the company's Research Laboratories in Warren, Michigan, spent three years analyzing this problem. She discovered that employees who worked for a division of GM that had both foreign and domestic branches usually adjusted comfortably upon their return, whereas employees of divisions that had only domestic branches often did not. Through interviews, Briody discovered the reason: workers returning to domestic divisions felt that their co-workers in the United States had little appreciation for their overseas work. They had difficulty readjusting because they were upset at being thought of as having contributed little to their home branch (Dunkel 1992:12).

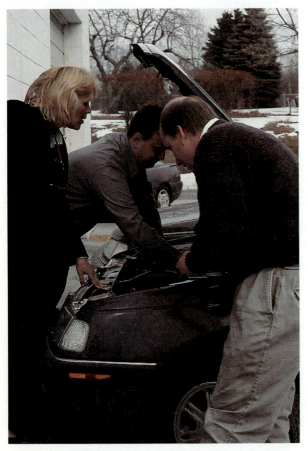

Some anthropologists use their training in anthropology to help private businesses to be more profitable. At a car dealership in Massachusetts, business anthropologist Kristina Cannon-Benventre reviews customer service procedures with the service manager. Her advice has helped the firm to win customer loyalty and repeat business.

apart from other aspects of behavior, the reverse is also true. We cannot understand a culture unless we understand its economic system.

SUMMARY

Economic anthropology is the study of how societies allocate their resources (means) to achieve their wants and needs (ends). It differs somewhat from the academic discipline of economics, which focuses on economic behavior observed in the West: pursuing profits, acquiring surpluses, and the like. Economic anthropologists question whether the theories and concepts of formal economics are all that useful for understanding the economic behavior of non-Westerners, for whom material gain may be relatively unimportant and the idea of saving for a rainy day unknown.

Both economists and economic anthropologists think of economic behavior as consisting of production, distribution, and consumption, which taken together add up to a society's economic system. Production, the transformation of resources into things people can use, is affected by what resources the environment provides, the technology available, the organization of the producers' labor, and their cultural values. Distribution, allocating products to those who need or want them, can take the form of moneyless giving and receiving called reciprocity (generalized, balanced, or negative); the pooling and disbursal of commodities, also moneyless, called redistribution; or a market system, in which transactions are negotiated with money and are impersonal instead of being based on descent, affinity, social position, or political relationships. Consumption is the use of products. It does not always take place merely to satisfy people's basic needs; frequently, in various kinds of economies, it also conveys prestige.

When economic changes are planned and executed at the national level, this is called economic development. The Vicos Project is a good example of an economic development project that resulted in improvements, at least in part because economic factors were understood holistically, in relation to other cultural and social factors. Not all economic development has been as successful, however, and anthropologists continue to argue about whether or not they should sacrifice some scientific objectivity in the attempt to improve people's lives, especially when improvement is not always the result.

Anthropologists are increasingly using their skills to help businesses improve their efficiency, an application of anthropology called business anthropology. Business anthropologists analyze the internal operations of companies, sometimes carrying out cultural audits; survey the market potential for products; and advise companies that conduct business abroad how they might interact more smoothly with customers and workers of different cultures.

KEY TERMS

balanced reciprocity
barter
business anthropology
capital
capitalist mode of production
consumption
cultural audit
dependency ratio
destructive potlatch
distribution
economic development
economic system
economy
ends
generalized reciprocity
general-purpose money
kin-oriented mode of production

market exchange
means
money
negative reciprocity
peripheral market
potlatch
price
production
reciprocity
redistribution
silent barter
special-purpose money
tributary mode of production

SUGGESTED READINGS

Leach, Jerry W., and Edmund Leach. 1983. *The Kula: New Perspectives on Massim Exchange.* Cambridge: Cambridge University Press. A thought-provoking collection of articles, remarkable for its comprehensive treatment of the kula. Provides new insights into the ideas and behavior associated with the kula as practiced by societies other than the Trobrianders.

Plattner, Stuart (ed.). 1989. *Economic Anthropology.* Stanford, CA: Stanford University Press. Twelve scholars discuss a wide range of economic topics in the context of gatherer-and-hunter, horticultural, peasant, and urban societies. An essay on the roles women play in economic institutions is particularly interesting.

Sackmann, Sonja A. 1991. *Cultural Knowledge in Organizations: Exploring the Collective Mind.* Newbury Park, CA: Sage. This contribution to our understanding of business anthropology shows how insights gained in cognitive anthropology can be applied to modern businesses.

Sahlins, Marshall. 1972. *Stone Age Economics.* New York: Aldine. A collection of essays about the economics of technologically simple societies. The first, "The Original Affluent Society," has been widely quoted and reprinted.

•••

T he tiny island of Grenada lies in the Caribbean Sea, near the tail of a curving chain of similarly tiny islands arching southward from Puerto Rico to the coast of South America. All of these islands, collectively called the Lesser Antilles, are spectacularly beautiful, but Grenada may be the most beautiful of all. Along its protected south-western coast, white sand beaches are interrupted only by clusters of coconut palms, and the sea, pale aqua at the shoreline, is a deep azure beyond. On the eastern coast, open to the Atlantic, green surf foams dramatically against dark volcanic crags. In the interior, steeply sided mountains, lushly green, shade banana and spice plantations.

To the tourist, whose dollars represent a major part of Grenada's economy, the island is a tropical paradise. But behind its upscale facade of tourist hotels, boutiques, bars, and restaurants lives a population only a few generations removed from plantation-based slavery, struggling daily with the same problems that beset other developing countries: poverty, rising expectations, inadequate public services, gender- and class-based inequalities. Half of this population lives in or near the capital, a pretty bayside town called St. George's, where no building exceeds three stories; the rest dwell in villages scattered along the coast and throughout the countryside. Grenada is so small that nobody lives more than an hour's bus ride from St. George's.

Jeannie, born in Grenada 22 years ago, has never left this miniature country of 110,000 people. A seasonally employed waitress at a large, American-owned, beachfront hotel, she commutes by bus from a village outside St. George's to work 60 hours a week during the 4-month tourist season. Despite the long hours, these are good times for Jeannie, for she earns the equivalent of about 150 U.S. dollars a month (about average by Grenadian standards). But when tourism slacks off, beginning in March and lasting until November, she takes other employment wherever she can find it. Over the last few years, she has worked off and on at domestic jobs and in several factories, where she has assembled electronic parts and put medicine tablets into bottles. Her wages during these months are low—in an average week she may make only 50–60 U.S. dollars, and when she can't find work, she earns nothing.

Jeannie has two good reasons for working at unrewarding jobs for long hours and low pay: her two little girls, aged 6 and 2. Since Jeannie has never married, she must support her daughters alone and must contribute to her household's income as well. Her 2-year-old's father, who is still her steady boyfriend, is a taxi driver who gives what he can to help out with the baby, but it's not much since he's also helping to support his mother and her several younger children. The father of Jeannie's 6-year-old left Grenada before the child was born to find work in Florida, and Jeannie hasn't seen him since.

She was disappointed but not surprised by his disappearance from her life. Jeannie thinks marriage is the ideal male-female partnership, but none of the young women she knows are married; most, like Jeannie, have had several boyfriends and assume there will be others, but don't expect a lifetime commitment from any of them. Since only about a third of unions in the Caribbean region are legal marriages, and two-thirds of all births are to unmarried women, no one thinks any the less of Jeannie for being a single mother. She has what is called a "visiting relationship" with her current boyfriend, and she is happy with it; he treats her and the baby well, and if he hasn't mentioned marriage, she thinks this is probably because he can't afford it.

Jeannie has been a mother since she was 16. If there is widespread social acceptance of single motherhood in her village, approval of teenage motherhood is less enthusiastic, and Jeannie's own mother, with whom she still lives, was angry and disappointed when Jeannie became pregnant the first time and had to leave school. Her mother wanted to know why Jeannie hadn't paid more attention in sex education class in school, why she hadn't gone to the free family-planning clinic at the health center, and what on earth she had been learning about in Sunday school.

Yet motherhood is highly valued in the Caribbean; 80 percent of women are mothers, and most eventually have three or more children. So Jeannie's mother, herself a mother at 15 and a grandmother at 31, was quick to forgive her when the baby came. After all, almost a quarter of teenage girls give birth region-wide.

Jeannie would be lost without her mother, now 37, the strong-willed head of a large household that includes three of Jeannie's step-siblings (the youngest only 3), three grandchildren, and her mother's current boyfriend. Jeannie's 20-year-old half-brother, her mother's second child, recently left Grenada to live with his father in Brooklyn, New York, where there is a big community of Grenadian immigrants. Like many young, unskilled Grenadian men, he thoroughly disliked the thought of staying in Grenada and "doing bush" (agricultural work). He has found a job as a janitor but hasn't sent any money home yet. Jeannie's 17-year-old sister, disappointed in love, plans to go to Canada to find work, leaving her year-old baby behind with her mother, but she hasn't got the airfare. If she left, that would mean more space in the sagging three-room, tin-roofed house for Jeannie's two girls and her two youngest half-brothers, 9 and 3, and only eight people for her mother to cook and clean for.

In Grenada, almost half of all households are headed by women. Anthropologists have termed the female-headed domestic unit the *matrifocal* family because within it women/mothers play a more important economic and social role than men/fathers. These women are economically independent of men and, at least within the family, demand and get considerable respect. But for Caribbean women, matrifocality is a mixed blessing, often involving early motherhood, incomplete education, a series of sexual partnerships (sometimes followed by relatively late marriage), children by several different fathers, delegation of child-care responsibilities (typically to a female relative), employment in a series of low-wage jobs, full or major economic responsibility for the household, and lack of upward mobility.

The economic position of most Caribbean women is weak. Across the region, the true proportion of working women is unknown, since much of women's work takes place in the informal sector—petty trading, for instance, or domestic work. But women's formal unemployment is higher than men's, and unemployment among young women is especially high. Women's wages are lower than men's, and women lack equal access to credit. In general, and especially at the lower end of the socioeconomic spectrum, Caribbean women's jobs—whether in restaurants and hotels, factories, or other people's homes—tend to make more use of traditional domestic skills than formal training. Thus, although many Caribbean women are economically independent, their constant struggle to make ends meet often makes higher education or entrepreneurship—which could eventually improve their economic situation—impossible, and in this way their poverty is repeated through the generations. Like Jeannie, whose employment is a matter of dire economic necessity, many poor Caribbean women lack the time, energy, or money to overcome this situation.

Jeannie's mother is not formally employed, but that is not to say she doesn't work. She keeps house, cooks, does the family laundry, tends chickens and a vegetable garden where much of the family's food comes from, and for a few dollars a week, takes other people's laundry to the community laundromat for them. She spends Sundays at church: first choir practice, then the service, then the social hour, then cleaning up. And all the while she looks after three grandchildren and her own two youngest sons. "Hard work is all I do," she complains, "and even so, sometimes we do without."

With so many women in the labor force, child-care arrangements other than parental care are widespread in the Caribbean. Female relatives are the most frequent source of child care, followed by neighbors or friends. Traditionally, a child's maternal grandmother was the preferred caretaker, but today many grandmothers are in the work force, so in many cases older children baby-sit. Jeannie is fortunate that her mother has a three-year-old since this keeps her at home. Institutionalized day care is becoming more common, although the quality of such arrangements is uneven, and impoverished governments may not monitor them adequately.

Although too slowly for Jeannie to be aware of it, the expectations and behavior associated with Caribbean matrifocality are changing. Caribbean men now in their twenties and thirties are more willing to be long-term, responsible sex partners and fathers than their fathers were. Caribbean women like Jeannie, now in their twenties and thirties, are less tolerant of men's promiscuous behavior than their mothers were. But outside of the household, where they may enjoy considerable authority, women's social status is still secondary to men's. One factor that directly affects women's well-being is that males often exert great influence over them. What would she respond if her current boyfriend asked her to have another child "for him," with no promise of continuing financial or emotional support? "I haven't decided my mind about that," says Jeannie.

CHAPTER 10

POLITICS AND SOCIAL CONTROL

Politics, the process by which societies regulate people's behavior, exists in all societies, and all societies have some way of designating political leaders. At their 1992 convention in New York, Democratic party delegates nominated the man who was later chosen, by voting, to be the next leader of the United States.

INTRODUCTION

Last spring, at the end of your freshman year in college, you decided to run for sophomore class president. It would be hard to say why, exactly. You were senior class treasurer in high school and enjoyed it; it was flattering to see your name at the head of a petition full of signatures; you'd like to be a member of the student-faculty senate next year, when you're a junior; and of course you really did think you could make a difference as class president. You're even considering politics as a career.

You won! It really wasn't hard. You're well known, you're not afraid of public speaking, you have a good feel for the issues that particularly interest your classmates, and—most important—you have a lot of friends. So for a few weeks you tacked up campaign posters, made a point of turning up at parties and athletic events, were especially friendly to everybody, did a few favors, and that's all there was to it. You were pleased that your support came from a wide variety of your classmates. Even the engineering students, who usually vote in a block for one of their own, pulled the lever for you.

That was then; this is now. At the moment, your whole class is up in arms about being denied permission to live off-campus, a privilege granted only to juniors and seniors. Ever the conscientious class president, you've already discussed this problem with the director of residence, who was totally inflexible. Sophomores have never been permitted off-campus apartments, and that's that. Since you got nowhere, you didn't bother to mention this meeting to your constituents.

Now there seems to be a spontaneous rally going on in front of the Administration Building. Unfortunately, it's beginning to get ugly. Insults are being tossed about—next it will be soda cans. What should you do? You could defuse the immediate situation by addressing the rally and suggesting you'll work to get the disputed policy overturned. This would probably get you some credit for calming things down, but your long-term credibility would be lost (along with your student-faculty senate aspirations) when it became clear that you have no authority to change the system. Or you could tell the sophomores that you already know from the director of residence that the matter is nonnegotiable. They might applaud the fact that you tried to negotiate on their behalf, but they will certainly notice that your efforts were ineffective. Or you could leave without putting in an appearance at the rally, but if you abdicate responsibility now, will you ever get future support? Politics, politics! Your head hurts.

This chapter is about **politics,** the process by which human groups regulate the behavior of their members by setting common goals, changing them, enforcing them, preventing and resolving conflict, and designating certain people to oversee the process. By definition, politics exists in every human society, and all societies have some kind of **political organization (po-**litical system)—some mechanism, formal or informal, for establishing and maintaining social control. Some societies, however, lack **governments**—formal organizations through which the political process is carried out—and so have no formalized political organizations.

◆◆◆◆◆◆◆◆◆◆◆◆◆◆◆◆◆◆◆◆◆◆◆◆◆◆◆◆◆◆◆◆◆◆◆◆◆◆

POLITICAL LEADERSHIP

Power and Authority

If individual members of a society were free to set their own agendas and behave as they liked, there could be no society, only anarchy. Every society, therefore, designates certain individuals (and often groups as well), by formal or informal means, to exercise leadership and control over others: to set and maintain the society's priorities (sometimes called policies); to prevent, limit, or resolve conflicts between individuals or groups; to dissuade or punish those who challenge the social order;

Power is the capacity to control others, whereas authority is the socially granted right to use power. Both are needed to maintain social order. During a credit union robbery in California, a gunman with power but without authority makes his getaway.

and to direct change. These individuals or groups assume or are granted power and authority denied to others.

Power is the capacity to control the behavior of others, using such means as education, persuasion, force or threat of force, punishment, or reward (Galbraith 1983). It may be based on physical strength, wealth, or efficient organization. Or it may be based on superior knowledge; in some societies, only certain people—priests or hereditary rulers, for instance—are allowed access to certain kinds of information. In still other cases, personal power is based on something much less tangible: **charisma,** which comes from a Greek word meaning "divine gift." Sociologist Max Weber (1963:48), who identified charisma as an important source of power in society, saw it as the very essence of leadership: a quality that makes charismatic people so dynamic, so extraordinary, that they naturally command agreement, inspire loyalty, and generate enthusiasm among their fellows.

Authority, in contrast, is the socially granted right to exercise power. Ordinarily it is conveyed to an individual through an **office**—a position in which a certain kind and amount of authority is inherent and which exists independently of its occupant at any given time. Theoretically, authority can exist without power, although it would be useless (e.g., a "lame-duck" president); and power can, of course, be exercised without authority. But for social order, both are needed.

Where does authority come from? It may be either inherited or earned. Inherited or **ascribed authority** is not a standard feature of North American political organization, yet it is very common around the world. The English throne, which Prince Charles will one day inherit from his mother, Queen Elizabeth, will give him ascribed authority. **Achieved authority,** in contrast, is earned. The office of U.S. senator, for example, won by securing a greater number of votes than one's competitors for the same office, conveys achieved authority on its incumbent. Achieved authority is a familiar idea not only to North Americans but also to members of many other societies, Western and non-Western. Like U.S. senators, village leaders among the Shavante of Brazil

◆ ASK YOURSELF

We all know of charismatic public figures, but do you know any charismatic individuals personally? Have you ever followed someone's lead mainly because of the force of that individual's personality?

Ascribed authority is inherited; achieved authority is earned. Among the Ashanti of Ghana, chiefly authority is ascribed; the current leader of the Ashanti, shown above sitting on his throne, inherited his office matrilineally.

◆◆◆

politics the process of regulating the behavior of members of a group

political organization (political system) a mechanism, formal or informal, for establishing and maintaining social control

government a formal organization through which the political process is carried out

power the capacity to control the behavior of others, using means such as education, persuasion, coercion, punishment, or reward

charisma personal magnetism capable of inspiring agreement, loyalty, and enthusiasm

authority the socially granted right to exercise power

office a position in which a certain kind and amount of authority is inherent and which exists independently of its occupant at any given time

ascribed authority authority that is inherited rather than earned

achieved authority authority that is earned

•••

How Charisma Can Change History

In Chapter 5 we mentioned the sudden explosion of religious zeal that in 1978 turned Iran—which the West had thought was one of the most stable of Muslim societies—on its head. One day Shah Reza Pahlevi's power and authority seemed invincible; by the next, a new leader, the Ayatollah Ruhollah Khomeini, was in control of the country.

Khomeini's great power was not a matter of physical might; in fact, before the shah's forced departure from Iran, Khomeini had no physical power at all, for his retinue was small and he had no military might. Nor did he have political authority since he held no political office. Instead, what toppled the once powerful shah was Khomeini's combination of charisma, leadership ability, and rhetorical skill. A brilliant speaker, Khomeini instinctively knew what quotes from the Koran could galvanize Iranians to action. He used his irresistible powers of persuasion to transform religious principles into the political doctrine of Muslim fundamentalism, a doctrine that may permanently change the face of the Middle East.

achieve their authority through a combination of hard work, skill, ambition, and luck.

Sometimes ascribed and achieved authority exist side by side in the same political organization. Among the Tetum, the office of village headman is inherited patrilineally, but a potential headman will inherit the office from his deceased father only if local villagers consider him just, ethical, and knowledgeable about tradition. Otherwise, another man—but one who is also related patrilineally to the former incumbent—will be installed as the new headman.

Politicians

In Western societies, successful politicians (usually men, perhaps for reasons we discussed in Chapter 8) must appear to be intelligent, well informed, honest, and hard-working, and it doesn't hurt to be good-looking and have plenty of charisma. But these attributes do not define the successful politician in all societies. Cross-culturally, no single set of attributes results in political success. Behavior that might go a long way toward ensuring success in one setting is almost guaranteed to result in failure in another. In some societies, marrying another wife or two would give a male politician more prestige, more followers, and thus more political influence, but certainly not in North American society. Politicians the world over must adapt themselves to particular political contexts.

A comparison of political leaders among the Tetum and Shavante demonstrates the wide variability in the qualities that can make (or break) a politician.

Among the Tetum, political offices are "owned" by patrigroups. The heads of these patrigroups wield influence more because of the authority vested in the office of patrigroup head than because of their leadership abilities. True, a leader needs certain qualities to be successful, but intelligence, dedication, and charisma—highly valued in some political systems—are not especially admired. Instead, the Tetum admire a man who has a thorough knowledge of his group's myths and how they can be applied in legal cases, patience and wisdom in negotiating disputes between members of his patrigroup, honesty, reliability, and the capacity to win the respect of his followers.

Rarely is this combination of attributes found in a single Tetum leader. Yet because inherited offices are traditional, a former patrigroup head's eldest son who exhibits only some of these qualities, and is not considered a weakling, is almost always asked to fill his father's shoes. Provided he does not abuse his office, he will be permitted to remain in it until he dies or leaves it voluntarily. Such is the respect given ascribed leadership that even a totally incompetent fellow sometimes holds office, although the real authority is exercised by men of his patrigroup acting on his behalf. This is because the Tetum distinguish between office and officeholder. The former endures and is respected always; the latter dies and is replaced, and may or may not be respected.

The Shavante, unlike the Tetum, are divided into **factions**—informal, mutually contentious political action groups that exist within larger units, such as political parties or villages. A typical Shavante village of one hundred to three hundred people is divided into two or three competing factions (Maybury-Lewis 1974). The individual considered to be the most effective politician in a faction is its leader. He does not inherit his position (in fact, the Shavante have no political offices), nor is he elected by other members of the faction; he is chosen by consensus. He owes his position entirely to his personal qualities and retains it only as long as he can maintain these qualities. When old age or ill health blunt his political skills or charisma, his personal hold over his faction weakens until a new and more dynamic person impresses its members as being more capable of leadership. At this point, the members of the faction switch allegiance.

The qualities that impress the Shavante enough to make them follow one politician rather than another are quite different from those the Tetum admire. Shavante demand that their leaders be truculent, assertive, and athletic. They must be successful hunters and display great oratorical skill. They must have no hesitation about killing political rivals if necessary, although the Shavante have more respect for a leader who uses persuasion than for one who is so weak that he has to resort to killing those whom he cannot sway verbally. The Tetum may tolerate a leader who is incompetent, but the Shavante follow only a leader who is dominant among men.

TYPES OF POLITICAL ORGANIZATIONS

Different kinds of societies have different kinds of political organizations. To help make sense of the differences as well as the similarities among political organizations, Elman R. Service (1962) has classified them into four categories: bands, tribes, chiefdoms, and states (see Table 10.1 on page 213).

These categories are admittedly generalizations to which many exceptions can be found, but they help us to understand politics in two important ways. First, when viewed from the synchronic perspective, they permit us to see how political organizations integrate holistically with other factors affecting social life, such as descent systems and forms of subsistence. Second, because they can be arranged according to their ever-increasing complexity, the categories are also useful diachronically. Al-

◆ ASK YOURSELF

Apart from the specific issues a politician may support, what are the personal qualities you admire in someone who is running for or holds a political office?

though it's not difficult to find exceptions, we can see a general trend, from bands to tribes to chiefdoms to states, toward increasing size and increasingly complex subsistence strategies and economic arrangements. The fact that the four categories can be ordered in this way attests to the usefulness of an underlying cultural evolutionary model of the kind mentioned in Chapter 4.

Bands

As discussed in Chapter 5, the band, the smallest-scale and least complex kind of political organization, is most often found among gatherers and hunters. A typical band contains only twenty five to fifty people, most of whom are closely related to one another by blood or marriage. Offices are nonexistent, so no one can achieve official authority over others. All adults of the same sex and approximate age enjoy roughly the same prestige, making bands the most egalitarian of all political organizations. Rights to private property are unusual: ordinarily, any property—a spear, for instance—may be taken up and used by anyone. The distribution of goods is through generalized reciprocity (see Chapter 9); successful gatherers and hunters share their spoils with everyone in the band, including those whose search for food has been fruitless and those who made no effort to find food. Land, too, belongs to the group.

With no one in authority, band members make political decisions informally, by consensus. When some activity must be performed in common, band members unite behind the person who most inspires their personal confidence, and then only for a clearly defined period of time. On a deer hunt, the most experienced hunter becomes the leader, the others following his orders only for the hunt's duration. Should the hunters decide to stay home and perform a ritual the next day, a different person—someone especially knowledgeable about ritual matters—organizes and leads the ritual. In contrast to the authority exercised in other categories of political organization, authority over a band is temporary and weak.

The band type of political organization integrates well with cognation, the descent system most typical of bands. Cognatic descent encourages both locational and social mobility. In bad times when food is hard to find, bands easily split up, with nuclear families going their own way for a time or perhaps moving in for awhile with relatives in other bands who have better access to

faction an informal, contentious political group existing within a larger unit, such as a political party or village

The smallest-scale and least complex kind of political organization, the band, is most often found among gatherers and hunters. At their camp in Australia, members of an aborigine band cook a sea turtle caught by one of their number.

food. Under such circumstances, having ties to both one's mother's and father's relatives is useful. (This kind of flexibility and mobility also appeals to people in societies with very different cultures and much larger memberships, including Western society, which, as noted in Chapter 6, is also cognatic.) The band type of political organization, informal and leaderless, accom-modates the frequent splintering and reforming of groups.

Tribes

A **tribe** consists of a few hundred to several thou-sand people who distinguish themselves from other

The Inuit of Angmagssalik

Angmagssalik, on the coast of Greenland near the North Pole, is such a harsh region that the Inuit band formerly living there had to alternate between two subsistence strategies to survive (Mauss 1979). Every winter, the band relied for its survival on seal hunting. Band members would move into stone long-houses on the seashore, their nuclear families uniting to form larger extended families. To gain authority over an extended family, a leader had to demonstrate a winning combination of qualities such as maturity, skill in hunting, wealth, or a reputation as a success-ful magician; his was thus the *achieved* type of au-thority. His duties included distributing seal meat af-ter a hunt, receiving strangers, and allotting seats for rituals in the longhouse. But his authority was lim-ited; he was not permitted to issue orders.

The adult members of the extended family col-lectively owned the longhouse, the site on which it stood, and all the tools and other artifacts in it. Food was also considered the property of the extended family. Any game captured belonged to the long-house of the successful hunter and was shared among all its residents.

At the beginning of summer, the Angmagssalik band would break up into nuclear families, which would then scatter across eastern Greenland to hunt animals that were themselves scattered. Artifacts and food now belonged to the individual families. Each family had a leader whose authority was of the *as-cribed* type, deriving from his position as senior male in his nuclear family rather than from any personal qualities. Family members were so dependent on this leader that if he died, they could not survive. His as-cribed authority carried more weight than did the achieved authority of the winter headman.

TABLE 10.1 TYPES OF POLITICAL ORGANIZATION AND TYPICALLY ASSOCIATED FEATURES

Type of Political Organization	Size and Complexity	Major Subsistence Strategy	Economy	Social Structure	Descent	Political System
Band	Smallest, least complex; 25 to 50 people	Gathering and hunting	Generalized reciprocity	Generally egalitarian	Cognatic	Noncentralized; no offices; temporary leaders; political decisions made informally, by consensus; few rights to personal property
Tribe	Larger, more complex than bands; few hundred to several thousand members	Horticulture; pastoralism	Balanced reciprocity	Personal inequality; weakly developed social classes	Lineal or cognatic	Noncentralized; offices rare; leadership attained informally; factions possible; warfare common
Chiefdom	Larger, more complex than tribes; population may number in the thousands	Nonmechanized agriculture	Balanced reciprocity; redistribution	Distinct social classes	Lineal or cognatic	Centralized authority; chief is officeholder; political decisions made formally
State	Largest, most complex political organization; tens of thousands to millions of members	Large-scale, technologically complex agriculture; industrial production	Market exchange; money	Highly stratified	Cognatic	Centralized government; authority based on law; rights of citizenship; complex bureaucracies

groups based on their common heritage, and often common ancestry as well. Typically, tribespeople are horticulturalists or pastoralists whose method of subsistence provides food more reliably and abundantly than gathering and hunting, so tribes can be larger than bands and their populations more concentrated. At the same time, horticulture and pastoralism *require* the cooperative labor of groups of people. A lone hunter can kill a seal, but a horticulturalist cannot clear the jungle for planting all by himself.

Horticultural tribespeople tend to live in permanent or semipermanent villages. Because these are relatively large, a variety of groups—descent groups, political factions, military associations (see Chapter 11)—can develop. Descent groups are especially important to tribal people since descent is a convenient way to orga-

◆◆◆

tribe a political organization often occuring among horticulturalists or herders who distinguish themselves from other groups by their common heritage and often common ancestry

When a tribe depends on horticulture for its subsistence, the tribespeople usually live in semipermanent or permanent villages like this one in Xishuan, China. Horticulture provides food reliably and abundantly enough to permit tribes to number in the hundreds or even the thousands.

nize labor. Sometimes descent groups or other groups cross-cut a number of villages, knitting local communities into a much larger society. This cannot happen among ever-shifting bands.

As in bands, tribal authority is noncentralized—that is, not concentrated in a single office. The various groups and factions have leaders, but their leadership is attained informally, and typically no especially rich or powerful individual heads the whole tribe. Instead, the leaders of the various factions and other groups come to-

◆◆◆

The Qashgai of Iran

The pastoralist Qashgai of western Iran, who were introduced in Chapter 5, number more than fifty individual tribes. A few of these are huge, containing many descent groups and several thousand families. Others are much smaller, some with as few as five or six families. The families, nuclear or extended, live in large, open-sided black tents made of goat hair, with an average of about ten people per tent (Beck 1980). Those who share a tent form an independent, cooperative economic unit.

The Qashgai migrate in a continual search for pastures to feed their extensive flocks of sheep and goats. Large extended families occupying thirty to one hundred tents migrate together, forming herding camps. In the winter, the Qashgai pitch their tents on land leased from settled people or owned by the tribespeople in common. In the spring, at the Iranian New Year, a long migration begins. Now the Qashgai, on foot or horseback, with camels and donkeys to carry their necessities, make their way northwestward through the foothills and into the uplands of the Zagros mountains, pasturing their flocks along the way. The trip may cover close to four hundred miles and take four to six weeks. After spending the summer in the mountains, the Qashgai migrate slowly back to their warmer winter quarters.

The political structure of Qashgai tribes is noncentralized. Each tribe is divided into clans, and each clan is divided into sections headed by an elder male (called a "white beard"). This leader is not elected but is chosen informally on the basis of his natural abilities as a leader. A council of "white beards" makes the important decisions that affect the migrating unit, such as when to migrate and when to pitch the tents. In this way, every member of every Qashgai family has an indirect say in decision making.

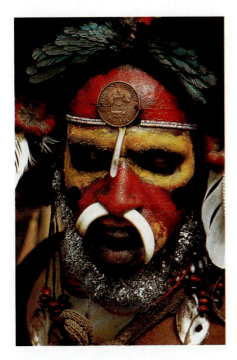

Political leaders called "big men" win their positions through charisma, eloquence, strength, political skill, and generosity. In the western highlands of New Guinea, a big man can be recognized by the wealth of ornaments he displays.

gether into a temporary coalition when necessary—in the face of a threat from the outside, for instance. Alliances are constantly being formed and broken.

Sometimes an informal leader emerges to settle conflicts among members or integrate the tribe's various groups in the face of an outside threat. This leader has no official mandate and occupies no formal office; his authority derives from his ability to coerce and persuade. Since people are of great value in tribal societies—it is their joint labor that provides food and their loyalty that gives a leader his influence—he "collects" people. He tries to win as many followers as possible and may marry many wives, thus associating himself with many lineages. For as long as his charisma lasts, he is respected and his advice is taken. As his charisma wanes, another leader takes his place.

◆◆◆

big man in Melanesia, a politician whose power depends on the influence he exerts over his followers rather than on a political office

chiefdom a relatively complex political organization controlling a large, sedentary population

On New Guinea and neighboring islands, political leaders who are charismatic, eloquent, physically powerful, politically skilled, and generous may achieve recognition as **big men.** They exhibit many of the characteristics of tribal leaders in other societies. A big man does not occupy an office; his power depends on the influence he exerts over his personal following. His generosity is particularly important, for making loans and gifts to supporters and potential supporters is essential for gaining leadership (Lederman 1990).

Chiefdoms

Chiefdoms, rare among gatherers and hunters, are relatively complex political organizations that control sedentary populations numbering in the thousands (Earle

A Tetum chief inherits his office patrilineally, but he needs wisdom, patience, honesty, reliability, and the respect of his followers to be successful. On the island of Timor, a Tetum chief shows off his wife and his badges of office.

◆◆◆

An African Chiefdom

In the early years of this century, the Azande—sedentary, nonmechanized cultivators who today still live in Central Africa—were divided into many "kingdoms." Each kingdom was intensely centralized and was itself divided into several provinces, whose administrative structure mirrored that of the kingdom. Provinces were led by princes, usually sons of a king; both offices were ascribed and transmitted patrilineally. Princes belonged to the royal rank, as did other members of their patriclans, and they controlled the lives of commoners (Evans-Pritchard 1971).

The king lived in a large central province and regarded the princes as his representatives in the outlying provinces. Since they enclosed his own province, those of the princes formed a buffer zone that protected the king's territory from attacks by other kings. Broad paths led from the king's headquarters to those of the princes, and along them tribute from the princes passed to the king. In their turn, the princes received tribute from their own subjects. Thus, millet, groundnuts, sweet potatoes, chickens, and beer passed continually from the level of the lowliest subject through the princes to the king.

Kings and princes were obligated to provide hospitality to their respective subjects when they visited and to give feasts. Thus much of the wealth that subjects gave their rulers in the form of tribute was returned to them as meals (Evans-Pritchard 1971).

Kings could have many wives. The more wives a king had, the greater the labor force available for his gardens and the more food his household could produce. The more food, the greater his hospitality and the larger the number of his followers. The larger his following, the greater his prestige and authority. The greater his prestige and authority, the greater the wealth he received, in the form of fines, fees, gifts, tribute, and the labor of his subjects (Evans-Pritchard 1971).

Kings and princes acted as supreme judges in courts of law in their own domains, and the king was also commander-in-chief of the forces of his kingdom, responsible for public order, communications, and intelligence for his realm. He did not interfere with the internal administration of any province except the one he lived in, unless a province rebelled or its leader proved too incompetent to govern. The king would then intervene quickly and violently (Evans-Pritchard 1971).

1989:84). They are almost always based on extensive nonmechanized cultivation. We do find a few exceptions here and there, one being the gatherers and hunters of the Northwest Coast, whose food supply was prodigious enough to support this complex form of political organization. But barring such special circumstances, only extensive cultivation can guarantee the regular and abundant supplies of food necessary for organizations as complex as chiefdoms to evolve.

In most chiefdoms, authority is centralized in the person of a chief, who oversees and coordinates various lower-level political units from his position at the political center of society. This officeholder's authority may be ascribed; his chieftaincy, for instance, may be inherited patrilineally or matrilineally. Or it may be achieved; he may be elected on the basis of personal qualities. Or the office of chief may be obtained partly as a result of

ascription and partly as a result of achievement, as among the Tetum. In any case, a chieftaincy is usually a permanent office.

Social classes, almost nonexistent in bands and only weakly developed in tribes, are much more common in chiefdoms, which therefore cannot be described as egalitarian. These societies are divided into classes such as royalty, aristocrats, commoners, and slaves. Usually the higher classes—royalty and aristocrats—control all political offices, from chief down to the lowest official. No one outside these elite classes can aspire to office.

A chief protects his people from external enemies; coordinates his subjects' labor; resolves disputes; and collects, stores, and redistributes much of his society's wealth. In some chiefdoms, he personally symbolizes the health and well-being of the society, so much so that should he become sick his subjects may fear for the welfare of the chiefdom. Some chiefs are even considered by their subjects to be divine (Feeley-Harnick 1985).

Chiefdoms can take many different forms. A particularly complex form, once common in Central and West Africa, was led by rulers whose ethnographers termed them "kings" rather than chiefs, and the leaders under them "princes." These were huge political organizations, their populations numbering in the tens of thousands. Although the descendants of these populations still live in Africa, African chiefdoms, like those in other parts of the world, no longer exist as independent political entities. All have been absorbed into states.

States

A **state** is a large, complex, autonomous political unit that includes many communities and, usually, hundreds of thousands of people. It has a centralized government, with authority and power to conscript labor, make and enforce regulations, collect taxes, and create and maintain institutions to support itself. The territory covered by a state has well-established boundaries, and its people enjoy rights of citizenship, though these rights may not necessarily be the same for everyone. To obtain the huge and reliable supply of food needed to sustain the population of a state, technologically complex agricultural methods must be used, such as irrigation, terracing, and animal or machine power.

Kinship frequently conveys authority in other types of political organizations, but authority in states is based on the **law,** a body of rules (called laws) that were created over time, are institutionalized (acknowledged society-wide or even internationally), and have been ratified by a society or its leaders. These laws permit the state to create and control complex bureaucracies such as armed services, a civilian police force, and a department of taxation, which give the state great power over individuals, their behavior, time, labor, money, and sometimes even their minds.

States often seek to extend their territories by encroaching on the boundaries of their neighbors—bands, tribes, chiefdoms, or less powerful states. Colonial ambitions of this kind are common in the West, especially among those states that have come to the fore in the last five hundred years.

The first states arose, apparently independently, beginning in the fourth millenium B.C.: Babylonian and Sumerian (Iraq), Egyptian (Egypt), Mayan (Central America), Incan (Peru), Aztec (Mexico), and possibly Harappan (Pakistan).[1] A number of theories have been proposed to explain their emergence. One is based on the concept of the **hydraulic society,** a society in which crops are watered not just by rainfall but also by a complex system of water management that includes irrigation, drainage, and flood control (Wittfogel 1957). Such a system requires a more complex organization of labor than agriculture that relies on rainfall, and this in turn affects other aspects of society. A huge number of workers must be supervised, so managers must be appointed. Once a complex water control system is installed, these managers must agree on how the water is to be distributed and how disputes between water users will be handled. To attain this managerial control, bureaucracies evolve. Sometimes the bureaucrats operating the system become extremely powerful.

In the past, anthropologist Karl Wittfogel (1957) argued, some hydraulic systems worked so well over such a long time that huge, dense populations developed, which required ever more bureaucrats to control them. The bureaucrats' authority increased so much that eventually those who authorized access to water and managed the labor force were able to concentrate political power in their own hands, giving rise to a highly stratified political organization. When some individuals managed to manipulate their way into positions of great power, despotism resulted. Since this kind of system appears to have reached an extreme form in China's Yellow River valley, Wittfogel termed the phenomenon **oriental despotism.**

One problem with Wittfogel's (1957) thesis is that

---

[1]Archaeologists are unsure whether or not the term *state* should be applied to the political organization of Harappan civilization.

◆◆

state a large, complex, autonomous political unit consisting of many communities and large numbers of people under a centralized government that can conscript labor, make and enforce laws, collect taxes, and create and maintain institutions to support itself

law an institutionalized body of rules, created over time and ratified by a society or its leaders

hydraulic society a society in which crops are watered by a complex system of water management

oriental despotism a kind of political system, highly developed in ancient China, in which some individuals achieved power by controlling water and labor

"The Law" and "Laws"

There has been considerable debate in anthropology over the meaning of the term *law*. Some definitions, frankly ethnocentric, are based on Western views of what constitutes law and reflect Western values, traditions, and procedures. Thus, for Radcliffe-Brown (1965:212), law is "social control through the systematic application of the force of politically organized society." Edward E. Evans-Pritchard (1940:162) sees law as existing where there is some "authority with power to . . . enforce a verdict." By either of these definitions, societies that lack "force" or the "power to enforce a verdict" would have to be viewed as lawless.

But even gatherer-and-hunter societies, where authority (when it exists) is noncentralized and temporary, have agreed-upon regulations that have evolved through time and to which people are expected to conform. We therefore prefer our simple definition of law, which ducks the question of enforcement while making the important point that laws are institutionalized, created over time, and ratified by a society or its leaders.

there doesn't have to be any connection between complex hydraulic systems and states. The Romans had a multi-layered bureaucracy without a sophisticated water control system, and the Makassai of Timor have an intricate water control system, including irrigated agricultural terraces, but no state system.

An alternative hypothesis (Carneiro 1970, 1978) covers such cases. Three factors, according to Carneiro, operate jointly to trigger state formation: physical limitation or "circumscription" (environmental or social), increasing population, and warfare. Narrow valleys, arid areas, oases, or small islands are examples of environmental circumscription; political units cannot expand geographically in such places. Social circumscription—

The Aztec State

The Aztec state, first known to Westerners in 1519, was begun by people who entered the Valley of Mexico about A.D. 1200. By the early fifteenth century, only three hundred years later, the Aztecs had expanded their realm from the Pacific Ocean to the Gulf of Mexico. Their capital, the ruins of which today lie under Mexico City, was called Tenochtitlan.

Aztec society recognized five classes: a royal class, which provided the Aztec ruler; a small class of nobles; a large middle class; a small lower class; and a slave class. Only royalty and nobles shared in the booty that flowed into Tenochtitlan from conquered neighboring states, although middle-class men whose service to the state was exceptional were sometimes elevated by the king into the nobility. Slaves and members of the lower class had no power and owned no land but carried out the bulk of the agricultural work. Most were unskilled laborers, barely able to support their own families.

The corn and other crops on which the Aztecs depended were planted and tended by hand on plots made by cutting water plants from the surfaces of rivers and lakes (an unusual method; in most early states, plows and draft animals were used in cultivation). These plants were piled up in thick layers to make floating "islands," anchored in place by willows planted along the edges of the canals that ran between them. Long dikes controlled flooding and ensured access to neighboring freshwater lagoons. This was a sophisticated kind of crop raising indeed. Since water management contributed to its agricultural success, the Aztec state is classified by anthropologists as a hydraulic society.

when neighbors prevent a population from emigrating, for example—can also prevent expansion.

When gatherers and hunters become horticulturalists, Carneiro (1970) argues, population increases. But their geographical expansion may be prevented by environmental or social circumscription. Since land is scarce, conflicts arise and war breaks out. The losers, unable to flee, are forced to submit to the victors, who demand tribute. To pay it, the losers intensify their production, employing new techniques and working harder. Their villages grow, eventually uniting to form chiefdoms. In time, one chiefdom conquers others, and a state is formed. However, like Wittfogel's (1957) hypothesis, Carneiro's thesis has not escaped criticism since there are examples of population increase within circumscribed environments that did not lead to state formation.

Elman R. Service (1971:32) sees state formation as the result of attempts by political leaders to obtain and hold power by organizing public works, redistributing wealth, and forming armies for their followers' benefit. Yet another explanation stresses the state-forming effects of long-distance trade (Polanyi et al. 1957). Each of these approaches—Wittfogel's, Carneiro's, Service's, and Polanyi's—gives us insights into how states may have originated, but none can be used to explain every case of state formation.

Some feminist anthropologists have tried to show that as states arise, women's authority and status decrease and a gender hierarchy (see Chapter 8) emerges. They argue that in "kinship societies"—bands, tribes, and chiefdoms, in which descent and marriage help determine access to positions of influence, authority, and power—women hold a greater share of these positions than they do in states, political organizations in which kinship usually has much less impact.

Christine Ward Gailey (1987:264) uses the Polynesian chiefdom of Tonga, where women traditionally wielded considerable influence, as a case study to make this point. In Gailey's view, as Westernization transformed the Tongan chiefdom into a state, activities over which women exercised control, such as births and marriages, fell increasingly under the domination of civil authorities representing the newly emerging state. At the same time, as the economy became more dependent on cash, goods traditionally produced by women lost their value to Tongans, and women's labor itself became devalued. Arguing on the opposite side of this hypothesis are other feminists who don't believe that the rise of the state necessarily brings about the subjugation of women (Silverblatt 1988:444–448).

CONFLICT CONTAINMENT AND RESOLUTION

The boundaries of acceptable behavior—what is permissible to do, say, or even think or look like—vary widely from society to society. In fact, these boundaries are not always the same for different people in the same society. Boundaries that are institutionalized are called laws; those that are informal are termed **norms.** Sometimes norms and laws are grounded in religion or mythology; in technologically simpler societies, people often say that their ancestors taught them how to behave.

Norms and laws protect the social order, without which societies could not exist. Still, they are often ignored or violated, and the result may be conflict—the disruption of the social order. Nonconformity with norms and laws takes many different shapes, ranging from victimless crimes (like using illegal drugs) to personal attacks (such as rape, theft, or murder) to political terrorism to larger-scale civil rebellions to wholesale revolutions and international disputes. To prevent, contain, or resolve such conflicts, societies have ways of encouraging and enforcing conformity with norms and laws and discouraging and punishing nonconformity. Some of these means are orderly (a North American legal trial, for example); others (like civil war) reflect a breakdown of the social order.

Orderly Means

Councils and Committees. Councils and committees are advisory groups found in many different kinds of societies. We have briefly mentioned **councils**

 ASK YOURSELF

Jews and Christians believe that their most important rules, the Ten Commandments, were given to them by God through the prophet Moses. Do you think this is true? If not, where do you think these social rules came from?

norm informal rule for behavior

council an advisory group, typical of simpler political organizations, that is usually informally appointed, meets in public, and resolves conflicts by consensus

Councils, advisory groups made up of informally appointed elders, meet in public and achieve resolutions to local problems by consensus. In Botswana, Africa, Tswana council members welcome a foreign dignitary to their outdoor meeting.

among the Shavante, Tetum, and Qashgai. They meet in public and are usually made up of informally appointed elders. **Committees** differ from councils in that they meet privately (Bailey 1965:20). Moreover, whereas councils are typical of simpler political organizations, committees are more characteristic of states. But the two kinds of groups can and often do coexist within the same political organization. When this occurs, councils are su-

Consensus in Pentrediwaith

In the small Welsh village of Pentrediwaith, everyone knows everyone else, and ties of descent, affinity, joint economic ventures, and religion bind individuals together (Frankenberg 1957). The open expression of conflict cannot be permitted to occur since it would create friction between individuals who *must* cooperate with their fellows. Hence, in their daily interaction, the villagers of Pentrediwaith, rather than resolving conflicts, go to great lengths to avoid them in the first place. A villager will not refuse an unreasonable request, but may forever delay fulfilling it. Issues of common concern are discussed in committee meetings, and decisions are arrived at by consensus of its members. But the minutes of these meetings are not taken down in detail, and the names of members who propose or second controversial motions are unrecorded.

Outsiders from England are sometimes brought into committees and maneuvered into bringing up topics that need to be discussed but are so controversial that local villagers do not wish to be associated with them. In this way, the blame for any resulting unpleasantness falls on outsiders rather than on villagers. Committee members are anxious to work out compromises, a desire springing from the realization that if a decision is not a compromise it will not be carried out.

Ronald Frankenberg (1957:94, 138) tells of an instance in which a committee in Pentrediwaith refused to seek consensus, insisting instead on taking a vote to reach a majority decision. The secretary of the committee, who was in the losing minority, "forgot" to write up the minutes and the decision was never implemented. In Pentrediwaith, consensus not only dampens disputes but resolves them, too (Bailey 1965:8).

perior to committees, whose tasks and powers are delegated to them by councils.

Councils tend to be consensus-seeking bodies, while committees are more apt to achieve agreement by voting (although either kind of body may reach decisions in either way). Consensus seeking is typical of small social groups whose members have frequent personal interaction. Once a council or committee increases to more than about fifty members, decision by consensus is no longer possible. Voting is typical of larger groups whose members do not see much of one another in daily life and who owe their main allegiance not to other group members but to people (perhaps many millions) outside the council or committee. Members may in fact represent these outside people, as is the case with the U.S. Congress (Bailey 1965).

Sanctions. A **sanction** is a reaction by society to approved or disapproved behavior (Radcliffe-Brown 1965:205). Reactions to approved behavior are called *positive sanctions;* reactions to disapproved behavior are called *negative sanctions.* The Nobel Prize and a round of applause are both positive sanctions; the death penalty, a $50 fine, and unflattering gossip are negative sanctions. We can now point out an additional difference between (institutionalized) laws and (informal) norms: laws are always backed up by sanctions; norms often are not.

Just as sanctions can be either positive or negative, so each kind can be either diffused or organized (see Figure 10.1). **Diffused sanctions** are spontaneous expressions of either approval or disapproval. Either way, they are informal and noninstitutionalized. A round of applause and unflattering gossip are both diffused sanctions—one positive, the other negative. **Organized sanctions,** in contrast, are formalized and institutionalized, like the Nobel Prize or the death penalty.

Thus, *diffused positive sanctions* are informal gestures of approval. Teachers who care for their students and who go out of their way to help them master and enjoy a course may receive thank-you notes at the end of the semester; these are diffused positive sanctions. *Diffused negative sanctions,* in contrast, are informal punishments. Often they are verbal: an offender may be labeled discourteous or dishonorable or may be ridiculed or even completely shunned, a severe negative sanction known as **ostracism.** *Organized positive sanctions* are formal gestures of approval given to individuals who

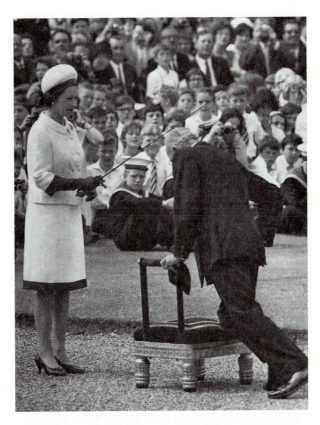

Knighthood, a formal gesture of approval given to people who have done something admirable, is an example of an organized positive sanction. Using a sword once belonging to Sir Francis Drake, the Queen of England bestows knighthood on Sir Francis Chichester, who distinguished himself by sailing around the world alone in a tiny sailboat.

committee an advisory group, most common in states, that meets in private and usually achieves agreement by voting

sanction a positive or negative reaction by society to approved behavior (positive sanction) or disapproved behavior (negative sanction)

diffused sanction a spontaneous expression of either approval or disapproval

organized sanction a formalized and institutionalized expression of approval or disapproval

ostracism a diffused sanction in which the offender is shunned

◆ **ASK YOURSELF**

Have you ever been sanctioned, positively or negatively, by a group of which you are a part? What did the sanction consist of? Was it diffused or organized? What was your reaction?

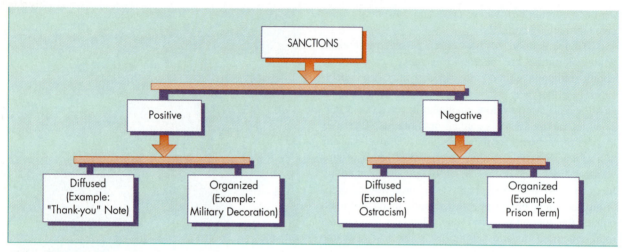

Figure 10.1
Types and Examples of Sanctions

have done something admirable—military or civilian decorations, for example. *Organized negative sanctions* are formal punishments, such as a spell in prison, administered to rule breakers or those who have neglected to fulfill their social obligations. Generally the most clearly defined of all sanctions, these differ from diffused negative sanctions in that they have the weight of society behind them.

Who is responsible for deciding what sanctions to apply and under what circumstances? In most societies, one or more people have the right and duty to sit in judgment of their fellows and decide what, if any, sanctions should be imposed. Depending on the society, such authority might be vested in the head of a simple family or a lineage, a village chief, a group of tribal elders, a king or emperor, or a jury.

Courts and Judges. In many societies, the identification of wrongdoers, the decision to punish them or not, and the method of punishment to be used are duties of a **court,** a group of people with the authority to hear the cases of disputants and their witnesses, to determine innocence or guilt, and to decide on punishment (Gulliver 1969:24). A court's members are not directly involved in the dispute. The head of a court is usually a

◆ **ASK YOURSELF**

Have you ever been responsible for deciding on someone's guilt or innocence or served as a mediator in a dispute? If so, what evidence did you consider in making your judgment?

judge, who acts on behalf of the community or a higher political authority. In societies with centralized political systems, the judge is typically backed up by the weight of the entire political system, for his office is a political position.

In Central Africa, a judge of the Lozi chiefdom relies in his decision making on a concept familiar to Westerners: that of the reasonable man (Gluckman 1969:367–371). The Lozi judge asks himself whether the accused behaved reasonably and in conformity with custom. If the offense involves an action that the defendant committed in his capacity as a father, for instance, the judge compares the defendant's behavior against Lozi norms for paternal behavior. Standards of accepted behavior are familiar to all Lozi individuals, and deviants know that if they are brought to court they will be judged according to their degree of conformity to these standards. Fear of the court serves as a sanction against deviant behavior, even behavior that does not actually break the law.

Instead of being vested in the person of a judge, the authority to sit in judgment may be combined with the other functions of a lineage head, ritual leader, village headman, senior kinsman, or other influential person (Gulliver 1969:25). When a dispute occurs, such a person may be pressed into temporary service as a **mediator**—a third party, neutral to the dispute, charged with negotiating a settlement. In contrast to the judge in a centralized political system, mediators may be little more than spokespersons for public opinion, summing up the consensus on the disputed matter (Gulliver

In a divination ritual, a past or future event is divined with help from supernatural agents. In Mali, a Dogon diviner (left, with crook) studies the pawprints of foxes as he attempts to foretell the future.

1969:25). Sometimes, when the contending parties agree to accept the mediator's decision as final and binding, the process of settling a dispute is called **adjudication.**

Some conflicts are handled in what might be termed *informal courts.* When a dispute occurs among the Arusha of East Africa, each disputant recruits a body of supporters and with them meets peacefully with his opponent and *his* supporters to negotiate a settlement. Supporters are recruited on the basis of patrilineal descent, similar age, and neighborhood. Each party seeks to win the support of influential men, such as members of lineage councils. These supporters, neither judges nor neutral mediators, negotiate with the other disputant's supporters to reach a compromise. Social pressures of every kind are brought to bear by each party on the other, and if an agreement is to be reached at all, each must give ground and accept a compromise. Enforcement is rarely a problem since both sides accept the compromise as the best solution available under the circumstances (Gulliver 1969:26).

Another alternative is for an entire community to act as its own court, with community consensus deciding the verdict. The Central Inuit require the disputants in a wife-stealing argument to confront each other in a public song contest (Hoebel 1964:93–99). Before the whole community, each disputant sings songs ridiculing the other. The man who manages to sing the wittiest, most satirical song receives the most applause from the assembled group and is judged the winner by community consensus.

Determining Innocence or Guilt. Whether a court exists or not, determining the innocence or guilt of accused individuals is basic to the enforcement of rules and norms. Evidence of either is required, but what manner of evidence is acceptable and who should assess its merits vary widely among societies. You are probably familiar with the North American system, in which a judge, jury, or both analyze the conflicting claims of both parties in a dispute, determine the facts of the matter, and proclaim guilt or innocence. If the accused is found guilty, a judge then imposes a penalty as determined by law. In other societies, other methods of establishing the facts, determining guilt or innocence, and specifying penalties may be used.

In societies other than our own, **divination** is sometimes used to determine innocence or guilt. In a divination, performed by a ritual specialist called a **diviner,** something that will happen in the future is fore-

◆◆◆

court a group of people with the authority to hear the cases of disputants and their witnesses, to determine innocence or guilt, and to decide on punishment

mediator a person who is neutral to a dispute and charged with negotiating its settlement

adjudication the process by which a dispute is settled after the disputants agree that a mediator's decision will be binding

divination a ritual designed to foretell the future or interpret the past, with the help of supernatural agents

diviner a person who performs a divination ritual

◆◆

The Goetz Case

In December 1985, a slim, shy electronics expert in his middle thirties joined other passengers on a New York subway train, taking his seat near four young men. Within minutes, one of the four approached the lone traveler and demanded five dollars, whereupon Bernhard Goetz pulled a gun from his clothing and shot his way to celebrity.

Under the laws of New York State, one may use deadly force in self-defense if this is what a "reasonable man" would do if he feared himself threatened in a similar way. But Goetz shot one of his assailants, 21-year-old Darryl Cabey, not once but twice, allegedly remarking to Cabey, "You seem to be all right, here's another." The second bullet severed Cabey's spine, causing paralysis from the waist down. Critics of Goetz thought his remark suggested a murderous coolness of mind rather than fear. Moreover, in New York—as in every state in the United

States—shooting a person after the immediate threat has passed is not considered legitimate self-defense (Berger 1987:B6). Goetz was charged with attempted murder.

It looked as if Goetz's words and actions might convict him. But Barry Slotnick, his attorney, convinced the jury that "no man is reasonable when he's surrounded by four thugs" (Berger 1987:B6), that even as he fired his second shot at Cabey, Goetz was acting under extreme stress brought about by fear. The verdict was not guilty.

In a curious footnote to the Goetz case, defense attorney Slotnick, leaving his office one day a month or so after the Goetz verdict, was himself attacked and robbed by a mugger. Slotnick was not carrying a gun. If he had been, one wonders whether or not he would have used it.

---

told, or something that happened in the past is revealed (divined) with the help of supernatural agents.

Another method of determining guilt or innocence is the **conditional curse,** a verbal formula containing a conditional phrase, something like "If I'm lying, may lightening strike me dead!" This is similar to the oath required of witnesses in North American courts, which obliges them to tell the truth "so help me God."

Mere words, however, are not a sufficient guarantee of the truth in all courts, as shown by the **trial by ordeal,** a physical test of the accused for the purpose of revealing the truth. In Europe, just a couple of centuries ago, the hands and feet of an accused witch were bound together, and she (or more rarely he) was tossed into a stream. Water symbolized purity, so if the accused sank to the bottom, it was believed she was free of witchcraft since the water had accepted her. If she floated, it was believed that the water had rejected her because she was polluted by witchcraft. It was a no-win situation for the accused!

Disorderly Means

Unfortunately, disputes are not always resolved in orderly fashion. Resolution within the prevailing system

of laws and norms may not be sought, may be sought but not achieved, or may be achieved only to break down in the face of renewed hostility. In the case of disputes between individuals, society may require the disputants, and only them, to resolve their differences in a physical contest—a spear fight, for example, or a boxing match. When groups rather than individuals are involved, the result may be feuds or wars.

Feuds. A **feud** is a prolonged but usually intermittent hostile relationship between two groups. Especially typical of tribes, feuding often occurs between two descent groups or factions. The way feuds are carried out differs among societies, but all feuds share three important characteristics (Pospisil 1974:3). First, despite the way the word is commonly used, feuds involve not individuals but groups, for whom injury to even one

◆◆◆

conditional curse a verbal formula containing a conditional phrase designed to establish innocence or guilt

trial by ordeal a physical test of an accused person for the purpose of revealing the truth

feud a prolonged but usually intermittent hostile relationship between two groups

Societies sometimes require or permit disputants to resolve their differences in one-on-one contests. In July 1804, U.S. Vice-President Aaron Burr shot and killed his political opponent, Alexander Hamilton, former secretary of the Treasury, in an unofficial and unsanctioned duel provoked by the political rivalry of the two men.

member is considered injury to all. Second, feuds are physical. Violence, even killing, is believed to be justified for either of two reasons: revenge on enemies or glory for one's own group. Typically, the violence follows a pattern: injury, reprisal, and counter-reprisal. Thus, once begun, feuds tend to continue, perhaps for generations. And third, feuding takes place within societies rather than between them, so feuding groups share the same cultural values, institutions, and expectations and observe the same set of rules (4).

Feuding is found more often in tribes than in bands, chiefdoms, or states because tribes are large

The Hatfields and the McCoys

In the late nineteenth century, many residents of the isolated, mountainous border between West Virginia and Kentucky—farmers, hunters, and illegal moonshiners by occupation—thumbed their noses at civil authority. Their children rarely attended school, so illiteracy was high. Religion had no more influence on most people's behavior than government or education. Opportunities for individuals to learn self-control in social situations were thus limited. Nuclear families tended to be large, with a dozen or more children, and extended families enormous. Family ties were strong, but boys grew up pursuing solitary activities such as hunting and fishing, "often . . . untempered by strong parental or social discipline" (Rice 1978).

During the warm afternoon of August 10, 1882, the body of Ellison Hatfield, stabbed repeatedly and shot in the back in a drunken fight between his kin and the hated McCoys, was lowered into its grave. The very next day, three coffins containing the bodies of Tolbert, Pharmer, and Randolph McCoy, riddled with bullets and found tied to some pawpaw bushes, were placed in a single grave. The McCoys had paid with their lives for Ellison's death. It was neither the first time nor the last that Hatfields and McCoys would kill each other in the longest-running and most notorious of a number of late nineteenth-century Appalachian feuds.

No one knows just what started the Hatfield-McCoy feud. It seems to have been rooted in everyday conflicts of the time: different opinions on the Civil War, political arguments, minor theft. The first killing, in 1865, followed an earlier exchange of gunfire, a couple of pig-stealing episodes, and some vandalism. A brief Romeo-and-Juliet episode, strongly opposed by both families, increased the enmity, and home-brewed liquor contributed to hot tempers on both sides. After a Hatfield was acquitted of pig-stealing charges, the McCoys refused to accept the decision of the court and "resorted to the law that might makes right" (Rice 1978:16). Soon afterward, a Hatfield was murdered.

In the decades that followed, the feud escalated. The two large extended families, increasingly active politically, won friends in official positions and even filled some of these positions themselves, but frequently they took matters into their own hands, ignoring the law. In the 1880s, threats, fights, beatings, arson, and murder were frequent occurrences. There were even rumors of cannibalism. As the century drew to a close, however, increasingly widespread education and technological development slowly drew the Appalachian mountain area into the American cultural mainstream. At the same time, it became more and more difficult to take the law into one's own hands and get away with it; local customs gave

In what may be America's most famous feud, the Hatfields and the McCoys—extended families living in Appalachia in the late nineteenth century—threatened, fought, and killed each other over a period of four decades. Above, Hatfield men pose with their guns in 1899.

way in the face of more strictly enforced state and national legal and political processes. Sometime during the early years of the twentieth century, the famous Hatfield-McCoy feud fizzled out.

enough to be divided up into special-interest groups but still small enough to be organized on the basis of kinship rather than some overarching principle of law. But feuding can occur even in states, including Western ones. Feuds are most common in societies that lack a central government (as well as other formal educational or religious institutions) or where the government exerts little influence or authority.

Warfare. Many Westerners are unfamiliar with feuds since our society does not ordinarily include the small but intimately related social and political groups that typically provide the stage for feuding. We are, however, all too familiar with war.

Two important features distinguish wars from feuds. First, warfare is conducted on a level above that of the local community; warring groups are usually either relatively large-scale elements within a single nation (civil war) or whole nations (international war). The

second difference lies in the relationship between the antagonistic parties. In a feud, the participating groups are part of the same relatively small-scale social system—for instance, antagonistic lineages within the same tribe. (If we consider the nineteenth-century Appalachian community of much-intermarried, white, western European immigrant farmers a "tribe," this is the situation in which the Hatfields and the McCoys found themselves.) In warfare, although the disputants may be covered by the same broad cultural umbrella (as were the combatants in the American Civil War), at a lower level they represent quite distinct political or social or economic organizations. This may be why they fight.

Modern wars are of three kinds—world wars; more geographically confined wars (which may nevertheless, like the Vietnam and Persian Gulf wars, include extraregional superpowers among the combatants); and smaller-scale, intraregional conflicts such as the recent war in Bosnia. Although there are obvious differences among them, their causes are similar. Values such as honor, freedom, or religious principles may be the avowed reasons for fighting, but social and economic inequalities between the combatants—the lack of territory, unevenly distributed natural resources, unequal influence in a larger political arena, unequal access to regional or world markets—are more likely to be the real causes. In the recent war between Iran and Iraq, young men on both sides went willingly to their deaths in the name of religion, even though this war was not so much about the ideological differences between two branches of Islam as it was about the region's underground oil riches.

How do anthropologists explain warfare? Many hypotheses have been suggested, but no consensus has been reached (see Ferguson and Farragher 1988). Some scholars claim that warfare is motivated by people's involuntary reactions to environmental, economic, or cultural forces (Robarchek 1989). One ecological argument suggests that warfare prevents population growth that would lead to the overexploitation and deterioration of resources (Vayda 1961:347). Yet there are many examples in human history in which populations have increased, causing natural resources to deteriorate, but war has not erupted (Hallpike 1973:457). A deterministic view of this kind implies that people are the helpless pawns of irresistible forces.

Functionalists have argued that warfare strengthens the internal solidarity of groups that engage in it. But it doesn't follow that the entire society of which a warring group is a part is also strengthened. In fact, many societies punish members who risk plunging their particular groups into war. Among the Konso of Ethiopia (Northeast Africa), if a man steals a goat from a man of another town, the elders of the thief's town, far from feeling obliged to support the thief (thereby, as the functionalists would insist, strengthening the solidarity of their town), force him to pay compensation (Hallpike 1973:460).

People aren't "passive machines pushed this way and that by ecological, biological, sociological, or even cultural determinants" (Robarchek 1989:903–904). At least some of the time, they make decisions among clear options and constraints in pursuit of a variety of goals. Another explanation for warfare, which we might call

◆ **ASK YOURSELF**

Can you think of possible causes of warfare in addition to the ones mentioned above?

the pragmatic, seems to fit this view as well as the realities of human history. Its most eloquent spokesperson, C. R. Hallpike (1973:459), rejects deterministic explanations of warfare. The desire for power, prestige, material wealth, and sex, and the envy of those who have them, are among the most powerful forces in human nature, Hallpike writes. To attain such goals, and to keep others from attaining them, is sufficient reason for warfare. "The human race has evolved few more definitive means of proving one's superiority over an enemy than by battering him to death and eating him, or by burning his habitation, ravaging his crops, and raping his wife" (459).

Warfare has changed through the ages and is now more technologically complex and more destructive of both property and human life than ever before. Moreover, it has moved from an activity involving only a few of a society's members (e.g., members of a military association) to one that can involve not only hundreds of thousands of professional combatants but millions of noncombatants as well. Various modern-day measures to contain warfare have either failed, like the League of Nations, or are still in their infancy, like the United Nations.

CONCLUSION

In this chapter we presented a cultural-evolutionary model of political organizations, pointing out that a general trend toward bigger populations and increasingly complex lifeways is evident between the first and the last of the four types of organizations discussed. Elsewhere (Chapter 4), we warned against interpreting increasing complexity as progress. You'll recall that neo-evolutionists prefer the term *process* to describe what happens to cultures through time since the word doesn't imply progress or, for that matter, any change at all. Here we'd like to take a quick look at modern states with these two notions in mind.

In every society, political power is unequally distributed; it rests largely in the hands of certain people who impose order, define and pursue society's goals, punish disobedience, direct change, and sometimes (depending on the size of the society) oversee bureaucracies made up of lesser officeholders. How do societies determine which individuals get to wield political power? Although room exists for some wrangling over leadership in every kind of society, the more complex the political organization, the more difficult it is for any given individual to be an important player on the political stage. In bands, experienced male heads of households typically get to be leaders, although other adults have their say in these highly egalitarian political organizations. In tribes and chiefdoms, many adults are ineligible for leadership for reasons of descent, sex, or class, and among those who are eligible there may be much jockeying for influence, power, wealth, and followers. Relatively few individuals wind up with real political power. The same was true in early state-level political organizations: only some people were eligible for political roles.

Today, in many state-level societies, every adult member is, in principle, eligible to participate in politics—even to become a leader. But states may have populations too large to permit more than a small proportion of their members to play any hands-on part in politics, much less to become leaders. Instead, states may claim to have instituted "representative" governments. They may further claim that representatives are selected democratically.

This kind of system is more ideal than real. In "representative" governments, who is represented, and how, varies. So does the process of "democratic" selection of leaders. Modern states commonly prevent certain categories of people from participating in politics: South Africa before 1991 is an example. Even in the United States, young adults whom society considers old enough to be pressed into military service to benefit the state but are still under the age of 21 are excluded from candidacy for office. These examples make it clear that the evolution of political organizations mentioned in this chapter doesn't necessarily imply improvement. No kind of society—except, perhaps, the band—has yet developed a political system in which everyone is assured a chance to participate.

◆◆◆

SUMMARY

This chapter is about politics, the ways in which human groups regulate the behavior of their members. Politics exists in every society, and all societies have some kind of political organization for establishing and maintaining social control. Every political organization has leaders, who set priorities; prevent, limit, or resolve conflicts; punish those who threaten the social order; and direct change. These leaders must have both power and authority. Power, the capacity to control the behavior of others, may be based on physical strength, wealth, organization, knowledge, charisma, or a combination of these. Authority, which may be either ascribed or

achieved, is the socially granted right to exercise power, and it is usually conveyed to an individual through an office that exists independently of its occupant.

Elman R. Service has described four types of political organizations. In order of increasing complexity, they are bands, tribes, chiefdoms, and states. In a very general way, these types, from the first to the fourth, have increasingly complex subsistence strategies, larger and larger size, and increasingly complex economic arrangements.

The simplest political organization, the band, is most common among gatherers and hunters. In bands, power and authority are noncentralized and allocated on an informal, temporary basis. In tribes—somewhat larger groups of horticulturalists or herders who distinguish themselves on the basis of their common heritage—power and authority are also noncentralized. Chiefdoms tend to be based on extensive cultivation; and power and authority, either achieved or ascribed, are centralized in or around chiefs. States, the largest and most complex political organizations of all, have centralized governments with the authority and power to conscript labor, make and enforce laws, collect taxes, and create and maintain institutions to support themselves. States are based on technologically sophisticated agriculture, the only way to obtain the huge food supply necessary to sustain a very large population. Authority in states is based on the law.

Several explanations for the emergence of states have been proposed. Wittfogel's is based on the idea that manufactured water control systems, which require more labor and more complex management than rainfall agriculture, encourage the development of powerful bureaucracies in which political power becomes concentrated. Carneiro sees environmental or social circumscription, increasing population, and warfare as jointly encouraging state formation. Service thinks state formation is the result of the attempts made by political leaders to obtain and hold power by organizing public works, redistributing wealth, and forming armies; and Polanyi stresses the effects of long-distance trade. But none of these explanations can explain every case of state formation.

The boundaries of acceptable behavior, which vary widely from society to society, may be either informal, in which case they are called norms, or formally recognized, in which case they are called laws. To prevent, contain, or resolve conflicts, all societies have ways, orderly or otherwise, of encouraging and enforcing conformity with norms and laws and discouraging and sometimes punishing nonconformity. Orderly means include dispute-resolving councils and committees. Councils meet in public and are typical of simpler political organizations; committees meet privately and are more characteristic of states.

Sanctions, society's reactions to behavior it approves or disapproves, may also be used to resolve conflicts in an orderly fashion. Some sanctions, such as applause, are positive; others, like jail terms, are negative. Sanctions may be diffused (informal and noninstitutionalized), or organized (formal and institutionalized). Yet another peaceful means of conflict resolution is the court, a group of people with the authority to determine innocence or guilt and to decide what punishment to mete out. Courts are headed by judges, officials authorized to act on behalf of society. Whether a court exists or not, establishing the guilt or innocence of an accused person is basic to social control. Sometimes the verdict is determined by a diviner, who seeks to discover the truth with the help of supernatural agents. The conditional curse is another way of determining guilt or innocence.

Disorderly methods of social control include feuds and wars. Feuds are prolonged, usually intermittent hostilities between two closely associated groups of people sharing the same larger cultural tradition. Most characteristic of tribes, feuds frequently occur between two clans or factions. Violence for revenge or glory follows a pattern of injury, reprisal, and counter-reprisal. Wars, in contrast, are associated with chiefdoms and states, are conducted by whole communities against other communities, and involve more participants and more widespread violence.

Some anthropologists claim that warfare is motivated by involuntary reactions to environmental, economic, or cultural forces. Others emphasize its function as a cohesive mechanism. A more pragmatic, less deterministic explanation may lie in universal human desires for power, prestige, material wealth, and revenge.

KEY TERMS

adjudication
achieved authority
ascribed authority
authority
big man
charisma
chiefdom
committee
conditional curse
council
court
diffused sanction
divination
diviner
faction
feud
government
hydraulic society
law
mediator
norm

office
organized sanction
oriental despotism
ostracism
political organization (political system)
politics
power
sanction
state
trial by ordeal
tribe

SUGGESTED READINGS

Bailey, F. G. 1991. *The Prevalence of Deceit*. Ithaca, NY: Cornell University Press. A study of how truth can be relative in political contexts and how power can depend on the ability of politicians to deceive their supporters. This well-written book illuminates the tactics and antics of those who would rule us.

Chagnon, Napoleon. 1992. *Yanomamo* (4th ed.). New York: Harcourt Brace Jovanovich. A graphic account of the causes and consequences of warfare among South American forest dwellers.

Conley, John M., and William M. O'Barr. 1990. *Rules versus Relationships: The Ethnography of Legal Discourse*. Chicago: University of Chicago Press. This book deals with law in the American legal system and contains a wealth of information on how the law actually works at the grass-roots level.

Gledhill, John, Barbara Bender, and Mogens Trolle Larsen (eds.). 1988. *State and Society*. London: Unwin Hyman. Scholars from different disciplines examine social hierarchies and political centralization in case studies that include chiefdoms and states. West Africa, Hawaii, the Valley of Mexico, and ancient Egypt are a few of the examples given.

Roberts, Simon. 1979. *Order and Dispute: An Introduction to Legal Anthropology*. New York: St. Martin's Press. A useful introduction to basic topics in the anthropology of social control. Examples include gatherer-and-hunter and pastoralist societies as well as states.

Starr, June, and Jane F. Collier (eds.). 1989. *History and Power in the Study of Law: New Directions in Legal Anthropology*. Ithaca, NY: Cornell University Press. A collection of case studies on topics ranging from the invention of legal ideas to the language of public executions in Norway to constitution making in Islamic Iran to the American love of litigation.

CHAPTER 11

GROUPS

Groups of people who share a common heritage and identify themselves as distinct from others are called ethnic groups. Often, two or more such groups are found side by side, as in Israel, where Palestinians' shared traditions, values, and style of dress distinguish them from the Israelis among whom they live and work. Near their mosque in Jerusalem, white-robed Palestinians argue with Israeli policemen after a dispute with Jewish worshippers.

INTRODUCTION

According to the admissions catalog of a big midwestern university, the on-campus living and social arrangements for undergraduates included about a dozen fraternities—more or less depending on how many of these all-male clubs had, at any given time, been placed on probation by the dean for infringements of academic or social rules. The admissions catalog conveyed the impression that these fraternities were all very much alike. Each was governed by a democratically elected president, vice-president, financial officer, and social affairs director. Each listed, among its reasons for existence, brotherhood, academic excellence, and worthy charitable goals. Each professed democratic ideals and pledged full cooperation with the university's goals and regulations as well as ongoing involvement in campus projects and issues. The catalog also gave the impression that although only about a third of the male undergraduates on campus actually belonged to a fraternity, becoming a member was simply a matter of deciding which one you liked best.

So it came as a surprise to many male freshmen to discover that what the catalog suggested about fraternities did not reflect the actual situation at all. In reality, these organizations were not alike. Instead, they were ranked, in the minds of everybody on campus, from best to worst. One fraternity had a high proportion of athletes and was widely acknowledged to be the most prestigious. Another, also high-ranking, contributed more than its share of officers to the student government and other campus organizations. Lower down in the ranking scheme was a fraternity considered to be made up of rich students with preppy tastes, and somewhere below that was one known for its wild parties and frequent confrontations with the campus cops. There was even a bottom-of-the-heap fraternity that consisted, in the view of most students, of members unacceptable to all the other fraternities.

Not only were the fraternities unequal in social status; applicants to the fraternities, too, quickly assumed different positions in a ranking system. Long before the end of the rush period, when students interested in joining fraternities made this choice known, a rigid "pecking order" of all freshman applicants had developed. This pecking order reflected the perceptions of all those involved in the selection process—freshmen hopefuls and upperclass fraternity members alike—about the relative desirability of various freshmen as fraternity brothers. It was based on the applicants' personalities,

◆ **ASK YOURSELF**

Do you think fraternities and sororities improve the college experience? If your college or university has fraternities and sororities, are you a member of one? If so, why, and if not, why not? If your institution has no fraternities or sororities, would you like to have them? Why or why not?

physical appearance and style of dress, participation in campus clubs and sports teams, and behavior at rush functions.

In earlier chapters, we mentioned descent and marriage as institutions that serve to classify individuals as members of particular groups. But these aren't the only means by which societies organize people into groups. Many other kinds of groups exist, defined by what it is that brings their members together and what these members have in common. Sex, relative social standing, and common interests are some of the attributes that bring North American students together into sororities or fraternities. In other societies these same attributes, plus age, occupation, ethnicity, and others, may create groups. This chapter describes some of the many ways in which the members of different societies are grouped, as well as some of the cross-culturally important customs and institutions created by these various systems.

Distinguishing among individuals or groups according to their different attributes is called **social classification,** and it's a human universal. The number of people grouped together may be small (e.g., the members of a nuclear family) or huge (e.g., ethnic Ukranians in the United States, a group tied together by common traditions and language). Like most of the things human beings do, classifying, or "pigeonholing," people serves a number of useful purposes. Simple identification is among the most important; when a person is classified as a member of a particular group, or a group is ranked relative to other groups, both the similarities and differences between that person or group and others are immediately known. But social classification serves other purposes as well. It may be used to allocate rights and duties on the basis of the category occupied, provide group members with mutual support, aid in social solidarity, or prevent discord.

A system of social classification may merely differentiate between individuals or groups viewed as social equals, or it may convey notions of superiority and inferiority. When the occupants of various pigeonholes in a system of social classification are viewed as unequal to one another, the result is **social stratification (social ranking).** In this case, people or groups are not only distinguished from one another but also hierarchically ordered. Like all classification systems, stratification systems may be formal and large-scale (like the hierarchical arrangement of ethnic groups in societies with many such groups, for example) or informal and individual (like the stratification of students in a grade-school classroom, in which every student knows just how all the others—sports heros, geniuses, dimwits, jokesters, daredevils, bullies—stand relative to one another). An organization of people emerges even in stuck elevators, where it soon becomes apparent who is the calm, capable leader and who the craven wretch! When people are classified hierarchically, like the layers of a many-tiered cake, their different positions are called **ranks.** We call a whole society that is divided up hierarchically a stratified or ranked society.

STATUS, ROLE, AND PRESTIGE

Individuals and groups occupying pigeonholes in a system of social classification often find that certain social attitudes and types of behavior are expected from them. They also find their fellows' reactions toward them to be fairly consistent. This raises two interesting questions: how do occupants of particular pigeonholes in social classification systems know how to behave in relation to the occupants of other pigeonholes and society at large, and how does society ensure the appropriate behavior by the occupants of these pigeonholes? Anthropologists analyze these interactions by using the concepts of status, role, and prestige.

The anthropological term for what we have been calling a pigeonhole is **status,** a word used in two ways in English. Status may refer to one of several interrelated positions in a social structure, or it may denote prestige. For the sake of clarity, we'll restrict our use of the word to the first sense: status is the place an individual occupies in a social structure. Every status is characterized by certain attitudes, and when interacting with his or her fellows an individual is actively expressing the attitudes associated with his or her status. When the attitudes linked with a given status and the behavior that expresses these attitudes are combined, they add up to a **role.** We may put the difference between status and role this way: an individual or group occupies a status but plays a role.

Inevitably among human beings, the occupant of a particular status sometimes fails to play the **role** society expects. Status and role are so closely linked that when this happens the offender may be forced out of his or her status. The role associated with the status of president of the United States involves obeying the Constitution. In the early 1970s, Richard Nixon failed to fulfill society's expectations for this role when he covered up information concerning the Watergate burglary from Congress. Subsequently, he lost his status as president.

Prestige involves social reputation and depends on people's evaluation of a status. It's thus a more subjective concept than either status or role. The higher the value placed on a status, the higher its prestige. Depending on the society, wealth, power, social origins, education, occupation, dress, body ornaments, religion, and personal achievement are all factors that make some statuses more prestigious than others.

People don't always agree on what qualities engender high or low prestige. In societies undergoing Westernization, values long supporting the superiority of the traditional aristocracy, such as descent, wealth, or race, may come under fire from members of lower classes, as new criteria for evaluating prestige emerge, such as education, white-collar employment, or Western styles of dress. The determinants of prestige in a society can change rapidly. In the late 1970s in Iran, Western clothes, goods, and music conveyed high prestige, particularly among the young. Almost overnight, however, these tokens of prestige were displaced by others: a traditional Muslim life-style, extreme forms of Muslim religious expression, and anti-Western sentiment.

Anthropologists studying social classification try to isolate the factors that determine prestige. Among the fraternity members described at the beginning of this chapter, good looks, a "cool" demeanor, and athletic ability were among the qualities contributing to high prestige; but in the broader context of North American society, wealth probably supercedes any of these as the major component of prestige. In contrast, the English consider prestige based on wealth to be somewhat crass. In England, prestige depends more on genealogy. If your

social classification a systematic way of distinguishing among individuals or groups according to their different attributes

social stratification (social ranking) a system of social classification in which the occupants of various statuses are viewed as unequal to one another

rank a position in a hierarchical system of social classification

status the place an individual occupies in the social structure

role the behavior that expresses the attitudes and behavior associated with a given status

prestige social reputation based on a subjective evaluation of social statuses relative to one another

Prestige depends on people's subjective evaluation of the status of others. In Tokyo, Japan, a visiting businessman, at left with briefcase, greets his host. The visitor's slightly lower bow shows that in this particular context he is inferior to his host.

family reckons its descent along aristocratic lines, then you, as an aristocrat, are granted higher prestige than any commoner. It matters not that you are poor and the commoner is a multimillionaire.

◆◆

SOCIAL STRATIFICATION

The sociologist Max Weber (1947:424–429; 1971:250–264), one of the first scholars to establish possible connections among power, prestige, and unequal access to resources, suggested that social inequality tends to develop in a society when

1. People have unequal access to whatever is considered valuable: natural resources, labor, money, or—especially in non-Western societies—intangibles such as ritual knowledge.
2. People are entitled to different degrees of prestige, depending on criteria such as descent, wealth, or race, or more recently, on education or westernization.
3. Some people enjoy more power, either physical or ideological (based on ideas or charisma), than others.

Such differences are both causes and characteristics of stratified societies.

Class

Inequality often presents itself in the form of social **classes.** These occur in many kinds of societies, from technologically simple to modern, and were described by Karl Marx as groups created and defined by economic production (see Chapter 9). In modern societies, production involves unequal control over what Marx called the "factors of production"—resources such as land, labor, and capital. Classes are distinguished by their different relationships to these factors. Those who exert the greatest control over resources belong to the upper classes; those whose control is limited or lacking altogether belong to the lower classes. Defined in this way, classes are more than just occupational groupings. The owners of a bookstore and a shoestore are members of the same class, while the salespeople employed in both of these establishments belong to a different class.

Marx's definition of class as an economic phenomenon assumes that in creating their own wealth the high-ranking classes will exploit the labor of the low-ranking classes. Marx also believed that conflict between different classes has been going on throughout human history and is therefore inevitable.

Some people recognize themselves as members of particular classes, holding common ideas and working together toward common goals (Fallers 1977). Others,

Maloh Class Stratification

One example of class stratification and its functions in a non-Western society is provided by the Maloh of Borneo. These agriculturalists were traditionally stratified into three social ranks: aristocrats, commoners, and slaves. The ranks were not unlike those that prevailed in the American South prior to the Civil War (King 1985:14).

Members of the different classes occupied very different positions in the process of production. The aristocrats controlled labor (the work of slaves as well as compulsory service from commoners); they had rights to more and better land than commoners; they accumulated agricultural surpluses and trading profits; and they translated part of these benefits into permanent forms of wealth, such as ritual objects. Commoners controlled their own land and labor, although from time to time they had to work for aristocrats and pay tribute to them. Slaves worked for their aristocratic owners rather than for themselves and could be exchanged for goods or used as sacrificial victims in rituals. Some slaves farmed independently, but they had no rights to land, and the products of their labor belonged to their masters.

Because their classes were traditionally based on unequal rights over resources used for production, the Maloh are a classic example of a class-stratified society as defined by Marx.

equally identifiable as members of classes according to Marx's definition, do not. Social scientists have long argued about whether class consciousness, people's self-identification as class members, is necessary for a group to be defined as a class. Marx himself did not answer this question, which remains unresolved.

In societies stratified by class, the lower classes often suffer while the upper classes prosper from their misery, as anyone who has seen pictures of luxurious high-rises towering over squatter settlements in cities from Lima to Lagos knows. But class distinctions do not always benefit only the upper classes.

In Peru, until the middle of this century, there were pronounced distinctions between a small, wealthy, white upper class of European ancestry and much larger classes of middle-income and poor people of native American or mixed native American and white ancestry. The prosperous whites, who controlled the country's

formal institutions (including the government, the church, and the schools), exploited the lower classes economically. At the same time, however, they provided employment, education, and health care to poorer Peruvians. The poor benefited from, and indeed came to depend on, this system of vertical patron-client relationships. When in need, they looked up the social ladder, seeking help from charities and other organizations created by the upper class (Stein 1985). Although this system has crumbled in recent years as Peru has become more and more industrialized, for many years it had some benefits for both the upper and lower classes.

Caste

In complex societies, jobs are often ranked according to the prestige granted to those who perform them. This is certainly true in our own society; no one is surprised when a member of the U.S. Senate is given more attention or more deference—in the press, say, or in a public setting such as a restaurant—than a night watchman. In some societies, certain occupations are regarded as being so lowly or degrading that only those of inferior social rank undertake them. Likewise, prestigious jobs may be performed only by members of a superior rank.

 ASK YOURSELF

In the context of North American society at large, what social class do you think you belong to—lower, middle, or upper? What attributes, your own or your family's, identify you as a member of this class? To which class would you assign the following well-known people: H. Ross Perot, Mike Tyson, Jacqueline Kennedy Onassis, Jimmy Carter, J. Paul Getty, Madonna?

class a group defined by the amount of control it exerts over factors of production

Traditional Hindu society in India, divided into four **varnas** ("colors"), illustrates this custom. The priestly (or Brahman) varna had the highest prestige. It was followed, in descending order, by the warrior varna (Ksatriya); merchants and cultivators (Vaisya); and craftsmen, laborers, and servants (Sudra). Traditionally, beneath all four varnas were a group of people so lowly they were considered outside this ranking system altogether: the untouchables. Well-defined sets of rights, duties, and rules of conduct were associated with each of the varnas and the untouchables. As a Hindu, just how you should behave, what treatment you could expect from others, and what you were responsible for depended on which group you had been born into (Tyler 1973:77).

Within each varna were numerous **castes,** hereditary social groups bound by specific rights, duties, and prohibitions, each occupying a permanent place in a hierarchy of similar groups and each associated with a specific occupation. The castes shared several well-defined features. Caste members inherited their membership patrilineally and were members for life. Castes were endogamous; members were required to marry someone from the same caste, although from a different patrilineage. Each caste occupied a permanent position in an overall hierarchy of castes, with each (except for those at the top and bottom) ranked as superior to as well as inferior to at least one other. An Indian village might contain residents belonging to a number of castes, each associated with one of the four varnas. Untouchables belonged to no caste.

If you had been a member of a caste in traditional India, only you and other members of your caste would have had the right to perform the traditional services "owned" by your caste. For example, only if you were a member of the Washerman caste could you have made clothing ritually clean. Anyone, of course, might physically have been able to launder clothing, but for Hindu society "ritually clean" meant that the washing had been done by an individual of the appropriate caste. Likewise, you would have had to be a member of the Astrologer caste to read horoscopes, or a Barber to cut hair. In addition, you could not have accepted food from, or have had sex with, a person of any caste that ranked below yours. Finally—as is often true of members of descent groups, too—you would probably have been prohibited from eating certain foods forbidden to members of your caste.

Specialists in Indian studies disagree about whether the caste system should be considered predominantly an economic or a religious institution. Actually, it contained features of both. From an economic perspective, castes were clearly occupational, but the hierarchical ordering of castes was based on a religious concept. At the core of Hinduism lies the notion of personal purity and pollution. One way these were determined was by one's varna; Brahmans were purer than Sudras, and this kind of purity or pollution was unchangeable. But a person could also be polluted by the biological functions of daily life—eating, excretion, sex, childbirth, or death—and such pollution was thought to be contagious. Thus, for example, sexual relations between individuals of unequal rank were considered highly polluting for the

◆◆◆

varna one of four traditional divisions of Hindu Indian society

caste a hereditary social group associated with a specific occupation; bound by specific rights, duties, and prohibitions; and occupying a permanent place in a hierarchy of similar groups

◆◆

Why "Caste"?

In the last few decades of the fifteenth century, Portuguese sailors landed on the coast of India. There they found that where people practiced the Hindu religion, everyone belonged to one or another of hundreds of nonlocalized, hierarchically arranged groups, most obviously distinguished from one another on the basis of occupation. In Hindi, these were called *jati.* The Portuguese had no such groups, so their language lacked a word for them. But since *jati* could be roughly translated as "species," it seemed to the foreigners to imply the notion of "breed," "family," or "tribe." The Portuguese word *casta* could mean any of these, so the sailors used *casta* when referring to the groups the Hindus called *jati.* In English, *casta* became *caste.*

Castes and Unions

One aspect of the traditional Indian caste system that strikes some Westerners as particularly unfair was that individuals had virtually no choice of occupation. A caste member did not have the right to hold whatever job he or she might want, the one that would earn the most money or make the best use of his or her talents. Instead, caste members had to perform the work to which membership in their particular caste entitled them.

In the West, we also recognize formal occupational groups, called labor unions. Granted, there are important differences between castes and labor unions. For one thing, membership in a union is not hereditary; for another, unions are not hierarchically arranged, as are castes. However, in both castes and unions group membership is associated with particular jobs. Here in the West, as in India, you often find that to be allowed to do a certain kind of construction work—bricklaying, for instance, or pipe fitting—you must be a member of the proper group. Otherwise, you are not permitted to work at that job.

higher-ranked partner. This is where the economic specialization of the caste system and the Hindu religion merged: the ranking of castes was based on the degree of purity or pollution associated with the job traditionally performed by members of a given caste.

The notion of caste is so foreign to Westerners that some might view the system as incomprehensible, irrational, or nonfunctional, but this would be ethnocentric. To this day some Indian Hindus still identify themselves as caste members, and those who do are aware of their position and function in the hierarchy and of what behavior is expected of them, both within their own caste and in relation to members of other castes. This

"provides a sense of security . . . if a man moves into a strange environment, he identif[ies] himself with his own caste group, where he feels secure and at ease" (Wiser and Wiser 1971:259–260). The system has another important function, too. By forcing people into dependence on one another's specialized services, it promotes their interaction and encourages cooperation among the groups to which they belong, thereby increasing the integration of the entire society.

Systems of social classification neither work perfectly nor remain unchanged, and the caste system is no exception. Over the last half century, the system has been considerably weakened, first by Western influences

Change in India

In his account of life in the southern Indian village of Gopalpur, Alan R. Beals (1980:82–83) describes how missionaries converted many members of the village's lower castes to Christianity, a religion in which all people are believed to be equal in the sight of God. Among those converted were some members of the lowly Chamar, or Leather Workers, caste.

One of the traditional jobs of Chamars was disposing of the carcasses of animals that had died in the village. One day, Beals writes, a water buffalo died in Gopalpur, but the Chamars refused to remove it on the grounds that they had rejected traditional ways and were no longer members of the Chamar caste. So the buffalo's corpse lay rotting in its stall. Eventually, unable to stand the stench (made all the worse by the fierce Indian heat) any longer, an angry committee of villagers belonging to other castes tied the animal's legs together, thrust a pole through them, and carted the carcass to the edge of the village. Only a generation before, this could never have happened, for non-Chamars would never have polluted themselves by performing such a defiling job.

and then by Indian law. The Indian government has tried to raise the status of members of low-ranking castes by encouraging them to change the occupations allocated to them by tradition, and this has allowed many Indians to break out of the system. William and Charlotte Wiser, who studied social relations in the Indian village of Karimpur between 1930 and 1960, returned there in 1970 and found that much had changed. "There are fewer caste restrictions than there used to be," reported the villagers, although they added that castes were still endogamous and that most of Karimpur's Hindus were still uncomfortable with the idea of accepting food from a member of a lower-ranking caste. But the villagers added, "these rules . . . have not interfered with our personal relationships with each other. [We have] friends in other castes and we think nothing of it. Friendship is more important than caste, anyhow" (Wiser and Wiser 1971:225).

In the two decades since the Wisers' return to Karimpur, the caste system has continued to decline in importance for many Indians. Yet because the system continues to be functional, it persists, despite the fact that discrimination based on caste is now illegal. If all the members of the Farm Laborers caste abandoned this occupation in favor of jobs traditionally owned by a higher-ranking caste—for example, the Farm Owners—there would be no one to weed and harvest, for an Indian farm owner cannot carry out all this work alone. The caste system is no longer as rigid as it once was, but especially in rural India the classification of some individuals along occupational lines continues.

Slavery

In a caste system, however polluting your occupation and however lowly your caste, at least you own your labor. Were you a slave, however, you would find your situation radically different. Slaves do not own their labor. On the contrary, they are themselves owned by other people.

Slaves in the American South, barred from marrying, often lived together as husband and wife until they were separated at the auction block. An 1861 print shows members of a slave family being sold at auction.

Throughout history slavery has taken many different forms. War captives and their descendants formed a class of slaves in some societies; in others, slaves were a commodity that could be bought and sold. The rights granted to a slave varied, too. In ancient Greece, a slave could marry a free person, but in the stratified society of the southern United States before the Civil War, slaves were not allowed even to marry each other because they were not permitted to engage in legal contracts. Still, slaves in the South often lived together as husband and wife throughout their adult lives, forming nuclear families that remained tightly knit until they were separated at the auction block (Henretta 1987:415).

In 1860, about 4 million blacks lived as slaves in the southern states. Slavery allowed their owners, most of whom were planters, to enforce a strict organization of slave labor. Work was specialized, and slaves could be severely disciplined if they failed to measure up to their owners' demands. The owner or his assistant, the overseer (usually a white man), divided his workers into "gangs," which were assigned specific jobs depending on the season. The overseers and their subordinates, slaves themselves, used the threat of the whip to force gangs into tight, coordinated units for plowing, hoeing, and picking crops (Henretta 1987:411).

Slavery was institutionalized in the American South largely for economic reasons. Plantation owners could not possibly have gotten free farm laborers to work at the pace or with the discipline they commanded from slaves, and free laborers would have had to be paid for their hard work. Even factoring in the expense involved in purchasing and maintaining slaves, slavery was much more economical for the whites than wage labor.

After slavery became established, the notion that slaves deserved their status took root and helped to maintain the institution. Both the planters and the politicians they voted into power insisted that blacks were an inferior race, forever unsuited for freedom and in need of rigorous social control. They also pointed out that slavery liberated whites from the most degrading types of work. Southerners thus regarded slavery as guaranteeing equality and freedom for whites, and they argued that the institution actually served to protect the highest values of the United States (Henretta 1987:414).

Apartheid

We have seen that stratification occurs when the things a society values are distributed unequally among its members. It is only a short step from this kind of inequality to the idea that some people are naturally infe-

◆ **ASK YOURSELF**

How many differences can you identify between the official South African policy of apartheid and the ways in which blacks were treated in the United States after the Civil War but prior to the civil rights movement of the 1960s? What about now?

Until its abolition in 1991, the official South African government policy of apartheid segregated nonwhites physically, politically, and economically from whites. In 1985, children played in the black township of Khayelitsha.

rior to others. This belief underlies **apartheid** ("apartness"), an official policy of the (white) government of South Africa from 1948 until 1991. The intent of apartheid was to maintain the social superiority of white people, and under its provisions the overwhelming majority of all South Africans, those with dark skins, were physically, politically, and economically segregated from the white-skinned minority. Not only were whites separated from nonwhites under apartheid; nonwhites (black Africans, Asians, and people of mixed race) were also separated from one another. They were prohibited from living or working in certain areas reserved for whites, to stay overnight in public accommodations, or to use public facilities. Whites and nonwhites were educated separately and to different standards, and nonwhites were not represented in government. Until the 1980s, nonwhites were required to carry identity cards authorizing their presence in white neighborhoods.

Apartheid was finally legally abolished in South Africa because of the increasing self-awareness of nonwhite South Africans; their access to the media; the work of the once-outlawed African National Congress (ANC), which represented the interests of blacks; demonstrations and strikes; international sanctions; and finally, reforms instituted by the government of South African President F. W. de Klerk. Still, residential and educational segregation, unequal access to resources, and the political underrepresentation of nonwhites remain. As we write this, the government is still run by whites, and it may take many years before others are adequately represented.

●●●

AGE GROUPS

Societies sometimes use age to create social groups that cut across other distinctions, such as different political affiliations or different religious convictions. A Cub Scout troop, this year's debutantes, the local Young Republicans Club, and the senior citizens' bowling league are North American examples of social classification by age. In each case a specific interest combines with age to unite members of the group, but common interest is not necessary for the classification of people by age. In some societies, people who are otherwise separate or even opposed to one another are brought together solely by age. Two common applications of age as a principle for social classification are the age grade and the age set.

Social groups called age groups, created solely on the basis of age, are common in many societies. In North America, there are similar groups, but age-group members, like these Atlanta debutantes, usually share some common interest as well.

••

Shavante Age Groups

The Shavante combine age grades and age sets. Here, boys leaving the age grade of childhood and entering the bachelor age grade are initiated into one of eight cyclical age sets.

Age grades and age sets are sometimes combined in the same society. Such combinations have several important functions, among them social identification, enculturation, mutual support, and protection. As members of particular age grades and age sets, individuals are not only efficiently enculturated as a group (a major function of age grades) but also form bonds of loyalty and affection with their age mates (an important function of age sets).

The Shavante of central Brazil provide an example. The two thousand or so Shavante are scattered among about a dozen villages, some of which lie many miles apart, and are politically independent. Counteracting the divisive nature of this political organization are interlocking age grades and age sets that cut right across Shavante villages because the same age grades and age sets occur in each. Adolescents from every village thus belong to the same age grade, and each age set has members in every village.

The Shavante have four age *grades* for males: children, bachelors, young men, and mature men (Maybury-Lewis 1974), each with specific rights and duties. Interlaced with these age grades is a cyclical system of eight age sets (Figure 11.1, page 242). A male becomes a member of an age set at the end of childhood as he becomes a bachelor, and his membership links him to Shavante bachelors not only in his own village but in every other village as well. He can thus expect hospitality and protection from his age-set fellows in any Shavante village to which he might travel.

Age Grades

An **age grade** is a period of life through which an individual passes as he or she grows older. We recognize the existence of age grades in our own society, calling them "infancy," "childhood," "adolescence," and so on. But our categories are vague compared with the age grades of other societies.

The most important characteristic of age grades is that they are fixed. No matter what the age grades are actually called, a person living an average life span must pass first through infancy, then childhood, then adolescence, followed by young adulthood, middle age, and ul-

•••

apartheid a former policy of the government of South Africa, under which nonwhite South Africans were physically, politically, and economically segregated from the white minority

age grade a period of life through which an individual passes as he or she grows older

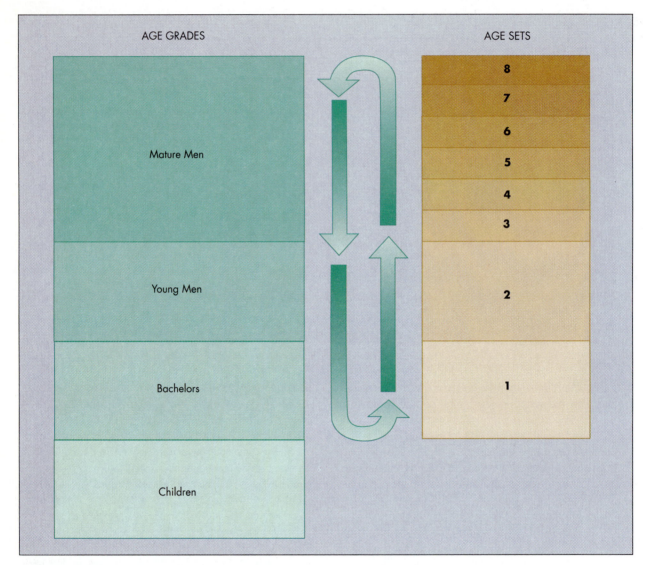

Figure 11.1
Shavante Age Grades and Sets. The interlocking system of Shavante age grades and age sets helps enculturate and integrate this society's members.

timately old age. It is the maturing individual who moves; the age grades remain static as the individual passes through them. We may thus conceptualize a system of age grades as a sort of immovable backdrop before which individuals pass as they grow older.

Like a school grade in our society, each age grade provides its members with a context in which they can learn the information and behavior appropriate for their age. Moreover, each age grade is associated with certain rights and duties, meaning that an individual in a particular age grade is expected to behave in certain ways and

to conform to certain rules. This is as true in our own society as it is in others: no infant is held to the same standards of hygiene as its parents, nor do we expect middle-

◆ **ASK YOURSELF**

Do you belong to any social group based primarily on age? If so, were you ineligible for membership in this group before you reached a certain age? When you are a few years older, will you again be ineligible for membership? Besides age, what are the qualifications for membership?

aged people to act like adolescents (even though they sometimes do) or grant adolescents the same rights as adults. Adolescents cannot vote or legally drink at bars; middle-aged people can.

Age Sets

Unlike age grades, **age sets** are not familiar to Westerners, but they are quite common, especially in East Africa and South America. Like age grades, age sets are groups of people of about the same age. But unlike age grades, which are fixed, age sets can be viewed as moving forward through time.

In societies with age sets, a person normally becomes a member of one of these groups when still a young child or around puberty. The other members of the same age set, who may or may not all be of the same sex, will be of roughly the same age. Usually age sets have names. If you were in an age set called the Lions, you and the other Lions would remain together as Lions as you got older. Age sets can thus be visualized as individual steps on a constantly moving escalator, with all the members of a given age set remaining on one step as the step moves forward through time. Membership in an age *set* does not convey specific rights and duties (like the right of adult age-*grade* members to drink in bars). Membership in an age set does, however, foster a sense of common identity with other members, just as being in a gang does for some American teenagers. This sense of identity is an important function of age sets.

The type of age-set system we have just described is known as a **lineal age set;** each age set remains a coherent entity through time, from its members' childhood to their old age. When all members have died, the set no longer exists. Lineal age sets are especially typical of East Africa. Kenya's Maasai, for example, classify all males born during the same four-year span as members of a particular age set. If, instead of a lineal system, a society has a **cyclical age set** system, an age set need not become extinct when its members die. Instead, its name is taken up by children who are just entering the age-set system, those in the lowest age grade. If the age set is called Lions, the new Lions repeat the path traced out several generations ago by earlier Lions, until they in their turn have passed through all of the age grades from infancy to old age. Then the name Lions begins its next cycle from the age grade of infancy.

A summary of the three principal differences between age grades and age sets may help you to keep these two closely related but nevertheless different age-based classificatory systems distinct. First, a person's age *grade* changes as she or he grows older, but once a person is drafted into an age *set* she or he remains in it for life. At age 7 you are in the age grade of childhood, and at 70 you are in the age grade of old age, but once a Lion, always a Lion. Second (and following from this first difference), age *grades* are immovable, whereas age *sets* move through time. Finally, unlike age *grades,* age *sets* are not associated with specific duties, rights, types of behavior, or attitudes.

ETHNIC GROUPS

In Chapter 1, we noted that groups whose members share cultural traditions and values and a common language, and who distinguish themselves from other groups (and are so distinguished by others), are called ethnic groups (Barth 1981:199–200). The term is often limited to **minorities,** groups that are smaller than the dominant group in their society.[1] The makeup of an ethnic group is not necessarily homogeneous; as with other kinds of groups, different life-styles or different levels of income or education may distinguish individuals within the same ethnic group from one another.

There may be many ethnic groups in one country or even in one city. The island nation of Madagascar, for example, has some eighteen different ethnic groups. New York City has even more. Because of their many ethnic groups, these can be termed **polyethnic** societies. In such societies, ethnicity is a means of social classification. People use ethnicity to anticipate, to evaluate,

---

[1]Some social scientists use the term *minority* even in societies where the "minority" is numerically larger than the dominant ethnic group. This is true of South Africa, where blacks outnumber whites but are still sometimes referred to as the minority.

---

age set a group of individuals of about the same age

lineal age set a system in which an age set ceases to exist when all of its members have died

cyclical age set a system in which an age set's name is continually recycled

minority an ethnic group typically numerically smaller than the dominant group in its society

polyethnic made up of different ethnic groups

China, the most populous country in the world, has 56 officially recognized ethnic groups. One, the Han, is so big that over 90 percent of the nation's people belong to it. Among the other 55, together totaling almost 70 million people, a few groups are very large, numbering as many as 10 million people. Others contain only a few thousand.

One mid-sized Chinese ethnic group is the Jingpo (also called the Kachin), consisting of more than half a million people who straddle the mountainous border between China and neighboring Burma. Until recently, relatively little was known about the 100,000 or so Jingpo on the Chinese side, for the area had been closed to the outside world since the Communists assumed power in China in 1949.

The Communists launched an ambitious nationwide program to modernize China's "underdeveloped" people, integrate them culturally with the rest of the country, and convert them to socialism. The first step was to identify and count China's ethnic minorities. Led by Communist party committees, teams of researchers traveled to minority areas all over China. Once the government officially recognized a minority, it worked to bring the group into what it considered the country's economic and cultural mainstream. It was a difficult task; minority groups often inhabited inaccessible areas and resisted some of the changes the government wished to impose, for they considered their traditional culture to be the very essence of their identity.

THE ANTHROPOLOGIST AT WORK

By 1984, the government had somewhat relaxed its largely unsuccessful efforts to institute reforms among minorities, and economic development was progressing, if slowly. That year, a Chinese scholar at the Yunnan Nationalities Research Institute, Zhusheng Wang, joined a team of social scientists sent to assess the progress of economic, social, and cultural change among the Jingpo (Wang 1991). The researchers found that sluggish economic development in the region where the Jingpo lived could be attributed to ineffective government policies. These policies themselves resulted from the central government's ignorance of Jingpo culture and its failure to acknowledge the ethnic distinctiveness of the Jingpo people.

Wang went back to southwest China in 1988–1989, this time as a graduate student in anthropology at an American university. Working in the Jingpo village of Dazhai, he recorded information on the people's systems of kinship and marriage, their politics, and their beliefs and rituals. He also documented the changes, initiated by the Communist government, that had been imposed on the village. Wang found the residents of Dazhai eager for economic development and modernization but at the same time insistent on preserving their ethnic identity. The road to change in Dazhai, he concluded, will be a long, rough one.

and—at least sometimes—to understand the behavior of others.

In addition to ethnic groups we also introduced the term *ethnicity,* the identification of individuals with particular ethnic groups, in Chapter 1. Members of ethnic groups may be proud of their ethnicity and may signal this pride and express their mutual solidarity by behaving in a distinctive manner, living near one another, attending special functions, performing rituals traditional to their group, or wearing particular clothes. But ethnicity may be a mixed blessing, for discrimination against members of ethnic groups (often caused by ethnocentrism) is common, especially for urban ethnic minorities.

The concept of ethnicity has proven useful to do-

mestic government agencies and international organizations seeking to help people in polyethnic societies to improve their lot. Rather than treating the inhabitants of a developing country as culturally homogeneous, for instance, most international aid agencies now try to take into account the values, institutions, and customs of various ethnic groups, targeting relief or aid to their particular needs.

COMMON-INTEREST GROUPS

In our discussion of urban migrants in Chapter 5, we introduced the term *voluntary association,* which we

Ethnic group members may demonstrate their feelings of pride in and solidarity with their group by wearing particular articles of clothing. In Iran, a Qashgai man proudly wears the traditional winged cap of his tribe.

defined as a mutual-aid society, usually formed for relatively well-defined, practical reasons and often, but not exclusively, found among urban immigrants. We described a typical voluntary association, a group of young mothers in an immigrant neighborhood in Lima, Peru, who formed a collective to combat malnutrition in their children by buying powdered milk in bulk.

Voluntary associations are one kind of **common-interest group,** a group defined not by descent, residence, affinity, sex, class, or age but by common needs and concerns. Although they occur in nonliterate and

◆ **ASK YOURSELF**

Do you identify yourself as a member of a particular ethnic group? Why or why not? If your ethnic heritage is dual (e.g., German Jewish mother, Italian Catholic father), with which ethnic group do you identify more strongly? Why?

peasant societies, such groups are more frequently found in urban societies, including North American society.

The functions of North American common-interest groups are varied. Some, like bridge clubs, garden clubs, or barbershop quartets, exist mainly to entertain their members. Some, like Little League teams, encourage athletic prowess and engender team spirit. Some, like the Girl Scouts, Boy Scouts, or Future Farmers of America, stress education and character building. Some, like Rotary Clubs or the Red Cross, exist largely for charitable purposes. Some, like doctors' or secretaries' professional associations, are related to jobs. Others, like the League of Women Voters, are political. And still others, called **ethnic associations,** are based on common ethnicity. Common-interest groups in non-Western societies fulfill these same functions.

One kind of common-interest group is based on sex. Because both women and men find advantages in participating in activities that relieve them of the cultural roles assigned them on the basis of sex, some of these groups are exclusively female or exclusively male. Others, although they exist for the benefit of one sex, may have members of both.

Women's Groups

Cross-culturally, women's groups seem to be less common than men's. One reason may be that women's child-rearing and domestic chores keep them at home, so they have less opportunity than men to organize their own groups. Or it may be that restricting women to the home, particularly in small-scale societies with extended families, creates domestic groups of related women, so women need not organize groups outside of the family to enjoy the company of other women. It may even be that—because in the past most ethnographers were males who had relatively little opportunity to glimpse women's side of society—women's groups are more common than we suppose. Though they may be fewer in number, however, women's groups exist in most societies and serve multiple functions, from self-help to charitable purposes to recreation.

In the 1960s, North American newspapers still advertised female and male jobs in separate columns; airlines hired stewardesses but not stewards, and fired

common-interest group a group defined by the common needs and concerns of its members

ethnic association a common-interest group based on ethnicity

Both women and men sometimes need a break from the constant companionship of the opposite sex, an idea institutionalized in some women's and men's common-interest groups. Above, women in Brooklyn, New York, meet weekly for quilting and companionship.

stewardesses who got married. Some states even prohibited women from waitressing at night. By the middle of the decade, however, many American women were questioning the roles society had traditionally allotted to them. In 1966 the National Organization for Women, better known as NOW, was founded. Seldom has a common-interest group grown so rapidly and to such size. Over the next twenty-five years, as hundreds of thousands of American women (and even some men) joined its ranks, the group raised both women's and men's awareness about gender inequities in American life and, through its advocacy of women's rights, helped bring about radical changes in many areas of public life. Thanks in large part to NOW, women not only entered the American labor market in greater numbers than ever before but also joined professions previously denied to them; moreover, they weakened the force of sexual discrimination in employment and in access to credit (Gross 1992:16).

American women are not the only ones who have grouped together to promote change. For decades, Caribbean women have been joining voluntary associations to improve their welfare (Ellis 1986:14). Today, the Caribbean Women's Association (CARIWA), a regional umbrella organization made up of nongovernmental women's groups, has a membership of more than 500 women's groups representing 12 Caribbean countries. Although all of these groups are dedicated to im-

Calypso Women

Calypso is a kind of music popular throughout the Caribbean for its lively, African-inspired beat and clever lyrics, which frequently offer pointed social or political commentary. Accompanied by a steel band, a good calypso singer never loses an opportunity to promote a politician, advocate a cause, or poke fun at a cultural institution.

Traditionally, calypso songs were written and sung by men, and in the past they often reflected Caribbean society's tolerance of men's macho behavior (Reyes 1986:120). Caribbean women were sometimes portrayed in calypso songs as scheming, promiscuous, or money-crazy (119). The lyrics of a calypso hit of some years ago advised men,

Every now and then, knock them down

They love you long, and they love you strong.

Recently, however, women have begun to compose and sing calypsos themselves, and to use them to promote women's causes. One popular song takes men to task for violence against women:

If I don't leave now
Is licks in the morning
In the evening.
I telling you flat
I done wit' dat.

Attitudes are often slow to change, and calypso music is no exception. But it appears that Caribbean women are beginning to use this traditional West Indian art form as a medium through which to protest ill treatment and lobby for a less sexist society.

Battered Women

One spin-off of the North American women's movement has been heightened awareness of the incidence and consequences of physical violence against women. In the 1960s, rape crisis centers were established, and in the 1970s their success inspired the establishment of shelters where women beaten by their husbands or boyfriends could seek protection (Hoffman 1992:25).

From this informal beginning as a loose coalition of emergency shelters, a battered women's movement has evolved, with the goal of combating domestic violence. Women in Duluth, Minnesota, developed a model program for battered women designed to ensure that police, prosecutors, judges, and probation officers all conveyed the message that the legal system will not tolerate domestic violence. In addition to providing safe havens for battered women, police officers are now required to arrest violent husbands or boyfriends regardless of whether or not their victims want them to, and men who assault women must receive treatment as well as punishment. One member of the Duluth battered women's group estimates that in Duluth alone at least five women are alive today who would otherwise have been killed (Hoffman 1992:25). The program has been widely imitated throughout the United States.

A similar program has recently begun in La Paz, Bolivia, where about a quarter of the population are native Americans called the Aymara. In the culture of the Aymara, a woman is the property of her husband, and wife beating is a test of manhood. Be-

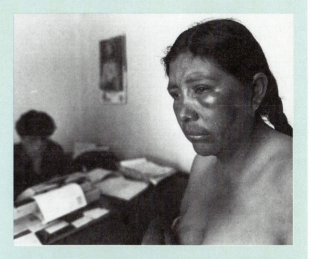

In the culture of the Aymara of Bolivia, a man's right to beat his wife has long been accepted, but recently Aymara wives have begun to organize to protect themselves from such abuse. Above, an Aymara beating victim seeks treatment at a government-sponsored shelter for battered women.

cause husbands are viewed as kings, their right to beat their wives is protected, sometimes by the wives themselves. But more and more Aymara women are "trying to organize and . . . assert their rights," according to an American sociologist in La Paz (Nash 1992). "These women have networks, organizations, and a lot of solidarity. They are trying to help each other." The Bolivian government's Office of Battered Women has recently opened a halfway house where abused women can receive treatment and respite.

---

proving the economic and social well-being of women (154), they have widely varying goals, from consciousness raising to preventing rape to increasing agricultural production.

Men's Groups

In some societies, men join together to set themselves apart from women, sometimes because (as we saw in Chapter 8), contact with women is thought to weaken them. The Etoro of New Guinea believe that each male has a limited quantity of "life force," some of

which he loses each time he has sex with a woman. Beliefs of this kind encourage the segregation of males from females, and it is not surprising that New Guinea is famous for its men's associations.

Other men's groups exist for different reasons. For example, **military associations,** common to many traditional and modern societies, are groups of males who have fought or may fight together. In some societies,

military association a group of males who have fought or may fight together

◆ **ASK YOURSELF**

Do you belong to a group that is composed exclusively of males or females? If so, do group members ever display negative feelings about members of the opposite sex? Why or why not? If you do not belong to any group based on sex, would you be interested in joining one? Why or why not?

military associations are combined with age grades. Among the Shavante, for example, the role of warrior belonged to the mature men's age grade. In other societies, military associations exist without age grades, although in any society men who go to war together are apt to be members of the same generation.

Military associations were an important part of the culture of the native Americans of the Great Plains of North America. Able-bodied Cheyenne men, for example, belonged to military associations with names like Fox, Hoof Rattle, Shield, Bowstring, and Northern Crazy Dogs (Hoebel 1978:40–42). When he felt he was ready to go to war, a Cheyenne boy joined whichever group he wished, often choosing the one to which his father or an older brother belonged. In addition to going to war against other Plains groups, Cheyenne military associations also policed tribal ceremonies and hunts and worked with the tribal council to make and enforce laws.

The prestige of a military association fluctuated, but there was no permanent hierarchy; these groups were organized internally in the same way and carried out the same activities. Only dress, dances, and songs distinguished them. Some, however, did have female members: the virgin daughters of tribal chiefs, who served as maids of honor. These young women joined the warriors in rituals and sat in the midst of the circle of war chiefs during council meetings. If a maid of honor lost her virginity before she married, she brought bad luck to her association's warriors.

CONCLUSION

Any society consists of various social groups based on sex, descent, marriage, relative social standing, age, occupation, ethnicity, or common interest—or in most cases, combinations of two or more of these criteria. These groups may intersect with one another, forming a multidimensional, interleaved matrix so complex

that every individual in the society can be fitted in somewhere. A person in North America may be a member of a particular family, a women's field hockey team, NOW, Students Against Drunk Driving, Delta Gamma sorority, the Democratic party, and the Presbyterian church, all at the same time.

Every group in which you, as an individual in a society, claim membership or to which you are assigned membership by society affects not only how others view you but also how you view yourself, what you think, how you feel about yourself, and how you behave. Without groups to identify, distinguish among, and influence the ideas and direct the behavior of individuals, there could be no society.

SUMMARY

Social classification, or distinguishing among people according to their different attributes, is a universal characteristic of human societies. It can be based on age, occupation, descent, sex, social standing, common interests, ethnicity, or other criteria; and it can serve a number of purposes, among them identification, allocating rights and duties, mutual aid, social solidarity, and preventing conflict.

Some systems of social classification distinguish between individuals or groups viewed as social equals, whereas others convey notions of superiority or inferiority. When people are viewed as unequal to one another, the result is termed social stratification, and the different layers into which society is divided are called ranks. Social stratification is based on differences in status, role, and prestige. A status is a place in the social structure, carrying with it society's expectations of a certain kind of behavior, whereas a role involves the behaviors associated with a specific status. Prestige is relative repute, a more subjective concept. It depends on people's evaluation of a status. It can be based on factors including wealth, power, social origins, education, occupation, dress, body ornaments, religion, and personal achievement.

In some stratified societies, people are divided into groups defined by economic production, called classes. In others, most notably Indian society, stratification is by castes, groups based mainly on occupation and notions of religious purity. Other social institutions found in some stratified societies are slavery, under which the members of one class, slaves, do not even own their own labor, and apartheid, under which South African nonwhites and whites were segregated from each other to promote and maintain the superior position of whites.

Some societies use age to create social groups. Two

widespread examples are age grades and age sets. An age grade is a period of life through which an individual passes as he or she grows older, while an age set (which can be either lineal or cyclical) is a group of individuals of about the same age who mature together. A system of age grades can be viewed as an immovable backdrop before which individuals pass as they grow older; a system of age sets can be viewed as a moving escalator, with each step occupied by a group of people of about the same age. In some societies, age grades and age sets are combined.

In polyethnic communities, ethnic group membership is a useful means of social classification since it enables community residents to anticipate, evaluate, and perhaps understand the behavior of others. But ethnicity may also provoke discrimination against members of particular ethnic groups.

Common-interest groups, such as the voluntary associations often found among urban immigrants, are based on members' common needs and concerns. In this chapter we focus on groups based on sex. Some women's groups, like the National Organization for Women (NOW), are dedicated to promoting change beneficial to women, whereas others serve charitable or recreational purposes. Women's groups occur in various parts of the world but don't seem to be as common as men's groups. Some men's groups exist to keep males apart from females, while others have more pragmatic goals. Military associations among the native Americans of the Great Plains, for example, filled a variety of functions, including conducting warfare and policing ceremonies and hunts.

The various groups in a society intersect with one another, forming a multidimensional web of statuses and roles into which every individual in the society can be fitted. Your particular place in this web affects how you think, how you behave, how you view yourself, and how others view you.

KEY TERMS

age grade
age set
apartheid
caste
class
common-interest group
cyclical age set
ethnic association
lineal age set
military association
minority
polyethnic
prestige
rank
role
social classification
social stratification (social ranking)
status
stratified (ranked) society
varna

SUGGESTED READINGS

Bernardi, Bernardo. 1985. *Age Class Systems: Social Institutions and Polities Based on Age* (David I. Kertzer, trans.). Cambridge: Cambridge University Press. An outstanding introduction to age systems, including discussions of the Shavante and Maasai.

Bradfield, Richard Maitland. 1973. *A Natural History of Associations: A Study in the Meaning of Community,* Vols. I and II. New York: International University Press. The Nuer, Trobrianders, and Hopi are among many cultures whose associations are discussed in these volumes. The author includes an extended discussion of ecology and social organization.

Hanson, Jeffery H. 1988. Age-set Theory and Plains Indian Age-grading: A Critical Review and Revision. *American Ethnologist* 15:349–364. Like the Shavante and Maasai, many native American groups also had age systems. Hanson attempts to explain the presence of age systems among native Americans of the Great Plains by correlating them with warfare and horses, among other variables.

di Leonardo, Micaela. 1984. *The Varieties of Ethnic Experience: Kinship, Class, and Gender among California Italian-Americans.* Ithaca, NY: Cornell University Press. The social conditions of Italian-American families in the San Francisco Bay area are the focus of this detailed ethnographic study of one of the most prominent minority groups in the United States.

Raheja, Gloria Goodwin. 1988. India: Caste, Kingship, and Dominance Reconsidered. In *Annual Review of Anthropology* 17:497–522 (Bernard J. Siegel, Alan R. Beals, and Stephen A. Tyler, eds.). Palo Alto, CA: Annual Reviews. A student who wants a brief yet comprehensive overview of this topic will find this an extremely useful introduction.

CHAPTER 12

BELIEF SYSTEMS

A religion provides those who practice it not only with a system of beliefs and a set of behavioral guidelines, but also with a sense of inner peace. In an ancient Hindu temple near Udaipur, India, a young man performs his daily prayers.

INTRODUCTION

Be it enacted by the General Assembly of the State of Tennessee, that it shall be unlawful for any teacher in any of the universities, normals and all other public schools of the State . . . to teach any theory that denies the story of the divine creation of man as taught in the Bible, and to teach instead that man has descended from a lower order of animals (quoted in Weinberg 1957:174–175).

People who believe that their religion's doctrines are all literally true are called fundamentalists. In 1925, Christian fundamentalists cheered when Tennessee passed a law requiring public schools to teach students, as truth, the account of the creation of human beings as presented in the Bible. They regarded the alternative theory—that human beings did not suddenly appear on earth in modern form but had evolved from earlier, ape-like creatures—as anti-religion, despite the fact that the theory of evolution was supported by a growing body of fossil evidence. In their successful efforts to incorporate their views into state law, they had been assisted by a famous politician and orator, William Jennings Bryan, himself an arch-fundamentalist.

Dismayed by Tennessee's new law, a 24-year-old evolutionist and high school biology teacher, John T. Scopes, together with some friends, hatched a plot to test its legality. Their plan called for Scopes to defy the law by teaching evolution openly in his Dayton, Tennessee, classroom. Scopes was promptly reported to the local authorities, arrested, and brought to trial.

The prosecution was spearheaded by fundamentalist Bryan himself. Opposing him and leading Scopes's defense was a renowned trial lawyer, Clarence Darrow. The jury chosen to sit in judgment on Scopes consisted of 12 males, 11 of whom were Christians and regular churchgoers (6 Baptists, 4 Methodists, and a member of the Disciples of Christ). Judge John T. Raulston presided.

Darrow opened the proceedings by roundly challenging the new law. He then asked the court's permission to put scientists who specialized in evolution on the witness stand, but Judge Raulston refused to allow such testimony. So, in a surprise countermove, Darrow requested permission to put an expert on the Bible on the stand—none other than Bryan, the prosecution's own attorney. The subsequent interchange between Darrow and Bryan provided an instructive, if at times irreverent, illustration of the impact of strong religious belief on people's ideas, emotions, and behavior (Weinberg 1957:209–227).

> *Darrow:* Did you ever read a book on primitive man? Like Tylor's *Primitive Culture,* or Boas, or any of the great authorities?
> *Bryan:* I don't think I ever read the ones you have mentioned.
> *Darrow:* Have you read any?
> *Bryan:* Well, I have read a little from time to time. But I didn't pursue it, because I didn't know I was to be called as a witness.

> *Darrow:* You have never in all your life made any attempt to find out about the other peoples of the earth—how old their civilizations are—how long they had existed on the earth, have you?
> *Bryan:* No, sir; I have been so well satisfied with the Christian religion that I have spent no time trying to find arguments against it.
> *Darrow:* Were you afraid you might find some? . . .
> *Bryan:* Your honor, I think I can shorten this testimony. The only purpose Mr. Darrow has is to slur at the Bible. . . .
> *Darrow:* I object to that.
> *Bryan:* (continuing) . . . to slur at it, and while it will require time, I am willing to take it.
> *Darrow* (angrily): I object . . . I am examining you on your fool ideas that no intelligent Christian on earth believes. (A few cheers; prolonged boos.)

The beliefs and opinions expressed so vehemently at the Scopes trial were significant not only to those individuals present in Dayton in the hot summer of 1925 but to all Americans, because religion is embedded in the very fabric of every society. The Scopes trial provides this chapter with its theme: that religious belief, behavior, and emotion are social as well as individual phenomena. In fact, in most technologically simpler societies, religion permeates every aspect of social life, from marriage to politics to trade, and actually helps to maintain the social order.

◆◆

ELEMENTS OF RELIGION

"Religion is the belief in Spiritual Beings" (Tylor 1873:424). This was one of the first definitions of religion, and its simplicity, along with its emphasis on belief, has made it a long-time favorite with anthropologists. Around the world, people who share a religion also share certain beliefs about spiritual beings, the origins of human beings, the meaning of life and death, and what happens to people after they die.

The religious beliefs of some major (or world) religions, such as Hinduism, Islam, Judaism, and Christianity, are organized into consistent doctrines, but this is not true of all religions. Ethnographers sometimes report asking questions about religion in small-scale societies and finding that no one seems able to put the ideas current in the society together into a coherent whole. Perhaps even more frustrating for the Westerner is the tendency for informants to contradict one another, and sometimes even themselves, when attempting to de-

*In a 1925 legal test of the Tennessee law that required schoolchildren to be taught the Bible's
version of the creation, defense attorney Clarence Darrow, in a court session held outdoors
because of hot weather, mercilessly grilled prosecuting attorney and Bible expert William Jennings
Bryan on the witness stand.*

scribe the attributes of the spirits they believe in, the nature of life after death, and the origin of the world.

The traditional beliefs of some native Americans demonstrate this kind of flexibility. The Crow religion, for instance, imposes no concrete doctrines, does not mandate any generally accepted rules of conduct, and does not oblige its followers to accept a fixed set of beliefs about the nature of the universe (Lowie 1970:30). No Crow individual would be denounced as a heretic because he or she rejected the current theory of creation, and in the absence of an official dogma on the subject there is nothing to prevent a variety of versions.

Whether religious beliefs are organized into a set of doctrines or are only loosely formulated, they are often associated with a code of moral behavior. For example, the Koran, the sacred book of Islam, contains many beliefs that taken together give the followers of Islam a guide for living a morally good life.

Religious beliefs are also associated with **rituals:** behaviors that use symbols to communicate meaning in repetitive, stereotypical ways. Not all rituals are religious; kneeling in a mosque (a religious act) and nodding one's head to signify agreement (a nonreligious act) are both rituals. Some rituals—kneeling and nodding are examples—are very simple, consisting of a single symbolic act, whereas others are complex, consisting of a combination of symbols of many kinds—including actions, words, sounds, colors, and scents—that have some special meaning and are repeated at specific times. A religious wedding is an example of a ritual in this broader sense.

Religious beliefs are frequently associated with **myths,** timeless stories that describe the origin of something—the world, a natural phenomenon, or some aspect of culture such as a particular custom or idea—and

•••

ritual stereotyped, repetitive behavior, either religious or nonreligious, that uses symbols to communicate meaning

myth a story describing the origins of the world, some natural phenomenon, or some aspect of culture, which contains at least one physically or humanly impossible event or situation

On the island of Flores in eastern Indonesia, men from different villages slash at each other with buffalo-hide whips in a ritual performed so that local spirits will make crops fertile. If blood is drawn, villagers believe that a good rice harvest will follow.

"confront us with at least one event or situation which is physically or humanly impossible" (Needham 1978:59). Some rituals are the dramatic reenactment of myths. Among the Tetum of Indonesia, the ritual performed at the birth of a child reenacts the birth of the first Tetum people from the "womb" of the earth goddess.

Anthropologists interested in religion (see Table 12.1) have noted that it has the capacity to inspire awe, fear, love, hatred, ecstasy, and other emotions among its followers. Basing his definition of religion on fieldwork among the Crow, Robert Lowie (1970:xvi) emphasized its emotional content, defining religion as a "sense of the Extraordinary, Mysterious, or Supernatural." Victor

Turner (1967) also stressed the importance of emotion—specifically, the emotional impact of symbols, such as the milk tree—on believers (Chapter 3). But other aspects of life also stir up emotions—politics, works of art, love—so we are not really justified in defining religion in emotional terms.

Émile Durkheim (1965), in seeking to define religion, first drew attention to the importance of the distinction between the terms *sacred* and *profane*. *Sacred*, he said, defined things set apart from ordinary life; *profane* described ordinary, secular things. This distinction made, Durkheim went on to define religion as "a unified system of beliefs and practices relative to sacred things

TABLE 12.1 SOME APPROACHES TO UNDERSTANDING RELIGION

Approach	Some Leading Advocates
Intellectual	Edward Tylor, James George Frazer
Emotional	Robert Lowie, Bronislaw Malinowski, Sigmund Freud
Sociological	Émile Durkheim, A. R. Radcliffe-Brown

. . . which unite into one single moral community, called a Church, all those who [follow] them" (62). The definition highlighted Durkheim's belief that religion is communal in nature; members of a society customarily acquire their religious beliefs, rituals, and even to some extent their emotional reactions to these as a result of enculturation. Because religious ideas express the very nature of the society in which they are embedded, they are necessarily valid for their particular societies. In tacit acknowledgement of the important anthropological concept of cultural relativity, Durkheim wrote, "there are no religions which are false. All are true in their own fashion; all answer, though in different ways, to the given conditions of human existence" (15).

Since religion is a social phenomenon, the values, ideas, and patterns of behavior evident in other areas of a society's culture appear also in its religion. For example: the pastoralist Nuer of Africa are divided into clans, which are in turn divided into lineages. These lineages are divided into smaller units, which themselves are divided into even smaller subunits. At the bottom of this complicated social hierarchy is the individual. Not surprisingly, Nuer ideas about spirits correspond exactly to this social structure (Evans-Pritchard 1974:117–119). The tribe, the largest social unit, is identified with the supreme Nuer god. Descending through the structural hierarchy, each Nuer clan has its own major spirit, inferior to this supreme god; each lineage has its own spirit, inferior to the clan spirit; and so on. Finally, each Nuer individual has a spirit, or soul, which occupies the lowest ranking in the hierarchy of spirits.

Durkheim went further with the notion that religion reflects other aspects of culture. He asserted that in effect, society is a god because it possesses godlike properties: it has absolute power over its members, gives them a feeling of perpetual dependence, and is the object of great respect. Religious beliefs, Durkheim concluded, are actually the ideas by which believers explain the nature of their society.

ORIGINS OF RELIGION

Archaeological Clues

No one knows how religion first began, although archaeology provides some clues about when. Some archaeologists interpret materials found at sites dating as far back as 70,000 years ago as evidence of religious be-

lief. Later, some 30,000 years ago, the Upper Palaeolithic Cro-Magnon people of western Europe seem to have been expressing religious feelings when they carved and painted bones, stones, and the walls of caves. The survival of these gatherers and hunters required that females reproduce abundantly and that hunting be successful. Both fertility and successful hunting are prominent themes in Cro-Magnon art. Statuettes called "Venus figurines" represent women with pregnant bellies and huge breasts; cave paintings include apparently pregnant animals and others with spears lodged in their bodies. Perhaps the hunters believed they could influence events by creating the image of a pregnant woman or animal or by portraying the killing of an animal, thus prompting life to imitate art. This requires a belief in agencies beyond the merely human.

Psychological Hypotheses

Beyond these archaeological clues to the origins of religion, scholars have proposed various hypotheses to explain how religion began. In the nineteenth century, Edward Tylor (1873) noticed that a belief in unseen beings was a common feature of religions. Perhaps, he suggested, this belief arose in prehistoric times because people known to have died are often encountered in dreams. Our ancestors, according to Tylor, reasoned that there must be some part of us that exists outside of our visible, tangible bodies and continues to live after the death of the body. If people had such "ghost-souls," perhaps trees or bodies of water or even the stars had them too. Early ideas about these nonphysical manifestations of physical entities evolved with the passage of time, in Tylor's view, into beliefs in nonphysical beings—spirits—that could exist quite independently of physical entities (see Figure 12.1).

Tylor gave the name **animism** to the belief that invisible beings inhabit the bodies of animals, plants,

 ASK YOURSELF

Do you think of yourself as religious? If so, do you practice your religion? How? In a world where there are so many religions, can we ever be sure which is the "true" one? Do you think it matters whether your own religion, if you practice one, is "true" or "false"?

animism the belief that souls or spirits inhabit animals, plants, or inanimate objects

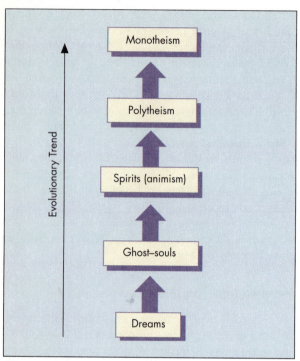

Figure 12.1
Edward Tylor's Ghost-Soul Hypothesis

religious rituals born. As time passed, people conjured up increasingly powerful spirits, and **polytheism**—the belief in the existence of many gods—evolved. Polytheism in turn evolved into **monotheism,** the belief that there is only one god. For Tylor, the modern notion of God was an extension of notions of ghost-souls and spirits.

Monotheism, of course, characterized the religion of Tylor's own society, Christianity. Tylor's view that monotheism was the result of a long evolutionary process was typical of many nineteenth-century anthropologists. It was ethnocentric since it implied that monotheism is somehow the logical end product of a process in which simpler beliefs were gradually replaced by more complex ones. Actually, there is no reason to think that monotheism is a more developed or more complex form of religion than beliefs in ghost-souls, spirits, or multiple gods.

We have already suggested another possible origin of religion: our human desire for some control over events in a world where things often seem to occur randomly. The Cro-Magnon cave dwellers may have been expressing this need when they painted their pictures of speared game animals. Similarly, someone who places a crucifix on the dashboard of a car believes, somewhere deep inside, that the crucifix can have some beneficial effect on what happens to the car and its occupants.

Another possible explanation for the existence of religion may lie in our need to understand how and why

and inanimate objects. Animism was, he claimed, the first religion. To win favors from ghost-souls or spirits, people began offering sacrifices to them, and thus were

Freud and Religion

Sigmund Freud proposed that a common human emotion, guilt, was the wellspring of religion. To illustrate the point, he relied on a variation of the Oedipus myth (see the discussion of incest in Chapter 7). Freud conjured up a scenario that he thought might have taken place in primeval times, when our ancestors supposedly lived in a group led by an elder male, who kept all of the females in the group for his own pleasure. Eventually the man's frustrated sons revolted, killing him and eating his body in a cannibalistic orgy. Later, overcome by pangs of guilt, the sons elevated their slain father to the status of a hero.

In the fullness of time, the dead elder's status was raised still higher, until he eventually became a god.

This tale is suggestive of two stages in today's Christian eucharist or mass, a ritual in which a priest or minister and congregation commemorate the death of Jesus and then symbolically consume his flesh and blood. The parallel between Freud's story and this symbolic behavior is striking; but whether or not Freud was influenced by Christianity, he got his anthropology all wrong. We have no evidence that any religion originated in this way.

Religion may be a response to our desire for control in a world where events often seem to occur randomly. On the dashboard of his car, a devout Hindu places marigold petals and incense before pictures of two Hindu gods in the belief that the gods, thus honored, will protect both car and driver.

things happen. Inexplicable things disturb us, and religion helps us to make sense of them. Our need to understand has by no means been eclipsed by the scientific discoveries of recent decades; although we now understand how the earth revolves around the sun, how diseases are transmitted, and how babies are conceived, mysteries concerning the human condition still exist, and we are still trying to understand them. A parent devastated by a child's death may be comforted by believing that the death was a part of God's plan.

Ethnographic Evidence

We may not know how the first religions originated, but ethnographic data show how religions have evolved in more recent times. Over the last several centuries, many small-scale societies have undergone social, economic, and political upheavals, often as a result of contact with other cultures. Under these circumstances, new religious beliefs and practices, or variations

◆ **ASK YOURSELF**

Do you wear a religious symbol or carry a lucky charm? Do you ever knock on wood, hold your breath when passing a cemetery, or avoid walking under a ladder? Why or why not?

on old ones, have sometimes emerged (Wallace 1985). These **revitalization movements** often take the form of popular movements for radical social change. They have political as well as religious implications and are often inspired by charismatic figures of the kind we mentioned in a political context in Chapter 10.

The "Handsome Lake" religion of the Iroquois of upper New York State is a telling example (Kehoe 1989:113–127). During the Revolutionary War, the Iroquois had supported the British, and after the American victory they had been dispersed in reservations as settlers took over their lands. By about 1800, the Iroquois were suffering under wretched social and economic conditions, and alcoholism was taking a heavy toll. In this context, Handsome Lake, an Iroquois chief, claimed to have experienced visions in which spirits warned him that the Iroquois would be destroyed unless they changed their ways. Forcefully preaching this message to his people, the charismatic Handsome Lake succeeded not only in initiating radical economic changes—

◆◆◆

polytheism the belief in the existence of many gods

monotheism the belief that there is only one god

revitalization movement a popular movement for radical change, led by a charismatic figure and usually prompted by social, economic, and political upheaval

A Javanese Toadstool

While the anthropologist Clifford Geertz (1966:16) was doing fieldwork in a village on the island of Java, Indonesia, a large toadstool of peculiar shape sprouted from the ground in a remarkably short time. So unusual was this phenomenon that people came from miles around to marvel at its strange and sudden appearance. Their fascination did not lie in the importance of toadstools in Javanese culture, for toadstools have no special significance in Java. Its odd shape and speedy growth were solely responsible for all the clamor it caused. It failed to fit into the usual Javanese categories for ordering things, thus challenging the islanders' ability to understand their world and raising the disagreeable possibility that their beliefs about nature were somehow inadequate.

So the villagers felt compelled to come up with some explanation. Several could have been proposed—that the toadstool was a fake, that it had been transplanted from somewhere else, that it was the result of unusually heavy rain. Rather than select a "scientific" explanation, however, the villagers settled on one from their religion. They decided that the toadstool had been created by spirits. Though based on faith rather than evidence, their explanation gave them comfort and satisfaction.

---

traditional Iroquois farming methods were replaced by European methods, for example—but also in founding a new religion based on traditional Iroquois beliefs and rituals.

One well-known kind of revitalization movement is the **millenarian movement,** a response made by a community to a situation of deprivation. The society's members anticipate and prepare for a coming period in which their hearts' desires will be fulfilled. Such movements have sprung up from time to time in Melanesia, where they are called **cargo cults.** The first one seems to have developed among troubled tribespeople in eastern New Guinea, where early in the twentieth century a charismatic visionary convinced his followers that the spirits of their dead ancestors would soon return to them. The spirits, who would arrive in ships loaded with valuable cargo, would kill the European invaders. In later years, Melanesians came to believe that certain rituals would make weapons, cars, food, and other Western goods—similar to those which they had seen in the pos-

session of American troops during World War II—appear as ships' cargo.

Revitalization movements—even those attended by some success, such as the Handsome Lake religion—are usually self-limiting because they are based on unrealistic expectations. When people realize that the new order they seek is not just around the corner, that their revered leader lacks the power to fulfill his claims, that the cargo will never arrive, the movement collapses.

RELIGIOUS PRACTITIONERS AND THEIR SOCIAL CONTEXTS

Most religions need someone to lead, guide, inspire, or interpret religious beliefs and expressions for others. The role of the religious specialist varies among religions, but three categories of religious specialist are especially important because we find them in many societies: shamans, prophets, and priests.

Shamans

The term **shaman,** borrowed from the vocabulary of a Siberian tribe, the Northern Tungus, can be translated as "one who is excited or moved." Shamans (also popularly known, especially in the movies, as "medicine men" or "witch doctors") are charismatic religious figures, believed to be chosen by spirits, who function as intermediaries between the world of spirits and human

 ASK YOURSELF

What parallels can be drawn between the revitalization movements described above and fundamentalist Christian sects in the United States, whose leaders exhort us on television to behave in certain ways in order to be saved? Would you call David Koresh's Branch Davidian cult a revitalization movement?

In Melanesia, followers of millenarian movements called cargo cults believe that certain ritual acts will ensure the eventual arrival of longed-for Western goods. On the island of Tanna, cult members drill with bamboo "rifles" in preparation for the day when their cargo will arrive.

beings (Lewis 1986:88–92). Thus inspired, shamans, sometimes said to be "masters of the spirits," often serve as healers. They may enter trance states in order to be "possessed" by spirits or to "leave" their bodies to visit spirits in the next world. Their relationship with spirits gives shamans power in the human world, which is increased by their skill at curing physical and mental illnesses. This they frequently do in seances with the help of "spirit guides." Shamans may be men or women or, in some societies, transvestites. Their healing talents are aided by the force of their strong personalities.

Cross-culturally, most shamans appear able to hallucinate or to enter trances, sometimes with the use of drugs and sometimes as a result of natural ability. At such times they are believed to be possessed by spirits whom they have invited into their bodies. Usually, before a shaman can practice "controlled" spirit posses-

sion, he or she must suffer the "uncontrolled" invasions of such beings. This traumatic experience, so overwhelming that a shaman who has successfully endured it is sometimes said to have died and been reborn, qualifies the shaman to cure others.

Trickery may also be part of a successful

millenarian movement a response made by a deprived community, characterized by anticipating a time when its hopes will be fulfilled

cargo cult a popular movement for social change in New Guinea, whose followers believe that certain rituals will bring ships loaded with valuable cargo

shaman a religious figure, believed to be chosen by spirits, who functions as an intermediary between the world of spirits and human beings

Shamans, charismatic religious figures believed to be chosen by spirits, serve as intermediaries between the spirit world and the world of the living. During a shamanistic performance in Korea, a female shaman shows she has been possessed by a spirit by balancing on a bowl.

shaman's talents. Like professional magicians in Western society, some are ventriloquists and others practice sleight of hand. In many societies, shamans are called on to perform the "sucking cure," in which they claim to suck "evil" out of the body of someone who is ill. In reality, the "evil" that is sucked out may be something like a splinter of wood that the shaman has tucked into his cheek before beginning the "cure."

Successful shamanism involves the shrewd manipulation of both information and props. However uncontrolled shamanistic behavior might seem at times, shamans must keep their wits about them to convince their clients that they know what they are doing. The

strangeness of shamans' behavior has encouraged some anthropologists to suggest that shamanism functions as a socially acceptable way for mentally ill people to resolve their problems, either by tuning out or acting out. In reality, however, people who are mentally ill lack the self-control to be good shamans.

Prophets

We have noted that when a society undergoes rapid social change its religion is likely to be affected. At such times, people may feel disillusioned, disenchanted, or dissatisfied, and their conservative, established religion may be incapable of changing to accommodate the needs of those who feel change is necessary. Under these circumstances, which may be associated with revitalization, a **prophet**—a charismatic leader, usually male, who offers solutions in times of extreme social unrest—may emerge. He usually undergoes some intense spiritual experience in which a spirit reveals to him new truths and new ways of behaving or perhaps urges him to return to traditional ways. As a result of this experience, the prophet typically feels he has a mission to fulfill among his fellows, and if he is convincing he may develop a following. In this way, a new religion may come into being.

The Iroquois chief Handsome Lake was such a figure. Another example is Jesus, who broke away from the religious orthodoxy prevailing at a time of social upheaval. He persuaded people to give up their livelihoods and become his lifelong disciples, and inspired a religion that provided answers to many people's perplexities. After his death, the church he founded continued under the noncharismatic leadership of Peter and eventually became an institution.

Priests

Unlike prophets, who emerge when the social order is changing rapidly, priests tend to have a well-established place in society. They are most often found in agricultural or technologically complex societies in which religion is practiced on a larger scale and more publicly than elsewhere.

Like the shaman or prophet, the **priest** is a religious specialist who mediates between humans and spirits, but here the similarity ends. The priest does not become a religious figure by entering trances or attracting a devoted following in times of social stress but rather as a result of learning doctrines and rituals from other,

Revitalization movements, typically under the leadership of charismatic figures, tend to emerge when people are socially and economically deprived. One such movement ended in tragedy in 1978, when members of the People's Temple in Jonestown, Guyana, followed their charismatic leader, Jim Jones, to death by suicide.

older priests. Personality and personal experience are much less relevant for priests than they are for shamans and prophets; instead, priests are officeholders whose authority is drawn from their official position.

RELIGIOUS BELIEFS AND RITUALS

Beliefs

Gods. Westerners are familiar with the concept of a supreme being who created the universe and everything in it. Not all societies conceive of such a god, and among those societies that do, a wide variety of attributes is associated with the god. This kind of god may be masculine or feminine and may reign alone or share his or her power with other gods.

The idea of an all-powerful earth goddess or earth mother appears in the religious thought of the ancient Babylonians, Sumerians, Assyrians, and Greeks, to

 ASK YOURSELF

In the popular book The Exorcist, *later made into a movie, an evil spirit takes possession of a young girl. The spirit is eventually expelled by exorcism, a rarely performed ritual of the Catholic church. Do you believe people can be possessed by spirits? If so, can exorcism expel spirits?*

prophet a charismatic leader who emerges after some intense spiritual experience

priest a religious specialist whose authority comes from the office he or she occupies

The Ghost Dance

Ghost dancing among the Sioux led to heightened tensions between these native Americans and U.S. military authorities charged with keeping the peace, and eventually to the massacre of the Sioux in 1890 by U.S. Army troops at Wounded Knee, South Dakota. Above, Sioux victims of this massacre are buried in a mass grave.

The idea of a culture hero who would one day lead his people to prosperity was an oft-repeated theme in the myths of native North Americans. Some groups believed the Great Spirit would soon transform the earth into a paradise; others thought their ancestors would return to life.

By the last decades of the nineteenth century, the native Americans of the Great Plains were undergoing considerable cultural deprivation. Their vast buffalo herds had been virtually wiped out, and their crops had repeatedly failed. White people had seized their lands and herded them onto reservations. Alcoholism, measles, and whooping cough, introduced by the whites, had ravished native American groups, killing thousands. The relentless westbound expansion of the pioneers left massacres and broken peace treaties in its wake, and native Americans grew increasingly desperate.

In this context, charismatic prophets emerged, predicting that the whites themselves would be wiped out, the buffalo would return, land would be recovered, and dead relatives would be restored to life (Kehoe 1989). If people would only follow them, the prophets claimed, their prayers would be answered. Sickness and death would disappear, and everlasting prosperity and happiness would be theirs. All that was needed to bring about the millennium was for the people to have faith, pray, and repeatedly perform a ritual called the Ghost Dance (see Chapter 1). Since such promises offered people their only hope, ghost dancing was widely practiced, but to no avail.

name only a few. A modern-day example is found in the religion of the Tetum, for whom the female earth goddess is contrasted with another, masculine, god who dwells in the sky. Humanity was created, say the Tetum, after the sky god had sex with the earth goddess. The sky god then retreated to his celestial home and has since played no part in human affairs. The earth goddess, however, has been worshiped ever since the first human beings emerged from holes in the ground (the goddess's body). The spirits and demons that occasionally haunt people's lives are thought of as being different forms of this goddess.

Other Supernaturals. In many religions there is a supernatural world inhabited by the souls of the dead, souls that have become transformed by time into ancestral ghosts, demons, and nature spirits. In the belief system of the !Kung San, for example, the universe is inhabited by a high god, a lesser god, and a host of minor animal spirits that bring good luck and misfortune, success and failure. Its principal figures, though, are the souls of recently deceased !Kung, who not long ago were the parents, kin, and friends of the living (Lee 1984:103). Now they hover near villages, and when serious misfortune strikes, the !Kung believe that these souls have caused it.

A belief in ancestral ghosts often accompanies patrisystems or matrisystems, in which ancestral ghosts may provide positive or negative sanctions. Among the Bara of southern Madagascar, for instance, ancestral ghosts and their living lineage agnates form a single religious congregation in which the living worship the dead (Huntington 1988:33). The ghosts control the behavior of their living agnates by threatening to inflict sickness if they disobey local laws. To avoid these sanctions, the living sacrifice cows as offerings to their dead agnates.

Life after Death. Religious beliefs are also extremely varied concerning life after death. The Shavante, for instance, have invented a colorful afterworld, which souls of the dead reach only after a long and perilous journey as far to the east as it is possible to travel (Maybury-Lewis 1974:289). On its way, a soul is guided by ancestral ghosts who have gone before it and who attempt to protect it from danger, for should a person's soul be killed before reaching the community of the dead, it would be obliterated forever. If it got lost, a soul might wander forever between the worlds of the living and the dead. Once in the world of the dead, though, the soul has entered a place of abundance, where life is easy and souls spend their time singing and dancing. Evil people never reach this much-hoped-for village of the dead.

Rituals

Rituals are a universal feature of social life. In North America, there are religious rituals to cleanse people of sin (like confession in the Catholic church), secular rituals to bring people together (such as Thanksgiv-

ing dinner), political rituals to sway public opinion (such as baby kissing by candidates), and many more. Other societies have curing rituals to restore health, agricultural rituals to make crops grow, fertility rituals to cause pregnancy, and death rituals to ensure the entry of the departed into the afterworld.

Several hypotheses have been suggested to explain why all cultures have rituals. The functionalist Malinowski (1954) proposed that faced with death or some other grave threat, people use rituals to control their anxiety. We never have all the knowledge required to overcome life's problems, Malinowski noted, and nonliterate people, especially, lack the technology needed to feel secure when faced with danger. Malinowski's Trobriand Islanders, who made perilous sea voyages in open canoes, performed rituals before setting out as a way to reduce the tension between their feelings of helplessness and the safety they would like to secure. Performing rituals brought about the same feeling of security they would have achieved with a greater knowledge of weather forecasting or superior navigational techniques. Trobrianders do not perform rituals before sailing in safe lagoons!

Another explanation, offered by Rodney Needham (1985:177), is that we perform rituals simply because we are programmed by our very natures to do so. "Considered in its most characteristic features, [ritual] is a kind of activity—like speech or dancing—that man as a 'ceremonial animal' happens naturally to perform."

Among the most common forms of religious ritual are sacrifices, rites of passage, and rituals of propitiation.

Sacrifices. **Sacrifices** are offerings made to spiritual beings. The term is also used for the sacrificial ritual itself. The person or group making the offering has some specific goal in mind, such as ensuring a productive agricultural season or appeasing the anger of an offended god.

The most dramatic kind of sacrifice, of course, is the sacrifice of a human being. It would be difficult to find an American elementary school student who did not know that the Aztecs of preconquest Mexico made gruesome human sacrifices to their bloodthirsty gods (Clendinnen 1991). But whether it is a human life, a sum of money, or merely a bit of food that is being offered, the give-and-take nature of a sacrifice bridges the gap

••

sacrifice an offering made to a spirit; the term also denotes the ritual itself

Aztec Human Sacrifice

The Aztecs of preconquest Mexico sacrificed human beings to their gods. In a contemporary illustration, an Aztec priest, standing before a temple, cuts the heart from one victim while another lies at the foot of the temple steps.

The most common sacrifice among the Aztecs was human sacrifice, and sacrificial killings were as likely to be carried out on the streets as in temples. Townspeople would prepare the victims, deliver them to the place of sacrifice, and dispatch and then dismember them. On special occasions, warriors carrying gourds full of human blood or dressed in the skins of their victims would run through the streets, to be ritually welcomed into dwellings; the flesh of the victims simmered in domestic cooking pots; human thighbones, scraped and dried, were put on dis-play in the courtyards of households (Clendinnen 1991:2).

Why this mass slaughter? Divine hunger may have been one reason. The Aztecs believed that humans had to pay debts, regularly and in human blood, to the earth, whose fruits they had enjoyed. Only sacrifice could fully extinguish these debts, by enabling the gods of the earth to feed on the bodies of human beings as human beings had fed on them (Clendinnen 1991:74–75).

between giver and receiver. The sacrifice creates a relationship, just as gift giving between humans establishes a bond of reciprocity (see Chapter 9). The individual making the sacrifice hopes that the spirit who receives it will feel obligated to help.

Rites of Passage. As we saw in Chapter 11, status is of great importance in many societies. Thus it is hardly surprising that when an individual moves from one social status to another, society often marks the transition with a special, usually public, ritual. Transitions of this kind are called **rites of passage**, a term invented by the Belgian anthropologist Arnold Van Gennep (1961) (see Figure 12.2).

A rite of passage transports a person from one social status to another. In a wedding ceremony, for example, a man and a woman move out of the unmarried state and enter the state of marriage, a condition viewed by

Gender and the Bible

As Durkheim would be the first to agree, the particular ideas and images a society uses to represent its religious beliefs are drawn from a larger fund of ideas and images current in the society. Naturally these help to mold the characteristics attributed to the gods and spirits who populate religious belief. Thus, in societies where men tend to be dominant, gods are usually represented as male. For example, Christianity, whose principles are contained in its major text, the Bible, incorporates and reflects Christians' notions about gender and validates the dominance of the male sex. References to the Christian god continually conjure up the image of a supreme being who is male.

In the gender-sensitive climate of American society in the late twentieth century, it was perhaps inevitable that attempts would be made to bring the Bible into line with modern attitudes about gender (Austin 1983). One such effort is reflected in a revised translation of Bible readings commissioned in 1983 by the United States National Council of Churches. In it, God is referred to as both the "father" and "mother" of "humankind," which seems quite logical to those who view God as sexually neutral. What is perhaps more surprising is that Jesus—who in the New Testament is indisputably a man—is also sexually neutral. In an old version of the Bible, for instance, John 3 contains this passage: "For God so loved the world that He gave His only Son, that whoever believes in Him should not perish, but have eternal life." The sexually neutered version reads, "For God so loved the world that God gave God's only Child, that whoever believes in that Child should not perish, but have eternal life."

When criticized for this awkward language, with its blatant obliteration of the sex of a historical figure, the translators defended themselves by pointing out that they resorted to sexual neutralization only in those passages that refer to Jesus as the messiah. When Jesus is referred to as a historical person, masculine pronouns are maintained.

---

society as fundamentally different from being single. Such transitions usually occur at birth, puberty, marriage, and death, and rituals performed at these times have a distinctive structure.

Moving from one status to another changes an individual's place in society. The rights and privileges, duties and responsibilities of an unmarried man, for example, change dramatically at marriage. No longer does society grant him the right to court unmarried women in public, but he now enjoys the right of exclusive sexual access to his wife. Likewise, he loses his self-sufficient status and picks up the jural and moral responsibility of helping to provide for the well-being of any children his wife may bear. Some societies consider this change in

◆ **ASK YOURSELF**

What moral difference, if any, do you see between priests' ritual sacrifice of human beings to feed hungry gods and Serbs' slaughter of their Muslim neighbors in Bosnia to bring about "ethnic cleansing"?

role so important that it must be marked by a public statement of the altered condition. Individuals moving from one state to another must be seen by society as being clearly removed from their prior positions and just as clearly repositioned in their new ones.

Rites of passage consist of three separate stages. In order of succession, they are separation, liminality, and incorporation. By moving through each of these stages in turn, the individual leaves his or her original status in society, is next isolated in some way, and then finally enters his or her new status.

The **separation** stage conveys the idea of severance from the old status, a theme communicated symbolically in actions and words. For example, in the separation stage of some male puberty rituals, circumcision symbolizes the cutting off of young men from boyhood.

---

rite of passage a ritual performed at a period of transition in the life cycle

separation first stage of a rite of passage, in which an individual is separated from an established status

Figure 12.2
Van Gennep's Three Stages in a Rite of Passage

Separation is followed by **liminality.** In this stage, individuals undergoing transition find themselves in a "neither here nor there" position, half way—physically, psychologically, or both—between the status they occupied before the ritual began and the one they will occupy at its end. Their lack of any clear-cut status may be symbolized by physical removal from society—for example, segregation in a special room or even banishment to the wilderness for a period of time, a common feature of puberty rituals in some non-Western cultures. In the traditional wedding ceremony of Western cultures, liminality is symbolized less drastically. Standing before the official who will transform her into a married woman, the bride is physically positioned between her father, representing the life she is about to leave, and her husband-to-be, symbol of the new life she is about to enter.

The final stage of a rite of passage, **incorporation,** may be expressed by a meal or a dance in which the person for whom the ritual has been held rejoins society, but in a new role. At a typical Western wedding, the joyful exit of the bride and groom, arm in arm, through a crowd of beaming family and friends symbolizes the reintegration of the man and woman, each in a new state, into society.

Rituals of Propitiation.   A **ritual of propitiation** is intended to appease the spirits. The most important ritual of the Inuit of Baffin Island is performed in the fall, when the goddess Sedna is believed ready to provide plenty of food if the community has observed her laws over the previous year (Hutchinson 1977). The Inuit gather around three shamans whose mission is to visit Sedna in her underwater home. Sending their souls into the underworld is considered the shamans' greatest feat. By this spiritual descent, they attempt to please their powerful goddess so they may live untroubled by famine, bad weather, and sickness. The shamans begin chanting, and soon their souls leave their bodies to descend to Sedna's house. There they ask her if the forth-coming year will bring health and plenty of food. Sedna then rebukes them for disobeying her laws but assures them that if they mend their ways she will grant them their desires. The souls of the shamans then return home with the good news—but also with Sedna's admonishment that in the future they must observe the laws.

MAGIC

Spiritual beings are usually involved in religious rituals, and if some beneficial result is desired it is usually they, not the person performing the ritual, who control nature or other people. **Magic,** in contrast, is designed to bring about some desired practical result without the intervention of spirits. A magician attempts to take direct control over some part of nature or of other people. Magic may occur either in association with religion—sometimes the two even occur in the same ritual—or independently of it.

This distinction between magic and religion was made by Sir James Frazer (1966:55–59, 65–69), who considered magic to have more in common with science than with religion. Instead of relying on spirits to grant what people wish, Frazer wrote, the magician attempts, like the scientist, to manipulate the laws of nature to achieve the desired result. From the Western point of view, the difference is that the laws of nature on which the scientist bases his or her actions are valid, while those on which the magician's actions are based are not. However, from the point of view of those who believe in magic, the laws of nature and those governing magic rituals are equally valid.

The interconnections among magic, religion, and science so fascinated Frazer (1966) that true to the Victorian tradition of seeking origins within the philosophical framework of cultural evolution, he proposed a hypothesis to explain how the three were diachronically linked (see Figure 12.3). In their intellectual evolution,

The Tetum Death Ritual

When a Tetum man breathes his last, his hair is immediately cut, his nails are pared, and his clothing is stripped from his body—three acts that symbolize his separation from life. At the same time, hair and fingernails are clipped from his close kin, whom the Tetum call "the people of death" because of their close association with the deceased. These activities signify that the intimate ties between the dead man and his relatives are now severed. The corpse is dressed in new clothes—the "clothing of death"— and is carried to a special "death house" on the edge of the hamlet, further symbolizing for the dead man's relatives and neighbors his separation from the everyday human world of Tetum society.

The dead villager's body lies in the death house for almost three days before being carried to the local cemetery. During this liminal period, the dead man is between the human world and the world of the dead. He is neither at home nor in his grave, neither alive among his relatives and neighbors nor buried in the ground among his ancestral ghosts. On the third day after death, the corpse is lowered into its grave, signifying the former villager's incorporation into the world of the dead. After the burial, the "people of death" share a meal with their village neighbors, an act that reintegrates the dead man's kin into Tetum society.

Frazer wrote, people first entered a stage of magic, seeking to manipulate objects and events without the help of spirits. When their efforts inevitably failed, they turned in hope to spirits to provide them with the things they desired, and the age of religion was born. Much later, skeptical individuals realized that religion could not provide all the answers they needed. Thus was born the age of science, in which Frazer saw himself and his fellow Victorians.

Frazer went on to distinguish between two types of magic (1966:12–14). To perform **imitative** (or homeopathic) **magic,** one imitates the desired effect, and it happens. The Azande prick the stalks of bananas with the teeth of crocodiles, hoping that the fruits will be as abundant as crocodiles' teeth (Evans-Pritchard 1985:450). To perform **contagious magic,** one obtains some object that was once in contact with someone— perhaps a tooth or an article of clothing—and does something to it in the belief that this action will affect the person with whom the object was once in contact. Cross-culturally, it's common for the hair clippings or nail parings cut off as part of a rite of separation to be carefully hidden lest some enemy get hold of them and burn them in a ritual of contagious magic designed to injure those from whom they were cut.

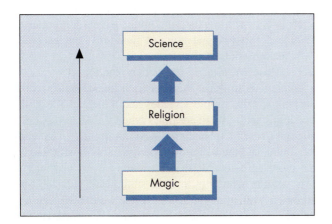

Figure 12.3
James George Frazer's Three Stages of Human Intellectual Development

liminality second stage of a rite of passage, in which an individual has no established status

incorporation final stage of a rite of passage, in which an individual is integrated into a new status in society

ritual of propitiation a ritual intended to appease a spirit

magic a ritual intended to bring about some desired practical result without the intervention of spirits

imitative magic a ritual that imitates the result desired

contagious magic magic based on the idea that even after they have been separated, things once in contact can influence each other

•••

Baseball Magic

To test Malinowski's hypothesis that people use magic in situations of uncertainty, George Gmelch (1985:231–235), an anthropologist and former professional baseball player, drew on his personal experiences of the game. Among baseball's three essential skills—pitching, hitting, and fielding—pitching involves the greatest degree of uncertainty. "The pitcher," noted Gmelch, "is the player least able to control the outcome of his own efforts." His best pitch may be hit for a home run; his worst may be hit directly into a teammate's glove. It's not uncommon for a pitcher to perform well and lose or to perform badly and win. He is dependent on the proficiency of his teammates, the ineptness of the opposing team, "and the supernatural (luck)."

Gmelch (1985), observing baseball pitchers, discovered a whole series of rituals, taboos, and "sacred" objects that together form a complex of "pitcher" magic. Rituals include tugging one's cap between pitches, touching the rosin bag after each bad pitch, and smoothing the dirt on the field. "Many baseball fans have observed this behavior never realizing that it may be as important to the pitcher as throwing the ball," wrote Gmelch. One common taboo involves the words "no-hitter." A pitcher who hears these words while a no-hitter is in progress believes that the no-hitter will be lost. Pitchers may also view articles of clothing as "sacred" objects. While playing for Spokane, pitcher Alan Foster forgot his baseball shoes on a road trip and borrowed a pair from a teammate. That night he pitched a no-hitter. Later he bought the shoes from his teammate, and they became his most prized possession.

With ethnographic data such as these, Gmelch demonstrated that Malinowski was correct. In baseball, magic is most prevalent in situations of chance and uncertainty. The uncertainty involved in pitching helps to explain the elaborate magical beliefs and rituals that accompany this activity, whereas fielders' high success rate in fielding, which involves much less chance, offers the best explanation for the absence of magic in this activity.

Good magic is carried out to achieve ends that society considers beneficial. A ritual to ensure safety at sea is good magic. "Bad magic," also called **sorcery,** is carried out to achieve ends that society regards as evil. A ritual to kill an innocent neighbor is an example of sorcery.

Magic is found in many nonliterate societies. Interestingly, a lot of the time it really seems to work! Sometimes this can be attributed to coincidence; one performs a magical ritual to restore one's sick mother to good health, and sure enough, she improves. Autosuggestion, too, may be involved: a patient who believes he or she will be restored to good health often is.

•••

WITCHCRAFT

Witchcraft, like magic, is a close relative of religion, especially the religions of technologically simpler societies. It is the belief that certain individuals called witches can injure others by psychic means. Everyone knows that evil exists, but it's a difficult concept to understand, especially when bad things happen to people who are "good" within the context of their societies. Personifying evil as a witch is one common way of explaining the existence of evil in the world. Where witchcraft is believed to exist, misfortune occurs not because people deserve it, and not just randomly, but because witches cause it to happen.

Most Westerners' instinctive reaction to such explanations is to reject them as foolishness. But in both technologically simple societies and those familiar with modern science, there are times when no satisfying, empirically based explanation for an unfortunate event can be found, and the belief that witches cause misfortune is no more unreasonable than attributing it to "bad luck." An Azande who trips over a stump and cuts his toe knows as well as anyone else that the wound was caused by the foot hitting the stump (Evans-Pritchard 1985). But why, they ask, did the man fail to spot the danger? They consider several possible reasons, such as carelessness, stupidity, a failure to observe the proper taboos, or

◆◆◆

Catemaco Magic

In the little seaside town of Catemaco, Mexico, the man they call the Infernal Goat earns his living by curing people's illnesses, improving their sexual potency, and casting spells (Golden 1992:A4). The Goat, really Jorge Jauregui, is a 41-year-old professional magician whose pharmacy containing dried tree bark, dead snakes, and bottled potions stands ready to assist him in his magical endeavors. In a typical treatment, the Goat might run an egg or a live toad over a patient's body, chant, and spit a green potion all over him or her.

The Goat is worried that when the North American Free Trade Agreement among the United States, Canada, and Mexico takes effect, the people of Catemaco will hear about "all kinds of inventions and things that we don't have here" in Catemaco and lose faith in his magical powers. So far, however, technology doesn't seem to be costing the Goat business. A woman from Mexico City who recently sought a consultation said she personally believes magic is quackery, but nothing else had helped her sick mother. Magic was her last resort. So the magic business, a mixture of herbalism, pre-Columbian religion, Christianity, and "mumbo jumbo" in which both God and the Devil may be invoked, is booming.

a failure to pay sufficient attention to one's ancestors. But if these can be ruled out, the Azande believe the accident may have been caused by witchcraft. A Westerner in the same situation might fall back on bad luck.

Women are labeled witches far more often than men. This was as true in colonial America and historic Europe as it is in many parts of the non-Western world today. In 1692, of 19 witches hanged on Witches' Hill in Salem, Massachusetts, 13 were women. In fifteenth-century Essex, England, most witches were women (MacFarlane 1990:230). Historian H. C. Erik Midelfort (1972) discovered that in sixteenth- and seventeenth-century southwest Germany the overwhelming majority of accused witches were women. According to Malinowski (1954), most Trobriand witches were women, and the flying witches feared by all sailors were always female. While witches among the Azande and some other African societies are as likely to be male as female, many other African groups, such as the Nupe, Tallensi, Yoruba, and Luvale, heavily stress the feminine nature of witchcraft. Not to be outdone, the Balinese have created as one of their most profound terrors the great female witch Rangda.

Why should women be particularly associated with evil? In addressing this question, scholars have exploited the various perspectives we have introduced in this book. Structural-functionalists, for example, point out that in most societies women, relative to men, are deprived of political and economic power. Attributing occult power to women "compensates" them for a lack of legitimate power.

One historian, seeking to account for the gender bias in witchcraft accusations in colonial New England, has taken a psychological approach (Demos 1983). He bases his argument on a study of infant development by Dorothy Dinnerstein (1990), who attempted to discover the origins of antifemale attitudes in Europe and North America. Dinnerstein begins by noting that no matter what its sex, an infant's first experiences are entirely of and with its mother. It is she who creates the baby's sense of security and provides milk, caresses, and soothing noises. Inevitably, however, she also withholds these delights. She can never gratify her infant's needs all the time nor satisfy its every craving. In the developing mind of the infant, therefore, the mother becomes ambiguous, both loving and rejecting.

The developing infant also becomes aware that it is dependent on its mother for its very existence and has no choice but to acknowledge her power over its life. At the same time, the infant finds it impossible to fully separate itself psychologically from its mother or to place

◆◆◆

good magic magic performed to achieve ends that society considers beneficial

sorcery bad magic, performed to achieve ends society regards as evil

witchcraft the belief that certain individuals, called witches, can injure others by psychic means

Azande Witchcraft

People who believe in witchcraft explain misfortune by blaming witches for it. Among the Azande of Central Africa, individuals who believe they have been attacked by witches sometimes consult a "witch doctor" to discover who is bewitching them.

Edward Evans-Pritchard (1985:18), the ethnographer of the Azande, describes how pervasive witchcraft is in the daily lives of these people.

> If blight seizes the groundnut crop, it is witchcraft; if the bush is vainly scoured for game, it is witchcraft; if termites do not rise when their swarming is due, and a cold, useless night is spent in waiting for the flight, it is witchcraft; if a prince is cold and distant with his subjects, it is witchcraft; if a magic rite fails to achieve its purpose, it is witchcraft; if, in fact, any failure or misfortune falls upon anyone at any time and in relation to any of the manifold activities of his life, it may be due to witchcraft.

her into a neat pigeonhole in a system of personal classification. As the infant becomes a child, it projects its mother's "unclassifiability" onto all women. Eventually, both males and females invest the female sex with what Dinnerstein calls the "magically formidable" qualities of all mothers: ambiguity, power, malevolence, and mysteriousness—the exact attributes of the New England witch.

The New Englanders' disinclination to stereotype males as witches can also be explained by Dinnerstein's analysis. By the time an infant realizes the existence of what has up until then been a marginal figure, its father, it will have already passed the earlier critical stage of growing self-awareness and will have grown completely accustomed to itself as an independent being. Secure in this feeling, the infant can classify the second person in its young life as a being much like itself. The father figure is not perceived as at all ambiguous or mysterious, nor are there any unpleasant experiences to cast a shadow on him.

Structural anthropologists might seek a more global explanation for the association between women and witches. They might remind us that there is a worldwide mental association of femaleness with the negative (or evil) side of experience and maleness with the positive (or good) side. Witches are evil, and so are primarily identified with females. What of those few societies that regard males as equally likely, or even more likely, to be witches? In such societies, ecological or cultural or social factors might outweigh these universal mental associations.

Since the 1960s, North America and England have witnessed the emergence of a movement whose followers, although they sometimes call themselves witches, usually refer to themselves as neopagans. Neopagans see themselves not as practitioners of rituals designed to inflict harm on others but as revivers of pagan beliefs and practices from the time of the pre-Christian religion called **wicca** or, more recently, **neopaganism.** Feminism and harmony with nature are strong features of modern-day neopaganism, as is a desire to seek alternative ways of curing sickness than those offered within the context of the typical physician-patient relationship in contemporary Western medicine (Orion, in press).

We close with the thought that some Western beliefs in unseen, inexplicable things—God or the Devil, for example, or extraterrestrials or the efficacy of astrol-

In both Western and non-Western societies in which people believe in witchcraft, witches are far more often female than male. Above, a "classic" European witch—an elderly female clad in a robe and pointed hat—flies through the air on a broomstick.

ogy—are no more (or less) intellectually justifiable than a belief in witches.

◆◆◆

CONCLUSION

Religion provides an order essential to both the individual and society, serves as an outlet for human emotions, acts as an agent of change, comforts people and brings them together socially, and satisfies the universal human need to explain the meaning of life and human misfortune.

Perhaps the greatest of all human misfortunes is

◆◆◆

wicca a pre-Christian European religion
neopaganism a modern revival of a pre-Christian religion

◆ ASK YOURSELF

Neopagans contend that Western women were traditionally attended by female midwives when they gave birth, until the male-dominated medical profession seized control of this crucial process and made it unnecessarily complicated and expensive. Do you think Americans give doctors too much control over their health care? Do you view the medical profession as male-dominated?

death. We may avoid other trials—sickness, accidents, social failures—for a long time, hoping our run of luck continues unabated, but our intellects force us to accept the inevitability of death. We know for sure that whether we die tomorrow or in 60 years' time, we *will* die sometime. Perhaps it is this certainty that prompts our endless speculation about what, if anything, comes after death.

Such panhuman interests help us understand how our ancestors came to imagine the existence of some kind of life after the death of the body and why many of us continue to cling to this notion. We have no evidence to suggest that modern-day people are ceasing to think about death and its possible aftermath or that twentieth-century science is succeeding in explaining this mystery to our full satisfaction. So people go on responding to what might almost be called a religious instinct. One way to interpret the universality of religion is to view it as an attempt to deny the dismal possibility of our own permanent extinction.

SUMMARY

Religion, a belief in spiritual beings, involves beliefs, rituals, and emotions that often contribute to social coherence, especially in technologically simpler societies. This chapter has given you a glimpse of the variability of religious beliefs and rituals, at the same time stressing those that constantly recur in human societies.

The earliest indications of religious belief date to the Middle and Upper Paleolithic periods. Among the many hypotheses proposed to explain how and why religion began, Tylor's is based on the notion of spirits encountered in dreams and trances; Freud's is based on people's supposed guilty feelings and their consequent elevation of father figures to the status of gods; Durkheim's stresses the nature of religion as a force for maintaining social order. Although none of these hypotheses provides a full understanding of religion, we do have ethnographic data to show how new religions have arisen and old ones have changed in recent times. Religious change in the form of revitalization movements of various kinds, such as cargo cults, seems to be a product of social, economic, and political upheaval.

In most religions, specialists lead, guide, inspire, or interpret religious belief. Shamans, most frequently found in small-scale societies, are thought to experience direct contact with spirits, often by entering trance states. Prophets, charismatic leaders who seem to have answers to people's problems, may emerge when society is changing rapidly. Priests, in contrast to both shamans and prophets, are officeholders who depend not on personal charisma, talent, or social stress so much as on traditional doctrines and rituals taught to them by older priests. Religious beliefs include those in gods, spirits, souls, and life after death. These may be justified in myths and expressed in a variety of rituals such as sacrifices, rites of passage, and rituals of propitiation.

Closely related to religion are magic and witchcraft. Magic, either imitative or contagious, is a way for people to bring about some desired practical result by assuming direct control over some part of nature or over other people without resorting to supernatural agents. Witchcraft is a way of accounting for unfortunate happenings when other explanations fail. Witchcraft as an explanation for unfortunate events resembles North American society's beliefs in unseen things such as bad luck, God, the Devil, extraterrestrials, or astrology. All are attempts to explain the otherwise inexplicable.

Women are labeled witches far more often than men, a phenomenon we examine from the structural-functionalist, psychological, and structuralist points of view. The relationship of gender to witchcraft is evident in the rise of neopaganism in North America and Britain, which has a strong feminist component.

The chapter concludes with a look at what is perhaps the most mysterious and troubling aspect of human existence, death. We suggest that it may be the certainty of death, and the horror of the idea of permanent extinction, that is responsible for the universality of religion.

KEY TERMS

animism
cargo cult
contagious magic
good magic
imitative magic
incorporation
liminality
magic
millenarian movement
monotheism
myth
neopaganism
polytheism
priest
prophet
revitalization movement
rite of passage
ritual
ritual of propitiation
sacrifice

separation
shaman
sorcery
wicca
witchcraft

••

SUGGESTED READINGS

Atkinson, Clarissa W., Constance H. Buchanan, and Margaret R. Miles (eds.). 1985. *Immaculate and Powerful: The Female in Sacred Image and Social Reality*. Boston: Beacon Press. Hinduism, Buddhism, and Catholicism are among the religions included in these 11 studies of how religious symbols represent women in different cultures.

Atkinson, Jane Monnig. 1992 (1989). *The Art and Politics of Wana Shamanship*. Berkeley: University of California Press. An ethnographic study of shamans in an eastern Indonesian society that treats the capacity of shamans to bring about cures, their role as mediators between the human and spirit worlds, and shamanistic ritual performances.

Bynum, Caroline Walker, Stevan Harrell, and Paula Richman. 1986. *Gender and Religion: On the Complexity of Symbols*. Boston: Beacon Press. A series of articles on how women use religious symbols differently from men in Buddhism and various other religions.

Lehman, Arthur C., and James E. Myers (eds.). 1989. *Magic, Witchcraft, and Religion: An Anthropological Study of the Supernatural* (2nd ed.). Mountain View, CA: Mayfield. Fifty articles covering a wide range of topics, including witchcraft, cargo cults, shamanism, ritual, and the Bible. Some contributions are classics in the field of religious anthropology; others, equally good, are less well known but deserve a careful reading.

Obeyesekere, Gananath. 1981. *Medusa's Hair: An Essay on Personal Symbols and Religious Experience*. Chicago: University of Chicago Press. This book contains a series of case studies based on interviews with religious practitioners in Sri Lanka, most of whom are women. Linking the ideas of Sigmund Freud and Max Weber, the author shows how symbols created by individuals are transformed into symbols accepted by communities. Emotion, belief, ritual, and society are brought into a single system.

Russell, Jeffrey B. 1980. *A History of Witchcraft: Sorcerers, Heretics, and Pagans*. London: Thames & Hudson. The most informative introduction yet to witchcraft. Russell surveys the gender bias against women in some detail.

PERSONALITY PROFILE

From time to time on Sunday he felt a tightness in his chest but had no difficulty dismissing it from his mind. On Monday the tightness had given way to intermittent jabs of pain, and he grew uneasy. By Tuesday afternoon, he had trouble taking even the mildest of breaths, and he was now apprehensive. When he woke during the darkness of Timor's predawn he was very frightened indeed. So before the sun had cleared the horizon, Rubi Loik, of the Tetum village of Vessa, had pulled a cloth wrap over his shoulders to keep the chill of early morning at bay and was already hastening to the home of a local shaman, whose diagnoses had always proved accurate in the past. When he reached the house, he was not surprised to see Hare Leki at her door, as though she had foreseen his visit.

Although a woman by sex, Hare Leki was by preference masculine. The way she carried herself, the males with whom she kept company, and the activities she pursued all bore witness to her unwillingness to remain a prisoner of nature. Since her earliest years she had chosen boys rather than girls as her playmates, and encouraged by the liberal norms of Tetum society, she was free to indulge her inclinations. To Hare Leki fellow villagers were not merely tolerant. They respected her skill at diagnosing sickness and admired her talent for communicating with the spirits. Her bisexuality filled her with a power an ordinary man or woman could not possess, because the Tetum believe that just as bisexual individuals partake of the worlds of men and of women, so they partake of the ordinary world of humanity and the extraordinary world of spirits. Like shamans everywhere, Hare Leki was an extremely powerful mediator between human beings and spirits and thus could bring her influence to bear on both.

Years ago Hare Leki had discovered within herself certain skills. One was to go into a trance with greater ease than anyone else in the community. She did this by chewing a mild narcotic called betel nut, and in this condition she would communicate with spirits who trusted her to look after their interests in the human world, mainly by persuading her fellow villagers to offer sacrifices of food and drink to them. A particular spirit might wish to take possession of her body and speak words in a language none in the community could understand apart from the shaman herself. In this way Hare Leki might learn the answers to the questions she would put to the spirit on behalf of a sick person.

Another skill was based on Hare Leki's sociability and cleverness at ferreting out information from other villagers. She always seemed to be in the company of someone, and so comfortable did people feel in her presence that likely as not the companion (male as well as female) would confide hitherto closely held secrets in exchange for the benefit of her counsel. She made it her business—as it literally was, of course—to learn all she could about all that went on in the local villages, including who was neglecting to offer sacrifices to spirits or to the ancestral ghosts, who was suspected of practicing witchcraft, and who was cheating on a spouse. As the years rolled by she combined this mix of qualities into the highly successful profession of shaman.

Thus, when people were sick they would search out Hare Leki to diagnose the cause of their complaint, a quest that usually meant finding out which spiritual agency—ghost, spirit, or witch—was causing it. This question in turn led to the search for the reason why the spiritual agency involved was punishing the invalid. Once the reason was known, the shaman would suggest a cure. The answers to all of these questions, however, depended on Hare Leki's communion with her favorite spirits, on which experience had taught her to rely. She needed them to succeed, so that her remarkable reputation for being the most reliable shaman around would not be lost. If it were, her clientele would abandon her for a rival shaman, for unsuccessful shamans do not exist in Tetum society. And so that morning Rubi Loik was entrusting his life to her.

The popular shaman welcomed him into her house, an unremarkable rectangular building no different from those of other villagers. There in the darkness at the rear the sick man urgently gave her the reason for his early visit. When he had finished telling her about his pains, she questioned him closely about his personal life over the last several months to find out if he might have deliberately (or innocently) antagonized someone (possibly a witch), broken some taboo, failed to perform a sacrifice to a spirit or ghost, or neglected to carry out some ritual obligation or legal responsibility appropriate to a man of his social status. He replied as best he could, but the shaman was not satisfied. She appeared to think he was keeping something back or that something had slipped from the network of his memory. She seized the least tidbit of information to probe for the vital evidence she needed. As soon as it seemed Rubi Loik had emptied his mind of all the knowledge he possessed, she quietly moved away from him, drew up the mat on which she sat when entering her trances, closed her eyes, and soon appeared deep in contemplation. She thought about all Rubi Loik had told her, looking for some pattern in his recent social and ritual activities that could help her discover what spiritual agency was causing his sickness and how he may have himself drawn down spiritual wrath.

Satisfied that she had explored every possibility and oblivious to the distressed man sitting on the floor before her, Hare Leki put betel nut in her mouth and began to chew and hum. It seemed to Rubi Loik that the shaman's eyes had been closed for a very long time indeed before her body quivered violently, and she began muttering a strange language in a voice that did not seem hers. He knew her soul was now communicating with a spirit that had possessed her body. This possession lasted only a few minutes,

and after a short period during which she remained motionless, Hare Leki shook her body, and her eyes fluttered open. She stared hard into Rubi Loik's eyes as though trying to see deep into his soul.

Scarcely daring to breathe, the man waited to learn his fate. Could she suggest anything that would make him better? Or was he doomed to die? Hare Leki told him that his sickness had been brought on by his failure to make a sacrifice to the ghosts of his patrilineage. This is an obligation every living man is bound to observe, and it is supposed to be carried out daily. Rubi Loik protested to her that he was scrupulous about performing the sacrifice, but she kept up her prosecutions until he recalled that, yes, he had on one occasion slipped up. This single omission, the shaman triumphantly informed him, had persuaded one of his lineage's ghosts to punish him. That ghost had possessed Hare Leki's body while she was in a state of trance.

Rubi Loik now knew the nature of his sickness, but he still needed to learn what he must do to be cured. The shaman commanded him to sacrifice the most desirable pig in his herd to the ghosts he had offended. She reminded him that duties must not be neglected if a person wished to have any hope of avoiding sickness, and she lectured him about not misbehaving in the future. His visit was almost over, but Hare Leki had one more thing to tell him. Payment for her services would be Rubi Loik's second-best pig.

Feeling a new man already, he was happy to agree. His sickness, he was convinced, would leave him after he had paid the shaman and had sacrificed his best pig to the neglected ancestors. And so it did.

CHAPTER 13

LANGUAGE

Apes' ability to learn sign language suggests a possible origin for human language. Koko, a female gorilla with a sign language vocabulary of some three hundred words, signs "cry" as primate researcher Francine Patterson shows her what "The Three Little Kittens" did when they lost their mittens.

INTRODUCTION

In February 1964, with the temperature hovering around 35 degrees below zero, a missionary from Illinois and his pregnant wife arrived in the Northwest Territories of Canada. During the next 14 months, Herb and Judy Zimmerman and their baby lived in an isolated encampment of tents and tiny huts in which all of the other occupants were native Americans called Dogribs. From the moment of their arrival, the Zimmermans worked at learning the Dogrib language, for as members of the Evangelical Free Church of America they considered it their divine mission to translate the Bible into Dogrib. Since this language had never been written down nor its grammatical rules defined, the missionaries were faced with a real linguistic challenge.

"Translating the Bible into another tongue is a difficult assignment," wrote a newspaper reporter who covered the missionaries' story, since the Zimmermans "must also translate the Bible into another culture" (Malcolm 1981:14). Isolated in the frigid Canadian wilderness, the Dogribs had of course never heard of many of the biblical objects and concepts familiar to Western-educated people. So the "three wise men" had to be translated into Dogrib words meaning the "three chiefs," and these "chiefs" were given horses to ride instead of camels. For people who had no farm animals and whose survival depended in part on killing any mountain sheep they came across, the metaphor of the "good shepherd"—one who cares spiritually for a flock of dependents—meant nothing to the Dogribs; so instead of "shepherd" the Zimmermans had to settle for the Dogrib word *gikedi,* which meant "communal baby sitter."

To make the Bible meaningful to the 2,500 Dogrib speakers, the Zimmermans needed a thorough understanding of Dogrib culture, aspects of which were reflected in their language. Unlike North Americans, for example, the villagers placed great emphasis on the communal ownership of property, at the same time devaluing individual property ownership. The dominance of community over individual rights was reflected in the Dogribs' use of possessive pronouns (*mine, yours, his, hers, ours, theirs*). These could be used only for parts of a person's own body and for relatives. Instead of saying, for instance, "my sled," as English speakers would, Dogrib speakers' looser sense of "ownership" was expressed through the use of prepositional phrases such as "this sled is to me."

Fortunately for the Zimmermans, the Dogribs were very friendly—so friendly that they considered it rude for newcomers to their community to wait for a formal invitation to visit their neighbors. In their view, visitors should immediately make a "walk-around" to every village home, beginning with that of the chief, to pay their respects. So it wasn't long before the Zimmermans found themselves socializing, and at the same time learning Dogrib customs and manners. They quickly discovered that participation in Dogrib daily life made

learning the language easier, so—like ethnographers using the participant observation field method (Chapter 2)—they immersed themselves in community activities, and their project was underway.

In every society there are close links between culture and language. Thus, anyone who wishes to understand a culture must understand the language spoken by its members. Only by learning the Dogrib language could the Zimmermans properly understand the way the Dogrib thought, why they behaved as they did, and how they viewed their world.

This chapter is about anthropological linguistics. Its focus is **language,** the primary medium of human interaction (Collinge 1990:xv). Language doesn't necessarily make use of speech; any means of communication between people that is systematic (that is, based on a set of rules) can be considered language, whether it employs vocalizations or only gestures and symbols. Language is the most complex kind of communication, and the only one with limitless variety and potential for elaboration and change. Many anthropologists think it is language that most sharply distinguishes human beings from other living creatures.

We begin by exploring the origins and development of the two main expressions of language, speech and writing. Next, we discuss the varied work of anthropological linguists. Some of them seek to understand contemporary languages, written or unwritten, studying the sounds and sound combinations making up a language and the ways in which these can be arranged to convey meaning. Others focus on the world's ancient languages. Some of these are represented by written texts, while others exist only in the form of a few words that managed to survive and were included in other languages. Finally, we examine the nature of the important links among language, thought, and culture.

Each of these areas of study is essential for understanding language. But the last one is of the most immediate importance to the ethnologist since language is the primary means of transmitting culture, from generation to generation within a society and also from one society to another.

◆◆◆

THE ORIGINS OF LANGUAGE

To help us to understand the origins of language, we can draw on evidence from several fields. Primatology has taught us something about how apes, our closest relatives among the world's animal species, communi-

Since many aspects of culture are reflected in language, understanding a culture involves understanding its language as well. Herb and Judy Zimmerman of Yellowknife, Northwest Territories, had to immerse themselves in Dogrib culture before they could accurately translate the Bible into the previously unwritten Dogrib language.

cate. Comparative anatomy has revealed the differences in the physical apparatus of language between humans and these close relatives. Physical anthropology has traced the evolution of human beings from prehuman creatures. Archaeology has documented some of the ways in which members of past human societies communicated symbolically. Finally, elementary education has contributed to our knowledge of how children learn to speak.

Speech

How Did Speech Evolve?   No one knows for sure when **speech**—communication through spoken words—evolved, although it is reasonable to suppose that it was a gradual outgrowth of the system of communication used by our prehuman ancestors. This may have been something like the "call system" of hoots and grunts used by apes in the wild. Such calls are mutually exclusive; they cannot convey two ideas at the same time. For example, there may be one call that means "food" and another that means "danger." If a chimp notices a ripe banana nearby but at the same time spots a hungry leopard waiting to pounce, it can send only one of these messages to its fellows, for a call system lacks a way of combining the messages "food" and "danger." Speech, however, permits such combinations. Even new

combinations, never uttered before, will be understood.

Some researchers think that prehuman creatures learned, over a long period of time, to combine two calls to produce a new one. Suppose one of our ancestors found herself simultaneously confronting food and danger, both important to her and her companions. Perhaps she uttered a unique cry incorporating the elements of both the "food" and "danger" calls, and the members of her troop successfully reached the food and avoided the danger. The association between the cry and successful food getting and danger avoidance had been made. Over time, she or other prehumans might have repeated the same cry, until it became recognized as meaning "food-*and*-danger." This may be the way speech evolved (see Landsberg 1988).

Other researchers have suggested that speech arose as an adaptation to a food-getting strategy based on group foraging (Parker and Gibson 1979). Successfully obtaining food in this way may have required planning and teamwork, which in turn required vocal communication about what kinds of food were located where.

An ape-sized brain is inadequate for this kind of

language the primary medium of human interaction

speech communication through spoken words

communication, but beginning about 2.5 million years ago, the brain size of early hominids (prehuman creatures) grew relatively rapidly. Archaeologists have shown that at the same time, prehumans were making stone tools. Physical anthropologists believe that tool-making and language involve some of the same mental processes, such as step-by-step planning and foresight. They hypothesize that brain enlargement, increased tool-making skills, and increased ability to communicate may all have stimulated one another simultaneously, even though the vocal apparatus of prehumans could not have produced speech as we know it (Lieberman 1984). This scenario remains hypothetical, but it does seem likely that by the time anatomically modern human beings emerged some 35,000 years ago, they could speak.

Communication through gestures has also been suggested as an avenue to speech. Gordon W. Hewes (1973) sees the basis of spoken language in hand and arm gestures. He suggests that apes' ability to use signs (Chapter 3) shows that prehumans could have developed a simple sign language. This evidence from primate behavior plus archaeological evidence of early tool using plus studies of the use of body language in human communication may suggest the pathway to vocalization.

Learning to Speak. Children, no matter what their parents' language, do not have to be taught any basic linguistic rules, such as correct word order. They just seem to pick up these rules automatically (Chomsky 1972; see also George 1989). Children learning English seem to know instinctively that "Mama go bye-bye" makes sense, whereas "bye-bye go Mama" does not. Children learning to speak other languages appear to be similarly endowed. Moreover, no matter how difficult or simple the language, children the world over all learn to speak at about the same time.

To explain these findings, some influential linguists have proposed the hypothesis that a natural grammatical ability, or **universal grammar,** is programmed in the brains of human beings from birth, and at the deepest mental levels the structure of all languages is therefore the same. The most prominent of such theorists is Noam Chomsky, whose controversial ideas converge with the theoretical approach we call cognitive anthropology (Chapter 4). Cognitive anthropologists believe the human brain contains "mental structures," fixed patterns of learning and thinking, so that the minds of human beings everywhere conform to the same patterns.

◆ ASK YOURSELF

In English, if someone is rushed we say "Where's the fire?" In Latin, we would say "Ubi ignis est?" This translates into English as "Where fire is?"— hardly a grammatical utterance. If linguistic rules are really innate, how would you explain differences in word order between languages?

Australopithecines, prehuman creatures with relatively small brains who lived some 2.5 million years ago, almost certainly could not speak, but they could probably make simple tools and communicate with gestures and vocalizations. In an artist's imaginary view, a female Australopithecine successfully communicates her needs to a male companion.

Writing

Notations and Calendars. **Writing** is the graphic or visual representation of language, using lines or other strokes on a two-dimensional surface, in media ranging from rock carving to laser printing. Writing cannot have been invented in a hurry. It must have been preceded by many different attempts by prehistoric human beings to map, demonstrate, illustrate, or record. But until quite recently, no one knew what those early attempts were or when or where they had taken place.

Until the 1960s, it was widely assumed that the earliest attempts at writing had been made sometime after the beginnings of agriculture, less than 10,000 years ago. In 1964, however, science writer Alexander Marshack made a startling suggestion: that engraved markings on pieces of bone and antler found in European archaeological sites, some of them as much as 35,000 years old, were really graphic representations of ideas, and thus ancestors of writing. Archaeologists had previously assumed that these markings were either decorations or grooves cut to improve one's grip on pieces of bone used as handles for tools. Bucking the tide of archaeological opinion, Marshack (1972) embarked on a quest for evidence in support of his hypothesis about prehistoric notations.

Much of Marshack's argument rests on techniques borrowed from the police laboratory. Using a microscope, he photographed otherwise invisible features on a number of engraved bones. Just as a gun leaves distinctive marks on bullets fired from its barrel, so each different stone tool used in carving a piece of bone leaves its own distinctive "signature." Through his microscope, Marshack observed again and again that the markings on one piece of bone were all made with different implements. He reasoned that if the markings had served merely as decorations or to "rough up" the bones to improve their grip, all the markings on a given bone would have been cut with a single tool. However, as many as 24 different tools had been used to make a single set of marks. This strongly suggests that the marks were cut on different occasions, which would be characteristic of record keeping.

On some of the artifacts Marshack studied, a long series of vertical lines was inscribed—usually 29, 30, or 31 in a row. Marshack believes these represent successive nights on which the moon was visible—in other words, a lunar month. To gatherers and hunters, the moon in its regular succession of phases was a sort of calendar in the sky, but people required graphic assistance to keep track of this calendar. The engraved artifacts seem to have served the purpose nicely. Notational systems closely resembling the European Ice Age devices were used until recently in parts of Australia, Siberia, and Africa, which lends support to Marshack's ideas.

Today, although many anthropologists agree with Marshack that our long-ago ancestors could and did make graphic representations, the very first attempt at writing is still undocumented. Perhaps someone's need to communicate her physical presence at a particular place by leaving marks on a rock or tree were the first "written" symbols, or perhaps a long-ago fisherman remembered a particularly plentiful catch by means of a tally stick onto which notches were carved. Maybe a hunter sought to provide his fellows with directions to where game animals were feeding by symbolically representing—on the dirt of the forest floor, with a pointed stick—the streams, swamps, and rock outcroppings they would need to pass. We'll never know. What is now clear from the work of Marshack and others is that by the last Ice Age, long before the development of agriculture, our ancestors were communicating with one another not only with speech but also with graphic symbols.

True Writing. Some 10,500 years ago, Middle Eastern farmers, landowners, and traders began keeping records of crop sales and real estate transactions by using little clay tokens of different shapes, such as spheres, cones, and disks, sometimes marked with lines or indentations. Each token represented a particular object or a certain quantity, and by lining up several tokens one could symbolically convey notions such as "five sheep" or "18 hectares of land."

 ASK YOURSELF

Imagine yourself in a world without calendars or timekeeping devices of any sort. What events would you most want to keep track of? How important to you would it be to know how many days had elapsed since the last full moon?

universal grammar a hypothetical grammatical ability inherent in all human beings from birth

writing the graphic or visual representation of language

American Sign Language (ASL)

Like spoken languages, sign languages allow their users to express an unlimited number of ideas, but they rely on hand and body gestures instead of sounds to convey meaning. In a scene from the movie Children of a Lesser God, *deaf actress Marlee Matlin uses sign language to communicate with actor William Hurt.*

About one in a thousand babies is born deaf or nearly so, which makes learning a spoken language very difficult. Indeed, children who are unable to hear a language find it almost impossible to speak it naturally since normal speech depends, to a great extent, on repeating what one hears. Special schools and programs train deaf or hearing-impaired children to understand the speech of others, but they can never understand as well as a hearing person because 75 percent of spoken English words cannot be accurately lip-read (Fromkin and Rodman 1988:383).

To solve this problem, various **sign languages,** which use hand and body gestures instead of sounds to express meaning, have been invented. Sign languages are fully developed languages, which like spoken languages allow their users to understand and create unlimited numbers of new sentences. Also like spoken languages, sign languages are grammatical, systematic, and change over time (Fromkin and Rodman 1988:383).

The success of sign languages provides an important insight into the nature of language, for it suggests that language acquisition does not depend on any specific ability to produce and hear sounds. In-stead, our capacity to use language seems to be grounded in a biologically determined cognitive ability. This confirms the hypothesis that language (but not speech) is biologically based. Another interesting finding is that deaf children of deaf parents learn sign language in stages that parallel those in which hearing children learn spoken language. Deaf children often "sign" themselves to sleep, just as children who can hear talk themselves to sleep. They sign to their dolls and stuffed animals and sometimes make gestural errors identical to slips of the tongue in spoken language. "Finger fumbles" amuse signers, just as tongue twisters amuse speakers (Fromkin and Rodman 1988:384–388).

The most common sign language in North America is **American Sign Language** (ASL), which includes not just words but also grammatical rules like those that structure spoken languages. The formal units of ASL, which correspond to the sounds of spoken languages, are called **primes.** Primes transmit their meaning in a number of ways, including the configuration of the hand (see Figure 13.1) and the motion of the hand(s) toward or away from the body (Fromkin and Rodman 1988:384).

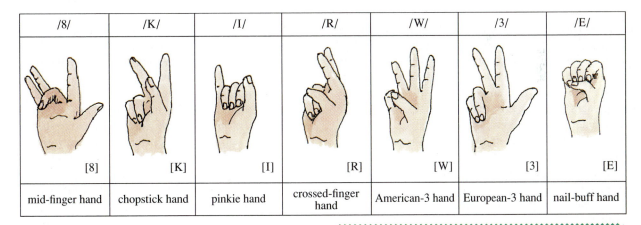

/B/	/A/	/G/	/C/	/5/	/V/
[B]	[A]	[G]	[C]	[5]	[V]
flat hand	fist hand	index hand	cupped hand	spread hand	V hand

/O/	/F/	/X/	/H/	/L/	/Y/
[O]	[F]	[X]	[H]	[L]	[Y]
O hand	pinching hand	hook hand	index-mid hand	L hand	Y hand

/8/	/K/	/I/	/R/	/W/	/3/	/E/
[8]	[K]	[I]	[R]	[W]	[3]	[E]
mid-finger hand	chopstick hand	pinkie hand	crossed-finger hand	American-3 hand	European-3 hand	nail-buff hand

Figure 13.1
Primes, the individual signs that make up American Sign Language (ASL), correspond to the individual sounds of spoken languages. Above are the hand configurations corresponding to ASL's primes in order of the frequency with which they are used. (Source: From Fromkin and Rodman 1988:385.)

sign language a language in which hand and body gestures, instead of sounds, are used to express meaning

American Sign Language (ASL) the most common sign language used by the deaf in North America

prime a formal unit of American Sign Language, corresponding to the sounds of spoken language

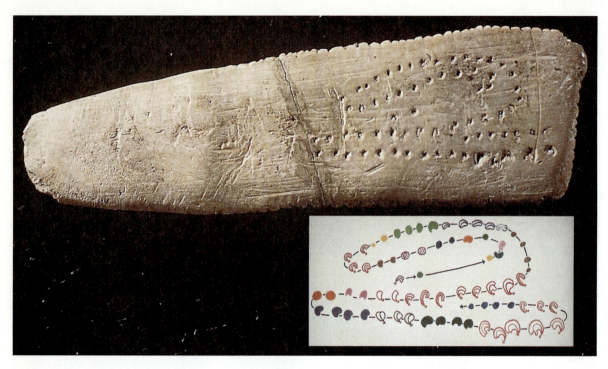

Before writing, people must have tried many ways of representing their ideas graphically. Science writer Alexander Marshack believes this piece of bone, which was found in a rock shelter in France and may be as much as 30,000 years old, is an ancient calendar. According to Marshack, the markings on the bone depict the cycles of the moon over a period of two and a half months.

Denise Schmandt-Besserat (1992), an expert in the ancient uses of clay, suggests that true writing evolved directly from the shapes produced when such tokens were pressed into wet clay. According to her, clay tablets found at Uruk, an ancient town in present-day Iraq, represent an evolutionary stage in a system of recording that had been in use in the Middle East since the first stages of the transition from a gatherer-and-hunter way of life to a more settled, agricultural life. She suggests that this new way of life required a record-keeping system.

Four principal stages marked the evolution of writing, according to Schmandt-Besserat (1992). The first occurred about 10,500 years ago, when tokens of specific shapes were used to represent items, such as bread, sheep, and clothes, that were traded among villages. These tokens seem to have served as invoices or bills of lading. Thus, a herder selling ten sheep to someone in another village might give a middleman transporting the shipment a sealed pouch containing ten to-

kens representing sheep—or perhaps one "sheep" token and one token representing the quantity 10. This document would have guaranteed the accuracy of the shipment when "read" by the buyer.

The second stage began about 5,500 years ago, with the enclosure of tokens in hollow clay spheres. The personal seal of the seller was pressed into the fresh, wet clay on the outside of each sphere. The clay subsequently hardened, so the sphere had to be broken open on delivery, revealing the tokens inside.

The third stage, following closely on the second, began when people found that the need to break open the clay spheres to check the record, perhaps during shipment, could be avoided if a duplicate record was made by pressing each token on the outside of the sphere while the clay was still wet. The characteristic shape of each token *inside* the sphere was thus recorded on its shell. Intact spheres have been found and opened, and the tokens inside them have corresponded exactly to the impressions on the outside. Schmandt-Besserat

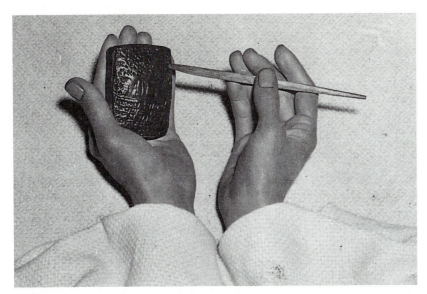

The characters that made up cuneiform writing, which spread throughout the Middle East some five thousand years ago, were impressed into wet clay with a pointed stick. Impressing was better than inscribing because inscribing—rather like snowplowing—gouged out curls of clay that tended to obscure the details of the symbol being inscribed.

(1992) suggests that these marks may be considered to be the crucial link between the old system of recording in three dimensions and writing.

The final stage occurred when the system of impressions became generally understood, about 5,200 years ago. The tokens themselves then became unnecessary, and fully fledged writing appeared. Instead of tokens, a pointed stick was used to inscribe the same symbols into clay. Schmandt-Besserat argues that new words, for which there had never been tokens, were subsequently added. Many of them were obviously **pictographs**—simple pictorial representations of the objects they stood for. A rising sun, for example, stood for "day."

Within a very few centuries, pictographic writing evolved into the more stylized **cuneiform,** in which an arrangement of tiny wedge-shaped dents impressed into wet clay produced a version of the earlier pictogram. Five thousand years ago, cuneiform writing quickly spread throughout the Middle East, making possible more complicated and codified systems of commerce, law, religion, history, literature, and science.

veloping world—have only recently been put into written form. What may be even more surprising is that there are still literally hundreds of languages in use that have never been written down. Thus, fieldworkers in both linguistics and cultural anthropology sometimes find themselves having to learn a spoken language that has no written form.

When this happens, the fieldworker must analyze the language, primarily so that he or she can learn it for fieldwork purposes but also so that the language can be taught to and learned by others. All the sounds of which the language is made up must be isolated, the precise meanings of all these sounds must be identified, its vocabulary must be listed, and its grammatical rules must be defined. Later, the language must be put into written form, using the alphabet of some written language. **Descriptive linguistics** is that branch of linguistics that aims to describe all the features of a language.

The descriptive linguist is trained to identify, describe, and analyze the components of languages. When the language is unwritten, it's a mind-boggling job. To give you an idea of what is required, imagine you're an

UNDERSTANDING LANGUAGES

Descriptive Linguistics

It may surprise you to learn that of the world's thousands of languages, many—particularly in the de-

pictograph a simple pictorial representation of an object

cuneiform ancient writing consisting of an arrangement of tiny wedge-shaped dents impressed into wet clay

descriptive linguistics the branch of linguistics that seeks to describe the features of languages

ethnographer who has just encountered a group of people among whom you would like to do fieldwork. You are, however, completely unprepared to talk with these people since their language has never been written down and they do not speak or write your language. It is with some misgivings, then, that you enter their village for the first time. With the use of gestures—smiles, waves, nods—you manage to communicate your friendly intentions. The villagers respond cheerfully, inviting you with gestures to sit down with them and make yourself as comfortable as the circumstances permit. A babble of unintelligible sounds surrounds you, not one of which is meaningful. Soon refreshments are fetched, and someone presents you with a suspicious-looking drink, accompanied by a smile and a brief remark. To you, the words sound like this:

ME-KAHM-KEH-SHOW-MAH-EEN-RA-DAS-TEE-BAH-SHEED[1]

Your linguistic problems begin. First, you do not know what the utterance means, although in the context of the situation you guess it probably has something to do with being offered a drink. Second, you can count 11 different sounds making up this utterance, but you have no idea how many individual words these 11 sounds represent, much less what their meanings might be. You don't even know whether they constitute a complete sentence or just a phrase.

The people point repeatedly at you, using the two syllables SHOW-MAH, so you infer that these two syllables together might translate into the English word *you.* That's a start. But you already know that languages are made up of a lot more than their vocabularies, and even if you were able to divide the utterance into the individual words that make it up and to translate those individual words, you do not know the grammatical rules according to which the words are arranged. In English, after all, the phrase "Steve loves Laura" is not at all the same as the phrase "Laura loves Steve." In our language and many others, word order is everything—and the rules governing word order are only some of the rules you need to speak and understand the language. You've got your work cut out for you.

Where to start? An important part of descriptive linguistics is understanding the various sounds used in a

language and the way that these sounds can be combined into meaningful words, phrases, and sentences. Your first task as a descriptive linguist, then, is to identify all the meaningful sounds used in the language—all the sounds that can make a difference in meaning. Doesn't every sound used in a language make a difference in meaning? Not necessarily. In English, for example, the sounds that the letters *t* and *th* make are meaningful sounds. They can change *tan* to *than.* But in other languages there may be no meaningful distinction between these two sounds. The smallest meaningful units of sound into which a language can be divided are called its **phonemes.** Studying them is called **phonology.**

You cannot assume that the sounds used in the new language are the same ones that make up English. Chances are, they're not. Over the next few weeks, you make a list of all the new language's phonemes. Some of them correspond to individual letters you are familiar with; there is an *s* sound, for instance, and a *b* sound. Some of them do not. There is, for example, a deep, throaty sound that you find yourself virtually incapable of repeating, and there doesn't seem to be a letter of the English alphabet that could be used to represent this sound. (Even in the English language, phonemes and letters do not equate to one another on a one-to-one basis. The letter *t* is a phoneme, and so is the letter *p*. These phonemes are responsible for the different meanings of the words *tan* and *pan.* But the two-letter combination *th* is also a phoneme since *tan* clearly does not mean the same thing as *than.*)

After having identified all the sounds that together make up the new language, your next task is to identify the larger combinations of sounds that mean something in this language. These are **morphemes,** the smallest combinations of sounds that have a meaning in a language. Studying them is called **morphology.** As phonemes often correspond to individual letters, so morphemes often correspond to individual words—but not always. In English, even a single letter—for example, the letter *s*—can change the meaning of a word. *Hat* is not the same as *hats,* so the English word *hats* is made up of not one but two morphemes, *hat* plus *s.* Languages vary widely in the number of morphemes their words contain. In English, most words contain only one or two, but in the new language you are learning, it becomes apparent that many morphemes can be strung together to form a single word.

Many weeks after being offered that first drink, you are able to divide ME-KAHM-KEH-SHOW-MAH-EEN-RA-

---

[1]This example is not, of course, taken from one of the world's still unwritten languages. If it were, it wouldn't be written here! The example is from Farsi, a language spoken by millions of Middle Easterners.

Anthropological linguists are trained to describe and analyze little-known languages, some of them unwritten. In the village of Kailga in the New Guinea highlands, linguistic fieldworker Alan Rumsey (right, with fern headdress) studies one of the 45 distinct languages spoken in Papua New Guinea.

DAS-TEE-BAH-SHEED into individual words, this way:

MEKAHM KEH SHOWMAH EENRA DASTEE BASHEED.

After you have mastered both the phonology and the morphology of your new language, you are ready to tackle the really hard part—the **syntax,** the rules governing the way the morphemes can be arranged in order to make sense. You must learn just what meaningful beginning morphemes (**prefixes**) and ending morphemes (**suffixes**) can be attached in what way to what kinds of words. You learn to **conjugate** the language's verbs—that is, to change the verbs to reflect different tenses, persons, moods, and so on—and to **decline** its nouns—to change them to reflect particular cases, numbers, or genders. After a few more months of study, you have figured out that

MEKAHM is a form of the verb meaning "to want" and consists of two morphemes: the verb stem, MEK-, and a morpheme indicating the first person singular in the present continuous tense, -AHM. It means "I am wanting."

phonemes the smallest meaningful units of sound into which a language can be divided

phonology the study of phonemes

morphemes linguistic units made up of the smallest combinations of sounds that have a meaning in a language

morphology the study of morphemes

syntax the rules governing the way morphemes can be arranged in order to make sense

prefix a morpheme that is added at the front of a word to alter its meaning

suffix a morpheme that is added to the end of a word to alter its meaning

conjugate to change a verb to reflect different tenses, persons, and moods

decline to change a noun to reflect case, number, or gender

KEH means "that," in the (English-language) sense of introducing a subordinate clause rather than serving as a demonstrative pronoun. Two phonemes make it up—the gutteral sound you have chosen to represent with the English letter *k*, plus a short *e* sound. The first of these two phonemes sometimes sounds to you like a *k* and sometimes more like a hard *g*, but although these two sounds are different phonemes in En-glish (changing *kill* to *gill*, for instance), they are only one phoneme in your new language.

SHOWMAH, as you correctly guessed on your very first day of fieldwork, means "you."

EENRA is translated by two English words, *this* and *thing*, but in the language you are studying it is only one word, meaning "this thing."

DASTE and BASHEED are the two parts of a compound verb. One is a form of the word for "have," and the other expresses the subjunctive mood. Together the two words mean "you should have."

Now you are finally able to translate the phrase you first heard so many months ago. The friendly fellow who presented you with a drink on that first day of your fieldwork was saying to you, "I want that you this thing should have," or loosely translated, "Here, have a [drink]." Lucky for you that your fieldwork preparation included some training in descriptive linguistics!

One problem in writing down the phonemes used in a particular language is that a phoneme and the letter used to represent it when transcribed may not always match up. The words *heed* and *head* both have the letter *e* as their second letters, but it's pronounced differently in the two words. So to avoid the possibility of making a mistake, linguists have developed a system of phonemic symbols, each of which represents one sound only. The most widely used system of phonemic symbols used today is that of the International Phonetic Association (IPA). Table 13.1 shows the phonemic symbols for the consonants and vowels of American English.

In addition to phonemes, morphemes, and syntax, human speech also uses voice effects. These include pitch, loudness, speed, and other vocal qualities, which may be used singly or in various combinations to convey meaning. We call these features of language **para-language.**

Let's take a look at how the meaning of a sentence changes when the intonation is changed:

He's coming, isn't he

If you say this in such a way that your voice falls on the

◆ ASK YOURSELF

An immigrant from China was recently fired from his job in the United States because his employer felt his accent did not present a good image for the company. In North America, British accents are considered charming, but other accents sometimes cause people to wonder, "What's wrong with this guy?" Do you speak English with an accent? If so, has this ever caused you problems? Do you find any particular accent more or less attractive than any other?

TABLE 13.1 A PHONETIC ALPHABET FOR AMERICAN ENGLISH PRONUNCIATION

Consonants				Vowels		
pʰ pill	tʰ till	kʰ kill		i beet	I bit
p spill	t still	k skill		e bait	ε bet
b bill	d dill	g gill		u boot	U foot
m mill	n nil	ring		o boat	bought
f feel	D rider	h high		æ bat	a pot
v veal	s seal	bottle		ˆ but	sofa
θ thigh	z zeal	l leaf		aj bite	aw bout
ꟗ thy	chill	r reef		ɔ boy	
§ shill	˘ Jill	j you			
‰ azure	• which	w witch			

Source: Fromkin & Rodman 1988:57.

Phonemes are the smallest meaningful units of sound into which a language can be divided. The English language is represented by more phonemic symbols than it has letters because one letter can represent several different sounds. Above are the phonemes of English as it is pronounced in America, with examples of how each sound is used in an actual word.

THE ANTHROPOLOGIST AT WORK

Linguistic research has contributed in important ways to finding solutions for social problems. Education, advertising, medicine, and the law have all benefited from the work of linguists.

In 1984, a threat to bomb a Pan-American Airlines plane at the Los Angeles airport was recorded on tape. A New York man was arrested for the crime and put on trial. After analyzing the taped threat, linguist William Labov (1988:170–181), called as a witness, concluded that it had been uttered not by a New Yorker but by a native New Englander. The California jurors who listened to the tape could not distinguish between New York and New England accents, but by comparing the vowels of the defendant with those of the real bomber, Labov was able to convince the judge that the defendant could not have made the call. Despite the circumstantial evidence against him, "the clarity and objectivity of the linguistic evidence" was compelling (180). The accused was acquitted.

second "he," you probably intend the utterance to be a flat statement, with which you expect your listener to agree. However, if you say these words so that the second "he" is uttered with a rising tone, your meaning changes. In this case, you are making a request for information (Crystal 1975:165–166).

Historical Linguistics

Historical (comparative) linguistics approaches the study of language diachronically rather than synchronically, as descriptive linguistics does. Historical linguists are interested in the histories of the world's "living" (currently used) languages, and they decipher "dead" or obsolete languages—something like breaking a secret code. They are also interested in the past and present relationships among languages (one reason why this subfield of anthropology is sometimes called comparative linguistics) and relationships among **dialects,** varieties of a language based on region, occupation, or class.

One of the greatest challenges a historical linguist faces is trying to reconstruct the ancestor of a known language, called its **protolanguage.** Searching for a protolanguage is often a speculative undertaking since such a language lacks any spoken or written examples. Thus, the protolanguage that is re-created is in the nature of a hypothesis rather than a certainty. But the historical linguist is aided in this seemingly impossible task by two facts. First, in any language there is a **core vocabulary,** made up of basic words (see Table 13.2). These include words for parts of the body, objects in the natural environment, and the numbers below ten. Some linguists think core words change very slowly because they are essential for social interaction; and when they do change, they appear to change in fairly systematic, predictable ways.

Reconstructing a "lost" language begins with a search among early written languages from the same general area of the world for **cognates,** words historically derived from the same source. In practice, this means finding words that are similar in appearance and meaning in different languages. The Farsi word for "brother," for instance, is *barodar,* which is quite similar to the English word *brother.*

In *any* two languages, there will be a certain number of overlapping or nearly overlapping words since a small percentage of every language's words are simply replications of the sounds these words are intended to convey. Bees the world around, for instance, say *buzz.* But there are other, genuine cognates among languages. These are apt to be core words, slow to change. Once

paralanguage the use of voice effects to convey meaning

historical (comparative) linguistics the study of the histories of languages, both living and dead, and the relationships between languages and dialects

dialect a variety of a language resulting from its speakers' region, occupation, or class

protolanguage a hypothetical language thought to be the ancestor of a known language

core vocabulary the most basic words of any language

cognate a word historically derived from the same source as another word

TABLE 13.2 BASIC CORE VOCABULARY

1	I	26	root	51	breasts	76	rain
2	you	27	bark	52	heart	77	stone
3	we	28	skin	53	liver	78	sand
4	this	29	flesh	54	drink	79	earth
5	that	30	blood	55	eat	80	cloud
6	who	31	bone	56	bite	81	smoke
7	what	32	grease	57	see	82	fire
8	not	33	egg	58	hear	83	ash
9	all	34	horn	59	know	84	burn
10	many	35	tail	60	sleep	85	path
11	one	36	feather	61	die	86	mountain
12	two	37	hair	62	kill	87	red
13	big	38	head	63	swim	88	green
14	long	39	ear	64	fly	89	yellow
15	small	40	eye	65	walk	90	white
16	woman	41	nose	66	come	91	black
17	man	42	mouth	67	lie	92	night
18	person	43	tooth	68	sit	93	hot
19	fish	44	tongue	69	stand	94	cold
20	bird	45	claw	70	give	95	full
21	dog	46	foot	71	say	96	new
22	louse	47	knee	72	sun	97	good
23	tree	48	hand	73	moon	98	round
24	seed	49	belly	74	star	99	dry
25	leaf	50	neck	75	water	100	name

Source: Renfrew 1987:114.

The core vocabulary of a language is made up of a limited number of basic words that some linguists believe change very slowly because they are essential for social interaction. The one hundred words above constitute an English core vocabulary.

identified, the systematic process by which the ancient core words came into existence can be mapped and their antecedents inferred. For example, the English word *hand* has cognates in German (*hand*), Dutch (*hand*), Swedish (*hand*), Danish (*haand*), and the now extinct Gothic language (*handus*) (Ruhlen 1987:6). From these cognates, the historical linguist can infer a common ancestral form in the lost language called Proto-Germanic. By collecting the ancestral forms of words in use today, historical linguists can attempt to reconstruct a protolanguage.

A once-promising technique for historical linguists, **glottochronology,** was popularized by Morris Swadesh in the 1960s. This was a method for pinpointing the time at which two languages branched off from a common ancestor. The technique was based on two assumptions. The first was that in every language, some

words fade from use and are replaced with new words, whereas others remain in use. Second, the "fading" of words takes place at a constant rate. Thus, two languages identical in vocabulary at the time their speakers go their separate ways will become increasingly different as time goes on, through word loss and innovation (Renfrew 1987:114–119). The greater the difference between two related languages, the greater the amount of time separating them from their common ancestor.

Promising as it seemed, this method has now been recognized as flawed in several respects. Most damagingly, there is no reason to assume that languages lose words at a constant rate. Social factors, such as whether a community is literate or not, certainly influence vocabulary. As the archaeologist Colin Renfrew (1987:117) has remarked, "glottochronology in its simple assumptions is just too good to be true."

The First Americans:
When and Where?

Most American archaeologists believe that the first people to populate the New World came from Asia, more than 10,000 years ago, by trekking across a bridge of land that once connected Siberia with Alaska. But whether this migration occurred just once or repeatedly has been a mystery. Now, historical linguists are helping to find the answer by searching the vocabularies of the six hundred existing native American languages for core words and then reconstructing the protolanguages from which the native American languages sprang. The number of native American protolanguages could be an important clue to the number of separate migrations from Asia as well as the origins of the migrants (Ruhlen 1987:6).

In 1954, the linguist Joseph Greenberg began a study of native American languages. Patiently collecting lists of words from as many New World languages as possible over a period of many years, Greenberg compared their cognates and hypothesized that there were only three separate American protolanguages: Eskimo-Aleut, Na-Dene, and Amerind. The geographical locations in which the languages derived from these three basic families are spoken suggest that three separate migrations took place from Asia into the New World (Ruhlen 1987:10).

Greenberg and other linguists discovered a small but significant number of global cognates, or word similarities between languages spoken in different parts of the world and thought to be totally unrelated to each other. This hints at a fascinating possibility: that all the languages in the world may ultimately be derived from a single protolanguage (Ruhlen 1987:10).

SOCIOLINGUISTICS

Language is an important vehicle through which people express their thoughts, beliefs, interests, and feelings. But can a language, in addition to performing this function, actually *affect* the thoughts, beliefs, interests, and feelings of its speakers? Can it encourage them to think in certain ways? Can it limit their imaginations in some ways and expand them in others? Can it channel their intellectual and emotional lives in certain directions rather than in others? **Sociolinguistics,** a branch of linguistics that studies all aspects of the relationship between language and society, offers important clues.

From Nonliteracy to Literacy

Some authorities contend that introducing writing into a nonliterate society alters not only the ways in which people absorb, retain, and transmit information but also the ways in which they think and arrange their social relationships (Goody 1981; Ong 1982). Thus, in certain significant ways (though not in every way), literate people may express themselves and view their world

differently from nonliterates. This argument is based in part on studies of poets and storytellers in present-day, nonliterate societies and in part on the analysis of the poetry of the great Greek bard, Homer, whose rich oral legacy was written down only after his death. Linguistic scholars have discovered that such oral texts are often shaped by their nonliterate contexts. Once literacy is introduced into a society and spoken texts begin to be written down, the stories and poems of the society change profoundly.

◆ ASK YOURSELF

Try to imagine living in a community where no one knows how to read or write and there is no electronic means of communication. How would this affect your studies? Your job? Your social life?

glottochronology a method for establishing the approximate time at which two languages branched off from a common ancestor

sociolinguistics a branch of linguistics that focuses on the relationship between language and society

The transition from a purely oral society to one in which most individuals are literate appears to provoke certain radical changes in culture. Literate people, for example, tend not to view their world as a unified system of categories or explain it in myth, as do many nonliterate people. As literacy develops, former nonliterate people reorder their world into fragmented subsystems, in which economics, art, religion, kinship, and politics are seen as separate matters instead of parts of one unified system. This is the kind of view we Westerners have created for ourselves. The philosopher Walter Ong (1982) proposes that the use of an alphabet (a limited series of characters that can be arranged meaningfully only in certain ways) transformed the consciousness of Westerners, who reconstructed their traditional view of the world to make it consistent with the way in which they organized their written language.

Literacy has features that contrast markedly with those of nonliteracy. Literacy stresses the *content* of a linguistic transaction (a tale, poem, or message); nonliteracy places greater emphasis on the *style* in which it is presented. Literacy also increases the psychological distance between the sender and the receiver of a linguistic transaction, often granting anonymity to the receiver (the reader). Listeners, in a nonliterate culture, are physically close to the sender, and this of course affects what the sender will say and the way he or she will say it. Finally, the use of print turns words into texts, which are tangible things, existing on flat surfaces at arm's reach, in marked contrast with the intangible intimacy of the world of sound that envelops the teller of tales in a nonliterate society. The form of language, in other words, affects human perception.

The Sapir-Whorf Hypothesis

The best-known attempt to demonstrate a relationship between language and perception is called the **Sapir-Whorf hypothesis** (or **Whorfian hypothesis**) after two linguists, teacher and student, who worked together on the idea that the language we learn as members of our society not only reflects our view of the world and makes it possible for us to express it but actually structures the way we perceive the world. Edward Sapir (1884–1939) first proposed that the "language habits" of a society shape its members' perception of reality. Later, Benjamin Whorf (1897–1941) expanded on the idea. Speakers of different languages, according to Sapir and Whorf, actually "see" the world quite differently.

Writing and reading create psychological distance between senders and receivers of words, but speaking and listening bring them physically and psychologically close. As she recounts a tale from Africa's rich oral tradition, Nongenile Masithathu Zenani, a master storyteller of South Africa's Xhosa people, uses her whole body to entertain and educate her audience.

Color Terms

Different languages have very different ways to describe colors and different numbers of basic color terms because the people who speak them use color terms for different purposes. The Nuba, cattle herders who live in the Sudan, in Africa, have no term at all meaning "color," so their ethnographer, James Faris, found it difficult to discuss the subject with them. Once, for example, when Faris asked about the color of palm leaves, he was given a word that he later learned means "crisp."

Faris discovered that the Nuba combine all the colors for which Westerners have separate words into only four terms, which roughly translate as the English words *black, white, red,* and *yellow* (Faris 1972:59). The Nuba term for *black* covers dark red, brown, purple, and blue. *White* is used for very light colors—pale blue, pale green, pink, and grey. *Red* suggests not only the various shades of what we would describe as red but pink and orange as well; and *yellow* refers to what we would call green, greenish yellow, yellow, and blue-green.

Of course, the Nuba see and distinguish shades of color as well as any other people. When they need to, they can describe the colors of objects accurately by using their four basic color terms together with other descriptive terms meaning, for instance, "dark" or "light." But making fine distinctions between different colors is not particularly important in the technologically simple life of the Nuba.

How is this possible? A language, Sapir and Whorf pointed out, consists of a great deal more than a long list of words, each standing for some particular object or concept and directly translatable into another language. If all that we had to work with, linguistically, were lists of words, we could communicate with one another in only a rudimentary way. There would be many concepts we would be unable to express: past, future, or hypothetical action, for example, or the idea of subject and object: which person or thing is acting and which is being acted upon. So in addition to its list of words, every language has a set of rules, called its **grammar.** Grammar regulates the order in which words should be spoken so that they make sense, what prefixes or suffixes should be added to words to convey precise meanings, and other, similar guidelines for speakers. Using correct grammar, speakers can convey the idea of action taking place in the future or of hypothetical action that *might* take place. They can make it clear what or whom is an actor and what or whom is being acted upon, or suggest possession or emphasis.

Sapir and Whorf thought that both our words and our grammar shape the way we see reality. Facts, objects, people, and events can be classified in many different ways. In English, for example, we refer to all our cousins by the same term, *cousin.* But this term includes a wide variety of people, of both sexes and from both sides of the family. Other languages lump together relatives that English separates and separate relatives English lumps together. In a matrisystem, you would probably call your mother's sister's daughter by a term different from that by which you refer to your father's sister's daughter. But you might call the former by the same term as that for your sister. Such verbal classifications are important; as we saw in Chapter 7, in some societies certain cousins are considered potential spouses, but in other societies they are prohibited as spouses.

Whorf's ideas came in part from his study of the language of the Hopi of the American Southwest. In the Hopi language, the past, present, and future tenses, as we use them in English, do not exist. Instead, Hopi speakers distinguish two different states of existence into which all events fit: the state of being, in terms of which they discuss things that have actually existed in the past or actually exist now, and the (potential) state of becoming, in terms of which they discuss things that

Sapir-Whorf hypothesis (Whorfian hypothesis) the idea that the way in which the members of a society order their world is conditioned by their language

grammar the rules governing word order, prefixes and suffixes, and other aspects of a language

will or might happen in the future. According to Whorf, the Hopi view of time differs noticeably from ours. We view time as a linear progression, he argued, because our language uses different tenses for verbs. The Hopi, because their language lacks these tenses, do not (Carrol 1956).

Over the years, there has been some anthropological support for the Sapir-Whorf hypothesis. Basing her work on Malinowski's data from the Trobriands, Dorothy Lee (1985) argues that English and Trobriand speakers have different worldviews because their languages are ordered by different grammars. Our world view is ordered *lineally*. Whenever possible, we impose lines on the world around us: we *draw* conclusions, *trace* relationships, and envision the present as having *developed* from the past. We think, in other words, in terms of causality, movement, and progress. Trobrianders see things differently. Rather than being lineally arranged, their world is based on the idea of eternal, self-contained patterns of objects, actions, and events. Since there is no past or present, one thing does not cause another. An action may be completed, but this doesn't mean it is over; "it may (still) be present or time-less" (Lee 1985:114). A yam, to the Trobrianders, is a yam, period. It does not *become* overripe. An overripe yam is another thing altogether. Events do not lead to other events; they form elements in patterned wholes. Tenses do not exist in the Trobriand language, which also lacks words to express causal relationships.

If we were to describe what is going on when we plant a coconut, we would probably use a time line and assume that specific actions produce specific results: "first we do action A, and then we do action B, which causes event C to happen." Here is a translation of a Trobriand description of what happens when a coconut is planted, with strings of words with hyphens between them representing single words in the Trobriand language:

> Thou-approach-there coconut thou-bring-here-we-plant-coconut thou-go-thou-plant our coconut. This-here it-emerge sprout. We-push-away this other coconut-husk-fiber together sprout it-sit together root.

The Trobrianders do not make lineal connections between the various steps involved in planting a co-conut, nor do they draw a causal relationship between the planting and the subsequent sprouting. Although this lack of a sense of action and reaction may seem peculiar to us, Lee discerns a good fit between the Trobrianders' language and their worldview. The Trobrianders are very intelligent, and they do perceive continuity, but

progress in our sense of the term is not important to them (or at least it wasn't in Malinowski's day). Value, in the Trobriand view of the world, lies in the sameness of things, in repeated patterns. What is good is that which is the same as it was in the past. As Whorf claimed for the Hopi language, the Trobriand language makes the past, present, and future one and the same. And it is in these terms that the Trobrianders view their world.

The Sapir-Whorf hypothesis is attractive to some anthropologists for its cultural relativity, but it has not won universal acceptance, partly because tests carried out to verify it have not always succeeded (Polomé 1990:462). Still, there doesn't seem to be any doubt that language influences the view a community has of the world it lives in and, as the Zimmermans discovered (Malcolm 1981), is intimately connected with other aspects of culture. In fact, words may not even be the most important aspect of a language. When we speak, we are doing more than simply trying to make a listener understand what we think and feel. We are also trying to define our relationship with the listener, to identify ourselves as a member of some social group, or to persuade the listener to accept some point of view. Like us, the speakers of other languages use words to convey a host of deeper cultural messages—perhaps to reinforce gender or class distinctions between people, for example, or to identify themselves with a particular social group or ideology.

Gender and Language

Sociolinguistics has found an important place in contemporary studies of gender (Todd and Fisher 1988). In an important though much criticized book, *Language and Woman's Place* (1975), feminist Robin Lakoff used the term *woman's language* for two things: (1) the language American women customarily use and (2) the language used in American society to describe women.

 ASK YOURSELF

The vocabulary of a language reflects the interests of the people who speak it. Thus, the world languages, such as English and Russian, incorporate numerous scientific and technological terms. What words might be found in languages spoken in nonliterate societies that are not found in the world languages?

Some linguists believe that American women are taught a different, more "polite" style of speech than men, which makes them seem uncertain and indecisive. In this conversation, the man at left does appear to have the upper hand, although age, status, or other factors besides gender may be the reason.

Both, Lakoff believes, can deprive a woman of her identity as a person.

The "polite" style of speech that American females are taught to use may, Lakoff suggests, encourage them to express uncertainty rather than decisiveness. In the following example, (A) may be either a man or woman, and (B) is a woman:

(A) "When will dinner be ready?"

(B) "Oh . . . around six o'clock . . . ?

Using the paralanguage typical of American women, (B) responds to the question with a rising intonation, indicated by the question mark. This suggests to Lakoff (1975:17) that the woman is seeking confirmation from (A), even though she is the person who has the requested information. (B) is placing herself in the position of requiring confirmation, even approval, from (A). She sounds unsure of herself, as if she were saying "Six o'clock, if that's OK with you." Lakoff argues that one result of this "polite" speech will be that (B) will be per-

ceived as someone who cannot be taken seriously or trusted with any real responsibility since "she can't make up her mind" and "isn't sure of herself." In short, her speech pattern is taken to reflect something about her character and abilities. Lakoff concludes that if (B) were a man, he would be much more likely to reply with something like this:

(B) "Six o'clock, and you'd better be here!"

Certain American linguistic conventions, Lakoff (1975:23) believes, may subtly denigrate women. For example, in a sentence in which either the word *woman* or the word *lady* might be used, the choice of *lady* may trivialize the subject under discussion. Lakoff describes a newspaper article that referred to its female subject as a "lady atheist." Using *lady* in this context, Lakoff thinks, reduces the woman's position to that of a scatterbrained eccentric, someone not to be taken seriously.

The hypothesis that American women speak more tentatively than men because they seek affirmation has been effectively challenged on two grounds: first, that Lakoff (1975) failed to support it with hard data, and second, that the hypothesis was grounded in feminist ideology, which caused Lakoff to assume an existing (but never demonstrated) link between a particular way of speaking and the absence of female assertiveness. Far from regarding this style of speaking as "weak," others see it as an attractive way of expressing oneself (Hamilton et al. 1992:104). Moreover, Lakoff ignores ethnographic evidence from Canada, the United Kingdom, and Australia, where some men habitually end sentences on a rising note (Cameron et al. 1989:75–76). The meanings of linguistic forms can be understood only if we also consider other factors, including the roles being played by the participants in an interaction, the objectives of the interaction, and the participants' status relative to one another and to the social context in which the interaction takes place (91–92). Gender is at best only one factor.

An alternative interpretation of "women's language" comes from psychological anthropology. In Chapter 8, we mentioned Carol Gilligan's hypothesis that middle-class American girls are enculturated differently from boys. While girls are urged to maintain ties with their families (particularly their mothers), boys are encouraged to sever these ties. Because of these differences in enculturation, women choose a different form of speech, a form in which they can express empathy—identification with the feelings and interests of others (Boe 1987). The lack of solid evidence that females have greater empathy than males weakens this hypothesis also, but it is an intriguing one all the same since it encourages ethnographers to look for possible connections between speech and upbringing.

Pidgins and Creoles

Sociolinguists are also interested in the social contexts in which new languages are created. Composite languages called pidgins and creoles provide examples of how new languages come into being (Holm 1989).

If you want to communicate with a person whose language is different from your own, but neither of you knows the other's native tongue, you may communicate by using elements from both tongues or even a third. In a **pidgin** language, the syntax and vocabulary of the "lender" languages are greatly simplified. Prepositions may be omitted, and tenses may be limited to the present. For example, if you were from one language com-

munity and wanted to comfort a person of another language community who had injured his leg, instead of declaring in your own language, "Your leg will get well again," you might say, in pigdin, "Bimeby [by and by] leg belong you he-all-right gain [again]." Or, to ask at a hardware store for a pan in which to cook bread, you might say, "Me like-im saucepan belong cook-im bread" (Hudson 1980:64).

Since pidgin languages tend to evolve from people's practical need to communicate, often for purposes of commerce, they are sometimes called *trade languages*. One famous pidgin language, from which the examples above are taken, is Neo-Melanesian Pidgin, or Tok Pisin (from *tok* meaning "talk," and *pisin* meaning "pidgin"). This has become the standard language of trade and administration in New Guinea, where many dozens of different languages are spoken. Using Tok Pisin, speakers of all these different languages can communicate.

Although a pidgin language tends to be something of a "minimum language," we must not think of pidgins as lacking rules of syntax. They do have syntactical rules, and linguists consider them real languages.

Should a pidgin language evolve to the point where it actually becomes the mother tongue of a community, we call it a **creole.** This process of "creolization" might occur, for example, in a setting in which husbands and wives, each with different native tongues, speak pidgin at home. Their children learn pidgin as their only and native language, so for them, their parents' pidgin has become their creole. This happened on a large scale among African slaves brought to the New World. Residents of several countries in the West Indies, for example, speak a creole language that combines English and French (the languages of the former slave owners) with elements of various African languages. Today, there are more speakers of creoles than of pidgins: 10 to 17 million, compared with between 6 and 12 million (Hudson 1980:66).

When a speaker switches from one language or dialect to another, according to whom he or she is speaking, this is called **code switching** (Heller 1988). If you sometimes need to use a pidgin language to make yourself understood, you are code switching. Some people do this easily and continually. In English speaking Caribbean countries, for instance, native-born people are skillful code switchers. Routinely speaking creole when conversing informally at home, they speak English, their official language and the one taught in schools, while they are at work. Being able to speak more than one language with equal, or roughly equal, competence is called **bilingualism.**

Black Vernacular English

The term **vernacular** denotes the standard language or dialect of a population. **Black Vernacular English (BVE)** is a dialect of English spoken by black youths involved in the street culture of the inner cities of the United States (Labov 1984:xiii). Linguist William Labov warns us not to confuse this dialect with *black English,* a term that refers to the entire range of linguistic forms used by black people in the United States, from the creole spoken in coastal South Carolina to the most formal literary style (xii). In its syntax, phonology, and vocabulary, BVE differs so much from the forms of English spoken by white, middle-class Americans that some have considered it unacceptable in the context of American society and have tried to discourage its use.

Labov (1984) has described some of the distinctive properties of BVE. For example, the form of the verb *to be* used in standard American English is omitted in certain constructions ("He a teacher"; "he happy"; "he with them"). The position of negatives is sometimes inverted ("Ain't nobody gon' hit you"). And the word *it* is sometimes used as a substitute for *there* ("It ain't nothin' happenin'").

Until the 1970s, when studies of BVE began to be published, such deviations from standard American English were believed by many authorities to be evidence that BVE was merely an inferior form of English. Black students who expressed themselves in BVE, and who failed to understand questions put to them by their teachers in standard American English, were regarded as less capable of learning than their white peers. A middle-class white teacher hearing a student say, "I don't want none" or "they hers" would sometimes consider the student to be suffering from "verbal deprivation" rather than speaking a legitimate dialect of English.

Recent research has proven that BVE is a legitimate form of English. Its syntax, phonology, and other linguistic features make up a linguistic system well suited for communication by those who know it. Today, enlightened teachers have come to realize that their goal should be to encourage black students to retain their skills at using BVE, the dialect they need to function in their home environment, and at the same time enable them to acquire the standard dialect of American English that they need to succeed in the wider society.

CONCLUSION

Think back for a moment to the plight of the Wild Boy of Aveyron, whom you met in Chapter 3. Unable to communicate with other human beings, he couldn't even participate in, much less enjoy or contribute to, human society. It's clear that we wouldn't be really human had we not been born into a cultural setting. Without language, culture—the most distinctive hallmark of human beings—is impossible. It could not exist, much less develop or be transmitted to others. Our conclusion has to be that nothing contributes more to making us human than language.

Not only is language a unique human ability; it is also a compelling human need. Human beings, it seems, *must* communicate—must put their feelings into forms that enable other humans to understand them. This is the most important way we have of coming together, of creating society. The social institutions we have discussed in earlier chapters, such as the different forms of marriage and different kinds of political organizations that human beings have developed, couldn't have come into being without language.

SUMMARY

We can approach language from several perspectives, both synchronic and diachronic. We can learn the individual sounds, vocabulary, and grammar of a specific language, written or unwritten, just as the Zimmermans did. We can study the history and development of language, expressed either vocally or graphically, as did Alexander Marshack and Denise Schmandt-Besserat. We can try to understand how human beings learn languages, as did Noam Chomsky. We can examine how language

pidgin a language in which the syntax and vocabulary of two other languages are simplified and combined

creole a pidgin language that has become the mother tongue of a community

code switching switching from one language or dialect into another

bilingualism being able to speak more than one language with equal, or roughly equal, competence

vernacular the standard language or dialect of a population

Black Vernacular English (BVE) a dialect of English spoken by black youths in the inner cities of the United States

...uences human thought and culture, as did Edward Sapir, Benjamin Whorf, and Walter Ong. Or we can see how human beings use language as an instrument of interaction, as did Robin Lakoff and Carol Gilligan.

We have by no means exhausted the list of what anthropological linguists do, but with these examples we have introduced the broad areas of study into which the subdiscipline of anthropological linguistics is divided. Descriptive linguistics includes the study of all the sounds and sound combinations that make up a given language and the ways in which these can be arranged in order to be meaningful. Historical linguistics deals with the history of the world's languages—how they developed, how they have changed through time, and how they are related to one another. Finally, sociolinguistics focuses on the ways in which language affects, and is affected by, thought and culture. Among many other issues, sociolinguists study the contrasting influences on culture of nonliteracy and literacy; how language structures the way we perceive the world (an idea called the Sapir-Whorf hypothesis); how language both reflects and expresses gender attitudes; how composite languages called pidgins and creoles develop; and the way in which dialects of standard English, such as Black Vernacular English, are used.

KEY TERMS

American Sign Language (ASL)
bilingualism
Black Vernacular English (BVE)
code switching
cognate
conjugate
core vocabulary
creole
cuneiform
decline
descriptive linguistics
dialect
glottochronology
grammar
historical (comparative) linguistics
language
morpheme
morphology
paralanguage
phoneme
phonology
pictograph
pidgin
prefix
prime
protolanguage
Sapir-Whorf hypothesis (Worfian hypothesis)
sign language
sociolinguistics
speech
suffix
syntax
universal grammar
vernacular
writing

SUGGESTED READINGS

Crystal, David. 1980. *A First Dictionary of Linguistics and Phonetics.* Boulder, CO: Westview Press. Many anthropologists find the linguistic branch of their discipline confusing because of its large technical vocabulary. This dictionary is an admirable solution to the problem. Its clarity and comprehensiveness make it indispensable to anyone wishing a command of linguistic terms, and we have relied on it heavily in this chapter.

Darnell, Regna. 1990. *Edward Sapir: Linguist, Anthropologist, Humanist.* Berkeley: University of California Press. A biography of the famous linguist whose studies of native American languages helped to establish the subfields of historical and descriptive linguistics.

Giglioli, Pier Paolo (ed.). 1986 (1972). *Language and Social Context.* Harmondsworth, England: Penguin Books. Fifteen articles, each by a different linguistic authority, give cross-cultural treatment to three topics: face-to-face interaction; the relationship among language, social structure, and cultural traits; and the relationship among language, conflict, and social change.

Graddol, David, and Joan Swann. 1989. *Gender Voices.* Oxford: Basil Blackwell. A well-reasoned cross-cultural comparison of how language and gender influence each other without the ideological bias that usually skews such studies.

Lyons, John. 1981. *Noam Chomsky.* New York: Viking. The famous linguist's own books and articles tend to be a bit weighty for nonlinguists. Lyons's review of Chomsky's work will make his interesting hypothesis clearer to students.

Renfrew, Colin. 1987. *Archaeology and Language: The Puzzle of Indo-European Origins.* Cambridge: Cambridge University Press. A fascinating and readable example of how linguistic analysis is used to trace population movements.

Trudgill, Peter. 1983 (1974). *Sociolinguistics: An Introduction to Language and Society* (rev. ed.). Harmondsworth, England: Penguin Books. Demonstrates how gender, class, and religion create differences within as well as between languages. The book also discusses the influence of language on the way people think and on the cultural traits they have created.

Walkerdine, Valerie, Cathy Urwin, and Carolyn Steedman (eds.). 1985. *Language, Gender and Childhood*. London: Routledge & Kegan Paul. A collection of eight essays on the ways in which language is central to the positions of women and girls in society and how such positions have come about.

EXPRESSIVE CULTURE

Folk art, produced in traditional ways by people in small-scale societies, is often highly sophisticated, both in execution and symbolic content. Woodcarvers in Cameroon, Africa, produce elaborate and highly symbolic reliefs, masks, and free-standing sculptures, sometimes for tourists but often for their own religious purposes.

INTRODUCTION

On the streets of the South Bronx in New York City, they were known as the Bombers. Depending on your point of view, they were either juvenile delinquents who expressed their social rebelliousness by spray-painting graffiti on city subway cars and other public property or gifted young artists stifled by an environment that failed to provide outlets for their creative urges. The Bombers' big, energetic, cartoon-like paint-ings, full of sweeping strokes, overlapping images, clashing colors, and personal names, expressed the young painters' confusion, anger, need for attention, and sense of alienation from their society.

Until recently, the Bombers were being accused (and frequently convicted) of vandalism. Now, thanks to a new city youth program, nine former graffiti painters have become legitimate artists under a contract in which they have agreed not to deface property in exchange for free art supplies and workspace. Trading their spray cans for paintbrushes and canvases has proven lucrative for several of the young artists, who have discovered that their subway-style graffiti has artistic merit, at least for some art lovers. At a recent exhibition, their works of art, which included traditional landscapes as well as "pop art style" graffiti graphics, sold for as much as $200 each, and several of the artists have received com-missions for future works (*New York Times* 1987).

Few aspects of culture challenge the anthropolo-gist's commitment to cultural relativism as much as the broad area of human endeavor popularly called art. One problem is that the Western system of classification dis-tinguishes between art and non-art. In many cultures, however, there is no such rigid distinction, and Western ethnographers sometimes find themselves studying ob-jects and behaviors that take them far beyond the realm of what they would ordinarily call art (Hardin 1988:36). One expert has gone so far as to argue that the category "art" does not exist outside of Western ideas (Anderson 1992).

Not surprisingly, therefore, a definition of art that will satisfy every anthropologist is hard to come by. Given that the category of objects and behaviors West-erners call art is itself an artifact of Western culture, we prefer to use the term *expressive culture* for the wide range of things we'll be discussing in this chapter. Where we do use the term *art,* it denotes specific cate-gories of expressive culture.

Expressive culture concerns aesthetics, a sense of what is beautiful (Coote and Shelton 1992). Aesthetic experience is highly individual, of course, but in addi-tion to being a subjective expression of individuals' imagination, it is also an expression of cultural values. For us, therefore, **expressive culture** is the purposeful arrangement of forms, colors, sounds, language, and/or body movements in ways that have meaning and/or are aesthetically appealing not only to those who do the ar-ranging but also, in most cases, to other members of their culture as well.

Aesthetic experience is highly subjective, and what is aestheti-cally appealing to one person may not be so appealing to oth-ers. On a wall on New York City's lower east side, graffiti memorializes a painter's dead friend. Some would call this "art"; others would not.

Various categories of expressive culture—paint-ing, drawing, sculpture, music, literature, drama, or dance, to name only a few—play central roles in every human society. Although not every society exploits every category, the universality of expressive behavior suggests that the urge to produce meaningful or pleasing creations is innate. And while the creative impulse may be an individual matter, culture plays a crucial part in artistic creation by determining which artistic media and styles a particular group of people will adopt as its dom-inant modes of artistic expression and suggesting what artistic themes will be pursued. As the Bombers' graffiti shows, expressive culture is often at one with the beliefs, ideas, institutions, and behaviors of the societies in

 ASK YOURSELF

Do you have a favorite way of expressing yourself through art?

which it is created—a culturally patterned reflection of society itself. This is what makes it so interesting to anthropologists.

These two observations—that humans have a strong natural impulse to express themselves artistically and that what they create is culturally patterned—give this chapter its main themes.

FORMS OF EXPRESSIVE CULTURE

We can't discuss in one chapter every category of expressive culture created by human beings. Instead, we'll focus on three of the most important: (1) the so-called plastic and graphic arts, such as sculpture and painting; (2) language, in both its spoken and written forms, when it is used as an artistic medium; and (3) music. Because two or more varieties of expressive culture often form part of a single artistic complex (as sound and language are combined in songs, for example), we'll also discuss forms that combine two or more artistic media.

The Plastic and Graphic Arts

Plastic art is three-dimensional art in which objects are created by modeling or molding a variety of materials, including wood, metal, clay, bone, ivory, and stone. Carving, sculpture, basket weaving and pottery making are all forms of plastic art. **Graphic art,** in contrast, is rendered on a two-dimensional surface, whether that surface is paper, a piece of canvas stretched across a wooden frame, or the rough stone wall of a cave. Drawing, painting, and stone incising are all forms of graphic art.

The Origins of Plastic and Graphic Art.   No one knows who first had the idea of creating something that wasn't practical (or at least not solely so) but was nevertheless worth the effort of its creation because it was aesthetically pleasing, meaningful, or both. We do know, however, that by Upper Paleolithic times, plastic and graphic art was an important aspect of human life and culture.

The earliest plastic and graphic art seems to have been created in western Europe, where as long as 30,000 years ago gatherers and hunters stroked colored pigments, obtained from rocks, on the walls of caves, using brushes made from grass or feathers. More rarely, they sculpted three-dimensional clay images (Pfeiffer 1982).

Their most common artistic theme was wild animals, which is hardly surprising since these people lived in a wilderness in which people were far outnumbered by wild cattle and horses, reindeer, ibex, and mammoths. (We mentioned in Chapter 12 that in cave paintings these animals were sometimes shown pierced by spears, an apparent attempt by artists to influence the hunt with sympathetic magic.) These first works of art often show great artistic sophistication. Cave artists, for instance, frequently used the natural unevenness of a rough cave wall to suggest the taut muscles of a charging bison or reindeer, and they clearly understood the use of shading to suggest depth.

From an anthropological point of view, perhaps the most interesting aspect of cave art is the motivation behind it. Early analysts suggested that the cave dwellers created works of art for the same reason that college students hang posters in their dorm rooms: for decoration. But this is now thought unlikely since most cave art is found in poorly ventilated chambers where smoke from the fires or oil lamps that would have been needed to provide light would have prevented habitation. It is more likely that cave dwellers lived not in the depths but in the mouths of caves, which were better lit and airier, and that the artworks they created deep inside the earth held some meaning beyond mere decoration.

Archaeologists recently learned more about the motivation for cave art by exploring the relationship between the animals drawn and the diets of the people who drew them (Rice and Paterson 1985). They discovered that there is no simple correlation between the number of bones of particular animals found in Upper Paleolithic sites and how frequently the same animals appear in artwork. In general, larger species, such as wild cattle, are overportrayed relative to the number of their bones found, and smaller ones, such as deer, are underportrayed. The archaeologists hypothesized that the cave artists portrayed either the animals they preferred (presumably the meatier species) or the ones they most feared. They identified the meatiest species by calculat-

---

expressive culture the purposeful arrangement of forms, colors, sounds, language, and/or body movements in ways that have meaning and/or are aesthetically appealing to those who do the arranging, and usually to others as well

plastic art sculpture and other three-dimensional forms of art

graphic art two-dimensional forms of art such as painting or drawing

Paintings of animals on the walls of caves in western Europe, among the earliest known works of art, are so realistic the animals must have seemed almost alive when viewed in the flickering light of oil lamps. The painter of this charging bull, found in Lascaux cave in France, has skillfully suggested great strength and headlong movement.

ing average animal weights and the most fearsome by assessing the amount of danger involved in hunting each animal. It turns out that *both* the meatier and the more dangerous species were consistently overportrayed in cave art relative to the number of bones found. It is clear that "the art is related to the importance of hunting" for the cave artists (98).

Similarities in Folk Art. **Folk art,** the art produced by traditional societies, is often termed "primitive," not because it is necessarily simple, either in conception or execution, but because it is produced in a technologically simple context. Both the ideas expressed and the techniques used in folk art may be highly sophisticated. Although these ideas and techniques vary through time and from culture to culture, the art of small-scale, traditional societies, expecially those little affected by Westernization, is apt to share certain similarities. For example, the pottery of America's prehistoric Pueblo people, with its striking black-and-white painted geometric decoration, is almost indistinguishable from the pottery of the ancient town of Shahr-i Sokhta in Iran (see Figure 14.1), yet these two cultures were located on different sides of the globe and were separated from each other by two thousand years.

Scholars interested in the anthropology of art have often asked why the people of different cultures, widely separated from one another in time and space, would produce similar works of art. Part of the explanation is

found in the artistic media used and the limited number of ways in which those media can be manipulated. The same media tend to be available to people living the same life-style, even if they are separated in time and space. The Pueblo people and the people of Shahr-i Sokhta were both simple horticulturalists. Most such people know very well that clay can be found in the ground, that it can be molded into various shapes, and that baking objects molded of clay will make them permanently hard and waterproof. One very practical application for this knowledge is making clay containers for food and drink. Not surprisingly, we find that clay pots, formed and fired in very similar ways, were used (and are still being used) in many horticultural societies.

If a particular medium (in this case, clay) suggests a particular artistic form, it also suggests a certain artistic style. The decorations on the pottery made by the Pueblo people and the people of Shahr-i Sokhta are nearly identical. Both societies favored angular designs, consisting of straight lines, triangles, and filled areas, in the same two colors, black and white. Anthropologists can suggest at least two reasons for the striking similarity between the decorated pottery of the two societies.

◆ **ASK YOURSELF**

Can you think of examples of purposeful, as opposed to merely decorative, graphic or plastic art in Western society?

Figure 14.1
People living the same life-style, even when widely separated in time and space, often use the same artistic media in the same ways. A pot created before 2,000 B.C. by the people of ancient Shahr-i Sokhta in Iran (left) is similar to one created around A.D. 1100 by the Pueblo people of the American Southwest (right).

First, in simple horticultural settings black and white paints are easily made from ash and powdered bone. Second, designs composed of straight lines can be easily made by hand, but curved designs are very difficult to paint on pottery unless you know the technique of the potter's wheel.

Another explanation for artistic similarities between cultures follows from the possible existence of "mental universals" (Chapter 4), fixed patterns of thought, more instinctive than learned, which some cognitive anthropologists believe are common to all people. The hypothesis that mental universals exist was proposed precisely because expressive culture in so many societies includes similar patterns and themes in myths, rituals, plastic art, and graphic art. According to this hypothesis, straight-lined black-and-white designs on simple clay pots are found all over the world because such designs are mental universals and thus hold some natural attraction for all human beings. But this hypothesis has yet to be proven.

Verbal Art

As long as people have been communicating with words, they have manipulated language—sometimes alone, sometimes in combination with other sounds (such as music) or body movements (as in drama)—to create pleasurable or meaningful works of art. In Western societies, art in the form of words is usually read silently from a printed page, with the exception of the

bedtime stories parents read to their children. But in nonliterate societies, art in the form of words is **oral art**, spoken (or sometimes sung) aloud. Even in some small-scale societies whose language is now written, verbal art is still primarily oral.

In traditional settings, art in the form of words is called *folklore,* which consists of stories, songs, poems, riddles, sayings, and other traditional oral expressions. The formal study of folklore grew out of the nineteenth-century interest in European peasants' verbal art. Later, when ethnographers began collecting data from traditional societies outside of Europe, the term came to be applied to their oral literature as well. In fact, folklore and cultural anthropology overlap so much in the area of expressive culture that folklorist Alan Dundes, today's leading authority on traditional verbal narrative, is a faculty member in a department of cultural anthropology.

Oral art is meant to be spoken or sung in the presence of an audience. Whereas the audience for a book in a Western society consists of an unrelated group of individuals separately reading something composed by an author they have in most cases never met, a non-Western audience consists of socially related individuals who not only listen to a work of oral art but may also become an important part of it. The artist (in contrast to the author of a book) becomes a performer. He or she is in di-

folk art the art produced by traditional societies

oral art art expressed in the form of speech

••

Human Remains or Works of Art?

Anthropologists have mixed opinions about the collection and display of folk art. On the one hand, art is an integral part of a society's culture, so that removing a work of art from its cultural context eliminates its capacity to contribute to the culture that created it. On the other hand, since works of art created from wood, cloth, fibers, and other perishable materials often decay quite rapidly in the environment in which they were created, collecting objects that would otherwise perish and preserving them in museums may prevent the loss of objects of great ethnographic as well as artistic value. No consensus on this controversy has yet emerged (MacClancy 1990; Price 1990).

The Maori of New Zealand, whose religion involves ancestor worship, preserve the heads of the deceased, decorating these relics with elaborate tattoos and revering them as religious objects. Not long ago, a London auction house announced that it had acquired one of these relics and was planning to sell it. The National Maori Council, supported by the government of New Zealand, began legal moves to stop the sale, but private collectors and art auctioneers who favored the sale argued that the piece merely used a skull as the basis for overmodeling, and "the result is a work of art rather than part of a human body" (Benthall 1988:1).

Anthropologists don't ordinarily involve themselves in commercial disputes, but when it comes to trading in art objects made from human remains, it is difficult for them to refrain, so England's Royal Anthropological Institute (RAI) weighed in to help. The

When an auction house in London made plans to sell the preserved, tattooed head of an ancestor of the Maori of New Zealand as an art object, the Maori, for whom such heads have religious meaning, objected. During the debate that ensued, a cartoon showing a Maori head tatooed with the symbol for the British pound appeared in a London newspaper.

RAI adopted the official position that selling human remains in any form is unethical when members of the society in which the remains originated object. The Maori community made it abundantly clear that they strongly objected to the proposed sale of an ancestral head (*Anthropology Today* 1988). The sale was canceled.

rect, ongoing contact with individuals who, by their open and instant reaction to the performance, stimulate and sometimes even guide the artist into composing what they wish to hear. This means the audience enters into the act of creation itself.

An audience may consist of only one particular group in a society, perhaps members of a lineage or age set or of a particular social rank. As a result, the theme, content, and purpose of a non-Western narrative may be changed to fit the particular social context in which it is recited. The words uttered by the non-Western teller of

tales will also change from recitation to recitation as the mood of the audience changes. And a story told to chil-

 ASK YOURSELF

How would you feel if your great-grandmother's bones were unearthed in an archaeological excavation and displayed in a museum? Do you feel the same way about the international sale of ancient Egyptian mummies and their display in museums?

A Teller of Tales as Performer and Creator

South African Nongenile Masithathu Zenani, whose picture appears on page 292, is a teller of traditional Xhosa tales who innovates and imitates at the same time (Zenani 1992). Basing her narratives on centuries-old traditional Xhosa stories well known to her audiences, she embellishes on these stories, using new similes, new metaphors, and new gestures to keep them fresh and interesting. Thus, although the basic outline of a given tale may be familiar to her listeners and its outcome predictable, every telling of it is new and commands not only the rapt attention but also the emotional involvement of its listeners.

Mrs. Zenani learned her tales the way all Xhosa storytellers do, by listening intently to stories told by others and by picking up their tricks over the course of a lifetime. She still listens to other storytellers, forever willing to improve her own performances by incorporating effective new stylistic devices and interesting details into her own repertoire. In this way,

Mrs. Zenani's performances combine the best features of all the oral performances she has ever witnessed.

As she begins a narrative, the tall, regal Mrs. Zenani seems almost disdainful of her audience, pulling a red cape about her and proceeding with her story despite the chatter of those around her. Absorbed in her own words, she alternately grimaces, frowns, and smiles, varying the pitch, intensity, and speed of her voice and using precise, controlled movements of her hands and body to illustrate and punctuate her story.

Mrs. Zenani's natural verbal ability, her powers of observation, and her formidable memory work together to produce original verbal masterpieces that reflect not only her personality but Xhosa culture as well. The result is apparent when you look at the faces of her audience. Her listeners become psychologically immersed in the performance.

---

dren will be told differently to adults. It's often misleading, then, to speak of a single, accurate version of a non-Western narrative because such narratives, folktales in particular, are flexible in content.

Anthropologists classify oral narratives as myths, legends, or folktales. The criteria used to define these categories overlap somewhat, so that a narrative that one anthropologist would classify as a folktale might be classified as a legend by a colleague. Still, these classifications can help us highlight themes that make one narrative different from another.

Myths. In Chapter 12 we defined myths as timeless stories explaining origins—of the world, of natural phenomena, of particular customs or ideas. The central character in a myth is often a culture hero, a larger-than-life person who lived in the distant past, and myths always include some event that is humanly impossible. Clan myths, for example, may describe how a clan's culture hero founded the group. Other common mythological themes include the origins of fire, of people and animals, of societies, of the sexual differences between women and men, of incest, of agriculture, and of death.

Every culture has such stories, although in some societies they are taken more literally than in others.

Perhaps the most famous myth in Western society describes the origins of humanity and of the differences between male and female—the story of Adam and Eve. The origin myth of the Eel clan of the Tetum of Indonesia (see Chapter 6) is a good example of an origin myth from a non-Western society. Both of these myths are religious narratives, describing improbable events that occurred at some distant mythological time, in order to provide explanations for things that are important in the present. The story of Adam and Eve explains, among other things, how evil entered the world, while the Eel story explains how certain rituals came to be invented.

Even as a particular myth may help to account for a particular ritual, so may a ritual physically reenact events related in a myth. This is not to say that every myth must be associated with a corresponding ritual; after all, the myth of Adam and Eve has no counterpart in ritual.

The structural anthropologist Claude Lévi-Strauss has been the world's best-known authority on myths for over four decades. Beginning in the 1950s with a wholly original interpretation of the Oedipus myth, Lévi-Strauss succeeded in reviving anthropology's all but extinct interest in the subject and in bringing to a wider academic audience facts about myths that most anthropologists now take for granted.

Lévi-Strauss's methods for analyzing myths are complex, and even experts in this field are sometimes baffled by his arguments, but many anthropologists have been impressed by at least two of his suggestions. First, since *all* versions of a myth must be taken into account before its meaning can be understood, it is fruitless to try to establish which version of a particular myth is the "true" one—a quest beloved by earlier generations of scholars. Second, insights into the meaning of a myth can be gained by searching for oppositions and analogies such as male/female, culture/nature, and right/left (we noted in Chapter 4 that opposition is an important tool of structural anthropology). Once he has understood the meaning of a myth by considering it in all its versions, Lévi-Strauss seeks to place it in its cultural context and to draw holistic conclusions about the culture.

Legends.   We use the word **legend** for narratives that tell of events set in specific places in the real world, at times less remote than the mythological past. Their chief characters are real people rather than gods, godlike humans, or animals, and they often revolve around great migrations, victories in battle, or the heroic deeds of ancient chiefs or kings. Many are based on some kernel of truth, a real event that may have been embellished over the generations. The story of George Washington's encounter with the cherry tree, a tale invented by a nineteenth-century parson long after Washington's time, might be considered an American legend.

Folktales.   **Folktales** are stories about the adventures of animals, humans, or both. Legends may be based on or even confused with reality, but folktales are acknowledged to be fiction. One country blessed with an abundance of folktales is Russia, and it was a Russian scholar, Vladimir Propp (1988), who pioneered the structural analysis of folktales in his book *Morphology of the Folktale,* originally published in Russian in 1928.

A familiar kind of folktale is the **fable,** a folktale that instructs those who hear or read it in some important moral lesson. Aesop's *Fables,* perhaps the most famous collection of fables in Western literature, includes a tale, "The Tortoise and the Hare," that tells how a slow-moving but determined tortoise plods its way to

George Washington and the Cherry Tree

The story of George Washington and the cherry tree, which recounts the deeds of a real person and which may be based on an actual event, qualifies as an American legend. In an 1867 engraving, the truthful young Washington confesses his vandalism to his forgiving father.

One day in eighteenth-century Virginia, according to legend, a small boy who was later to become the first president of the United States discovered an ax. Yielding to an irresistible temptation to see what this instrument could do, George Washington began to hack away at an ornamental cherry tree, a favorite of his father.

George's father, upon discovering that one of his prize trees had been vandalized, angrily demanded to know who was responsible. Young George spoke up, for even at his tender age this future personification of our national integrity could not tell a lie. His father, legend has it, was so impressed by George's honesty that he forgave the boy immediately.

The Monkey and the Shark

Once upon a time, Shark and Monkey jointly owned a garden, which Monkey selfishly desired to control for himself. Knowing Shark was a sea creature, crafty Monkey suggested he and his gardening partner compete in a footrace, with the garden as the prize.

Shark realized he was no match for speedy Monkey, so the night before the race, he dove down to his home in the sea to have a chat with his three brothers. By the time the race started the next morning, the brothers had devised a plan for outwitting Monkey. Monkey dashed into the lead, as expected, but when he turned the first corner of the racetrack, he saw Shark plodding slowly along ahead of him! Amazed he had not seen Shark pass him, Monkey did not know that the runner ahead of him was really one of Shark's look-alike brothers. Determined to win, Monkey rushed forward, overtook his rival, and sped off, leaving the first Shark brother in the dust. Whipping around the next turn, however, the astounded Monkey again could scarcely believe his eyes. Ahead of him yet again was Shark! Monkey surged forward more furiously than ever, once more gaining the lead. Zooming around the final turn, he knew he had won. But as the finish line came into view, there was Shark just crossing it!

"The garden's all mine now, Monkey," said Shark. "Your selfishness has caused you to lose everything. From now on, I'll cooperate only with my true brothers."

---

victory in a race against a much speedier but overly confident and frequently side-tracked rabbit. Because they are instructive, folktales may serve as tools for educating young people in their culture's attitudes, values, and standards. "The Monkey and the Shark," a Tetum folktale (see box above), teaches the value of cooperation among kin.

Music

Music is a form of expressive culture whose medium consists of sounds, patterned in different rhythmic combinations. The elements of music are tones, percussion, and rhythm. A **tone** is a sound that has a certain duration, quality, and (most important) a certain highness or lowless, determined by the frequency of its sound vibrations (a tone's highness or lowness is called its **pitch**). **Percussion** consists of toneless sounds made by striking something. When a series of consecutive tones of various pitches are assembled in coherent sequence, the result is a melody. Music is made up of patterned combinations of tones (usually assembled into melodies), toneless percussive sounds, and rhythms. These patterned combinations differ among societies, and studying them within a specific cultural context or cross-culturally is called **ethnomusicology.**

The sounds out of which human beings make music can be produced in two different ways. First, the human body can be used as a sound-producing instrument. The human voice can produce an enormous range of dif-

 ASK YOURSELF

The Tetum folktale "The Monkey and the Shark" bears a close resemblance to the Western fable "The Tortoise and the Hare," in that both rest on the same theme: "slowly but surely wins the race." To what do you attribute this similarity?

legend a narrative that describes events set in a specific place in the real world, at a time less remote than the mythological past

folktale a fictional story about the adventures of animals or of animals and human beings

fable a category of folktale that teaches some important moral lesson

tone a sound of distinct duration, quality, and pitch

pitch the highness or lowness of a musical sound, largely determined by the frequency of its sound vibrations

percussion toneless sounds made by striking something

ethnomusicology the study of music in its cultural context, either in a single society or cross-culturally

ferent tones, and percussive sounds can be made by clapping the hands, stamping the feet, or slapping the thighs, all elements of music frequently encountered cross-culturally. Second, music can be produced by instruments, which range in complexity and musical potential from simple rattles made from dried gourds to technologically complex electric organs and sound synthesizers.

Defined as a form of expressive culture consisting of patterned sounds, music is found in every contemporary society. Moreover, even though music (like language) was until recently an ephemeral art—meaning that works of musical art disappeared as soon as they were performed—we can assume that music (like oral art) was an important part of ancient cultures, too. Like other forms of art, it appears to be a human universal. The evidence for this belief is not just that every culture known today creates music; there are also archaeological hints distributed worldwide: ancient instruments such as whistles, flutes, drums, rattles, and **bullroarers** (elongated pieces of bone or other materials, which when attached to cords and whirled about the head produce an eerie, prolonged tone).

Like other forms of art, music is culturally patterned and therefore differs widely among societies. Most North Americans were introduced to the music of the Western cultural tradition as babies, so this is the music we find most appealing; in fact, we may be downright uncomfortable listening to, say, Asian music. The two kinds of music are different because they order the world of sounds very differently. More specifically, they separate tones from one another in different ways. In the fixed set of tones (or **scale**) on which Western music is based, each tone is separated from its nearest neighbor on the basis of how many more or fewer vibrations it comprises. Divided from one another in this way, the tones on which Western music is based make up an **octave,** a set of eight primary tones. To the Western ear, music based on the octave sounds "correct" and pleasing. But in Japan, where the set of tones on which traditional music is based does not conform to the octave, Western music may sound unmusical. The important point here is that the two very different kinds of music are equally pleasing in the context of their own cultures.

In every society, music is an important part of social life. In North American society, for instance, it almost always accompanies parties, weddings, and funerals. On the island of Bali and in other parts of Indonesia, music is a traditional accompaniment for oral literature as well. There, orchestras called **gamelans** provide music for the repeated enactment of local legends, as important a part of Balinese social life as the yearly Christmas holiday is to some Westerners. A gamelan may contain up to 75 instruments played by as many as 30 musicians (Dalton 1988:160–162). Most of the sounds come from bronze and wooden xylophones shaped like

On the island of Bali in Indonesia, orchestras called gamelans, *made up mostly of drums and xylophones, play traditional music which many Westerners find unmelodic. Here, members of a gamelan orchestra play at a Balinese funeral.*

•••

The Physiology of Trance States

Not much is known about the physiological state of dancers in a trance, except that the brain waves of such dancers are patterned like those of epileptics just before a seizure. It seems likely, therefore, that not only a dancer's state of consciousness but also his or her physiological state is altered during a dance-induced trance.

Despite the lack of scientific studies, anthropologists and other students of the dance have repeatedly observed that a combination of certain stimuli often produces a trance. In the ritual Balinese witch-killing dance just described, these stimuli include rhythmic drumming, rapid breathing resulting from exertion, dizziness produced by whirling around, and perhaps self-hypnotic suggestion. In other rituals performed by members of other societies, inhaled smoke or some other narcotic, flickering light, and self-inflicted deprivations (such as fasting before dancing) may also play a part in inducing a trance. Whatever the physical changes these stimuli produce, the result is the same. Dancers "tune out," hallucinate, experience muscular spasms or actual seizures, and sometimes faint. Later, they often report having had a religious vision or an out-of-body sensation or being possessed.

---

discs or cylinders and from bulbous, hollow bowls beaten with hammers. The tonal system employed by a gamelan is made up of scales divided into intervals different from those in Western music. The resulting music is soft, mellow, and liquid, though perhaps unmelodic to many Western ears.

Combined Art Forms

In Western as in other societies, there are a number of categories of artistic expression in which not one but several artistic media—form, color, sound, language, and/or body movement—are arranged in pleasurable or meaningful ways. Drama, for example, combines language with body movement. In opera, perhaps the most elaborate of the Western combination art forms, all five media are arranged into what for some is pure pleasure and for others a sensory overload.

Yet another combined art form is dance, which combines body movement with music or, in some societies, only with percussive sound. Members of almost all societies dance, but the reasons for this behavior differ. In the West, we dance (or watch others dance) primarily for the pleasure of it and sometimes for the feelings of social solidarity this form of expression conveys. In other, non-Western, societies, dancing may be a form of religious or political expression.

Sometimes the combination of sound, movement, and religious belief is so potent that non-Western dancers fall into trance states (Winkleman 1986; Ward 1989; Shaara and Strathern 1992). A particularly dramatic example comes from Bali, Indonesia, where religious rituals often incorporate dancing. One such ritual reenacts a violent knife fight between the power of fear, represented by an elaborately costumed "witch" dancer, and the power of life, represented by several dancers dressed up as a "dragon." During the dance, in which body movement and persistent, rhythmic drumming converge to create a highly emotionally charged atmosphere, the dancers—each wielding a long knife called a kriss—fall into a trance. Holding their krisses so that the sharp points press against their chests, the dancers whirl wildly about in time to the beat of the drums. Remarkably, no one gets hurt; overly violent dancers are gently restrained by onlookers, and their knives are taken away. At the end of the ritual, the onlookers help the perform-

•••

bullroarer an elongated piece of bone or other material, which when whirled about on a cord produces a tone

scale a fixed set of tones on which music is based

octave a set of eight primary tones

gamelan an Indonesian orchestra containing as many as seventy-five different instruments

◆◆

Bar'a Dancing

A dance called bar'a *is performed on festive occasions by men in the Middle Eastern country of Yemen. In al-Ahjur in rural Yemen,* bar'a *dancers, accompanied by drums, symbolize their tribe's ability to function cooperatively by circling energetically while brandishing traditional tribal daggers.*

A dance called *bar'a* is performed on religious holidays, at weddings, and on other festive occasions by tribal people in the Middle Eastern country of Yemen. Accompanied by the beat of drums, *bar'a* dancers, always men, perform closely together in an open circle, moving forward and backward with a variety of hops, knee bends, and turns while brandishing daggers in their right hands (Adra 1985:70). One dancer, the leader, directs the movements and timing of the others, who try to remain in step with the beat of the drums. The basic *bar'a* dance step is not in itself complicated, but maintaining close coordination between dancers and drummers is tricky; and with many dancers crowded together, each wielding a dagger, a misstep can result in injury.

Following Bateson's (1972) hypothesis that "the patterning of a work of art can provide information on the underlying value system of the culture in which it is produced," anthropologist Najwa Adra went to Yemen in the late 1970s to study the *bar'a* dance. She discovered that the *bar'a* is a metaphor for Yemeni tribesmen's concept of tribalness. By performing the *bar'a,* dancers are symbolizing, for par-

ticipants and spectators alike, "the coherence of the tribe, its ability to function cooperatively, and the strength and endurance of its members." Adra (1984:75) concluded that "the dance and other arts can be a valuable source of information on the motivating value system of the culture that produces them."

In 1990, the political situation in Yemen changed dramatically with the unification of North and South Yemen, never previously under one rule, into a single country. One effect of this unification has been the increasing importance to Yemenis of the concept of nationhood. In an attempt to forge a new Yemeni identity, tribal symbols have been taken up by urbanites. People who are not of tribal origin genealogically are now wearing tribal dress, eating tribal foods, and carrying tribal daggers. Not surprisingly, the *bar'a* dance has changed too. Once a localized, rural art form, it is now increasingly popular in cities. Once performed by tribesmen, it is now danced by nontribal Yemenis. Suddenly, *bar'a* has became not a tribal but a Yemeni art form (Adra 1992).

In addition to their aesthetic appeal, works of art can also symbolize social institutions and depict values. Norman Rockwell's painting of children gathered around their teacher in an old-fashioned country schoolhouse expresses the simple, rural values many Americans cherish.

ers to emerge from the trance with fragrant incense and a sprinkling of holy water.

FUNCTIONS OF EXPRESSIVE CULTURE

If the main function of expressive culture is the individual creation of something new, meaningful, or pleasurable, it also has a number of important social functions. Through expressive culture, ideas can be expressed, social institutions symbolized, values portrayed in concrete form, and order imposed on the external world—and perhaps on the internal world of the mind as well.

Reflecting a Society's View of the World

A society's expressive culture can mirror its general perception of the world. Norman Rockwell's hugely popular and very American mid-twentieth-century paintings, for instance, portray the comfortable, rural, child-oriented, patriotic, optimistic, God-fearing America that Americans believed they had secured through their contribution to the allied victory in World War II.

A non-Western example of this same phenomenon comes from West Africa, an area of the world that has produced some of the world's most varied, plentiful, and elaborate art, most notably in the form of wood carvings. Using a structural approach, anthropologist James Fernandez (1971) analyzed the wood sculptures of the West African Fang people of Gabon and Cameroon. Fernandez discovered that these works of art reflect, to a remarkable degree, the Fang view of the world. The Fang envision the world as a series of complementary oppositions, of which the most common are right/left, northeast/southwest, and male/female. In each pair, one of the partners (e.g., "male") balances its complementary but opposed partner (e.g., "female"), which sets up an even tension between the two partners. To the Fang way of thinking, this tension imparts vitality and balance.

In a reflection of this preference for harmonic tension between complementary opposites, numerous features of Fang social life are similarly arranged into pairs of complementary oppositions. Villages, for instance, consist of two rows of huts facing each other. A settlement consisting of only one row of houses is considered neither pleasing nor functional. Indeed, a collection of buildings like this isn't considered a real village at all (Fernandez 1971:366–367). Similarly, in the men's council house, two rows of benches face each other, and from these opposed benches the parties to disputes face each other on an equal footing.

Fang woodcarvings of human figures and faces are very much a part of the society in which they are produced. Since Fang people say that balance and vitality give them pleasure, we would expect them to feel that objects reflecting these qualities are beautiful. Fang artists strive to express balance and vitality in their carved figures' arms, legs, and ears—all parts of these figures that are in complementary opposition to each other. When the Fang compare wooden statues of their ancestors for their artistic merits, these are the qualities they find most desirable.

Affirming Social Organization and Group Solidarity

The native American groups of the Northwest Coast were stratified into many different social ranks, whose members were much concerned with questions of relative status and prestige. Their potlatches (see Chapter 9) involved the exchange, and sometimes even the destruction, of material goods by rival chiefs for the purpose of increasing their prestige. Many of the objects exchanged or destroyed at potlatches were works of art—painted wooden chests, conical hats, woven blankets—all elaborately and distinctively decorated. The most prized objects of all were "coppers," large, shield-like copper plaques considered to be the highest form of wealth and owned only by men who had given extraordinary potlatches. A chief's prestige could best be increased if he showed utter disdain for his wealth, behaving as if much more were available. So chiefs sometimes destroyed great quantities of coppers and other art objects during potlatches.

Not surprisingly, much of this art, which was created in a variety of media and remains among the most distinctive of any society, symbolized and confirmed its owners' social rank, status, and prestige. Among a magnificent array of art objects, perhaps most notable were totem poles—tall, elaborately carved cedar tree trunks that rose, sometimes to a height of 60 feet, beside chiefs' houses (Stewart 1993). They bore carved images of beavers, frogs, hawks, eagles, and wolves, as well as thunderbirds and other creatures who lived only in peo-

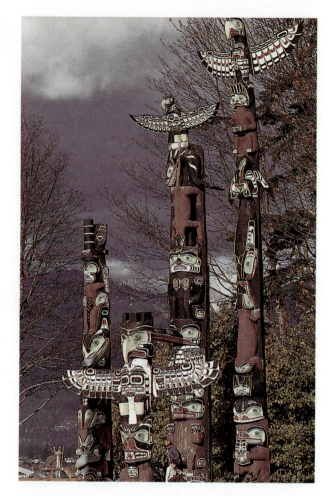

The art of native Americans of the Northwest Coast reflected their intense concern with status and prestige. The three rings around the hat at the top of the totem pole on the left, each representing a successful potlatch given by a particular chief, are a visual reminder of the chief's prestige.

ple's imaginations. Perched atop a pole would often be a human figure wearing a hat. A series of rings around this hat represented successful potlatches given by the chief who owned the house. The greater the number of rings, the greater the chief's prestige. Totem poles were dramatic visual reminders of the hierarchical structure of Northwest Coast society.

Expressive culture can also bring about social solidarity, the comforting sense of individuals that they are accepted members of a single social group. Iranian girls knotting carpet threads on the same loom, a group of tourists standing in awe before Michaelangelo's famous

Inuit Artists

The Inuit of Alaska live in a natural environment so demanding and hostile we might suppose they lack the time, materials, or energy for artistic creativity. Nevertheless, they produce art of considerable sensitivity and widespread appeal. In fact, producing art is one of their most commonly enjoyed and widely admired activities.

Tagoonarak is an elderly Inuit stonecarver who is uncertain of his exact age, where he was born, or how to spell his name in English (Malcolm 1979:A13). Most days, he gets up before dawn and walks to the local high school. In the art room, together with a handful of other equally elderly Inuit artists, he saws, files, and polishes stone all day, producing elegant carvings of animals, birds, fish, and sometimes human figures.

Like all traditional Inuit carvers, Tagoonarak studies each piece of stone carefully before he starts to carve. Sometimes it takes hours for him to sense what kind of spirit is trapped in the stone, waiting for its release. The result is almost always a powerful and aesthetically pleasing piece of work. Reflecting his view of the world, Tagoonarak is most interested in portraying the shape and bulk of animal and human forms in stone. Details are few; facial features are often merely scratched in. Human beings, engaged in everyday tasks, are never smiling. Frequently they are leaning forward, as if they are bearing some heavy burden or perhaps countering a strong wind.

If his eyes don't fail him, Tagoonarak can complete a small sculpture in a single day. When it is finished, he wraps it gently in a plastic bag and takes it to a cooperative outlet for the work of local artists. If his piece is carved and polished finely enough, it may fetch $10. In a good week, after paying his stone bill

Before they begin work, Alaska's Inuit stonecarvers carefully study pieces of stone to determine what kind of spirit they conceal. They then carve works of art of great aesthetic and, today, commercial appeal. In a government-sponsored art studio, Inuit craftsman Tagoonarak works on a stone swan.

of 50 cents per pound, Tagoonarak earns between $20 and $30. He'll never get rich, but he says no amount of money could buy the joy he gets from carving, from creating something with his hands out of the memories of long-ago hunts and ancient tales (Malcolm 1979:A13).

David, the congregation of an American church singing an Easter hymn, Nuba men applying paint and ash to one another's faces, American moviegoers watching a James Cameron film—all are brought solidly, if temporarily, into social relationships with their fellows through an artistic medium.

Influencing Events

Art can be a potent agent for culture change (see Chapter 16), not only reflecting but also affecting what happens in the world. This is particularly true of Western art, which is more apt to express nonconformist or countercultural ideas and values than the traditional art of small-scale societies. By challenging prevailing ideas and values and encouraging audiences to reorient their ways of looking at the world, Western painters, writers, sculptors, dancers, dramatists, and musicians have helped to bring about social changes ever since the Renaissance. Art that generates new ideas and values is called **revolutionary art.**

Western art is more revolutionary than the art of other societies because the social context in which Western art is created encourages artists to produce works of originality and individuality, to explore their society's beliefs, and to challenge its institutions. Possibly, too, the continual replacement of older Western artistic styles with newer ones is "an evolutionary paradigm . . . related to [Western] patterns of politics, war, and a theory of history" (Pasztory 1989:37). In other words, Westerners' general outlook on life, which incorporates expectations of continuous evolutionary change (biological, social, and historical), may be reflected in continuous artistic change.

A classic example of Western revolutionary art is Western rock music of the 1950s and 1960s. When it first burst on the musical scene in mid-century North America, rock music flew in the face of some firmly ingrained ideas about personal behavior and morality. The activities, ideas, and values its lyrics championed, as well as the way of life its artists seemed to espouse, were frowned on under the widely accepted model of moral rectitude and personal success current at the time. According to this model, conformity, self-denial, self-discipline, and teamwork were highly valued. Because of its apparent call for self-indulgence and individuality, rock was viewed by many as dangerously immoral—an image that its performers, true revolutionary artists, skillfully perpetuated. Rock music had its intended effect: by the post-Vietnam 1970s, some of the values it celebrated, such as unfettered sexual expression or the freedom to "do one's own thing," had won broad acceptance in Western culture.

In nonliterate societies, the potential of art to encourage change tends to be more limited because individual creativity and stylistic innovation, with their implicit or explicit challenge to existing value systems, are usually not so highly prized. **Conservative art** is often preferred in these societies. Artists seek to maintain the existing order rather than to overthrow it and replace it with a new one.

We don't mean to suggest that traditional, non-Western artists never try to influence what happens in the world. To the contrary, in non-Western societies works of art are often created with the express purpose of affecting or changing things, but these are apt to be particular, immediate events rather than fundamental alterations in value systems. People might create carvings or paintings, for instance, specifically to help ensure success in hunting.

Expressing Political Themes

Expressive culture can also have profound political significance, challenging people's ideas and values, symbolizing political institutions, or adding weight to political causes. In societies with centralized political organizations (chiefdoms and states), it can serve as potent propaganda, confirming and strengthening the authority of political leaders. Under Hitler, Germany's Third Reich created a government arts institution, the Reichskulturkammer, to oversee and control the work of German painters, sculptors, and architects. At its height, this institution supported as many as 23,000 German artists, encouraging them, through their works of art, to idealize German family life in paintings of pastoral scenes and to legitimize and glorify German military efforts in statues of intrepid German warriors (Adam 1992).

In the area of West Africa that is now Ghana, the king of the Ashanti, a confederacy of African cities that united about 1701, owns numerous works of art, many made of solid gold. Possessing these objects demonstrates that the king is the most powerful individual in his kingdom. Each successive Ashanti king inherits from his predecessor a variety of ritual objects symbolizing his supremacy in the confederacy. Of these objects, the Golden Stool is the most sacred (Fraser 1972).

The boxlike Golden Stool, a container for the soul of the nation and a symbol of the new union of cities, is believed by the Ashanti to have fallen from heaven, at the bidding of the head priest, into the first Ashanti king's lap. Before he called the Golden Stool down from heaven, however, the head priest demanded that various other symbols of the individual cities, which consisted

 ASK YOURSELF

Recently, a self-described New York artist produced an unusual "work of art": he arranged for three nude couples to caress and kiss each other in public. When asked whether this was really art, he replied, "It's art because I'm an artist and I say it's art." Do you agree?

Rock stars often champion individuality and self-indulgence, which are counter to more traditional Western values such as conformity and self-discipline. Truth or Dare *(1991), a documentary film about Madonna, shows this hardworking performer taking life easy and downplays the effort that goes into actually producing rock music.*

of other stools, shields, and swords, be surrendered to him. These he buried in a riverbed, so no art object in the new nation could claim a longer history than the Golden Stool and hence be considered superior to it. This action also disposed of the powerful symbols of the former independence of the cities. To ensure that all the newly unified cities accepted the Golden Stool as the symbol of their single king, the priest commanded that locks of hair, nail parings, and rings belonging to the most important chiefs be collected and put inside it.

These events occurred almost three hundred years ago, but even today the Golden Stool of the Ashanti retains its powerful symbolism. Credited with supernatural powers, the stool must never be allowed to touch the bare ground, and when displayed in public, it always rests on a silver-plated throne. The Golden Stool must be fed at regular intervals, for were it to suffer hunger, it might sicken and die, and with it the soul of the Ashanti nation. (The story of how the Golden Stool arrived from heaven is, of course, an origin myth explaining how the single nation of the Ashanti came to be.)

Sometimes members of a society "invent" an artistic "tradition" by proclaiming that certain symbols, ideas, or customs, actually of recent origin, are traditional parts of their culture, a phenomenon called **invented tradition** (Hobsbawm and Ranger 1992). For example, a clan might invent or embroider on an origin myth to justify its current political aims.

Transmitting Culture

Art, as we suggested earlier, may also function as a learning tool through which information can be transmitted. The Tetum folktale about the monkey and the shark recounted earlier in this chapter, for example, incorporates an important moral lesson. Likewise, the *Mahabharata,* a long epic poem told repeatedly over the last two thousand years in India, contains an Indian history lesson, recounting the struggles for dynastic succession in an ancient kingdom.

For literate Indians, the lessons of the *Mahabharata* have long been transmitted in written form, but to this day they continue to be passed along by word of mouth in rural Indian villages, where nonliterate storytellers can recite and sing passages from the *Mahabharata* for hours on end (Weisman 1987:C17). Nowadays, Indians buy tape cassettes of this work of oral art, listening to them as avidly as some Western rock fans listen to U2. Indian children read colorful comic-book

revolutionary art art that generates new ideas and values

conservative art art that sustains the existing social order

invented tradition symbols, ideas, or customs that members of a society claim as traditional parts of their culture but which in reality are of more recent origin

versions describing the fabulous adventures of the super-heros of the poem, much as Western children read about Superman, and adults and children alike watch *Maha-bharata* TV serials with the same enthusiasm that some Westerners watch "General Hospital." The *Maha-bharata* is one way in which the lessons and values of the Indian past are made accessible to present generations.

Expressing Gender Relationships

Affirming the relationship of males and females in a society is another way in which expressive culture becomes social commentary. Folklorist Alan Dundes (1989:152ff.) analyzes an eastern European folktale, told, or sometimes sung, in several variations in peasant communities in Hungary, Bulgaria, Romania, Greece, Albania, and Serbia. "The Building of Skadar" recounts an attempt by a group of men, sometimes described as brothers, to build a castle, bridge, or monastery. Because of a supernatural spell, whatever the builders manage to erect during the course of a day is magically undone at night. In a dream, the builders learn that the spell can be broken if the first woman to arrive at the site the next day is walled up in the foundation. The men agree not to inform their wives, who daily bring their husbands' lunches, so that the victim may be selected by fate. However, all the men but one break this agreement and inform their wives.

The next day, the wife of the worker who honored his promise arrives at the construction site carrying food for her husband and learns that she is to be entombed. In some versions of the tale, she is tricked into entering the unfinished building when her husband throws his wedding ring into the foundation and then asks her to retrieve it. When she tries to do so, the builders wall her up. In some versions, she begs the men to leave a small opening, "a window at her breasts," so that she may suckle her infant son.

How are we to interpret this sad tale? The story, Dundes (1989) suggests, is a symbolic expression of women's role in this part of eastern Europe. Beginning, as a structural anthropologist would, by searching for oppositions and analogies, Dundes notes that in eastern Europe, men work outside the home whereas women work inside: thus, men are to women as outside is to inside. In this story about the relationship between men and women in marriage and the impact of marriage on women's lives, women must be sacrificed so that men can accomplish their work. For a woman, marriage is

like being locked up until death. This aspect of gender relations is symbolized by the husband's dropping his wedding ring into the construction site, for it is in pursuit of a wedding ring that the wife enters her tomb. In versions of the story in which the wife retains a window on the outside world so that she may feed her son, the message is that the welfare of a male child is the only reason not to shut her away completely.

The treachery of the men who warn their wives not to be the first on the scene, Dundes (1989) argues, again refers to the male-female opposition in eastern Europe. The trusting man who places his faith in his fellow men causes not his own death but the death of a female. The wife is walled up not because of any fault of her own but because of the perfidy of men. Women, Dundes concludes, must pay for the offenses of men. Seeking support for his analysis in the local ethnography, Dundes found that brides in Serbia live within their husband's households and have little or no status until they produce offspring, preferably male. Local wedding songs commonly include images of marriage as death.

The art of other societies may express a more harmonious relationship between the sexes. The Shoshone Indian Sun Dance has been described as a beautiful symbol of the cooperation between males and females in a society in which subsistence work is divided between women who gather food and men who hunt. The song that accompanies the Sun Dance is begun by a male, whose opening phrase is repeated by other men accompanying themselves on drums. After this repetition of the opening phrase, women join the singing. Midway through the final repetition, the men stop singing and drumming and the women finish the song (Vander 1989:7).

THE FUTURE OF FOLK ART

The Yolngu, a small-scale, clan-based society of Northeast Arnhem Land, Australia, produce intricate paintings on bark. These portray natural objects—animals, birds, human figures, rivers, trees, clouds—and often include intricately patterned fields of fine, cross-hatched lines. Most Yolngu paintings represent either mythological events or topographical features, although the distinction between the two is not always clear-cut since the Yolngu see topographical features as "a continuing manifestation of ancestral events" (Morphy 1991:218).

Prior to European contact, these works of art were intended solely for, and confined to, Yolngu society. In the 1930s, however, Europeans established a mission in Northeast Arnhem Land. In response, the Yolngu began to produce new paintings to fit new contexts. Today, Yolngu make paintings both for their own rituals and for sale to Westerners. New and different meanings are contained in these paintings; the ways in which meanings are expressed have changed, and the ways the paintings are used have also changed. Yolngu art has gradually become incorporated into the postcolonial Australian market economy, and, later, the world market economy, and it can now be found in art galleries not only in Australia but also around the world (Morphy 1991:2). Yolngu today live in a world that includes both Western and aboriginal institutions, systems, knowledge, and languages, and their contemporary art is clearly influenced by both (4).

Sometimes, traditional and Western-influenced artistic forms are combined to produce a new, unified artistic tradition. The two original forms must be close enough to each other to be joined into a single tradition. In the Caribbean, for example, Western and African music have combined to produce a new musical category called reggae, which is pleasing within the context of both musical traditions. The blending of two or more cultural traditions into a single new one is called **syncretism.** Since Western music is very different from, say, North American Indian music, syncretism is much less apt to occur between these two musical categories. A native American child may learn to play the clarinet at school while learning traditional Indian music at home. Since no blending is possible, the child must keep the two types of music separate for different occasions.

Flexibility does not characterize all traditional, non-Western art. Earlier in this chapter, we described the Inuit stone carver Tagoonarak. Over the last twenty-five years, Tagoonarak's world has changed dramatically because of the enormous, and not universally welcomed, impact of external changes on traditional Inuit life. Cigarettes, alcohol, and television have entered his people's lives. Children have drifted away from traditional Inuit behaviors and expectations, and even the elderly find it difficult to continue their old lifeways in the confusion of conflicting values and disrupted patterns of behavior. A younger generation of Inuit, unfamiliar with traditional ways, is largely uninterested in carving. When the elderly stone carvers like Tagoonarak are gone, the production of traditional Inuit art will come to

Traditional artists in Australia paint animals, birds, human figures, and natural objects on bark, both for their own rituals and for sale to Western museums, galleries, and private collectors. This bark painting shows two kangaroos in traditional style, with open areas filled with patterned fields of fine, cross-hatched lines.

an end (Malcolm 1979:A13). If a non-Western artistic technique or tradition cannot accommodate itself to the social changes inevitably taking place around it, it comes to an end.

syncretism the blending of two or more cultural traditions into a single new one

CONCLUSION

Although both Western art and art created in nonliterate societies are vehicles for the expression of cultural ideas and values, an important contrast can be drawn between them. In Western societies, artistic efforts are often set apart from other occupations. Works of art are most likely to be created by individuals such as ballet dancers, movie producers, rock stars, novelists, sculptors, painters, and opera singers whose main role in the economic system is to produce artistic creations. Moreover, Western art is apt to be self-justifying rather than a means to some practical end. It is appreciated, enjoyed, and understood for itself rather than as a method of achieving a particular, immediate goal.

In nonliterate societies, we also find specialists who produce works of art—basket weavers or pottery makers, for example—but their art is not as self-justifying; it often has some practical purpose beyond its aesthetic appeal. And in nonliterate societies we are much more apt to find artists whose creations are inspired by motivations beyond artistic expression, and whose art is thus a byproduct of some other goal. A Hopi shaman creates a sand painting because this is part of a curing ritual, and an African storyteller recounts legends to educate candidates in tribal lore for an initiation ceremony. Non-Western art, in short, is more likely than Western art to be closely integrated with economic production, religion, politics, the law, descent, and other aspects of social life.

SUMMARY

Expressive culture—the purposeful manipulation by human beings of a limited number of media (including form, color, sound, language, and body movement) into arrangements that are pleasurable, meaningful, or both—is a human universal. But the forms, the extent, and the significance of expressive culture are by no means uniform across societies. These are very largely determined by two factors. First is the culture of which they are a part. Like other aspects of human life, artistic expression is shaped by its cultural context. Second, the particular artistic media that cultures have available greatly affect their expressive culture. Artistic media are limited, both in number and in potential, which perhaps helps explain why

works of art from societies widely separated from one another in space or time may look so much alike. If cognitive anthropologists are right about mental universals, these might also help to explain artistic similarities among cultures.

Of the many ways in which human beings can express themselves artistically, we have been able to focus on only a few in this chapter, but the art forms we have discussed are among the most common cross-culturally: the plastic and graphic arts, verbal art (such as legends, folktales, and myths), and music. We also briefly addressed combined artistic forms, such as dance. We observed that the functions of these and other forms of art are numerous and include mirroring a society's view of the world, affirming a particular social organization and people's sense of social solidarity, influencing future events, expressing political ideas, transmitting culture, and expressing gender relationships.

Most small-scale societies today are a product of both traditional and recent Western influences, and over time their art has changed to reflect this. Sometimes, in a process of syncretism, traditional and Western-influenced artistic forms combine to produce a new, unified artistic tradition. However, the artistic traditions of some non-Western societies have proven less flexible and are threatened with extinction.

KEY TERMS

bullroarer
conservative art
ethnomusicology
expressive culture
fable
folk art
folktale
gamelan
graphic art
invented tradition
legend
octave
oral art
percussion
pitch
plastic art
revolutionary art
scale
syncretism
tone

SUGGESTED READINGS

Anderson, Richard L. 1992. *Art in Small-scale Societies* (2nd ed.). Englewood Cliffs, NJ: Prentice-Hall. A comprehensive overview of the visual art of nonliterate societies, which provides an authoritative introduction to its meaning, creation, and creators.

Brunvand, Jan Harold. 1981. *The Vanishing Hitchhiker: American Urban Legends and Their Meanings*. New York: W. W. Norton. Stories about grandmothers' runaway corpses, batter-fried rats, and other oddities are reproduced here as modern American folktales.

Corbin, George A. 1988. *Native Arts of North America, Africa, and the South Pacific*. New York: Harper & Row. Magnificent photographs accompany this introduction to the plastic and graphic arts of the peoples of New Guinea, the Inuit, the Ashanti, the Trobrianders, the Australian aborigines, and the Maori, whose artistic efforts include masks, body decoration, sculptures, and shields.

Myers, Helen (ed.). 1992. *Ethnomusicology: An Introduction*. The Norton/Grove Handbooks in Music. New York: W. W. Norton. An excellent collection of essays dealing with almost every aspect of ethnomusicology, including gender and music, dance, and a vast number of other topics of interest to contemporary anthropology.

Rosman, Abraham, and Paula G. Rubel. 1990. Structural Patterning in Kwakiutl Art and Ritual. *Man* 25:620–640. By means of a structural analysis, the authors show that the art of the Kwakiutl of the Northwest Coast expresses certain religious ideas.

CHAPTER 15

In both Western and non-Western societies, it's common for people to make permanent changes to the outward appearance of their bodies, but both the changes themselves and the cultural messages they convey differ. Here a colorful tattooed dragon slinks across the shoulder of a North American man.

INTRODUCTION

The professor in a big introductory course in anthropology at a state university often illustrated his lectures with ethnographic films. Most of these films portrayed events in the lives of people living in small-scale societies in faraway parts of the world. Over the course of the semester, students in the class saw Inuit hunters celebrating a successful seal hunt with drumming, dancing, and singing; a group of Middle Eastern nomads walking hundreds of miles to take their sheep to new pastures; Balinese dancers performing a religious drama to the eerie accompaniment of strange-looking stringed instruments; and opposing groups of Pacific islanders, wearing elaborate feather headdresses, fighting bitterly with homemade spears. The reaction of the students to these films was mixed. Some viewers were intrigued, others were bored, and still others admitted that at times they were shocked or even repelled. In general, however, the students were more struck by the strangeness of what they saw on the movie screen than by similarities between the filmed scenes and events in their own lives.

One day, toward the end of the semester, the professor dimmed the lecture hall lights for yet another film. This one, like several of the others, began with a darkened screen and the heavy thump of distant drumming, and some students groaned inwardly at the thought of having to sit through what they anticipated would be another strange, incomprehensible, or even repellent dance, drama, sacrifice, or other ritual. As the screen slowly brightened, shadowy human figures became visible—moving shapes with flapping clothing and grotesque, voluminous hairdos. Smoke swirled around the silhouetted figures, who bounced up and down rhythmically to the faint but steady beat of the drums.

As the sound track gradually grew louder and musical tones surfaced above the percussive thumping, the students began to listen more intently, for they thought they recognized something familiar. Soon the screen brightened, and they began to laugh, for this footage, far from showing a primitive rite filmed in some remote land, had been filmed at a popular nightclub near the campus, and the mysterious figures gyrating rhythmically to the music were none other than the students themselves.

In their physical appearance, human beings, unlike all other living things, are much more than just the products of particular sets of genes. True, each person inherits a genetic legacy that very largely determines the gross body form in which he or she must remain for life. But beyond what is biologically determined, one of the important ways in which human beings are fundamentally different from all other organisms on earth is that only they constantly and purposefully alter their outward appearance. (We use the term *purposefully* to distinguish people from other animals, such as chameleons or weasels, that change their outward appearance in automatic response to specific external stimuli.) Our bodies are like painters' canvases on which different cultural and personal beliefs, attitudes, ideals, and preferences are presented to the world through particular kinds of dress, jewelry, cosmetics, or hairdos; through other forms of body alteration or adornment, like piercing, scarring, or tattooing; and through body movements such as gestures, postures, and facial expressions.

In Chapter 14, we discussed expressive culture, pointing out that in every society aesthetic expression has both individual functions (creating something new, personally meaningful, or pleasurable) and social functions (expressing ideas and values, symbolizing social institutions). This chapter is also about aesthetic expression, but here we focus specifically on the human body as a vehicle for expressive culture. We look cross-culturally at what people do with and to their bodies in order to change their appearance and express a variety of cultural messages. We investigate some of the ways in which people alter, adorn, or modify their bodies; how body movements convey different messages in different cultural settings; and how attitudes toward the body— what is acceptable, what is forbidden, what is ugly, what is beautiful—vary from culture to culture.[1] By examining what motivates people to choose particular forms of body expression and how these forms fit holistically into their cultural contexts, we illustrate what can be learned about a culture from studying its people's physical appearance.

◆◆

BODY ADORNMENT

By the term *body adornment,* we mean a specific category of changes that people make to the outward appearance of their bodies: those that are both voluntary and reversible (as opposed to permanent). These changes include the wearing of clothing and jewelry, the use of cosmetics (which in many societies are applied to the body as well as to the face), and the styling and coloring of the hair.

---

[1]This chapter does not by any means exhaust the subject of the anthropology of the body. The relationship between the body and the mind, for example, or the patterns of body movement involved in dancing are fascinating topics for anthropological treatment. But this is an introductory textbook, so we must leave these and related areas of anthropological inquiry for more advanced texts.

Clothing

Human beings almost completely lack the external physical protection from the natural environment that other animals enjoy, such as tough hides, hard shells, layers of feathers, or thick coats of fur. Even people living in tropical climates, where no insulation against cold weather is needed, must protect their bodies from the sun, rain, stinging insects, thorny vegetation, or rough surfaces. No doubt for this reason, the vast majority of people wear clothes. The native people of Australia, called the Aborigines, were an exception; most were naked when first contacted by Westerners. But for practical reasons, we know of very few societies in the past, and none today, that completely lack a tradition of clothing the body.

The garments people wear protect them, but clothes have another, equally important function as well: to convey messages, both about individual clothes wearers and about the culture or subculture of which they are a part (Kaiser 1990; Barnes and Eicher 1992). One of these is the message of sexual identity. Few societies depend totally on natural differences to distinguish males from females. In most, different styles of clothing confirm the differences between the two sexes. Contemporary Western society is unusual in that certain items of casual wear, such as jeans, T-shirts, and jogging shoes, are considered appropriate for both males and females. In India, women wear saris, men wear dhotis—never the reverse.

Wearing clothes seems not to depend on any innate human sense of modesty, for there is no universal agreement about which parts of the body should be kept hidden from view. In many (but by no means all) societies, the sexual organs, especially those of adults, are kept covered, but in other societies they are intentionally exposed. Sometimes clothing both covers and accentuates simultaneously; Western women's bras and Pacific men's penis sheaths both conceal and emphasize parts of the body. Depending on the society, other parts of the

Although adults' sexual organs are kept hidden by clothing in most societies, in some they are intentionally exposed or accentuated. In western New Guinea, a Dani man wears a traditional penis sheath.

body—the hair, the lower part of the face, the ankles, the female midsection (to name just a few)—are either well hidden or intentionally exposed to public view.

Another message clothes convey is self-identity. If you were shown close-up photographs of the faces—and only the faces—of two young males, you might be able to determine their approximate ages, ethnic origins, states of health, and moods, but you would have trouble determining which was the face of a punk rocker and which a preppy. Whole-body photographs of the same two males, however—one in a metal-studded leather jacket, combat boots, and spiked hairdo; the other in an oxford-cloth shirt, madras slacks, deck shoes, and short, slicked-down hair—would give you a great deal of information about the different interests and values of these two individuals, provided the cultural context was one with which you were familiar.

The interests and values expressed by the appearances of these two individuals are not merely personal.

◆ **ASK YOURSELF**

American football uniforms have heavily padded shoulders and codpieces to provide protection for their wearers. These same uniform features, of course, also accentuate players' size and masculinity. Is this intentional or not? Do other kinds of Western sports uniforms intentionally emphasize players' size, strength, or other attributes?

Clothing reflects cultural as well as personal beliefs and ideals, and it is the cultural rather than the personal aspects of clothing that most interest us here. What can we learn about the worldview of a given society from the way its members dress? In what values do the society's members collectively believe? What can clothes tell us about who is socially, politically, or economically dominant in the society and who isn't? About the relationships between the sexes in the society and the attitudes of members of one sex toward members of the other? About the people's sense of national or ethnic identity, their conservative or liberal inclinations, even their religious beliefs?

Head coverings are a good example of the range of ideas that can be conveyed by a single item of clothing. The custom of covering the head, and sometimes the face as well, with a piece of cloth is widespread among females in Middle Eastern societies. Women wear headcloths ranging in size from small kerchiefs to large, enveloping semicircles of cloth that cover the entire body, including the head and sometimes much of the face. These veils, as they are called in English, are the external expression of deeply rooted Middle Eastern customs and collective ideas (Fernea and Fernea 1987), some of which find their origins in the Muslim religion.

The Middle Eastern custom of veiling originated in the time of the prophet Muhammad (A.D. 570–632), founder of Islam, as an outward symbol of religious identity. Muhammad's wives, so the story goes, were once mistaken for slaves—a grievous insult. To avoid future confusion, female followers of Muhammad began to wear veils (Fernea and Fernea 1987:106). But if its first cultural message was one of religious identity, veiling soon began to send a message about social status as well. Because it obstructed both movement and vision, the veil made performing certain tasks very difficult. A poor woman obliged to labor in the fields could not wear one. Thus wearing this garment soon began to suggest a privileged life-style and high social status. This notion remains widely held today.

Veiling delivers other cultural messages too. Many Middle Easterners believe that females have strong sexual appetites and that their sexual behavior reflects directly on the honor of their families. For some, a family's honor rests in part on controlling women's sexuality (Lindholm and Lindholm 1985:234). To protect women from sexual temptation, and males from the uncontrollable lust of dangerous women who might ruin their good names, the physical seclusion of women, a custom known as **purdah,** has been practiced since the

Middle Eastern women in purdah wear garments that hide both their faces and bodies. Faces may be shielded by light fabric through which women can see enough to get about, heavier fabric in which eyeholes have been cut, or full masks of leather or even metal. Above, a Muslim woman in purdah waits with her sick child at a village health clinic.

time of Muhammad. Houses may be surrounded by high walls, and women may spend their entire lives virtually imprisoned behind them. Wrapping a woman in a garment that conceals her body from public view is another reflection of the same idea. Today, a Middle Eastern woman wearing a veil on a public street is signaling "hands off!" A man who approaches a veiled woman invites serious trouble, for he is shaming both the woman and her family. This doesn't mean that a woman wearing a veil is necessarily repressed, inhibited, or even ultraconservative. A modern Muslim woman's veil may conceal a T-shirt, jeans, and sneakers.

Another cultural notion associated with veiling is modesty. Among the Bedouin, Arabic-speaking nomads of the Middle East, modesty is an essential component of personal honor and respectability (Abu-Lughod 1986, 1987). The honorable person keeps his or her distance from members of the opposite sex (except for close relatives); casts the eyes shyly downward; moves with formality; and refrains from eating, smoking, talking, or laughing in certain social situations. Young, unmarried women show that they are modest and respectable by wearing kerchiefs on their heads. Married women wear black headcloths that can be drawn protectively across the face when they are in the presence of certain men, such as in-laws. To display one's modesty in this way is a matter of pride for the Bedouin, who consider this behavior "a sign of respect for the social and moral system" (1987:29).

These examples show that in the Middle East, the cultural meanings attached to wearing a veil (or not wearing one) are many. Depending on where and in what style it is being worn, the veil can symbolize a woman's faith, the idea of protection (both from danger and from temptation), the notion of women as temptresses who must not be allowed to distract men, status and wealth, and personal modesty. And although we have been discussing the veil as an article of female apparel, among the Tuareg, camel pastoralists of North Africa, men wear veils because lips are considered obscene.

Westerners, too, convey messages with their clothing. In church, a woman's hat or kerchief is a mark of her religious faith; at a party, her expensive beaded dress suggests her wealth and thus her social status. Her white bridal gown symbolizes her purity, and her bridal veil her modesty. When she wears a bikini she does so not to express faith, wealth, social status, purity, or modesty but rather to show off her attractive body. Her message is one of good health, self-discipline, self-esteem, and interest in attracting the attention of the opposite sex.

Jewelry

You're no doubt aware that in North American culture, certain kinds of jewelry—rings, for instance—convey specific messages. A graduate's high school or

◆ ASK YOURSELF

How do you feel about our society's custom of veiling brides? What cultural message(s) do you think a bridal veil conveys? If you marry, will a veil be part of your wedding?

When introduced in 1945, this kind of bathing suit was considered nothing short of atomic, so it was named after Bikini Atoll, an atomic bomb test site. But Roman women were wearing similar garments as early as A.D. 300. In the hunting lodge of emperor Maximilian Herculius are found mosaics of goddesses, heros, jungle animals—and bikini-clad women (Swindells 1987:23).

college ring denotes both educational status and institutional affiliation; a married person's wedding ring reveals his or her marital status; and a football player's Superbowl ring testifies to his athletic prowess, not to mention his membership in a very exclusive athletic group. Men's lapel pins and tie tacks are another class of jewelry often intended to signal professional, religious, political, or social affiliations or to reflect their wearers' interests in particular sports or hobbies. Other items of

purdah the physical seclusion of women, a custom common in the Middle East

THE ANTHROPOLOGIST AT WORK

The high-fashion industry is thriving in North America, Europe, and most recently Japan. We don't know of any anthropologists working in this industry, but why not? Since clothing is so expressive of its wearers' beliefs, attitudes, and ideals, we think an anthropologist would have a lot to contribute to the design and marketing of clothes.

Understanding the cultural or personal messages that particular kinds of dress convey, or how attitudes about revealing or concealing certain parts of the body are changing, might help to sell a lot of clothes. If you're considering a career in the world of fashion, perhaps you can think of ways that majoring in anthropology might make you uniquely employable.

jewelry worn in our society convey less intentional or even unconscious messages. A woman's sparkling diamond cocktail ring may suggest wealth and thus social status, but she may claim she wears it only as an ornament.

Jewelry reflects status, group membership, or personal interests in other societies, too. When a young Zulu woman falls in love, she makes a beaded necklace resembling a close-fitting collar with a flat panel attached, which she gives to her boyfriend. Depending on the colors and patterns of the beads, this necklace can convey a host of different romantic messages. A combination of pink and white beads in a certain pattern, for instance, might mean "you are poor . . . but I love you" (Dubin 1987:134). Some Zulu men wear multiple necklaces, each a gift from a different girlfriend. Together they prove their wearers' attractiveness to the opposite sex: the more necklaces, the more girlfriends. A married man's necklaces may show how many wives he has. With other items of beaded jewelry—belts, bracelets, and anklets—young Zulu women let the world know whether they are romantically involved with someone or still available, the same message that engagement rings convey in our own society.

In addition to proclaiming social, educational, or marital status, group affiliation, or personal interests, jewelry is sometimes worn to ensure good luck or protect its wearer from harm. In North America, jewelry bearing religious symbols is common, and many wearers refuse to remove such jewelry for fear of bad luck.

Cosmetics

Another way in which people adorn their bodies is by temporarily decorating their skin with **cosmetics,** the general term for preparations designed to improve the appearance of the body, or part of it, by directly but tem-

porarily applying them to the skin. In Western society, cosmetics take the form of various mass-produced, petroleum-based, colored creams, oils, or powders. These are usually applied to the face and are much more fre-

Zulu women give their boyfriends beaded collars with flat panels that convey different romantic messages, depending on their colors and patterns. The white beads in this panel stand for love and purity, and red sometimes symbolizes weeping, but the exact message imparted by the red diamond pattern is a private one, understood only by the couple involved.

quently used by females than by males. In other societies, the term *cosmetics* may refer to body as well as
face paints, usually made by combining animal or vegetable oils with colored powders made from naturally
occurring minerals.

The extent to which cosmetics are used in human
societies—from the remote jungles of South America to
the high-fashion capitals of western Europe—suggests
that the notion of adorning or enhancing the surface of
the body, like the idea of covering it with clothing,
comes close to being a human universal. There are differences of placement, emphasis, and extent among various traditions of cosmetic use, but the reasons for wearing cosmetics are similar.

In every society with a cosmetic tradition, including our own, bodies are often decorated to enhance
them, to make them appear more perfectly in accord
with society's ideals of beauty (although, as we shall see
at the end of this chapter, what is considered attractive
varies widely from society to society). But in some societies, the use of cosmetics quite consciously conveys
other benefits as well. It may keep people from harm,
express their social status, or identify them as members
of particular classes or families. Benefits of this kind are
probably part of the reason behind Western cosmetic use
also, although the wearers of cosmetics may not be
aware of it.

If Westerners differ little from members of other
societies in our primary motivations for applying cosmetics, we differ from some in the relatively modest extent to which we decorate ourselves. Cosmetic use in
some societies is so extensive it would make the heavy-
handed application of cosmetics to a female American
screen star by a Hollywood makeup artist seem moderate.

A well-turned-out Nuba male from Kordofan
Province in the Sudan of northern Africa is literally
painted from head to foot. Among the Nuba, body painting begins in infancy, when a baby's scalp is decorated
with either red or yellow paint, depending on its family
membership (Faris 1972:30). Thereafter, body painting
is used to suggest one's social and physical status as
well as to beautify, and it becomes more and more complex with advancing age. A young Nuba boy, for example, wears simple, inconspicuous, red and greyish white
decorations on his scalp, gradually earning the right to
use increasingly more elaborate, colorful, and extensive
designs as he matures (38). Each change of age and status means a new kind of decoration for the boy, as with
advancing years he earns the right to use more products

*Cosmetics are universally used to beautify people, protect
them from harm, express their social status, or identify them
as members of particular groups. In Liberia, a Bassa girl being initiated into the Sande, an all-female secret society, is
elaborately decorated with a chalky white clay.*

in a wider range of colors and designs. (Westerners, too,
sometimes use cosmetics as an age marker, as when an
American girl is forbidden by her parents to wear lip-
stick until she has reached a certain age.)

The scalp, face, chest, back, arms, and legs of a
young adult Nuba male may literally be covered with
colorful designs (Faris 1972:18–19, 62), both purely
decorative (straight and curved lines, dots, triangles,
crosshatching) and representational (animals, airplanes,

cosmetics preparations designed to improve the appearance of
the body, or part of it, by directly but temporarily applying
them to the skin

lightening, stars—even English words, which may or may not be intelligible to the Nuba). Often these designs are asymmetrically placed on the face or body and are strikingly modern looking. They may take up to an hour to apply and may be redone daily.

Decorating the body as well as the face with cosmetics is by no means limited to rural or small-scale societies. Some modern, urban girls and women in North Africa, the Middle East, and South Asia decorate their skin with henna, an orange-red dye made from leaves. Urban Moroccan women, for example, may be decorated on suitable occasions with fine lines and dots forming intricate designs. These are typically applied to the hands and feet, which then look as if they are clad in lace gloves or stockings. Henna is applied at a "henna party," to which the person to be decorated invites her friends, a professional henna artist, and sometimes professional musicians or other entertainers. During the long and careful process of decorating, the guests eat, sing songs, tell jokes, and dance around the woman being decorated (Messina 1988).

Moroccan women who use henna say they apply it for a variety of reasons. A girl or woman may be decorated in preparation for a religious festival, in celebration of her marriage, to cheer her up in late pregnancy, to soften her skin, to prevent spirits called "jinni" from causing illness or misfortune, or to calm her nerves. Whatever the reason, applying henna is cause for celebration; a henna party provides a "lively departure" from formal Islamic expectations of proper female behavior (Messina 1988:46). People from different regions admire different designs, and styles of decoration change constantly, but the designs themselves have no explicit meanings.

Hairdressing

Hair is perhaps the physical feature most frequently used for self-expressive purposes. After all, it is the most easily manipulated feature. Another reason is that hair (like fingernails) grows continually, which suggests to some people that it has life and power of its own—just like individuals.

This combination of life and power sometimes suggests the fertility of crops or of human beings. In a ritual performed by the Rindi of Sumba, Indonesia, hair is clipped from the front of men's heads or from the back of women's to ensure the fertility of rice crops (Forth 1981:167–168). The hair clippings are discarded like useless rice chaff, which is similarly thrown away.

The hair that remains on people's heads symbolizes rice that has been harvested and which, of course, feeds the Rindi villagers. The idea behind the ritual is that by getting rid of what is useless and retaining that which is essential, the rice crop next season will also be maintained.

Cross-culturally, clippings of hair commonly symbolize the individual from which they have been taken. Moreover, hair can be seen as a sort of extension of the human body, a notion that adds to its usefulness as a symbol for the individual or even the entire society. Thus we find that in many societies the act of cutting the hair is a symbol for surrendering power, as in the biblical story of Samson.

Hair may also symbolize the possibilities for sex, the prohibition of sex, or merely the control of unrestrained sex. For the Rindi, hair worn long symbolizes unrestrained sexuality and fertility, whereas hair fastened into a topknot or bun symbolizes restrained sexuality and controlled fertility. The people in this society demonstrate their control over sexual behavior either by cutting their hair, which suggests an absolute restriction, or by binding it, which suggests sexual restraint (Forth 1981:159).

Psychological anthropologist Gananath Obeyesekere (1984:33–51) uses hair symbolism to demonstrate links between culture and personality in Sri Lanka, where some people allow their hair to grow into long, dirty, matted locks. In Chapter 4, we described how Obeyesekere was able to link the long locks of matted hair worn by priestesses of a Hindu-Buddhist cult to snakes, and snakes to anxiety about castration. Obeyesekere showed that personal symbols such as individuals' matted hair can become symbols that are accepted by whole communities. His study demonstrates once again that the physical properties of hair make it highly suitable for expressing changes in an individual's ritual, social, or sexual status.

The symbolism of hair is not altogether unfamiliar to Westerners. A little boy's first trip to the barber to have his baby curls shorn is an important event to some Western families. The toddler's father snaps photographs, his mother cries, and bystanders exclaim what

 ASK YOURSELF

Compared with females, North American males use cosmetics only rarely. How do you feel about cosmetic use among males? What message is a man who uses a bronzing lotion conveying? A man who uses eye shadow?

In many societies, having one's hair cut symbolizes the relinquishment of personal power. In what has become a traditional rite of passage in the U.S. military, new Marines are shorn of their hair as their training begins.

a "big boy" he has suddenly become. An 11-year-old girl who cuts off her braids is announcing that she feels ready for adulthood. Hair fashions—different choices about cut, color, and curl—identify both male and female teenagers as belonging to one or another social or ethnic group, as being bold or shy, or as conforming to traditional values or rejecting them. Middle-aged men and women are exhorted to "wash away that grey" in order to project youth and vitality. In Western culture as in others, hair conveys a wide range of cultural messages.

BODY ALTERATION

Altering the outward appearance of the body by making permanent, nonreversible changes may sound drastic, but this is widely practiced in Western as well as non-Western societies. Westerners are familiar with pierced ears and tattoos and in the 1970s even grew accustomed to the punk fad of piercing the cheeks with safety pins (although relatively few individuals actually did this). But similar customs, also intended to improve the appearance of the body by changing it permanently, may seem distasteful to Westerners. Piercing a hole through the septum of the nose to insert a piece of bone or shell, for example, or soldering a tall stack of iron rings around the neck might make some of us shudder. Repeatedly puncturing the skin in an intricate pattern to produce permanent, decorative scarring (**cicatrization**) might make us glad we don't live in a culture where such demands are imposed. In fact, Westerners may

think of these kinds of body alteration as deformation or mutilation instead of decoration. But are they really so very different from ear piercing or tattooing?

In our own and other societies, permanent body alteration may be practiced for a number of reasons: for purely decorative purposes, for religious expression, for imagined health benefits, or to announce changes in social or physical status.

Labrets

Gê-speaking tribes in Brazil—including the Kayapó, whom we have mentioned before—provide an interesting example of permanent body alteration (T. S. Turner 1987). In some Gê societies, when a young man becomes a father for the first time, he is seen as having officially passed from boyhood to manhood. This important transition is symbolized by a permanent physical change. A small plug (**labret**) that was inserted through the flesh of his lower lip when the new father was himself an infant is replaced by a much larger, saucerlike plate, which may reach a diameter of 4 inches.

Doesn't inserting this disc hurt? Of course, but so does inserting, tightening, and removing dental braces in Western society. Many Westerners consider this pain quite bearable, given the aesthetic benefits of orthodon-

cicatrization a form of scarification in which the skin is repeatedly punctured in an intricate pattern

labret a plug inserted through the flesh of the lower lip

Sometimes sexual and social status are both symbolized by a single bodily alteration or artifact. Among the Kayapó of Brazil, a lip disc called a labret symbolizes masculine strength, maturity, and leadership.

tia. Similarly, no respectable Kayapó male would want to save himself the pain of inserting the lip disc since he feels the long-range cultural benefits outweigh the short-term pain. The ornament symbolizes manhood, and more. Once a father, a man is entitled to speak his mind on matters of concern to his village. In fact he must, if he is to earn the respect of other villagers. Silence is not considered a virtue. Verbally assertive, mature males, and they alone, command the political respect that permits them to preside over village life. The lip disc symbolizes not only fatherhood but also a male's status as a mature, strong, verbally aggressive village leader. Sexual and social status are thus combined in this single symbolic artifact. Women are never entitled to wear the labret because of its strong associations with male characteristics (T. S. Turner 1987).

Scarification

The personal artistic tradition of the Nuba of the Sudan, whose elaborate body painting we described earlier, also includes **scarification.** The term refers to designs made by the intentional wounding and subsequent healing and scarring of the skin. (Cicatrization, mentioned above, is one form of scarification.) A young Nuba girl's body is decorated with its first scars when puberty begins, usually when she is nine or ten (Faris 1972:32). The skin on the abdomen is repeatedly hooked with a sharp thorn, pulled away from the body, and sliced with a small metal knife. Later, when the girl begins to menstruate, this first series of scars is comple-

mented by a second, extending from beneath the breasts to the back and covering the torso. Finally, after she has given birth and has weaned her first child, she is again scarred, this time over the rest of her back, neck, the backs of her arms, buttocks, and the backs of her legs.

It hurts. Nuba girls try to remain stoic, but some pass out from the pain and loss of blood. Yet the cultural benefits of scarification outweigh its painful penalties. The Nuba see scarification primarily as a "beauty treatment" (Faris 1972:36), but it is also a symbol of sexual status, proclaiming that a female has begun to develop sexually, is sexually mature and thus marriageable, or has become a mother. Nuba boys are not decorated with body scars, though both males and females are scarred above the eyes and on the temples. Again, this is done mainly for the sake of beauty, but the Nuba also believe that facial scars will improve one's vision and prevent headaches.

Mutilation

Pain and suffering are carried to greater extremes in societies that practice actual **mutilation** of the body. The term refers to altering any healthy part of the body in a permanently irreversible way, and we find it practiced in non-Western and Western and in small-scale and large-scale societies. In the name of God, Muslims in Middle Eastern countries may sever the hands of those found guilty of theft. Whereas most Westerners might find such customs distasteful, we have grown quite accustomed to the removal of other healthy tissues in the name of religion, health, or beauty. Infant boys routinely undergo circumcision for religious, health, or cosmetic reasons. And Western medical practitioners increasingly perform surgeries such as liposuction (removal of fat from under the skin), breast reduction, and rhinoplasty (the surgical restructuring of the nose) to improve patients' appearance.

The Dani of western New Guinea carry out what may seem to Westerners a particularly grim ritual mutilation. The religion of the Dani is a form of ancestor worship. When an enemy from a neighboring village kills a Dani, the ancestral ghosts of the victim's community require its members not only to avenge the death by killing an enemy but to carry out a ritual as well. This ritual includes severing the top of a finger from a young female relative of the victim (Heider 1979:124–126). The rite of passage for the dead person may require as many as three girls, between about three and six years old, to sacrifice a finger joint. Some undergo this painful experience for more than one dead relative.

The mutilation is performed by a ritual specialist, who first ties a string tightly around the upper arm of the chosen girl. He numbs her fingers by striking them hard against a rock, then severs one or two fingers at the first joint with a blow from a stone ax. Someone quickly bandages the girl's wounds with leaves, and afterward she sits quietly for the rest of the day, probably in a state of shock, holding her bloody hand upright so healing can begin.

In other circumstances, the Dani seem eager to avoid causing pain to children, which suggests that their reason for hand mutilation—that it helps lessen the anger of their long-dead ancestors, now ghosts—is very important to them. The girl's pain is apparently thought of as a sacrificial offering to these phantoms. Going beyond the Dani's own explanation, a structural-functionalist might argue that mutilation is a symbolic way of integrating Dani females into the otherwise all-male intertribal cycle of killing and revenge. Whatever the reason behind the practice, the result is that many Dani women go through life with mutilated hands. Interestingly, however, they perform their many household tasks with little trouble. Many can knit and weave with great skill.

We have already mentioned another kind of mutilation, circumcision, which is much more common cross-culturally than the severing of fingers or hands. In contemporary Western societies, only males are circumcized, but a similar procedure was performed on females in the United States and Europe up until Victorian times,

Scarification *is a general term for designs made by intentionally wounding the skin, and* cicatrization *refers specifically to puncturing the skin repeatedly to produce a permanent decorative pattern. On a Korongo girl in the Sudan, Africa, cicatrization advertises sexual maturity and marital status.*

usually as a medical treatment for masturbation (see Masson 1986). As you know from Chapter 2, circumcision is still performed on females in some non-Western societies, although not to "cure" masturbation (Abdalla 1982; Lightfoot-Klein 1986). Over much of Africa, in parts of the Muslim world, and elsewhere, circumcision of both males and females is a customary part of ceremonies marking the official entry of boys and girls into adulthood.

Female circumcision can involve several different operations. Most medical authorities distinguish be-

◆◆◆

scarification designs made by the intentional wounding and subsequent healing and scarring of the skin

mutilation any irreversible alteration of a healthy human body

•••

Ancient Evidence for Hand Mutilation

In the last chapter we mentioned the cave art of the Cro-Magnon people, Ice Age ancestors of today's western Europeans, which consisted largely of lively and often strikingly realistic images of the wild animals on which these hunters depended for their livelihood. In several of the caves decorated with such artwork, another kind of image appears: mutilated human hands.

The images were obviously created by using real hands rather than by drawing imaginary ones. They were made by placing a hand firmly against a cave wall and then blowing a mouthful of paint at it to produce a smudgy, haloed outline. (This may remind you of the "spatter-painting" technique with which North American kindergarteners are familiar, except that today's young artists are discouraged from taking mouthfuls of paint and are taught to spatter it from toothbrushes instead.) Many of the hands are missing all their fingers. Others lack only a single digit or just a couple of fingertips. Although an artist could conceivably produce such a painting by bend-

ing under one or more fingers of a healthy hand at the second joint, it is impossible to fold under one's fingertips at the first joint and still produce an image as sharp as those in the cave paintings. There is no doubt that at least some of the paintings were made with deformed hands.

We'll probably never know with certainty why the gatherers and hunters of northern Spain may have intentionally mutilated themselves. Perhaps chopping off fingers was intended to please the ghosts of long-dead ancestors, as among the Dani, or perhaps it was a form of punishment, like the removal of a hand in the Middle East today. Deformed hands may even have been considered beautiful, as are the small, straight noses of Westerners who have had bone and flesh removed by plastic surgeons. Possibly the deformities were not intentional; they may have resulted from frostbite, infection in cuts acquired during stone toolmaking, or some crippling disease. Unintentional or not, however, the ancient Ice Age hunters left a purposeful record of their deformities.

---

tween two main types. **Clitoridectomy** is the partial or complete removal of the clitoris and sometimes the labia minora as well. **Infibulation** includes clitoridectomy but refers more specifically to the process of stitching together the two sides of the vaginal opening (the term comes from the custom of the ancient Romans of fastening a pin, or fibula, through the labia majora to prevent women from committing adultery). More important for our purposes than the different physical procedures performed, however, is an understanding of their cultural explanations. In many cultures, circumcision of both males and females is performed to promote physical or psychological health, as a mark of social status, or frequently to make a symbolic statement about sexual identity and the different roles of men and women. In circumcising males, for instance, people may say they are removing the female part, and in circumcising females they may say they are removing the male part.

Among some Somalians in Northeast Africa, girls are infibulated between the ages of 6 and 12. While

older women gather around to restrain the girl and offer advice and encouragement, a female specialist performs the operation with a razor. No antiseptics or anaesthetics are used to protect the girl from pain or infection (Abdalla 1982:18). Why are girls in Somalia forced to endure what strikes most Westerners as a very severe ordeal? First, circumcision is a rite of passage. In the Somali view, it transforms a girl into a marriageable woman—a desirable social status. Second, virginity is highly valued in Somali society, and infibulation provides visual proof that an unmarried female is a virgin (52). The smaller the entrance to the bride's vagina, the greater her reputation, the higher her value in the marriage market, and the more honorable her family (20).

You may find it difficult to understand how a society, whatever its religious beliefs or social customs, could tolerate causing pain to children. But remember that here in the West little boys are routinely circumcised, in what is undoubtedly a painful and occasionally hazardous operation. Often this is done for reasons simi-

Among the Dani, fingers from the hands of young girls are sacrificed to the spirits of the dead. Above, a Dani girl (center), her hand wrapped in banana leaves, recovers from her sacrifice.

lar to those of non-Western societies—tradition, religious belief, and status. Some Western parents and pediatricians have recently rejected male circumcision on the grounds that its possible health benefits are outweighed by the pain it causes and the potential risk of bleeding or infection it entails. But the custom is deeply ingrained among Americans, and some 60 percent of American male infants are still routinely circumcised (Lindsey 1988). Health and hygiene are the explanations generally given to justify this particular form of mutilation in North America, but religious tradition is the justification for North American Jews; and many non-Jewish parents approve of circumcision for their infant sons because they think most other boys are circumcised and they don't want their sons to be embarrassed in the locker room later on in life. The force of custom is very strong.

BODY LANGUAGE

The movements of our bodies and faces are among the media we use to communicate with other members of our culture (Vargas 1986). **Body language (kinesics)** consists of nonverbal ways of conveying ideas, feelings, and intentions through body movements and facial expressions. Unlike body adornment and alteration, body language may be unintentional or even unconscious. It includes universally employed facial gestures such as smiles or frowns, completely reflexive movements such as the involuntary enlargement of the pupils of our eyes when we see something attractive, and conscious movements such as squaring our shoulders before we enter a roomful of people. Whether involuntary or controllable, body language can send many kinds of messages.

Let's look at a few examples of body language. You've failed a test and now sit in your professor's office twisting your ring around and around on your finger. Whether you are conscious of doing this or not, your action says, "I'm nervous." Later, you lurch into a tough-looking character on a moving bus, and your involuntary, tight grin, executed with your teeth clenched, says, "that was purely accidental, not an aggressive move on my part." Safe at home at last, you argue with your younger brother, whose arms are folded across his chest. His defiant stance signifies, "I'm not going to give in to you on this one!" Body language is so important a part of human behavior that studying it is considered by some to be a science.

Imagine the very different postures, gestures, and facial expressions of the following people: someone who is violently angry and ready to fight, someone who is grief-stricken after getting devastating news, someone who feels obliged to listen to a dull lecture, and someone

clitoridectomy the partial or complete removal of the clitoris and sometimes the labia minora as well

infibulation the process of stitching together the two sides of the female vaginal opening

body language (kinesics) nonverbal communication through body movements or facial expressions

who has just caught a touchdown pass or pitched a no-hitter. You'll have no trouble in appreciating the extent to which our body language can mirror intentions, feelings, or states of mind. The body language that conveys most basic emotions, whether anger, grief, boredom, or joy, is similar all over the world.

However, body language we can control, as opposed to involuntary actions that we cannot, may have one meaning in one culture and an entirely different meaning in another. In parts of Latin America, tapping the head with a forefinger means "I'm thinking," but in North America it can mean "you're crazy." The "A-OK" gesture of circled thumb and index finger, so familiar in North America, is considered vulgar in Brazil. In Finland, people who fold their arms are thought to be arrogant, but in Fiji, the same gesture conveys disrespect (Axtell 1985:43-47). In traditional Tibet, a low-status person, upon encountering a higher-status person on the street, sticks his tongue out at his superior as a symbol of respect. Controllable body language, like verbal language, comes from culture rather than nature.

Sexual messages conveyed by the body demonstrate the combination of involuntary and controllable behaviors that make up body language. In all cultures, children learn the behavior appropriate to members of their sex, mostly without being aware they are learning it. Little girls imitate their mothers or older females; little boys imitate their fathers or older males. (In the West, this imitation is often based on the behavior of characters on television or in the movies in addition to or instead of family members.) But the nonverbal ways of communicating that are learned in this fashion vary widely from one culture to another.

Western adults often use their bodies to signal sexual interest (Hall and Hall 1987). A woman may lower her chin, glance briefly upward at a man, and look away; or she may look directly at him, narrowing her eyes and slightly parting her lips. Either way, her eyes will seem brighter than usual because her pupils are dilated, an unconscious physiological response to her feelings. She is likely to make what students of animal behavior call "preening gestures": touching the back of her hair, straightening her back, crossing her legs if she is seated. She may place her hand on her thigh or stroke the inside of her wrist as she talks, showing the palm of her hand. A man, to attract a particular woman, may place his hands in his pockets or hook his thumbs through his belt, movements that raise and square his shoulders, making them look larger. When he catches her eye, he may hold her glance a little longer than is usual in our

society. If he receives an encouraging smile, he may move toward her, standing within her "personal space" (the space beyond which casual conversation always takes place in our culture), and engage in playful talk. His preening gestures may include straightening his tie or cuffs or smoothing his hair (88).

The body language with which both males and females in Western culture signal sexual interest is thus partly conscious and intentional and partly unconscious and unintentional. Either way, it is usually relatively easily deciphered by members of the same culture who are of the opposite sex. However, the body language with which we are familiar may be misinterpreted by members of other cultures, and vice versa. In Latin America, people engaged in ordinary conversation typically stand closer to each other than do people in North America, so the relative lack of personal space between two people who are speaking to each other does not in itself signal sexual interest.

ATTITUDES TOWARD THE BODY

Attitudes toward the body include concepts of what is beautiful versus what is ugly, what is healthy versus what is unfit, what is sexy versus what isn't, and what suggests high moral character versus low. Opinions on these matters differ from society to society. To the Classic Maya, who lived in Mexico, Guatemala, and Belize about a thousand years ago, flat, elongated heads, achieved by pressing children's heads between boards, were considered beautiful. In traditional China, short female feet were considered so desirable that the feet of upper-class girls were tightly bound so they would not grow normally but remain forever child-sized. In North America, the slimness of women's feet, rather than their shortness, is valued and is accentuated with uncomfortable pointed shoes. The body paintings and other decorations worn by the Nuba people would certainly strike

 ASK YOURSELF

Do you ever feel "crowded" while standing and conversing with someone? If so, what do you usually do about it? How does the physical distance between you and someone you're speaking with affect you? How do you feel about conversational partners who occasionally touch your arm or shoulder?

Body language is a combination of intentional and involuntary behaviors. To signal sexual interest, a woman may intentionally narrow her eyes, part her lips, and touch her hair, while her pupils dilate in an unconscious physiological response to her feelings.

us as extremely colorful but not attractive in the same way as they are to other Nuba.

Although the focus of this chapter is on how people alter their bodies to express cultural messages, we'd like to make the point here that femaleness or maleness itself can symbolize cultural values. In South Africa, the Tswana people regard the female body as being "open" to whatever hostile forces plague Tswana life. In con-

Lionesses in the Corporate Jungle

The impact of body language on women's careers was the subject of a recent TV program in England (McKee 1990). Its producers videotaped bank employees, both male and female, then analyzed their body language to discover "whether men speak a language women don't—the language of power."

The answer, it seems, is yes. Film clips show men . . . stretching like lazy lions, stalking majestically about to define their space, and pawing their female counterparts patronizingly in displays of dominance. The women, on the other hand—even those of equal rank to the male managers—huddle together like sheep . . . or hover in doe-like deference to the species they plainly perceive as . . . superior. . . .The men confer like a war council—upright, arrogant, with bold gestures—while the women, even if they're talking business, appear to gossip in girlish camaraderie.

The program noted that some women in positions of power, such as former British Prime Minister Margaret Thatcher, have recently changed their style of moving and speaking. Men, the show prophesied, will have to "start learning the submissive body language of subordinates as more lionesses begin to prowl the business jungle."

trast, the bodies of males are "closed," making males more able to resist such forces (Comaroff 1985:67–68, 81). "Open" female bodies are classified as "hot," and "closed" male bodies are "cool." Since heat is unstable and liable at any moment to spill over into other individuals, women are seen as dangerous to men, whose coolness makes them more socially stable. These distinctions (and you'll recognize them as the sort of oppositions with which structural anthropology concerns itself) fit neatly into a holistic picture of Tswana culture. To take Tswana subsistence activities as an example, horticulture (a risky, uncertain enterprise) is best suited to the "unstable" female sex; pastoralism (far more predictable and controllable) is best suited to the "steadier" male sex.

Thus, among the Tswana, not only do bodies themselves have symbolic meaning; body symbolism is also integrated with other aspects of Tswana culture. Likewise, in a provocative examination of the symbolism surrounding femaleness in North America, Emily Martin (1992) argues that American female bodies also serve as metaphors that affect how American women view themselves and their world. American women's bodies, Martin suggests, are seen both as systems controlled by the brain and as factories for the production of babies. Depending in part on their socioeconomic status, American women both accept and resist the cultural meanings these metaphors impose on female body processes such as menstruation, birth, and menopause.

Thinness and Fatness

In contemporary North America, thinness is considered by most people to be more attractive than fatness. In fact, so important is thinness in our current ideal of feminine attractiveness that many women are prepared to endure the discomfort of continuous dieting in order to stay slim. Some even develop an unrealistic view of themselves as too fat, become hooked on the habit of starving themselves, and suffer dangerous and occasionally fatal weight loss, a mental and physical condition known as **anorexia nervosa.** Although now considered a disease, anorexia seems to be as much a product of attitudes toward the body as it is a pathology of mind or body (Wolf 1991).

Anorexia was first identified as a disease by the English physician Sir William Gull over a hundred years ago, in 1873, but outside of the medical community its existence was not widely recognized until the middle of this century. Previously, people whose eating habits kept them in a state of semistarvation—the Duchess of Windsor is an example—were usually not diagnosed as suffering from any disease. But many were undoubtedly anorexic, for the hallmark of this disease is not so much the appearance of the body or the meagerness of the diet but the fact that starvation is not required to adapt successfully to a career or social position. In contrast to those with anorexia, thin jockeys or high-fashion female models are not usually considered anorexic because their professions require extreme thinness.

Various anthropological explanations for anorexia have been suggested. One is that it is a "symbolic struggle" against male power and authority (B. S. Turner 1984:202). That power is in some way involved in anorexia is also suggested in a recent study by Naomi Wolf (1991), who takes a feminist stance. Imposing impossible standards of thinness, she asserts, is society's way of "punishing" women for their newfound political power. Perhaps more convincing and certainly less political is the view expressed by Aimee Liu in an autobiographical account of her anorexia. Extreme dieting, she wrote, was her first "totally independent exhibit of power" (B. S. Turner 1984:194).

Stoutness has also been fashionable in many societies, including our own. Portraits of past American presidents Grover Cleveland, Benjamin Harrison, the assassinated William McKinley, his successor Theodore Roosevelt, and William Howard Taft show that at the end of the nineteenth century and the beginning of the twentieth big men were deemed best suited for big jobs. All of these presidents were what would be regarded today as unfashionably (and unhealthily) overweight, but at the time corpulence was considered proof of having dined often and well—and therefore of having the wealth necessary to do so. Americans felt they could place their trust and confidence in a beefy president. The ideal late Victorian woman, too, was as handsomely solid and well upholstered as her furniture (Lurie 1981:119).

 ASK YOURSELF

What in your opinion are the physical attributes that make a male body attractive? A female body? Are the attributes you listed universally agreed upon within your culture? Can you think of any widely agreed-upon attribute of attractiveness that you do not find attractive, in either males or females?

••

That Was Then; This Is Now

Grover Cleveland, a Democrat who was both the twenty-second and the twenty-fourth president of the United States, steered the U.S. government between 1885 and 1889 and again between 1893 and 1897. Cleveland was a huge man with chubby cheeks, an extra chin or two, and a barrel-shaped body from which not even a well-cut suit could distract the observer's notice.

The straight-laced, hard-working Cleveland has not become one of our better-known presidents, but what might seem remarkable to us now is that he was ever elected to the presidency in the first place. In our own era, which has been described as obsessed with fitness and in which the corpulent are often looked down on as unattractive, undisciplined, and even self-aggrandizing, Cleveland looks positively unfit for the job of president. Both President Clinton and former President Bush, recognizing that a politician with a waistline like Cleveland's might have a hard time even getting himself heard, jogged daily and publicly during the 1992 presidential campaign. In the fashion of the present day, fitness, not fatness, conveys the impression of personal and moral rigor and dedication that today's successful politician must project. But in his own time, Cleveland appeared to be the ideal man for the job: big, successful, and confident.

Most North Americans view stoutness as unfashionable and unhealthy, but a century ago it was admired. By today's standards, President Grover Cleveland looks unfit for the presidency, but when photographed in 1888 he appeared the ideal man for the job: big, successful, and confident.

Today, slimness is by no means admired everywhere. In Indonesia, where David Hicks carried out fieldwork, local people claim they can assess the wealth and social importance of a man by the size of his waistline. The fatter a man is, the more likely he is to be a leader. Ordinary villagers tend to be skinny, headmen rather less so, local district leaders distinctly pudgy, civil servants of higher rank downright fat, and so on up the financial and social scale. But Indonesians know that corpulence is only an ideal body type. The body shape of many individual officeholders does not conform to this image.

highly erotic in the context of one culture may be unacceptable, unattractive, or even sexually repellent in another. When it comes to notions about what is beautiful versus what is ugly about the human body, there are probably few attributes that are more culture-bound than body hair.

The amount and distribution of hair on the body varies greatly in human beings, both between the sexes and among and within ethnic groups. But some societies are not content to leave the existence, let alone the amount, of body hair entirely at the mercy of nature. Each society has its (often unrealistic) ideals, but these

Body Hair

Notions of physical attractiveness are highly culture-bound; what is acceptable or attractive or even

••

anorexia nervosa a mental and physical disorder characterized by an unrealistic view of oneself as too fat, self-induced starvation, and severe weight loss are often very different cross-culturally. Most young North American women scrupulously shave the hair from their underarms and legs, but some of their European counterparts allow underarm hair to grow and make no effort to conceal it. One American male wrote:

> Several years ago, I was in Berlin having dinner with a German [male] friend. A beautiful woman entered the restaurant, [and was] escorted to the next table. She wore furs and a sleek dress—she was a sensation. But when she removed her cloak, I could see her hairy underarms. I was instantly turned off. I told my friend, who said it turned him on (he was visibly titillated). Now that's culture shock! (Herdt and Stoller 1986:411)

To be beautiful, an Indian bride must have any hair on her forearms shaved before the wedding, but North American brides have no such ideal. Within societies, ideals can vary between the sexes. Facial hair is not only acceptable on North American men, it is often viewed as attractive. Facial hair on women is unacceptable.

Teeth

In Western society, to be considered really attractive, people must have a full set of teeth, and the teeth themselves must be straight and near white. Altering the natural appearance of the teeth to achieve these standards, by straightening, capping, or bleaching, is common. Decorating one or more teeth by embedding a precious stone and capping or replacing natural teeth with gold ones are somewhat less common procedures but by no means unheard of in Western culture. Westerners are not so different from most other societies in this regard; cross-culturally, changing the natural appearance of the teeth is common. Depending on the society, teeth may be shaped artificially, inlaid with substances such as jade or gold, or removed altogether (Milner and Larsen 1991:357).

Beauty is the most common reason for such alterations. While North Americans are whitening or straightening their teeth, the Krīkatí of Brazil are filing theirs to attractive points, and the Balinese are blunting theirs since long teeth are considered dog-like and ugly. Another reason is health. While Americans are having their decayed teeth filled, people in the West Indian nation of Dominica, lacking modern dental services, are having them extracted. In Dominica, a few gaps between teeth is not considered unattractive. A third reason for altering the teeth is social status. While some North Americans are having their front teeth capped with gold or inlaid with diamonds, young men in East Africa are having theirs removed in rites of passage marking their new, adult status (Milner and Larsen 1991:363).

CONCLUSION

All human beings start out in infancy with bodies that are quite similar physically and that proceed to grow and change in fairly predictable ways. But we human beings are not content to let nature dictate our physical appearance. Universally, we alter our appearance with clothing, jewelry, hairdressings, cosmetics, or more permanent physical changes, and we adopt a wide range of physical stances and gestures as well. After these changes have been made, our outward appearances may be quite different from those nature originally provided. Adorning our bodies temporarily or altering them permanently thus transforms what were once completely natural objects into what we may certainly regard as cultural artifacts. Could any behavior be more cultural, more human, than this?

SUMMARY

The human body is used as a medium of expression in all cultures. In this chapter, we liken the body to a canvas on which beliefs, attitudes, ideals, and preferences are reflected through adornment with clothing, jewelry, cosmetics, and hairdos; more permanent forms of body alteration such as scars, tattoos, circumcision, or other forms of mutilation; and body language, consisting of gestures, postures, and facial expressions.

After investigating some of the ways in which human beings adorn, alter, and modify their bodies, this chapter discusses cultural variations in attitudes toward the body. Obesity is frowned on in some societies and highly valued in others. There is similar cross-cultural variation in attitudes toward the ideal amount and distribution of hair on the body and toward the presence or absence and alteration of the teeth.

No matter what the society, some of the messages that manipulating the body's natural form can communicate are (1) social, economic, political, or religious status; (2) group membership; (3) the wish to be more attractive; (4) the wish to conform to the tastes and expectations of others in one's culture; (5) the wish *not* to conform; (6) distinguishing maleness from femaleness; and (7) the projection of inner states—modesty, mourning, pride, and many others.

KEY TERMS

anorexia nervosa
body language
cicatrization
clitoridectomy
cosmetics
infibulation
labret
mutilation
purdah
scarification

SUGGESTED READINGS

Barnes, Ruth, and Joanne B. Eicher (eds.). 1992. *Dress and Gender*. New York: Berg. The essays in this book, one of the series *Cross-Cultural Perspectives on Women*, show how clothing functions as an expression of social identity in Indonesia, Guatemala, India, Israel, Nigeria, and other cultures including the West.

Blacking, John (ed.). 1977. *The Anthropology of the Body*. Association of Social Anthropology, Monograph 15. London: Academic Press. Essays dealing with the body in a wide range of contexts. Subjects include kinesics, health, sexuality, and dance.

Lightfoot-Klein, Hanny. 1986. *Prisoners of Ritual.* New York: Haworth Press. An overview of female genital circumcision in Africa, written by a social psychologist.

Marwick, Arthur. 1988. *Beauty in History: Society, Politics, and Personal Appearance, c. 1500 to the Present.* London: Thames & Hudson. A scholarly history of Western standards of beauty from 1500 to the present.

Verswijver, Gustaaf (ed.). 1993. *Kaiapó, Amazonia: The Art of Body Decoration.* Seattle: University of Washington Press. Gorgeous photographs of body paintings, feather ornaments, bracelets, necklaces, ear decorations, headdresses, and adornments worn by the Kaiapó (or Kayapó) of central Brazil provide a vivid summary of how expressive culture can transform the human body into a work of art.

Wolf, Naomi. 1991. *The Beauty Myth.* New York: Morrow. A look at America's attitudes toward the female body from a feminist perspective. The book suggests that setting nearly impossible standards of thinness is society's way of "punishing" women for their newfound political power.

CHAPTER 16

CULTURE CHANGE AND ANTHROPOLOGY'S RESPONSE

Because people are incessantly experimenting and innovating, change is a constant in human life, and often it results in improvements to the well-being of societies and individuals. In Alaska, Inuit load caribou meat onto their snowmobile for transport to a village some 40 miles away.

INTRODUCTION

Where Western rock music once blared from the doorways of record stores, silence now prevails. Where working women once wore high-fashion, off-the-rack dresses designed in New York and made in Hong Kong, lengths of dark-colored cloth now envelop them from head to toe. Where laborers once lined up to buy pints of vodka at the end of a long workday, sweetened tea now revives the weary. Where high noon once came and went with little interruption in the bustle of city life, hundreds of thousands now stop whatever they are doing, unroll their prayer rugs, and kneel facing the direction of Mecca when they hear the Muslim call to prayer. Teheran is not the same city it once was.

The change in Iran is countrywide, and occurred with dramatic swiftness. Disenchanted with the enthusiasm with which their hereditary ruler, Shah Reza Pahlavi, embraced Western technology and culture, and demoralized by the abuses that accompanied his great wealth and power, the Iranian people, traditional Muslims at heart, decisively rejected the shah in 1978, throwing their allegiance behind an elderly Muslim cleric—a religious fundamentalist and cultural conservative. The Iranian upheaval was only one of a number of profound, sudden, state-level cultural changes that have taken place in the recent past. The collapse of communism in eastern Europe and of official apartheid in South Africa are others.

In small-scale societies, as in modern nations, change is a constant in human life. Forever thinking, organizing, experimenting, and innovating, we human beings continually challenge established patterns of thought, and in so doing change our cultures for better or for worse.

This chapter approaches culture diachronically, focusing on why and how culture change occurs, what happens when it does, and how anthropologists can—or if they should—get involved. Should they restrict themselves merely to documenting and explaining what people in other cultures do, or should they try to influence the course of change?

CULTURE CHANGE

In Chapter 4, in which we defined cultural evolution as a gradual, continuous process of adaptive change, we mentioned the neoevolutionary idea that change need not imply forward progress or improvement, only process. Occasionally, features of a culture become simpler; for instance, the agricultural system in the American South after the Civil War became less, not more, complex. Yet even though the passage of time does not always bring increased cultural complexity, history has witnessed a general movement in this direction. For a good example, recall the political developmental model in Chapter 10: bands, tribes, chiefdoms, and states.

Broadly speaking, we can detect general movement through history in the direction of increasing political complexity, from bands to tribes to chiefdoms to states.

Internal Change

Anthropologists distinguish between two types of culture change: internal and external. **Internal change** comes from within a society; **external change** comes from without.

For most of the history of humankind, cultures existed in some degree of isolation from one another. Widespread cultural contact is a relatively recent development, certainly no older than the Neolithic revolution. As recently as the nineteenth century, hundreds of remote societies still existed in South America, Africa, Asia, the Arctic, and the Pacific. Thus, during the infancy of anthropology as an academic discipline, scholars could observe small-scale societies and their cultures in relative isolation from one another. This isolation didn't mean that these societies hadn't changed, only that whatever changes had occurred were more apt to have come from within rather than from the outside.

So far as we know, there no longer exists, anywhere on earth, a society that is changing *only* from within, one that has never been contacted and influenced by some other culture. All formerly existing "living laboratories," as isolated societies have been called, have been influenced to one degree or another by other cultures.

The Influence of the Natural Environment. One reason cultures change from within is in response to changing conditions in their natural environment. These may be relatively short-term climatic events, like the severe drought in the early 1990s that disrupted agriculture in southern Africa and forced many farmers to leave their homes and migrate to cities in search of food.

 ASK YOURSELF

If a heretofore totally isolated society should be discovered living in some remote part of our planet, what do you think the world's reaction would be? What should it be? Would the situation be different if a society of humans or humanlike creatures were discovered living on another planet?

The Tasaday

In 1971, a tiny group of cave-dwelling gatherers and hunters, the Tasaday, was reported to be living in the dense interior rain forest of the Philippine island of Mindanao (Headland 1992). They were thought by some to be the last uncontacted, totally isolated human group on earth. To protect the Tasaday as a valuable cultural treasure, Philippine government officials soon staked out a vast forest zone in which the little group could live in isolation from outside influences.

Fifteen years later, after Philippine President Ferdinand Marcos had fallen from power, anthropologists visiting the Tasaday discovered much evidence of culture change. Some Tasaday were wearing Western T-shirts; others were using steel-bladed knives and smoking cigars. "We're seeing a textbook case of social change, compressed in time," said one of the anthropologists (Mydans 1986). Others, however, were not so sure. In fact, some claimed that the Tasaday were not the world's last previously uncontacted group at all but a hoax created by Marcos so that he and his supporters could mine, log, and farm the rich interior of Mindanao, free of outside interference (Iten 1986).

A recent review of the evidence concludes that although the Tasaday weren't "rain forest phonies who were paid or coaxed to move into the forest and masquerade as Stone Age cavemen," neither were they never-before-contacted foragers (Headland 1992:215). Instead, they seem to be an indigenous group that had been living for a long time in the region in some degree of cultural isolation. Just how much isolation has never been determined; although living in a cave when discovered, they had iron knives, glass beads, and tin cans (216). And they *were* manipulated by the Marcos government; for ex-

When they came to the world's attention in 1971, the cave-dwelling Tasaday of the Philippines were touted as an uncontacted, totally isolated human group, but later some said they were a hoax. Above, Tasaday find food by breaking open hard fruits with rattan-tied stone axes.

ample, they were asked to wear clothing made from leaves instead of commercially manufactured cloth when visitors arrived.

In spite of the many unanswered questions surrounding the Tasaday, their rights and lands should undoubtedly be protected. This concern is at least as important as the still-debated details of their past and present life (Headland 1992:222–223).

Other environmental changes, however, take place over much longer periods of time. The retreat of glaciers from northern Europe at the end of the Upper Paleolithic caused a gradual warming trend and a slow replacement of forests by grasslands. These changes resulted in a decrease in the big-game animals on which the region's cave-dwelling gatherers and hunters depended. Slowly but completely, their way of life changed in response.

internal change change originating within a society

external change change originating outside a society

Inventions. A second and more frequent cause of internal change is invention. The changes resulting from new ideas, born of the unique capacity of humans for insight and experimentation, may be material (like the idea of propelling a sharply tipped shaft of wood with the help of a taut bowstring rather than human muscle alone) or nonmaterial (like a newly invented folktale). In either case, inventions are the products of the creative abilities of members of a society, individually or collectively. They may be responses to pressing needs, products of the human creative impulse and enough leisure to exploit it, chance associations of ideas, or even the result of the urge to find an aesthetically pleasing order. The discoverers of the structure of DNA, James D. Watson and Francis Crick, hoped that the physical shape of the molecule they were seeking would prove to be "pretty," and so it did: a double helix.

The old saying, "necessity is the mother of invention," is apparently only rarely true. Necessity is more apt to be the mother of development or improvement of what is already known. Historians of technology have suggested that metallurgy (the science of extracting useful metals from their ores) may have come about not because our ancestors needed to make knives for domestic work or arrowheads for war but because they wished to express themselves artistically by fashioning metal beads or armbands. Likewise, pottery may have been accidentally invented when it was discovered that figurines or counting beads, fashioned of soft clay, would harden if left near a fire. Our ancestors may have been cultivating flowers for pleasure long before this hobby was translated into planting grain for food, and playing with pets may have given them the idea of domesticating animals for subsistence.

Invention does not necessarily produce internal change, for every novel idea has to win acceptance and some societies accept innovation more readily than others. Here the personality of the innovator can be decisive. A charismatic innovator is more likely to win approval among his or her colleagues than someone who is disliked. The idea that a single forceful individual can cause major change is called the **great man theory** of history. There is less general agreement about its validity than about the proposition that a climate of openness to new ideas greatly affects culture change.

Anthropologist Leslie White (1971), who has written at length about culture change, uses the fourteenth-century B.C. Egyptian pharaoh Ikhnaton (sometimes spelled Akenaton) to illustrate the relative effects on culture change of individual greatness and the cultural cli-

mate in which change occurs. It was Ikhnaton who first devised the idea of monotheism. In the process of promoting this new philosophy, he swept away his people's old polytheistic religion, reorganized their government, and revitalized Egyptian art. The cultural impact of this one man can still be felt today.

Yet ancient hieroglyphic texts and portraits suggest that Ikhnaton was physically unattractive and may have suffered some illness that deformed his body. Thus, White argues, something besides personal attractiveness and physical strength must have encouraged the ancient Egyptians to accept his revolutionary ideas. White (1971:280) concludes that great men such as Ikhnaton are products of cultural forces and historical circumstances, which are what really bring about culture changes. The great man is "best understood as an effect" rather than as a primary cause (190). As culture advances, the great man becomes less and less significant in culture change, and the "community of scientific and technological workers" becomes more and more important (224–225).

At first glance, internal culture change seems to occur at a much slower rate in technologically simpler societies than in industrialized, Western ones. But this observation may be misleading, resulting from the nature of the evidence. Archaeologists have shown that during the almost inconceivably long period in which all human beings lived as gatherers and hunters, their subsistence economy, technology, and material culture changed relatively little in comparison with the rate of change since the food-producing revolution. The archaeological record is full of examples of cultural conservatism, the retention of old ideas, artifacts, and institutions. But caution is needed here, for although the material, physical world of some early gatherers and hunters may have changed very little over a long span of time, many kinds of changes may have taken place among them without leaving traces for archaeologists to discover. We do not know what innovations may have been introduced into ancient gatherers and hunters' languages, descent systems, or other nonmaterial aspects of their cultures.

In the nineteenth and early twentieth centuries, the impression that technologically simpler people were culturally conservative, sticking steadfastly to their traditional ideas and customs, was reinforced by anthropologists' fieldwork among groups of gatherers and hunters. Sometimes, compared with what was happening in the West as the result of the Industrial Revolution, these groups appeared to be hanging on to obsolete ways of

The Egyptian pharoah Ikhnaton, an example of the great-man theory, revolutionized Egyptian culture in the fourteenth century B.C., yet contemporary reliefs portray him as physically deformed. Here the long-faced, large-eared, pot-bellied pharoah and his queen make offerings to Aton, the sun god.

living. Some ethnographers, unable to observe much evidence of technological development, assumed that other aspects of these cultures hadn't changed much either. Later fieldworkers showed that nonliterate communities do change internally, sometimes—as revitalization movements (Chapter 12) demonstrate—very rapidly. In general, however, the rate of change in nonliterate societies does tend to be slower than in our own fast-paced society.

External Change

External culture change comes from outside society as the result of **cultural diffusion,** the spread of ideas and technology between cultures. The process is so common it has inspired **diffusionism,** the idea that much culture change can be explained by contacts between representatives of different cultures. In the early decades of the twentieth century, diffusionism was championed in perhaps its most extreme form by diffusionists who implausibly argued that the roots of all civilizations lay in the culture of ancient Egypt. We now accept the more reasonable idea that diffusion is a powerful impetus to culture change but is far from being its only agent.

Direct and Indirect Diffusion. Anthropologists distinguish two types of cultural diffusion: **direct diffusion** and **indirect diffusion.** When a Christian missionary succeeds in his or her evangelical work among a previously non-Christian group, we can say that Christianity diffused directly from the missionary's own culture to another. Not all new ideas or artifacts diffuse so directly, however. Some spread from one society to another through an intermediary culture. When Christianity diffuses from a culture into which it was first introduced from the outside to yet another culture, this is indirect diffusion.

Diffusion and Adaptation. Sometimes, rather than accepting a diffused idea or complex of ideas in its entirety, people use it selectively. They may, for example, adapt and change a good idea to suit their own special needs. Sequoia, a native American of the Cherokee tribe who observed the many advantages Europeans enjoyed as a result of knowing how to read and write, adapted the English alphabet to suit his own language.

◆◆◆

great man theory the idea that a single forceful individual can cause major change in a society

cultural diffusion the spread of ideas and technology between cultures

diffusionism the idea that culture change can be explained by intercultural contacts

direct diffusion the diffusion of an idea or custom from one culture to another without passing through an intermediary culture

indirect diffusion the diffusion of an idea or custom from one culture to another after passing through an intermediary culture

Change in Western Society

Western anthropology has tended to suggest that technologically simpler societies are more reluctant to incorporate internal change than Western society. Actually, Western society offers many examples of new ideas that were slow to catch on, or even rejected at first, because of ignorance, prejudice, personal dislike of an inventor, a strong commitment to tradition, or plain disinterest.

The economist Thorstein Veblen noted that nineteenth-century Britain, reliant on steam power, was so slow to convert to electricity that its iron and steel industry was quickly outstripped by those of Germany and the United States (Barrett 1991:103–104). Similarly, when Charles Darwin (1809–1882) proposed natural selection as an explanation for the existence and physical form of human beings, the idea was greeted with great skepticism. Only later, after earlier theories had been disproven, was the idea accepted as valid. And just in case you are tempted to believe that the nineteenth century saw the end of closed minds, recall the Scopes monkey trial (Chapter 12). New ideas, even in twentieth-century Western society, are not always welcome.

The work of Christian missionaries where Christianity has previously been unknown is an example of direct diffusion, the spread of ideas or customs directly from one culture to another. In a scene from the movie At Play in the Fields of the Lord, *two missionaries confront their intended converts.*

Tobacco's Rapid Spread

The custom of smoking spread by both direct and indirect diffusion. In 1586, Sir Walter Raleigh returned to England from the colony of Virginia with tobacco, which native Americans had shown him how to grow and use. Smoking tobacco was an immediate hit with the English, a case of direct diffusion. Some four years later, English medical students introduced the practice to the Dutch in Holland; Dutch sailors then exported it into the countries of northern Europe, thus spreading the custom by indirect diffusion. It was then introduced into Spain by seafarers, from where it spread across the Mediterranean into the Near East. By 1605, less than two decades after Raleigh, it had reached far-off Japan. Smoking is now universal.

Changing some letters and inventing new ones, Sequoia gave his people their own alphabet. Alternatively, people sometimes use only some elements of a diffused idea, blending these with elements from their own cultural tradition to produce a new idea well suited to their particular cultural context. In Chapter 14, we used reggae music to illustrate syncretism, the blending of elements from two cultural traditions. Reggae combines elements of both Western and African music to produce an entirely new musical category. But syncretism is not just a musical phenomenon; it can take place in any area of culture.

Beneficial versus Destructive Diffusion. When a new idea or artifact diffuses into a society, its members will obviously accept it only if they think it will benefit them. But good ideas in the context of one culture often work well in others too. The Mattapoisett Indians showed the Pilgrims of Plymouth Colony how to plant corn, an instance of beneficial diffusion that resulted in the harvest celebrated at the first Thanksgiving. In our late twentieth-century world of rapid and relatively easy global communication, beneficial diffusion is commonplace. Japanese improvements to cameras and cars mean that Americans can have better photographs and more efficient transportation, Middle Eastern oil powers western European generators, and AIDS test kits produced in the United States protect supplies of blood in Latin American hospitals.

Yet as members of one village in India discovered, diffusion can have unexpected or even destructive social, cultural, and economic results. Recently a solar-powered water pump was hooked up to a village well in India (Wicker 1987). Freed from the time-consuming task of drawing water by hand, village women found

The blending of elements from two or more cultural traditions into a single new one is called syncretism. In Zimbabwe, southern Africa, followers of a syncretic religion combining Christianity with traditional beliefs pray together in the rocky, uninhabited countryside outside the capital, Harare.

◆◆

Inuit Computers

Even the Inuit need freezers (Wren 1986). In Canada's Northwest Territories, the Baffin Island Regional Council, made up of representatives from 14 isolated Inuit communities, is installing walk-in freezers in remote Inuit hamlets to store the game that Inuit hunters shoot. The Inuits' need for modern technology doesn't end with freezers. The council also plans to computerize the contents of each community's freezer, so that if one hamlet finds itself with plenty of caribou meat but few seal, it can easily locate a hamlet with an excess of seal and trade one kind of meat for the other.

Soon, computers will also be used to help Inuit communities communicate with one another. Distances between villages are daunting in the Arctic, making it difficult for community representatives to come together to present their common interests to the government. The harsh climate and difficult terrain slow down the mail. The telephone system, which uses a satellite, is excellent, but Inuit settlements are poor, and people can't call long-distance as often as they might wish. Flying community representatives to Baffin Island Regional Council meetings in Frobisher Bay would be even more expensive than phone calls.

Computers with telephone modems would be an ideal way to solve the area's communication problems. Both the hardware and software will have to be user-friendly since many Inuit have little formal education and not all of them speak English. The council has chosen the Apple Macintosh, which uses images rather than words to execute commands. A local teacher has written a software program made up of the lines and circles of the Inuit alphabet.

To equip every Inuit community with a Macintosh and a modem will take time and money, but computers are already being used at council headquarters to monitor budgets, draw up reports, store information, and communicate by modem with the outside world. The cold climate has created some problems; computer operators have found, for instance, that the Macintosh will not read frozen diskettes. But even temperatures of 50 degrees below zero have not kept the Inuit from benefiting from modern technology. When frozen diskettes are allowed to thaw out, the new computer system works just fine.

---

they were spending much less time chatting with one another around the well. Village boys whose job had been to draw water from the well in buckets now had nothing to do, and with time on their hands and nothing to occupy them, some turned to petty crime. Soon the easy availability of water had attracted hoards of unwanted wanderers from outside the village. Meanwhile, the gap between rich and poor widened. The rich, who owned land, could use the pump for irrigation, but the poor had no land to irrigate. The well was definitely a mixed blessing. When discontent reached its peak, women of the village intentionally broke the pump so they could once more gather around the well that had been the center of their social lives.

Resisting or Rejecting Diffusion. For all its power to alter cultures, for worse as well as for better, diffusion is by no means impossible to resist. Many societies have energetically preserved their traditional ways rather than accept "progress" in the form of ideas or technologies invented elsewhere. Small-scale societies are sometimes able to secure the best of both the traditional and modern worlds. Native Americans may live in modern brick houses, drive station wagons, watch television, cook in microwave ovens, and speak English in addition to their native Navajo or Choctaw. At the same time, their homes may be decorated with native American crafts, they may visit traditional healers when sick, and their food (like that of their ancestors) may be home-grown.

Sometimes people sample ideas and artifacts that have diffused into their culture but then reject them. In Zaire in Central Africa, the gathering-and-hunting Mbuti tried horticulture, then rejected it. Persuaded by Belgian

Cultural diffusion, the spread of ideas and technology between cultures, has sometimes been aided by sea travel. On the high seas near Micronesia, sailors steer their tiny craft much as their ancestors, who brought new cultural elements and languages all the way from Asia, must have done.

administrators to plant crops, the Mbuti were competent farmers but experienced too many unwanted changes in the rest of their culture to accept this novelty. Gathering and hunting had given meaning to their lives, but as farmers, "they degenerated socially and physically at an alarming rate, losing all sense of individual or family responsibility and dying from sunstroke and stomach disorders" (Turnbull 1965:313). So they turned down horticulture and returned to gathering and hunting.

Barriers to Diffusion.   Mountain ranges, glaciers, swamps, and forests have since prehistoric times provided natural barriers to cultural exchange between different populations. For example, the Indonesian island of Timor, although small, is home to more than

◆ **ASK YOURSELF**

A businessman bought a hand-held tape recorder with which to record notes and remember appointments, only to find he never used it. Jotting down appointments and notes with pencil and paper was easier and faster. Have you ever had a similar experience?

twelve different language groups; the island's mountainous landscape proved an effective barrier to intercultural communication. In contrast, the oceans that cover our planet have sometimes provided a means of relatively easy communication, as linguistic similarities between North America and England demonstrate.

Increasingly through history, natural and cultural barriers have fallen to cultural inventions. To get his troops across the Alps into Italy in the third century B.C., the Carthaginian general Hannibal used elephants, common enough in the context of his own North African culture but no doubt an astonishing sight to the Italians. Today, highways, ships, planes, telephones, and satellites are only some of the ways in which intercultural contact can be made and maintained. Contact is so powerful a force for change that when political leaders don't want changes to occur, they try to prohibit it. Following World War II, in an attempt to keep Western values from diffusing to their own citizens, the leaders of the Soviet Union did their best to cut off channels of communication with the West, a policy that prompted Winston Churchill's famous remark that "an iron curtain has fallen down upon eastern Europe."

Naming the Yucatan

When the Spanish conquistadores landed in the Yucatan peninsula of what is now Mexico in 1517, they were greeted by a people different from any they had ever seen, whose language was different from any they had ever heard. The Spaniards greeted the local people and asked them what their homeland was called, but of course the native Americans didn't understand the question, for they spoke Maya, not Spanish. They therefore responded, in Maya, "*uic athan*," which means "we don't understand you." The Spaniards, believing their question to have been answered, from then on called the place Yucatan (Clendinnen 1987). This was only the first in a long series of tragic failures in communication between these native Americans and their eventual conquerers.

THE STATUS OF SMALL-SCALE SOCIETIES

Although culture change takes place continually in all societies, today small-scale societies are more apt to be its victims than its beneficiaries. Perhaps no global trend is more dismaying to anthropologists than the increasing rate at which the world's remaining small-scale societies are being weakened or even exterminated. When the members of such societies realize that their cultural individuality is threatened, some strongly resist efforts to bring their aims, values, and ways of life into line with other, usually national, ideologies. Instead, they may strive to protect their cultural traditions from **Westernization,** the diffusion of technologies, ideas, values, and customs from the West. The Yanomamo of Brazil, whose culture and ancestral territory are seriously threatened by Western mining and logging interests, illustrate how forced development can threaten to extinguish a people's whole way of life (Bodley 1988:409).

But you don't have to go to an exotic place to find people trying to preserve their cultural heritage. Wales is part of Great Britain, and many Welsh people speak both English and their native Welsh language. If you traveled in Wales some years ago, perhaps you observed that the road signs were entirely in English. If you've been to Wales recently, however, you surely noticed a change; most highway signs are now in both English and Welsh. This change is the result of an increasingly strong movement among the Welsh people for the preservation of their ancient language and culture. Some of them are even lobbying and demonstrating for their country's complete political separation from Great Britain.

The Welsh are an ethnic group, which we defined in Chapter 11 as a self-perpetuating group distinguished by others (and whose members distinguish themselves) by their shared traditions, values, and language. Termed *ethnic minorities* when they are smaller than other groups within their larger society, ethnic groups are parts of nations and their members may participate fully in national events, yet they take pride in their unique cultural traditions. Tribal groups like the Yanomamo

Like the members of many other societies, the Welsh are struggling to preserve their language, culture, and identity. Some even advocate the political separation of Wales from Great Britain. Near Conwy in northern Wales, separatist graffiti incorporates the word Cymru, *the Welsh term for "Wales."*

also have distinct cultural traditions, but unlike ethnic groups they are less integrated into the nations in which they are found. The two kinds of groups confront similar problems in the face of culture change.

Some ethnic and tribal groups face an uphill battle because their interests and values are not those of the governments of the countries within whose borders they live. What usually happens is that governments attempt to absorb these less powerful groups into the national culture, typically for political reasons. In trying to create the nation of Iran, Reza Shah (the father of the shah overthrown by Khomeini) found himself at odds with the tribal Qashgai, who refused to recognize his authority and whose nomadic pastoralist way of life was not "modern" enough for the new Iran he planned. The shah tried to convert the nomads into peasants and bring them into the mainstream of twentieth-century Iranian culture. Using tanks and planes to cut off their migration routes, he bullied the nomads into building huts and settling down in villages. It didn't work. After Reza Shah abdicated in 1941, most Qashgai burned their huts and resumed their transhumant existence.

From the point of view of national leaders, attempting to absorb tribal or ethnic minorities makes sense for several reasons. First, at the national level minorities may be thought "backward," and the leaders of countries struggling for economic development may find their presence an embarassment. Second, the health and education of minorities are often poor, and governments' attempts to bring modern health care and education—"progress"—to all their people may be weakened by the determination of minority groups to maintain their traditional ways. Third, national leaders realize that the more strongly people feel about their ethnic identity, the less loyalty they have toward their country. This makes it difficult, for example, to conscript soldiers to fight for the country's interests. Leaders may thus see it as their mission to force members of ethnic or tribal groups to follow their agenda.

Taken to extremes, the forceful attempt to assimilate an ethnic or tribal group becomes **ethnocide,** the deliberate attempt to destroy a group's culture. If this attempt includes trying to destroy the people themselves, it is called **genocide.** The most notorious case of both ethnocide and genocide in this century was the Nazi attempt, declared an official policy of the German state in 1942, to exterminate the Jewish people and their culture. The "ethnic cleansing" of Bosnian Muslims by Serbs in the former Yugoslavia reminds us that attempts to exterminate people and their culture continue even today.

ANTHROPOLOGY'S ROLE IN SOLVING GLOBAL PROBLEMS

Earth's human population is increasing at a tremendous rate, while people consume its resources ever more hungrily. Related problems affecting both our natural and cultural environments are environmental pollution; the disregard of human rights, particularly among minority groups; the poor health and nutritional status of many of the world's people; large-scale warfare and other, smaller-scale, regional and ethnic hostilities and the refugees they create; and glaring economic inequalities among individuals, groups, and nations. These and other global problems cause anthropologists and nonanthropologists alike to wonder about the future of *Homo sapiens sapiens,* and present anthropologists and others with continuing opportunities and challenges. Increasingly, anthropology's response has been to address such problems head-on, in either of two ways: through development anthropology or advocacy.

Development Anthropology

In Chapter 1, we introduced a subfield of anthropology called applied cultural anthropology, the use of anthropological ideas (especially holism and cultural relativity) and methods (especially participant observation and field interviewing) to achieve practical ends in areas such as government, business, medicine, and law. In that context we briefly discussed **development anthropology,** anthropologists' contribution to a broad range of efforts to improve the well-being of people in "developing" countries by helping them solve specific problems of health care, education, agriculture, and so on. Later, in Chapter 9, we again touched on development anthropology in describing economic development.

Westernization the process by which non-Western societies become more like Western ones by adopting Western technologies, ideas, values, and customs

ethnocide the deliberate attempt to destroy the culture of an ethnic group

genocide the deliberate attempt to exterminate the members of a culture

development anthropology efforts by anthropologists to improve the well-being of people in the "developing" countries in areas such as health care, education, and agriculture

Contemporary Ethnocide

In 1975, the Indonesian army invaded East Timor, and thousands of Tetum and other citizens were massacred. Sixteen years later, at a ceremony commemorating one of the dead, troops again opened fire, killing and wounding hundreds. Above, mourners gather up the victims' bloodstained clothes.

Although not as well publicized as the Nazi atrocities or the more recent "ethnic cleansing" in the former Yugoslavia, the attempts by the government of Indonesia since 1975 to eradicate the traditional cultures of East Timor have been no less horrifying. Until 1975, East Timor, occupying half of the island of Timor, was a colony of Portugal, and adjacent West Timor was part of Indonesia. When the Portuguese gave up control of East Timor, its political leaders declared it an independent country. But East Timorese independence was to last for only about a month. On December 7, 1975, President Suharto of Indonesia ordered an invasion of the new country—home to the Tetum, mentioned in previous chapters—by his armed forces.

As a result of this order, an unkown number of Tetum and other citizens of East Timor were killed. Many were massacred by the Indonesian military; many others died of starvation following the fighting. A conservative estimate put the death toll at over 100,000 out of a total population of no more than 500,000—20 percent of the population. East Timor was quickly incorporated into the Republic of Indonesia as a mere province. Since then, the Indonesians have forcibly imposed their own customs, beliefs, and values on the Timorese, some of whom continue a guerilla struggle to preserve their traditions and regain their former independence.

Development anthropology is part of a broad, multidisciplinary field called **international development,** a comprehensive term for many different kinds of efforts by anthropologists and other specialists to improve human welfare, particularly in developing countries. In addition to individuals, institutions in both industrialized and developing countries contribute to this work. They include world bodies like the United Nations, national

Among the most acute of contemporary world problems, mass starvation challenges anthropologists to help through development efforts or advocacy. A starving child is force-fed by a local relief worker in Baidoa, Somalia, in 1992.

governments, and public and private agencies. These employ experts of all kinds, including social scientists, doctors, teachers, and agronomists (see Skar 1985).

Perhaps the most daunting challenge to international development in general, and development anthropology in particular, is suggesting ways to satisfy what development workers term "basic human needs" and to provide basic services for those who lack them. These basic needs and services include food and shelter, primary health care, and education. Closely tied to their provision are such goals as increased economic production, technological improvements, a more equal distribution of resources, and preservation of the natural environment. Thus an international development project in a developing country might have as its goal improving the management of the country's public health system, resettling refugees fleeing war or drought, introducing new and more productive crops and better agricultural techniques to farmers, recording a body of oral literature that is fast being forgotten, building a new road or sewage system, retraining unemployed rural women in marketable skills, or informing teenagers about AIDS.

Anthropologists' best chance to be of service may lie in helping governments and international agencies better understand the cultures of the people whose needs

◆ **ASK YOURSELF**

What do you consider the single major global problem we face today? What solutions can you think of to solve it?

they wish to meet. Development efforts affect different cultures and different social groups in those cultures in different ways, and what works for one culture or group may not be suitable for all. A development project might raise the standard of living of one group but lower it for another. Development that benefits men may not provide the same advantages for women. An anthropologist knowledgeable about the ethnographic details of a particular culture and aware of it as a holistic entity is ideally placed to point out to governments and international organizations how certain changes, while benefiting some, may at the same time make the lives of others even more difficult.

Despite anthropology's potential to contribute to development projects, the jury is still out on this subject. Some critics, both within and outside the discipline, doubt that Western outsiders are morally entitled to interfere in the lives of non-Western people, even if their intentions are the best. Others point out that national leaders in developing countries have been known to ignore the wishes of local communities in pushing through "progressive" reforms, and money earmarked for improvements sometimes vanishes into the pockets of government officials. Still others question whether anthropologists, as social scientists, are justified in relinquishing their scientific objectivity and committing themselves to change.

◆◆

international development a comprehensive term for international efforts to improve the well-being of the world's people

A Philosophy of International Development

One guiding premise of international development today is that both its narrower practical goals and its broader scientific aims are best achieved at the invitation and with the cooperation of the communities involved. Another is that development projects should be **sustainable:** their intended beneficiaries should be able to continue to achieve the desired results after development assistance ends. These two premises may seem obvious enough, but they were often lacking in development projects in the past. Both were arrived at after trial and error.

In its formative period in the years following World War II, international development consisted largely of donations of money, facilities, or equipment from rich nations to poor ones. Sometimes the recipients put these resources to good use, but all too frequently such donations did not have the intended results. Equipment given to hospitals might work as advertised for awhile but later require servicing or parts unavailable in a developing country. A newly introduced crop might not find a local market because local people preferred their customary food. As our example of the unwelcome effects of a solar-powered water pump in a rural Indian village showed, technological changes sometimes have adverse side effects.

This early approach to development assistance, called the **top-down approach** because donations and assistance were imposed by outsiders without the full participation of the local people they were intended to benefit, proved ineffective and unsustainable. Today, people in developing countries often initiate and manage much of their own development, actively participating in designing, implementing, and evaluating development projects. International organizations such as the World Bank, government agencies like USAID, and private agencies like the Rockefeller Foundation continue to give money and provide technical assistance to developing countries. But they don't do it alone; they rely for their success on the active participation of people in the countries in which they work, from government officials to the residents of local communities.

A long-delayed but welcome addition to the practice of development anthropology has been the growing recognition over the last decade or two of the importance of women in developing countries (Young 1993). For too long, development anthropologists and other development "experts" saw women primarily as mothers or, when their economic role outside the household was recognized at all, as providers of services: domestics, teachers, nurses. Today, recognizing the enormous variety of women's economic as well as cultural contributions to their societies, development workers are more aware of such issues as women's rights and the impact of traditional gender hierarchies. Without taking women's roles into account at every level of development thinking, planning, and implementation, sustainable development is impossible (147).

The Anthropologist as Advocate

A second way in which anthropologists can involve themselves in world problems is through advocacy: using their influence and expertise to aid a cause. A number of anthropologists now serve as advocates for small-scale societies and ethnic minorities. Although the distinction between development anthropology and advocacy is a fine (at times even an indistinguishable) one, in general advocacy is a somewhat less hands-on although no less valuable anthropological strategy for helping to solve world problems.

One of anthropology's best-known advocates is David Maybury-Lewis, whose fieldwork among the Shavante convinced him that this society needed and wanted help in retaining its identity and defending its interests

Let Tribal People Choose!

The aim of organizations like Cultural Survival is not necessarily to encourage minorities to "be true to their traditions," a romantic notion that may not serve minority groups well, but instead to assist people who request help to maintain those aspects of their culture they themselves regard as important (Maybury-Lewis 1988:380). Such organizations reject the paternalistic notion that tribal people need to be told what to preserve or how to respond to change.

In southern Brazil, a tribal group was recently offered what for them was a huge amount of money to grant lumber companies the right to cut down trees on their land (Maybury-Lewis 1988:386). The tribespeople thought the impact of the lumbering on what they considered an inexhaustible resource would be trivial. Anthropologists acting as advocates tried to persuade them to decline the offer, but they decided to accept it nonetheless. At that point, the anthropologists ceased their opposition to the project. They felt they had made its ecological consequences clear and were confident the local people had all the information that was available on which to base a decision. The future was theirs to choose.

---

against the encroachments of big business and the Brazilian government. In 1972, Maybury-Lewis founded a nonprofit organization called Cultural Survival, to encourage tribal peoples' participation in national market economies, to secure their land rights, and to fund projects designed and carried out by the people themselves. Cultural Survival also keeps Westerners informed about tribal groups and ethnic minorities by publishing information that results from its research.

Organizations like Cultural Survival are founded in the belief that some tribal and ethnic groups are being wronged and that their rights should be protected (Maybury-Lewis 1988:376). Adopting the stance of cultural relativism, anthropologists in their role as advocates examine, analyze, and attempt to understand the goals of minorities and the factors that might prevent these goals from being achieved, and work to develop effective strategies for dealing with specific injustices. Maybury-Lewis stresses that it is the minority groups themselves, not anthropologists, who determine the kind of cultural survival for which he and like-minded anthropologists strive.

Addressing World Problems

In this section, we consider only three of the major global problems that anthropologists, through development work or advocacy, can help solve: uncontrolled population growth, the planetary loss of species diversity, and poor health and nutrition.

Stemming Overpopulation. Between 1801 and 1974, the world's population grew from 1 billion to 4 billion people. By 1992, it was over 5 billion, and it is projected to reach 7 billion by the year 2000. Although some of the more industrialized countries have made great strides in this century in slowing, halting, or even reversing their rate of population growth, many other countries, despite the family planning efforts of national and international organizations, have yet to do so. Mexico, for example, grew from 28 million people to almost 86 million people in the 40 years between 1950 and 1991. The problem is that earlier population booms in some countries resulted in huge increases in the number of women now of reproductive age. These women are having fewer babies each year than their mothers did, but since there are so many of them, the total number of children they will bear is much greater than the total born to their mothers.

Some of the implications of unchecked population growth are obvious. Overpopulation often means there isn't enough food, health care, or employment to go around, so more people are likely to be undernourished, sick, and unemployed or underemployed. Other conse-

sustainability the capacity of the beneficiaries of a development project to continue to achieve results after development assistance ends

top-down approach in international development, providing assistance to local people without their full participation

Particularly in some developing nations, rapid population growth rates are alarming, since they may result in future urban overcrowding, insufficient public assistance funds, and shortages of food, housing, health care, and employment opportunities. Despite the family-planning efforts of national and international organizations, families as large as this one are still common in many countries.

quences are more subtle but also pose serious problems, especially for the poorer nations of the world. The changing age structure of a country's labor force may drain its public assistance and social security funds; the depletion of local resources may encourage rural-urban migration, placing heavy demands on urban housing and services.

Opportunities for anthropologists to help stem the tide of uncontrolled population growth are many. As employees of governments, international aid agencies, religious or other cultural organizations, or private charitable foundations, anthropologists are increasingly involved in population projects ranging from social mar-

keting studies of family planning devices to helping formulate national population policies.

Preserving Biodiversity. In Chapter 5, we described the environmental adaptation of Maasai cattle pastoralists in Tanzania, which showed that environmental conservation and the subsistence needs of small-scale societies are not necessarily incompatible. But in some parts of the world, governments and international agencies find themselves facing a knotty question: which is more important, people or nature? If nature is to be left undisturbed, how are people who depend on natural resources to obtain their subsistence?

Of the many natural resources on which people depend, few are more important than tropical rain forests. These tracts of unspoiled land, with their enormous diversity of species (**biodiversity**), have been described as the lungs of the planet, for they convert the huge quantities of carbon dioxide produced by cars and factories into oxygen. Destroying rain forests removes the planet's best means of removing carbon dioxide from the atmosphere and greatly contributes to global warming through the greenhouse effect. Rain forests are also home to plant and animal species found nowhere else, some of which are of proven or potential medicinal or other value.

Yet an estimated 50 million acres of rain forest are being wiped out every year—1½ acres per second (Survival International 1990). Prominent among the causes are large-scale tree cutting by the logging industry and slash-and-burn agriculture by indigenous people. As a response, and with the help of anthropologists, international conservation and development organizations such as the World Wildlife Fund and USAID have developed plans and provided funds for protecting rain forests. Economic development may be prohibited in forested regions, and local populations may be either relocated or prohibited form exploiting newly protected animal and plant resources as they once did.

An example is Ranomafana National Park in Madagascar, a huge island lying off the southeast coast of Africa. So extensive and remote that parts of it have yet to be explored, Ranomafana is one of the richest, yet at the same time most endangered, natural areas in the world. By 1985, hunting by local people, as well as deforestation resulting from fuel collecting and industrial logging, had seriously endangered the existence of Ranomafana's lemurs, rare primates that exist nowhere else in the world. An international conservation conference was called to help the government of Madagascar decide

Ranomafana National Park in Madagascar, one of the richest yet most endangered natural areas in the world, is home to an internationally funded development project to protect its environment and rare animal species. At the same time, the project is providing the local people with schools, health clinics, cooperatives, and agricultural assistance. Here, development workers join local Betsileo people at a party in the village of Ambato Lahy.

how the forest and the lemurs could best be protected. Participants realized they needed to establish policies that would simultaneously preserve the land and its species and help satisfy the economic needs of the local people, the Tanala and Betsileo.

When anthropologist Patricia Wright was appointed director of the Ranomafana National Park Project, she realized that any conservation plan that failed to win the cooperation of the Tanala and Betsileo in maintaining the park would be doomed to failure. To learn what the villagers' needs would be if the use of their traditional lands was denied to them, she led a survey team on foot over rugged hillsides to Tanala and Betsileo villages. In each village, the team first met with the elders, then called a general meeting of village members at which their need for schools, health clinics, women's cooperatives, and technical assistance with agriculture could be discussed. As the team listened, the scope of the project increased (Wright 1992:28).

Their survey completed, Wright and her team were able to recommend to the government sustainable alternatives to villagers' environmentally destructive practices such as slash-and-burn agriculture and cattle herding in the forest. These alternatives included beekeeping, raising fish in ponds, and cultivating wet rice. Subsequently, studies of the need for health care, pri-

mary education, and technical assistance with agricultural and forestry projects were carried out. The team realized that **ecotourism**—tourism based on viewing wildlife—was an excellent prospect for Ranomafana, one of very few places where lemurs can be seen in their natural habitat. Already, some villagers have given up traditional but ecologically harmful subsistence activities to work as tourist guides.

Improving Health and Nutrition. Anthropologists are also at work in international health, studying the customs and attitudes that lead to illness, the impact

◆ ASK YOURSELF

If you are majoring not in anthropology but in one of the natural sciences, humanities, or a social science other than anthropology, can you think of possible ways you might apply your expertise to help alleviate global problems mentioned in this chapter, as some anthropologists hope to do?

◆◆◆◆◆◆◆◆◆◆◆◆◆◆◆◆◆◆◆◆◆◆◆◆◆◆◆◆◆◆◆◆◆◆◆◆◆◆◆

biodiversity the diversity of species

ecotourism tourism based on viewing wildlife

THE ANTHROPOLOGIST AT WORK

In the small country of Yemen on the Arabian peninsula, virtually all adult men wear daggers at their waists. Many of these daggers have handles carved from rhinocerous horn, the traditional material (Varisco 1989:215). Rhinos are not native to Yemen, so horn for dagger handles is imported from East Africa. But the rhino is a gravely endangered species. Unless the killing of rhinos for their horns ceases, these creatures will soon become extinct. In 1982, in response to this problem, the Yemeni government banned the importation of rhino horn, but some Yemenis value it so highly that international smuggling of rhino horns continues.

In 1987, anthropologist Dan Varisco, working for the World Wildlife Fund, went to Yemen to study the cultural significance of the Yemeni dagger, assess local awareness of the plight of the rhino, and develop a strategy to reduce the demand for rhino horn and thus help promote conservation of these endangered animals. Varisco found that wearing a dagger symbolizes a Yemeni man's honor and ability to defend himself and serves as a "potent symbol of Yemeni identity" (Varisco 1989:217). Although there seems to be no intrinsic reason why a dagger's handle should be made of rhino horn, this material is valued because it becomes translucent with age, eventually resembling highly prized amber. Thus daggers with rhino horn handles, expensive (at around $1,500) to begin with, increase in value with age. Even though younger Yemeni males are not as interested in daggers as their fathers were, most fathers still want to purchase rhino horn daggers for their sons because of their increasing value in a part of the world where there are relatively few safe investments. Varisco predicts that rhino horn will be in great demand in Yemen for some time to come.

He also predicts that it will be impossible to stop the trade in rhino horn until alternative materials acceptable to the local people are promoted. Warning that there are no easy, short-term solutions to the problem, he has proposed a multistep plan to help save the rhinocerous. The steps include developing a synthetic alternative to rhino horn and promoting efforts to conserve Yemen's own wildlife species, an initiative that would raise awareness of the value of conservation and might eventually create a climate more favorable for reducing the demand for rhino horn. But perhaps the most important step is education. Most Yemenis do not even realize the rhino is in danger of extinction.

---

of illness on cultures, and how health care is provided in developing countries (Hull 1991; Pillsbury 1991).

The close link between AIDS and various aspects of culture has made this socially transmitted disease a focus of much anthropological attention. Some anthropologists are helping to identify cultural factors that may inhibit or promote the spread of AIDS. For example, in Indonesia, people needing medicine prefer to take it by injection rather than orally. In view of the well-known impact of needle use on the spread of AIDS, Indonesian society may be at more risk of an AIDS epidemic than societies in which injections are not favored. Applied anthropologists are also helping to identify the social changes that result when AIDS strikes and possible measures to prevent this terrible disease.

Economic growth may raise local standards of living at the same time it brings about **diseases of affluence,** such as cancer, heart ailments, and diabetes. Poor nutrition, lack of exercise, stress, smoking, and overindulging in alcohol are some of the culprits. Non-Western societies are no longer exempt from diseases of affluence. In some Pacific island nations, the customary diet is changing from one based on high-fiber, low-fat foods like root crops, fresh fish, green leaves, and coconuts to one based on white flour or rice, canned meat, fish, and large quantities of sugar and salt. In Fiji, the

 ASK YOURSELF

A tropical rain forest contains medicinal plants known to cure AIDS. The people who live in the forest regard these plants as so sacred they refuse to allow them to be gathered. Should their national government ignore these people's religious beliefs to harvest plants that could save the lives of millions? Or should government adopt a hands-off policy? Do you see any other options?

In San Antonio, western Belize, Mayan herb gatherer Antonio Cuk prepares a medicinal herb for a traditional therapist. North Americans searching for ways to cure cancer, heart disease, and AIDS have recently begun to study the curative properties of plants used by non-Western healers.

proportion of total energy deriving from less nutritious imported foods has steadily increased: high enough at 43 percent in 1977, it had risen to 63 percent by 1981 (Hull 1990:25).

Some anthropologists are contributing to improved health through **ethnobotany,** the study of the way cultures classify local plants. Until recently, North American medical researchers paid little attention to the curative properties of the plants used in non-Western societies. Now they are increasingly turning to these plants in their quest for cures for AIDS, cancer, and heart disease. Pharmaceutical companies, scientists, governments, environmental conservationists, and indigenous healers are coming together in an unusual coalition in which all parties might profit.

CONCLUSION

Anthropologists are often tempted to view their discipline as one of the bricks in an ivory tower. Many still regard their work as a pure quest for scientific information, considering attempts to apply anthropology to practical ends as somehow unsuited to this lofty aim. One of our themes in this book has been that theoretical studies should be pursued alongside considerably more practical activities. Neither interest need suffer. This isn't a new idea; mixing theory with practice has had a long and respectable history within cultural anthropology. Franz Boas, who thought a knowledge of other cultures could be an antidote to racism, was an anthropological activist as early as 1919.

Anthropology can be put to work for both theoretical and applied purposes in every culture and subculture. Its research methods, its analytical techniques, and the huge wealth of empirical data anthropologists have accumulated give us a unique perspective on small-scale and large-scale societies, both Western and non-Western, past and present; on females and males; on rural people and urbanites; on the newly socialized and the elderly.

But whether we are able to take advantage of what anthropology offers depends on our ability to suspend value judgments arising from ethnocentrism. Sometimes it's hard to reject the view that our modern, industrialized, twentieth-century way of life is somehow "better" than that of other cultures. Most of us feel that despite the costs associated with energy use, houses with central heating make "better" homes than houses built around open fires because we're more comfortable breathing clean air in 72 degree surroundings than we would be in a cooler or smokier environment. Most of us also think passenger jets are "better" for transportation than donkeys because jets move people from place to place much faster. Not everyone would agree. And no such value judgments can be applied to other aspects of culture. No one can say whether the languages we speak, the ideas and beliefs we hold, or the customs we have devised to order our social lives represent improvements over the

diseases of affluence diseases that result from a rise in living standards

ethnobotany the study of the ways cultures classify local plants

languages, ideas, and customs of other cultures, past or present.

A conscious suspension of ethnocentricity is one of the best ways to put an education in cultural anthropology to use.

◆◆

SUMMARY

The word *change,* when applied to cultures, implies only difference; it does not imply improvement or even movement in the direction of greater complexity, which is why anthropologists prefer to view change as a process rather than equate it with progress. However, in the evolution of culture, there *has* been a general movement toward increasing complexity and (for Westerners, at least) improvement in at least one aspect of culture, the material.

Change can come from within a culture (internal change) or from outside it (external change). In ancient times, when cultures were more isolated from one another than they have been throughout the twentieth century, change was more apt to be internal—a product of environmental shifts or invention—than external. In more recent times, culture change has mainly resulted from contact between societies and has occurred very rapidly. The mechanism through which external change comes about is diffusion: the spread of ideas, customs, artifacts, or language from one culture to another, directly or indirectly.

Some changes are beneficial, some destructive. When beneficial, changes are often modified by the society that receives them. When destructive, they are sometimes resisted or rejected.

Small-scale societies are more apt to be victims than beneficiaries of "progress," and anthropologists are concerned about the plight of these societies as their cultures are eroded by ethnocide and their members face extermination by genocide. Contemporary ethnocide is taking place in Bosnia and on the island of Timor; and the Nazi attempt to exterminate the Jews was a notorious instance of genocide. Among the reasons for both policies is the desire of states to make all the residents within their frontiers conform to a single national ideology.

Development anthropologists are applied anthropologists involved in international development, a multidisciplinary effort intended to improve the well-being of the world's people, especially in the "developing" world. Development anthropology's aims, mainly practical ones, include assisting in international efforts to provide such basic needs as food, shelter, and health care. Beyond these fundamental goals are broader ones, such as increased economic production, improved technology, a more equitable distribution of resources, and environmental conservation.

This chapter concludes with a description of how development anthropologists concern themselves with three global problems: overpopulation, the loss of biodiversity, and poor health and nutrition. In helping to solve these and other problems, anthropologists can play an important part in the modern world.

◆◆

KEY TERMS

biodiversity
cultural diffusion
development anthropology
diffusionism
direct diffusion
diseases of affluence
ecotourism
ethnobotany
ethnocide
external change
genocide
great man theory
indirect diffusion
internal change
international development
top-down approach
Westernization

◆◆

SUGGESTED READINGS

Bodley, John H. 1985. *Anthropology and Contemporary Human Problems* (2nd ed.). Palo Alto, CA: Mayfield. An anthropological look at some of the most urgent problems we face today. The author discusses overconsumption, hunger, war, overpopulation, and the depletion of natural resources.

Bodley, John H. (ed.). 1988. *Tribal Peoples and Development Issues: A Global Overview.* Mountain View, CA: Mayfield. An outstanding collection of 39 articles yielding theoretical insights about cultural change and development and a wealth of empirical case studies from societies throughout the world.

Bodley, John H. 1990. *Victims of Progress* (3rd ed.). Mountain View, CA: Mayfield. This book gauges the impact of change on the indigenous cultures of the world. Among the many topics discussed are ethnocide, the effect of tourism on tribal people, progress and the quality of life, technological change, diseases of development, and ethnocentrism.

Cernea, Michael M. 1985. *Putting People First: Sociological Variables in Rural Development.* New York: Oxford University Press for the World Bank. A collection of articles on problems resulting from development projects in various countries. The editor is a noted social scientist affiliated with the World Bank.

Denslow, Julie Sloan, and Christine Padock (eds.). 1988. *People of the Tropical Rain Forest.* Berkeley: University of California Press. Twenty-three experts collaborated on this multidisciplinary study of how human beings use and misuse one of our most important natural resources. Case studies from Indonesia, Brazil, Africa, Thailand, Central America, and other regions are combined with more theoretical discussions on big business, logging, sustainability, resettlement, and native Americans' rights in Amazonia. Anthropologists are well represented.

West, Patrick C., and Steven R. Bechin (eds.). 1991. *Resident Peoples and National Parks: Social Dilemmas and Strategies in International Conservation.* Tucson: University of Arizona Press. Over two dozen articles dealing with the human problems raised by creating environmentally protected areas in South Korea, the United States, Nepal, Costa Rica, Israel, and other countries.

REFERENCES

Abdalla, Raqiya Haji Dualeh
    1982. *Sisters in Affliction: Circumcision and Infibulation of Women in Africa.* London: Zed Press.

Abu-Lughod, Lila
    1986. *Veiled Sentiments.* Berkeley: University of California Press.
    1987. Bedouin Blues. *Natural History* 98(7):24–32.

Ackroyd, Anne V.
    1984. Ethics in Relation to Informants, the Profession, and Governments. In Roy F. Ellen (ed.), *Environment, Subsistence, and System: The Ecology of Small-scale Social Formations,* pp. 133–154. Cambridge: Cambridge University Press.

Adam, Peter
    1992. *Art of the Third Reich.* New York: Abrams.

Adra, Najwa
    1985. Achievement and Play: Opposition in Yemeni Tribal Dancing. In *The Consulting Symposium on the Collecting and Documenting of the Traditional Music and Dance of the Arabian Gulf,* pp. 69–75. Doha, Qatar: Arab Gulf States Folklore Centre.
    1992. Personal communication.

Agar, Michael H.
    1980. *The Professional Stranger: An Informal Introduction to Ethnography.* New York: Academic Press.

American Anthropological Association
    1971. *Principles of Professional Responsibility.* Washington, DC: American Anthropological Association.

Anderson, Richard L.
    1992. *Art in Small-scale Societies* (2nd ed.). Englewood Cliffs, NJ: Prentice Hall.

Anthropology Today
    1988. News 4(3):29.

Ardrey, Robert
    1961. *African Genesis.* New York: Atheneum.

Arens, W.
    1981 (1976). Professional Football: An American Symbol and Ritual. In W. Arens and Susan P. Montague (eds.), *The American Dimension: Cultural Myths and Social Realities,* pp. 3–14. Sherman Oaks, CA: Alfred Publishing Co.

Århem, Kaj
    1985. *Pastoral Man in the Garden of Eden: The Maasai of Ngorongoro Conservation Area, Tanzania.* Uppsala, Sweden: University of Uppsala.

Armstrong, W. E.
    1967. Rossel Island Money: A Unique Monetary System. In George Dalton (ed.), *Tribal and Peasant Economies: Readings in Economic Anthropology,* pp. 246–253. Garden City, NY: American Museum of Natural History Press.

Austin, Charles
    1983, October 15. New Bible Text Makes God Male and Female. *New York Times,* pp. 1, 8.

Axtell, Roger E. (ed.)
    1985. *Dos and Taboos Around the World.* New York: Wiley.

Bachtiar, Harsja
1967. *Negri* Taram: A Minangkabau Village Community. In Koentjaraningrat (ed.), *Villages in Indonesia.* Ithaca, NY: Cornell University Press.

Bailey, F. G.
1965. Decisions by Consensus in Councils and Committees. In Michael Banton (ed.), *Political Systems and the Distribution of Power.* ASA Monographs 2. London: Tavistock Publications.

Barnes, J. A.
1981. Ethical and Political Compromise in Social Research. Ms. quoted and cited in Ackroyd (1984:154).

Barnes, Ruth, and Joanne B. Eicher (eds.)
1992. *Dress and Gender: Making and Meaning.* New York: Berg.

Barrett, Richard A.
1991. *Culture and Conduct* (2nd ed.). Belmont, CA: Wadsworth.

Barringer, Felicity
1992, July 17. Rates of Marriage Continue Decline. *New York Times,* p. A20.

Barth, Frederik (ed.)
1981. Ethnic Groups and Boundaries. *Process and Form in Social Life,* Vol. I, pp. 198–227. London: Routledge & Kegan Paul.

Bateson, Gregory (ed.)
1972. Style, Grace and Information in Primitive Art. *Steps to an Ecology of Mind: Collected Essays in Anthropology, Psychiatry, Evolution, and Epistemology,* pp. 128–152. San Francisco: Chandler Publishing.

Beals, Alan R.
1980. *Gopalpur: A South Indian Village.* New York: Holt, Rinehart & Winston.

Beck, L.
1980. Herd Owners and Hired Shepherds: The Qashgai of Iran. *Ethnology* 19(3):327–351.

Bender, Barbara
1975. *Farming in Prehistory: From Hunter-Gatherer to Food Producer.* London: John Baker.

Benedict, Ruth
1989 (1934). *Patterns of Culture.* Boston: Houghton Mifflin.

Benthall, Jonathan
1988. The Bonham's Head Affair. *Anthropology Today* 4(4):1–2.

Berger, Joseph
1987, June 18. Goetz Verdict: Race, Fear, and the Nature of Urban Life. *New York Times,* p. 6B.

Berman, Paul (ed.)
1992. *Debating P.C.: The Controversy over Political Correctness on College Campuses.* New York: Laurel/Dell.

Boas, Franz
1897. *The Social Organization and the Secret Societies of the Kwakiutl Indians.* Report of the U.S. National Museum, 1895. Washington, DC: U.S. National Museum.

1966. *Kwakiutl Ethnography* (Helen Codère, ed.). Chicago: University of Chicago Press.
1973 (1919). Scientists as Spies. In Thomas Weaver (ed.), *To See Ourselves: Anthropology and Modern Social Issues,* pp. 51–52. Glenview, IL: Scott, Foresman.

Bock, Philip K.
1988 (1980). *Rethinking Psychological Anthropology: Continuity and Change in the Study of Human Action.* New York: W. H. Freeman.

Bodley, John H.
1988. The World Bank Tribal Policy: Criticisms and Recommendations. In John H. Bodley (ed.), *Tribal Peoples and Development Issues: A Global Overview,* pp. 406–413. Mountain View, CA: Mayfield.

Boe, S. Kathryn
1987. Language as an Expression of Caring in Women. *Anthropological Linguistics* 29(3):271–285.

Bott, Elizabeth
1971. *Family and Social Networks* (2nd ed.). London: Tavistock Publications.

Boyer, Paul, and Stephen Nissenbaum
1974. *Salem Possessed: The Social Origins of Witchcraft.* Cambridge, MA: Harvard University Press.

Brandes, Stanley
1985. Women of Southern Spain: Aspirations, Fantasies, Realities. In David D. Gilmore and Gretchen Gwynne (eds.), Sex and Gender in Southern Europe: Problems and Prospects. *Anthropology* 3(1–2):111–128.

Brooke, James
1991, 19 November. Brazil Creates Reserve for Imperiled Amazon Tribe. *New York Times,* p. A3.

Burkhalter, S. Brian
1986, June. The Anthropologist in Marketing. In Hendrick Serrie (ed.), *Anthropology and International Business,* pp. 113–124. Studies in Third World Societies, Publication No. 28. Williamsburg, VA: Department of Anthropology, College of William and Mary.

Burton, Michael, Lilyan Brudner, and Douglas White
1977. A Model of the Sexual Division of Labor. *American Ethnologist* 4(2):227–251.

CNP (Consejo Nacional de Poblacion)
1984. *Guia Demografica y Socioeconomica.* Lima, Peru: CNP.

Callender, Charles, and Lee M. Kochems
1983. The North American Berdache. *Current Anthropology* 24(4):443–470.

Cameron, Deborah
1989. Lakoff in Context: The Social and Linguistic Functions of Tag Questions. In Jennifer Coates and Deborah Cameron (eds.), *Women in Their Speech Communities: New Perspectives on Language and Sex,* pp. 74–93. White Plains, NY: Longman.

Campbell, J. K.
1964. *Honour, Family, and Patronage: A Study of Institutions and Moral Values in a Greek Mountain Community.* Oxford: Clarendon Press.

Carneiro, Robert L.
1970. A Theory of the Origin of the State. *Science* 69:733–738.
1978. Political Expansion as an Expression of the Principle of Competitive Exclusion. In

Ronald Cohen and Elman R. Service (eds.), *Origins of the State: The Anthropology of Political Evolution,* pp. 205–223. Philadelphia: Institute for the Study of Human Issues.

Carrier, J. M.
1980. Homosexual Behavior in Cross-Cultural Perspective. In Judd Marmor (ed.), *Homosexual Behavior,* pp. 100–122. New York: Basic Books.

Carroll, J. B. (ed.)
1956. *Language, Thought and Reality: Selected Writings of Benjamin Lee Whorf.* Cambridge, MA: M.I.T. Press.

Chagnon, Napoleon
1983. *Yanomamo: The Fierce People* (3rd ed.). New York: Holt, Rinehart & Winston.
1992. *Yanomamo* (4th ed.). Orlando: Harcourt Brace Jovanovich.

Chodorow, Nancy
1974. Family Structure and Female Personality. In Michelle Rosaldo and Louise Lamphere (eds.), *Women, Culture, and Society,* pp. 43–66. Stanford, CA: Stanford University Press.

Chomsky, Noam
1972. *Language and Mind* (2nd ed.). New York: Harcourt Brace Jovanovich.

Clammer, John
1984. Approaches to Ethnographic Research. In Roy Ellen (ed.), *Ethnographic Research: A Guide to General Conduct,* pp. 63–85. ASA Research Methods in Social Anthropology No. 1. London: Academic Press.

Clatts, Michael
1991. Order and Change in a Southeast Asian Community: An Ethnographic Perspective on Development Initiatives. Ph.D. dissertation, Department of Anthropology, State University of New York at Stony Brook.

Clendinnen, Inga
1987. *Ambivalent Conquests: Maya and Spaniard in Yucatan, 1517–1570.* Cambridge: Cambridge University Press.
1991. *Aztecs: An Interpretation.* Cambridge: Cambridge University Press.

Clifford, James, and George E. Marcus (eds.)
1986. *Writing Culture: The Poetics and Politics of Ethnography.* Berkeley: University of California Press.

Cohen, A. P.
1984. Types of Informant. In Roy Ellen (ed.), *Ethnographic Research: A Guide to General Conduct,* pp. 63–85. ASA Research Methods in Social Anthropology No. 1. London: Academic Press.

Cohen, Ronald, and Elman R. Service (eds.)
1978. Classical and Modern Theories of the Origins of Government. *Origins of the State: The Anthropology of Political Evolution,* pp. 21–34. Philadelphia: Institute for the Study of Human Issues.

Coles, Catherine, and Beverly Mack (eds.)
1991. *Hausa Women in the Twentieth Century.* Madison: University of Wisconsin Press.

Collinge, N. E. (ed.)
1990. *An Encyclopaedia of Language.* London: Routledge.

Comaroff, Jean
    1985. *Body of Power, Spirit of Resistance: The Culture and History of a South African People.* Chicago: University of Chicago Press.

Coote, Jeremy, and Anthony Shelton (eds.)
    1992. *Anthropology, Art and Aesthetics.* Oxford: Clarendon Press.

Corwin, Miles
    1984, December 7. It's Only a Cardboard Box—But It's Home to Them. *Los Angeles Times,* Part 1, pp. 3, 24.

Crystal, David
    1975. Paralinguistics. In Jonathan Benthall and Ted Polhemus (eds.), *The Body as a Medium of Expression,* pp. 162–174. New York: E. P. Dutton.

Cushing, Frank Hamilton
    1896. *Outlines of Zuni Creation Myths.* Bureau of American Ethnology Annual Report, No. 16. Washington, DC: Smithsonian Institute.
    1990. *Cushing at Zuni: The Correspondence and Journals of Frank Hamilton Cushing, 1879–1884,* Jesse Green, ed. Albuquerque: University of New Mexico Press.

D'Emilio, John, and Estelle B. Freedman
    1988. *Intimate Matters: A History of Sexuality in America.* New York: Harper & Row.

Dahlberg, Frances (ed.)
    1981. *Woman the Gatherer.* New Haven, CT: Yale University Press.

Dalton, Bill
    1988. *Indonesia Handbook* (4th ed.). Chico, CA: Moon Publications.

Dalton, George
    1968. Economic Theory and Primitive Society. In Edward E. LeClair and Harold K. Schneider (eds.), *Economic Anthropology: Readings in Theory and Analysis,* pp. 143–167. New York: Holt, Rinehart & Winston.

Delmonaco, Joe
    1986. "Communicative Tension" in Rural Greece: Toward a General Theory of the Evil Eye. Unpublished manuscript.

Demos, John Putnam
    1983. *Entertaining Satan: Witchcraft and the Culture of Early New England.* New York: Oxford University Press.

Dentan, Robert Knox
    1979. *The Semai: A Nonviolent People of Malaya.* New York: Holt, Rinehart & Winston.

Dinnerstein, Dorothy
    1990 (1976). *The Mermaid and the Minotaur: Sexual Arrangements and Human Malaise.* New York: Harper Perennial.

Doughty, Paul L.
    1987. Vicos: Success, Rejection, and Rediscovery of a Classic Program. In Elizabeth M. Eddy and William L. Partridge (eds.), *Applied Anthropology in America* (2nd ed.), pp. 433–459. New York: Columbia University Press.

Dover, K. J.
    1989. *Greek Homosexuality.* Cambridge, MA: Harvard University Press.

DuBois, Cora
> 1961 (1944). *The People of Alor: A Social-Psychological Study of an East Indian Island.* New York: Harper Torchbooks.

Dubin, Lois Sherr
> 1987. *The History of Beads.* New York: Abrams.

Dundes, Alan
> 1968. The Number Three in American Culture. In Alan Dundes (ed.), *Every Man His Way: Readings in Cultural Anthropology,* pp. 401–424. Englewood Cliffs, NJ: Prentice-Hall.
> 1981. *The Evil Eye: A Casebook.* New York: Garland Publ.
> 1989. *Folklore Matters.* Knoxville: University of Tennessee Press.

Dunkel, Tom
> 1992, January 13. A New Breed of People Gazers. *Insight,* pp. 10–13.

Durkheim, Émile
> 1938 (1895). *The Rules of the Sociological Method* (S. Solovay and J. Meuller, trans.). New York: Free Press.
> 1965 (1915). *The Elementary Forms of the Religious Life.* New York: Free Press.

Earle, Timothy
> 1989. The Evolution of Chiefdoms. *Current Anthropology* 30(1):84–88.

Ellen, Roy
> 1982. *Environment, Subsistence, and System: The Ecology of Small-scale Social Formations.* Cambridge: Cambridge University Press.
> 1984. *Ethnographic Research: A Guide to General Conduct.* ASA Research Methods in Social Anthropology 1. London: Academic Press.

Ellis, Pat (ed.)
> 1986. *Women of the Caribbean.* London: Zed Books.

Escobar, Arturo
> 1991. Anthropology and the Development Encounter: The Making and Marketing of Development Anthropology. *American Ethnologist* 18:658–682.

Evans-Pritchard, E. E.
> 1940. *The Nuer.* Oxford: Clarendon Press.
> 1951. *Social Anthropology.* London: Cohen & West.
> 1962. *Essays in Social Anthropology.* London: Faber & Faber.
> 1965. *Theories of Primitive Religion.* Oxford: Clarendon Press.
> 1971. *The Azande: History and Political Institutions.* Oxford: Clarendon Press.
> 1974 (1956). *Nuer Religion.* Oxford: Clarendon Press.
> 1985 (1937). *Witchcraft, Oracles and Magic Among the Azande* (Abridged, with an introduction by Eva Gillies). Oxford: Clarendon Press.

Fallers, Lloyd
> 1977. Equality and Inequality in Human Societies. In Sol Tax and L. Freeman (eds.), *Horizons of Anthropology* (2nd ed.), pp. 257–268. Chicago: Aldine.

Farb, Peter
> 1978. *Humankind.* Boston: Houghton Mifflin.

Faris, James C.
> 1972. *Nuba Personal Art.* Toronto: University of Toronto Press.

Feeley-Harnick, Gillian
> 1985. Issues in Divine Kingship. In *Annual Review of Anthropology* 14:273–313.

Ferguson, R. Brian, and Leslie Farragher
    1988. *The Anthropology of War: A Bibliography.* New York: Harry Frank Guggenheim Foundation.

Fernandez, James
    1971. Principles of Opposition and Vitality in Fang Aesthetics. In Carol F. Jopling (ed.), *Art and Aesthetics in Primitive Societies,* pp. 356–373. New York: E. P. Dutton.

Fernea, Elizabeth W., and Robert A. Fernea
    1987. Behind the Veil. In James P. Spradley and David W. McCurdy (eds.), *Conformity and Conflict: Readings in Cultural Anthropology* (6th ed.), pp. 104–112. Boston: Little, Brown.

Firth, Raymond
    1950. The Peasantry of South East Asia. *International Affairs* 26(4):503–514.
    1963 (1936). *We the Tikopia* (Abridged by the author). Boston: Beacon Press.

Fisher, Helen
    1992. *Anatomy of Love: The Natural History of Monogamy, Adultery, and Divorce.* New York: W. W. Norton.

Flannery, Kent V.
    1973. The Origins of Agriculture. *Annual Review of Anthropology* 2:271–310.

Ford, Clellan S., and Frank A. Beach
    1951. *Patterns of Sexual Behavior.* New York: Harper and Brothers, and Paul B. Hoeber, Inc., Medical Books.

Forde, Daryll
    1961. The Governmental Roles of Associations among the Yako. *Africa* 31(4):309–323.

Forth, Gregory L.
    1981. *Rindi: An Ethnographic Study of a Traditional Domain in Eastern Sumba.* Verhandelingen van het Koninklijk Instituut voor Taal-, Land- En Volkenkunde 93. The Hague: Martinus Nijhoff.

Fortune, R. F.
    1989 (1932). *Sorcerers of Dobu.* Prospect Heights, Illinois: Waveland, Inc.

Foster, George M.
    1965. Peasant Society and the Image of the Limited Good. *American Anthropologist* 67:293–315.
    1972. A Second Look at the Limited Good. *Journal of American Folklore* 83:304–317.

Fox, Robin
    1983 (1967). *Kinship and Marriage: An Anthropological Perspective.* New York: Cambridge University Press.

Frankenberg, Ronald
    1957. *Village on the Border.* London: Cohen & West.

Fraser, Douglas
    1972. The Symbols of Ashanti Kingship. In Douglas Fraser and Herbert M. Cole (eds.), *African Art and Leadership,* pp. 137–152. Madison: University of Wisconsin Press.

Frayser, Suzanne G.
    1985. *Varieties of Sexual Experience: An Anthropological Perspective on Human Sexuality.* New Haven: HRAF Press.

Frazer, Sir James George
  1966 (1922). *The Golden Bough: A Study in Magic and Religion* (abridged ed.). New York: Macmillan.

Freedman, Maurice
  1967. *Rites and Duties, or Chinese Marriage.* London: G. Bell & Sons.
  1970. Ritual Aspects of Chinese Kinship and Marriage. In Maurice Freedman (ed.), *Family and Kinship in Chinese Society,* pp. 163–187. Stanford, CA: Stanford University Press.

Freud, Sigmund
  1918. *Totem and Taboo.* New York: A. A. Brill.

Friedl, Ernestine
  1984. *Women and Men: An Anthropologist's View*. Prospect Heights, IL: Waveland Press.
  1985 (1978). Society and Sex Roles. In David E. K. Hunter and Phillip Whitten (eds.), *Anthropology: Contemporary Perspectives* (4th ed.), pp. 228–232. Boston: Little, Brown.

Fromkin, Victoria, and Robert Rodman
  1988. *An Introduction to Language* (4th ed.). Forth Worth, TX: Holt, Rinehart & Winston.

Gailey, Christine Ward
  1987. *Kinship to Kingship: Gender Hierarchy and State Formation in the Tongan Islands.* Austin: University of Texas Press.

Galbraith, John Kenneth
  1983. *The Anatomy of Power.* Boston: Houghton Mifflin.

Gardner, John, and John Maier
  1985. *Gilgamesh* (trans. from the Sin-leqi-unnini version). New York: Vintage Books.

Geertz, Clifford
  1966. Religion as a Cultural System. In Michael Banton (ed.), *Anthropological Approaches to the Study of Religion.* A.S.A. Monographs 3. London: Tavistock Publications.
  1973. *The Interpretation of Cultures.* New York: Basic Books.

George, Alexander (ed.)
  1989. *Reflections on Chomsky.* Oxford: Basil Blackwell.

Gilligan, Carol
  1982. *In a Different Voice: Psychological Theory and Women's Development.* Cambridge, MA: Harvard University Press.

Gilmore, David D., and Gretchen Gwynne (eds.)
  1985. *Sex and Gender in Southern Europe: Problems and Prospects.* Anthropology Special Issues #3. Stony Brook: Department of Anthropology, State University of New York.

Givens, David B., and Susan N. Skomal
  1992. The Four Fields: Myth or Reality? *Anthropology Newsletter* 33(7):1,17.

Gluckman, Max
  1969. Concepts in the Comparative Study of Tribal Law. In Laura Nader (ed.), *Law in Culture and Society,* pp. 349–373. Chicago: Aldine.

Gmelch, George
  1985 (1971). Baseball Magic. In Arthur C. Lehman and James E. Myers (eds.), *Magic, Witchcraft, and Religion: An Anthropological Study of the Supernatural* (2nd ed.), pp. 231–235. Mountain View, CA: Mayfield.

Gmelch, George, and Walter P. Zenner (eds.)
1980. *Urban Life: Readings in Urban Anthropology.* New York: St. Martin's Press.

Golden, Tim
1992, June 11. Catemaco Journal: Magic That Gives Both God and Devil Their Due. *New York Times,* p. A4.

Goldman, Irving
1980. Boas on the Kwakiutl: The Ethnographic Tradition. In Stanley Diamond (ed.), *Theory and Practice: Essays Presented to Gene Weltfish.* The Hague: Mouton.

Goldstein, Melvyn C.
1987. When Brothers Share a Wife. *Natural History* 96(3):39–48.

Gombrich, E. H.
1979a, September 27. Letter. *The New York Review of Books.*
1979b. *The Sense of Order.* Ithaca, NY: Cornell University Press.

Gonzalez, Nancie L.
1972. Patron-Client Relationships at the International Level. In Arnold Strickon and Sidney M. Greenfield (eds.), *Structure and Process in Latin America,* pp. 179–210. Albuquerque: University of New Mexico Press.
1974. The City of Gentlemen: Santiago de los Caballeros. In George M. Foster and Robert V. Kemper (eds.), *Anthropologists in Cities,* pp. 19–40. Boston: Little, Brown.
1984. The Anthropologist as Female Head of Household. *Feminist Studies* 10(1):97–114.

Goody, Jack (ed.)
1981. *Literacy in Traditional Society.* New York: Cambridge University Press.

Goody, Jack, and S. J. Tambiah
1973. *Bridewealth and Dowry.* Cambridge: Cambridge University Press.

Gough, Kathleen
1962. Nayar: Central Kerala. In David M. Schneider and Kathleen Gough (eds.), *Matrilineal Kinship,* pp. 298–384. Berkeley: University of California Press.

Gregory, James R.
1975. Image of Limited Good, or Expectation of Reciprocity? *Current Anthropology* 16:73–92.

Grönewald, Sylvia
1972. Did Frank Hamilton Cushing Go Native? In Solon T. Kimball and James B. Watson (ed.), *Crossing Cultural Boundaries.* New York: Chandler & Sharp.

Gross, Jane
1992, March 1. Does She Speak for Today's Women? *New York Times Magazine,* pp. 16–19, 38, 54.

Gulliver, P. H.
1969. Dispute Settlement without Courts: The Ndendeuli of Southern Tanzania. In Laura Nader (ed.), *Law in Culture and Society,* pp. 24–68. Chicago: Aldine.

Haas, Jack
1984. A Study of High Steel Ironworkers' Reactions to Fear and Danger. In Herbert Applebaum (ed.), *Work in Market and Industrial Societies,* pp. 103–119. Albany: State University of New York Press.

Hadingham, Evan
1979. *Secrets of the Ice Age.* New York: Walker and Co.

Hall, Edward T., and Mildred Reed Hall
    1987 (1971). The Sounds of Silence. In James P. Spradley and David W. McCurdy (eds.),
    Conformity and Conflict: Readings in Cultural Anthropology (6th ed.), pp. 80–92.
    Boston: Little, Brown.

Hallpike, C. R.
    1973. Functionalist Interpretations of Primitive Warfare. *Man* 8:451–470.

Hamilton, David. L.
    1991. Stereotypes and Language Use. In Gun R. Semin and Klaus Fiedler (eds.), *Language, Interaction and Social Cognition,* pp. 102–128. London: Sage.

Hardin, Kris L.
    1988. Aesthetics and the Cultural Whole: A Study of Kono Dance Occasions. *Empirical Studies of the Arts* 6(1):35–57.

Harris, Marvin
    1968. *The Rise of Anthropological Theory.* New York: Thomas Y. Crowell.
    1993. *Culture, People, Nature* (6th ed.). New York: HarperCollins.

Headland, Thomas N. (ed.)
    1992. *The Tasaday Controversy: Assessing the Evidence.* AAA Scholarly Series Special Publication No. 28. Washington, DC: American Anthropological Association.

Heider, Karl
    1979. *Grand Valley Dani: Peaceful Warriors.* New York: Holt, Rinehart & Winston.

Heller, Monica (ed.)
    1988. *Codeswitching: Anthropological and Sociolinguistic Perspectives.* New York: Mouton de Gruyter.

Henretta, James, W. Elliot Brownlee, David Brody, and Susan Ware
    1987. *America's History.* Chicago: Dorsey Press.

Henry, Jules
    1964. *Jungle People: A Kaingáng Tribe of the Highlands of Brazil.* New York: Random House.

Herdt, Gilbert, and Robert J. Stoller
    1986. *Intimate Communications: Erotics and the Study of Culture.* New York: Columbia University Press.

Herzfeld, Michael
    1985. Gender Pragmatics: Agency, Speech and Bride-Theft in a Cretan Mountain Village. *Anthropology* IX(1–2):25–44.

Hewes, Gordon W.
    1973. Primate Communication and the Gestural Origin of Language. *Current Anthropology* 14(1–2):5–24.

Hicks, David
    1984. Getting into the Field and Establishing Routines. In Roy Ellen (ed.), *Ethnographic Research: A Guide to General Conduct,* pp. 192–197. ASA Research Methods in Social Anthropology No. 1. London: Academic Press.
    1988 (1976). *Tetum Ghosts and Kin.* Prospect Heights, IL: Waveland Press.
    1990. *Kinship and Religion in Eastern Indonesia.* Gothenburg: Acta Universitatis Gothenburgensis.
    1991. The Timor Civil War. Manuscript.

Hobsbawm, Eric, and Terence Ranger (eds.)
1992. *The Invention of Tradition.* Cambridge: Cambridge University Press.

Hoebel, E. Adamson
1964. *The Law of Primitive Man.* Cambridge, MA: Harvard University Press.
1978. *The Cheyennes: Indians of the Great Plains.* New York: Holt, Rinehart & Winston.

Hoffman, Jan
1992, February 23. When Men Hit Women. *New York Times Magazine,* pp. 22–27, 65–66, 72.

Holm, John
1989. *Pidgins and Creoles* (2 vols.). New York: Cambridge University Press.

Holy, Ladislav
1984. Theory, Methodology and the Research Process. In Roy F. Ellen (ed.), *Ethnographic Research: A Guide to General Conduct,* pp. 13–34. ASA Research Methods in Social Anthropology 1. London: Academic Press.

Horowitz, I. L. (ed.)
1967. *The Rise and Fall of Project Camelot: Studies in the Relationship between Social Science and Practical Politics.* Cambridge, MA: M.I.T. Press.

Hudson, R. A.
1980. *Sociolinguistics.* Cambridge: Cambridge University Press.

Hull, Valerie
1991. Health and Development: Seeking the Best of Both Worlds. *Cultural Survival Quarterly* 15(2):24–27.

Huntington, Richard
1988. *Gender and Social Structure in Madagascar.* Bloomington and Indianapolis: Indiana University Press.

Hutchinson, Ellen
1977. Order and Chaos in the Cosmology of the Baffin Island Eskimo. *Anthropology* I(2):120–138.

Itard, Jean-Marc-Gaspard
1962 (1932). *The Wild Boy of Aveyron.* New York: Appleton-Century-Crofts.

Iten, Oswald
1986, June. The Tasaday: A Stone Age Swindle. *Swiss Review of World Affairs,* pp. 14–19.

Jacobs, Norman
1966. *The Sociology of Development: Iran as an Asian Case Study.* New York: Praeger.

Jankowiak, William R., and Edward F. Fisher
1992. A Cross-Cultural Perspective on Romantic Love. *Ethnology* 31:149–155.

Kaiser, Susan B.
1990. *The Social Psychology of Clothing* (2nd ed.). New York: Macmillan.

Kardiner, Abram
1945. *The Psychological Frontiers of Society.* New York: Columbia University Press.

Kehoe, Alice Beck
1989. *The Ghost Dance: Ethnohistory and Revitalization.* New York: Holt, Rinehart & Winston.

Kelly, Raymond
1976. Witchcraft and Sexual Relations. In P. Brown and G. Buchbinder (eds.), *Man and Woman in the New Guinea Highlands,* pp. 36–53. Special Publications No. 8. Washington, DC: American Anthropological Association.

Kennedy, John
1966. Peasant Society and the Image of the Limited Good: A Critique. *American Anthropologist* 68:1212–1225.

King, Victor T.
1985. *The Maloh of West Kalimantan: An Ethnographic Study of Social Inequality and Social Change among an Indonesian People.* Verhandelingen van het Koninklijk Instituut voor Taal-, Land-en Volkenkunde 108. Dordrecht-Holland: Cinnaminson-U.S.A. Floris Publications.

Kinsey, Alfred C., Wardell B. Pomeroy, and Clyde E. Martin
1948. *Sexual Behavior in the Human Male.* Philadelphia: W. B. Saunders.

Kinsey, Alfred C., Wardell B. Pomeroy, Clyde E. Martin, and Paul H. Gebhart
1953. *Sexual Behavior in the Human Female.* Philadelphia: W. B. Saunders.

Kuper, Adam
1985. *Anthropology and Anthropologists: The Modern British School* (rev. ed.). Boston: Routledge & Kegan Paul.

Labov, William
1984 (1972). *Language in the Inner City: Studies in the Black English Vernacular.* Philadelphia: University of Pennsylvania Press.
1988. The Judicial Testing of Linguistic Theory. In Deborah Tannen (ed.), *Linguistics in Context: Connecting Observation and Understanding: Advances in Discourse Processes,* p. 24. Norwood, NJ: Ablex.

Ladurie, Emmanuel LeRoy
1979. *Montaillou: The Promised Land of Error* (Barbara Bray, trans.). New York: Vintage Books.

Lakoff, Robin
1975. *Language and Woman's Place.* New York: Harper & Row.

Landsberg, Marge E.
1988. *The Genesis of Language: A Different Judgement of Evidence.* New York: Mouton de Gruyter.

Lavi, Zvi
1990. *Kibbutz Members Study Kibbutz Children.* New York: Greenwood Press.

Leach, Edmund
1963. *Rethinking Anthropology.* London: Athlone Press.

Lederman, Rena
1990. Big Men, Large and Small? Towards a Comparative Perspective. *Ethnology* 19(1):3–15.

Lee, Dorothy
1985 (1950). How Languages Code Reality. In David E. K. Hunter and Phillip Whitten (eds.), *Anthropology: Contemporary Perspectives* (4th ed.), pp. 108–115. Boston: Little, Brown.

Lee, Richard
    1969 (1966). !Kung Bushman Subsistence: An Input-Output Analysis. In A. P. Vayda
    (ed.), *Environment and Cultural Behavior.* New York: Natural History Press.
    1984. *The Dobe !Kung.* New York: Holt, Rinehart & Winston.

Lehman, Arthur C., and James E. Myers (eds.)
    1989. *Magic, Witchcraft, and Religion: An Anthropological Study of the Supernatural*
    (2nd ed.). Mountain View, CA: Mayfield.

Lerner, Gerda
    1986. *The Creation of Patriarchy.* New York: Oxford University Press.

Lévi-Strauss, Claude
    1969 (French ed., 1949). *The Elementary Structures of Kinship.* Boston: Beacon Press.
    1983 (1967). *Structural Anthropology.* Chicago: University of Chicago Press.

Lewis, I. M.
    1986. *Religion in Context: Cults and Charisma.* Cambridge: Cambridge University Press.
    1989. *Ecstatic Religion: An Anthropological Study of Spirit Possession and Shamanism*
    (2nd ed.). London: Routledge.

Lewis, Oscar
    1961. *The Children of Sanchez: Autobiography of a Mexican Family.* New York: Ran-
    dom House.
    1966a. The Culture of Poverty. *Scientific American* 215:19–25.
    1966b. *La Vida: A Puerto Rican Family in the Culture of Poverty—San Juan and New
    York.* New York: Random House.

Lieberman, Philip
    1984. *The Biology and Evolution of Language.* Cambridge, MA: Harvard University
    Press.

Liebow, Elliot
    1967. *Tally's Corner.* Boston: Little, Brown.

Lightfoot-Klein, Hannie
    1989. *Prisoners of Ritual: An Odyssey into Female Genital Circumcision in Africa.* New
    York and London: Haworth Press.

Lindholm, Cherry, and Charles Lindholm
    1985 (1980). Life Behind the Veil. In David E. K. Hunter and Phillip Whitten (eds.), *An-
    thropology: Contemporary Perspectives* (4th ed.), pp. 233–236. Boston: Little, Brown.

Lindsey, Robert
    1988, February 1. Circumcision under Criticism as Unnecessary to Newborn. *New York
    Times,* p. A1, 20.

Little, Kenneth
    1982. The Role of Voluntary Associations in West African Urbanization. In Johnetta B.
    Cole (ed.), *Anthropology for the Eighties: Introductory Readings,* pp. 174–194. New
    York: Free Press.

Livingstone, Frank
    1969. Genetics, Ecology, and the Origins of Incest and Exogamy. *Current Anthropology*
    10:45–62.

Locke, John
    1979 (1690). *An Essay Concerning Human Understanding* (Peter H. Nidditch, ed.). Ox-
    ford: Clarendon Press.

Lorenz, Konrad
  1963. *On Aggression* (Marjorie Kerr Wilson, trans.). New York: Harcourt, Brace & World.

Lowie, Robert H.
  1970 (1948). *Primitive Religion.* New York: Liveright.

Lurie, Alison
  1981. *The Language of Clothes.* New York: Random House.

MacClancy, Jeremy
  1990. Primitive Thinking about Sophisticated Art. *Anthropology Today* 6(4):1–2.

Macfarlane, Alan
  1990. *Witchcraft in Tudor and Stuart England: A Regional and Comparative Study.* Prospect Heights, IL: Waveland Press, Inc.

Malcolm, Andrew H.
  1979, October 23. In Hands of Stone Carvers, Eskimo Tradition Clings to Life. *New York Times,* p. A13.
  1981, February 1. A Dogrib Bible, "Enitl'e-cho," Takes Shape in Canada. *New York Times,* p. 14.

Malinowski, Bronislaw
  1927. *Sex and Repression in Savage Society.* London: Routledge & Kegan Paul.
  1954 (1948). *Magic, Science, and Religion.* New York: Doubleday.
  1962 (1929). *The Sexual Life of Savages in Northwestern Melanesia.* New York: Harcourt, Brace and World.
  1965 (1935). *Coral Gardens and Their Magic. Vol. I: Soil-Tilling and Agricultural Rites in the Trobriand Islands.* Bloomington: Indiana University Press.
  1978 (1926). *Crime and Custom in Savage Society.* London: Routledge and Kegan Paul.
  1984 (1922). *Argonauts of the Western Pacific.* Prospect Heights, IL: Waveland Press.

Mangin, William
  1979. Thoughts on Twenty-four Years of Work in Peru: The Vicos Project and Me. In George M. Foster, Thayer Scudder, Elizabeth Colson, and Robert V. Kemper (eds.), *Long-Term Field Research in Social Anthropology,* pp. 65–84. New York: Academic Press.

Marcus, E. George, and Dick Cushman
  1982. Ethnographies as Texts. *Annual Review of Anthropology* 11:25–69.

Margolis, Maxine
  1984. *Mothers and Such: American Views of Women and How They Changed.* Berkeley: University of California Press.

Marshack, Alexander
  1972. *The Roots of Civilization: The Cognitive Beginnings of Man's First Art, Symbol and Notation.* New York: McGraw-Hill.

Martin, Emily
  1987. *The Woman in the Body: A Cultural Analysis of Reproduction.* Boston: Beacon Press.

Martin, M. Kay, and Barbara Voorhies
  1975. *Female of the Species.* New York: Columbia University Press.

Martinez-Alier, Juan, and Eric Hershberg
  1992, March. Environmentalism and the Poor: The Ecology of Survival. *Items* 46(1):1–5. New York: Social Science Research Council.

Masson, Jeffrey Moussaieff (ed. and trans.)
1986. *A Dark Science: Women, Sexuality and Psychiatry in the Nineteenth Century.* New York: Farrar, Straus & Giroux.

Masters, William H., Virginia E. Johnson, and Robert C. Kolodny
1985. *Human Sexuality* (2nd ed.). Boston: Little, Brown.

Mattoon, Mary Ann
1981. *Jungian Psychology in Perspective.* New York: Free Press.

Mauss, Marcel
1979 (1950). *Seasonal Variations of the Eskimo: A Study in Social Morphology* (in collaboration with Henri Beuchat; James J. Fox, trans.). London: Routledge & Kegan Paul.
1990 (1920). *The Gift: Forms and Functions of Exchange in Archaic Societies* (W. D. Halls, trans.). London: Routledge.

Maybury-Lewis, David
1974 (1967). *Akwē-Shavante Society.* Oxford: Clarendon Press.
1988. A Special Sort of Pleading: Anthropology at the Service of Ethnic Groups. In John H. Bodley (ed.), *Tribal Peoples and Development Issues: A Global Overview,* pp. 375–390. Mountain View, CA: Mayfield.

McConochie, Roger P.
1992. Personal communication.

McKee, Lauris
1992. Men's Rights/Women's Wrongs: Domestic Violence in Ecuador. In Dorothy Ayers Counts et al. (eds.), *Sanctions and Sanctuary: Cultural Perspectives on the Beating of Wives,* pp. 139–156. Boulder, CO: Westview Press.

McKee, Victoria
1990, March 5. With My Body I Thee Threaten. *London Times,* p. 17.

Mead, Margaret
1963 (1935). *Sex and Temperament in Three Primitive Societies.* New York: Morrow.

Messina, Maria
1988. Henna Party. *Natural History* 97(9):40–46.

Midelfort, H. C. Erik
1972. *Witch Hunting in Southwestern Germany, 1562–1684: The Social and Intellectual Foundations.* Stanford, CA: Stanford University Press.

Milner, George R., and Clark Spencer Larsen
1991. Teeth as Artifacts of Human Behavior: Intentional Mutilation and Accidental Modification. In Marc A. Kelley and Clark Spencer Larsen (eds.), *Advances in Dental Anthropology,* pp. 357–378. New York: Wiley-Liss.

Mitchell, J. Clyde
1984. Social Network Data. In Roy Ellen (ed.), *Ethnographic Research: A Guide to General Conduct,* pp. 13–34. ASA Research Methods in Social Anthropology 1. London: Academic Press.

Money, John, and A. A. Ehrhardt
1977. *Man and Woman, Boy and Girl: The Differentiation and Dimorphism of Gender Identity from Conception to Maturity.* Baltimore: Johns Hopkins University Press.

Montagu, Ashley (ed.)
1968. *Man and Aggression.* New York: Oxford University Press.

Morphy, Howard
  1991. *Ancestral Connections: Art and an Aboriginal System of Knowledge.* Chicago: University of Chicago Press.

Morrill, Warren T., and Alice V. James
  1990. Modernization and Household Formation on St. Bart: Continuity and Change. *Human Ecology* 18(4):457–474.

Morris, Desmond
  1967. *The Naked Ape.* New York: McGraw-Hill.

Mother Earth News
  1984. Barter Mania 89:108.

Moynihan, Patrick
  1965. *The Negro Family: The Case for National Action.* Washington, DC: U.S. Government Printing Office.

Ms.
  1982, September. The Barter Brokers: From Backyard to Boardroom, pp. 70–72.

Mukhopadhyay, Carol C., and Patricia J. Higgins
  1988. Anthropological Studies of Women's Status Revisited: 1977–1988. *Annual Reviews of Anthropology* 17:461–495.

Murdock, George P.
  1957. World Ethnographic Sample. *American Anthropologist* 59:664–687.

Murphy, Gardner
  1966 (1947). *Personality: A Biosocial Approach to Origins and Structure.* New York: Harper & Brothers.

Murphy, William P.
  1978. Oral Literature. *Annual Review of Anthropology* 7:113–136.

Mydans, Seth
  1986, May 13. The Tasaday Revisited: A Hoax or Social Change at Work? *New York Times,* p. C3.
  1987, December 27. From Forest to Manila, Stranger in a Strange Land. *New York Times,* p. A16.

Nash, Nathaniel C.
  1992, March 30. Bolivia Is Helping Its Battered Wives to Stand Up. *New York Times.*

Nation's Business.
  1985. Barter Boom. 73:18–25.

Needham, Rodney
  1970. "Introduction." In Arthur Maurice Hocart, *Kings and Councillors: An Essay in the Comparative Anatomy of Human Society.* Chicago: University of Chicago Press.
  1974. *Remarks and Inventions: Skeptical Essays About Kinship.* London: Tavistock Publications.
  1975 (1963). Introduction to Durkheim, Émile, and Mauss, Marcel. In Rodney Needham (trans. and ed.), *Primitive Classification* (5th impression). Chicago: University of Chicago Press.

1978. *Primordial Characters.* Charlottesville: University Press of Virginia.

1979. *Symbolic Classification.* Santa Monica, CA: Goodyear Publishing Company.

1985. *Exemplars.* Berkeley: University of California Press.

Newsday

1979, August 2. Brother and Sister Guilty of Marrying Incestuously, p. 13.

New York Times

1986, March 11. Secrets of Bearing a Burden.

1986, March 27. Zimbabwe Still Divided on Rights for Women, p. A17.

1987, August 18. Town in Montana Endures as an Outpost of Polygamy, p. A18.

1987, September 20. India Seizes Four After Immolation, p. A15.

1987, November 22. From Subway Graffiti to the Canvas: Bronx Program Transforms Vandals, p. 68.

Obeyesekere, Gananath

1981. *Medusa's Hair: An Essay on Personal Symbols and Religious Experience.* Chicago: University of Chicago Press.

Offir, Carole W.

1982. *Human Sexuality.* New York: Harcourt Brace Jovanovich.

Ong, Walter

1982. *Orality and Literacy: The Technologizing of the Word.* London: Methuen.

Orion, Loretta Lee

In press. *Never Again the Burning Time: Paganism Revived.* Prospect Heights, IL: Waveland Press.

Parker, Sue Taylor, and Kathleen Rita Gibson

1979. A Developmental Model for the Evolution of Language and Intelligence in Early Hominids. *Behavioral and Brain Sciences* 2(3):83–85.

Pasztory, Esther

1989. Identity and Difference: The Uses and Meanings of Ethnic Styles. In Susan J. Barnes and Walter S. Melion (eds.), *Cultural Differentiation and Cultural Identity in the Visual Arts,* pp. 15–37. Hanover: University Press of New England.

Paul, Robert A.

1989. Psychoanalytic Anthropology. *Annual Review of Anthropology,* vol. 18, pp. 177–202. Palo Alto, CA: Annual Reviews.

Pfeiffer, John E.

1982. *The Creative Explosion: An Inquiry into the Origins of Art and Religion.* New York: Harper & Row.

Piddock, Stuart

1965. The Potlatch System of the Southern Kwakiutl: A New Perspective. *Southwestern Journal of Anthropology* 21:244–264.

Piker, Steven

1966. The Image of the Limited Good: Comments on an Exercise in Description and Interpretation. *American Anthropologist* 68:1202–1211.

Pilbeam, David

1972. *The Ascent of Man.* New York: Macmillan.

Pillsbury, Barbara L. K.
1991. International Health: Overview and Opportunities. In Carole E. Hill (ed.), *Training Manual in Applied Medical Anthropology,* pp. 54–87. Washington, DC: American Anthropological Association.

Plattner, Stuart (ed.)
1989. *Economic Anthropology.* Stanford, CA: Stanford University Press.

Podolefsky, Aaron
1984. Contemporary Warfare in the New Guinea Highlands. *Ethnology* 23(2):73–87.

Pohorecky, Zenon
1992. Personal communication, University of Saskatchewan, Saskatoon.

Polanyi, Karl
1971. The Economy as Instituted Process. In George Dalton (ed.), *Primitive, Archaic, and Modern Economies: Essays of Karl Polanyi,* pp. 139–174. Boston: Beacon Press.

Polanyi, Karl, Conrad M. Arensberg, and Harry W. Pearson
1957. *Trade and Market in the Early Empires.* Glencoe, IL: Free Press.

Polomé, Edgar C.
1990. Language and Behaviour: Anthropological Linguistics. In N. E. Collinge (ed.), *An Encyclopaedia of Language,* pp. 458–484. London: Routledge.

Pospisil, Leopold
1974. *Anthropology of Law: A Comparative Theory.* New Haven, CT: HRAF Press.

Price, Sally
1990. *Primitive Art in Civilized Places.* Chicago: University of Chicago Press.

Propp, Vladimir
1988 (1958). *Morphology of the Folktale* (Laurence Scott, trans.; 2nd ed., Louis A. Wagner, ed.). Austin: University of Texas Press.

Pryor, Frederic L.
1986. The Adoption of Agriculture: Some Theoretical and Empirical Evidence. *American Anthropologist* 88(4):879–897.

Quinn, Naomi
1977. Anthropological Studies on Women's Status. *Annual Review of Anthropology,* vol. 6, pp. 181–225. Palo Alto, CA: Annual Reviews.

Radcliffe-Brown, A. R.
1965 (1952). *Structure and Function in Primitive Society: Essays and Addresses.* New York: Free Press.

Redfield, Robert
1956. *Peasant Society and Culture.* Chicago: University of Chicago Press.

Renfrew, Colin
1987. *Archaeology and Language: The Puzzle of Indo-European Origins.* Cambridge: Cambridge University Press.

Reyes, Elma
1986. Women in Calypso. In Pat Ellis (ed.), *Women in the Caribbean,* pp. 119–121. London: Zed Books.

Rice, Otis K.
1978. *The Hatfields and the McCoys.* Lexington: University Press of Kentucky.

Rice, Patricia C., and Ann L. Paterson
1985. Cave Art and Bones: Exploring the Relationships. *American Anthropologist* 87(1):94–100.

Robarchek, Clayton A.
1989. Primitive Warfare and the Ratomorphic Image of Mankind. *American Anthropologist* 91(4):903–920.

Rosaldo, Michelle, and Louise Lamphere (eds.)
1974. *Women, Culture, and Society.* Stanford, CA: Stanford University Press.

Ruhlen, Merritt
1987. Voices from the Past. *Natural History* 96(3):6–10.

Sahlins, Marshall
1968 (1965). On the Sociology of Primitive Exchange. In Michael Banton (ed.), *The Relevance of Models for Social Anthropology* (2nd impression), pp. 139–236. London: Tavistock Publications.
1974. *Stone Age Economics.* London: Tavistock.

Saibull, Ole Solomon
1981. *Herd and Spear: The Masaai of East Africa.* London: Collins and Harvill Press.

Saitoti, Ole Tepilit
1988 (1986). *The Worlds of a Maasai Warrior.* Berkeley: University of California Press.

Sangren, P. Steven
1992 (1988). Rhetoric and the Authority of Ethnography. In Sydel Silverman (ed.), *Inquiry and Debate in the Human Sciences,* pp. 277–306. Chicago and London: University of Chicago Press.

Sarsby, Jacquie
1984. Gender Orientations in Fieldwork. In Roy Ellen (ed.), *Ethnographic Research,* pp. 118–132. London: Academic Press.

Schmandt-Besserat, Denise
1992. *Before Writing.* Austin: University of Texas Press.

Serrie, Hendrick (ed.)
1986. *Anthropology and International Business.* Studies in Third World Societies No. 28. Williamsburg, VA: Department of Anthropology, College of William and Mary.

Service, Elman R.
1971. *Primitive Social Organization: An Evolutionary Perspective.* 2nd edition. New York: Random House.

Shaara, Lila, and Andrew Strathern
1992. A Preliminary Analysis of the Relationship Between Altered States of Consciousness, Healing and Social Structure. *American Anthropologist* 94(1):145–160.

Shanin, Teodor (ed.)
1971. *Peasants and Peasant Societies.* Baltimore: Penguin.
1973. Peasantry: Delineation of a Sociological Concept and a Field of Study. *European Journal of Sociology* 12:289–300.

Shepher, Joseph
1983. *Incest: A Biosocial View.* New York: Academic Press.

Shoumatoff, Alex
    1985. *The Mountain of Names: A History of the Human Family.* New York: Simon & Schuster.

Silverblatt, Irene
    1988. Women in States. In *Annual Review of Anthropology,* Vol. 17, pp. 427–460. Palo Alto, CA: Annual Reviews.

Skar, Harald O.
    1985. *Anthropological Contributions to Planned Change and Development.* Gothenburg Studies in Social Anthropology, No. 8. Atlantic Highlands, NJ: Humanities Press.

Smith, Cyril Stanley
    1975. Aesthetic Curiosity—The Root of Invention. *New York Times,* August 24, 1975.

Spradley, James P.
    1970. *You Owe Yourself a Drunk: An Ethnography of Urban Nomads.* Boston: Little, Brown.

Stansell, Christine
    1987 (1986). *City of Women: Sex and Class in New York, 1789–1860.* Urbana: University of Illinois Press.

Stein, Steve
    1985. Health and Poverty within the Sociopolitical Context of Peru, 1985. Unpublished manuscript, Department of History, University of South Florida, Coral Gables.

Steward, Julian
    1955. *Theory of Culture Change.* Urbana: University of Illinois Press.

Stewart, Hilary
    1993. *Looking at Totem Poles.* Seattle: University of Washington Press.

Stewart, Jon
    1980. Every Man a Saint: Archives Beneath the Rocky Mountains. *Saturday Review* 7:8–9.

Stoller, Robert J.
    1968. *Sex and Gender.* New York: Science House.

Sturo, Roberto
    1992, May 26. For Women, Varied Reasons for Single Motherhood. *New York Times,* p. A12.

Survival International
    1990, October. *Survival for Tribal Peoples* (newsletter). Washington, DC: Survival International USA.

Sweet, Ellen
    1980, December. A Tune-up for a Haircut, and Other Bartering Miracles. *Ms.,* p. 86.

Swindells, Neil
    1987, January 17. Uncovered—The Roman Bikini! *Daily Mail* (London), p. 23.

Talmon, Yonina
    1964. Mate Selection in Collective Settlements. *American Sociological Review* 29:491–508.

Todd, Alexandra Dundas, and Sue Fisher (eds.)
    1988. *Gender and Discourse: The Power of Talk.* Norwood, N.J.: Ablex.

Turnbull, Colin
   1965. The Mbuti Pygmies of the Congo. In J. C. Gibbs, Jr. (ed.), *Peoples of Africa,*
   pp. 281–317. New York: Holt, Rinehart & Winston.

Turner, Bryan S.
   1984. *The Body and Society: Explorations in Social Theory.* Oxford: Basil Blackwell.

Turner, Terence S.
   1987 (1969). Cosmetics: The Language of Bodily Adornment. In James P. Spradley and
   David W. McCurdy (eds.), *Conflict and Conformity: Readings in Cultural Anthropology*
   (6th ed.), pp. 93–103. Boston: Little, Brown.

Turner, Victor
   1967. *The Forest of Symbols: Aspects of Ndembu Ritual.* Ithaca, NY: Cornell University
   Press.

Tyler, Stephen A.
   1973. *India: An Anthropological Perspective.* Pacific Palisades, CA: Goodyear Publishing.

Tylor, Sir Edward Burnett
   1873. *Primitive Culture* (2 vols.). London: John Murray.
   1889. On a Method of Investigating the Development of Institutions. *Journal of the Royal
   Anthropological Institute* 18:245–272.

U.S. News
   1976, April 19. Unsolved Mystery: Who'll Get the Riches Howard Hughes Left Behind?
   U.S. News & World Report 80:21–23.

Valentine, Charles
   1968. *Culture and Poverty: Critique and Counter-Proposals.* Chicago: University of
   Chicago Press.

Vander, J.
   1989. From the Musical Experience of Five Shoshone Women. In R. Keeling (ed.),
   Women in North American Indian Music: Six Essays. Bloomington, IN: Society for Ethnomusicology.

Van Gennep, Arnold
   1961. *The Rites of Passage.* Chicago: University of Chicago Press.

Van Willigen, John
   1986. *Applied Anthropology: An Introduction.* South Hadley, MA: Bergin & Garvey.

Vargas, Marjorie Fink
   1986. *Louder than Words: An Introduction to Nonverbal Communication.* Ames: Iowa
   State Press.

Varisco, Daniel Martin
   1989. Beyond Rhino Horn: Wildlife Conservation for North Yemen. *Oryx*
   23(4):215–219.
   1992. Personal communication.

Vaughan, J. Daniel
   1984. Tsimshian Potlatch and Society: Examining a Structural Analysis. In Jay Miller
   and Carol M. Eastman (eds.), *The Tsimshian and Their Neighbors of the North Pacific
   Coast,* pp. 58–68. Seattle: University of Washington Press.

Vayda, Andrew P.
  1961. Expansion and Warfare among Swidden Agriculturalists. *American Anthropologist* 63:346–358.

Vayda, Andrew P., and Bonnie J. McCay
  1975. New Directions in Ecology and Ecological Anthropology. *Annual Review of Anthropology* 4:293–306. Palo Alto, CA: Annual Reviews.

Wallace, Anthony F. C.
  1985. Nativism and Revivalism. In Arthur C. Lehman and James E. Myers (eds.), *Magic, Witchcraft, and Religion: An Anthropological Study of the Supernatural* (2nd ed.), pp. 340–345. Mountain View, CA: Mayfield.

Wallman, Sandra, and Yvonne Dhooge
  1984. Approaches to Ethnographic Research. In Roy Ellen (ed.), *Ethnographic Research: A Guide to General Conduct,* pp. 257–267. ASA Research Methods in Social Anthropology No. 1. London: Academic Press.

Wang, Zhusheng
  1991. Road of Change: A Jingpo Village on China's Border. Ph.D. dissertation, Department of Anthropology, State University of New York at Stony Brook.

Ward, Colleen A. (ed.)
  1989. *Altered States of Consciousness and Mental Health: A Cross-Cultural Perspective.* Newbury Park, CA: Sage.

Watson, James L.
  1982. Of Flesh and Bones: The Management of Death Pollution in Chinese Society. In Maurice Bloch and Jonathan Parry (eds.), *Death and the Regeneration of Life.* Cambridge: Cambridge University Press.

Watson, James L., and Evelyn S. Rawshi (eds.)
  1990 (1988). *Death Ritual in Later Imperial and Modern China.* Berkeley and Los Angeles: University of California Press.

Weaver, Thomas (ed.)
  1973. *To See Ourselves: Anthropology and Modern Social Issues.* Glenview, IL: Scott, Foresman.

Weber, Anne
  1986, December. Anthropologists Look at the Office. *Business Monthly,* pp. 40–42.

Weber, Max
  1947. *The Theory of Social and Economic Organization.* New York: Free Press.
  1963 (1922). *The Sociology of Religion.* Boston: Beacon Press.
  1971. Class, Status and Party. In K. Thompson and J. Tunstall (eds.), *Sociological Perspectives,* pp. 250–264. Harmondsworth, England: Penguin Books.

Weinberg, Arthur (ed.)
  1957. *Attorney for the Damned.* New York: Simon & Schuster.

Weiner, Annette B.
  1976. *Women of Value, Men of Renown.* Austin: University of Texas Press.
  1988. *The Trobrianders of Papua New Guinea.* New York: Holt, Rinehart & Winston.

Weisman, Steven R.
  1987, October 27. Many Faces of the Mahabharata. *New York Times,* p. C17.

Westermarck, Edward
  1922 (1891). *History of Human Marriage.* New York: Allerton Book Co.

White, Douglas R., Michael L. Burton, Lilyan A. Bradner, and Joel D. Gunn
1975. *Implicational Structures in the Sexual Division of Labor.* Social Science Working Paper No. 83. Irvine: School of Social Science, University of California.

White, Leslie A.
1971 (1949). *The Science of Culture: A Study of Man and Civilization.* New York: Farrar, Straus & Giroux.

Whiting, John W. M., Richard Kluckhohn, and Albert Anthony
1958. The Function of Male Initiation Ceremonies at Puberty. In Eleanor E. Maccoby, T. M. Newcomb, and E. L. Hartley (eds.), *Readings in Social Psychology,* pp. 359–370. New York: Henry Holt and Co.

Wicker, Tom
1987, September 14. The Pump on the Well. *New York Times.*

Wilkerson, Isabel
1987, December 20. New Studies Zeroing in on Poorest of the Poor. *New York Times,* p. 26.

Williams, Walter L.
1986. *The Spirit and the Flesh: Sexual Diversity in American Indian Culture.* Boston: Beacon Press.

Winkelman, M. J.
1986. Trance States: A Theoretical Model and Cross-Cultural Analysis. *Ethos* 14:174–203.

Wiser, William H., and Charlotte Viall Wiser
1971. *Behind Mud Walls: 1930–1960* and *The Village in 1970.* Berkeley: University of California Press.

Wittfogel, Karl
1957. *Oriental Despotism: A Comparative Study of Total Power.* New Haven, CT: Yale University Press.

Wolf, Eric R.
1955. Types of Latin American Peasantry: A Preliminary Discussion. *American Anthropologist* 57:452–471.
1957. Closed Corporate Peasant Communities in Mesoamerica and Central Java. *Southwestern Journal of Anthropology* 57:451–471.
1966. *Peasants.* Englewood Cliffs, NJ: Prentice-Hall.
1982. *Europe and the People without History.* Berkeley: University of California Press.

Wolf, Margery
1992. *A Thrice-Told Tale: Feminism, Postmodernism, and Ethnographic Responsibility.* Stanford, CA: Stanford University Press.

Wolf, Naomi
1991. *The Beauty Myth.* New York: Morrow.

Wren, Christopher S.
1986, March 27. Computer Age Comes to Eskimos in Canada. *New York Times,* p. A15.

Wright, Patricia
1992. Primate Ecology, Rainforest Conservation and Economic Development: Building a National Park in Madagascar. *Evolutionary Anthropology* I(1):25–33.

Young, Gayle
    1986, June 12. Anthropologists Wade into the Dark Mystery of the Corporate Jungle. *Chicago Tribune,* Sect. 5, p. 4.

Young, Kate
    1993. *Planning Development with Women: Making a World of Difference.* New York: St. Martin's Press.

Zenani, Nongenile Masithathu
    1992. *The World and the Word: Tales and Observations from the Xhosa Oral Tradition* (Harold Scheub, ed.). Madison: University of Wisconsin Press.

Zubrow, Ezra B. W.
    1975. *Prehistoric Carrying Capacity: A Model.* Menlo Park, CA: Cummings Publishing Co.

GLOSSARY

acculturation the process by which important changes take place in a culture as the result of contact with another culture

achieved authority authority that is earned

adaptation a complex of ideas, activities, and technologies that add up to a particular way of making a living

adjudication the process by which a dispute is settled after the disputants agree that a mediator's decision will be binding

affinal alliance ties, created by marriage, between affines

affines relatives by marriage

affinity relationships created by marriage

age grade a period of life through which an individual passes as he or she grows older

age set a group of individuals of about the same age

agnates (patrikin) consanguines who trace their descent from a common male ancestor

ambilineal descent the kind of descent in which an individual may choose to join either the father's or the mother's side of the family

ambilocal residence the residence pattern in which couples choose whether to live with the husband's relatives or the wife's

American Sign Language (ASL) the most common sign language used by the deaf in North America

animism the belief that souls or spirits inhabit animals, plants, or inanimate objects

anorexia nervosa a mental and physical disorder characterized by an unrealistic view of oneself as too fat, self-induced starvation, and severe weight loss

anthropological linguistics (linguistic anthropology) the field of anthropology that focuses on languages

anthropological perspectives different viewpoints from which anthropologists try to understand culture

anthropological specialties topical areas in which major groups of anthropologists have done interesting and important research

apartheid a former policy of the government of South Africa, under which nonwhite South Africans were physically, politically, and economically segregated from the white minority

applied anthropology the use of anthropological ideas and methods to achieve practical ends outside of the academic community

archaeology the field of anthropology that focuses on the material remains of people of the past

armchair anthropologist an anthropologist who analyzes data from documents written by others rather than carrying out fieldwork

artifact any material thing created by people

ascribed authority authority that is inherited rather than earned

authority the socially granted right to exercise power

avunculocal residence the residence pattern in which male ego resides with his mother's brother

balanced reciprocity the immediate (or fairly prompt) return of goods equal in value to what has been given

band a group of gatherers and hunters

barter economic transactions in which goods and services are swapped without the use of money

berdache in some midwestern and western native American societies, a transvestite and perhaps also transsexual male who was prompted by visions to dress and behave like a woman

bifurcate merging kinship terminology a terminology in which F and FB are known by the same term, whereas MB is known by a different term, and where M and MZ are known by the same term, whereas FZ is known by a different term

big man in Melanesia, a politician whose power depends on the influence he exerts over his followers rather than on a political office

bilineal descent (double descent) a combination of patriliny and matriliny

bilingualism being able to speak more than one language with equal, or roughly equal, competence

biodiversity the diversity of species

Black Vernacular English (BVE) a dialect of English spoken by black youths in the inner cities of the United States

body language (kinesics) nonverbal communication through body movements or facial expressions

bride-capture (bride-theft) the forcible and frequently symbolic carrying off of a bride

bride-service an arrangement in which a son-in-law is obliged to work for his father-in-law as a way of compensating the father-in-law for the loss of his daughter's services

bridewealth (bride-price) property transferred from a groom's family to his bride's at marriage

bullroarer an elongated piece of bone or other material, which when whirled about on a cord produces a tone

business anthropology the kind of anthropology undertaken by anthropologists who study workers and workplaces and act as consultants to management

camp a temporary residential site for gatherers and hunters

capital resources not used up in the process of production

capitalist mode of production a system of production in which capital is controlled by capitalists, and workers, denied access to ownership of capital, must sell their labor to the capitalists to make a living

cargo cult a popular movement for social change in New Guinea, whose followers believe that certain rituals will bring ships loaded with valuable cargo

carrying capacity the maximum number of people who can live indefinitely within a given area at a given level of technology

case study a detailed ethnographic study focusing on a single individual or episode

caste a hereditary social group associated with a specific occupation; bound by specific rights, duties, and prohibitions; and occupying a permanent place in a hierarchy of similar groups

casual informant an informant from whom an ethnographer obtains information from time to time

charisma personal magnetism capable of inspiring agreement, loyalty, and enthusiasm

chiefdom a relatively complex political organization controlling a large, sedentary population

cicatrization a form of scarification in which the skin is repeatedly punctured in an intricate pattern

clan a descent group (patriclan, matriclan) whose members believe they are descended from (or in some special way related to) the same founder

class a group defined by the amount of control it exerts over factors of production

clitoridectomy the partial or complete removal of the clitoris and sometimes the labia minora as well

closed peasant society a type of peasant society characterized by production for household use, old-fashioned technology, isolation from mainstream city life, and resistance to change

code switching switching from one language or dialect into another

cognate a word historically derived from the same source as another word

cognation (cognatic descent) a form of descent reckoned through both males and females

cognitive anthropology a specialty whose practitioners attempt to explain cultures by examining the different categories people create to organize their universe

committee an advisory group, most common in states, that meets in private and usually achieves agreement by voting

common-interest group a group defined by the common needs and concerns of its members

conditional curse a verbal formula containing a conditional phrase designed to establish innocence or guilt

confusion explanation an explanation for the incest taboo that emphasizes the confusion that would result in the classification of relatives if incest occurred

conjugate to change a verb to reflect different tenses, persons, and moods

consanguines (consanguinal kin) individuals related by ties of consanguinity

consanguinity a relationship based on the tie between parents and children that also includes more distant relatives

conservative art art that sustains the existing social order

consumption all the ways in which the goods, services, and nonmaterial things produced in a society are used

contagious magic magic based on the idea that even after they have been separated, things once in contact can influence each other

control group a group similar in size and composition to a group under study, used for comparison or as a cross-check on the data provided by the study group

cooperation explanation an explanation for the incest taboo that emphasizes the social advantages that come from obliging members of the same family to marry outside of it

core vocabulary the most basic words of any language

cosmetics preparations designed to improve the appearance of the body, or part of it, by directly but temporarily applying them to the skin

council an advisory group, typical of simpler political organizations, that is usually informally appointed, meets in public, and resolves conflicts by consensus

court a group of people with the authority to hear the cases of disputants and their witnesses, to determine innocence or guilt, and to decide on punishment

creole a pidgin language that has become the mother tongue of a community

cross cousins children of siblings of the opposite sex

cross cousin marriage a marriage between two cross cousins

Crow terminology a bifurcate merging terminology sometimes accompanying matrilineal descent in which, among other identifications, FZ = FZD

cultural anthropology the anthropological study of contemporary and historic people

cultural audit in business anthropology, a study of discrepancies between the ideal and actual conduct of business in a company

cultural diffusion the spread of ideas and technology between cultures

cultural ecology a materialist perspective focusing on the natural environment as a factor influencing culture

cultural evolution the notion that in human culture there is a gradual, continuous process of adaptive change

cultural materialism the idea that concrete, measurable things, such as the natural environment or technology, are more responsible for specific aspects of culture than other factors

cultural pluralism the meeting of many cultural traditions in a society, particularly a large-scale, modern society

cultural process what happens to cultures through time, whether this means change or stability, increasing or decreasing complexity

cultural relativity a central idea in modern cultural anthropology—that a culture must be evaluated in terms of its own values, not according to the values of another culture

culture everything that people collectively do, think, make, and say

culture and personality an area of special interest in anthropology whose practitioners see a significant link between culture and human psychology

culture hero a mythological being, animal, or inanimate object thought to be associated with the origins of a clan

culture of poverty the ideas and behavior of poor people in some capitalist societies

culture shock the sense of confusion and disorientation fieldworkers may experience on entering the field

cuneiform ancient writing consisting of an arrangement of tiny wedge-shaped dents impressed into wet clay

cyclical age set a system in which an age set's name is continually recycled

decline to change a noun to reflect case, number, or gender

dependency mentality a feeling of powerless dependency on some superior person or group such as a landlord or a charitable organization

dependency ratio the number of people in a nation's work force compared with the number who are too young or too old to work

descent a relationship defined by a connection to an ancestor through a series of parent-child links

descent group a group made up of individuals who trace their descent to a common ancestor

descriptive linguistics the branch of linguistics that seeks to describe the features of languages

destructive potlatch a variety of potlatch in which Kwakiutl hosts destroyed their most valued possessions

development anthropology efforts by anthropologists to improve the well-being of people in the "developing" countries in areas such as health care, education, and agriculture

diachronic approach the study of societies and cultures as they move through time

dialect a variety of a language resulting from its speakers' region, occupation, or class

diffused sanction a spontaneous expression of either approval or disapproval

diffusionism the idea that culture change can be explained by intercultural contacts

direct diffusion the diffusion of an idea or custom from one culture to another without passing through an intermediary culture

diseases of affluence diseases that result from a rise in living standards

distribution the way in which goods and services are allotted in a society

divination a ritual designed to foretell the future or interpret the past, with the help of supernatural agents

diviner a person who performs a divination ritual

domestic (private, household) domain the social sphere that centers on the home and is associated with such activities as child rearing and food preparation for household consumption

double standard the notion that within a single society the rules governing sexual behavior should be different for males and females

dowry goods given by a bride's family to the family of her groom

economic development strategies for improving national economies based on the assumption that they will lead to improvements in human welfare

economic system the interrelated production, distribution, and consumption of goods and services in a society

economy in the most general sense, all the ways in which the members of a society satisfy their wants and needs

ecotourism tourism based on viewing wildlife

egalitarianism a condition in which all people of the same sex and age have a roughly equal social position

ego the individual from whose perspective a kinship diagram is drawn

ego-centered network a network centering on a particular individual and including all the links between this person and others in his or her community

enculturation the process by which an individual absorbs the details of his or her particular culture, starting from birth

endogamy the custom in which one's spouse must be chosen from within one's own group

ends the goals achieved by expending resources

Eskimo terminology a terminology, found in many cognatic societies, in which members of the nuclear family are distinguished from other relatives

ethnic association a common-interest group based on ethnicity

ethnic group a group whose members share basic cultural traditions and values and a common language and who identify themselves (and are identified by others) as distinct from other such groups

ethnicity the identification of individuals with particular ethnic groups

ethnobotany the study of the ways cultures classify local plants

ethnocentrism the belief that one's own society or culture is superior to all others

ethnocide the deliberate attempt to destroy the culture of an ethnic group

ethnographer an anthropologist in the process of doing ethnography

ethnography the process of collecting and recording information within a particular society

ethnology an alternative term for cultural anthropology

ethnomusicology the study of music in its cultural context, either in a single society or cross-culturally

exogamy the social rule that one must marry someone from outside one's own group, however that group is defined

expressive culture the purposeful arrangement of forms, colors, sounds, language, and/or body movements in ways that have meaning and/or are aesthetically appealing to those who do the arranging, and usually to others as well

extended family a larger family group than the nuclear, whose membership is more variable

external change change originating outside a society

fable a category of folktale that teaches some important moral lesson

faction an informal, contentious political group existing within a larger unit, such as a political party or village

family two or more individuals who consider themselves related, who are economically interdependent, and who share responsibility for rearing any children they have

feud a prolonged but usually intermittent hostile relationship between two groups

fieldwork the process of collecting information about people, ancient or modern, where they live or lived

focus group a small group of informants brought together to shed light on a particular topic

folk art the art produced by traditional societies

folktale a fictional story about the adventures of animals or of animals and human beings

fraternal polyandry the custom whereby two or more of a polyandrous woman's husbands are brothers

functionalism the idea that aspects of culture function to fulfill the biological and psychological needs of individuals

gamelan an Indonesian orchestra containing as many as seventy-five different instruments

gathering and hunting the nonproducing method of subsistence

gender learned maleness or femaleness, as reflected in "sexual orientation" and sex roles

gender hierarchy a ranking of cultural notions of maleness and femaleness, as opposed to a ranking of individual males and females

gender identity an individual's self-identification as male or female

genealogy a record of a person's relationships by descent or marriage

general-purpose money currency that can be used to buy anything available for purchase

generalized reciprocity gift giving with the expectation that sooner or later this act will be reciprocated

genetic explanation an explanation for the incest taboo that emphasizes the genetic advantages of marrying outside the family

genocide the deliberate attempt to exterminate the members of a culture

ghost marriage the custom in which the ghost of a man who has died "marries" and is considered able to father a child

glottochronology a method for establishing the approximate time at which two languages branched off from a common ancestor

good magic magic performed to achieve ends that society considers beneficial

government a formal organization through which the political process is carried out

grammar the rules governing word order, prefixes and suffixes, and other aspects of a language

graphic art two-dimensional forms of art such as painting or drawing

great man theory the idea that a single forceful individual can cause major change in a society

Great Tradition the wider, literate culture in which peasants exist

group marriage a form of marriage involving two or more men and two or more women as marriage partners at the same time

Hawaiian terminology a terminology, found in many cognatic societies, in which all relatives of the same sex in the same generation are included under the same term

herding camp the pastoralist residence, consisting of the temporary homes of families that herd and travel together

hermaphrodite an individual who has both male and female physical characteristics

hijada in northwestern India, a man who cross-dresses, begs for charity, and entertains like a woman at ceremonies

historical (comparative) linguistics the study of the histories of languages, both living and dead, and the relationships between languages and dialects

historical particularism the idea that every culture, because it is the product of specific historical circumstances, is unique

horticulture a method of subsistence based on growing crops with simple tools and technologies

human ecology the study of the relationship between human beings and their environment

hydraulic society a society in which crops are watered by a complex system of water management

hypothesis a reasonable statement about some phenomenon or the relationship among phenomena that is based on, and does not contradict, theory

illiterate lacking the ability to read and write while living in a literate society

image of the limited good the view that the world is a place in which there are not enough good things to go around

imitative magic a ritual that imitates the result desired

incest taboo the prohibition of sex between relatives

incorporation final stage of a rite of passage, in which an individual is integrated into a new status in society

indirect diffusion the diffusion of an idea or custom from one culture to another after passing through an intermediary culture

infibulation the process of stitching together the two sides of the female vaginal opening

informant an individual who provides an anthropological researcher with information

instinct explanation an explanation for the incest taboo that suggests that members of the same family instinctively find one another sexually unappealing

internal change change originating within a society

international development a comprehensive term for international efforts to improve the well-being of the world's people

interpretive anthropology the view that the ethnographer's

job is to describe and interpret what members of the culture being studied find meaningful

interview a conversation between an ethnographer and one or more informants

invented tradition symbols, ideas, or customs that members of a society claim as traditional parts of their culture but which in reality are of more recent origin

Iroquois terminology a bifurcate terminology associated with unilineal descent in which the matrilateral cross cousin and patrilateral cross cousin are known by the same term, which may sometimes be the same term as that for spouse

key informant an informant on whom, because of specialized knowledge or influence, an ethnographer relies heavily

kibbutz an agricultural collective in Israel whose main features include communal living, collective ownership of property, and communal child rearing

kin-oriented mode of production a system of production in which labor is organized according to descent and marriage

kindred a group of relatives who have at least one living relative, ego, in common

kinship (relationship) term a word specifying a specific category of relative

kinship (relationship) terminology the complete set of terms by which relatives are known

labret a plug inserted through the flesh of the lower lip

language the primary medium of human interaction

law an institutionalized body of rules, created over time and ratified by a society or its leaders

legend a narrative that describes events set in a specific place in the real world, at a time less remote than the mythological past

levirate the custom in which a widow marries her dead husband's brother

life history an informant's story of his or her life and the influences on it

liminality second stage of a rite of passage, in which an individual has no established status

lineage a descent group (patrilineage, matrilineage) made up of consanguines who can trace their precise genealogical links, through known ancestors, to a founding ancestor

lineal age set a system in which an age set ceases to exist when all of its members have died

magic a ritual intended to bring about some desired practical result without the intervention of spirits

market exchange the kind of exchange in which transactions are impersonal rather than based on descent, marriage, social position, or political relationships

marriage a socially sanctioned contract spelling out the domestic and civic rights and duties of the people who enter into it

material culture the physical things people create

matriarchy a society in which women dominate men politically and economically

matrigroup a matrilineal descent group, whether matriclan or matrilineage

matrikin (uterine kin) consanguines who trace their descent from a common female ancestor

matrilateral cousin a cousin on the mother's side

matrilateral cousin marriage a man's marriage to his mother's brother's daughter or a woman's marriage to her father's sister's son

matrilateral parallel cousin marriage a man's marriage to his mother's sister's daughter or a woman's marriage to her mother's sister's son

matriliny (matrilineal descent) a system of descent in which females provide the links by which property descends to the next generation

matrilocal residence residence for a husband near or with his wife's parents

means all the material and nonmaterial resources people use to fulfill their wants and needs

mediator a person who is neutral to a dispute and charged with negotiating its settlement

mental universals fixed patterns of thought believed to be common to human beings all over the world

military association a group of males who have fought or may fight together

millenarian movement a response made by a deprived community, characterized by anticipating a time when its hopes will be fulfilled

minority an ethnic group typically numerically smaller than the dominant group in its society

modal personality in any culture, the personality type that is statistically the most common

money objects accepted by a society's members as tokens of specific amounts of worth

monogamy the marriage of one husband and one wife

monotheism the belief that there is only one god

morphemes linguistic units made up of the smallest combinations of sounds that have a meaning in a language

morphology the study of morphemes

multiculturalism another term for cultural pluralism

multilineal evolution the notion that different cultures evolve along multiple, if similar, lines, depending on their natural and cultural environments

mutilation any permanently irreversible alteration of a healthy part of the body

myth a story describing the origins of the world, some natural phenomenon, or some aspect of culture, which contains at least one physically or humanly impossible event or situation

negative reciprocity an economic interaction between hostile parties in which each tries to get the better of the other

neo-evolutionism any of several twentieth-century variations on cultural evolution

Neolithic revolution the shift in human subsistence from collecting to producing subsistence needs

neolocal residence residence for a married couple in a location separate from the residences of their families

neopaganism a modern revival of a pre-Christian religion

network analysis gathering and organizing data by focusing on individuals or small groups and their interrelationships in order to establish patterns of association

nomads pastoralists who travel constantly throughout the year, within a large area, to provide their animals with grazing land

nonliterate lacking a tradition of reading and writing

nonmechanized agriculture agriculture using wooden or metal plows, pulled by animals

norm informal rule for behavior

nuclear (elementary or simple) family a social unit consisting of a father, a mother, and unmarried children

octave a set of eight primary tones

office a position in which a certain kind and amount of authority is inherent and which exists independently of its occupant at any given time

Omaha terminology a bifurcate merging terminology sometimes accompanying patrilineal descent in which, among other identifications, MB = MBS = MBSS

open peasant society a type of peasant society characterized by substantial participation in a national or international economy

opposition thinking in terms of opposed categories

oral art art expressed in the form of speech

organized sanction a formalized and institutionalized expression of approval or disapproval

oriental despotism a kind of political system, highly developed in ancient China, in which some individuals achieved power by controlling water and labor

origin myth a story describing the origins of some feature of the physical environment, of a society, or of a culture; often describes the appearance of a clan's culture hero and how the clan was founded

ostracism a diffused sanction in which the offender is shunned

paralanguage the use of voice effects to convey meaning

parallel cousins children of siblings of the same sex

parallel cousin marriage a marriage between two parallel cousins

participant observation cultural anthropology's major research tool—sharing in people's lives as well as observing them (see Chapter 2)

pastoralists those who practice a method of subsistence based on herd animals

patriarchy a society in which men dominate women politically and economically

patrigroup a patrilineal descent group, whether patriclan or patrilineage

patrilateral cousin a cousin on the father's side

patrilateral cross cousin marriage a man's marriage to his father's sister's daughter or a woman's marriage to her mother's brother's son

patrilateral parallel cousin marriage a man's marriage to his father's brother's daughter or a woman's marriage to her father's brother's son

patriliny (patrilineal descent) a system of descent in which males provide the links by which property descends to the next generation

patrilocal residence residence for a husband near or with his father after marriage

peasants typically agricultural people who share the same general cultural tradition as members of the larger and more technologically complex societies in which they live

percussion toneless sounds made by striking something

peripheral market a market of relatively little economic importance, in which only objects, as opposed to land or labor, are bought and sold

personal survey a survey undertaken personally by a researcher

phonemes the smallest meaningful units of sound into which a language can be divided

phonology the study of phonemes

physical (biological) anthropology the field of anthropology that focuses on the biological aspects of being human

physical (natural) science the more objective kind of science in which the researcher and the phenomena being observed are more clearly separated than is usual in the social sciences

pictograph a simple pictorial representation of an object

pidgin a language in which the syntax and vocabulary of two other languages are simplified and combined

pitch the highness or lowness of a musical sound, largely determined by the frequency of its sound vibrations

plastic art sculpture and other three-dimensional forms of art

political organization (political system) a mechanism, formal or informal, for establishing and maintaining social control

politics the process of regulating the behavior of members of a group

polyandry marriage between a wife and more than one husband

polyethnic made up of different ethnic groups

polygamy a general term that covers both polyandry and polygyny

polygyny marriage between a husband and more than one wife

polytheism the belief in the existence of many gods

postmodernism an anthropological specialty, developed in the 1980s, that encourages anthropology to focus on the analysis of ethnographies, examining them from a reflexive point of view

potlatch among native Americans of the Northwest coast, a form of institutionalized consumption consisting of a huge party given by a chief for a rival chief and for all the villagers under the sway of both chiefs

power the capacity to control the behavior of others, using means such as education, persuasion, coercion, punishment, or reward

prefix a morpheme that is added at the front of a word to alter its meaning

prestige social reputation based on a subjective evaluation of social statuses relative to one another

price the worth, expressed in the form of some agreed-on medium of exchange, of goods and services

priest a religious specialist whose authority comes from the office he or she occupies

prime a formal unit of American Sign Language, corresponding to the sounds of spoken language

production transforming natural resources into things people want and need

prophet a charismatic leader who emerges after some intense spiritual experience

protolanguage a hypothetical language thought to be the ancestor of a known language

psychoanalytic explanation an explanation for the incest taboo that suggests its origin in an attempt to control the unconscious desire of children to have sex with the parent of the opposite sex

psychological anthropology an anthropological specialty focusing on the relationship between culture and the psychological makeup of individuals and groups

public domain the social sphere that centers on the wider social world outside of the home and is associated with political and economic activity above the household level

purdah the physical seclusion of women, a custom common in the Middle East

race a term commonly used to identify groups of people supposedly sharing certain specific physical attributes or, alternatively, physical plus cultural similarities. The word is not useful for distinguishing either biological or cultural categories of people

racism the belief that some "races" are inherently superior to others

rank a position in a hierarchical system of social classification

realistic ethnography an ethnography that claims to represent a "real" portrait of a culture or society

reciprocity a mutual exchange of gifts or services

redistribution a way of distributing goods in which the goods are gathered into the possession of a particular individual or group and then parceled out among the members of a society

reflexivity the feedback process by which ethnographers and informants mutually affect one another

respondent a person who provides information for a respondent survey

respondent survey a survey consisting of a prearranged series of questions, in questionnaire form, asked of respondents

revitalization movement a popular movement for radical change, led by a charismatic figure and usually prompted by social, economic, and political upheaval

revolutionary art art that generates new ideas and values

rite of passage a ritual performed at a period of transition in the life cycle

ritual stereotyped, repetitive behavior, either religious or non-religious, that uses symbols to communicate meaning

ritual of propitiation a ritual intended to appease a spirit

role the behavior that expresses the attitudes and behavior associated with a given status

romantic love any intense and sexual attraction in which the person loved is an object of idealization, with the expectation that the feeling will last for some time into the future

sacrifice an offering made to a spirit; the term also denotes the ritual itself

sampling using a small part of something to represent a larger whole

sanction a positive or negative reaction by society to approved behavior (positive sanction) or disapproved behavior (negative sanction)

Sapir-Whorf hypothesis (Whorfian hypothesis) the idea that the way in which the members of a society order their world is conditioned by their language

scale a fixed set of tones on which music is based

scarification designs made by the intentional wounding and subsequent healing and scarring of the skin

science the attempt to discover the laws of nature

self the individual person as the object of his or her own perception

separation first stage of a rite of passage, in which an individual is separated from an established status

serial monogamy consecutive marriages to a number of different spouses

set-centered network a network based on groups of individuals linked to one another

sex the biological category into which a person is born, male or female, as determined by chromosomal and anatomical characteristics

shaman a religious figure, believed to be chosen by spirits, who functions as an intermediary between the world of spirits and human beings

sign language a language in which hand and body gestures, instead of sounds, are used to express meaning

silent barter a kind of barter in which the trading partners never meet each other face to face

sister exchange marriage marriage in which the men of two nuclear families or descent groups exchange women in marriage; sometimes called direct exchange

social anthropology especially in England, the brand of anthropology focusing on societies rather than on culture

social classification a systematic way of distinguishing among individuals or groups according to their different attributes

social explanation an explanation for the incest taboo that suggests it arose to prevent family disintegration

social science the more subjective kind of science in which the researcher and the phenomena being observed may not be distinctly separated

social stratification (social ranking) a system of social classification in which the occupants of various statuses are viewed as unequal to one another

social structure the web of relationships binding members of a society together

society a group of people whose members live in the same place and whose lives and livelihoods are interdependent

sociocultural anthropology a term for cultural anthropology that emphasizes society

sociolinguistics a branch of linguistics that focuses on the relationship between language and society

sorcery bad magic, performed to achieve ends society regards as evil

sororal polygyny the custom in which two or more of a polygynous man's wives are sisters

sororate the custom in which a widower marries his dead wife's sister; alternatively, the custom in which the husband of a barren wife marries her sister, and any ensuing children are considered the children of the first wife

special-purpose money objects of value that can be used to purchase only specific goods and services

speech communication through spoken words

state a large, complex, autonomous political unit consisting of many communities and large numbers of people under a centralized government that can conscript labor, make and enforce laws, collect taxes, and create and maintain institutions to support itself

status the place an individual occupies in the social structure

STD sexually transmitted disease

structural anthropology an anthropological specialty whose followers attempt to discover orderly patterns common to languages, myths, kinship systems, and other aspects of culture

structural-functionalism an anthropological perspective in which aspects of culture are viewed in terms of the part they play in maintaining the social structure

subculture a small group, within a larger one, whose members distinguish themselves (or who are distinguished by others) as culturally different from others

subsistence all the ways in which people get the things they need to subsist

Sudanese terminology a terminology often associated with unilineal descent, with separate terms for F, FB, MB, MZ, FZ, siblings, and cousins

suffix a morpheme that is added to the end of a word to alter its meaning

survey the counting and classifying of items, events, or opinions

sustainability the capacity of the beneficiaries of a development project to continue to achieve results after development assistance ends

swidden, slash-and-burn, or shifting cultivation a form of horticulture in which a plot of land is cultivated for some years and then abandoned in favor of a new one

symbol something that stands for something else

symbolic anthropology the anthropological study of symbols

synchronic approach the study of how aspects of societies and cultures fit together at any given time

syncretism the blending of two or more cultural traditions into a single new one

syntax the rules governing the way morphemes can be arranged in order to make sense

theory a statement about some observable, testable phenomenon that has been examined repeatedly and is widely accepted as true

tone a sound of distinct duration, quality, and pitch

top-down approach in international development, providing assistance to local people without their full participation

totem a plant, animal, or object from which members of a clan are believed to have descended or which plays some central role in its history

transhumance a pastoral way of life in which people move with their herds according to the seasons

transsexual an individual who adopts the social role of the sex opposite to his or her anatomical one

transvestite (cross-dresser) a man who dresses like a woman or a woman who dresses like a man

trial by ordeal a physical test of an accused person for the purpose of revealing the truth

tribe a political organization often occuring among horticulturalists or herders who distinguish themselves from other groups by their common heritage and often common ancestry

tributary mode of production a system of production in which producers must pay tribute to people who control the things needed for production in order to gain access to them

unilineal descent a line of descent that runs through either males or females but not both

unilineal evolution the notion that all cultures follow the same trajectory, from savagery to civilization

universal grammar a hypothetical grammatical ability inherent in all human beings from birth

urban anthropology the anthropological study of urban dwellers

varna one of four traditional divisions of Hindu Indian society

vernacular the standard language or dialect of a population

voluntary association a self-help group

Westernization the process by which non-Western societies become more like Western ones by adopting Western technologies, ideas, values, and customs

wicca a pre-Christian European religion

witchcraft the belief that certain individuals, called witches, can injure others by psychic means

writing the graphic or visual representation of language

PHOTO CREDITS

Unless otherwise acknowledged, all photographs are the property of Scott, Foresman and Company.

ington Post/Woodfin Camp & Associates; **262**: Montana Historical Society; **264**: Library of Congress; **270**: Anthro-Photo; **271**: Free Library of Philadelphia.

CHAPTER 13
277: The Gorilla Foundation; **279**: Andrew H. Malcolm/NYT Pictures; **282**: PhotoFest; **285**: Museum of Science and Industry, Chicago; **287**: Anthro-Photo; **292**: by Harold Scheub used with permission © by Harold Scheub; **295**: Jeff Guerrant.

CHAPTER 14
301: Berry/Magnum Photos; **302**: Photo Researchers; **304**: FPG; **306**: By Peter Brookes from *The London Times,* 6 June 1988; **310**: Woodfin Camp & Associates; **312**: Najwa Adra; **313**: "A Country School" by Norman Rockwell, 1946. Courtesy The Norman Rockwell Museum, Stockbridge; **314**: Wing/Stock Boston; **315**: Andrew H. Malcolm/NYT Pictures; **317**: PhotoFest; **319**: The Metropolitan Museum of Art, The Michael C. Rockefeller Memorial Collection.

CHAPTER 15
323: Maxine Hicks Photo; **325**: Bagish/Anthro-Photo; **326**: Robert Frerck/Odyssey Productions, Chicago; **327**: McIntyre/Photo Researchers; **328**: From *The History of Beads* by Dubin; **329**: Charles D. Miller III; **331**: Campion/Sygma; **332**: Anthro-Photo; **333**: George Rodger/Magnum Photos; **335**: Michael Rockefeller Film Study Center, Harvard University; **337**: Tom Campbell; **339**: Library of Congress.

CHAPTER 16
343: Steve McCutcheon/AlaskaStock Images; **345**: Nance/Magnum Photos; **347**: The Metropolitan Museum of Art; **348**: The Kobal Collection; **349**: M. A. Gwynne; **351**: Nicholas DeVore III; **352**: J. T. Gwynne; **354**: Reuters/UPI/Bettmann; **355**: AP/Wide World; **358**: Bob Daemmrich; **359**: Patricia Wright; **361**: Michael J. Balik, New York Botanical Garden.

NAME INDEX

SUBJECT INDEX

Note: Page numbers in italics indicate references to figures.